GEOMETRY

for Enjoyment and Challenge

NEW EDITION

You are invited to cross the bridge into the exciting world of geometry, for enjoyment and challenge.

GEOMETRY

for Enjoyment and Challenge

NEW EDITION

Richard Rhoad
New Trier High School
Winnetka, Illinois

George Milauskas
Illinois Mathematics and
Science Academy
Aurora, Illinois

Robert Whipple
New Trier High School
Winnetka, Illinois

McDougal Littell
A HOUGHTON MIFFLIN COMPANY

Evanston, Illinois ◆ Boston ◆ Dallas

Reviewers

Karen Ardner
Waite High School
Toledo, Ohio

William Duncker
Midland Independent School District
Midland, Texas

Rosanne Hornyak
Wethersfield High School
Wethersfield, Connecticut

Don Nagel
John Marshall High School
Rochester, Minnesota

Irene Norde
Kettering High School
Detroit, Michigan

Sarah Steinmetz
Corona del Sol High School
Tempe, Arizona

Roberta Simonson
Grissom High School
Huntsville, Alabama

Credits

Cover

Cover collage: Carol Tornatore, photograph by Tom Petrillo

1: © Peter Mauss/Esto, Mamaronock, New York, all rights reserved; 2,5,6,13,15: © Chip Clark, Washington, D.C.; 3,7,8,12: Adrienne McGrath, North Barrington, Illinois; 4,10: (detail) Reprinted by Permission of E.P. Dutton, New York; 9: (detail) Reprinted with Permission of *Better Homes and Gardens* ®, Des Moines, Iowa, American Patchwork and Quilting; 11: JPL, NASA's Regional Planetary Image Facilities, Pasadena, California; 14: Ric Ergenbright, Bend, Oregon.

Fine Art and Photography

Frontispiece: *Suspension Bridge, Kaibab Trail, Grand Canyon, Arizona,* Paul A. Otto, Lake St. Louis, Missouri

2: *Open Book,* 1930, Paul Klée, Guggenheim Museum, New York; 35: Courtesy of Wendell Griffen; 48: © 1985 Sidney Harris, New Haven, Connecticut; 60: Richard Sullivan, Los Angeles; 81: J. Nettis/H. Armstrong Roberts, Chicago; 94: Stember Photography, Lawrenceville, New Jersey; 110: *Sheba,* 1980, Dorothea Rockburne, National Museum of Women in the Arts, Washington, D.C., Holladay Collection; 130: Norman McGrath, New York; 137: Courtesy of Dorothy Washburne; 168: Algimantas Kezys, Stickney, Illinois; 175: *Ad Parnassum,* 1932, Paul Klée, Kunstmuseum, Bern, Switzerland; 191: (all) E.D. Getzoff/Scripps Clinic and Research Foundation, LaJolla, California; 194: Carmine Fantasia, Chicago; 197: Historical Pictures Service, Chicago; 198: Algimantas Kezys, Stickney, Illinois; Credits continued on p. 769

ISBN 0-86609-965-4
1997 Impression
Copyright © 1991 by McDougal, Littell & Company
Box 1667, Evanston, Illinois 60204

99/15 14 13

CONTENTS

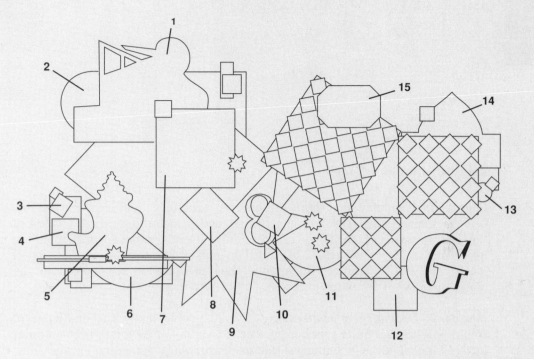

1. Café at Parc de la Villette, Paris
2, 13. Cuban tree snails
3, 8, 12. Pythagorean Theorem proofs
4, 10. Pieced quilt, Broken Dishes variation, silk, made by Susan Simpson, New Jersey, c. 1870
5. Miraculous Thatcheria, a marine snail from Taiwan
6. Round blue topaz
7. Amusement-park ride
9. Amish quilt, Star of Bethlehem pattern
11. Saturn's B- and C-rings
14. Hazart Ali Shrine, Mazari-i-Sharif, Afghanistan
15. Malaya, a variety of garnet, from East Africa

LETTER TO STUDENTS

Why Study Geometry?

Reason 1: Geometry is useful. Engineers, architects, painters, carpenters, plumbers, teachers, electricians, machinists, and homebuilders are only a few of the people who use geometry in their daily lives. Geometric principles are important in the construction of buildings and roads, the design and use of machinery and scientific instruments, the operation of airplanes, and the planning of new inventions plus many other activities.

Reason 2: Geometry is challenging. Many people enjoy the challenge of solving riddles and other types of puzzles. The study of geometry offers similar intriguing challenges—challenges that are particularly appealing because they involve visible figures as well as words and ideas.

Here's a first challenge for you. How many squares are in the figure shown? (The answer is upside down at the bottom of the next page.)

Reason 3: Geometry is logical. As we become educated, we learn to rely more on reason and proof and less on superstition, prejudice, and guesswork. One of the main purposes of this book is to help you appreciate the power of logic as a tool for understanding the world around you. For this reason, the first six chapters focus on the concept of proof. Although proofs may seem difficult to you for a few weeks, with reasonable effort on your part the feeling of difficulty will soon pass. You will be amazed at your skill in forging a chain of reasoning and will appreciate as never before the uses of logic in mathematics and in your daily life.

Reason 4: Geometry gives visual meaning to arithmetic and algebra. Here is a problem that does so:

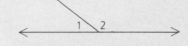

If angle 2 is five times as large as angle 1, what is the size of each of the angles?

A little thought might lead us to write the equation

$$x + 5x = 180$$

which we can use to solve the problem. (Where do you think the x, the 5x, and the number 180 came from?)

The important ideas of geometry must be developed gradually. Almost every day, your geometry homework will include a few problems involving areas, perimeters, and the measures of angles and segments. You will begin to learn about the significant concepts of probability, rotation, and reflection in Chapter 1. In Chapter 2, you will review and begin to extend what you have learned about coordinate graphs in your algebra studies. As you progress, you will become more and more familiar with these topics.

You will find that some of the problems in this book can be solved in your head, some require paper and pencil, and some are most easily solved with the aid of a scientific calculator.

The geometry course on which you are about to begin is one that we hope you will find fun, exciting, and powerful. We, the authors, wish you well on the year's journey.

Richard Rhoad   *George Milauskas*   *Robert Whipple*

There are nine squares in the figure.

INTRODUCTION TO GEOMETRY

This painting, *Open Book* by Paul Klee, incorporates geometric shapes and relationships.

1.1 GETTING STARTED

Objectives

After studying this section, you will be able to
- Recognize points
- Recognize lines
- Recognize line segments
- Recognize rays
- Recognize angles
- Recognize triangles

Part One: Introduction

Points

In the diagram at the right, five **points** are represented by five dots. The names of the points are A, B, C, D, and E. (We use capital letters to name points.)

.A   .B

.C   .E

.D

Lines

The diagram below represents three **lines.** Lines are made up of points and are straight. The arrows on the ends of the figures show that the lines extend infinitely far in both directions.

All lines are straight and extend infinitely far in both directions.

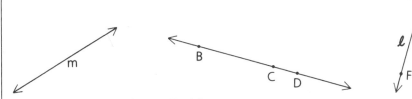

- The line on the left is called line m.
- Since we can name a line in terms of any two points on it, the line in the middle can be called by a variety of names.

$$\overleftrightarrow{BD} \quad \overleftrightarrow{BC} \quad \overleftrightarrow{CD} \quad \overleftrightarrow{CB} \quad \overleftrightarrow{DB} \quad \overleftrightarrow{DC}$$

- The line on the right can be called by any of three names.

$$\text{line } \ell \quad \overleftrightarrow{EF} \quad \overleftrightarrow{FE}$$

In algebra you learned that a **number line** is formed when a numerical value is assigned to each point on a line.

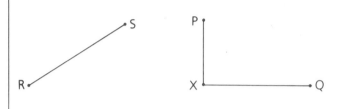

The coordinate of A is -2. The coordinate of B is $1\frac{1}{2}$.

Line Segments

The following diagram represents several **line segments,** or simply **segments.** Like lines, segments are made up of points and are straight. A segment, however, has a definite beginning and end.

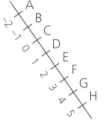

A segment is named in terms of its two **endpoints**

- The segment on the left can be called either $\overline{RS}$ or $\overline{SR}$.
- In the middle figure there are two segments. The vertical (up-and-down) segment can be called either $\overline{PX}$ or $\overline{XP}$. The horizontal (crosswise) segment can also be named in two ways. Can you name these two ways?
- How might we name the segment whose endpoints have coordinates 3 and 0 in the figure on the right?

Rays

In the diagram below, three **rays** are represented. Rays, like lines and segments, are made up of points and are straight. A ray differs from a line or a segment in that it begins at an endpoint and then extends infinitely far in *only one* direction.

When we name a ray, we must name the endpoint first so that it is clear where the ray begins.

- The ray on the left is called $\overrightarrow{AB}$.
- The ray in the middle can be called $\overrightarrow{CD}$ or $\overrightarrow{CE}$. (As long as the endpoint is given first, any other point on the ray can be used in its name.)
- The ray on the right can be named in only one way. Do you know what its name is?

Angles

Two rays that have the same endpoint form an *angle*.

Definition   An *angle* is made up of two rays with a common endpoint. This point is called the *vertex* of the angle. The rays are called *sides* of the angle.

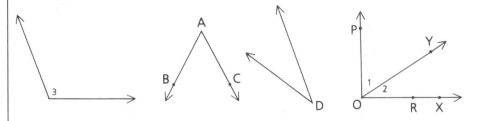

- In the diagram above, the angle on the left is called ∠3. The 3 placed inside the angle near the vertex names it.
- The second angle in the diagram can be called by any of three names.

∠BAC   ∠CAB   ∠A

    (Notice that when we use three letters, the vertex must be named in the middle.)
- The third angle is called ∠D.
- In the last figure above, there are three angles. Can you tell which angle is ∠O? Because names might refer to more than one angle in a diagram, we *never name an angle in a way that could result in confusion.*

    ∠1 can also be called ∠POY or ∠YOP.

    ∠2 can also be called ∠YOR, ∠YOX, ∠ROY, or ∠XOY.

    The other angle in this figure can be named ∠POR. See if you can find three other names for this angle.

Triangles

We shall call the following figure *triangle* ABC (△ABC).

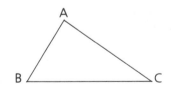

A triangle has three segments as its sides. You may wonder whether we can talk about an ∠B in the triangle, since there are no arrows in the diagram. The answer is yes. We shall often talk about rays, lines, and angles in a diagram of a triangle. So a triangle not only has three sides but has three angles as well. Can you name the angle at the top of the triangle shown on the preceding page in three ways?

The triangle is the **union** (∪) of three segments.

$$\triangle ABC = \overline{AB} \cup \overline{BC} \cup \overline{AC}$$

The **intersection** (∩) of any two sides is a **vertex** of the triangle.

$$\overline{AB} \cap \overline{BC} = B$$

Part Two: Sample Problems

Problem 1

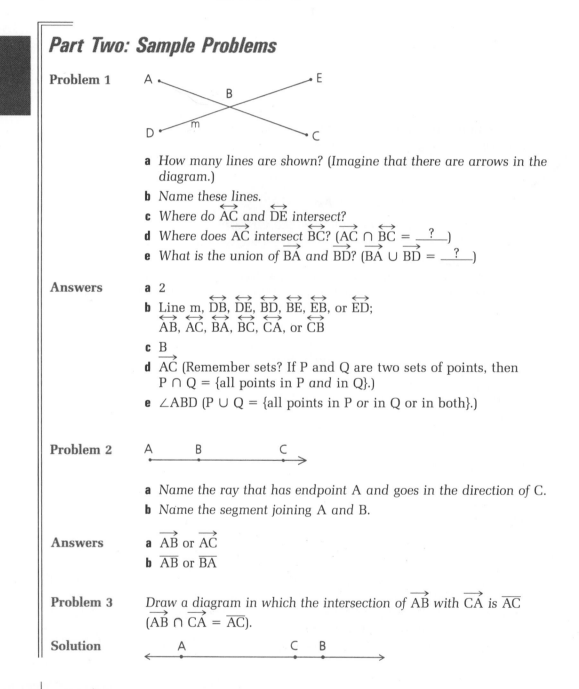

a How many lines are shown? (Imagine that there are arrows in the diagram.)

b Name these lines.

c Where do $\overleftrightarrow{AC}$ and $\overleftrightarrow{DE}$ intersect?

d Where does $\overrightarrow{AC}$ intersect $\overleftrightarrow{BC}$? ($\overrightarrow{AC} \cap \overleftrightarrow{BC} = \underline{\ ?\ }$)

e What is the union of $\overrightarrow{BA}$ and $\overrightarrow{BD}$? ($\overrightarrow{BA} \cup \overrightarrow{BD} = \underline{\ ?\ }$)

Answers

a 2

b Line m, $\overleftrightarrow{DB}$, $\overleftrightarrow{DE}$, $\overleftrightarrow{BD}$, $\overleftrightarrow{BE}$, $\overleftrightarrow{EB}$, or $\overleftrightarrow{ED}$; $\overleftrightarrow{AB}$, $\overleftrightarrow{AC}$, $\overleftrightarrow{BA}$, $\overleftrightarrow{BC}$, $\overleftrightarrow{CA}$, or $\overleftrightarrow{CB}$

c B

d $\overrightarrow{AC}$ (Remember sets? If P and Q are two sets of points, then P ∩ Q = {all points in P *and* in Q}.)

e ∠ABD (P ∪ Q = {all points in P *or* in Q *or* in both}.)

Problem 2

$$\overset{A \qquad B \qquad\quad C}{\longrightarrow}$$

a Name the ray that has endpoint A and goes in the direction of C.

b Name the segment joining A and B.

Answers

a $\overrightarrow{AB}$ or $\overrightarrow{AC}$

b $\overline{AB}$ or $\overline{BA}$

Problem 3 Draw a diagram in which the intersection of $\overrightarrow{AB}$ with $\overrightarrow{CA}$ is $\overline{AC}$ ($\overrightarrow{AB} \cap \overrightarrow{CA} = \overline{AC}$).

Solution

$$\overset{\qquad A \qquad\qquad\qquad C \quad B}{\longleftrightarrow}$$

Problem 4   *Draw a diagram in which △ABC ∩ $\overrightarrow{DE}$ = F.*

Solution

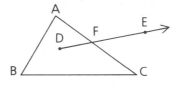

There are other correct answers, and a lot of wrong ones.

Part Three: Problem Sets

Problem Set A

In the back of the book, you will find answers to many of the problems. It will help you learn to check your answer in the back after you solve a problem. Then rethink your work if necessary.

1 What are three possible names for the line shown?

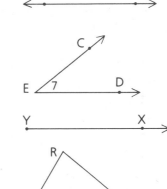

2 What are four possible names for the angle shown?

3 Can the ray shown be called $\overrightarrow{XY}$?

4 Name the sides of △RST.

5 a $\overline{AB}$ ∩ $\overline{BC}$ = ___?___
  b $\overrightarrow{EC}$ ∪ $\overrightarrow{EA}$ = ___?___
  c $\overleftrightarrow{AC}$ ∩ $\overleftrightarrow{DB}$ = ___?___
  d $\overline{DC}$ ∩ $\overline{AB}$ = ___?___
  e $\overrightarrow{AC}$ ∩ $\overrightarrow{EC}$ = ___?___
  f $\overrightarrow{BA}$ ∪ $\overrightarrow{BC}$ = ___?___
  g $\overline{EC}$ ∪ $\overline{CB}$ ∪ $\overline{BE}$ = ___?___

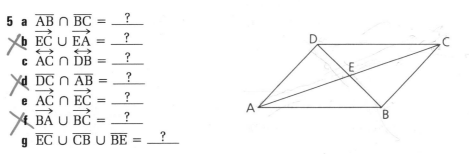

6 a Name ∠OPR in all other possible ways.
  b What is the vertex of ∠TOS?
  c How many angles have vertex R?
  d Name ∠TSP in all other possible ways.
  e How many triangles are there in the figure?

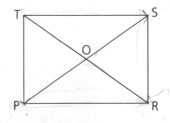

Problem Set A, *continued*

7 Figure 1 shows the reflection of the letter F over a line. Copy Figure 2 and draw the reflections of the letters *P*, *A*, and *J* over the given line.

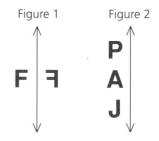

8 a A line is made up of ___?___.

b An angle is the union of two ___?___ with a common ___?___.

9 Draw a number line and label points F, G, H, and J with the coordinates $-4\frac{2}{3}$, 2, 5, and 3.5 respectively. One of these points is the *midpoint* (the halfway point) between two others. Which is it?

10 Given a rectangle with sides 2.5 cm and 8.6 cm long, find

a The rectangle's area

b The rectangle's perimeter (the distance around it)

Problem Set B

11 a In △HJK, $\overline{HJ}$ is twice as long as $\overline{JK}$ and exactly as long as $\overline{HK}$. If the length of $\overline{HJ}$ is 15, find the perimeter of (the distance around) △HJK.

b If the length of $\overline{HJ}$ were 4x, the length of $\overline{HK}$ were 3x, the length of $\overline{JK}$ were 2x, and the perimeter of △HJK were 63, what would the length of $\overline{HJ}$ be?

12 Draw a diagram in which $\overline{AB} \cap \overline{CD} = \overline{CB}$.

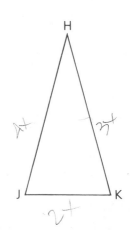

Problem Set C

13 Draw a diagram in which the intersection of ∠AEF and ∠DPC is $\overrightarrow{ED}$.

14 a What percentage of the triangles in the diagram have $\overline{CT}$ as a side?

b What percentage have $\overline{AC}$ as a side?

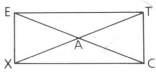

MEASUREMENT OF SEGMENTS AND ANGLES

Objectives

After studying this section, you will be able to
- Measure segments
- Measure angles
- Classify angles by size
- Name the parts of a degree
- Recognize congruent angles and segments

Part One: Introduction

Measuring Segments

We measure segments by using such instruments as rulers or metersticks. We may use any convenient length as a unit of measure. Some of the units that are currently in common use are inches, feet, yards, millimeters, centimeters, and meters. To indicate the measure of $\overline{AB}$, we write AB.

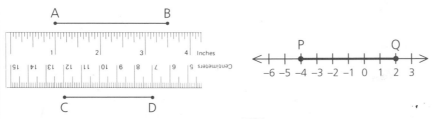

On the ruler shown, find the length of $\overline{AB}$ in inches and the length of $\overline{CD}$ in centimeters. On the number line, find PQ.

Measuring Angles

Angles are commonly measured by means of a *protractor*. (The diagram at the top of the next page shows how a protractor can be used to measure a 117° angle.) We shall measure angles (∠s) in *degrees* (°). In later courses, you may use other units, such as radians or grads.

The *measure*, or size, of an angle is the amount of turning you would do if you were at the vertex, looking along one side, and then turned to look along the other side. (A surveyor's transit works in much the same way.)

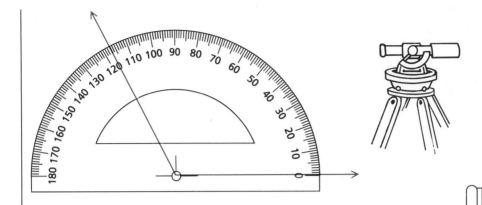

Surveyor's Transit

If you turned all the way around (to face your starting direction), you would turn 360°. You can use this fact to estimate the size of an angle.

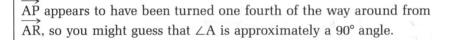

$\overrightarrow{AP}$ appears to have been turned one fourth of the way around from $\overrightarrow{AR}$, so you might guess that ∠A is approximately a 90° angle.

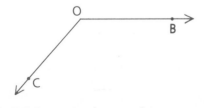

Angle 1 required less than a quarter turn. A good guess would be that it is a 60° angle.

Angle BOC required more than a quarter turn, so its size could be estimated at 130°.

Some math courses deal with negative angles, zero angles, and angles greater than 180°. In this course, you will usually be working with angles greater than 0° and less than or equal to 180°.

$$0 < \text{angle measure} \leq 180$$

Classifying Angles by Size

As shown below, we classify angles into four categories according to their measures.

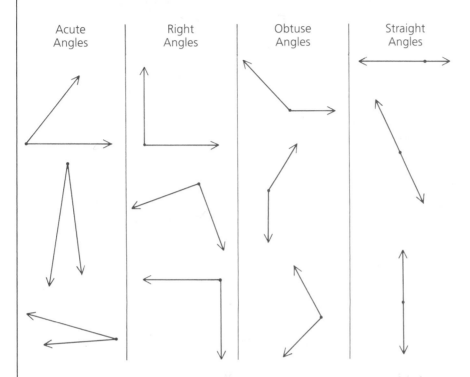

| Acute Angles | Right Angles | Obtuse Angles | Straight Angles |

Definitions

An *acute angle* is an angle whose measure is greater than 0 and less than 90.

A *right angle* is an angle whose measure is 90.

An *obtuse angle* is an angle whose measure is greater than 90 and less than 180.

A *straight angle* is an angle whose measure is 180. (As you can see, a straight angle forms a straight line.)

Parts of a Degree

As you know, each hour of the day is divided into 60 minutes, and each minute is divided into 60 seconds. Similarly, each degree (°) of an angle is divided into 60 *minutes* ('), and each minute of an angle is divided into 60 *seconds* (").

$60' = 1°$ (60 minutes equals 1 degree.)
$60'' = 1'$ (60 seconds equals 1 minute.)

Thus, $87\frac{1}{2}° = 87°30'$
$60.4° = 60°24'$
$90° = 89°60'$ (since $60' = 1°$)
$180° = 179°59'60''$ (since $60'' = 1'$ and $60' = 1°$)

Study the following examples closely.

Example 1   *Change $41\frac{2}{5}°$ to degrees and minutes.*

Since there are 60′ in 1°, $\frac{2}{5}°$ is $\frac{2}{5}(60)$ minutes, or 24′.

Hence, $41\frac{2}{5}° = 41°24′$.

Example 2   *Given: ∠ABC is a right angle.*
                  ∠ABD = 67°21′37″

Find: ∠DBC

Subtract 67°21′37″ from 90° as follows.

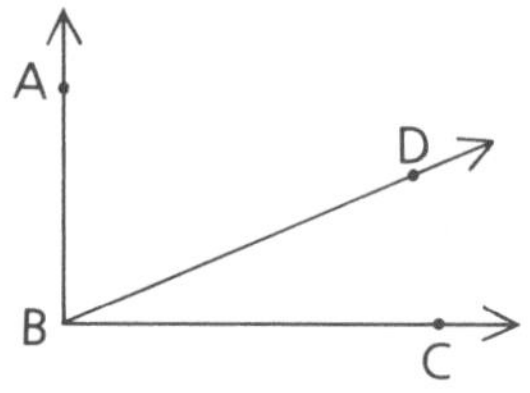

$$89°59′60″ \quad (90° = 89°59′60″)$$
$$-\,67°21′37″$$
$$\overline{22°38′23″}$$

Example 3   *Change 60°45′ to degrees.*

We must change 45′ to a fractional part of a degree. Since 60′ = 1°, 45 is divided by 60, and the fraction is reduced.

$$\frac{45}{60} = \frac{3}{4} \qquad \text{So } 60°45′ = 60\frac{3}{4}°.$$

Congruent Angles and Segments

In the diagram below, ∠s A, B, and C are ***congruent***. We write ∠A ≅ ∠B ≅ ∠C.

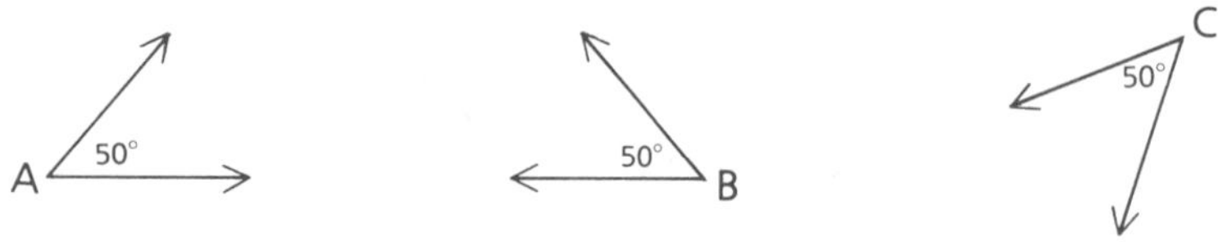

Definition   *Congruent (≅) angles* are angles that have the same measure.

In a similar way, segments can be congruent.

Definition   *Congruent (≅) segments* are segments that have the same length.

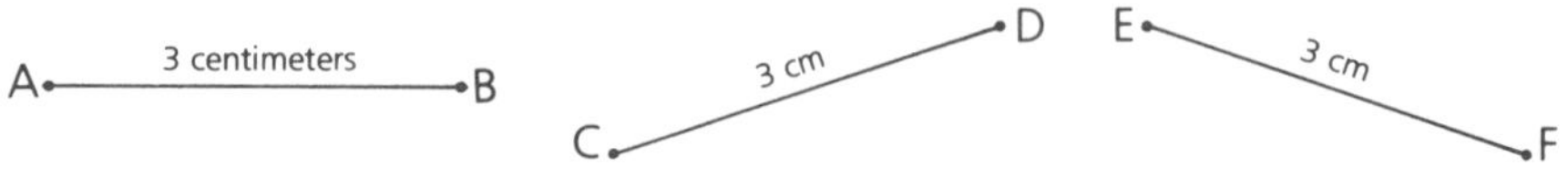

In the diagram above, segments $\overline{AB}$, $\overline{CD}$, and $\overline{EF}$ are congruent. We write $\overline{AB} ≅ \overline{CD} ≅ \overline{EF}$.

Often, we use identical ***tick marks*** to indicate congruent angles and segments. In the following diagram, the identical tick marks indicate that there are four pairs of congruent parts. Can you name them?

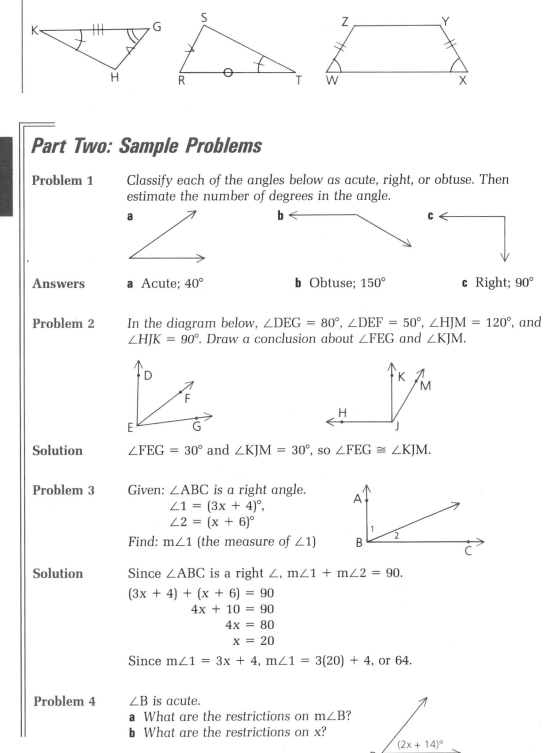

Part Two: Sample Problems

Problem 1   *Classify each of the angles below as acute, right, or obtuse. Then estimate the number of degrees in the angle.*

a   **b**   **c**

Answers   **a** Acute; 40°   **b** Obtuse; 150°   **c** Right; 90°

Problem 2   *In the diagram below, ∠DEG = 80°, ∠DEF = 50°, ∠HJM = 120°, and ∠HJK = 90°. Draw a conclusion about ∠FEG and ∠KJM.*

Solution   ∠FEG = 30° and ∠KJM = 30°, so ∠FEG ≅ ∠KJM.

Problem 3   *Given:* ∠ABC *is a right angle.*
                ∠1 = (3x + 4)°,
                ∠2 = (x + 6)°
                Find: m∠1 *(the measure of* ∠1)

Solution   Since ∠ABC is a right ∠, m∠1 + m∠2 = 90.
                (3x + 4) + (x + 6) = 90
                             4x + 10 = 90
                                   4x = 80
                                     x = 20
                Since m∠1 = 3x + 4, m∠1 = 3(20) + 4, or 64.

Problem 4   ∠B *is acute.*
                a *What are the restrictions on* m∠B?
                b *What are the restrictions on x?*

                (2x + 14)°
                B

Solution

a Since ∠B is acute, m∠B > 0 and
m∠B < 90 (0 < m∠B < 90).

b 2x + 14 > 0   and   2x + 14 < 90
2x > −14   and   2x < 76
x > −7   and   x < 38

Thus, −7 < x < 38.

Problem 5   *Find the angle formed by the hands of a clock at each time.*

a 4:00   **b** 5:15

Solution   **a** Since 360° is divided into 12 inter-   **b** Remember that the hour hand is
vals on a clock, each interval is 30°.   on 5 only when the minute hand
From 12 to 4 there are 4 intervals, so   is on 12. At 5:15 the hour hand is
the angle is 4(30°), or 120°.   one fourth of the way from 5 to 6.
Since $\frac{1}{4}(30°) = 7\frac{1}{2}°$, the hands form
an angle of $60 + 7\frac{1}{2}$, or $67\frac{1}{2}$ degrees.

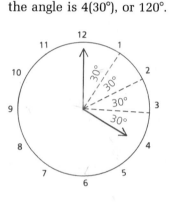

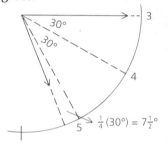

Part Three: Problem Sets

Problem Set A

1 Change each of the following to degrees and minutes.

a $61\frac{2}{3}°$ **b** 71.7°

2 Change each of the following to degrees.

a 132°30′   **b** 19°45′

3 Which two of the angles below *appear* to be congruent?

4 a $\overrightarrow{QV} \cap \overleftrightarrow{TS} = $ ___?___
  b $\overline{WP} \cap \overline{VR} = $ ___?___
  c $\overrightarrow{WP} \cup \overrightarrow{VR} = $ ___?___
  d $\overrightarrow{SQ} \cup \overrightarrow{SR} = $ ___?___
  e How many angles have vertex Q?

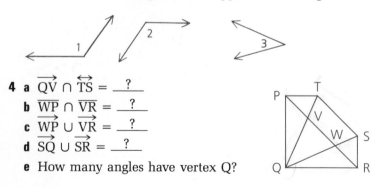

5 a Evaluate $49°32'55'' + 37°27'15''$.

b Evaluate $123°15' - 40°26'$.

6 There is a right angle at each corner of PRST. (Later in the course you will learn that PRST is a rectangle.)

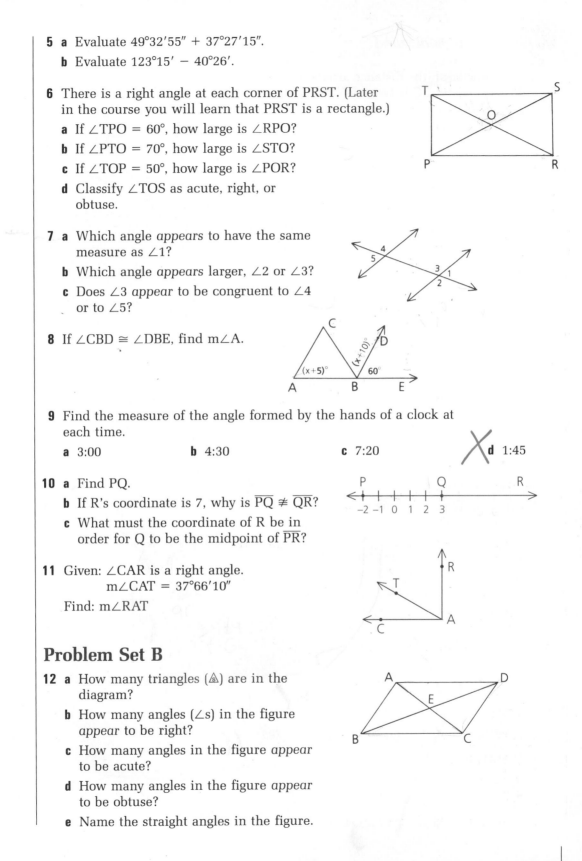

a If $\angle TPO = 60°$, how large is $\angle RPO$?

b If $\angle PTO = 70°$, how large is $\angle STO$?

c If $\angle TOP = 50°$, how large is $\angle POR$?

d Classify $\angle TOS$ as acute, right, or obtuse.

7 a Which angle *appears* to have the same measure as $\angle 1$?

b Which angle *appears* larger, $\angle 2$ or $\angle 3$?

c Does $\angle 3$ *appear* to be congruent to $\angle 4$ or to $\angle 5$?

8 If $\angle CBD \cong \angle DBE$, find m$\angle A$.

9 Find the measure of the angle formed by the hands of a clock at each time.

a 3:00   **b** 4:30   **c** 7:20   **d** 1:45

10 a Find PQ.

b If R's coordinate is 7, why is $\overline{PQ} \not\equiv \overline{QR}$?

c What must the coordinate of R be in order for Q to be the midpoint of $\overline{PR}$?

11 Given: $\angle CAR$ is a right angle.
         m$\angle CAT = 37°66'10''$

Find: m$\angle RAT$

Problem Set B

12 a How many triangles (△) are in the diagram?

b How many angles ($\angle$s) in the figure *appear* to be right?

c How many angles in the figure *appear* to be acute?

d How many angles in the figure *appear* to be obtuse?

e Name the straight angles in the figure.

Problem Set B, *continued*

13 The perimeter of (the distance around) ABCD is 66, and $\overline{DC}$ is twice as long as $\overline{CB}$. How long is $\overline{AB}$?

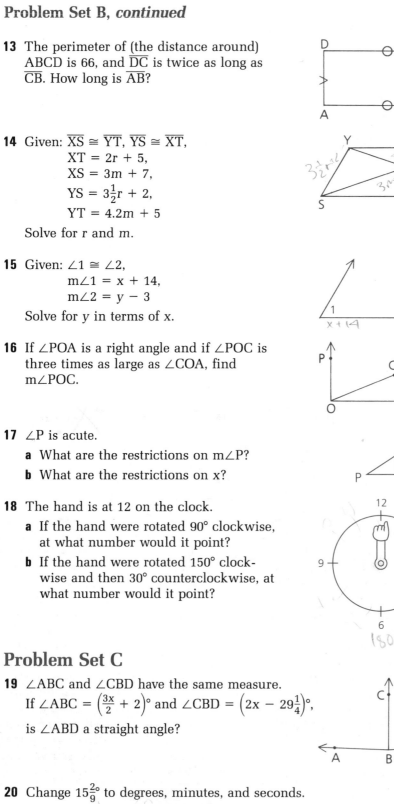

14 Given: $\overline{XS} \cong \overline{YT}$, $\overline{YS} \cong \overline{XT}$,
XT = 2r + 5,
XS = 3m + 7,
YS = $3\frac{1}{2}r + 2$,
YT = 4.2m + 5

Solve for *r* and *m*.

15 Given: ∠1 ≅ ∠2,
m∠1 = x + 14,
m∠2 = y − 3

Solve for *y* in terms of *x*.

16 If ∠POA is a right angle and if ∠POC is three times as large as ∠COA, find m∠POC.

17 ∠P is acute.

a What are the restrictions on m∠P?

b What are the restrictions on x?

18 The hand is at 12 on the clock.

a If the hand were rotated 90° clockwise, at what number would it point?

b If the hand were rotated 150° clockwise and then 30° counterclockwise, at what number would it point?

Problem Set C

19 ∠ABC and ∠CBD have the same measure. If ∠ABC = $\left(\frac{3x}{2} + 2\right)°$ and ∠CBD = $\left(2x - 29\frac{1}{4}\right)°$, is ∠ABD a straight angle?

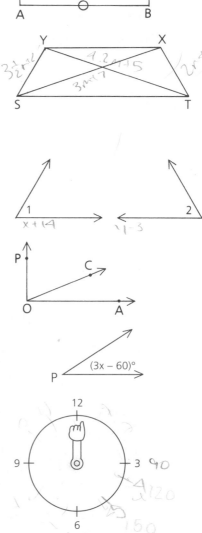

20 Change $15\frac{2}{9}°$ to degrees, minutes, and seconds.

21 Given: ∠TRS is a straight angle.
    ∠TRX is a right angle.
    m∠TRS = 2x + 5y,
    m∠XRS = 3x + 3y

Solve for x and y.

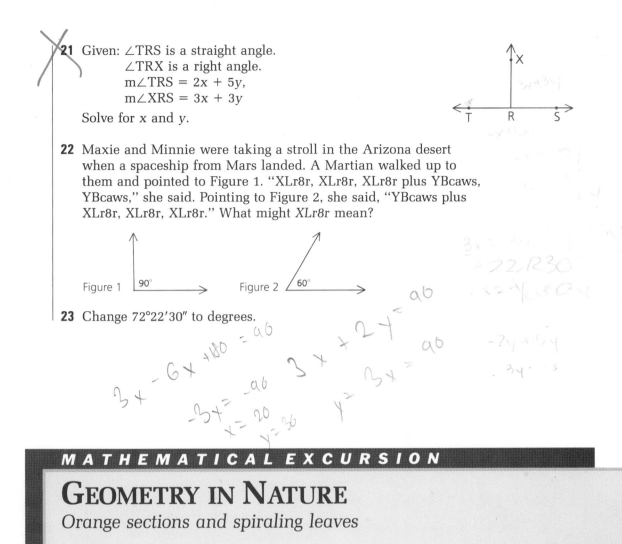

22 Maxie and Minnie were taking a stroll in the Arizona desert when a spaceship from Mars landed. A Martian walked up to them and pointed to Figure 1. "XLr8r, XLr8r, XLr8r plus YBcaws, YBcaws," she said. Pointing to Figure 2, she said, "YBcaws plus XLr8r, XLr8r, XLr8r." What might *XLr8r* mean?

Figure 1 90°   Figure 2 60°

23 Change 72°22′30″ to degrees.

GEOMETRY IN NATURE
Orange sections and spiraling leaves

If you cut a cross section of an orange, you will see that it is divided into sections that together form a 360° angle. The mathematician Johannes Kepler (1571–1630) thought that all fruits and flowers that grew on trees had five sections or petals. You can see that this isn't true, but the sections of an orange do appear to be the same size and shape.

Flower petals, and leaves on stems grow in a spiral pattern and form angles of consistent sizes.

Phyllotaxis is the distribution of leaves around the stem of a plant. The measure of the angle formed by any two leaves in succession on a stem is equal to the measure of the angle between any two other leaves in succession.

The most common angles seem to be 144° and 135°. A 144° angle is characteristic for rose leaves. Suppose you draw a series of 144° angles with a protractor, using one of the sides of the last angle you drew for each new angle and proceeding in a clockwise direction. You will see that the angles eventually divide a circle into five equal parts.

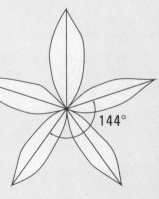

144°

Botanists say that these angles exist because each bud grows where it will have the most room between the bud before it and the one that will come after it.

COLLINEARITY, BETWEENNESS, AND ASSUMPTIONS

Objectives

After studying this section, you will be able to
- Recognize collinear and noncollinear points
- Recognize when a point can be said to be between two others
- Recognize that each side of a triangle is shorter than the sum of the other two sides
- Correctly interpret geometric diagrams

Part One: Introduction

Collinearity

It is often useful to know that a group of points lie on the same line.

Definition Points that lie on the same line are called ***collinear***. Points that do not lie on the same line are called ***noncollinear***.

COLLINEAR POINTS   NON-COLLINEAR POINTS

In the diagram at the right, R, S, and T are collinear points. P, O, and X are also collinear. M, O, X, and Y are noncollinear.

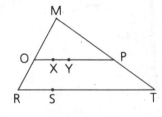

Betweenness of Points

In order for us to say that a point is between two other points, all three of the points must be collinear.

T is between A and R   We do *not* say O is between X and Y

Triangle Inequality

For any three points, there are only two possibilities:

1 They are collinear. (One point is between the other two. Two of the distances add up to the third.)
2 They are noncollinear. (The three points determine a triangle.)

Notice that in the triangle, $14 + 11 > 24$. This is an example of an important characteristic of triangles: *The sum of the lengths of any two sides of a triangle is always greater than the length of the third.*

Assumptions from Diagrams

You may wonder what you should and should not assume when you look at a diagram. The chart below gives the general rules you should follow as you work with this book. (There are, however, occasional exceptions, as in Section 1.2, problem 19.)

How to Interpret a Diagram	
You Should Assume	**You Should Not Assume**
Straight lines and angles	Right angles
Collinearity of points	Congruent segments
Betweenness of points	Congruent angles
Relative positions of points	Relative sizes of segments and angles

The following example will help you understand what assumptions can be made.

Example *Given: Diagram as shown*

Question: What should we assume?

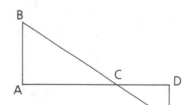

The following are some of the many valid interpretations.

Do Assume	**Do Not Assume**
$\overleftrightarrow{ACD}$ and $\overleftrightarrow{BCE}$ are straight lines.	$\angle BAC$ is a right $\angle$.
$\angle BCE$ is a straight angle.	$\overline{CD} \cong \overline{DE}$
C, D, and E are noncollinear.	$\angle B \cong \angle E$
C is between B and E.	$\angle CDE$ is an obtuse angle.
E is to the right of A.	$\overline{BC}$ is longer than $\overline{CE}$.

Reread and study the chart and the example carefully, for it is important that you know what to assume from a diagram.

Part Two: Sample Problems

Problem 1   *For each diagram, tell whether X is between P and R. (Answer Yes or No.)*

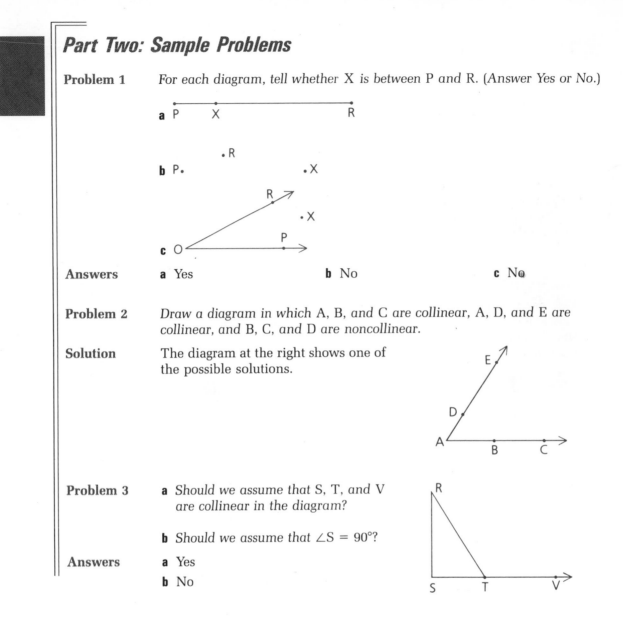

a P   X   R

b P•   •R   •X

c (diagram with rays from O, points R, X, P)

Answers   **a** Yes   **b** No   **c** No

Problem 2   *Draw a diagram in which A, B, and C are collinear, A, D, and E are collinear, and B, C, and D are noncollinear.*

Solution   The diagram at the right shows one of the possible solutions.

Problem 3   **a** *Should we assume that S, T, and V are collinear in the diagram?*

b *Should we assume that ∠S = 90°?*

Answers   **a** Yes

b No

Part Three: Problem Sets

Problem Set A

1 Find m∠ABC (the measure of ∠ABC).

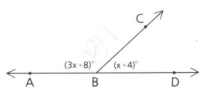

$(3x+8)°$ $(x+4)°$

2 Draw a diagram showing four points, no three of which are collinear.

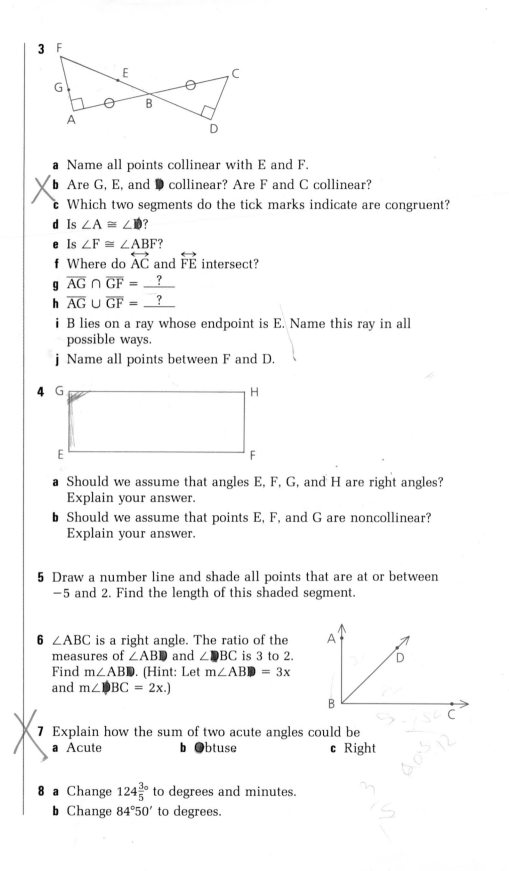

3

a Name all points collinear with E and F.

b Are G, E, and D collinear? Are F and C collinear?

c Which two segments do the tick marks indicate are congruent?

d Is $\angle A \cong \angle D$?

e Is $\angle F \cong \angle ABF$?

f Where do $\overleftrightarrow{AC}$ and $\overleftrightarrow{FE}$ intersect?

g $\overline{AG} \cap \overline{GF} = \underline{\quad ? \quad}$

h $\overline{AG} \cup \overline{GF} = \underline{\quad ? \quad}$

i B lies on a ray whose endpoint is E. Name this ray in all possible ways.

j Name all points between F and D.

4

a Should we assume that angles E, F, G, and H are right angles? Explain your answer.

b Should we assume that points E, F, and G are noncollinear? Explain your answer.

5 Draw a number line and shade all points that are at or between −5 and 2. Find the length of this shaded segment.

6 $\angle ABC$ is a right angle. The ratio of the measures of $\angle ABD$ and $\angle DBC$ is 3 to 2. Find m$\angle ABD$. (Hint: Let m$\angle ABD = 3x$ and m$\angle DBC = 2x$.)

7 Explain how the sum of two acute angles could be

    a Acute   **b** Obtuse   **c** Right

8 a Change $124\frac{3}{5}°$ to degrees and minutes.

    b Change 84°50′ to degrees.

Problem Set A, *continued*

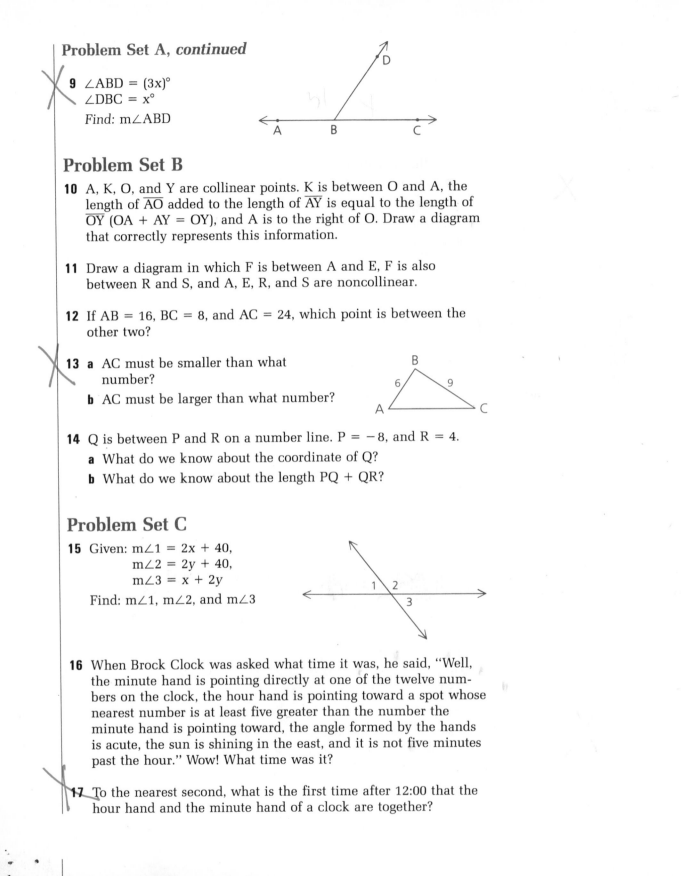

9 ∠ABD = (3x)°
∠DBC = x°

Find: m∠ABD

Problem Set B

10 A, K, O, and Y are collinear points. K is between O and A, the length of $\overline{AO}$ added to the length of $\overline{AY}$ is equal to the length of $\overline{OY}$ (OA + AY = OY), and A is to the right of O. Draw a diagram that correctly represents this information.

11 Draw a diagram in which F is between A and E, F is also between R and S, and A, E, R, and S are noncollinear.

12 If AB = 16, BC = 8, and AC = 24, which point is between the other two?

13 a AC must be smaller than what number?

b AC must be larger than what number?

14 Q is between P and R on a number line. P = −8, and R = 4.

a What do we know about the coordinate of Q?

b What do we know about the length PQ + QR?

Problem Set C

15 Given: m∠1 = 2x + 40,
m∠2 = 2y + 40,
m∠3 = x + 2y

Find: m∠1, m∠2, and m∠3

16 When Brock Clock was asked what time it was, he said, "Well, the minute hand is pointing directly at one of the twelve numbers on the clock, the hour hand is pointing toward a spot whose nearest number is at least five greater than the number the minute hand is pointing toward, the angle formed by the hands is acute, the sun is shining in the east, and it is not five minutes past the hour." Wow! What time was it?

17 To the nearest second, what is the first time after 12:00 that the hour hand and the minute hand of a clock are together?

1.4 BEGINNING PROOFS

Objective

After studying this section, you will be able to
■ Write simple two-column proofs

Part One: Introduction

Much of the enjoyment and challenge of geometry is found in "proving things." In this section, we shall give examples of *two-column proofs.* The two-column proof is the major type of proof you will use as you study this book.

We shall also introduce our first *theorems*.

Definition   A *theorem* is a mathematical statement that can be proved.

This section also illustrates a procedure that we shall use numerous times in this textbook:

Theorem Procedure

1 We present a theorem or theorems.
2 We prove the theorem(s).

   Note   Although all theorems presented can be proved, we shall omit the proofs of certain theorems.

3 We use the theorems to help prove sample problems.
4 You are then given the challenge of using the theorems to prove homework problems. Theorems will save you much time if you learn them and then use them.

We now present our first two theorems.

Theorem 1   *If two angles are right angles, then they are congruent.*

Given: ∠A is a right ∠.
      ∠B is a right ∠.
Prove: ∠A ≅ ∠B

Proof:

Statements	Reasons
1 ∠A is a right angle.	1 Given
2 m∠A = 90	2 If an angle is a right angle, then its measure is 90.
3 ∠B is a right angle.	3 Given
4 m∠B = 90	4 Same as 2
5 ∠A ≅ ∠B	5 If two angles have the same measure, then they are congruent. (See steps 2 and 4.)

Theorem 2   *If two angles are straight angles, then they are congruent.*

Given: ∠ABC is a straight angle.
      ∠DEF is a straight angle.
Prove: ∠ABC ≅ ∠DEF

Proof:

Statements	Reasons
1 ∠ABC is a straight angle.	1 Given
2 m∠ABC = 180	2 If an angle is a straight angle, then its measure is 180.
3 ∠DEF is a straight angle.	3 Given
4 m∠DEF = 180	4 Same as 2
5 ∠ABC ≅ ∠DEF	5 If two angles have the same measure, then they are congruent. (See steps 2 and 4.)

   Now that we have presented and proved two theorems, we are ready to use them to help prove some sample problems.
   We will use the theorems themselves as reasons in our proofs. You should also use the theorems as reasons in your homework problems.
   Remember, the purpose of a theorem is to shorten your work. Therefore, when doing homework problems, do not use the proofs of theorems as a guide. Use the sample problems as a guide.

Part Two: Sample Problems

Problem 1 Given: ∠A is a right angle.
∠C is a right angle.

Conclusion: ∠A ≅ ∠C

Proof

Statements	Reasons
1 ∠A is a right angle.	1 Given
2 ∠C is a right angle.	2 Given
3 ∠A ≅ ∠C	3 If two angles are right angles, then they are congruent.

You probably recognize that reason 3 is Theorem 1. Although it may seem easier merely to write "Theorem 1," *do not do so!* Eventually, such a shortcut would make it harder for you to learn the concepts of geometry.

Problem 2 Given: Diagram as shown

Conclusion: ∠EFG ≅ ∠HFJ

Proof

Statements	Reasons
1 Diagram as shown	1 Given
2 ∠EFG is a straight angle.	2 Assumed from diagram
3 ∠HFJ is a straight angle.	3 Assumed from diagram
4 ∠EFG ≅ ∠HFJ	4 If two angles are straight angles, then they are congruent.

Problem 3 Given: ∠RST = 50°,
∠TSV = 40°;
∠X is a right angle.

Prove: ∠RSV ≅ ∠X

Proof

Statements	Reasons
1 ∠RST = 50°	1 Given
2 ∠TSV = 40°	2 Given
3 ∠RSV = 90°	3 Addition (50° + 40° = 90°)
4 ∠RSV is a right angle.	4 If an angle is a 90° angle, it is a right angle.
5 ∠X is a right angle.	5 Given
6 ∠RSV ≅ ∠X	6 If two angles are right angles, then they are congruent.

Part Three: Problem Sets

Problem Set A

**In problems 1 and 2, copy the figure and the incomplete proof.
Then complete the proof by filling in the missing reasons.**

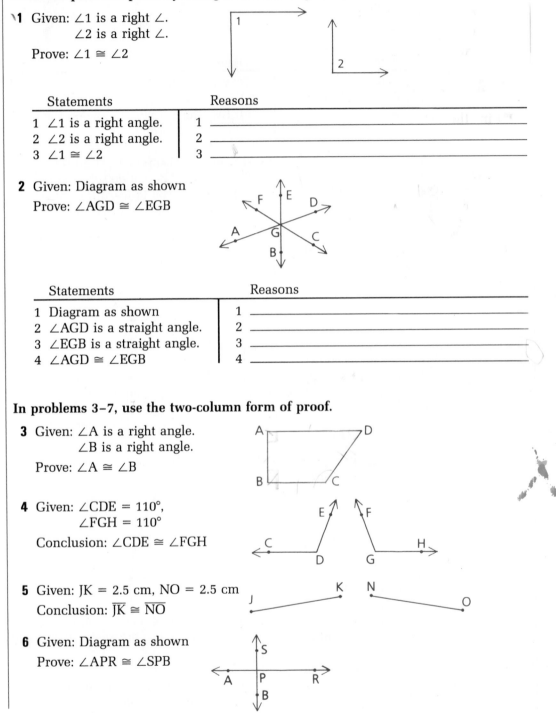

1 Given: ∠1 is a right ∠.
∠2 is a right ∠.

Prove: ∠1 ≅ ∠2

Statements	Reasons
1 ∠1 is a right angle.	1 _____
2 ∠2 is a right angle.	2 _____
3 ∠1 ≅ ∠2	3 _____

2 Given: Diagram as shown
Prove: ∠AGD ≅ ∠EGB

Statements	Reasons
1 Diagram as shown	1 _____
2 ∠AGD is a straight angle.	2 _____
3 ∠EGB is a straight angle.	3 _____
4 ∠AGD ≅ ∠EGB	4 _____

In problems 3–7, use the two-column form of proof.

3 Given: ∠A is a right angle.
∠B is a right angle.

Prove: ∠A ≅ ∠B

4 Given: ∠CDE = 110°,
∠FGH = 110°

Conclusion: ∠CDE ≅ ∠FGH

5 Given: JK = 2.5 cm, NO = 2.5 cm
Conclusion: $\overline{JK}$ ≅ $\overline{NO}$

6 Given: Diagram as shown
Prove: ∠APR ≅ ∠SPB

7 Given: $\angle 1 = 20°$,
$\angle 2 = 40°$,
$\angle 3 = 30°$

Prove: $\angle XYZ$ is a right angle.

8 Draw the figure ABCDEF.
  a Draw its reflection over $\overleftrightarrow{AF}$.
  b Draw its reflection over $\overleftrightarrow{AB}$.
  c Draw a 90° clockwise rotation of the figure about B.

9 Find the angle formed by the hands of a clock at 11:40.

10 The square has a perimeter of 42.
  a Solve for x.
  b If the perimeter were greater than 42, what would we know about the value of x?

Problem Set B

11 Given: $\angle ABD = 10°$,
$\angle ABC = 100°$,
$\angle EFY = 70°20'$,
$\angle XFY = 19°40'$

Prove: $\angle DBC \cong \angle XFE$

12 Point P has a coordinate of 7 on a number line. If you "slide" P 15 units in the negative direction, what are the coordinates of the resulting point P′?

13 a Draw a number line, labeling points A = (−1) and B = (5). Then label point A′, the reflection of A over B.
  b Does AB = BA′?
  c What do we know about point B?

Problem Set C

14 The measure of an obtuse angle is 5y + 45. What are the restrictions on y?

15 Given: $\angle 1 = (x + 7)°$,
$\angle 2 = (2x - 3)°$,
$\angle ABC = (x^2)°$,
$\angle D = (5x - 4)°$

Show that $\angle ABC \cong \angle D$.

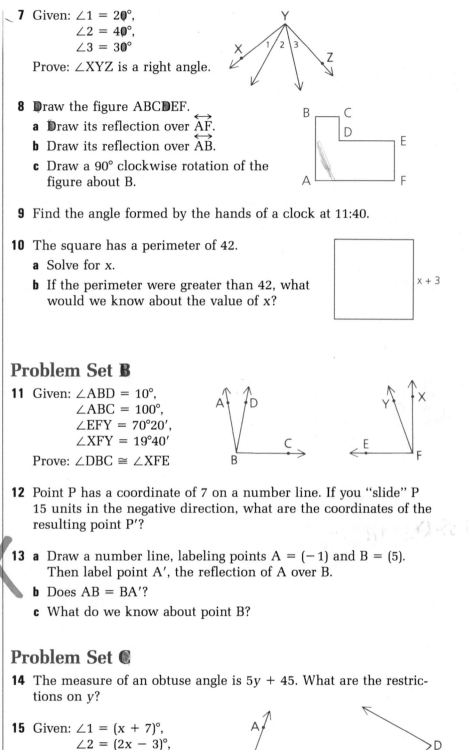

DIVISION OF SEGMENTS AND ANGLES

Objectives

After studying this section, you will be able to
- Identify midpoints and bisectors of segments
- Identify trisection points and trisectors of segments
- Identify angle bisectors
- Identify angle trisectors

Part One: Introduction

Midpoints and Bisectors of Segments

We shall often work with segments that are divided in half.

Definition   A point (or segment, ray, or line) that divides a segment into two congruent segments **bisects** the seg-
ment. The bisection point is called the **midpoint** of
the segment.

X is not a midpoint   Y is not a midpoint

Only segments have midpoints. It does not make sense to say
that a ray or a line has a midpoint. Do you understand why?

How many midpoints does $\overline{PQ}$ have?
How many bisectors could $\overline{PQ}$ have?

Study the following examples.

Example 1   If $\overrightarrow{XY}$ bisects $\overline{AC}$ at B, what conclusions can we draw?
Conclusions:
  B is the midpoint of $\overline{AC}$.
  $\overline{AB} \cong \overline{BC}$

Example 2   If D is the midpoint of $\overline{FE}$, what conclusions can we draw?
Conclusions:
  $\overline{FD} \cong \overline{DE}$
  Point D bisects $\overline{FE}$.
  $\overline{DG}$ bisects $\overline{FE}$.

Example 3 If $\overline{OK} \cong \overline{KP}$, *what conclusions can we draw?*

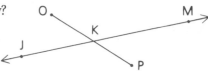

Conclusions:
K is the midpoint of $\overline{OP}$.
$\overleftrightarrow{JM}$ is a bisector of $\overline{OP}$.
Point K bisects $\overline{OP}$.

Trisection Points and Trisecting a Segment

A segment divided into *three* congruent parts is said to be **trisected**.

Definition Two points (or segments, rays, or lines) that divide a segment into three congruent segments **trisect** the segment. The two points at which the segment is divided are called the **trisection points** of the segment.

Again, only segments have trisection points; rays and lines do not have trisection points.

Example 1 If $\overline{AR} \cong \overline{RS} \cong \overline{SC}$, *what conclusions can we draw?*

Conclusions:
R and S are trisection points of $\overline{AC}$.
$\overline{AC}$ is trisected by R and S.

Example 2 *If E and F are trisection points of $\overline{DG}$, what conclusions can we draw?*

Conclusions:
$\overline{DE} \cong \overline{EF} \cong \overline{FG}$
$\overline{HE}$ and $\overline{HF}$ are trisectors of $\overline{DG}$.

Angle Bisectors

An angle, like a segment, can be bisected.

Definition A ray that divides an angle into two congruent angles **bisects** the angle. The dividing ray is called the **bisector** of the angle.

If $\angle ABD \cong \angle DBC$, then $\overrightarrow{BD}$ (not $\overrightarrow{DB}$) is the bisector of $\angle ABC$.

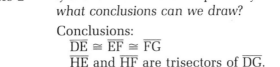

If $\angle NOP \cong \angle POR$ and $\overrightarrow{OQ}$ bisects $\angle POR$, then $\overrightarrow{OP}$ (not $\overrightarrow{PO}$) is the bisector of $\angle NOR$, and $\angle 1 \cong \angle 2$.

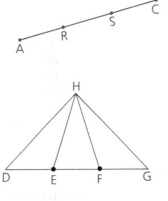

Angle Trisectors

Two rays can divide an angle into three equal parts.

Definition   Two rays that divide an angle into three congruent angles *trisect* the angle. The two dividing rays are called *trisectors* of the angle.

If ∠ABC ≅ ∠CBD ≅ ∠DBE, then $\overrightarrow{BC}$ and $\overrightarrow{BD}$ trisect ∠ABE.

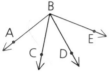

If $\overrightarrow{SV}$ and $\overrightarrow{SX}$ are trisectors of ∠TSY, then ∠TSV ≅ ∠VSX ≅ ∠XSY.

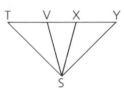

Part Two: Sample Problems

Problem 1   *The tick marks indicate that* $\overline{RS} \cong \overline{ST}$. *Is S the midpoint of* $\overline{RT}$?

Answer   No, the points are not collinear.

Problem 2   *If* $\overrightarrow{BD}$ *bisects* ∠ABC, *does* $\overrightarrow{DB}$ *bisect* ∠ADC?

Answer   No. We need more information.

Problem 3   *If B and C trisect* $\overline{AD}$, *do* $\overrightarrow{EB}$ *and* $\overrightarrow{EC}$ *trisect* ∠AED?

Answer   No! It is true that $\overline{AB} \cong \overline{BC} \cong \overline{CD}$, but the fact that the *segment* has been trisected does not mean that the *angle* has been trisected.

Problem 4   *Given:* $\overrightarrow{PS}$ *bisects* ∠RPO.
Prove: ∠RPS ≅ ∠OPS

Proof

Statements	Reasons
1 $\overrightarrow{PS}$ bisects ∠RPO.	1 Given
2 ∠RPS ≅ ∠OPS	2 If a ray bisects an angle, it divides the angle into two congruent angles.

Problem 5   Given: $\overleftrightarrow{CM}$ bisects $\overline{AB}$ (*In Chapter 3 we shall call* $\overline{CM}$ *a median of the triangle.*)

Conclusion: $\overline{AM} \cong \overline{MB}$

Proof

Statements	Reasons
1 $\overleftrightarrow{CM}$ bisects $\overline{AB}$.	1 Given
2 $\overline{AM} \cong \overline{MB}$	2 If a line bisects a segment, it divides the segment into two congruent segments.

Problem 6   Given: $\overline{DH} \cong \overline{HF}$

Prove: H is the midpoint of $\overline{DF}$.

Proof

Statements	Reasons
1 $\overline{DH} \cong \overline{HF}$	1 Given
2 H is the midpoint of $\overline{DF}$.	2 If a point divides a segment into two congruent segments, it is the midpoint of the segment.

Problem 7 $\overline{EH}$ is divided by F and G in the ratio $5:3:2$ from left to right. If EH = 30, find FG and name the midpoint of $\overline{EH}$.

Solution   According to the ratio, we can let EF = 5x, FG = 3x, and GH = 2x. First we draw a diagram and place the algebra on it as part of the solution.

$$5x + 3x + 2x = 30$$
$$10x = 30$$
$$x = 3$$

Thus, FG = 3(3), or 9. Since EF = 15 and FH = 15, F is the midpoint of $\overline{EH}$.

Problem 8   Given: $\overrightarrow{KO}$ bisects $\angle JKM$.

$\angle JKM = 41°37'$

Find: $m\angle OKM$

Solution $\frac{1}{2}(41°37') = 20\frac{1}{2}°18\frac{1}{2}'$

$= 20°48\frac{1}{2}'$ (since $\frac{1}{2}° = 30'$)

$= 20°48'30''$ (since $\frac{1}{2}' = 30''$)

Part Three: Problem Sets

Problem Set A

1 Name the congruent segments.

    a O is the midpoint of $\overline{CD}$.

    b $\overline{SW}$ bisects $\overline{XV}$.

2 Name the congruent angles.

    a $\overrightarrow{RO}$ bisects ∠NRP.

    b $\overrightarrow{XT}$ and $\overrightarrow{XV}$ trisect ∠SXW.

3 Name the angle bisector.

    a

    b m∠POK = m∠MOK

4 Find ∠XTZ if $\overrightarrow{TZ}$ bisects ∠XTY and ∠XTY equals

    a 60°

    b 48°50′

    c $36\frac{1}{2}°$

    d 85°74′

5 B and C trisect $\overline{AD}$.

    a Find the coordinates of B and C.

    b Find AC.

6 Given: OM = x + 8,
           MP = 2x − 6,
           OP = 44

    Is M the midpoint of $\overline{OP}$?

7 Given: m∠FGJ = 3x − 5,
           m∠JGH = x + 27;
           $\overrightarrow{GJ}$ bisects ∠FGH.

    Find: m∠FGJ

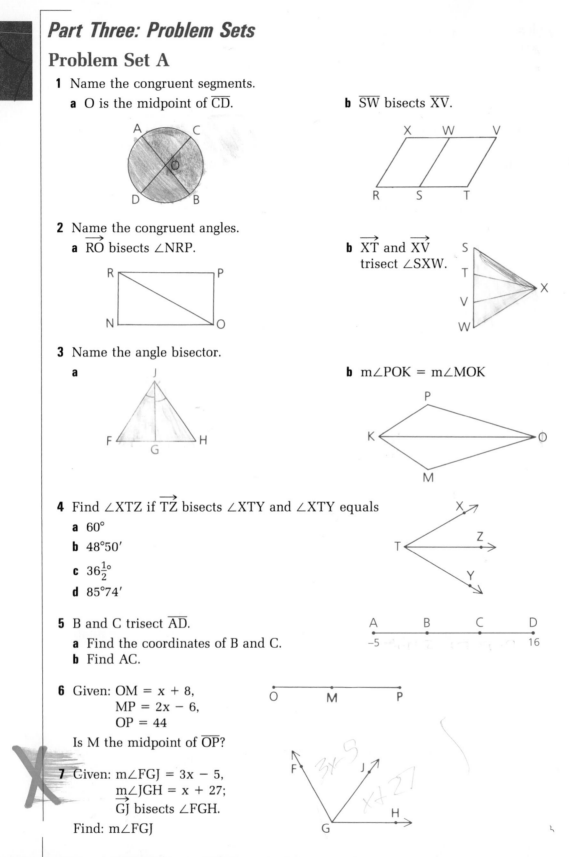

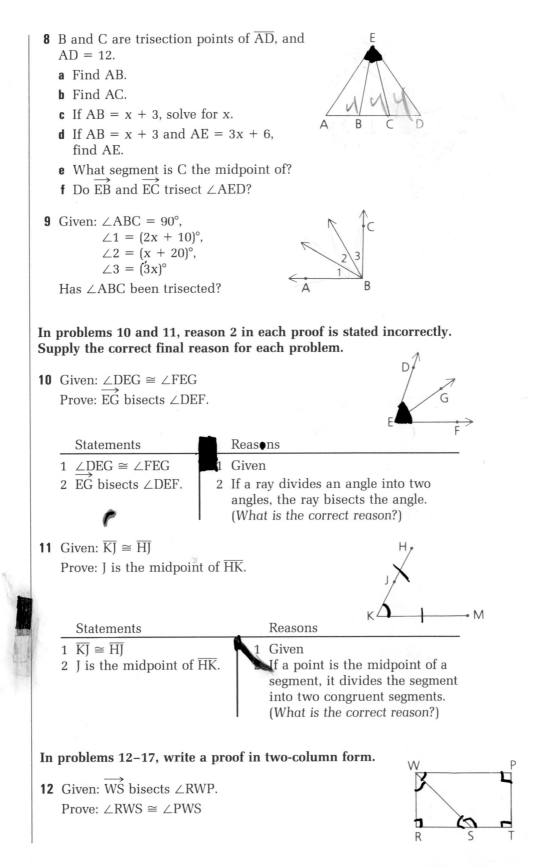

8 B and C are trisection points of $\overline{AD}$, and AD = 12.

  a Find AB.

  b Find AC.

  c If AB = x + 3, solve for x.

  d If AB = x + 3 and AE = 3x + 6, find AE.

  e What segment is C the midpoint of?

  f Do $\overrightarrow{EB}$ and $\overrightarrow{EC}$ trisect ∠AED?

9 Given: ∠ABC = 90°,
         ∠1 = (2x + 10)°,
         ∠2 = (x + 20)°,
         ∠3 = (3x)°

  Has ∠ABC been trisected?

In problems 10 and 11, reason 2 in each proof is stated incorrectly. Supply the correct final reason for each problem.

10 Given: ∠DEG ≅ ∠FEG
    Prove: $\overrightarrow{EG}$ bisects ∠DEF.

Statements	Reasons
1 ∠DEG ≅ ∠FEG	1 Given
2 $\overrightarrow{EG}$ bisects ∠DEF.	2 If a ray divides an angle into two angles, the ray bisects the angle. (*What is the correct reason?*)

11 Given: $\overline{KJ}$ ≅ $\overline{HJ}$
    Prove: J is the midpoint of $\overline{HK}$.

Statements	Reasons
1 $\overline{KJ}$ ≅ $\overline{HJ}$	1 Given
2 J is the midpoint of $\overline{HK}$.	2 If a point is the midpoint of a segment, it divides the segment into two congruent segments. (*What is the correct reason?*)

In problems 12–17, write a proof in two-column form.

12 Given: $\overrightarrow{WS}$ bisects ∠RWP.
    Prove: ∠RWS ≅ ∠PWS

Problem Set A, *continued*

13 Given: $\overline{XY} \cong \overline{YZ}$
Prove: Y is the midpoint of $\overline{XZ}$.

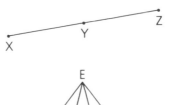

14 Given: $\angle AEB \cong \angle BEC \cong \angle CED$
Conclusion: $\overrightarrow{EB}$ and $\overrightarrow{EC}$ trisect $\angle AED$.

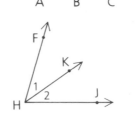

15 Given: $\angle 1 \cong \angle 2$
Conclusion: $\overrightarrow{HK}$ bisects $\angle FHJ$.

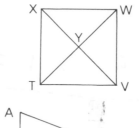

16 Given: $\angle TXW$ is a right angle.
$\angle TYV$ is a right angle.
Prove: $\angle TXW \cong \angle TYV$

17 Given: B is the midpoint of $\overline{AC}$.
Prove: $\overline{AB} \cong \overline{BC}$

Problem Set B

18 $\overrightarrow{OG}$ and $\overrightarrow{OH}$ divide straight angle FOJ into three angles whose measures are in the ratio 4:3:2. Find m$\angle$FOG.

19 Given: $\overleftrightarrow{TP}$ bisects $\overline{VS}$ and $\overline{MR}$.
$\overline{VM} \cong \overline{SR}$,
MP = 9, VT = 6,
perimeter of MRSV = 62
Find: VM

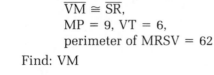

20 $\overrightarrow{PR}$ and $\overrightarrow{PS}$ trisect $\angle QPT$.
 a If m$\angle$RPS = 23°50′,
 find m$\angle$QPT.
 b If m$\angle$QPT = 120°48′30″,
 find m$\angle$QPS.

21 a Find the value of x.

  b Is Q the midpoint of $\overline{PR}$?

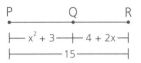

Problem Set C

22 Given: $\overrightarrow{OP}$ and $\overrightarrow{OR}$ trisect $\angle NOS$.

  $m\angle NOP = 3x - 4y$,

  $m\angle POR = x - y$,

  $m\angle ROS = y - 10$

Find: $m\angle ROS$

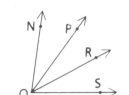

23 $\angle BAC = 120°$, and points D, E, and F are in the interior of $\angle BAC$ as shown. $\overrightarrow{AD}$ bisects $\angle BAF$. $\overrightarrow{AE}$ bisects $\angle CAF$. Find $m\angle DAE$.

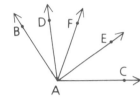

24 The measures of two angles are in the ratio 5:3. The measure of the larger angle is 30 greater than half the difference of the angles. Find the measure of each angle.

1.6 | PARAGRAPH PROOFS

Objective

After studying this section, you will be able to
▪ Write paragraph proofs

Part One: Introduction

Although most of the proofs you will encounter this year will be in two-column form, you also need to be familiar with ***paragraph proofs***. They are important because the proofs in journals, more-advanced mathematics courses, and other areas of study are usually in paragraph form.

The sample problems that follow demonstrate how to write paragraph proofs, as well as how to show that a particular conclusion cannot be proved true or can be proved false.

Part Two: Sample Problems

Problem 1   Given: $\angle O = 67\frac{1}{2}°$,
$\angle P = 67°30'$
Prove: $\angle O \cong \angle P$

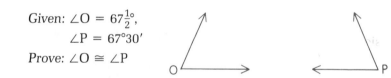

Proof   Since there are 60 minutes in 1 degree, $67°30'$ equals $67\frac{1}{2}°$.
Since $\angle O$ and $\angle P$ have the same measure, they are congruent.

Problem 2   Given: *Diagram shown*
Prove: $\angle DBC \cong \angle E$

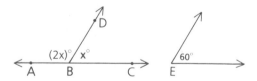

Proof   According to the diagram, $\angle ABC$ is a straight angle. Therefore,

$$2x + x = 180$$
$$3x = 180$$
$$x = 60$$

Since $\angle DBC = 60°$ and $\angle E = 60°$, the angles are congruent.

36 | Chapter 1   Introduction to Geometry

Problem 3   Given: ∠1 *is acute.*
                            ∠2 *is acute.*
                 Conclusion: ∠1 ≅ ∠2

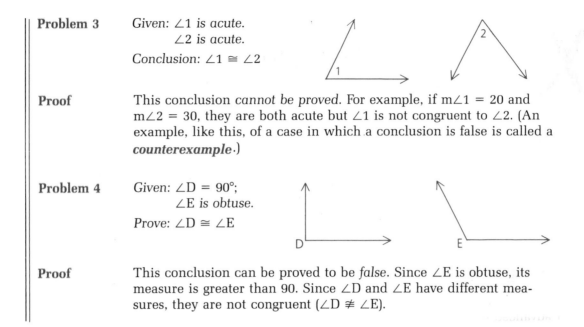

Proof   This conclusion *cannot be proved.* For example, if m∠1 = 20 and
                 m∠2 = 30, they are both acute but ∠1 is not congruent to ∠2. (An
                 example, like this, of a case in which a conclusion is false is called a
                 ***counterexample*.**)

Problem 4   Given: ∠D = 90°;
                            ∠E *is obtuse.*
                 Prove: ∠D ≅ ∠E

Proof   This conclusion can be proved to be *false.* Since ∠E is obtuse, its
                 measure is greater than 90. Since ∠D and ∠E have different mea-
                 sures, they are not congruent (∠D ≇ ∠E).

Part Three: Problem Sets

Problem Set A

In problems 1–6, write paragraph proofs.

1 Given: ∠V = $119\frac{2}{3}$°,
            ∠S = 119°40′
      Conclusion: ∠V ≅ ∠S

2 Given: Diagram shown
      Prove: ∠FEH ≅ ∠JKM

3 Given: Diagram shown, ∠OPT = 90°
      Prove: The measure of ∠VAY is twice that
             of ∠RPT.

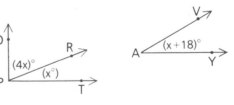

4 Given: AB = x + 4,
            BC = 2x,
            AC = 16
      Conclusion: $\overline{AB} ≅ \overline{BC}$

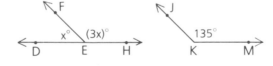

Problem Set A, *continued*

5 Given: ∠D is obtuse.
    ∠C is greater than 90° (∠C > 90°).
Conclusion: ∠D ≅ ∠C

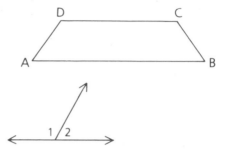

6 Given: ∠1 is obtuse.
    ∠2 is acute.
Prove: ∠1 ≅ ∠2

Problem Set B

In problems 7–9, write paragraph proofs.

7 Prove that if ∠1 ≅ ∠2, they are both
right angles.

8 Prove the following statement: "If an obtuse angle is bisected,
each of the two resulting angles is acute."

9 Given: $\overrightarrow{CE}$ bisects ∠BCD.
    ∠A is a right angle.
    m∠BCE = 45
Prove: ∠A ≅ ∠BCD

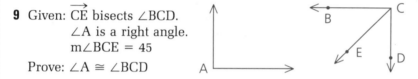

Problem Set C

In problems 10 and 11, write paragraph proofs.

10 Given: Diagram shown;
    $\overrightarrow{AC}$ bisects ∠BAD.
    $\overrightarrow{AE}$ bisects ∠DAF.
Prove: ∠CAE is a right angle.

11 Given: m∠J + m∠H + m∠JKH = 180
Prove: **a** m∠1 = m∠J + m∠H
    b m∠1 > m∠J

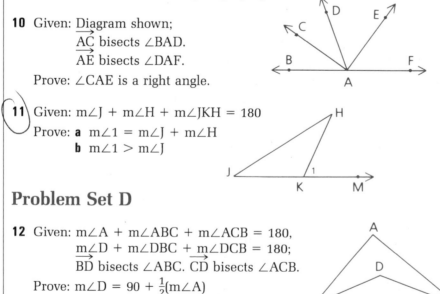

Problem Set D

12 Given: m∠A + m∠ABC + m∠ACB = 180,
    m∠D + m∠DBC + m∠DCB = 180;
    $\overrightarrow{BD}$ bisects ∠ABC. $\overrightarrow{CD}$ bisects ∠ACB.
Prove: m∠D = $90 + \frac{1}{2}$(m∠A)
    (Write a paragraph proof.)

1.7 DEDUCTIVE STRUCTURE

Objectives

After studying this section, you will be able to
- Recognize that geometry is based on a deductive structure
- Identify undefined terms, postulates, and definitions
- Understand the characteristics of theorems and the ways in which they can be used in proofs

Part One: Introduction

The Structure of Geometry

You have just spent a few days writing two-column proofs and paragraph proofs. Since you have learned how to prove a few statements, you may be interested in knowing something about the theory of proofs.

Geometry is based on a ***deductive structure***—a system of thought in which conclusions are justified by means of previously assumed or proved statements. Every deductive structure contains the following four elements.

- Undefined terms
- Assumptions known as ***postulates***
- Definitions
- Theorems and other conclusions

Undefined Terms, Postulates, and Definitions

Undefined terms, postulates, and definitions form the foundation on which the rest of a deductive structure is based. Examples of the undefined terms you have already encountered are *point* and *line*. Although we have not defined these terms, we have described points and lines, so that everyone should have a fairly clear idea of what they are.

As yet, we have not formally presented any postulates. We have, however, used some algebraic postulates in solving problems.

Definition   A ***postulate*** is an unproved assumption.

The postulates presented in this book will be preceded by the heading **Postulate**.

You have already seen a number of definitions, such as the definitions of *acute angle*, *right angle*, *obtuse angle*, and *straight angle*.

Definition   A *definition* states the meaning of a term or idea.

In this book, important definitions are identified by the heading **Definition**.

One very important characteristic of definitions is that they are *reversible*. For example, the definition of *midpoint* (of a segment) can be expressed in either of two ways:

1 If a point is the midpoint of a segment, then the point divides the segment into two congruent segments.
2 If a point divides a segment into two congruent segments, then the point is the midpoint of the segment.

In some problems, form 1 of the definition of *midpoint* must be used. In other problems the definition must be *reversed*, as in form 2 above.

Notice that this definition is stated in the form

"If p, then q"

where p and q are declarative statements. Such a sentence is called a *conditional statement* or an *implication*. The "if" part of the sentence is called the *hypothesis*. The "then" part of the sentence is called the *conclusion*. "If p, then q" can be symbolized $p \Rightarrow q$ (also read "p implies q").

The *converse* of $p \Rightarrow q$ is $q \Rightarrow p$. To write the converse of a conditional ("If . . . , then . . . ") statement, you reverse parts p and q. The converse of "If p, then q" is "If q, then p," so forms 1 and 2 of the definition of *midpoint* are converses of each other.

Theorems

As you have seen, a theorem is a mathematical statement that can be proved. Almost all the theorems presented in this book will be numbered for ease of reference. Each theorem will be preceded by a heading such as the following:

Theorem 78

You will prove some theorems and other relationships as homework problems. As you work, remember that you must prove conclusions by using conclusions previously assumed or proved. Thus, you cannot use Theorem 1 in order to prove Theorem 1.

Theorems and postulates are not always reversible. For example, "If two angles are right angles, then they are congruent" is true. The converse statement, "If two angles are congruent, then they are right angles," is false.

Remember,

- *Definitions* are always reversible
- *Theorems* and *postulates* are not always reversible

If you are to be successful in writing proofs, you must memorize postulates, definitions, and theorems. There is no easier way.

A complete mastery of the deductive structure of geometry is not possible in a short time. However, we do wish to point out the most common error that students make—using the converse of a statement at the wrong time.

It is important to pay attention to the direction of the flow of logic in order to avoid this error. The theorem "If two angles are right angles, then they are congruent" means that whenever we encounter right angles, we can conclude that they are congruent. There is a flow from *right angles* to *congruent*.

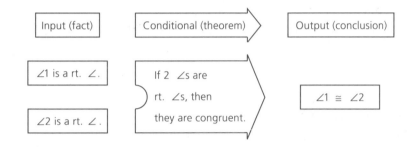

In this case, the flow works in only one direction—the converse of the statement, "If two angles are congruent, then they are right angles" is not true. *Remember, only definitions are always reversible. Theorems and postulates are not always reversible.*

The major purpose of this section and the next is to acquaint you with some terminology. As you study Chapter 2 and Chapter 3, you will grow to appreciate and understand these sections even more. The homework problems in these sections are rather different from those you have been solving, and we think you will enjoy them.

Part Two: Sample Problem

Problem   *State the converse of each of the following statements and tell whether the converse is true or false.*

a *If an angle contains 90 degrees, it is a right angle.*
b *If Mary received a B on her history test, then she passed the test.*

Answers   **a** *If an angle is a right angle, it contains 90 degrees. (True)*
b *If Mary passed her history test, she received a B on the test. (False)*

Part Three: Problem Sets

Problem Set A

1 What four elements are found in any deductive structure?

2 Which of the following kinds of statements are always reversible?

   a Definitions   **b** Theorems   **c** Postulates

3 Answer each question Yes or No.

   a Do we prove theorems?   **b** Do we prove definitions?

4 Tell whether each of the following statements is a theorem or a definition.

   a If two angles are right angles, then they are congruent.   **b** If a ray bisects an angle, it divides the angle into two congruent angles.

5 a Write the converse of each of the following statements.

     i If A, then B.
     ii Rain $\Rightarrow$ wet
     iii If an angle is a 45° angle, then it is acute.
     iv If a point is the midpoint of a segment, it divides the segment into two congruent segments.

   b Discuss the truth of each of the converses in part **a**.

In problems 6 and 7, comment on the reasoning used.

6 The school colors are orange and black, so I'll wear my orange skirt to the game and everyone will notice me.

7 I've flipped this silver dollar five times and the toss has come up heads each time. Thus, the odds are greater than 50–50 that the toss will come up tails next time.

Problem Set B

In problems 8–12, study each of the arguments and state whether or not the conclusion is deducible. If it is not, comment on the error in the reasoning.

8 If a student at Niles High has room 303 as his or her homeroom, the student is a freshman. Joe Jacobs is a student at Niles High and has room 303 as his homeroom. Therefore, Joe Jacobs is a freshman.

9 If the three angles of a triangle are acute, then the triangle is acute. In triangle ABC, angle A and angle B are acute. Therefore, triangle ABC is acute.

10 All school buses stop at railroad crossings. A vehicle stopped at the Santa Fe railroad crossing. Therefore, that vehicle is a school bus.

11 All cloudy days are depressing. Therefore, since I was depressed on Thursday, Thursday was cloudy.

12 If two angles of a triangle are congruent, then the sides opposite them are congruent. In △ABC, ∠A ≅ ∠B. Therefore, in △ABC, $\overline{BC} \cong \overline{AC}$.

Problem Set C

13 Study the following five statements.

1 Spoof is the set of all purrs.
2 Spoof contains at least two distinct purrs.
3 Every lilt is a set of purrs and contains at least two distinct purrs.
4 If A and B are any two distinct purrs, there is one and only one lilt that contains them.
5 No lilt contains all the purrs.

a Show that each of the following statements is true.
   i There is at least one lilt.
   ii There are at least three purrs.
   iii There are at least three lilts.

b If the lilt "girt" contains the purr "pil" and the purr "til" and if the lilt "mirt" contains the purr "pil" and the purr "til" then the lilt "girt" is the same as the lilt "mirt" except in one case. What is this case?

14 The Bronx Zoo has a green lizard, a red crocodile, and a purple monkey. They are the only animals of their kind in existence. One violently windy Saturday, their name tags blew off, and their keeper's journal was torn to shreds. Inasmuch as they were to appear on television at 7:30 Sunday morning, the night watchman had to replace their name tags. He managed to piece together the following information from the mangled journal.

1 Wendy cannot get along with the lizard.
2 Katie playfully took a bite out of the monkey's ear one month ago.
3 Wendy never casts a red reflection in the mirror.
4 Jody has the personality of a crocodile, but she isn't one.

Match the animals with their names.

STATEMENTS OF LOGIC

Objective

After studying this section, you will be able to
- Recognize conditional statements
- Recognize the negation of a statement
- Recognize the converse, the inverse, and the contrapositive of a statement
- Use the chain rule to draw conclusions

Part One: Introduction

Review of Conditional Statements

In this section, we will review and extend the discussion of conditional statements in Section 1.7. Recall that a conditional statement is a sentence that is in the form "If . . ., then . . ." Many declarative sentences can be rewritten in conditional form.

Declarative Sentence:
- Two straight angles are congruent.

Conditional Form:
- If two angles are straight angles, then they are congruent.

Remember that
- The clause following the word *if* is called the hypothesis
- The clause following the word *then* is called the conclusion
- The conditional statement "If p, then q" can be written in symbols as $p \Rightarrow q$

Negation

The ***negation*** of any statement p is the statement "not p." (Thus, the negation of "It is raining" is "It is not raining.") The symbol for "not p" is $\sim p$. Notice also that the negation of "It is not raining" is "It is raining"—in general, not (not p) = p, or $\sim \sim p = p$.

Converse, Inverse, and Contrapositive

Every conditional statement "If p, then q" has three other statements associated with it. (You have already been introduced to the first of these—the converse).

1 A converse (If q, then p.)
2 An ***inverse*** (If $\sim p$, then $\sim q$.)
3 A ***contrapositive*** (If $\sim q$, then $\sim p$.)

Example *Find the converse, the inverse, and the contrapositive of the statement "If you live in Atlanta, then you live in Georgia."*

The statement is in the form "If *p*, then *q*," with *p* being "You live in Atlanta" and *q* being "You live in Georgia."

Converse: "If you live in Georgia, then you live in Atlanta."
        (If *q*, then *p*.)

Inverse: "If you don't live in Atlanta, then you don't live in Georgia."
        (If ~*p*, then ~*q*.)

Contrapositive: "If you don't live in Georgia, then you don't live in Atlanta." (If ~*q*, then ~*p*.)

You may have noticed that some of the statements in the preceding example are not necessarily true, although the original statement is true. A useful tool for determining whether or not a conditional statement is true or false is a **Venn diagram**. Assume that the following statement is true: "If Jenny lives in Atlanta, then Jenny must live in Georgia."

All the people who live in Georgia are represented by points on the large circle and in its interior (G).

All the people who live in Atlanta are represented by points on the small circle and in its interior (A).

Notice that every person in set A, including Jenny (J), is also in set G.

The Venn diagram for this conditional statement may be used to test whether its converse, inverse, and contrapositive are true or false.

Converse: "If Jenny lives in Georgia, then she must live in Atlanta."

This statement is not necessarily true, as shown by the diagram. Notice that point J may lie in G but not in A. This means that Jenny could live in Georgia and yet not live in Atlanta.

In general, the converse of a conditional statement is not necessarily true. Try a similar argument with the same Venn diagram to convince yourself that the inverse of a conditional statement is also not necessarily true.

Contrapositive: "If Jenny does not live in Georgia, then she does not live in Atlanta."

This time point J lies outside of G, so it *cannot* lie in A. Any point that is not in G is also not in A. Therefore, the contrapositive is true.

This analysis suggests the following important theorem:

Theorem 3   **If a conditional statement is true, then the contra-positive of the statement is also true.**
(If p, then q ⟺ If ~q, then ~p.)

In other words, a statement and its contrapositive are *logically equivalent.*

Chains of Reasoning

Each proof that you do involves a series of steps in a logical sequence. In many cases, the sequence will take the following form.

If $p \Rightarrow q$ and $q \Rightarrow r$, then $p \Rightarrow r$.

This is called the **chain rule**, and a series of conditional statements so connected is known as a **chain of reasoning**.

Example   *If we accept the two statements "If you study hard, then you will earn a good grade" ($p \Rightarrow q$) and "If you earn a good grade, then your family will be happy" ($q \Rightarrow r$), what can we conclude?*

We can conclude that $p \Rightarrow r$—that is, if you study hard, then your family will be happy.

Part Two: Sample Problems

Problem 1   *Write the converse, the inverse, and the contrapositive of the following true statement: "If two angles are right angles, then they are congruent."*

Solution   Converse: "If two angles are congruent, then they are right angles." (The converse is false; for example, each angle may have a measure of 60.)

Inverse: "If two angles are not right angles, then they are not congruent." (The inverse is also false.)

Contrapositive: "If two angles are not congruent, then they are not right angles." (The contrapositive is true—the statements are logically equivalent.)

Problem 2   *Draw a conclusion from the following statements:*

If gremlins grow grapes, then elves eat earthworms.
If trolls don't tell tales, then wizards weave willows.
If trolls tell tales, then elves don't eat earthworms.

Solution   First, we rewrite the statements in symbolic form.

(1) $g \Rightarrow e$
(2) $\sim t \Rightarrow w$
(3) $t \Rightarrow \sim e$

To complete the chain of reasoning, we can rearrange the statements and use contrapositives as needed to match symbols. Thus,

(1) $g \Rightarrow e$
(3) $e \Rightarrow \sim t$ ($t \Rightarrow \sim e$ is equivalent to $e \Rightarrow \sim t$.)
(2) $\sim t \Rightarrow w$
∴ $g \Rightarrow w$ (The symbol ∴ means "therefore.")

Hence, if gremlins grow grapes, then wizards weave willows.

Part Three: Problem Sets

Problem Set A

1 Write each sentence in conditional ("If . . ., then . . .") form.

  a Eighteen-year-olds may vote in federal elections.

  b Opposite angles of a parallelogram are congruent.

2 Write the converse, the inverse, and the contrapositive of each statement. Determine the truth of each of the new statements.

  a If each side of a triangle has a length of 10, then the triangle's perimeter is 30.

  b If an angle is acute, then it has a measure greater than 0 and less than 90.

3 If a conditional statement and its converse are both true, the statement is said to be *biconditional*. Which of these statements is biconditional?

  a If two angles are congruent, then they have the same measure.

  b If two angles are straight angles, then they are congruent.

4 Draw a Venn diagram for the true conditional statement "If a person lives in Chicago, then the person lives in Illinois." Assuming that each of the following "Given . . ." statements is true, determine the truth of the conclusion.

  a Given: Penny lives in Chicago.
    Conclusion: Penny lives in Illinois.

  b Given: Benny lives in Illinois.
    Conclusion: Benny lives in Chicago.

  c Given: Kenny does not live in Chicago.
    Conclusion: Kenny must live in Illinois.

  d Given: Denny does not live in Illinois.
    Conclusion: Denny lives in Chicago.

Problem Set A, *continued*

5 Write a concluding statement for each of the following chains of reasoning.

a $a \Rightarrow b$ **b** $p \Rightarrow \sim q$
    $d \Rightarrow \sim c$ $r \Rightarrow q$
    $\sim c \Rightarrow a$ $s \Rightarrow r$
    $b \Rightarrow f$

c If weasels walk wisely, then cougars call their cubs.
    If goats go to graze, then horses head for home.
    If cougars call their cubs, then goats go to graze.
    If bobcats begin to browse, then weasels walk wisely.

Problem Set B

6 Write the converse, the inverse, and the contrapositive of "If M is the midpoint of $\overline{AB}$, then M, A, and B are collinear." Are these statements true or false?

7 Rewrite the following sentence in conditional form and find its converse, inverse, and contrapositive: "A square is a quadrilateral with four congruent sides."

8 Write the converse, the inverse, and the contrapositive of each statement.

a If a ray bisects an angle, it divides the angle into two congruent angles.

b If two sides of a triangle are congruent, then the angles opposite those sides are congruent.

9 What conclusion can be drawn from the following?

$\sim c \Rightarrow \sim f$ $g \Rightarrow b$ $p \Rightarrow f$ $c \Rightarrow \sim b$

Problem Set C

10 What conclusion can be drawn from the following?

    If the line is long, then Quincy will go home.
    If it is morning, then Quincy will not go home.
    If the line is long, then it is morning.

PROBABILITY

IF YOU HAVE 5 DOGS, 3 WILL BE ASLEEP

1.9 | PROBABILITY

Objective

After studying this section, you will be able to
- Solve probability problems

Part One: Introduction

A knowledge of *probability* is obviously important to an insurance company, to a card player or a backgammon expert, and to an operator of a gambling casino. Moreover, setting up and solving probability problems requires the precision and the organized, ordered thinking needed by secretaries, accountants, doctors, filing clerks, computer programmers, and geometry students.

    Although probability is not one of the major topics in this book, you will occasionally encounter probability problems in the problem sets. You can analyze such problems by following a simple two-step procedure.

Two Basic Steps for Probability Problems

1 Determine all possibilities in a logical manner. Count them.
2 Determine the number of these possibilities that are "favorable." We shall call these *winners*.

You can then calculate the probability by means of the following formula.

$$\text{Probability} = \frac{\text{number of winners}}{\text{number of possibilities}}$$

Part Two: Sample Problems

Problem 1   *If one of the four points is picked at random, what is the probability that the point lies on the angle?*

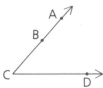

| **Solution** | We follow the two basic steps by listing all the possibilities and circling the winners. |

$$\circledA \quad \circledB \quad \circledC \quad \circledD$$

$$\frac{\text{Winners}}{\text{Possibilities}} = \frac{4}{4} = 1$$

Problem 2   *If two of the four points are selected at random, what is the probability that both lie on* $\overrightarrow{CA}$?

Solution   We follow the two basic steps by listing all the possibilities and circling the winners. (Notice how we have attempted to list the possibilities in an orderly manner.)

$$\text{\textcircled{AB}} \qquad \text{\textcircled{BC}} \qquad CD$$
$$\text{\textcircled{AC}} \qquad BD$$
$$AD$$

$$\frac{\text{Winners}}{\text{Possibilities}} = \frac{3}{6} = \frac{1}{2}$$

Problem 3   *If three of the four points are selected in a random order, what is the probability that the ordered letters will correctly name the angle shown?*

Solution   We follow the two basic steps by listing all the possibilities and circling the winners. (This problem is harder than the first two examples because the *order* of the points is important. Notice how we have listed the possibilities in an orderly manner.)

ABC	BAC	CAB	DAB
ABD	BAD	CAD	DAC
ACB	BCA	CBA	DBA
⟨ACD⟩	⟨BCD⟩	CBD	DBC
ADB	BDA	CDA	⟨DCA⟩
ADC	BDC	CDB	⟨DCB⟩

$$\frac{\text{Winners}}{\text{Possibilities}} = \frac{4}{24} = \frac{1}{6}$$

Problem 4   *A point Q is randomly chosen on* $\overline{AB}$. *What is the probability that it is within 5 units of C?*

Solution   Even though there are infinitely many points on the segment, we can find the probability by comparing the length of the "winning" region with the total length of $\overline{AB}$.

A ├─ 5 ─┼─ 5 ─┤ B
  C
3   11   15
├─ 5 ─┼─ 4 ─┤

The "winning" region is 9 (not 10) units long. $\overline{AB}$ is 12 units long.

Probability $= \dfrac{9}{12} = \dfrac{3}{4}$

Part Three: Problem Sets

Problem Set A

In problems 1–4, refer to the following diagram.

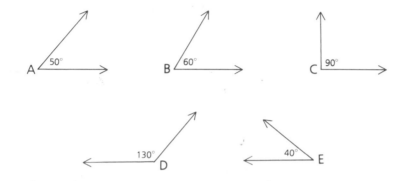

1 If one of the five angles is selected at random, what is the probability that the angle is acute?

2 If one of the five angles is selected at random, what is the probability that the angle is right?

3 If one of the five angles is selected at random, what is the probability that the angle is obtuse?

4 If one of the five angles is selected at random, what is the probability that the angle is straight?

5 If a point is randomly chosen on $\overline{PR}$, what is the probability that it is within 2 units of R?

P
•
4   6   8   10
R

Problem Set B

In problems 6–9, use the five angles shown at the beginning of Problem Set A.

6 If two of the five angles are selected at random, what is the probability that both are acute?

7 If two of the five angles are selected at random, what is the probability that one of them is obtuse?

8 If two of the five angles are selected at random, what is the probability that one is right and the other is obtuse?

Problem Set B, *continued*

9 An angle is selected at random from the five angles and then replaced. A second selection is then made at random. (Thus, the same angle might be selected twice.) What is the probability that an acute angle is selected both times?

10 If a point B is chosen on $\overline{AC}$, what is the probability that $-5 \le B \le 7$?

A
−20   −5   7 10
C

11 The second hand of a clock sweeps continuously around the face of the clock. What is the probability that at any random moment the second hand is between 7 and 12?

Problem Set C

12 If two of the five angles shown in Problem Set A are selected at random, what is the probability that neither angle is acute?

13 If the four points shown are to be labeled with the letters A, B, C, and D in such a way that A and two of the other points are collinear, in how many different ways can the diagram be labeled?

14 Consider points A, B, C, D, and E as shown.

E   D   C

A   B

a If two of these points are selected at random, what is the probability that they are collinear?

b If three of these points are selected at random, what is the probability that they are collinear?

c If four of these points are selected at random, what is the probability that they are collinear?

15 If a point is chosen at random in rectangle ABCD, what is the probability that

a It is in square SQUA?

b It is not in square SQUA?

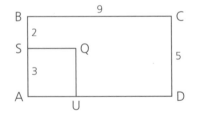

CHAPTER SUMMARY

CONCEPTS AND PROCEDURES

After studying this chapter, you should be able to
- Recognize points, lines, segments, rays, angles, and triangles (1.1)
- Measure segments and angles (1.2)
- Classify angles and name the parts of a degree (1.2)
- Recognize congruent angles and segments (1.2)
- Recognize collinear and noncollinear points (1.3)
- Recognize when a point is between two other points (1.3)
- Apply the triangle-inequality principle (1.3)
- Correctly interpret geometric diagrams (1.3)
- Write simple two-column proofs (1.4)
- Identify bisectors and trisectors of segments and angles (1.5)
- Write paragraph proofs (1.6)
- Recognize that geometry is based on a deductive structure (1.7)
- Identify undefined terms, postulates, and definitions (1.7)
- Understand the characteristics and application of theorems (1.7)
- Recognize conditional statements and the negation, the converse, the inverse, and the contrapositive of a statement (1.8)
- Use the chain rule to draw conclusions (1.8)
- Solve probability problems (1.9)

VOCABULARY

acute angle (1.2)
angle (1.1)
bisect, bisector (1.5)
chain rule (1.8)
collinear (1.3)
conclusion (1.7)
conditional statement (1.7)
congruent angles (1.2)
congruent segments (1.2)
contrapositive (1.8)
converse (1.7)
counterexample (1.6)
deductive structure (1.7)
definition (1.7)
endpoint (1.1)
hypothesis (1.7)

implication (1.7)
intersection (1.1)
inverse (1.8)
line (1.1)
line segment (1.1)
measure (1.2)
midpoint (1.5)
minute (1.2)
negation (1.8)
noncollinear (1.3)
number line (1.1)
obtuse angle (1.2)
paragraph proof (1.6)
point (1.1)
postulate (1.7)
probability (1.9)

protractor (1.2)
ray (1.1)
right angle (1.2)
second (1.2)
segment (1.1)
straight angle (1.2)
theorem (1.4)
tick mark (1.2)
triangle (1.1)
trisect, trisectors (1.5)
trisection points (1.5)
two-column proof (1.4)
union (1.1)
Venn diagram (1.8)
vertex (1.1)

REVIEW PROBLEMS

Problem Set A

1 a Name in all possible ways, the line containing A, R, and D.

b Name the sides of ∠ABC.

c What side do ∠2 and ∠4 have in common?

d Name the horizontal ray with end-point C.

e Estimate the sizes of ∠BAD, ∠2, and ∠ABC.

f Are angles FCD and DCE different angles?

g Which angle in the figure is ∠B?

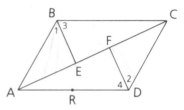

h $\overrightarrow{EC} \cup \overrightarrow{FA} =$ ___?___

i $\overrightarrow{EC} \cap \overrightarrow{FA} =$ ___?___

j $\overrightarrow{BA} \cup \overrightarrow{BE} =$ ___?___

k $\overleftrightarrow{AC} \cap \overleftrightarrow{DR} =$ ___?___

l ∠AFD ∩ $\overline{CE}$ = ___?___

2 Tell whether each of the following angles *appears* to be acute, right, obtuse, or straight. Which angle's classification can be assumed from the diagram?

a ∠H

b ∠G

c ∠GFE

d ∠DEF

e ∠HDF

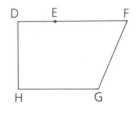

3 a 43°15′17″ + 25°49′18″ = ___?___

b 90° − 39°17″ = ___?___

4 a Change $46\frac{7}{8}°$ to degrees, minutes, and seconds.

b Change 132°6′ to degrees.

5 a According to the diagram, which two segments are congruent?

b According to the diagram, which two angles are congruent?

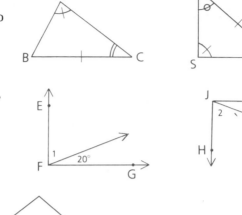

6 a If ∠EFG is obtuse and ∠HJK is right, is ∠1 ≅ ∠2?

b If ∠EFG ≅ ∠HJK, is ∠1 ≅ ∠2?

7 If ∠A ≅ ∠B, find m∠A.

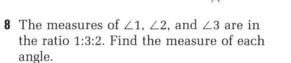

8 The measures of ∠1, ∠2, and ∠3 are in the ratio 1:3:2. Find the measure of each angle.

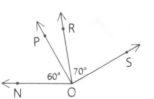

9 Is it possible for both ∠NOR and ∠POS to be right angles?

In problems 10 and 11, copy each figure and incomplete proof. Then complete the proof by filling in the missing reasons.

10 Given: Diagram as shown

Prove: ∠EFG ≅ ∠HJK

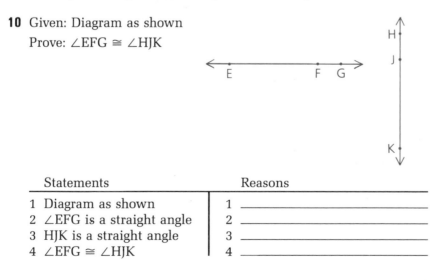

Statements	Reasons
1 Diagram as shown	1 _____
2 ∠EFG is a straight angle	2 _____
3 HJK is a straight angle	3 _____
4 ∠EFG ≅ ∠HJK	4 _____

11 Given: ∠ABC = 130°,
    ∠ABD = 60°

Prove: ∠DBC is acute.

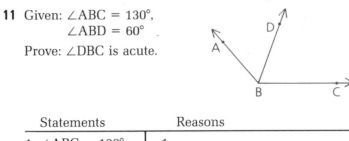

Statements	Reasons
1 ∠ABC = 130°	1 _____
2 ∠ABD = 60°	2 _____
3 ∠DBC = 70°	3 _____
4 ∠DBC is acute	4 _____

In problems 12–15, write each proof in two-column form.

12 Given: ∠X is a right angle.
    ∠Y is a right angle.

Prove: ∠X ≅ ∠Y

13 Given: $\overline{AB} \cong \overline{BC}$
    Prove: B is the midpoint of $\overline{AC}$.

14 Given: $\overrightarrow{DF}$ and $\overrightarrow{DG}$ trisect ∠EDH.
    Conclusion: ∠EDF ≅ ∠FDG ≅ ∠GDH

15 Given: $\overrightarrow{TW}$ bisects ∠VTX.
    Prove: ∠VTW ≅ ∠XTW

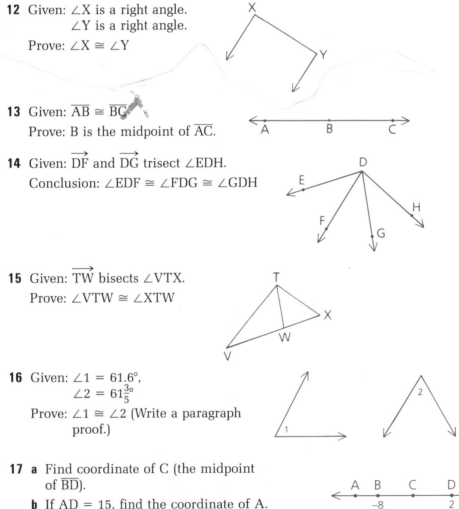

16 Given: ∠1 = 61.6°,
    ∠2 = $61\frac{3}{5}°$

Prove: ∠1 ≅ ∠2 (Write a paragraph
    proof.)

17 a Find coordinate of C (the midpoint
    of $\overline{BD}$).

   b If AD = 15, find the coordinate of A.

18 Copy the diagram and draw △A′B′C′, the reflection of △ABC, over ℓ₂. What is the length of A′B′?

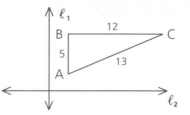

19 a If one of the five labeled points is selected at random, what is the probability that it is a midpoint?

b If two of the five points are randomly chosen, what is the probability that both are midpoints?

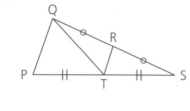

20 Given: $\overrightarrow{OR}$ and $\overrightarrow{OS}$ trisect ∠TOP.
$$∠TOP = 40.2°$$
Find: m∠POR

21 Find the angle formed by the hands of a clock at each time.
  a 1:00   **b** 11:20   **c** 4:45

22 Write the converse, the inverse, and the contrapositive of the statement "If the time is 2:00, then the angle formed by the hands of a clock is acute." Are these statements true or false?

Problem Set B

23 The perimeter of PRST is 10 more than 5(RS). If PR = 26, find RS.

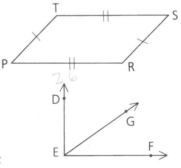

24 Given: ∠DEG = $(x + 3y)°$,
  ∠GEF = $(2x + y)°$;
  ∠DEF is a right angle.
  a Solve for y in terms of x.
  b If ∠DEG ≅ ∠GEF, find the values of x and y.

25 Given: WY = 25;
  The ratio of WX to XY is 3:2.
  Find: WX

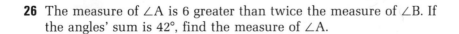

26 The measure of ∠A is 6 greater than twice the measure of ∠B. If the angles' sum is 42°, find the measure of ∠A.

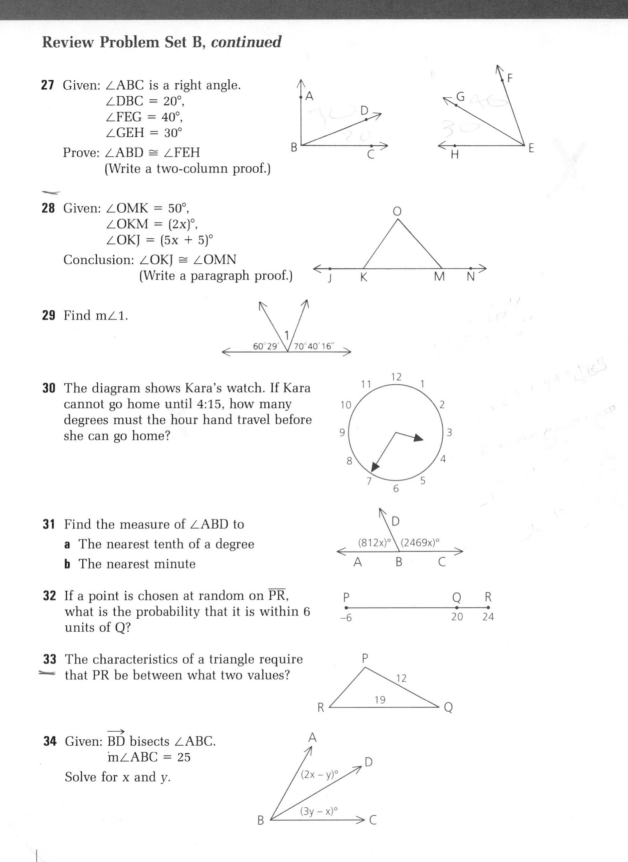

27 Given: ∠ABC is a right angle.
  ∠DBC = 20°,
  ∠FEG = 40°,
  ∠GEH = 30°
Prove: ∠ABD ≅ ∠FEH
  (Write a two-column proof.)

28 Given: ∠OMK = 50°,
  ∠OKM = (2x)°,
  ∠OKJ = (5x + 5)°
Conclusion: ∠OKJ ≅ ∠OMN
  (Write a paragraph proof.)

29 Find m∠1.

30 The diagram shows Kara's watch. If Kara cannot go home until 4:15, how many degrees must the hour hand travel before she can go home?

31 Find the measure of ∠ABD to
  a The nearest tenth of a degree
  b The nearest minute

32 If a point is chosen at random on $\overline{PR}$, what is the probability that it is within 6 units of Q?

33 The characteristics of a triangle require that PR be between what two values?

34 Given: $\overrightarrow{BD}$ bisects ∠ABC.
  m∠ABC = 25
  Solve for x and y.

35 ∠Q is obtuse.

    a What are the limitations on m∠Q? (Write two inequalities.)

    b What are the restrictions on x?

36 Given that ∠R is a right angle, solve for x.

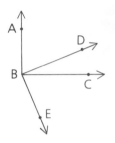

37 The perimeter of a rectangle is 20. If the rectangle's length is less than 4, what is the range of possible values of its width?

Problem Set C

38 Given: ∠ABC is a right angle.
              ∠DBE is a right angle.

    Prove: ∠ABD ≅ ∠CBE
            (Write a paragraph proof.)

39 Draw a diagram in which $\overleftrightarrow{AB}$ and $\overleftrightarrow{CD}$ intersect at E but in which ∠AEC does not appear to be congruent to ∠DEB.

40 Jennie's teacher told her to select two problems from a list of two C-level problems, five B-level problems, and one A-level problem. If she selected at random, what is the probability that she selected two B-level problems?

41 At 3:00 the hands of a clock form an angle of 90°. To the nearest second, at what time will the hands of the clock next form a 90° angle?

Problem Set D

42 If six points are represented on a sheet of paper in such a way that any four of them are noncollinear,

    a What is the maximum number of lines determined?

    b What is the minimum number of lines determined?

43 To the nearest second, what is the first time after 2:00 that the hands of a clock will form an angle $2\frac{1}{2}$ times as great as the angle formed at 2:00?

2 BASIC CONCEPTS AND PROOFS

P eople encounter the geometric concepts of perpendicularity, complementary angles, and supplementary angles on a leisurely stroll.

PERPENDICULARITY

Objectives

After studying this chapter, you will be able to
- Recognize the need for clarity and concision in proofs
- Understand the concept of perpendicularity

Part One: Introduction

A Look Back and a Look Ahead

If you feel somewhat confused at this time, you need not feel discouraged. Some confusion is inevitable at the start of geometry. Be patient! Read the lessons carefully, study the sample problems closely, and the confusion will begin to go away. Also, see your teacher for help as you need it.

In Chapter 1, you concentrated on two-column proofs but were also exposed to paragraph proofs. When writing either type, remember that understanding what you are trying to say is the most important element.

From now on, when you write a two-column proof, try to state each reason in a single sentence or less. To help you, the problems in Problem Set A of this section and the next will include a hint when a proof requires more than two steps.

This chapter contains more definitions and theorems for you to memorize and use. Toward the end of the chapter, the proofs will begin to get a little longer. As the proofs become more challenging, you will find more satisfaction in completing them.

Perpendicular Lines, Rays, and Segments

Perpendicularity, right angles, and 90° measurements all go together.

Definition   Lines, rays, or segments that intersect at right angles are **perpendicular** ($\perp$).

Below are some examples of perpendicularity.

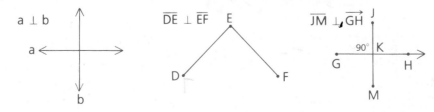

In the figure at the right, the mark inside the angle (¬) indicates that ∠B is a right angle. It is also true that $\overline{AB} \perp \overline{BC}$ and ∠B = 90°.

Do not assume perpendicularity from a diagram! In △DEF it appears that $\overline{DE} \perp \overline{EF}$, but we may not assume so.

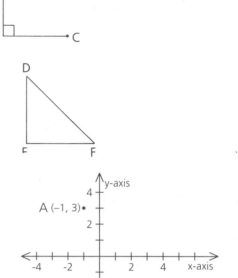

In your algebra studies, you learned that two perpendicular number lines form a two-dimensional coordinate system, or coordinate plane. (The horizontal line is called the **x-axis**; the vertical line, the **y-axis**.) Each point on the plane can be represented by an ordered pair in the form (x, y). The values of x and y in the pair, called the point's **coordinates**, represent the point's distances from the y-axis and the x-axis respectively. In the diagram, point A is represented by (− 1, 3).

The intersection of the axes is called the **origin**. Its coordinates are (0, 0).

Part Two: Sample Problems

Problem 1   Given: $\overline{AB} \perp \overline{BC}$,
          $\overline{DC} \perp \overline{BC}$

          Conclusion: ∠B ≅ ∠C

Proof

Statements	Reasons
1 $\overline{AB} \perp \overline{BC}$	1 Given
2 ∠B is a right angle.	2 If two segments are ⊥, they form a right angle.
3 $\overline{DC} \perp \overline{BC}$	3 Given
4 ∠C is a right angle.	4 Same as 2
5 ∠B ≅ ∠C	5 If angles are right angles, they are ≅.

The braces joining steps 1 and 2 emphasize the logical flow of reasoning from one step to the other. There is a similar logical flow from step 3 to step 4.

Problem 2   Given: $\overleftrightarrow{EH} \perp \overleftrightarrow{HG}$
          Name all the angles you can prove to be right angles.

Answer   Only ∠EHG (Why not ∠EFH and ∠HFG?)

Problem 3 Given: $\overrightarrow{KJ} \perp \overrightarrow{KM}$;
$\angle JKO$ is four times as large as $\angle MKO$.
Find: m$\angle JKO$

Solution Since $\overrightarrow{KJ} \perp \overrightarrow{KM}$, m$\angle JKO$ + m$\angle MKO$ = 90.

$4x + x = 90$
$\ \ \ \ 5x = 90$
$\ \ \ \ \ \ x = 18$

Substituting 18 for x, we find that m$\angle JKO$ = 72.

Problem 4 Given: a $\perp$ b,
c $\not\perp$ d (c is not $\perp$ to d.)
Conclusion: $\angle 1 \cong \angle 2$

Solution This conclusion is false. Since a $\perp$ b,
$\angle 1 = 90°$. Since c $\not\perp$ d, $\angle 2 \neq 90°$.
Since $\angle 1$ and $\angle 2$ have different
measures, $\angle 1 \not\cong \angle 2$.

Problem 5 Given: $\overline{EC}$ ∥ to x-axis
$\overline{RT}$ ∥ to x-axis
Find: Area of rectangle RECT

Solution The remaining coordinates are
$T = (7, -2)$ and $E = (-4, 3)$. So
$RT = 11$ and $TC = 5$ as shown. We
shall concentrate on area in Chapter
12, but from previous courses you
should know how to find a rectangle's area.

Area of rectangle = base × height
$A = bh$
$\ \ \ = 11(5)$
$\ \ \ = 55$
The area of RECT is 55 square units.

Part Three: Problem Sets

Problem Set A

1 Name all the angles in the figures to the
right that appear to be right angles.

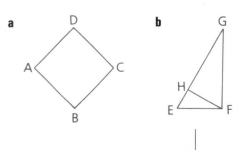

2 In each of the following, name the angles that can be *proved* to be right angles.

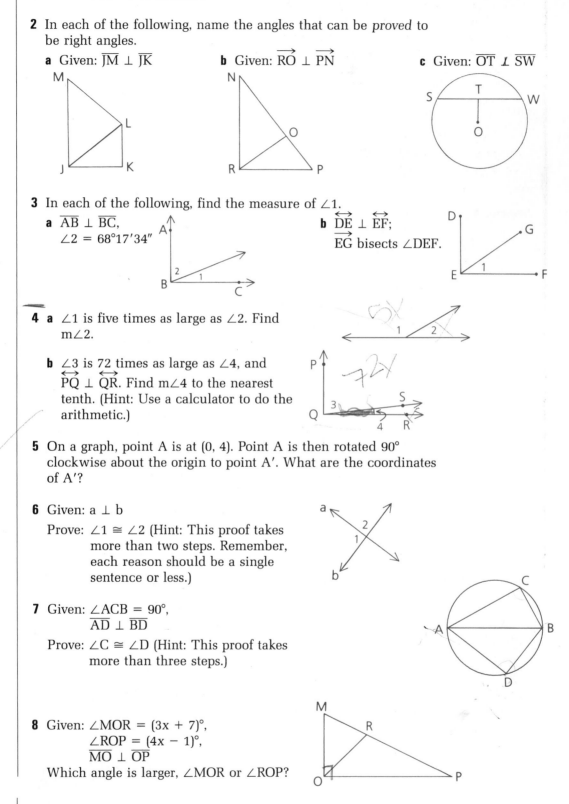

a Given: $\overline{JM} \perp \overline{JK}$

b Given: $\overrightarrow{RO} \perp \overrightarrow{PN}$

c Given: $\overline{OT} \perp \overline{SW}$

3 In each of the following, find the measure of ∠1.

a $\overline{AB} \perp \overline{BC}$, ∠2 = 68°17′34″

b $\overleftrightarrow{DE} \perp \overleftrightarrow{EF}$; $\overrightarrow{EG}$ bisects ∠DEF.

4 **a** ∠1 is five times as large as ∠2. Find m∠2.

b ∠3 is 72 times as large as ∠4, and $\overleftrightarrow{PQ} \perp \overleftrightarrow{QR}$. Find m∠4 to the nearest tenth. (Hint: Use a calculator to do the arithmetic.)

5 On a graph, point A is at (0, 4). Point A is then rotated 90° clockwise about the origin to point A′. What are the coordinates of A′?

6 Given: a ⊥ b

Prove: ∠1 ≅ ∠2 (Hint: This proof takes more than two steps. Remember, each reason should be a single sentence or less.)

7 Given: ∠ACB = 90°, $\overline{AD} \perp \overline{BD}$

Prove: ∠C ≅ ∠D (Hint: This proof takes more than three steps.)

8 Given: ∠MOR = (3x + 7)°, ∠ROP = (4x − 1)°, $\overline{MO} \perp \overline{OP}$

Which angle is larger, ∠MOR or ∠ROP?

9 You are the engineer for the development of a new subdivision in your town. When you design your street intersections, is it better to make the intersections perpendicular or oblique? Explain why.

Note When two lines intersect and are not perpendicular, they are called *oblique lines.*

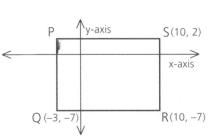

Street Intersections

Perpendicular   Oblique

10 PQRS is a rectangle.

  a Find the coordinates of point P.

  b Find the area of the rectangle.

P ↑ y-axis   S(10, 2)

x-axis

Q (−3, −7)   R(10, −7)

Problem Set B

11 $\overleftrightarrow{AB} \perp \overleftrightarrow{BC}$ and angles 1, 2, and 3 are in the ratio 1:2:3. Find the measure of each angle.

A
1
2
3
B   C

12 Line DE is perpendicular to line EF. The resulting angle is trisected, then one of the new angles is bisected, and then one of the resulting angles is trisected. How large is the smallest angle?

13 Given: ∠HGJ = 37°20′,
          ∠KGJ = 52°40′,
          $\overline{KJ} \perp \overline{HJ}$

Conclusion: ∠HGK ≅ ∠HJK (Use a paragraph proof.)

G   K

H   J

Problem Set C

14 Given: $\overline{AB} \perp \overline{BC}$,
          ∠ABO = (2x + y)°,
          ∠OBC = (6x + 8)°,
          ∠AOB = (23y + 90)°,
          ∠BOC = (4x + 4)°

Find: m∠ABO

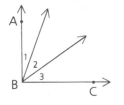

15 If a ray, $\overrightarrow{BD}$, is chosen at random between the sides of ∠ABC, where m∠ABC = 100, what is the probability that

  a ∠ABD is acute?

  b ∠DBC is acute?

  c Both ∠ABD and ∠DBC are acute?

2.2 COMPLEMENTARY AND SUPPLEMENTARY ANGLES

Objective

After studying this section, you will be able to
- Recognize complementary and supplementary angles

Part One: Introduction

We frequently see pairs of angles whose measures add up to a right angle or a straight angle. In this section we will study such pairs of angles—those with sums of 90° and 180°.

Definition   ***Complementary angles*** are two angles whose sum is 90° (a right angle). Each of the two angles is called the ***complement*** of the other.

The following are examples of pairs of complementary angles.

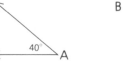

∠A and ∠B are complementary.

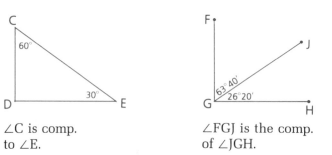

∠C is comp. to ∠E.

∠FGJ is the comp. of ∠JGH.

In the first diagram, ∠A is the complement of ∠B, and ∠B is the complement of ∠A. In the second diagram, two angles of a triangle, ∠C and ∠E, are complementary. In the third diagram, you can see how two complementary angles can share a side to form a right angle.

66   Chapter 2   Basic Concepts and Proofs

Definition   ***Supplementary angles*** are two angles whose sum is 180° (a straight angle). Each of the two angles is called the ***supplement*** of the other.

The following are examples of pairs of supplementary angles.

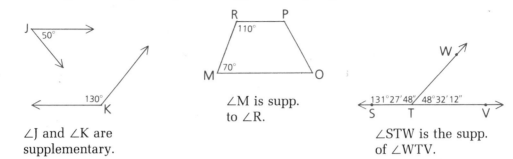

∠J and ∠K are supplementary.

∠M is supp. to ∠R.

∠STW is the supp. of ∠WTV.

In the first diagram, ∠J is the supplement of ∠K, and vice versa. In the middle diagram, which angle is the supplement of ∠M?

Sometimes, two supplementary angles will form a straight angle by sharing a side. See if you can verify that ∠STW + ∠WTV = 180°.

Part Two: Sample Problems

Problem 1   Given: ∠TVK is a right ∠.
Prove: ∠1 is comp. to ∠2.

Proof

Statements	Reasons
1 ∠TVK is a right ∠.	1 Given
2 ∠1 is comp. to ∠2.	2 If the sum of two ∠s is a right ∠, they are comp.

Problem 2   Given: Diagram as shown
Conclusion: ∠1 is supp. to ∠2.

Proof

Statements	Reasons
1 Diagram as shown	1 Given
2 ∠ABC is a straight angle.	2 Assumed from diagram
3 ∠1 is supp. to ∠2.	3 If the sum of two ∠s is a straight ∠, they are supp.

Problem 3   *The measure of one of two complementary angles is three greater than twice the measure of the other. Find the measure of each.*

Solution   Draw the angles and place your algebra on the figure.

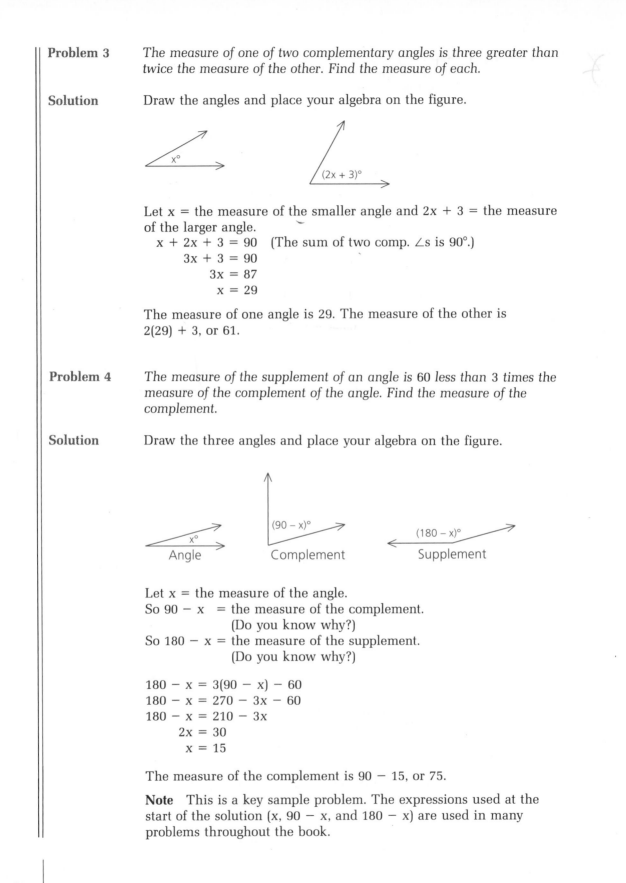

Let x = the measure of the smaller angle and 2x + 3 = the measure of the larger angle.

$$x + 2x + 3 = 90 \quad \text{(The sum of two comp. } \angle\text{s is } 90°.)$$
$$3x + 3 = 90$$
$$3x = 87$$
$$x = 29$$

The measure of one angle is 29. The measure of the other is 2(29) + 3, or 61.

Problem 4   *The measure of the supplement of an angle is 60 less than 3 times the measure of the complement of the angle. Find the measure of the complement.*

Solution   Draw the three angles and place your algebra on the figure.

Let x = the measure of the angle.
So 90 − x = the measure of the complement.
        (Do you know why?)
So 180 − x = the measure of the supplement.
        (Do you know why?)

$$180 - x = 3(90 - x) - 60$$
$$180 - x = 270 - 3x - 60$$
$$180 - x = 210 - 3x$$
$$2x = 30$$
$$x = 15$$

The measure of the complement is 90 − 15, or 75.

Note   This is a key sample problem. The expressions used at the start of the solution (x, 90 − x, and 180 − x) are used in many problems throughout the book.

Part Three: Problem Sets

Problem Set

1 Which two angles are complementary?

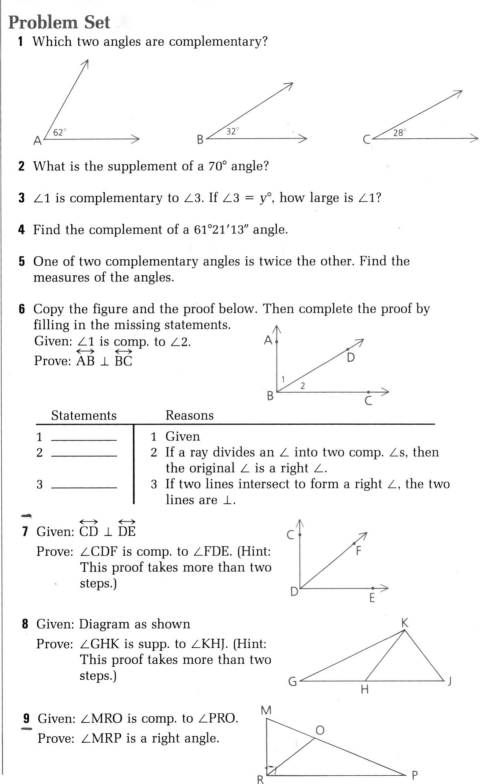

2 What is the supplement of a 70° angle?

3 ∠1 is complementary to ∠3. If ∠3 = y°, how large is ∠1?

4 Find the complement of a 61°21′13″ angle.

5 One of two complementary angles is twice the other. Find the measures of the angles.

6 Copy the figure and the proof below. Then complete the proof by filling in the missing statements.
Given: ∠1 is comp. to ∠2.
Prove: $\overleftrightarrow{AB} \perp \overleftrightarrow{BC}$

Statements	Reasons
1 _____	1 Given
2 _____	2 If a ray divides an ∠ into two comp. ∠s, then the original ∠ is a right ∠.
3 _____	3 If two lines intersect to form a right ∠, the two lines are ⊥.

7 Given: $\overleftrightarrow{CD} \perp \overleftrightarrow{DE}$

Prove: ∠CDF is comp. to ∠FDE. (Hint: This proof takes more than two steps.)

8 Given: Diagram as shown

Prove: ∠GHK is supp. to ∠KHJ. (Hint: This proof takes more than two steps.)

9 Given: ∠MRO is comp. to ∠PRO.

Prove: ∠MRP is a right angle.

Problem Set A, *continued*

10 Find the measure of ∠XVS.

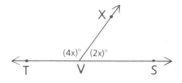

11 One of two supplementary angles is 70° greater than the second. Find the measure of the larger angle.

Problem Set B

12 a Point P is reflected over the y-axis to point A. Find the coordinates of A.

b Point P is reflected over the origin to point B. Find the coordinates of B.

c If C is the midpoint of $\overline{PA}$, find the coordinates of C.

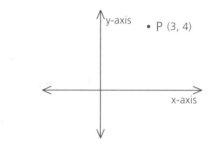

13 Complete each of the following conditional statements and justify your completion with an explanation.

a If two angles are supplementary and congruent, then ___?___.

b If two angles are complementary and congruent, then ___?___.

14 Find the measures of ∠AOC and ∠COB in the graph.

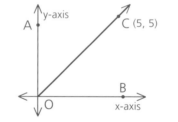

15 Find, to the nearest hundredth, the area of the rectangle.

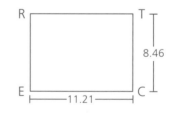

16 Two supplementary angles are in the ratio 11:7. Find the measure of each.

17 Write a paragraph proof to show that ∠ABF is complementary to ∠EBD.

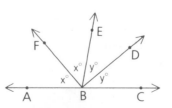

18 The larger of two supplementary angles exceeds 7 times the smaller by 4°. Find the measure of the larger angle.

19 One of two complementary angles added to one-half the other yields 72°. Find half the measure of the larger.

20 Given: $\overline{XY} \perp \overline{YW}$,
$\quad\quad\quad \overline{AB} \perp \overline{BC}$

Find: m∠DBC

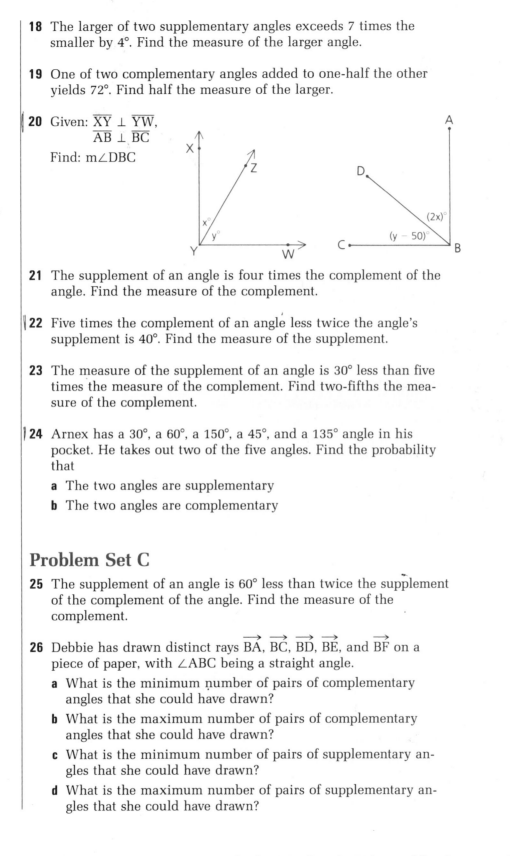

21 The supplement of an angle is four times the complement of the angle. Find the measure of the complement.

22 Five times the complement of an angle less twice the angle's supplement is 40°. Find the measure of the supplement.

23 The measure of the supplement of an angle is 30° less than five times the measure of the complement. Find two-fifths the measure of the complement.

24 Arnex has a 30°, a 60°, a 150°, a 45°, and a 135° angle in his pocket. He takes out two of the five angles. Find the probability that

a The two angles are supplementary

b The two angles are complementary

Problem Set C

25 The supplement of an angle is 60° less than twice the supplement of the complement of the angle. Find the measure of the complement.

26 Debbie has drawn distinct rays $\overrightarrow{BA}$, $\overrightarrow{BC}$, $\overrightarrow{BD}$, $\overrightarrow{BE}$, and $\overrightarrow{BF}$ on a piece of paper, with ∠ABC being a straight angle.

a What is the minimum number of pairs of complementary angles that she could have drawn?

b What is the maximum number of pairs of complementary angles that she could have drawn?

c What is the minimum number of pairs of supplementary angles that she could have drawn?

d What is the maximum number of pairs of supplementary angles that she could have drawn?

DRAWING CONCLUSIONS

Objective

After studying this section, you will be able to
- Follow a five-step procedure to draw logical conclusions

Part One: Introduction

There wouldn't be much progress in this world if all we did was justify conclusions that someone else had already drawn. Neither will you make much progress as a student of geometry if all you can do is justify conclusions the textbook has already stated. Although the following procedure may not work every time, it will be helpful to you in drawing conclusions.

Procedure for Drawing Conclusions
1 Memorize theorems, definitions, and postulates.
2 Look for key words and symbols in the given information.
3 Think of all the theorems, definitions, and postulates that involve those keys.
4 Decide which theorem, definition, or postulate allows you to draw a conclusion.
5 Draw a conclusion, and give a reason to justify the conclusion. Be certain that you have not used the *reverse* of the correct reason.

Example   Given: $\overrightarrow{AB}$ bisects $\angle CAD$.
Conclusion: ___?___

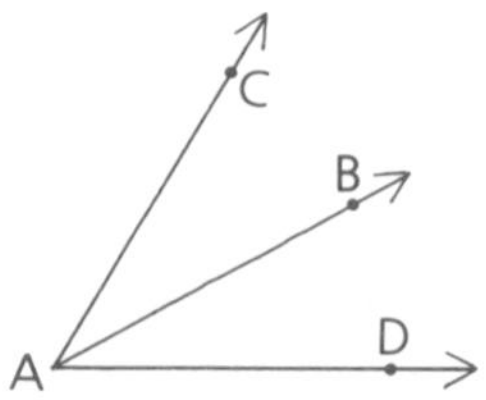

Thinking Process:

The key word is *bisects.*
The key symbols are $\rightarrow$ and $\angle$.
The definition of *bisector* (of an angle) contains those keys.
An appropriate conclusion is that $\angle CAB \cong \angle DAB$.

Statements	Reasons
1 $\overrightarrow{AB}$ bisects ∠CAD.	1 Given
2 ∠CAB ≅ ∠DAB	2 If a ray bisects an ∠, then it divides the ∠ into two ≅ angles.

Note The "If . . ." part of the reason matches the given information, and the "then . . ." part matches the conclusion being justified. *Be sure not to reverse that order.*

Part Two: Sample Problems

For each of these problems, we will write a two-column proof, supplying a correct conclusion and reason.

Problem 1   *Given: ∠A is a right angle.*
                            ∠B is a right angle.
           Conclusion: ___?___

Proof

Statements	Reasons
1 ∠A is a right angle.	1 Given
2 ∠B is a right angle.	2 Given
3 ∠A ≅ ∠B	3 If two ∠s are right ∠s, then they are ≅.

Problem 2   *Given: E is the midpoint of $\overline{SG}$.*
           Conclusion: ___?___

Proof

Statements	Reasons
1 E is the midpoint of $\overline{SG}$.	1 Given
2 $\overline{SE}$ ≅ $\overline{EG}$	2 If a point is the midpoint of a segment, the point divides the segment into two ≅ segments.

Problem 3   *Given: ∠PRS is a right angle.*
           Conclusion: ___?___

Proof

Statements	Reasons
1 ∠PRS is a right ∠.	1 Given
2 $\overleftrightarrow{PR}$ ⊥ $\overleftrightarrow{RS}$	2 If two lines intersect to form a right ∠, they are ⊥ .

In sample problem 3, we could have drawn a different conclusion. Do you know what that other conclusion is?

Part Three: Problem Sets

Problem Set

In problems 1–7, write a two-column proof, supplying your own correct conclusion and reason.

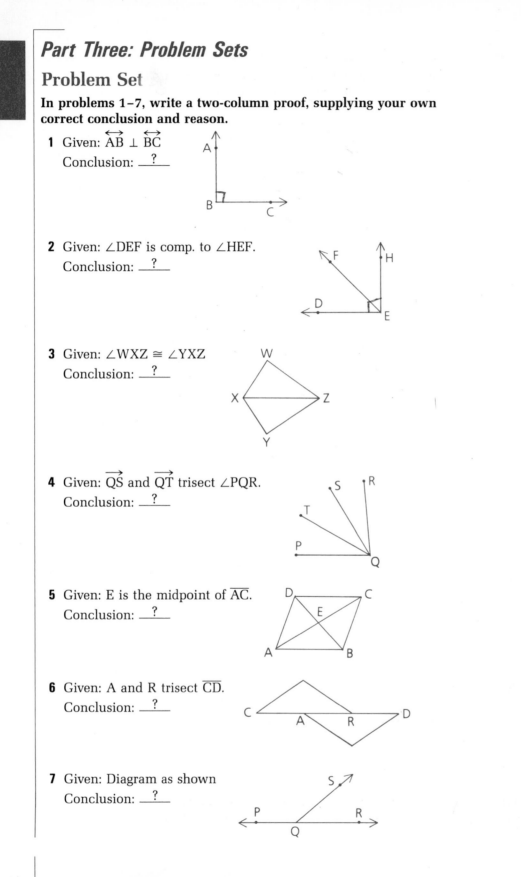

1 Given: $\overleftrightarrow{AB} \perp \overleftrightarrow{BC}$

Conclusion: ___?___

2 Given: $\angle DEF$ is comp. to $\angle HEF$.

Conclusion: ___?___

3 Given: $\angle WXZ \cong \angle YXZ$

Conclusion: ___?___

4 Given: $\overrightarrow{QS}$ and $\overrightarrow{QT}$ trisect $\angle PQR$.

Conclusion: ___?___

5 Given: E is the midpoint of $\overline{AC}$.

Conclusion: ___?___

6 Given: A and R trisect $\overline{CD}$.

Conclusion: ___?___

7 Given: Diagram as shown

Conclusion: ___?___

Problem Set

In problems 8–12, draw at least two conclusions for each "given" statement, and give reasons to support them in two-column-proof form.

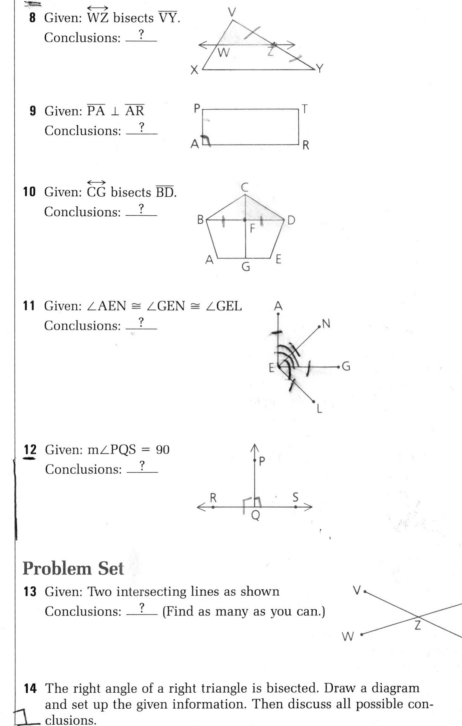

8 Given: $\overleftrightarrow{WZ}$ bisects $\overline{VY}$.

Conclusions: ___?___

9 Given: $\overline{PA} \perp \overline{AR}$

Conclusions: ___?___

10 Given: $\overleftrightarrow{CG}$ bisects $\overline{BD}$.

Conclusions: ___?___

11 Given: $\angle AEN \cong \angle GEN \cong \angle GEL$

Conclusions: ___?___

12 Given: $m\angle PQS = 90$

Conclusions: ___?___

Problem Set

13 Given: Two intersecting lines as shown

Conclusions: ___?___ (Find as many as you can.)

14 The right angle of a right triangle is bisected. Draw a diagram and set up the given information. Then discuss all possible conclusions.

CONGRUENT SUPPLEMENTS AND COMPLEMENTS

Objective

After studying this section, you will be able to
  Prove angles congruent by means of four new theorems

Part One: Introduction

In the diagram below, ∠1 is supplementary to ∠A, and ∠2 is also supplementary to ∠A.

How large is ∠1? Now calculate ∠2. How does ∠1 compare with ∠2? Your results will illustrate (but not prove) the following theorem.

Theorem 4   *If angles are supplementary to the same angle, then they are congruent.*

Given: ∠3 is supp. to ∠4.
     ∠5 is supp. to ∠4.
Prove: ∠3 ≅ ∠5

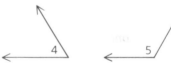

Proof: ∠3 is supp. to ∠4, so m∠3 + m∠4 = 180.
    Therefore, m∠3 = 180 − m∠4.
    ∠5 is supp. to ∠4, so m∠5 + m∠4 = 180.
    Therefore, m∠5 = 180 − m∠4.
    Since ∠3 and ∠5 have the same measure, ∠3 ≅ ∠5.

A companion to Theorem 4 follows.

Theorem 5   *If angles are supplementary to congruent angles,*
                   then they are congruent.

Given: ∠F is supp. to ∠G.
        ∠H is supp. to ∠J.
        ∠G ≅ ∠J
Conclusion: ∠F ≅ ∠H

The proof of Theorem 5 is similar to that of Theorem 4.

Two similar theorems apply to complementary angles.

Theorem 6   *If angles are complementary to the same angle,*
                   then they are congruent.

Theorem 7   *If angles are complementary to congruent angles,*
                   then they are congruent.

When studying the definitions of such terms as *right angle*, *bisect*,
midpoint, and *perpendicular*, you will master the concepts more
quickly if you try to understand the ideas involved without memorizing the definitions word for word. The theorems in this section,
however, are different. Unless you *memorize* Theorems 4–7, you will
have difficulty remembering the concepts they contain.

     Therefore, before you begin your homework,
       1 Memorize Theorems 4–7
       2 Read the sample problems carefully, so that you understand
         which of the theorems is used in each type of problem

Part Two: Sample Problems

Problem 1   Given: ∠1 is supp. to ∠2.
               ∠3 is supp. to ∠4.
               ∠1 ≅ ∠4
         Conclusion: ∠2 ≅ ∠3

Proof

Statements	Reasons
1 ∠1 is supp. to ∠2.	1 Given
2 ∠3 is supp. to ∠4.	2 Given
3 ∠1 ≅ ∠4	3 Given
4 ∠2 ≅ ∠3	4 If angles are supplementary to ≅ angles, they are ≅. (Short form: Supplements of ≅ ∠s are ≅.)

Problem 2 Given: ∠A is comp. to ∠C.
 ∠DBC is comp. to ∠C.
Conclusion: ___?___

Proof

Statements	Reasons
1 ∠A is comp. to ∠C.	1 Given
2 ∠DBC is comp. to ∠C.	2 Given
3 ∠A ≅ ∠DBC	3 If angles are complementary to the same angle, they are ≅. (Short form: Complements of the same ∠ are ≅.)

Problem 3 Given: Diagram as shown
Prove: ∠HFE ≅ ∠GFJ

Proof

Statements	Reasons
1 Diagram as shown.	1 Given
2 ∠EFG is a straight ∠.	2 Assumed from diagram
3 ∠HFE is supp. to ∠HFG.	3 If two ∠s form a straight ∠, they are supplementary.
4 ∠HFJ is a straight ∠.	4 Same as 2
5 ∠GFJ is supp. to ∠HFG.	5 Same as 3
6 ∠HFE ≅ ∠GFJ	6 If angles are supplementary to the same angle, they are ≅. (Short form: Supplements of the same ∠ are ≅.)

Problem 4 Given: $\overline{KM} \perp \overline{MO}$,
 $\overline{PO} \perp \overline{MO}$,
 ∠KMR ≅ ∠POR
Prove: ∠ROM ≅ ∠RMO

Proof

Statements	Reasons
1 $\overline{KM} \perp \overline{MO}$	1 Given
2 ∠KMO is a right ∠.	2 If segments are ⊥, they form right ∠s.
3 ∠RMO is comp. to ∠KMR.	3 If two ∠s form a right ∠, they are complementary.
4 In a similar manner, ∠ROM is comp. to ∠POR.	4 Reasons 1–3
5 ∠KMR ≅ ∠POR	5 Given
6 ∠ROM ≅ ∠RMO	6 If angles are complementary to ≅ angles, they are ≅. (Short form: Complements of ≅ ∠s are ≅.)

Part Three: Problem Sets

Problem Set A

Before starting the assignment, memorize Theorems 4–7. The key to the use of these theorems is to look for the double use of the word *complementary* or *supplementary* in a problem.

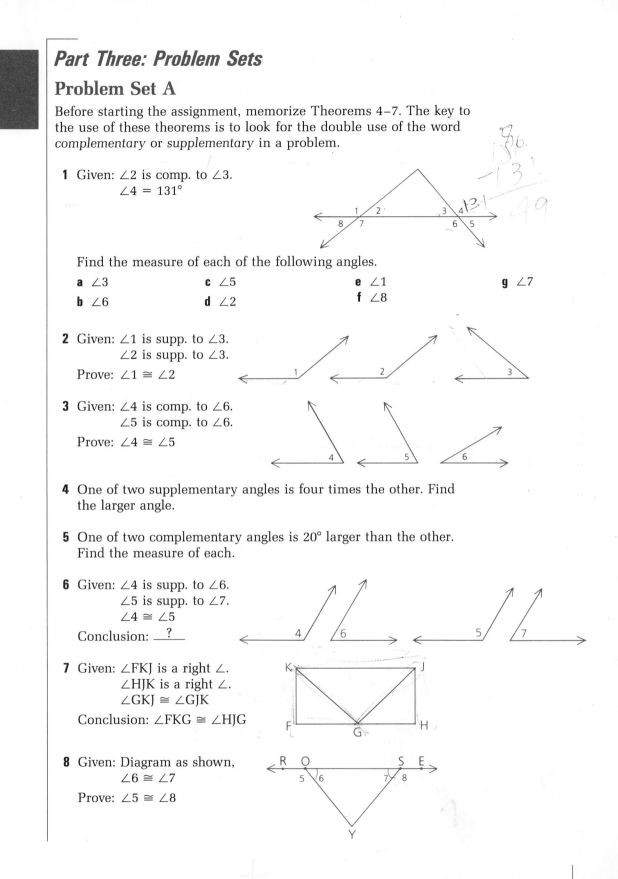

1 Given: ∠2 is comp. to ∠3.
∠4 = 131°

Find the measure of each of the following angles.

a ∠3 **c** ∠5 **e** ∠1 **g** ∠7

b ∠6 **d** ∠2 **f** ∠8

2 Given: ∠1 is supp. to ∠3.
∠2 is supp. to ∠3.
Prove: ∠1 ≅ ∠2

3 Given: ∠4 is comp. to ∠6.
∠5 is comp. to ∠6.
Prove: ∠4 ≅ ∠5

4 One of two supplementary angles is four times the other. Find the larger angle.

5 One of two complementary angles is 20° larger than the other. Find the measure of each.

6 Given: ∠4 is supp. to ∠6.
∠5 is supp. to ∠7.
∠4 ≅ ∠5
Conclusion: ___?___

7 Given: ∠FKJ is a right ∠.
∠HJK is a right ∠.
∠GKJ ≅ ∠GJK
Conclusion: ∠FKG ≅ ∠HJG

8 Given: Diagram as shown,
∠6 ≅ ∠7
Prove: ∠5 ≅ ∠8

Problem Set A, *continued*

9 Given: $\overrightarrow{SV}$ bisects ∠RST.
Conclusion: ∠RSV ≅ ∠TSV

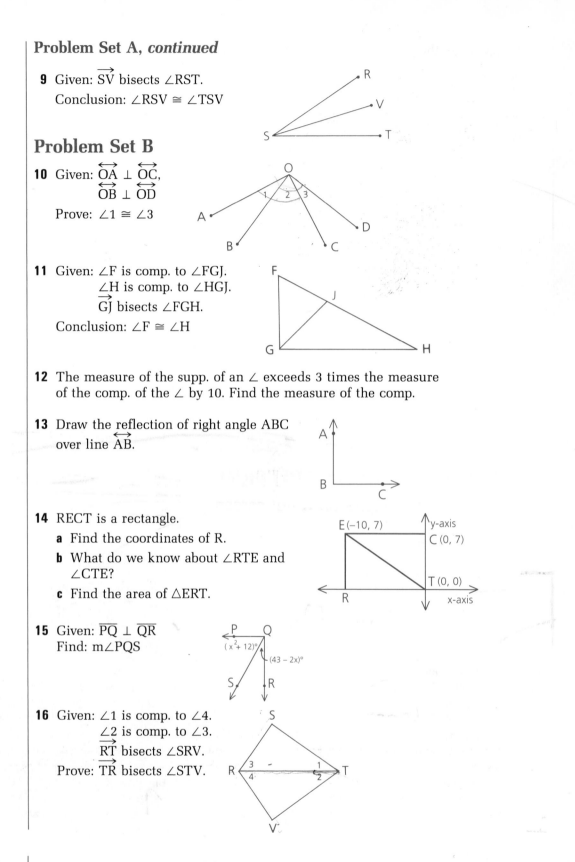

Problem Set B

10 Given: $\overleftrightarrow{OA} \perp \overleftrightarrow{OC}$,
$\overleftrightarrow{OB} \perp \overleftrightarrow{OD}$
Prove: ∠1 ≅ ∠3

11 Given: ∠F is comp. to ∠FGJ.
∠H is comp. to ∠HGJ.
$\overrightarrow{GJ}$ bisects ∠FGH.
Conclusion: ∠F ≅ ∠H

12 The measure of the supp. of an ∠ exceeds 3 times the measure of the comp. of the ∠ by 10. Find the measure of the comp.

13 Draw the reflection of right angle ABC over line $\overleftrightarrow{AB}$.

14 RECT is a rectangle.
  a Find the coordinates of R.
  b What do we know about ∠RTE and ∠CTE?
  c Find the area of △ERT.

15 Given: $\overline{PQ} \perp \overline{QR}$
Find: m∠PQS

16 Given: ∠1 is comp. to ∠4.
∠2 is comp. to ∠3.
$\overrightarrow{RT}$ bisects ∠SRV.
Prove: $\overrightarrow{TR}$ bisects ∠STV.

17 If three times the supp. of an $\angle$ is subtracted from seven times the comp. of the $\angle$, the answer is the same as that obtained by trisecting a right $\angle$. Find the supplement.

18 Given: $\angle WXZ \cong \angle VXY$

Conclusion: $\angle 1 \cong \angle 3$

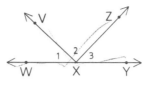

19 Given: $\angle PQR$ supp. $\angle QRS$, $\angle QRS$ supp. $\angle TWX$,
$\angle PQR = (5x - 48)°$, $\angle TWX = (2x + 30)°$

Find: m$\angle QRS$

Problem Set C

20 Given: $\angle 1 = (x^2 + 3y)°$,
$\angle 2 = (20y + 3)°$,
$\angle 3 = (3y + 4x)°$

Find: m$\angle 1$

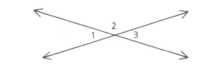

21 The ratio of an angle to its supplement is $3:7$. Find the ratio of the angle to its complement.

MATHEMATICAL EXCURSION

GEOMETRY IN COMPUTERS
Three-Dimensional views on a flat screen

Designers, architects, and draftspeople are putting away their T squares and doing more of their work with computers. A wide variety of software for computer-aided drafting and design (CADD) has made it possible to do accurate work on a computer screen. Using a computer makes exploring solutions to design problems, as well as making corrections and revising, more efficient. A computer also performs calculations and offers a system for filing alternative versions of a plan.

One of the most exciting features of CADD software is that it allows you to create a three-dimensional design and then rotate it on the screen, still in three dimensions. This enables an architect or designer to see, with the press of a key or the click of a mouse, how his or her design would look from any direction or angle.

Using a CADD program, you can see the measure of an angle displayed as you draw the angle. You can instruct the program to automatically bisect an angle you have drawn.

Simpler geometric drawing programs such as The Geometric Supposer offer some of the drawing and measuring capabilities of the CADD programs, including the opportunity for experimenting with geometric concepts such as angle sizes and relationships.

ADDITION AND SUBTRACTION PROPERTIES

Objectives

After studying this section, you will be able to
- Apply the addition properties of segments and angles
- Apply the subtraction properties of segments and angles

Part One: Introduction

Addition Properties

In the diagram below, AB = CD. Do you think that AC = BD? Suppose that BC were 3 cm. Would AC = BD? If AB = CD, does the length of BC have any effect on whether AC = BD?

7 cm	3 cm	7 cm
A	B C	D

Your answers should be that AC = BD in each case and the length of BC does not effect that equality. This is a geometric application of the algebraic Addition Property of Equality (AB + BC = CD + BC).

Theorem 8   ***If a segment is added to two congruent segments, the sums are congruent. (Addition Property)***

Given: $\overline{PQ} \cong \overline{RS}$

Conclusion: $\overline{PR} \cong \overline{QS}$ P   Q   R   S

Proof: $\overline{PQ} \cong \overline{RS}$, so by definition of congruent segments, PQ = RS. Now, the Addition Property of Equality says that we may add QR to both sides, so PQ + QR = RS + QR. Substituting, we get PR = QS. Therefore, $\overline{PR} \cong \overline{QS}$ by the definition of *congruent segments* (reversed).

Does a similar relationship hold for angles? Is ∠EFH necessarily congruent to ∠JFG?

The next theorem confirms that the answer is yes. Its proof is like that of Theorem 8.

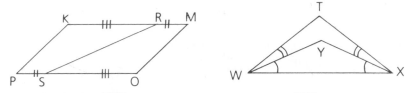

Theorem 9   *If an angle is added to two congruent angles, the sums are congruent. (**Addition Property**)*

In the figures below, identical tick marks indicate congruent parts.

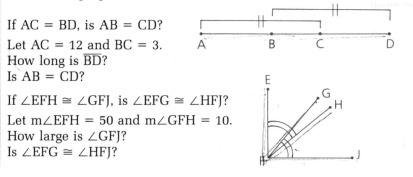

Do you think that $\overline{KM}$ is necessarily congruent to $\overline{PO}$? In the right-hand diagram, is ∠TWX necessarily congruent to ∠TXW? The answer to these questions is yes.

These congruencies are established by the following two theorems. Their proofs are similar to that of Theorem 8.

Theorem 10   *If congruent segments are added to congruent segments, the sums are congruent. (**Addition Property**)*

Theorem 11   *If congruent angles are added to congruent angles, the sums are congruent. (**Addition Property**)*

Subtraction Properties

We now have four addition properties. Because subtraction is equivalent to addition of an opposite, we can expect four corresponding subtraction properties.

If AC = BD, is AB = CD?

Let AC = 12 and BC = 3.
How long is $\overline{BD}$?
Is AB = CD?

If ∠EFH ≅ ∠GFJ, is ∠EFG ≅ ∠HFJ?

Let m∠EFH = 50 and m∠GFH = 10.
How large is ∠GFJ?
Is ∠EFG ≅ ∠HFJ?

If KO = KP and NO = RP,
is KN = KR?

Try this on your own and
see what you think.

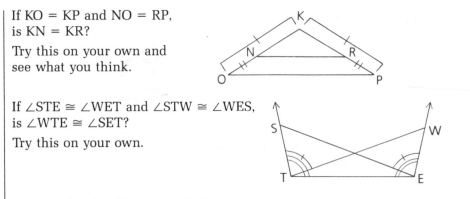

If ∠STE ≅ ∠WET and ∠STW ≅ ∠WES,
is ∠WTE ≅ ∠SET?

Try this on your own.

Your results should agree with the next two theorems.

Theorem 12   *If a segment (or angle) is subtracted from congruent segments (or angles), the differences are congruent. (Subtraction Property)*

Theorem 13   *If congruent segments (or angles) are subtracted from congruent segments (or angles), the differences are congruent. (Subtraction Property)*

Using the Addition and Subtraction Properties in Proofs

1 An addition property is used when the segments or angles in the conclusion are *greater than* those in the given information.

2 A subtraction property is used when the segments or angles in the conclusion are *smaller than* those in the given information.

Part Two: Sample Problems

Problem 1   Given: $\overline{AB} \cong \overline{FE}$,
$\overline{BC} \cong \overline{ED}$

Prove: $\overline{AC} \cong \overline{FD}$

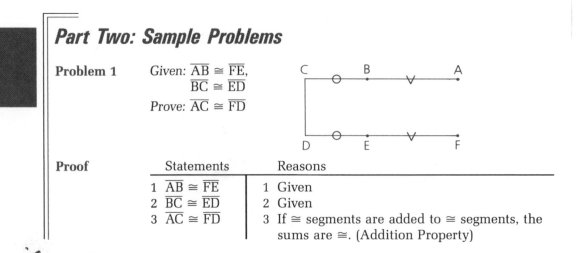

Proof

Statements	Reasons
1 $\overline{AB} \cong \overline{FE}$	1 Given
2 $\overline{BC} \cong \overline{ED}$	2 Given
3 $\overline{AC} \cong \overline{FD}$	3 If ≅ segments are added to ≅ segments, the sums are ≅. (Addition Property)

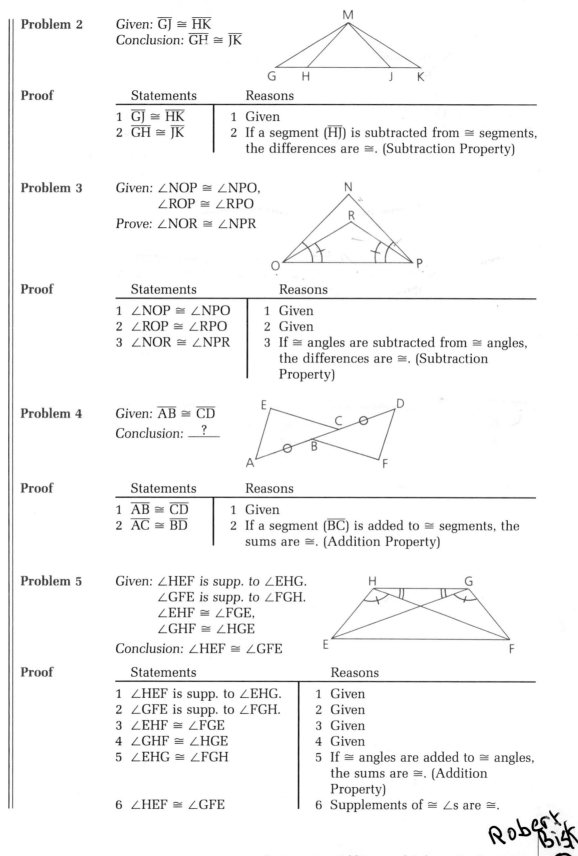

Problem 2 *Given:* $\overline{GJ} \cong \overline{HK}$
Conclusion: $\overline{GH} \cong \overline{JK}$

Proof

	Statements		Reasons
1	$\overline{GJ} \cong \overline{HK}$	1	Given
2	$\overline{GH} \cong \overline{JK}$	2	If a segment ($\overline{HJ}$) is subtracted from $\cong$ segments, the differences are $\cong$. (Subtraction Property)

Problem 3 *Given:* $\angle NOP \cong \angle NPO$,
$\angle ROP \cong \angle RPO$
Prove: $\angle NOR \cong \angle NPR$

Proof

	Statements		Reasons
1	$\angle NOP \cong \angle NPO$	1	Given
2	$\angle ROP \cong \angle RPO$	2	Given
3	$\angle NOR \cong \angle NPR$	3	If $\cong$ angles are subtracted from $\cong$ angles, the differences are $\cong$. (Subtraction Property)

Problem 4 *Given:* $\overline{AB} \cong \overline{CD}$
Conclusion: ____?____

Proof

	Statements		Reasons
1	$\overline{AB} \cong \overline{CD}$	1	Given
2	$\overline{AC} \cong \overline{BD}$	2	If a segment ($\overline{BC}$) is added to $\cong$ segments, the sums are $\cong$. (Addition Property)

Problem 5 *Given:* $\angle HEF$ *is supp. to* $\angle EHG$.
$\angle GFE$ *is supp. to* $\angle FGH$.
$\angle EHF \cong \angle FGE$,
$\angle GHF \cong \angle HGE$
Conclusion: $\angle HEF \cong \angle GFE$

Proof

	Statements		Reasons
1	$\angle HEF$ is supp. to $\angle EHG$.	1	Given
2	$\angle GFE$ is supp. to $\angle FGH$.	2	Given
3	$\angle EHF \cong \angle FGE$	3	Given
4	$\angle GHF \cong \angle HGE$	4	Given
5	$\angle EHG \cong \angle FGH$	5	If $\cong$ angles are added to $\cong$ angles, the sums are $\cong$. (Addition Property)
6	$\angle HEF \cong \angle GFE$	6	Supplements of $\cong$ $\angle$s are $\cong$.

Part Three: Problem Sets

Problem Set A

Throughout this problem set, think of addition when you are asked to prove that segments or angles are larger than the given segments or angles. Think of subtraction when you are asked to prove that segments or angles are smaller than the given segments or angles.

1 Name the angles or segments that are congruent by the Addition Property.

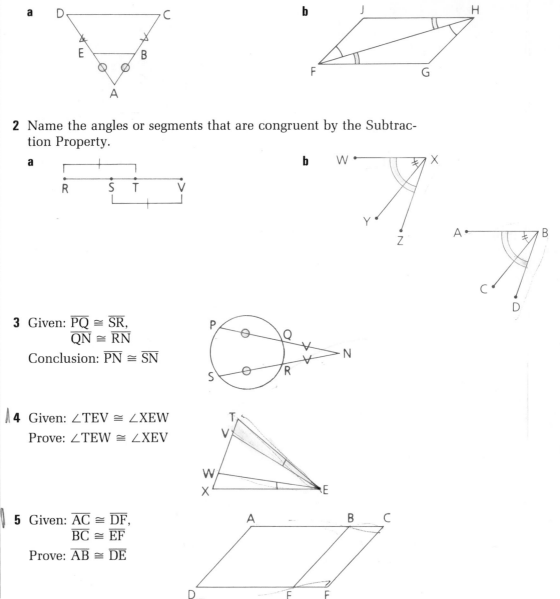

a

b

2 Name the angles or segments that are congruent by the Subtraction Property.

a

b

3 Given: $\overline{PQ} \cong \overline{SR}$,
   $\overline{QN} \cong \overline{RN}$
   Conclusion: $\overline{PN} \cong \overline{SN}$

4 Given: $\angle TEV \cong \angle XEW$
   Prove: $\angle TEW \cong \angle XEV$

5 Given: $\overline{AC} \cong \overline{DF}$,
   $\overline{BC} \cong \overline{EF}$
   Prove: $\overline{AB} \cong \overline{DE}$

6 Given: $\overline{GH} \cong \overline{JK}$, GH = x + 10,
HJ = 8, JK = 2x − 4
Find: GJ

7 Given: ∠PNO ≅ ∠PON,
∠1 ≅ ∠2
Conclusion: ___?___

8 Given: ∠T is comp. to ∠W.
∠X is comp. to ∠Z.
∠Z ≅ ∠W
Prove: ___?___

9 Given: $\overline{QR} \cong \overline{ST}$, QS = 5x + 17,
RT = 10 − 2x, RS = 3
Find: QS and QT

10 Given: ∠BAD is a right ∠.
$\overline{CA} \perp \overline{AE}$
Prove: ∠BAC ≅ ∠EAD

Problem Set

11 Given: ∠BAD ≅ ∠FAD;
$\overrightarrow{AD}$ bisects ∠CAE.
Conclusion: ∠BAC ≅ ∠FAE

12 Given: J and K are trisection
points of $\overline{HM}$.
$\overline{GH} \cong \overline{MO}$
Conclusion: $\overline{GJ} \cong \overline{KO}$

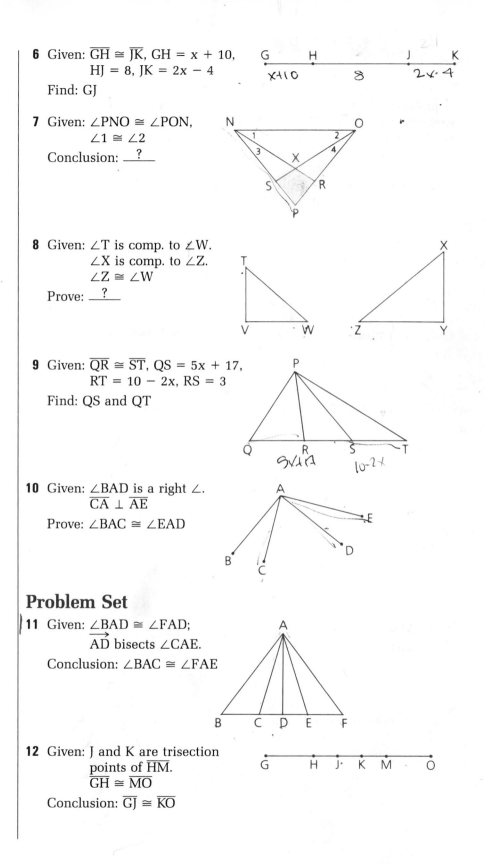

Problem Set B, *continued*

13 Given: $\angle$NPR is a right $\angle$.
$\overline{WE} \perp \overline{ET}$,
$\angle$SPR $\cong$ $\angle$XET
Prove: $\angle$NPS $\cong$ $\angle$WEX

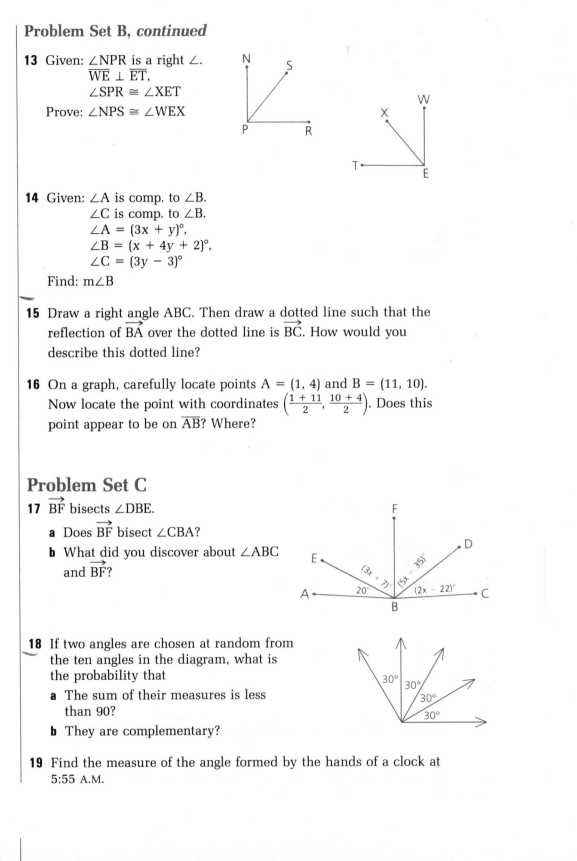

14 Given: $\angle$A is comp. to $\angle$B.
$\angle$C is comp. to $\angle$B.
$\angle$A = $(3x + y)°$,
$\angle$B = $(x + 4y + 2)°$,
$\angle$C = $(3y - 3)°$
Find: m$\angle$B

15 Draw a right angle ABC. Then draw a dotted line such that the reflection of $\overrightarrow{BA}$ over the dotted line is $\overrightarrow{BC}$. How would you describe this dotted line?

16 On a graph, carefully locate points A = (1, 4) and B = (11, 10). Now locate the point with coordinates $\left(\frac{1 + 11}{2}, \frac{10 + 4}{2}\right)$. Does this point appear to be on $\overline{AB}$? Where?

Problem Set C

17 $\overrightarrow{BF}$ bisects $\angle$DBE.

a Does $\overrightarrow{BF}$ bisect $\angle$CBA?

b What did you discover about $\angle$ABC and $\overrightarrow{BF}$?

18 If two angles are chosen at random from the ten angles in the diagram, what is the probability that

a The sum of their measures is less than 90?

b They are complementary?

19 Find the measure of the angle formed by the hands of a clock at 5:55 A.M.

MULTIPLICATION AND DIVISION PROPERTIES

Objective

After studying this section, you will be able to
  Apply the multiplication and division properties of segments and
  angles

Part One: Introduction

In the figure below, B, C, F, and G are trisection points.

A   B   C   D   E   F   G   H

  If AB = EF = 3, what can we say about $\overline{AD}$ and $\overline{EH}$?

  If $\overline{AB} \cong \overline{EF}$, is $\overline{AD}$ congruent to $\overline{EH}$?

In the figure at the right, $\overrightarrow{KO}$ and $\overrightarrow{PS}$ are
angle bisectors.

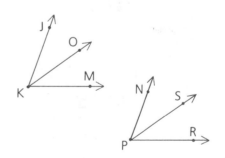

  If m∠JKO = m∠NPS = 25, what can we
  say about ∠JKM and ∠NPR?

  If ∠JKO ≅ ∠NPS, is ∠JKM congruent to
  ∠NPR?

The examples above illustrate a property whose proof is similar to
the proof of Theorem 8.

Theorem 14   *If segments (or angles) are congruent, their like*
               multiples are congruent. (Multiplication Property)

Also, because division is equivalent to multiplication by the reciprocal of the divisor, it is easy to prove the next theorem.

Theorem 15 *If segments (or angles) are congruent, their like divisions are congruent. (Division Property)*

Using the Multiplication and Division Properties in Proofs

1 Look for a double use of the word *midpoint* or *trisect* or *bisects* in the given information.

2 The Multiplication Property is used when the segments or angles in the conclusion are *greater than* those in the given information.

3 The Division Property is used when the segments or angles in the conclusion are *smaller than* those in the given information.

Part Two: Sample Problems

Problem 1 Given: $\overline{MP} \cong \overline{NS}$;
O *is the midpoint of* $\overline{MP}$.
R *is the midpoint of* $\overline{NS}$.

Prove: $\overline{MO} \cong \overline{NR}$

Proof

Statements	Reasons
1 $\overline{MP} \cong \overline{NS}$	1 Given
2 O is the midpoint of $\overline{MP}$.	2 Given
3 R is the midpoint of $\overline{NS}$.	3 Given
4 $\overline{MO} \cong \overline{NR}$	4 If segments are $\cong$, their like divisions (halves) are $\cong$. (Division Property)

Problem 2 Given: $\angle TRY \cong \angle ABE$;
$\overrightarrow{RW}$ *and* $\overrightarrow{RX}$ *trisect* $\angle TRY$.
$\overrightarrow{BC}$ *and* $\overrightarrow{BD}$ *trisect* $\angle ABE$.

Conclusion: $\angle TRW \cong \angle CBD$

Proof

Statements	Reasons
1 $\angle TRY \cong \angle ABE$	1 Given
2 $\overrightarrow{RW}$ and $\overrightarrow{RX}$ trisect $\angle TRY$.	2 Given
3 $\overrightarrow{BC}$ and $\overrightarrow{BD}$ trisect $\angle ABE$.	3 Given
4 $\angle TRW \cong \angle CBD$	4 If angles are $\cong$, their like divisions (thirds) are $\cong$. (Division Property)

Problem 3   Given: $\overline{MK} \cong \overline{FG}$;
$\overline{KG}$ bisects $\overline{MJ}$ and $\overline{FH}$.
Prove: $\overline{MJ} \cong \overline{FH}$

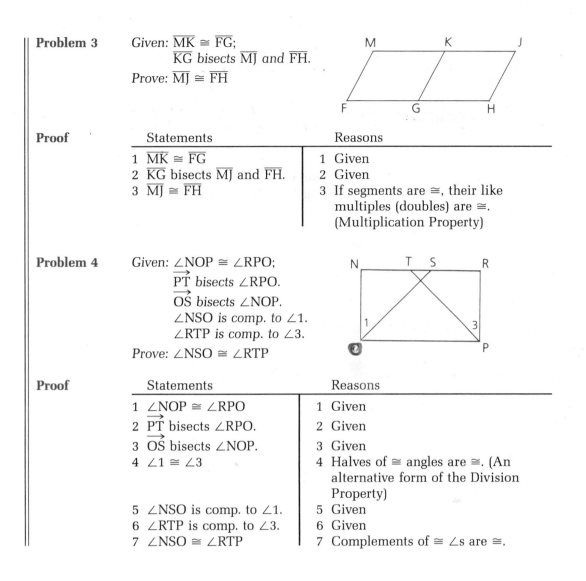

Proof

Statements	Reasons
1 $\overline{MK} \cong \overline{FG}$	1 Given
2 $\overline{KG}$ bisects $\overline{MJ}$ and $\overline{FH}$.	2 Given
3 $\overline{MJ} \cong \overline{FH}$	3 If segments are $\cong$, their like multiples (doubles) are $\cong$. (Multiplication Property)

Problem 4   Given: $\angle NOP \cong \angle RPO$;
$\overrightarrow{PT}$ bisects $\angle RPO$.
$\overrightarrow{OS}$ bisects $\angle NOP$.
$\angle NSO$ is comp. to $\angle 1$.
$\angle RTP$ is comp. to $\angle 3$.
Prove: $\angle NSO \cong \angle RTP$

Proof

Statements	Reasons
1 $\angle NOP \cong \angle RPO$	1 Given
2 $\overrightarrow{PT}$ bisects $\angle RPO$.	2 Given
3 $\overrightarrow{OS}$ bisects $\angle NOP$.	3 Given
4 $\angle 1 \cong \angle 3$	4 Halves of $\cong$ angles are $\cong$. (An alternative form of the Division Property)
5 $\angle NSO$ is comp. to $\angle 1$.	5 Given
6 $\angle RTP$ is comp. to $\angle 3$.	6 Given
7 $\angle NSO \cong \angle RTP$	7 Complements of $\cong$ $\angle$s are $\cong$.

Part Three: Problem Sets

Problem Set A

Before starting the proofs in this problem set, reread the chart on page 90.

1 Given: $\angle KMR \cong \angle VTW$;
$\overrightarrow{MR}$ and $\overrightarrow{MP}$ trisect $\angle KMO$.
$\overrightarrow{TX}$ and $\overrightarrow{TW}$ trisect $\angle STV$.
Prove: $\angle KMO \cong \angle STV$

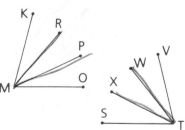

2 Use the given information to find the value of x.

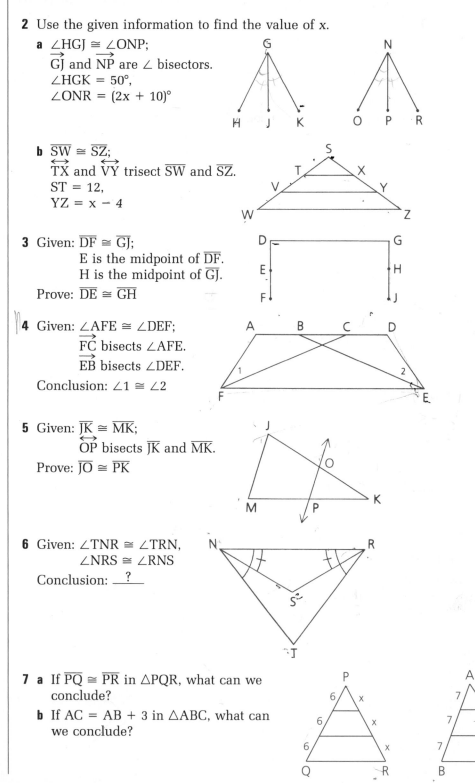

a ∠HGJ ≅ ∠ONP;
$\overrightarrow{GJ}$ and $\overrightarrow{NP}$ are ∠ bisectors.
∠HGK = 50°,
∠ONR = (2x + 10)°

b $\overline{SW} \cong \overline{SZ}$;
$\overleftrightarrow{TX}$ and $\overleftrightarrow{VY}$ trisect $\overline{SW}$ and $\overline{SZ}$.
ST = 12,
YZ = x − 4

3 Given: $\overline{DF} \cong \overline{GJ}$;
E is the midpoint of $\overline{DF}$.
H is the midpoint of $\overline{GJ}$.
Prove: $\overline{DE} \cong \overline{GH}$

4 Given: ∠AFE ≅ ∠DEF;
$\overrightarrow{FC}$ bisects ∠AFE.
$\overrightarrow{EB}$ bisects ∠DEF.
Conclusion: ∠1 ≅ ∠2

5 Given: $\overline{JK} \cong \overline{MK}$;
$\overleftrightarrow{OP}$ bisects $\overline{JK}$ and $\overline{MK}$.
Prove: $\overline{JO} \cong \overline{PK}$

6 Given: ∠TNR ≅ ∠TRN,
∠NRS ≅ ∠RNS
Conclusion: ___?___

7 a If $\overline{PQ} \cong \overline{PR}$ in △PQR, what can we
conclude?
b If AC = AB + 3 in △ABC, what can
we conclude?

8 Given: M is the midpoint of $\overline{GH}$.
   Conclusion: $\overline{GM} \cong \overline{MH}$

9 Given: $(x_1, y_1) = (5, 1)$,
   $(x_2, y_2) = (9, 3)$
   Find: $\left(\dfrac{x_1 + x_2}{2}, \dfrac{y_1 + y_2}{2} \right)$

10 Copy the diagram and the proof. Then complete the proof by filling in the missing reasons.
   Given: $\overline{VW} \cong \overline{AB}$, $\overline{WX} \cong \overline{BC}$;
         X is the midpt. of $\overline{VZ}$.
         C is the midpt. of $\overline{AD}$.
   Prove: $\overline{VZ} \cong \overline{AD}$

Statements	Reasons
1 $\overline{VW} \cong \overline{AB}$	1 _____
2 $\overline{WX} \cong \overline{BC}$	2 _____
3 $\overline{VX} \cong \overline{AC}$	3 _____
4 X is the midpt. of $\overline{VZ}$.	4 _____
5 C is the midpt. of $\overline{AD}$.	5 _____
6 $\overline{VZ} \cong \overline{AD}$	6 _____

Problem Set B

11 Given: $\overline{SZ} \cong \overline{ST}$,
         $\overline{XY} \cong \overline{VW}$;
         Y is the midpt. of $\overline{ZX}$.
         V is the midpt. of $\overline{TW}$.
   Prove: $\overline{SX} \cong \overline{SW}$

12 Given: $\overrightarrow{PR}$ bisects $\angle QPS$.
         $\overrightarrow{KO}$ bisects $\angle JKM$.
         $\angle 1$ is supp. to $\angle JKM$.
         $\angle 1$ is supp. to $\angle QPS$.
   Conclusion: $\angle 2 \cong \angle 3$

13 Given: $\angle 1 \cong \angle 2$;
         $\overrightarrow{BG}$ bisects $\angle ABF$.
         $\overrightarrow{CE}$ bisects $\angle FCD$.
   Prove: $\angle 3 \cong \angle 4$

Problem Set B, *continued*

14 If four times the supplement of an angle is added to eight times the angle's complement, the sum is equivalent to three straight angles. Find the measure of the angle that is supplementary to the complement.

Problem Set C

15 Point T is located on the graph so that $\overleftrightarrow{RT}$ is perpendicular to the x-axis and $3 < RT < 5$. Find the restrictions on the coordinates of T.

• R(–5, 1)

y-axis

x-axis

16 Given: $\angle 1 \cong \angle 2$,
$\overrightarrow{PE}$ bis. $\angle APN$,
$\overrightarrow{NE}$ bis. $\angle ANP$
Prove: $\angle XPE \cong \angle ENY$

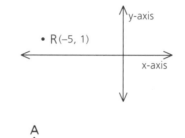

TRANSITIVE AND SUBSTITUTION PROPERTIES

Objectives

After studying this section, you will be able to
- Apply the transitive properties of angles and segments
- Apply the Substitution Property

Part One: Introduction

Transitive Properties

Suppose that $\angle A \cong \angle B$ and $\angle A \cong \angle C$. Is $\angle B \cong \angle C$?

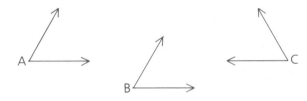

The transitive property of algebra can be used to prove this general rule.

Theorem 16	***If angles (or segments) are congruent to the same angle (or segment), they are congruent to each other. (Transitive Property)***

Theorem 16 can be used twice to prove the next theorem.

Theorem 17	***If angles (or segments) are congruent to congruent angles (or segments), they are congruent to each other. (Transitive Property)***

Substitution Property

In your algebra studies and in some of the problems you have worked this year, you have solved for a variable such as x and then *substituted* the value you found for that variable.

Example   *If ∠A ≅ ∠B, find m∠A.*

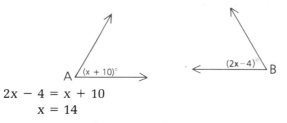

$$2x - 4 = x + 10$$
$$x = 14$$

We can now substitute 14 for x in m∠A = x + 10 to find that
m∠A = 14 + 10 = 24.

The Substitution Property can also be applied when no variables are involved.

If ∠1 is comp. to ∠2 and ∠2 ≅ ∠3, then ∠1
is comp. to ∠3 by **substitution.**

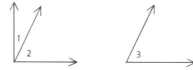

Part Two: Sample Problems

Problem 1   *Given:* $\overline{FG} \cong \overline{KJ}$,
          $\overline{GH} \cong \overline{KJ}$
     Prove: $\overleftrightarrow{KG}$ *bisects* $\overline{FH}$.

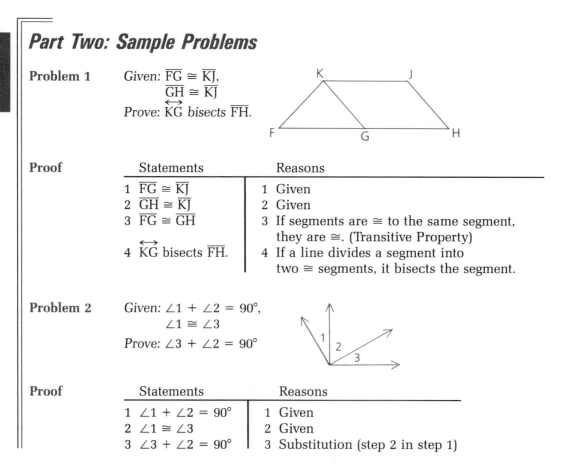

Proof

Statements	Reasons
1 $\overline{FG} \cong \overline{KJ}$	1 Given
2 $\overline{GH} \cong \overline{KJ}$	2 Given
3 $\overline{FG} \cong \overline{GH}$	3 If segments are ≅ to the same segment, they are ≅. (Transitive Property)
4 $\overleftrightarrow{KG}$ bisects $\overline{FH}$.	4 If a line divides a segment into two ≅ segments, it bisects the segment.

Problem 2   *Given:* ∠1 + ∠2 = 90°,
          ∠1 ≅ ∠3
     Prove: ∠3 + ∠2 = 90°

Proof

Statements	Reasons
1 ∠1 + ∠2 = 90°	1 Given
2 ∠1 ≅ ∠3	2 Given
3 ∠3 + ∠2 = 90°	3 Substitution (step 2 in step 1)

Problem 3   If ∠P ≅ ∠R and ∠Q ≅ ∠R, express
m∠Q in terms of x and a.

Solution
$$2y + a = x + y + a$$
$$2y = x + y$$
$$y = x$$

$$m\angle P = x + y + a = x + x + a$$

$$m\angle Q = 2x + a$$

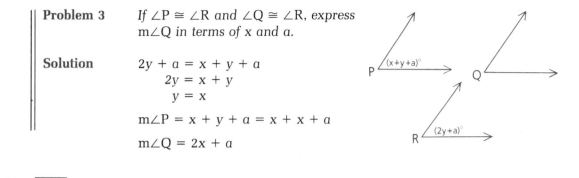

Part Three: Problem Sets

Problem Set A

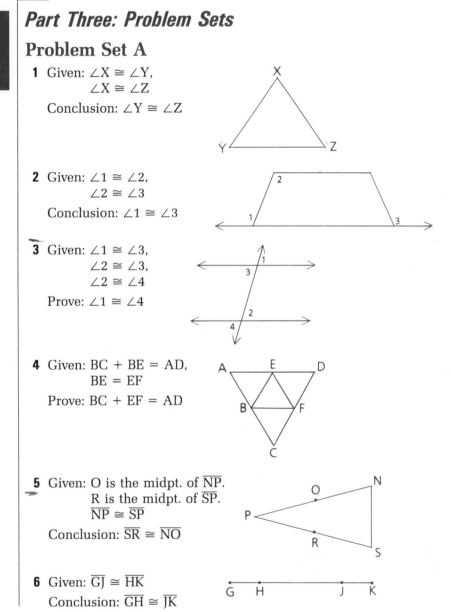

1 Given: ∠X ≅ ∠Y,
∠X ≅ ∠Z
Conclusion: ∠Y ≅ ∠Z

2 Given: ∠1 ≅ ∠2,
∠2 ≅ ∠3
Conclusion: ∠1 ≅ ∠3

3 Given: ∠1 ≅ ∠3,
∠2 ≅ ∠3,
∠2 ≅ ∠4
Prove: ∠1 ≅ ∠4

4 Given: BC + BE = AD,
BE = EF
Prove: BC + EF = AD

5 Given: O is the midpt. of $\overline{NP}$.
R is the midpt. of $\overline{SP}$.
$\overline{NP} \cong \overline{SP}$
Conclusion: $\overline{SR} \cong \overline{NO}$

6 Given: $\overline{GJ} \cong \overline{HK}$
Conclusion: $\overline{GH} \cong \overline{JK}$

Problem Set A, *continued*

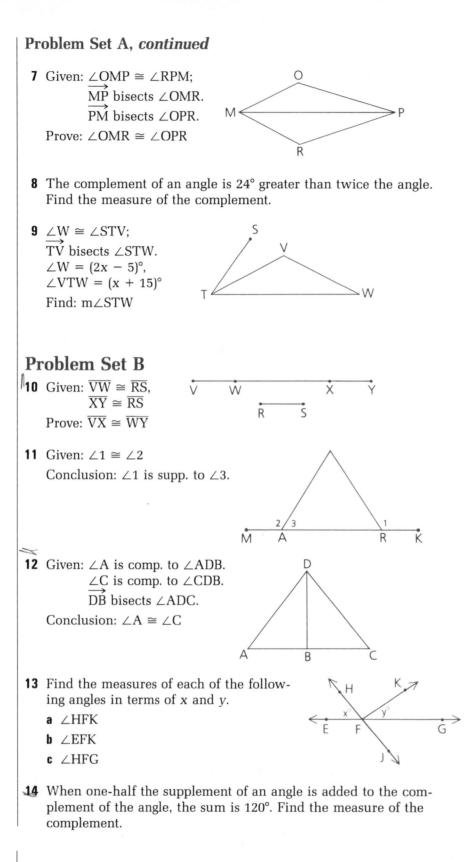

7 Given: ∠OMP ≅ ∠RPM;
   $\overrightarrow{MP}$ bisects ∠OMR.
   $\overrightarrow{PM}$ bisects ∠OPR.
Prove: ∠OMR ≅ ∠OPR

8 The complement of an angle is 24° greater than twice the angle. Find the measure of the complement.

9 ∠W ≅ ∠STV;
   $\overrightarrow{TV}$ bisects ∠STW.
   ∠W = (2x − 5)°,
   ∠VTW = (x + 15)°
Find: m∠STW

Problem Set B

10 Given: $\overline{VW}$ ≅ $\overline{RS}$,
   $\overline{XY}$ ≅ $\overline{RS}$
Prove: $\overline{VX}$ ≅ $\overline{WY}$

11 Given: ∠1 ≅ ∠2
Conclusion: ∠1 is supp. to ∠3.

12 Given: ∠A is comp. to ∠ADB.
   ∠C is comp. to ∠CDB.
   $\overrightarrow{DB}$ bisects ∠ADC.
Conclusion: ∠A ≅ ∠C

13 Find the measures of each of the following angles in terms of x and y.
   a ∠HFK
   b ∠EFK
   c ∠HFG

14 When one-half the supplement of an angle is added to the complement of the angle, the sum is 120°. Find the measure of the complement.

15 Given: ∠A is a right ∠.
       ∠B is a right ∠.
       ∠B ≅ ∠D

Prove: ∠A ≅ ∠D

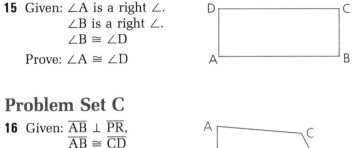

Problem Set C

16 Given: $\overline{AB} \perp \overline{PR}$,
       $\overline{AB} \cong \overline{CD}$

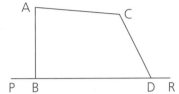

Fool Proof said that since $\overline{AB} \perp \overline{PR}$ and $\overline{AB} \cong \overline{CD}$, he could prove that $\overline{CD} \perp \overline{PR}$ by substitution. What is wrong with Fool's proof?

17 Given: $\overline{AB} \perp \overline{BC}$,
       ∠1 ≇ ∠3

Prove: ∠DBE is a right angle.

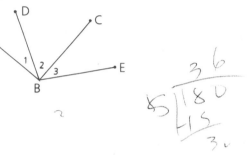

Problem Set D

18 $\overleftrightarrow{AB}$ and $\overleftrightarrow{CD}$ intersect at E, and the ratio of m∠AEC to m∠AED is 2:3. Write an argument to show that it is impossible for m∠DEB to be 80.

19 If two of the four nonstraight angles formed by the intersection of $\overleftrightarrow{FH}$ and $\overleftrightarrow{JK}$ are selected at random, what is the probability that the two angles are congruent?

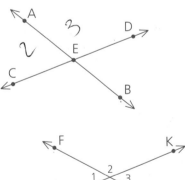

20 Find all possible values of x if x is the measure of an angle that satisfies the following set of conditions:

The angle must have a complement, and three fourths of the supplement of the angle must have a complement.

VERTICAL ANGLES

Objectives

After studying this section, you should be able to
- Recognize opposite rays
- Recognize vertical angles

Part One: Introduction

Opposite Rays

$\overrightarrow{AB}$ and $\overrightarrow{AC}$ are ***opposite rays.***

$\overrightarrow{ED}$ and $\overrightarrow{EF}$ are also opposite rays, as are $\overrightarrow{EG}$ and $\overrightarrow{EH}$.

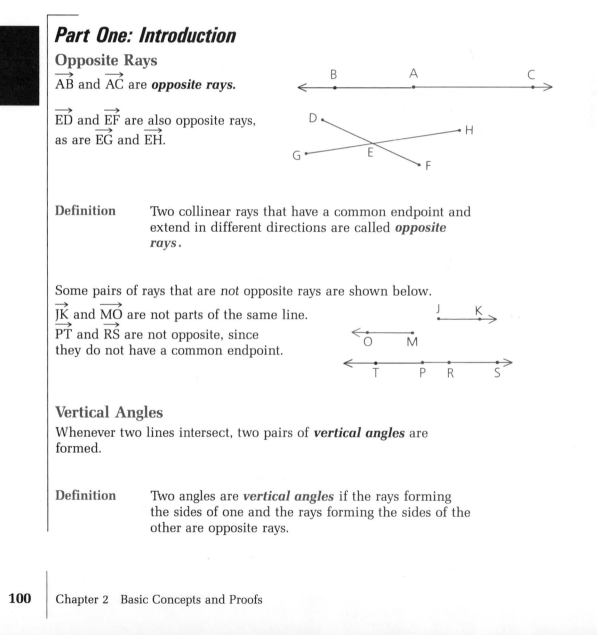

Definition   Two collinear rays that have a common endpoint and extend in different directions are called ***opposite rays.***

Some pairs of rays that are *not* opposite rays are shown below.

$\overrightarrow{JK}$ and $\overrightarrow{MO}$ are not parts of the same line.
$\overrightarrow{PT}$ and $\overrightarrow{RS}$ are not opposite, since they do not have a common endpoint.

Vertical Angles

Whenever two lines intersect, two pairs of ***vertical angles*** are formed.

Definition   Two angles are ***vertical angles*** if the rays forming the sides of one and the rays forming the sides of the other are opposite rays.

∠1 and ∠2 are vertical angles.
∠3 and ∠4 are vertical angles.

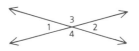

Are ∠3 and ∠2 vertical angles? How do vertical angles compare in size?

Theorem 18   *Vertical angles are congruent.*

Given: Diagram as shown
Prove: ∠5 ≅ ∠7

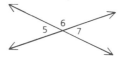

We proved Theorem 18 in Section 2.4, sample problem 3.

Part Two: Sample Problems

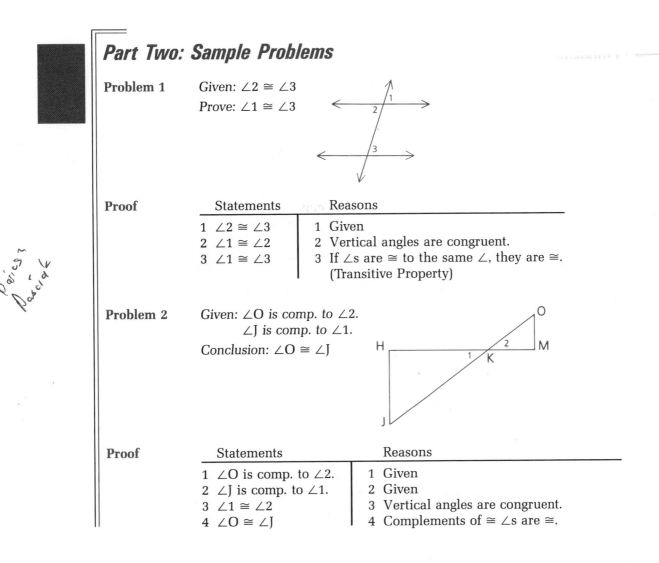

Problem 1   Given: ∠2 ≅ ∠3
                  Prove: ∠1 ≅ ∠3

Proof

Statements	Reasons
1 ∠2 ≅ ∠3	1 Given
2 ∠1 ≅ ∠2	2 Vertical angles are congruent.
3 ∠1 ≅ ∠3	3 If ∠s are ≅ to the same ∠, they are ≅. (Transitive Property)

Problem 2   Given: ∠O is comp. to ∠2.
                       ∠J is comp. to ∠1.
                  Conclusion: ∠O ≅ ∠J

Proof

Statements	Reasons
1 ∠O is comp. to ∠2.	1 Given
2 ∠J is comp. to ∠1.	2 Given
3 ∠1 ≅ ∠2	3 Vertical angles are congruent.
4 ∠O ≅ ∠J	4 Complements of ≅ ∠s are ≅.

Problem 3   Given: m∠4 = 2x + 5,
                        m∠5 = x + 30
                 Find: m∠4

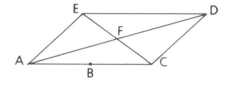

Solution   2x + 5 = x + 30
                        x = 25

                 Therefore, m∠4 = 2(25) + 5, or 55.

Part Three: Problem Sets

Problem Set A

1 a Name three pairs of opposite rays in
       the diagram.

b Name two pairs of vertical angles.

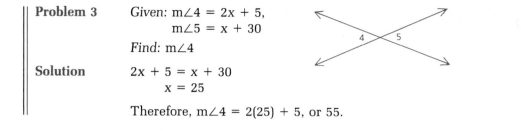

2 Given: ∠1 = 60°32′
    Find: **a** ∠2
          b ∠3
          c ∠4

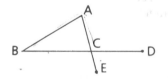

3 Given: ∠5 = (2x + 7)°,
           ∠6 = (x + 25)°
    Find: m∠5

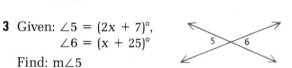

4 Given: ∠A ≅ ∠ACB
    Prove: ∠A ≅ ∠DCE

5 Given: ∠1 ≅ ∠4
    Conclusion: ∠2 ≅ ∠3

6 Given: $\overline{FH} \cong \overline{GJ}$
    Prove: $\overline{FG} \cong \overline{HJ}$

7 Is this possible?

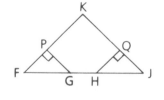

8 Given: $\angle 4 \cong \angle 6$

Prove: $\angle 5 \cong \angle 6$

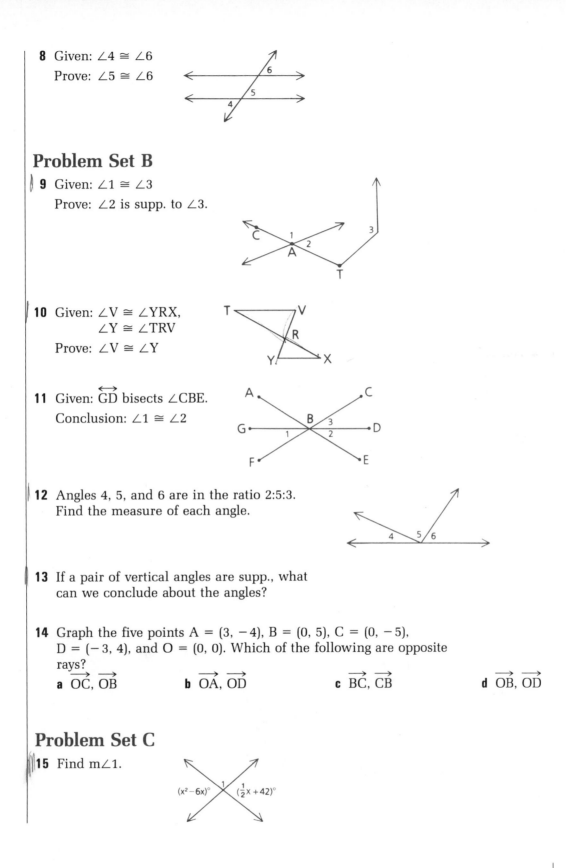

Problem Set B

9 Given: $\angle 1 \cong \angle 3$

Prove: $\angle 2$ is supp. to $\angle 3$.

10 Given: $\angle V \cong \angle YRX$,

$\angle Y \cong \angle TRV$

Prove: $\angle V \cong \angle Y$

11 Given: $\overleftrightarrow{GD}$ bisects $\angle CBE$.

Conclusion: $\angle 1 \cong \angle 2$

12 Angles 4, 5, and 6 are in the ratio 2:5:3. Find the measure of each angle.

13 If a pair of vertical angles are supp., what can we conclude about the angles?

14 Graph the five points A = (3, −4), B = (0, 5), C = (0, −5), D = (−3, 4), and O = (0, 0). Which of the following are opposite rays?

a $\overrightarrow{OC}, \overrightarrow{OB}$
b $\overrightarrow{OA}, \overrightarrow{OD}$
c $\overrightarrow{BC}, \overrightarrow{CB}$
d $\overrightarrow{OB}, \overrightarrow{OD}$

Problem Set C

15 Find $m\angle 1$.

$(x^2 - 6x)^\circ$ $(\frac{1}{2}x + 42)^\circ$

CHAPTER SUMMARY

CONCEPTS AND PROCEDURES

After studying this section, you should be able to
- Recognize the need for clarity and concision in proofs (2.1)
- Understand the concept of perpendicularity (2.1)
- Recognize complementary and supplementary angles (2.2)
- Follow a five-step procedure to draw logical conclusions (2.3)
- Prove angles congruent by means of four new theorems (2.4)
- Apply the addition properties of segments and angles (2.5)
- Apply the subtraction properties of segments and angles (2.5)
- Apply the multiplication and division properties of segments and angles (2.6)
- Apply the transitive properties of angles and segments (2.7)
- Apply the Substitution Property (2.7)
- Recognize opposite rays (2.8)
- Recognize vertical angles (2.8)

VOCABULARY

complement (2.2)
complementary angles (2.2)
coordinates (2.1)
oblique lines (2.1)
opposite rays (2.8)
origin (2.1)
perpendicular (2.1)

substitute (2.7)
substitution (2.7)
supplement (2.2)
supplementary angles (2.2)
vertical angles (2.8)
x-axis (2.1)
y-axis (2.1)

REVIEW PROBLEMS

Problem Set A

1 Given: $\overline{JK} \perp \overline{KM}$
Prove: $\angle JKO$ is comp. to $\angle OKM$.

2 Given: $\overline{PV} \cong \overline{PR}$,
$\overline{VT} \cong \overline{RS}$
Conclusion: $\overline{PT} \cong \overline{PS}$

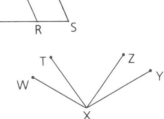

3 Given: $\angle WXT \cong \angle YXZ$
Prove: $\angle WXZ \cong \angle TXY$

4 Given: $\overline{FG} \cong \overline{JH}$;
N is the midpt. of $\overline{FG}$.
O is the midpt. of $\overline{JH}$.
Prove: $\overline{NG} \cong \overline{OH}$

5 Given: $\overline{RV}$ and $\overline{SW}$ trisect $\overline{PT}$ and $\overline{PX}$.
$\overline{ST} \cong \overline{WX}$
Conclusion: $\overline{PT} \cong \overline{PX}$

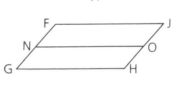

6 Given: Diagram as shown,
$\angle 1 \cong \angle 4$
Prove: $\angle 2 \cong \angle 3$

7 Point E divides $\overline{DF}$ into segments in a
ratio (from left to right) of 5:2.
If DF = 21 cm, find EF.

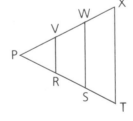

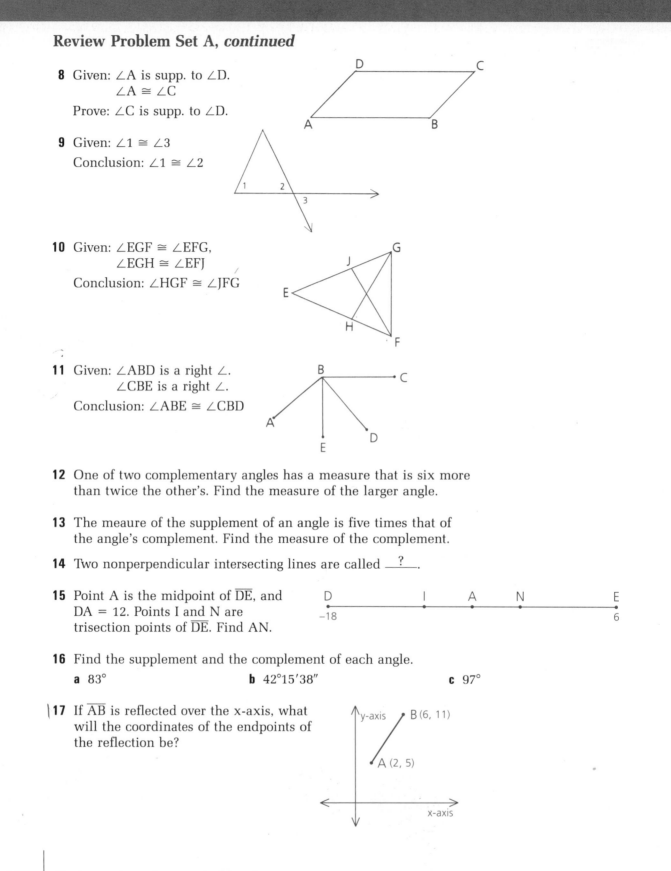

8 Given: ∠A is supp. to ∠D.
   ∠A ≅ ∠C
Prove: ∠C is supp. to ∠D.

9 Given: ∠1 ≅ ∠3
Conclusion: ∠1 ≅ ∠2

10 Given: ∠EGF ≅ ∠EFG,
     ∠EGH ≅ ∠EFJ
Conclusion: ∠HGF ≅ ∠JFG

11 Given: ∠ABD is a right ∠.
     ∠CBE is a right ∠.
Conclusion: ∠ABE ≅ ∠CBD

12 One of two complementary angles has a measure that is six more than twice the other's. Find the measure of the larger angle.

13 The meaure of the supplement of an angle is five times that of the angle's complement. Find the measure of the complement.

14 Two nonperpendicular intersecting lines are called ___?___.

15 Point A is the midpoint of $\overline{DE}$, and DA = 12. Points I and N are trisection points of $\overline{DE}$. Find AN.

16 Find the supplement and the complement of each angle.
   a 83°   **b** 42°15′38″   **c** 97°

17 If $\overline{AB}$ is reflected over the x-axis, what will the coordinates of the endpoints of the reflection be?

18 A point, R, was rotated about the origin, first 180° clockwise and then 90° counterclockwise. It ended at R' = (5, 0). Find the coordinates of point R.

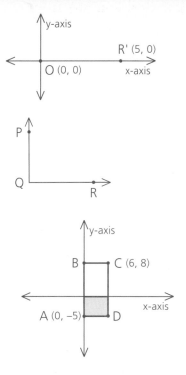

19 ∠PQR is a right angle. If $\overrightarrow{QS}$ is drawn at random between the sides of ∠PQR, what is the probability that

a ∠PQS and ∠SQR are complementary?
b ∠PQS is between 0° and 45°?

20 ABCD is a rectangle.

a Find the coordinates of B and D.
b If a point within ABCD is picked at random, what is the probability that it is in the shaded region?

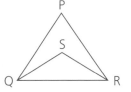

21 Given: ∠PQR ≅ ∠PRQ;
  $\overrightarrow{QS}$ bisects ∠PQR.
  $\overrightarrow{RS}$ bisects ∠PRQ.
  ∠PQR = 87°26′
Find: ∠PRS

Problem Set B

22 Given: ∠1 is comp. to ∠3.
  ∠4 is comp. to ∠2.
Conclusion: ∠1 ≅ ∠4

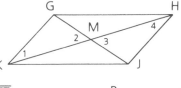

23 Given: O is the midpoint of $\overline{NP}$.
  $\overline{RN} \cong \overline{PO}$
Conclusion: $\overline{RN} \cong \overline{NO}$

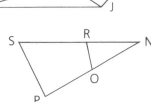

24 Given: ∠F ≅ ∠1,
  ∠J ≅ ∠2,
  $\overline{FK} \perp \overline{KH}$,
  $\overline{GK} \perp \overline{KJ}$
Prove: ∠F ≅ ∠J

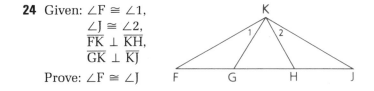

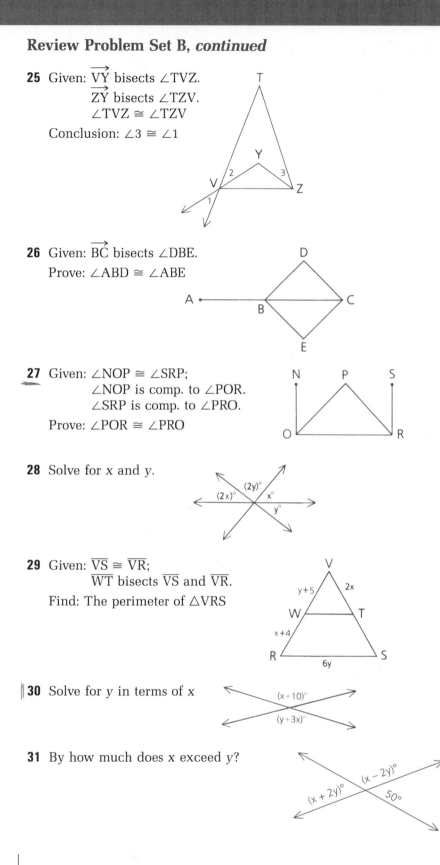

25 Given: $\overrightarrow{VY}$ bisects $\angle TVZ$.
$\quad\quad\quad \overrightarrow{ZY}$ bisects $\angle TZV$.
$\quad\quad\quad \angle TVZ \cong \angle TZV$

Conclusion: $\angle 3 \cong \angle 1$

26 Given: $\overrightarrow{BC}$ bisects $\angle DBE$.
$\quad\quad$ Prove: $\angle ABD \cong \angle ABE$

27 Given: $\angle NOP \cong \angle SRP$;
$\quad\quad\quad \angle NOP$ is comp. to $\angle POR$.
$\quad\quad\quad \angle SRP$ is comp. to $\angle PRO$.
$\quad\quad$ Prove: $\angle POR \cong \angle PRO$

28 Solve for x and y.

29 Given: $\overline{VS} \cong \overline{VR}$;
$\quad\quad\quad \overline{WT}$ bisects $\overline{VS}$ and $\overline{VR}$.
$\quad\quad$ Find: The perimeter of $\triangle VRS$

30 Solve for y in terms of x

31 By how much does x exceed y?

32 The measure of the supplement of an angle exceeds twice the measure of the complement of the angle by 20. Find the measure of half of the complement.

33 $\overrightarrow{BD}$ bisects $\angle ABC$.

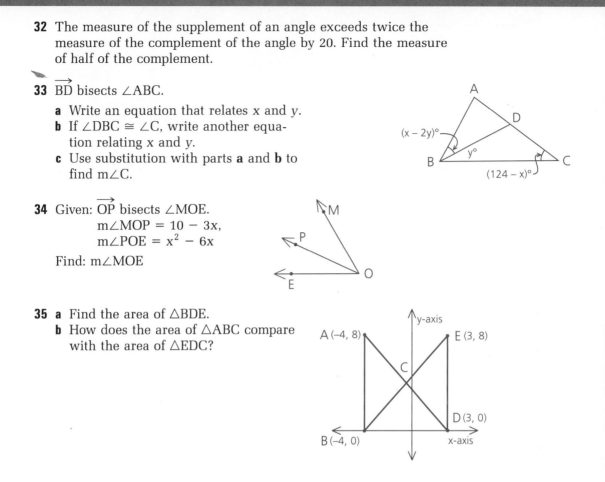

    a Write an equation that relates x and y.
    b If $\angle DBC \cong \angle C$, write another equation relating x and y.
    c Use substitution with parts **a** and **b** to find $m\angle C$.

34 Given: $\overrightarrow{OP}$ bisects $\angle MOE$.
             $m\angle MOP = 10 - 3x$,
             $m\angle POE = x^2 - 6x$
    Find: $m\angle MOE$

35 **a** Find the area of $\triangle BDE$.
    b How does the area of $\triangle ABC$ compare with the area of $\triangle EDC$?

Problem Set C

36 With respect to the origin, point $A = (1, 2)$ is rotated 100° clockwise, then 80° counterclockwise, then 210° clockwise, and finally 50° counterclockwise to point B.

    a Find the coordinates of point B.
    b After which of the four rotations was the point in Quadrant I?

37 Tippy Van Winkle is awakened from a deep sleep by the cuckoo of a clock that sounds every half hour. Before Tippy can look at the clock, his brother Bippy enters the room and offers to bet $10 that the hands of the clock form an acute angle. Assuming that the hands have not moved since the cuckoo sounded, how much should Tippy put up against Bippy's $10 so that it is an even bet?

38 Given: $\angle ABD$ is supp. to $\angle EDB$.
           $\overrightarrow{BC}$ bisects $\angle ABD$.
           $\overrightarrow{DC}$ bisects $\angle BDE$.
    Prove: $\angle CBD$ is comp. to $\angle BDC$.
           (Use a paragraph proof.)

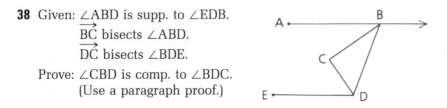

CONGRUENT TRIANGLES

C ongruent triangles create a geometric design
in this painting by Dorothea Rockburne.

WHAT ARE CONGRUENT FIGURES?

Objectives

After studying this section, you will be able to
- Understand the concept of congruent figures
- Accurately identify the corresponding parts of figures

Part One: Introduction

Congruent Figures

Although you learned a bit about the art of proof in Chapters 1 and 2, you may still be uneasy about proofs. You will, however, find your confidence growing as you work with triangles in this chapter. What you discover about congruent triangles will help you understand the characteristics of the other geometric figures you will meet in your studies.

In general, two geometric figures are congruent if one of them could be placed on top of the other and fit exactly, point for point, side for side, and angle for angle. *Congruent figures have the same size and shape.*

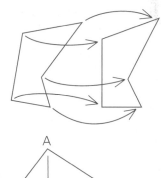

Every triangle has six parts—three angles and three sides. When we say that $\triangle ABC \cong \triangle FED$, we mean that $\angle A \cong \angle F$, $\angle B \cong \angle E$, and $\angle C \cong \angle D$ and that $\overline{AB} \cong \overline{FE}$, $\overline{BC} \cong \overline{ED}$, and $\overline{CA} \cong \overline{DF}$.

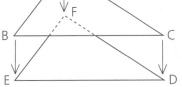

Definition   *Congruent triangles* $\Longleftrightarrow$ all pairs of corresponding parts are congruent.

Remember, an arrow symbol ($\Longrightarrow$) means "implies" ("If . . ., then . . ."). If the arrow is double ($\Longleftrightarrow$), the statement is reversible.

Would the statement △ABC ≅ △DEF be correct? The answer is no! Corresponding letters must match in the correspondence.

To say that △ABC ≅ △DEF is incorrect because △ABC cannot be placed on △DEF so that A falls on D, B on E, and C on F. Would it be correct to say that △EDF ≅ △BCA?

In later chapters we will use the following definition.

Definition   *Congruent polygons* ⟺ all pairs of corresponding parts are congruent.

Writing proofs involving congruent triangles will be unnecessarily tedious unless we shorten some of the reasons. From now on, therefore, we will refer to many theorems and postulates in proofs only by the names or abbreviations we have assigned. You may wish to review the following properties, presented in Chapter 2:

Addition Property   Multiplication Property   Transitive Property
Division Property   Subtraction Property   Substitution Property

More About Correspondences
Notice that △KET is a *reflection* of △KIT over $\overline{KT}$.

∠I reflects onto ∠E.
∠1 reflects onto ∠2.
∠3 reflects onto ∠4.
$\overline{KI}$ reflects onto $\overline{KE}$.
$\overline{IT}$ reflects onto $\overline{ET}$.

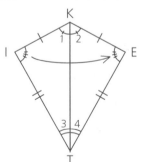

Notice also that $\overline{KT}$ is the sixth corresponding part. $\overline{KT}$ reflects onto itself. In fact, it is actually a side shared by the two triangles. We often need to include a shared side in a proof. Whenever a side or an angle is shared by two figures, we can say that the side or angle is congruent to itself. This property is called the *Reflexive Property.*

Postulate   *Any segment or angle is congruent to itself.*
              (Reflexive Property)

∠PQR, in △PQR, is congruent to ∠SQT, in △SQT, by the Reflexive Property.

Notice that ∠SQT and ∠PQR are actually different names for the same angle. We used different names so that you could see that the angle belonged to two different triangles.

The two figures shown are congruent.

$$PQRST \cong VWXYZ$$

The correspondence is evident if we **slide** PQRST onto VWXYZ.

The triangles at the right are congruent. To determine the correspondence of the triangles, we can **rotate** △FGH onto △LKH about H.

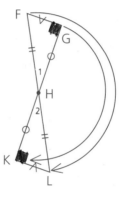

Angle 1 at H rotates onto angle 2 at H.

Thus, all six pairs of corresponding parts are congruent.

Part Two: Sample Problems

In the following two problems, try to justify each conclusion with one of the properties presented in Chapter 2 and in this section.

Problem 1 Given: M *and* N *are midpoints.*
$\overline{DC} \cong \overline{AB}$, $\overline{AB} \cong \overline{DB}$,
∠1 ≅ ∠4, ∠2 ≅ ∠3

Conclusions: **a** ∠ADC ≅ ∠ABC
b $\overline{CM} \cong \overline{AN}$
c $\overline{BD} \cong \overline{DB}$
d $\overline{DC} \cong \overline{DB}$

Answers **a** Addition Property
b Division Property
c Reflexive Property
d Transitive Property

Problem 2   Given: $\overrightarrow{FP}$ and $\overrightarrow{GP}$ are angle bisectors.
∠5 is an acute angle.
∠5 ≅ ∠7, $\overline{PF}$ ≅ $\overline{PG}$, $\overline{QG}$ ≅ $\overline{FR}$

Conclusions: **a** ∠QFG ≅ ∠RGF
b $\overline{QP}$ ≅ $\overline{PR}$
c ∠7 is an acute angle.
d ∠FER ≅ ∠GEQ

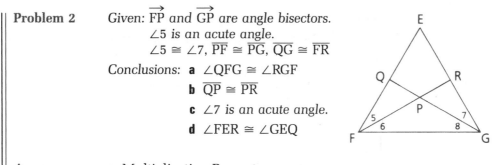

Answers   **a** Multiplication Property
b Subtraction Property
c Substitution
d Reflexive Property

Part Three: Problem Set

In problems 1–3, indicate which triangles are congruent. Be sure to have the correspondence of letters correct.

1 △ERC ≅ ___?___
Why is $\overline{RC}$ ≅ $\overline{RC}$?

2 E is the midpt. of $\overline{TP}$.
△SPE ≅ ___?___

3 △BOW ≅ ___?___
Why is ∠1 ≅ ∠2?

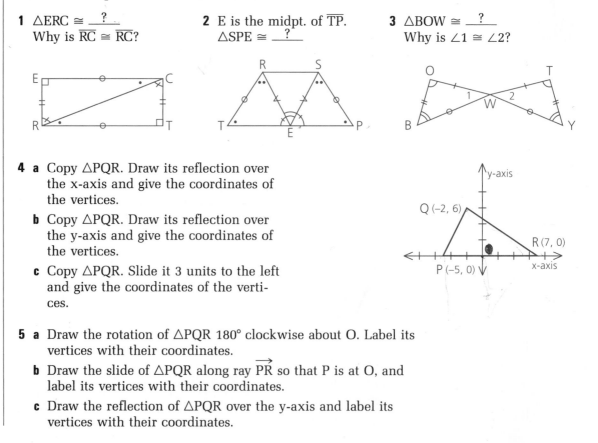

4 a Copy △PQR. Draw its reflection over the x-axis and give the coordinates of the vertices.
b Copy △PQR. Draw its reflection over the y-axis and give the coordinates of the vertices.
c Copy △PQR. Slide it 3 units to the left and give the coordinates of the vertices.

5 a Draw the rotation of △PQR 180° clockwise about O. Label its vertices with their coordinates.
b Draw the slide of △PQR along ray $\overrightarrow{PR}$ so that P is at O, and label its vertices with their coordinates.
c Draw the reflection of △PQR over the y-axis and label its vertices with their coordinates.

THREE WAYS TO PROVE TRIANGLES CONGRUENT

3.2

Objectives

After studying this section, you will be able to
- Identify included angles and included sides
- Apply the SSS postulate
- Apply the SAS postulate
- Apply the ASA postulate

Part One: Introduction

Included Angles and Included Sides

In the figure at the right, ∠H is ***included*** by the sides $\overline{GH}$ and $\overline{HJ}$. Side $\overline{GH}$ is included by ∠H and ∠G. Can you name the sides that include ∠G? Can you name the angles that include side $\overline{HJ}$?

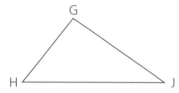

The SSS Postulate

Proving triangles congruent could be a very tedious task if we had to verify the congruence of every one of the six pairs of corresponding parts. Fortunately, triangles have some special properties that will enable us to prove two triangles congruent by comparing only three specially chosen pairs of corresponding parts. One of these sets of pairs consists of the corresponding sides.

This is the triangle that Jill built.

These are the three sticks that make up the triangle that Jill built.

Jill knows that there is only one triangle that can be constructed from three given sticks. In other words, if Jack has three sticks that are the same size as Jill's sticks, the only triangle he can build is one congruent to the triangle that Jill built.

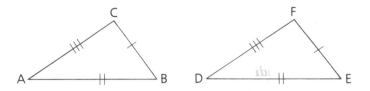

The tick marks on △ABC and △DEF show sufficient conditions for us to know that △ABC ≅ △DEF. This special property of triangles can be expressed as a postulate, which we will refer to as the SSS postulate. Each S stands for a pair of congruent corresponding sides, such as $\overline{AC}$ and $\overline{DF}$.

Postulate   *If there exists a correspondence between the vertices of two triangles such that three sides of one triangle are congruent to the corresponding sides of the other triangle, the two triangles are congruent. (SSS)*

The SSS relationship can be proved by methods that are not part of this course; we shall assume it and use the abbreviation SSS in proofs.

In the figure, is △GHJ congruent to △GKJ by SSS? The tick marks give us *two* pairs of congruent sides, but that is not enough. However, since $\overline{GJ}$ is a common side of both triangles, $\overline{GJ} \cong \overline{GJ}$ by the Reflexive Property. So we actually do have SSS!

The following diagram illustrates the flow of logic that proves that △GHJ and △GKJ are congruent.

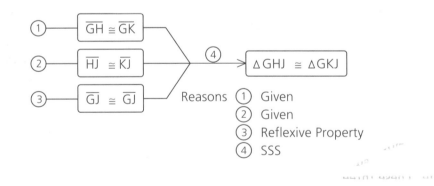

The SAS Postulate

It can also be shown that only two pairs of congruent corresponding sides are needed to establish the congruence of two triangles if the angles included by the sides are known to be congruent.

Postulate	*If there exists a correspondence between the vertices of two triangles such that two sides and the included angle of one triangle are congruent to the corresponding parts of the other triangle, the two triangles are congruent. (SAS)*

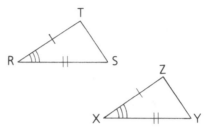

The fact that the *A* is between the *S*'s in SAS should help you remember that the congruent angles in the triangles must be the angles *included by* the pairs of congruent sides. Although this relationship, like SSS, can be proved, we shall assume it and use the abbreviation SAS in proofs.

The ASA Postulate

The following postulate will give us a third way of proving triangles congruent.

Postulate	*If there exists a correspondence between the vertices of two triangles such that two angles and the included side of one triangle are congruent to the corresponding parts of the other triangle, the two triangles are congruent. (ASA)*

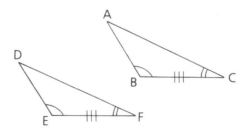

Again, ASA can be proved, although we shall assume it. The arrangement of the letters in *ASA* matches the arrangement of marked parts in the triangles; the congruent sides must be the ones included by the pairs of congruent angles.

If you are curious, you may be wondering whether SSS, SAS, and ASA are the only shortcuts for proving that triangles are congruent. Not quite. These three postulates, however, are enough to get us started on proofs that triangles are congruent.

Study the sample problems carefully before you attempt the problem sets. Notice that we call SSS, SAS, and ASA methods of proof. Any definition, postulate, or theorem can be called a method if it is a key reason in proofs.

Part Two: Sample Problems

In problems 1–3 and 5, you are given the congruent angles and sides shown by the tick marks. Name the additional congruent sides or angles needed to prove that the triangles are congruent by each specified method.

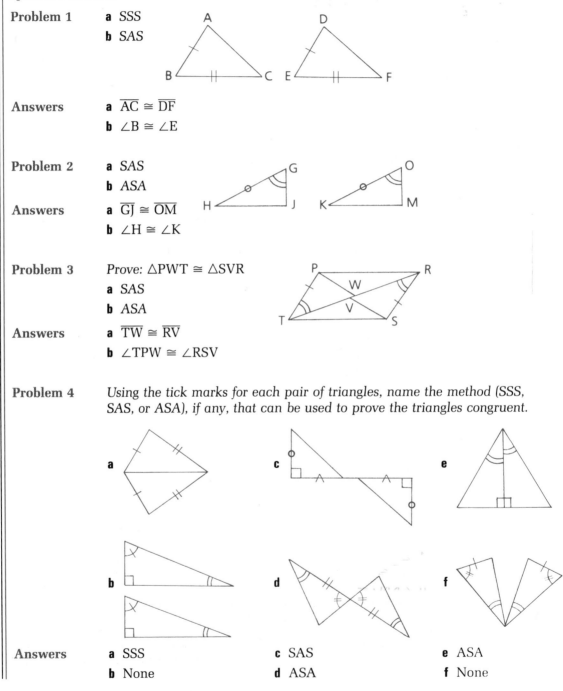

Problem 1   **a** SSS
            b SAS

Answers   **a** $\overline{AC} \cong \overline{DF}$
            b $\angle B \cong \angle E$

Problem 2   **a** SAS
            b ASA

Answers   **a** $\overline{GJ} \cong \overline{OM}$
            b $\angle H \cong \angle K$

Problem 3   Prove: $\triangle PWT \cong \triangle SVR$
            a SAS
            b ASA

Answers   **a** $\overline{TW} \cong \overline{RV}$
            b $\angle TPW \cong \angle RSV$

Problem 4   Using the tick marks for each pair of triangles, name the method (SSS, SAS, or ASA), if any, that can be used to prove the triangles congruent.

Answers   **a** SSS   **c** SAS   **e** ASA
            b None   **d** ASA   **f** None

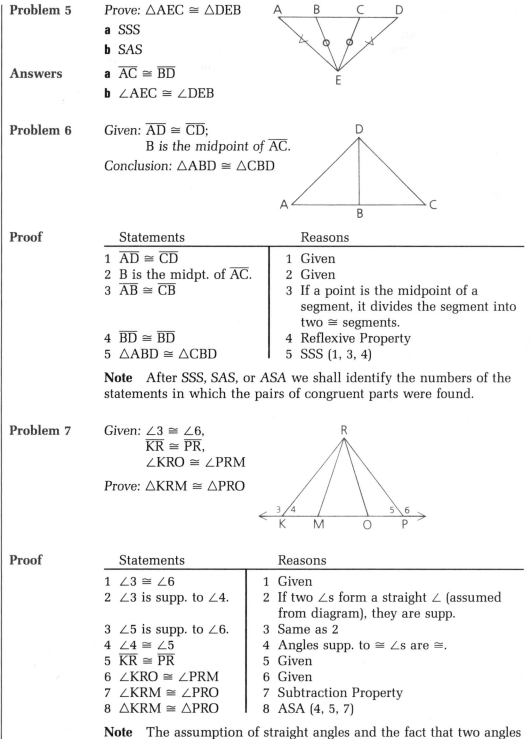

Problem 5   *Prove:* △AEC ≅ △DEB

           a *SSS*

           b *SAS*

Answers   **a** $\overline{AC} \cong \overline{BD}$

           b ∠AEC ≅ ∠DEB

Problem 6   *Given:* $\overline{AD} \cong \overline{CD}$;

                  B is the midpoint of $\overline{AC}$.

           Conclusion: △ABD ≅ △CBD

Proof

Statements	Reasons
1 $\overline{AD} \cong \overline{CD}$	1 Given
2 B is the midpt. of $\overline{AC}$.	2 Given
3 $\overline{AB} \cong \overline{CB}$	3 If a point is the midpoint of a segment, it divides the segment into two ≅ segments.
4 $\overline{BD} \cong \overline{BD}$	4 Reflexive Property
5 △ABD ≅ △CBD	5 SSS (1, 3, 4)

Note   After *SSS*, *SAS*, or *ASA* we shall identify the numbers of the statements in which the pairs of congruent parts were found.

Problem 7   *Given:* ∠3 ≅ ∠6,

                  $\overline{KR} \cong \overline{PR}$,

                  ∠KRO ≅ ∠PRM

           Prove: △KRM ≅ △PRO

Proof

Statements	Reasons
1 ∠3 ≅ ∠6	1 Given
2 ∠3 is supp. to ∠4.	2 If two ∠s form a straight ∠ (assumed from diagram), they are supp.
3 ∠5 is supp. to ∠6.	3 Same as 2
4 ∠4 ≅ ∠5	4 Angles supp. to ≅ ∠s are ≅.
5 $\overline{KR} \cong \overline{PR}$	5 Given
6 ∠KRO ≅ ∠PRM	6 Given
7 ∠KRM ≅ ∠PRO	7 Subtraction Property
8 △KRM ≅ △PRO	8 ASA (4, 5, 7)

Note   The assumption of straight angles and the fact that two angles that form a straight angle are supplementary may now be combined in one step (as in step 2 above).

Part Three: Problem Sets

Problem Set

1 Study the congruent sides and angles shown by the tick marks, then identify the additional information needed to support the specified method of proving that the indicated triangles are congruent.

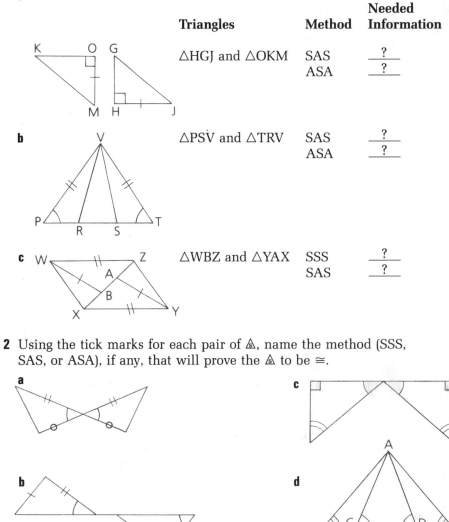

	Triangles	Method	Needed Information
	△HGJ and △OKM	SAS ASA	? ?
b	△PSV and △TRV	SAS ASA	? ?
c	△WBZ and △YAX	SSS SAS	? ?

2 Using the tick marks for each pair of △, name the method (SSS, SAS, or ASA), if any, that will prove the △ to be ≅.

a

c

b

d

△ABD and △AEC

3 Given: $\overline{AB} \cong \overline{CB}$,
　　　　∠ABD ≅ ∠CBD
Prove: △ABD ≅ △CBD

Given: $\angle 1 \cong \angle 2$,
$\overline{EF} \cong \overline{HF}$

Prove: $\triangle EFJ \cong \triangle HFG$

5 Given: $\overline{RO} \perp \overline{MP}$,
$\overline{MO} \cong \overline{OP}$

Prove: $\triangle MRO \cong \triangle PRO$

6 Given: $\overrightarrow{SV}$ bisects $\angle TSB$.
$\overrightarrow{VS}$ bisects $\angle TVB$.

Prove: $\triangle TSV \cong \triangle BSV$

7 Given: $\overline{TV} \cong \overline{XW}$,
$\overline{VA} \cong \overline{WA}$,
$\overline{TA} \cong \overline{XA}$

Prove: $\triangle TVA \cong \triangle XWA$

8 Given: $\overline{BC} \cong \overline{FE}$,
$\overline{DC} \cong \overline{DE}$,
$\angle 5 \cong \angle 6$

Prove: $\triangle BDG \cong \triangle FDG$

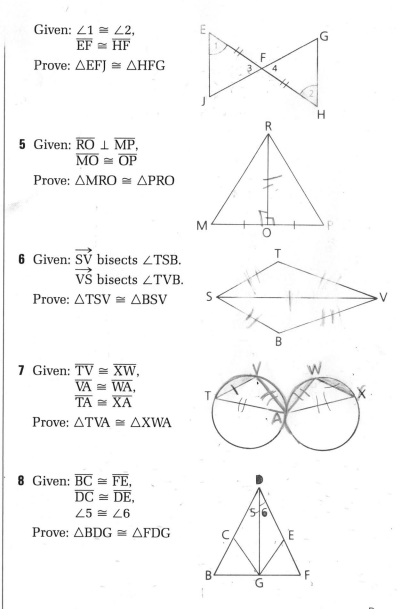

9 Two triangles are standing up on a table-top as shown. $\overline{PA} \cong \overline{PC}$ and $\overline{BA} \cong \overline{BC}$.

Prove: $\triangle PBA \cong \triangle PBC$

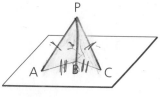

10 The perimeter of ABCD is 85. Find the value of x. Is $\triangle ABC$ congruent to $\triangle ADC$?

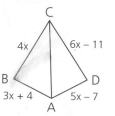

Problem Set A, *continued*

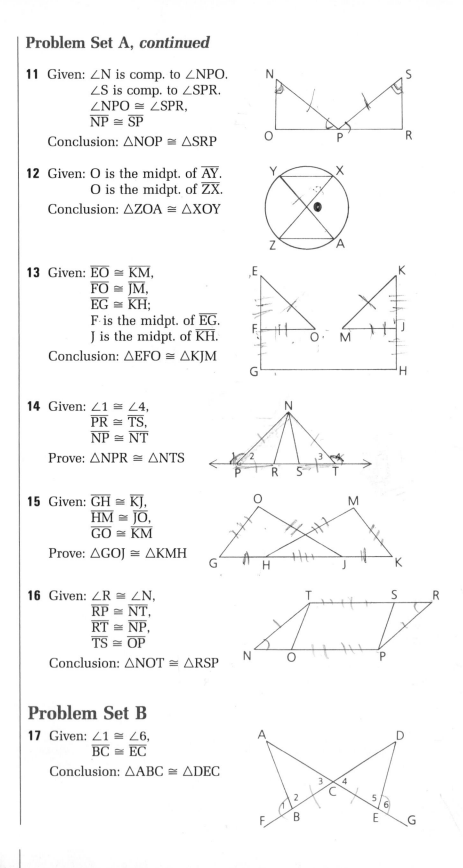

11 Given: ∠N is comp. to ∠NPO.
∠S is comp. to ∠SPR.
∠NPO ≅ ∠SPR,
$\overline{NP} \cong \overline{SP}$

Conclusion: △NOP ≅ △SRP

12 Given: O is the midpt. of $\overline{AY}$.
O is the midpt. of $\overline{ZX}$.

Conclusion: △ZOA ≅ △XOY

13 Given: $\overline{EO} \cong \overline{KM}$,
$\overline{FO} \cong \overline{JM}$,
$\overline{EG} \cong \overline{KH}$;
F is the midpt. of $\overline{EG}$.
J is the midpt. of $\overline{KH}$.

Conclusion: △EFO ≅ △KJM

14 Given: ∠1 ≅ ∠4,
$\overline{PR} \cong \overline{TS}$,
$\overline{NP} \cong \overline{NT}$

Prove: △NPR ≅ △NTS

15 Given: $\overline{GH} \cong \overline{KJ}$,
$\overline{HM} \cong \overline{JO}$,
$\overline{GO} \cong \overline{KM}$

Prove: △GOJ ≅ △KMH

16 Given: ∠R ≅ ∠N,
$\overline{RP} \cong \overline{NT}$,
$\overline{RT} \cong \overline{NP}$,
$\overline{TS} \cong \overline{OP}$

Conclusion: △NOT ≅ △RSP

Problem Set B

17 Given: ∠1 ≅ ∠6,
$\overline{BC} \cong \overline{EC}$

Conclusion: △ABC ≅ △DEC

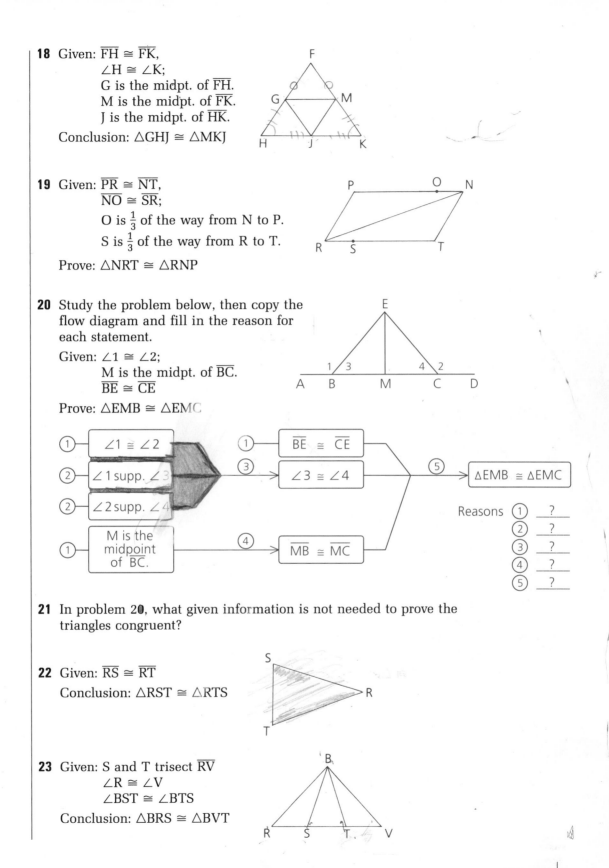

18 Given: $\overline{FH} \cong \overline{FK}$,
  $\angle H \cong \angle K$;
  G is the midpt. of $\overline{FH}$.
  M is the midpt. of $\overline{FK}$.
  J is the midpt. of $\overline{HK}$.
Conclusion: $\triangle GHJ \cong \triangle MKJ$

19 Given: $\overline{PR} \cong \overline{NT}$,
  $\overline{NO} \cong \overline{SR}$;
  O is $\frac{1}{3}$ of the way from N to P.
  S is $\frac{1}{3}$ of the way from R to T.
Prove: $\triangle NRT \cong \triangle RNP$

20 Study the problem below, then copy the flow diagram and fill in the reason for each statement.
Given: $\angle 1 \cong \angle 2$;
  M is the midpt. of $\overline{BC}$.
  $\overline{BE} \cong \overline{CE}$
Prove: $\triangle EMB \cong \triangle EMC$

① $\angle 1 \cong \angle 2$

② $\angle 1$ supp. $\angle 3$

② $\angle 2$ supp. $\angle 4$

① M is the midpoint of $\overline{BC}$.

① $\overline{BE} \cong \overline{CE}$

③ $\angle 3 \cong \angle 4$

④ $\overline{MB} \cong \overline{MC}$

⑤ $\triangle EMB \cong \triangle EMC$

Reasons ① ___?___
  ② ___?___
  ③ ___?___
  ④ ___?___
  ⑤ ___?___

21 In problem 20, what given information is not needed to prove the triangles congruent?

22 Given: $\overline{RS} \cong \overline{RT}$
Conclusion: $\triangle RST \cong \triangle RTS$

23 Given: S and T trisect $\overline{RV}$
  $\angle R \cong \angle V$
  $\angle BST \cong \angle BTS$
Conclusion: $\triangle BRS \cong \triangle BVT$

Problem Set B, *continued*

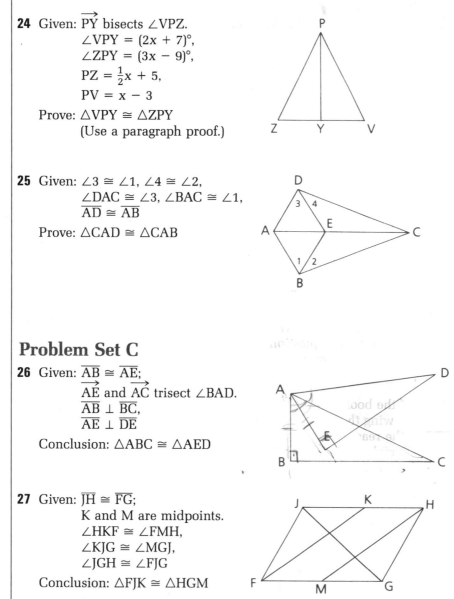

24 Given: $\overrightarrow{PY}$ bisects $\angle VPZ$.
  $\angle VPY = (2x + 7)°$,
  $\angle ZPY = (3x - 9)°$,
  $PZ = \frac{1}{2}x + 5$,
  $PV = x - 3$
Prove: $\triangle VPY \cong \triangle ZPY$
(Use a paragraph proof.)

25 Given: $\angle 3 \cong \angle 1$, $\angle 4 \cong \angle 2$,
  $\angle DAC \cong \angle 3$, $\angle BAC \cong \angle 1$,
  $\overline{AD} \cong \overline{AB}$
Prove: $\triangle CAD \cong \triangle CAB$

Problem Set C

26 Given: $\overline{AB} \cong \overline{AE}$;
  $\overrightarrow{AE}$ and $\overrightarrow{AC}$ trisect $\angle BAD$.
  $\overline{AB} \perp \overline{BC}$,
  $\overline{AE} \perp \overline{DE}$
Conclusion: $\triangle ABC \cong \triangle AED$

27 Given: $\overline{JH} \cong \overline{FG}$;
  K and M are midpoints.
  $\angle HKF \cong \angle FMH$,
  $\angle KJG \cong \angle MGJ$,
  $\angle JGH \cong \angle FJG$
Conclusion: $\triangle FJK \cong \triangle HGM$

28 Consider two triangles, $\triangle ABC$ and $\triangle FDE$, with vertices
A = (0, 7), B = (−4, 0), C = (0, 0), D = (2, 3), E = (2, −1), and
F = (9, −1). Draw a diagram and explain why $\triangle ABC \cong \triangle FDE$.

CPCTC AND CIRCLES

Objectives

After studying this section, you will be able to
- Apply the principle of CPCTC
- Recognize some basic properties of circles

Part One: Introduction

CPCTC

Suppose that in the figure △ABC ≅ △DEF. Is it therefore true that ∠B ≅ ∠E? If you refer to Section 3.1, you will find that we have already answered yes to this question in the definition of *congruent triangles*.

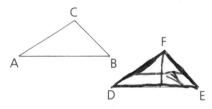

In the portions of the book that follow, we shall often draw such a conclusion *after* knowing that some triangles are congruent. We shall use CPCTC as the reason. *CPCTC* is short for "*Corresponding Parts of Congruent Triangles are Congruent.*" By corresponding parts, we shall mean only the matching angles and sides of the respective triangles.

Introduction to Circles

Point O is the center of the circle shown at the right. By definition, every point of the circle is the same distance from the center. The center, however, is not an element of the circle; the circle consists only of the "rim." A circle is named by its center: this circle is called circle O (or ⊙O).

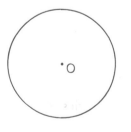

Points A, B, and C lie on circle P (⊙P).
$\overline{PA}$ is called a *radius*.
$\overline{PA}$, $\overline{PB}$, and $\overline{PC}$ are called *radii*.

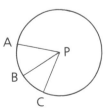

From previous math courses you may remember formulas for the area and the circumference of a circle:

$$A = \pi r^2$$
$$C = 2\pi r$$

By pressing the $\boxed{\pi}$ key on a scientific calculator, you can find that $\pi \approx 3.141592654$.

Theorem 19   ***All radii of a circle are congruent.***

Part Two: Sample Problems

Problem

Given: ⊙P

Conclusion: $\overline{AB} \cong \overline{CD}$

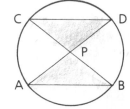

Proof

	Statements		Reasons
1	⊙P	1	Given
2	$\overline{PA} \cong \overline{PB} \cong \overline{PC} \cong \overline{PD}$	2	All radii of a circle are ≅.
3	$\angle CPD \cong \angle APB$	3	Vertical angles are ≅.
4	$\triangle CPD \cong \triangle APB$	4	SAS (2, 3, 2)
5	$\overline{AB} \cong \overline{CD}$	5	CPCTC (Corresponding parts of congruent triangles are congruent.)

Problem 2

Given: ⊙O;
   ∠T is comp. to ∠MOT.
   ∠S is comp. to ∠POS.

Prove: $\overline{MO} \cong \overline{PO}$

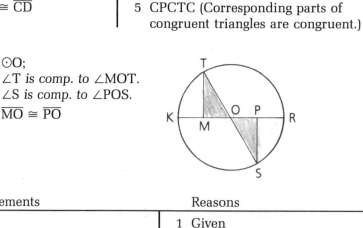

Proof

	Statements		Reasons
1	⊙O	1	Given
2	$\overline{OT} \cong \overline{OS}$	2	All radii of a circle are ≅.
3	∠T is comp. to ∠MOT.	3	Given
4	∠S is comp. to ∠POS.	4	Given
5	$\angle MOT \cong \angle POS$	5	Vertical angles are ≅.
6	$\angle T \cong \angle S$	6	Complements of ≅ ∠s are ≅.
7	$\triangle MOT \cong \triangle POS$ (Watch the correspondence.)	7	ASA (5, 2, 6)
8	$\overline{MO} \cong \overline{PO}$	8	CPCTC

Part Three: Problem Sets

Problem Set

1 Given: $\overline{AB} \cong \overline{DE}$,
$\overline{BC} \cong \overline{EF}$,
$\overline{AC} \cong \overline{DF}$

Prove: $\angle A \cong \angle D$

2 Given: $\angle HGJ \cong \angle KJG$,
$\angle KGJ \cong \angle HJG$

Conclusion: $\overline{HG} \cong \overline{KJ}$

3 Given: $\odot O$,
$\overline{RO} \perp \overline{MP}$

Prove: $\overline{MR} \cong \overline{PR}$

4 Given: T and R trisect $\overline{SW}$.
$\overline{XS} \cong \overline{XW}$,
$\angle S \cong \angle W$

Prove: $\overline{XT} \cong \overline{XR}$

5 Given: $\angle B \cong \angle Y$;
C is the midpt. of $\overline{BY}$.

Conclusion: $\overline{AB} \cong \overline{YZ}$

6 Given: $\odot O$,
$\overline{CD} \cong \overline{DE}$

Prove: $\angle COD \cong \angle DOE$

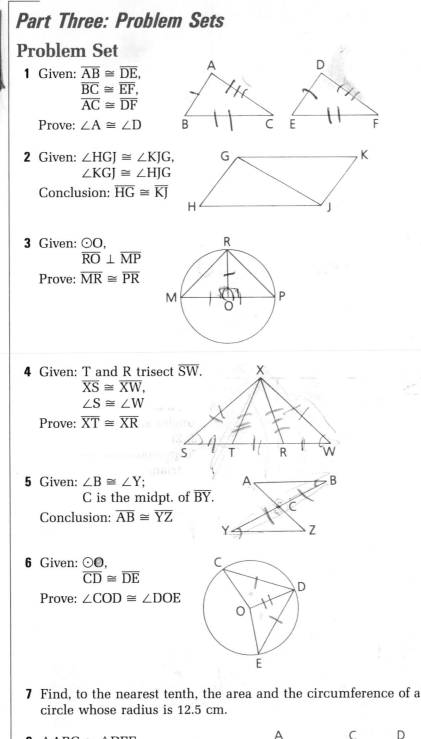

7 Find, to the nearest tenth, the area and the circumference of a circle whose radius is 12.5 cm.

8 $\triangle ABC \cong \triangle DEF$,
$\angle A = 90°$, $\angle B = 50°$, $\angle C = 40°$,
$m\angle E = 12x + 30$, $m\angle F = \frac{y}{2} - 10$,
$m\angle D = \sqrt{z}$

Solve for x, y, and z.

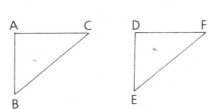

Problem Set A, *continued*

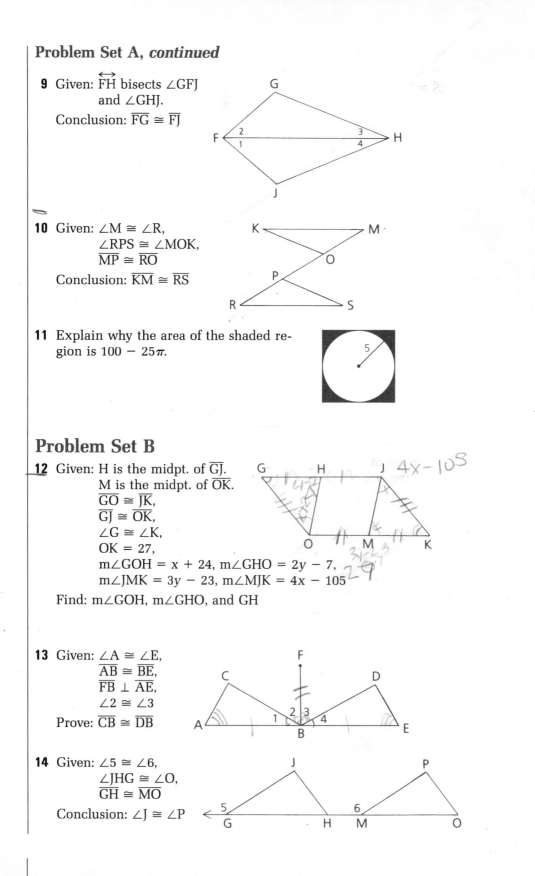

9 Given: $\overleftrightarrow{FH}$ bisects $\angle GFJ$
and $\angle GHJ$.

Conclusion: $\overline{FG} \cong \overline{FJ}$

10 Given: $\angle M \cong \angle R$,
$\angle RPS \cong \angle MOK$,
$\overline{MP} \cong \overline{RO}$

Conclusion: $\overline{KM} \cong \overline{RS}$

11 Explain why the area of the shaded region is $100 - 25\pi$.

Problem Set B

12 Given: H is the midpt. of $\overline{GJ}$.
M is the midpt. of $\overline{OK}$.
$\overline{GO} \cong \overline{JK}$,
$\overline{GJ} \cong \overline{OK}$,
$\angle G \cong \angle K$,
$OK = 27$,
$m\angle GOH = x + 24$, $m\angle GHO = 2y - 7$,
$m\angle JMK = 3y - 23$, $m\angle MJK = 4x - 105$

Find: $m\angle GOH$, $m\angle GHO$, and GH

13 Given: $\angle A \cong \angle E$,
$\overline{AB} \cong \overline{BE}$,
$\overline{FB} \perp \overline{AE}$,
$\angle 2 \cong \angle 3$

Prove: $\overline{CB} \cong \overline{DB}$

14 Given: $\angle 5 \cong \angle 6$,
$\angle JHG \cong \angle O$,
$\overline{GH} \cong \overline{MO}$

Conclusion: $\angle J \cong \angle P$

15 Given: ∠RST ≅ ∠RVT,
　　　　　 ∠RVS ≅ ∠TSV
　　Conclusion: $\overline{RS} \cong \overline{VT}$

16 Given: ∠7 ≅ ∠8,
　　　　　 $\overline{ZY} \cong \overline{WX}$
　　Prove: ∠W ≅ ∠Y

17 Given: ∠AEC ≅ ∠DEB,
　　　　　 $\overline{BE} \cong \overline{CE}$,
　　　　　 ∠ABE ≅ ∠DCE
　　Prove: $\overline{AB} \cong \overline{CD}$

18 Given: $\overline{KG} \cong \overline{GJ}$,
　　　　　 ∠2 ≅ ∠4,
　　　　　 ∠1 is comp. to ∠2.
　　　　　 ∠3 is comp. to ∠4.
　　　　　 ∠FGJ ≅ ∠HGK
　　Conclusion: $\overline{FG} \cong \overline{HG}$

19 a Find the coordinates of point P.
　　b Find the area of the circle.

20 Given: ⊙O,
　　　　　 $\overline{PQ} \cong \overline{QR}$
　　Prove: $\overrightarrow{QO}$ bisects ∠PQR.

Problem Set C

21 Given: $\overline{AE} \cong \overline{FC}$,
　　　　　 $\overline{FB} \cong \overline{DE}$,
　　　　　 ∠CFB ≅ ∠AED
　　Prove: ∠1 ≅ ∠2

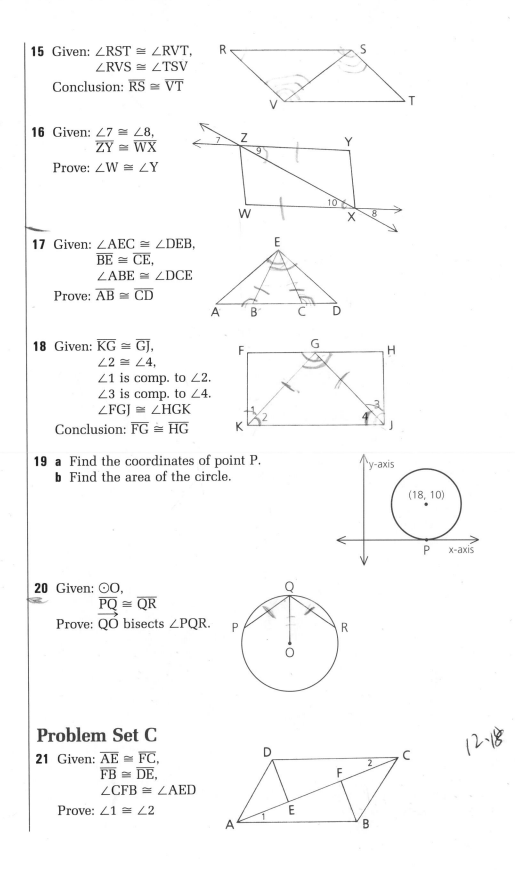

12-18

22 Prove that if $\overline{GJ}$ and $\overline{KH}$ bisect each other, then ∠MHO is larger than ∠K. (Write a paragraph proof.)

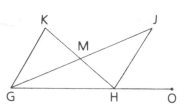

23 A radio antenna is kept perpendicular to the ground by three wires. They are staked at three points on a circle whose center is at the base of the antenna. Justify that the wires are equal in length.

STRUCTURAL CONGRUENT TRIANGLES
Humanizing skyscrapers

The structural engineer William Le Messurier (born 1926) is a pioneer who has used geometric shapes to make taller, lighter, and more spacious skyscrapers that are structurally sound. One of his techniques is to use congruent triangles. In the 915-foot-tall Citicorp Center in Manhattan, he used triangles to more efficiently distribute the downward pressure exerted by each of the building's vertical sections. Each triangle absorbs the stress—the straining forces resulting from weight and gravity—from its section of the building and transfers it to a vertical column down the center of that side of the building. While we might take for granted the congruence of the triangles, it is important to the design of this building. If the triangles were not congruent, then the building's stress would be distributed unevenly. That would make it difficult to predict what would happen to the building as gravity acted upon it over time, or in extreme conditions, such as high winds.

The building's design and structural efficiency make possible the sunken, skylit plaza that sits underneath it, an inviting place to visit. Thus, congruent triangles contribute not only to safety but also to making our cities more pleasant and livable.

3.4 BEYOND CPCTC

Objectives

After studying this section, you will be able to

- Identify medians of triangles
- Identify altitudes of triangles
- Understand why auxiliary lines are used in some proofs
- Write proofs involving steps beyond CPCTC

Part One: Introduction

Medians of Triangles

Three **medians** are shown:

$\overline{AD}$ is a median of $\triangle ABC$.
$\overline{EH}$ is a median of $\triangle EFG$.
$\overline{FJ}$ is a median of $\triangle EFG$.

Every triangle has three medians.

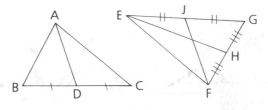

Definition   A **median** of a triangle is a line segment drawn from any vertex of the triangle to the midpoint of the opposite side. (A median divides into two congruent segments, or bisects the side to which it is drawn.)

Altitudes of Triangles

In the first diagram below, $\overline{AD}$ and $\overline{BE}$ are altitudes of $\triangle ABC$.

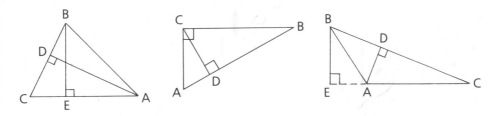

In the middle diagram, $\overline{AC}$ and $\overline{BC}$ and $\overline{CD}$ are altitudes of $\triangle ABC$. Notice that in this case, two of the altitudes are sides of the triangle.

In the diagram on the right, $\overline{AD}$ and $\overline{BE}$ are altitudes of $\triangle ABC$. Notice that altitude $\overline{BE}$ falls outside the triangle. Where does the third altitude lie?

Every triangle has three altitudes.

1-6, (0, 11

Definition   An *altitude* of a triangle is a line segment drawn from any vertex of the triangle to the opposite side, extended if necessary, and perpendicular to that side. (An altitude of a triangle forms right [90°] angles with one of the sides.)

Could an altitude of a triangle be a median as well?

Auxiliary Lines

Consider the following problem.

Given: $\overline{AB} \cong \overline{AC}$,
$\overline{BD} \cong \overline{CD}$

Conclusion: $\angle ABD \cong \angle ACD$

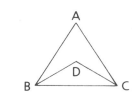

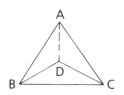

This proof would be easy if a line segment were drawn from A to D. We could then proceed to prove that $\triangle ABD \cong \triangle ACD$ (by SSS) and that $\angle ABD \cong \angle ACD$ (by CPCTC).

You will find that many proofs involve lines, rays, or segments that do not appear in the original figure. These additions to diagrams are called *auxiliary lines.* Most auxiliary lines connect two points already in the diagram, although you will see other types of auxiliary lines later in the course. Whenever we use an auxiliary line in a proof, we must be able to show that such a line can be drawn.

It is a postulate that *one and only one line, ray, or segment can be drawn through any two distinct points.*

Postulate   ***Two points determine a line (or ray or segment).***

The word *determine* indicates that there *is* a line through the given points and there is *no more than one* such line.

Steps Beyond CPCTC

Consider the following problem.

Given: $\overline{AD} \cong \overline{CD}$,
$\angle ADB \cong \angle CDB$

Prove: $\overline{DB}$ is the median to $\overline{AC}$.

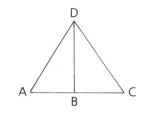

In this problem, we can prove that $\triangle ABD \cong \triangle CBD$ by SAS. Do you see how? Therefore, $\overline{AB} \cong \overline{CB}$ by CPCTC. Now we shall go one step beyond CPCTC. Since $\overline{AB} \cong \overline{CB}$, we may call $\overline{DB}$ a median of $\triangle ACD$, and the proof is complete.

Many proofs involve steps beyond CPCTC. By using CPCTC first, we can identify altitudes, angle bisectors, midpoints, and so forth. You will see some examples in the sample problems to follow.

A fascinating type of proof involves showing that one pair of triangles are congruent and then using CPCTC to show that another pair of triangles are congruent. Such proofs, called *detour proofs*, are explained in detail in Chapter 4.

Part Two: Sample Problems

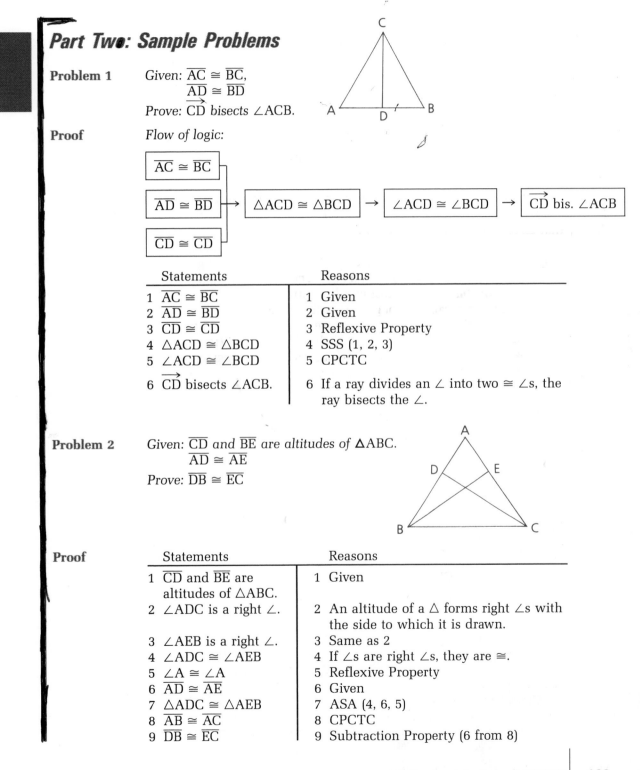

Problem 1   Given: $\overline{AC} \cong \overline{BC}$,
                              $\overline{AD} \cong \overline{BD}$
                  Prove: $\overrightarrow{CD}$ bisects $\angle ACB$.

Proof   *Flow of logic:*

$\overline{AC} \cong \overline{BC}$

$\overline{AD} \cong \overline{BD}$ → $\triangle ACD \cong \triangle BCD$ → $\angle ACD \cong \angle BCD$ → $\overrightarrow{CD}$ bis. $\angle ACB$

$\overline{CD} \cong \overline{CD}$

Statements	Reasons
1 $\overline{AC} \cong \overline{BC}$	1 Given
2 $\overline{AD} \cong \overline{BD}$	2 Given
3 $\overline{CD} \cong \overline{CD}$	3 Reflexive Property
4 $\triangle ACD \cong \triangle BCD$	4 SSS (1, 2, 3)
5 $\angle ACD \cong \angle BCD$	5 CPCTC
6 $\overrightarrow{CD}$ bisects $\angle ACB$.	6 If a ray divides an $\angle$ into two $\cong$ $\angle$s, the ray bisects the $\angle$.

Problem 2   Given: $\overline{CD}$ and $\overline{BE}$ are altitudes of $\triangle ABC$.
                              $\overline{AD} \cong \overline{AE}$
                  Prove: $\overline{DB} \cong \overline{EC}$

Proof

Statements	Reasons
1 $\overline{CD}$ and $\overline{BE}$ are altitudes of $\triangle ABC$.	1 Given
2 $\angle ADC$ is a right $\angle$.	2 An altitude of a $\triangle$ forms right $\angle$s with the side to which it is drawn.
3 $\angle AEB$ is a right $\angle$.	3 Same as 2
4 $\angle ADC \cong \angle AEB$	4 If $\angle$s are right $\angle$s, they are $\cong$.
5 $\angle A \cong \angle A$	5 Reflexive Property
6 $\overline{AD} \cong \overline{AE}$	6 Given
7 $\triangle ADC \cong \triangle AEB$	7 ASA (4, 6, 5)
8 $\overline{AB} \cong \overline{AC}$	8 CPCTC
9 $\overline{DB} \cong \overline{EC}$	9 Subtraction Property (6 from 8)

Problem 3   Given: G is the midpt. of $\overline{FH}$.

$\overline{EF} \cong \overline{EH}$

Prove: $\angle 1 \cong \angle 2$

Proof

Statements	Reasons
1 G is the midpt. of $\overline{FH}$.	1 Given
2 $\overline{FG} \cong \overline{HG}$	2 If a point is the midpt. of a segment, it divides the segment into two $\cong$ segments.
3 $\overline{EF} \cong \overline{EH}$	3 Given
4 Draw $\overline{EG}$.	4 Two points determine a segment.
5 $\overline{EG} \cong \overline{EG}$	5 Reflexive Property
6 $\triangle EFG \cong \triangle EHG$	6 SSS (2, 3, 5)
7 $\angle EFG \cong \angle EHG$	7 CPCTC
8 $\angle 2$ is supp. to $\angle EFG$.	8 If two $\angle$s form a straight $\angle$, they are supplementary.
9 $\angle 1$ is supp. to $\angle EHG$.	9 Same as 8
10 $\angle 1 \cong \angle 2$	10 Supplements of $\cong$ $\angle$s are $\cong$.

Problem 4   Given: $\angle T \cong \angle Y$,

$\angle SVZ \cong \angle SXZ$,

$\overline{TV} \cong \overline{YX}$

Conclusion: $\overline{SZ}$ is the median to $\overline{TY}$.

Proof

Statements	Reasons
1 $\angle T \cong \angle Y$	1 Given
2 $\angle SVZ \cong \angle SXZ$	2 Given
3 $\angle SVZ$ is supp. to $\angle TVZ$.	3 If two $\angle$s form a straight $\angle$, they are supplementary.
4 $\angle SXZ$ is supp. to $\angle YXZ$.	4 Same as 3
5 $\angle TVZ \cong \angle YXZ$	5 Supplements of $\cong$ $\angle$s are $\cong$.
6 $\overline{TV} \cong \overline{YX}$	6 Given
7 $\triangle TVZ \cong \triangle YXZ$	7 ASA (1, 6, 5)
8 $\overline{TZ} \cong \overline{YZ}$	8 CPCTC
9 $\overline{SZ}$ is the median to $\overline{TY}$.	9 If a segment from a vertex of a $\triangle$ divides the opposite side into two $\cong$ segments, it is a median.

Part Three: Problem Sets

Problem Set A

1 For the following figures, identify $\overline{AD}$ as a median, an altitude, neither, or both according to what can be proved.

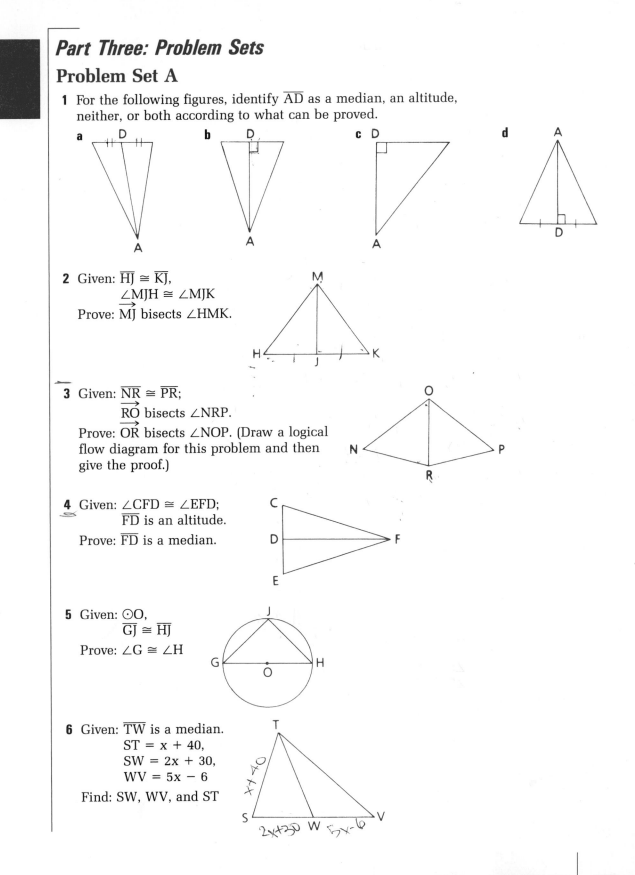

2 Given: $\overline{HJ} \cong \overline{KJ}$,
  $\angle MJH \cong \angle MJK$
Prove: $\overrightarrow{MJ}$ bisects $\angle HMK$.

3 Given: $\overline{NR} \cong \overline{PR}$;
  $\overrightarrow{RO}$ bisects $\angle NRP$.
Prove: $\overrightarrow{OR}$ bisects $\angle NOP$. (Draw a logical flow diagram for this problem and then give the proof.)

4 Given: $\angle CFD \cong \angle EFD$;
  $\overline{FD}$ is an altitude.
Prove: $\overline{FD}$ is a median.

5 Given: $\odot O$,
  $\overline{GJ} \cong \overline{HJ}$
Prove: $\angle G \cong \angle H$

6 Given: $\overline{TW}$ is a median.
  $ST = x + 40$,
  $SW = 2x + 30$,
  $WV = 5x - 6$
Find: SW, WV, and ST

Problem Set A, *continued*

7 Given: $\overline{KP}$ is a median.
     $\overline{MK} \cong \overline{RK}$

Conclusion: $\angle 3 \cong \angle 4$

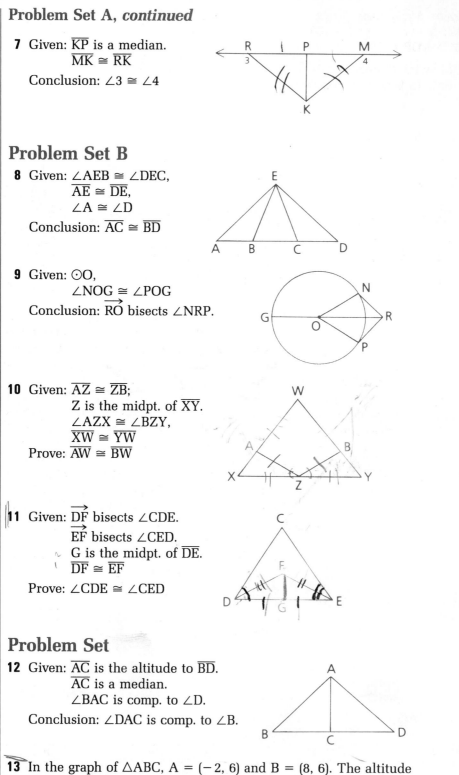

Problem Set B

8 Given: $\angle AEB \cong \angle DEC$,
     $\overline{AE} \cong \overline{DE}$,
     $\angle A \cong \angle D$

Conclusion: $\overline{AC} \cong \overline{BD}$

9 Given: $\odot O$,
     $\angle NOG \cong \angle POG$

Conclusion: $\overrightarrow{RO}$ bisects $\angle NRP$.

10 Given: $\overline{AZ} \cong \overline{ZB}$;
     Z is the midpt. of $\overline{XY}$.
     $\angle AZX \cong \angle BZY$,
     $\overline{XW} \cong \overline{YW}$

Prove: $\overline{AW} \cong \overline{BW}$

11 Given: $\overrightarrow{DF}$ bisects $\angle CDE$.
     $\overrightarrow{EF}$ bisects $\angle CED$.
     G is the midpt. of $\overline{DE}$.
     $\overline{DF} \cong \overline{EF}$

Prove: $\angle CDE \cong \angle CED$

Problem Set

12 Given: $\overline{AC}$ is the altitude to $\overline{BD}$.
     $\overline{AC}$ is a median.
     $\angle BAC$ is comp. to $\angle D$.

Conclusion: $\angle DAC$ is comp. to $\angle B$.

13 In the graph of $\triangle ABC$, A = $(-2, 6)$ and B = $(8, 6)$. The altitude from C is 5. Where is point C located?

14 Given: ⊙O and ⊙P;
Perimeter of △AOP = 80.
OC + DP = 16;
$\overline{CD}$ is 2 units longer than $\overline{OC}$.

Find: OB + BP

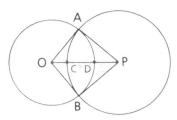

15 Given: $\overline{AB} \cong \overline{AC}$,
$\overline{BD} \cong \overline{CE}$

Prove: ∠1 ≅ ∠2

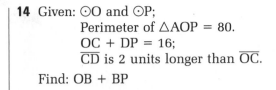

SYMMETRY UNLOCKS CULTURE
Dorothy Washburn uses patterns to decode the past

Archaeologists have traditionally classified decorative basket, cloth, and pottery patterns through reference to the design elements of the patterns. Archaeologist Dorothy Washburn decided to take a different approach. She explains her theory: "Structure is important in every culture. Instead of focusing on design elements I decided to look at the underlying *structure* of

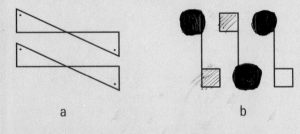

a   b

the patterns. It appeared that one fundamental rule guiding artists in their choices of patterns was pattern structure, so I proposed using symmetry as a basis for pattern classification."

Using Washburn's system, the two designs above would have identical classifications, since each has 180° (bifold) rotational symmetry. "We've uncovered a remarkable consistency in the choice of symmetries within a given cultural group. In my study of the Anasazi people of the American Southwest, I found that at most sites at least 50 percent of their decorative patterns were structured just by bifold rotational symme-

try." Most cultural groups use a small number of symmetries, sometimes for hundreds of years. If the group undergoes some major upheaval, the artists might then adopt a new series of symmetries.

Washburn majored in American history at Oberlin college, but one day she overheard another student discussing an upcoming archaeological dig. "Can I come along?" she inquired. Her future was altered. She joined a summer dig in Wyoming, then entered graduate school at Columbia University, where she earned her doctorate in anthropology. Today she is a research associate in anthropology at the University of Rochester.

Which strip patterns display bifold rotational symmetry?

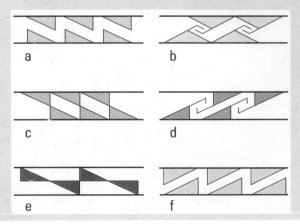

a   b

c   d

e   f

OVERLAPPING TRIANGLES

Objective

After studying this section, you will be able to
- Use overlapping triangles in proofs

Part One: Introduction

Consider the following problem.

Given: $\overline{DB} \cong \overline{AC}$,
$\overline{AD} \cong \overline{BC}$

Conclusion: $\angle D \cong \angle C$

At first glance you would probably think of showing that
$\triangle ADE \cong \triangle BCE$, thus proving that $\angle D \cong \angle C$ by CPCTC.

Soon you would realize that there is not enough information to
prove that $\triangle ADE \cong \triangle BCE$. There must be another way.

In this case the problem can be solved by finding two other
triangles to which $\angle D$ and $\angle C$ belong. We can prove that the overlapping triangles ABD and BAC are congruent by SSS, and thus that
$\angle D \cong \angle C$ by CPCTC.

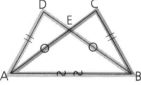

At first, you may have trouble recognizing which triangles to use
in a proof. You may want to outline triangles in color, as in the
sample problems. Just be willing to draw figures several times to find
the triangles that serve best.

Almost all the problems in this section involve overlapping
triangles. Elsewhere, the triangles of interest may or may not
overlap.

Part Two: Sample Problems

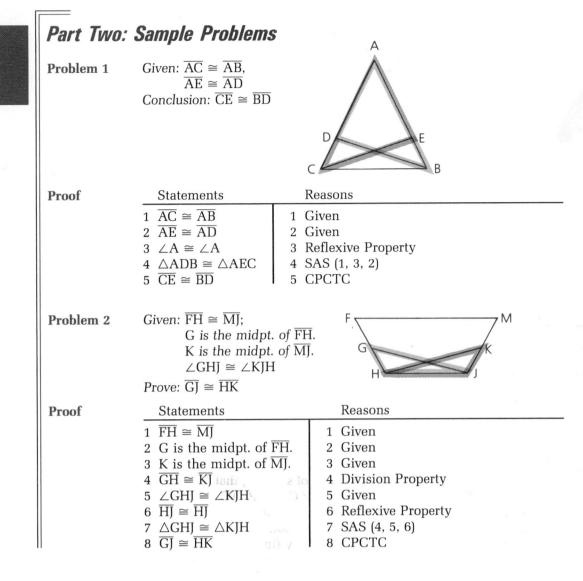

Problem 1   Given: $\overline{AC} \cong \overline{AB}$,
                         $\overline{AE} \cong \overline{AD}$
                 Conclusion: $\overline{CE} \cong \overline{BD}$

Proof

Statements	Reasons
1 $\overline{AC} \cong \overline{AB}$	1 Given
2 $\overline{AE} \cong \overline{AD}$	2 Given
3 $\angle A \cong \angle A$	3 Reflexive Property
4 $\triangle ADB \cong \triangle AEC$	4 SAS (1, 3, 2)
5 $\overline{CE} \cong \overline{BD}$	5 CPCTC

Problem 2   Given: $\overline{FH} \cong \overline{MJ}$;
                         G is the midpt. of $\overline{FH}$.
                         K is the midpt. of $\overline{MJ}$.
                         $\angle GHJ \cong \angle KJH$
                 Prove: $\overline{GJ} \cong \overline{HK}$

Proof

Statements	Reasons
1 $\overline{FH} \cong \overline{MJ}$	1 Given
2 G is the midpt. of $\overline{FH}$.	2 Given
3 K is the midpt. of $\overline{MJ}$.	3 Given
4 $\overline{GH} \cong \overline{KJ}$	4 Division Property
5 $\angle GHJ \cong \angle KJH$	5 Given
6 $\overline{HJ} \cong \overline{HJ}$	6 Reflexive Property
7 $\triangle GHJ \cong \triangle KJH$	7 SAS (4, 5, 6)
8 $\overline{GJ} \cong \overline{HK}$	8 CPCTC

Part Three: Problem Sets

Problem Set A

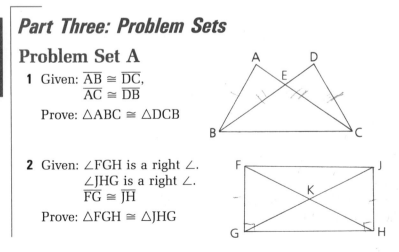

1 Given: $\overline{AB} \cong \overline{DC}$,
                $\overline{AC} \cong \overline{DB}$
        Prove: $\triangle ABC \cong \triangle DCB$

2 Given: $\angle FGH$ is a right $\angle$.
                $\angle JHG$ is a right $\angle$.
                $\overline{FG} \cong \overline{JH}$
        Prove: $\triangle FGH \cong \triangle JHG$

Problem Set A, *continued*

3 Given: $\overline{PM} \cong \overline{RM}$,
$\angle SPM \cong \angle ORM$
Prove: $\triangle PSM \cong \triangle ROM$

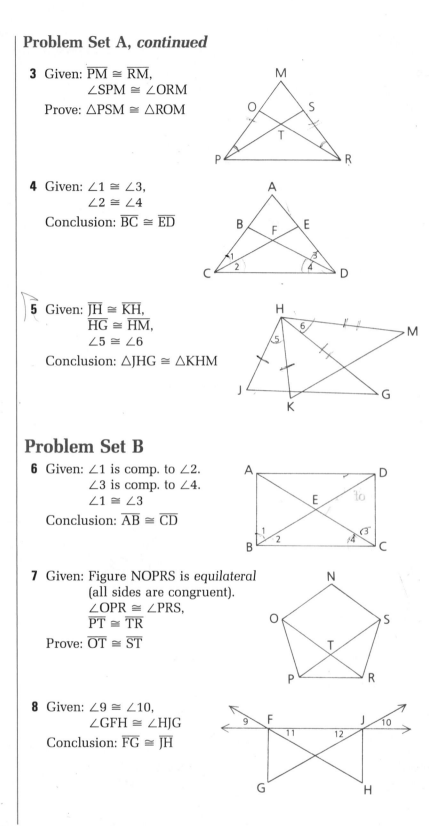

4 Given: $\angle 1 \cong \angle 3$,
$\angle 2 \cong \angle 4$
Conclusion: $\overline{BC} \cong \overline{ED}$

5 Given: $\overline{JH} \cong \overline{KH}$,
$\overline{HG} \cong \overline{HM}$,
$\angle 5 \cong \angle 6$
Conclusion: $\triangle JHG \cong \triangle KHM$

Problem Set B

6 Given: $\angle 1$ is comp. to $\angle 2$.
$\angle 3$ is comp. to $\angle 4$.
$\angle 1 \cong \angle 3$
Conclusion: $\overline{AB} \cong \overline{CD}$

7 Given: Figure NOPRS is *equilateral*
(all sides are congruent).
$\angle OPR \cong \angle PRS$,
$\overline{PT} \cong \overline{TR}$
Prove: $\overline{OT} \cong \overline{ST}$

8 Given: $\angle 9 \cong \angle 10$,
$\angle GFH \cong \angle HJG$
Conclusion: $\overline{FG} \cong \overline{JH}$

9 Given: $\overline{YW}$ bisects $\overline{AX}$.
  $\angle A \cong \angle X$,
  $\angle 5 \cong \angle 6$
Conclusion: $\overline{ZW} \cong \overline{YW}$

10 Given: B is the midpt. of $\overline{AC}$.
   E is the mdpt. of $\overline{AD}$.
   $\angle 7 \cong \angle 8$,
   $\angle ECD \cong \angle BDC$
Prove: $\overline{AC} \cong \overline{AD}$

11 Given: Two triangles, joined along $\overline{PQ}$
   and standing on a desktop,
   $\overline{PS} \cong \overline{PR}$, $\angle QPS \cong \angle QPR$
Prove: $\overline{QR} \cong \overline{QS}$

Problem Set C

12 Given: $\overline{HO} \cong \overline{MO}$,
   $\overline{JO} \cong \overline{KO}$;
   $\overline{HJ}$ is an altitude of $\triangle HJK$.
   $\overline{MK}$ is an altitude of $\triangle MKJ$.
Prove: $\angle 1 \cong \angle 2$

13 Given: $\overline{NR} \cong \overline{NV}$;
   P and Q are midpoints.
   $\angle R \cong \angle V$,
   $\overline{PX} \cong \overline{QX}$
Prove: $\triangle XST$ is *isosceles* (at least two
   sides are $\cong$).

14 Given: $\overline{YD} \cong \overline{ZD}$,
   $\overline{BD} \cong \overline{CD}$;
   E is the midpt. of $\overline{YZ}$.
Conclusion: $\angle BYZ \cong \angle CZY$

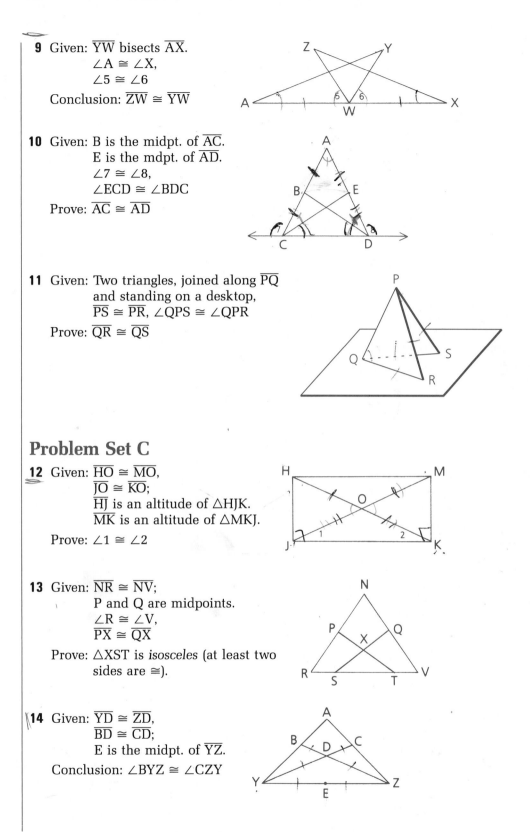

TYPES OF TRIANGLES

Objective

After studying this section, you will be able to
- Name the various types of triangles and their parts

Part One: Introduction

A number of names are used to distinguish triangles having special characteristics.

Definition   A *scalene triangle* is a triangle in which no two sides are congruent.

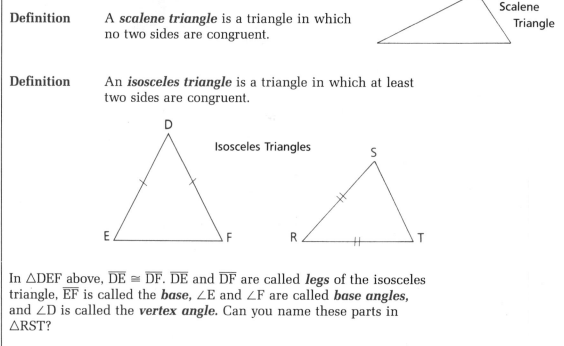

Scalene Triangle

Definition   An *isosceles triangle* is a triangle in which at least two sides are congruent.

Isosceles Triangles

In △DEF above, $\overline{DE} \cong \overline{DF}$. $\overline{DE}$ and $\overline{DF}$ are called *legs* of the isosceles triangle, $\overline{EF}$ is called the *base,* ∠E and ∠F are called *base angles,* and ∠D is called the *vertex angle.* Can you name these parts in △RST?

Definition   An *equilateral triangle* is a triangle in which all sides are congruent.

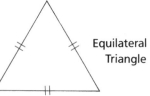

Equilateral Triangle

The word *equilateral* can be applied to any figure in which all sides are congruent.

Definition   An *equiangular triangle* is a triangle in which all angles are congruent.

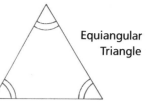

Equiangular Triangle

The word *equiangular* can be applied to any figure in which all angles are congruent.

Looking at the diagrams, you may wonder if there is any real difference between an equilateral triangle and an equiangular triangle. You will find out in Section 3.7, where you will also learn whether any differences exist between equilateral and equiangular figures of other numbers of sides.

Definition   An *acute triangle* is a triangle in which all angles are acute.

Acute Triangle

Definition   A *right triangle* is a triangle in which one of the angles is a right angle. (The side opposite the right angle is called the *hypotenuse.* The sides that form the right angle are called *legs.*)

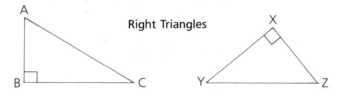

Right Triangles

In △ABC above, $\overline{AB}$ and $\overline{BC}$ are the legs, and $\overline{AC}$ is the hypotenuse. Can you name these parts in △XYZ?

Definition   An *obtuse triangle* is a triangle in which one of the angles is an obtuse angle.

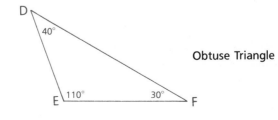

Obtuse Triangle

Part Two: Sample Problems

Problem 1   Given: ∠CBD = 70°
Prove: △ABC is obtuse.

Proof   ∠CBD = 70° and ∠ABD is a straight angle, so ∠ABC = 110°. Since △ABC contains an obtuse angle, it is an obtuse triangle.

Problem 2   Given: EG = FH,
EF > EG
Prove: △EFG is scalene.

Proof   Since EG = FH and $\overline{FH}$ is clearly longer than $\overline{FG}$, $\overline{EG}$ is also longer than $\overline{FG}$. It is given that EF > EG, so $\overline{EF}$ is also longer than $\overline{FG}$. Since no two sides of △EFG are congruent, the triangle is scalene.

Problem 3   Given: ∠1 ≅ ∠3,
∠2 ≅ ∠4,
$\overline{JP}$ ≅ $\overline{PO}$
Prove: △KPM is isosceles.

Proof

Statements	Reasons
1 ∠1 ≅ ∠3	1 Given
2 ∠2 ≅ ∠4	2 Given
3 ∠JKM ≅ ∠OMK	3 Addition Property
4 $\overline{KM}$ ≅ $\overline{KM}$	4 Reflexive Property
5 △JKM ≅ △OMK	5 ASA (2, 4, 3)
6 $\overline{JM}$ ≅ $\overline{KO}$	6 CPCTC
7 $\overline{JP}$ ≅ $\overline{PO}$	7 Given
8 $\overline{KP}$ ≅ $\overline{MP}$	8 Subtraction Property
9 △KPM is isosceles.	9 If at least two sides of a △ are congruent, the △ is isosceles.

Part Three: Problem Sets

Problem Set A

1 If the perimeter of △EFG is 32, is △EFG scalene, isosceles, or equilateral?

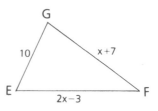

2 Classify each of the triangles as scalene, isosceles, or equilateral.

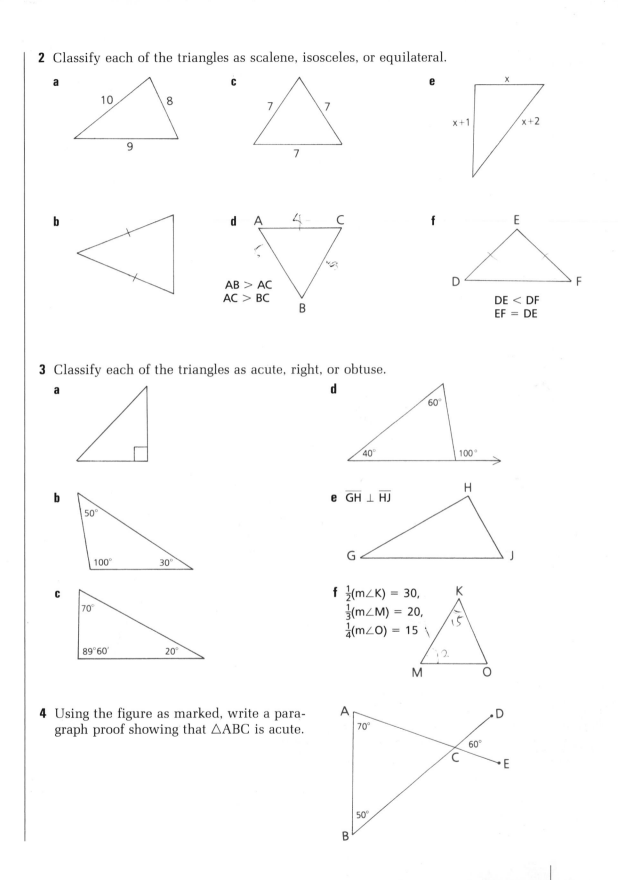

a
10 8
9

c
7 7
7

e
x
x+1 x+2

b

d A C
B
AB > AC
AC > BC

f E
D F
DE < DF
EF = DE

3 Classify each of the triangles as acute, right, or obtuse.

a

d
60°
40° 100°

b
50°
100° 30°

e $\overline{GH} \perp \overline{HJ}$
H
G J

c
70°
89°60' 20°

f $\frac{1}{2}(m\angle K) = 30,$
$\frac{1}{3}(m\angle M) = 20,$
$\frac{1}{4}(m\angle O) = 15$
K
M O

4 Using the figure as marked, write a paragraph proof showing that △ABC is acute.

A D
70°
60°
C E
50°
B

Problem Set A, *continued*

5 Given: ⊙O

Prove: △COD is isosceles.

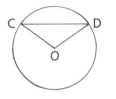

6 If △HJK is equilateral, what are the values of x and y?

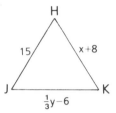

Problem Set B

7 Given: $\overline{AD}$ and $\overline{CD}$ are legs of isosceles △ACD.

B is the midpt. of $\overline{AC}$.

Prove: ∠A ≅ ∠C

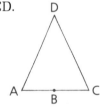

8 Given: $\overline{BI} ≅ \overline{RD}$, $\overline{RI} ≅ \overline{BD}$;

∠3 is comp. to ∠2.

Prove: △RIB is a right △.

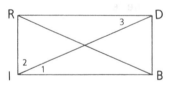

9 Given: $\overline{JF} ≅ \overline{JG}$;

F and G trisect $\overline{EH}$.

∠EFJ ≅ ∠HGJ

Conclusion: △EHJ is isosceles.

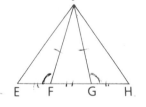

10 In △RST, RS = x + 7, RT = 3x + 5, and ST = 9 − x. If △RST is isosceles, is it also equilateral?

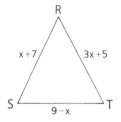

11 If △VSY is isosceles and its perimeter is less than 45, which side of △VSY is the base?

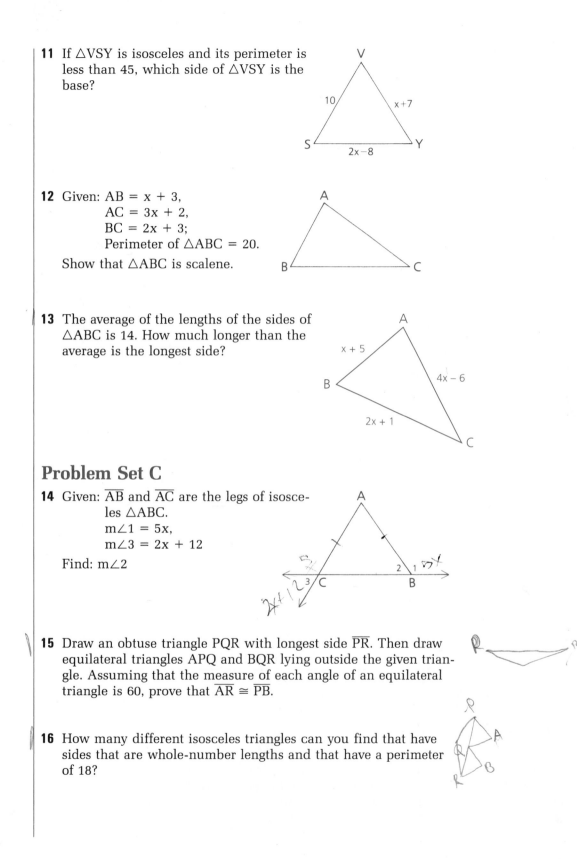

12 Given: AB = x + 3,
　　　 AC = 3x + 2,
　　　 BC = 2x + 3;
　　　 Perimeter of △ABC = 20.
　　Show that △ABC is scalene.

13 The average of the lengths of the sides of △ABC is 14. How much longer than the average is the longest side?

Problem Set C

14 Given: $\overline{AB}$ and $\overline{AC}$ are the legs of isosceles △ABC.
　　　 m∠1 = 5x,
　　　 m∠3 = 2x + 12
　　Find: m∠2

15 Draw an obtuse triangle PQR with longest side $\overline{PR}$. Then draw equilateral triangles APQ and BQR lying outside the given triangle. Assuming that the measure of each angle of an equilateral triangle is 60, prove that $\overline{AR} \cong \overline{PB}$.

16 How many different isosceles triangles can you find that have sides that are whole-number lengths and that have a perimeter of 18?

ANGLE-SIDE THEOREMS

Objective

After studying this section, you will be able to
- Apply theorems relating the angle measures and side lengths of triangles

Part One: Introduction

It can be shown that the base angles of any isosceles triangle are congruent.

Theorem 20   *If two sides of a triangle are congruent, the angles opposite the sides are congruent. (If △, then △.)*

Given: $\overline{AB} \cong \overline{AC}$
Prove: $\angle B \cong \angle C$

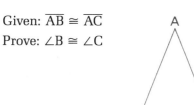

Proof:

Statements	Reasons
1 $\overline{AB} \cong \overline{AC}$	1 Given
2 $\overline{BC} \cong \overline{BC}$	2 Reflexive Property
3 $\triangle ABC \cong \triangle ACB$	3 SSS (1, 2, 1)
4 $\angle B \cong \angle C$	4 CPCTC

You should be accustomed to proving that one triangle is congruent to another triangle. But notice that to prove the preceding theorem, we proved that a triangle is congruent to itself (its mirror image). We shall use the same type of proof to show that the converse of Theorem 20 is also true.

Theorem 21 *If two angles of a triangle are congruent, the sides opposite the angles are congruent. (If △, then △.)*

Given: ∠D ≅ ∠E
Conclusion: $\overline{DF} \cong \overline{EF}$

Proof:

Statements	Reasons
1 ∠D ≅ ∠E	1 Given
2 $\overline{DE} \cong \overline{DE}$	2 Reflexive Property
3 △DEF ≅ △EDF	3 ASA (1, 2, 1)
4 $\overline{DF} \cong \overline{EF}$	4 CPCTC

Theorem 21 tells us that a triangle is isosceles if two or more of its angles are congruent. We now have two ways of proving that a triangle is isosceles.

Ways to Prove That a Triangle Is Isosceles

1 If at least two sides of a triangle are congruent, the triangle is isosceles.
2 If at least two angles of a triangle are congruent, the triangle is isosceles.

The inverses of Theorems 20 and 21 are also true. (Recall that the inverse of "If *p*, then *q*" is "If not *p*, then not *q*.") In fact, it can be proved that inequalities of sides and angles are related as shown in the diagram.

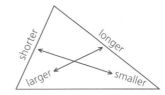

Theorem *If two sides of a triangle are not congruent, then the angles opposite them are not congruent, and the larger angle is opposite the longer side. (If △, then △.)*

Theorem *If two angles of a triangle are not congruent, then the sides opposite them are not congruent, and the longer side is opposite the larger angle. (If △, then △.)*

These theorems will be restated and proved in Chapter 15.

Let us now consider a question we raised in Section 3.6: Is an equilateral triangle also equiangular?

Given: $\overline{GH} \cong \overline{HJ} \cong \overline{GJ}$

Is $\angle H \cong \angle J \cong \angle G$?

If $\overline{GH} \cong \overline{HJ}$, which two angles must be congruent? If $\overline{HJ} \cong \overline{GJ}$, which two angles must be congruent? Do we therefore know that $\triangle GHJ$ is equiangular? Can we also prove that an equiangular triangle is equilateral?

Because of their equivalence, the terms *equilateral triangle* and *equiangular triangle* will be used interchangeably throughout this book. We cannot, however, use the words *equilateral* and *equiangular* interchangeably when we apply them to other types of figures. For example, figure ABCD is equilateral but not equiangular. Figure EFGH, on the other hand, is equiangular but not equilateral.

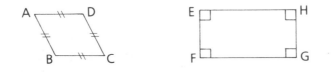

Part Two: Sample Problems

Problem 1   Given: AC > AB,
           $m\angle B + m\angle C < 180$,
           $m\angle B = 6x - 45$,
           $m\angle C = 15 + x$

What are the restrictions on the value of x?

Solution   Since AC > AB, $m\angle B > m\angle C$.

$$6x - 45 > 15 + x$$
$$5x > 60$$
$$x > 12$$

We also know that $m\angle B + m\angle C < 180$.

$$6x - 45 + 15 + x < 180$$
$$7x < 210$$
$$x < 30$$

Therefore, x must be between 12 and 30.

Problem 2   Prove: *The bisector of the vertex angle of an isosceles triangle is also the median to the base.*

Proof   For a problem like this, we must set up the proof and supply the diagram.

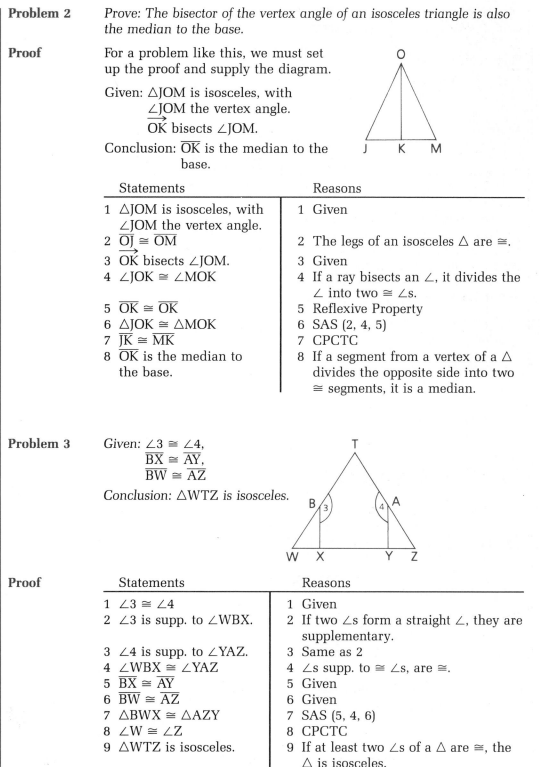

Given: △JOM is isosceles, with
∠JOM the vertex angle.
$\overrightarrow{OK}$ bisects ∠JOM.

Conclusion: $\overline{OK}$ is the median to the base.

Statements	Reasons
1 △JOM is isosceles, with ∠JOM the vertex angle.	1 Given
2 $\overline{OJ} \cong \overline{OM}$	2 The legs of an isosceles △ are ≅.
3 $\overrightarrow{OK}$ bisects ∠JOM.	3 Given
4 ∠JOK ≅ ∠MOK	4 If a ray bisects an ∠, it divides the ∠ into two ≅ ∠s.
5 $\overline{OK} \cong \overline{OK}$	5 Reflexive Property
6 △JOK ≅ △MOK	6 SAS (2, 4, 5)
7 $\overline{JK} \cong \overline{MK}$	7 CPCTC
8 $\overline{OK}$ is the median to the base.	8 If a segment from a vertex of a △ divides the opposite side into two ≅ segments, it is a median.

Problem 3   Given: ∠3 ≅ ∠4,
$\overline{BX} \cong \overline{AY}$,
$\overline{BW} \cong \overline{AZ}$

Conclusion: △WTZ is isosceles.

Proof

Statements	Reasons
1 ∠3 ≅ ∠4	1 Given
2 ∠3 is supp. to ∠WBX.	2 If two ∠s form a straight ∠, they are supplementary.
3 ∠4 is supp. to ∠YAZ.	3 Same as 2
4 ∠WBX ≅ ∠YAZ	4 ∠s supp. to ≅ ∠s, are ≅.
5 $\overline{BX} \cong \overline{AY}$	5 Given
6 $\overline{BW} \cong \overline{AZ}$	6 Given
7 △BWX ≅ △AZY	7 SAS (5, 4, 6)
8 ∠W ≅ ∠Z	8 CPCTC
9 △WTZ is isosceles.	9 If at least two ∠s of a △ are ≅, the △ is isosceles.

Problem 4   *Given:* $\angle E \cong \angle H$,
$\overline{EF} \cong \overline{GH}$

Conclusion: $\overline{DF} \cong \overline{DG}$

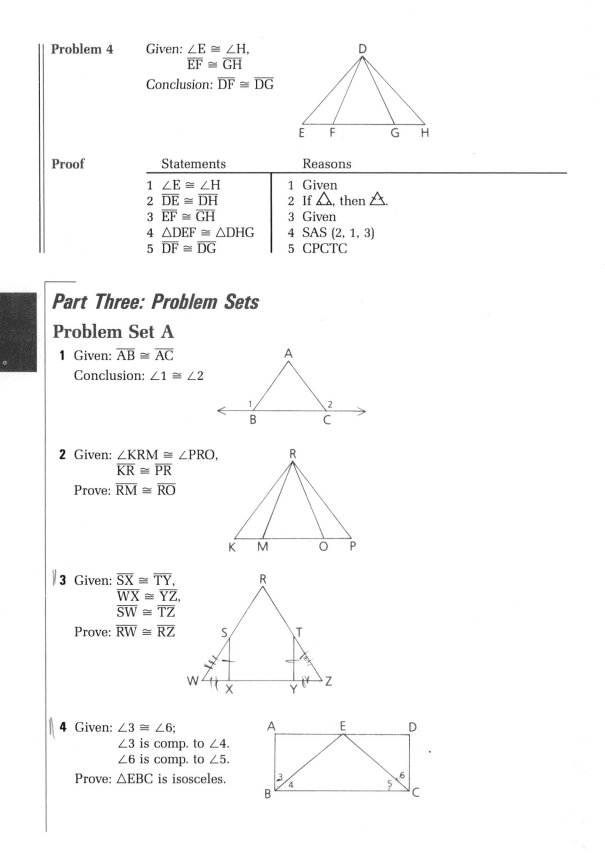

Proof

	Statements		Reasons
1	$\angle E \cong \angle H$	1	Given
2	$\overline{DE} \cong \overline{DH}$	2	If △, then △.
3	$\overline{EF} \cong \overline{GH}$	3	Given
4	$\triangle DEF \cong \triangle DHG$	4	SAS (2, 1, 3)
5	$\overline{DF} \cong \overline{DG}$	5	CPCTC

Part Three: Problem Sets

Problem Set A

1 *Given:* $\overline{AB} \cong \overline{AC}$
Conclusion: $\angle 1 \cong \angle 2$

2 *Given:* $\angle KRM \cong \angle PRO$,
$\overline{KR} \cong \overline{PR}$
Prove: $\overline{RM} \cong \overline{RO}$

3 *Given:* $\overline{SX} \cong \overline{TY}$,
$\overline{WX} \cong \overline{YZ}$,
$\overline{SW} \cong \overline{TZ}$
Prove: $\overline{RW} \cong \overline{RZ}$

4 *Given:* $\angle 3 \cong \angle 6$;
$\angle 3$ is comp. to $\angle 4$.
$\angle 6$ is comp. to $\angle 5$.
Prove: $\triangle EBC$ is isosceles.

5 Given: $\overline{FH} \cong \overline{GJ}$;
   $\triangle FKJ$ is isosceles, with $\overline{FK} \cong \overline{JK}$.
   Prove: $\triangle FKH \cong \triangle JKG$

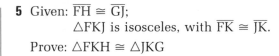

6 Given: $\angle 5 \cong \angle 6$;
   $\overline{JG}$ is the altitude to $\overline{FH}$.
   Prove: $\triangle FJH$ is isosceles.

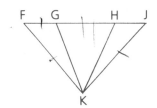

7 In $\triangle ABC$, $AC > BC > AB$. List the three angles in order of size, from largest to smallest.

8 Given: $m\angle P + m\angle R < 180$.
   $PQ < QR$

Write an inequality to describe the restrictions on x.

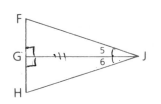

9 Given: $\overline{OP} \cong \overline{RS}$,
   $\overline{KO} \cong \overline{KS}$;
   M is the midpt. of $\overline{OK}$.
   T is the midpt. of $\overline{KS}$.
   Prove: $\overline{MP} \cong \overline{TR}$

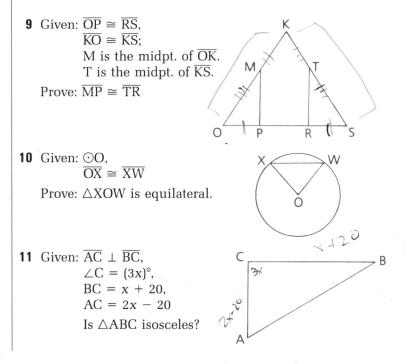

10 Given: $\odot O$,
   $\overline{OX} \cong \overline{XW}$
   Prove: $\triangle XOW$ is equilateral.

11 Given: $\overline{AC} \perp \overline{BC}$,
   $\angle C = (3x)°$,
   $BC = x + 20$,
   $AC = 2x - 20$
   Is $\triangle ABC$ isosceles?

Problem Set B

12 Given: $\odot$Q,
$\overline{PS} \perp \overline{SR}$,
$\angle P = 36°$

Find: **a** $\angle PSQ$
b $\angle R$

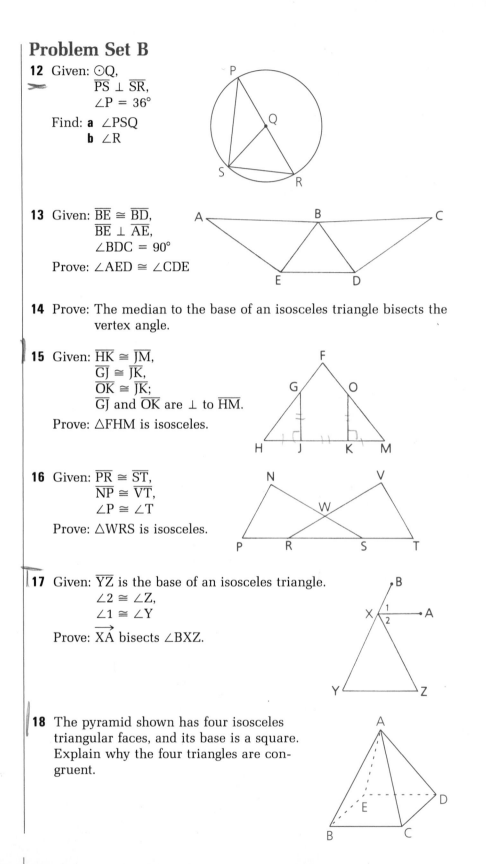

13 Given: $\overline{BE} \cong \overline{BD}$,
$\overline{BE} \perp \overline{AE}$,
$\angle BDC = 90°$

Prove: $\angle AED \cong \angle CDE$

14 Prove: The median to the base of an isosceles triangle bisects the vertex angle.

15 Given: $\overline{HK} \cong \overline{JM}$,
$\overline{GJ} \cong \overline{JK}$,
$\overline{OK} \cong \overline{JK}$;
$\overline{GJ}$ and $\overline{OK}$ are $\perp$ to $\overline{HM}$.

Prove: $\triangle FHM$ is isosceles.

16 Given: $\overline{PR} \cong \overline{ST}$,
$\overline{NP} \cong \overline{VT}$,
$\angle P \cong \angle T$

Prove: $\triangle WRS$ is isosceles.

17 Given: $\overline{YZ}$ is the base of an isosceles triangle.
$\angle 2 \cong \angle Z$,
$\angle 1 \cong \angle Y$

Prove: $\overrightarrow{XA}$ bisects $\angle BXZ$.

18 The pyramid shown has four isosceles triangular faces, and its base is a square. Explain why the four triangles are congruent.

19 Given: $\overline{HJ} \cong \overline{MK}$,
         $\angle HJK \cong \angle MKJ$

   Conclusion: $\triangle JOK$ is isosceles.

20 Given: $\angle A$ is the vertex of an isosceles $\triangle$.
         The number of degrees in $\angle B$ is
         twice the number of centimeters
         in $\overline{BC}$.
         The number of degrees in $\angle C$ is
         three times the number of centi-
         meters in $\overline{AB}$.
         $m\angle B = x + 6$,
         $m\angle C = 2x - 54$

   Find: The perimeter of $\triangle ABC$

21 Given: $\overline{CE} \cong \overline{CF}$,
         $\angle F \cong \angle 3$;
         $\angle E$ is supp. to $\angle 5$.

   Prove: $\triangle CDG$ is isosceles.

Problem Set C

22 Given: $\overline{FG} \cong \overline{JH}$,
         $\angle FGH \cong \angle JHG$

   Conclusion: $\triangle FKJ$ is isosceles.

23 Given: $\odot O$,
         $\odot P$;
         $\overleftrightarrow{AB}$ bisects $\angle$s OAP and OBP.

   Prove: Figure AOBP is equilateral.

24 Given: Figure XSTOW is equilateral and
         equiangular.

   Prove: $\triangle YTO$ is isosceles.

25 Given: $\triangle FED$ is equilateral.
         $\overline{GE} \perp \overline{DE}$,
         $m\angle FEG = x + y$,
         $m\angle D = 3x - 6$,
         $m\angle F = 6y + 12$

   Find: x, y, and $\angle F$

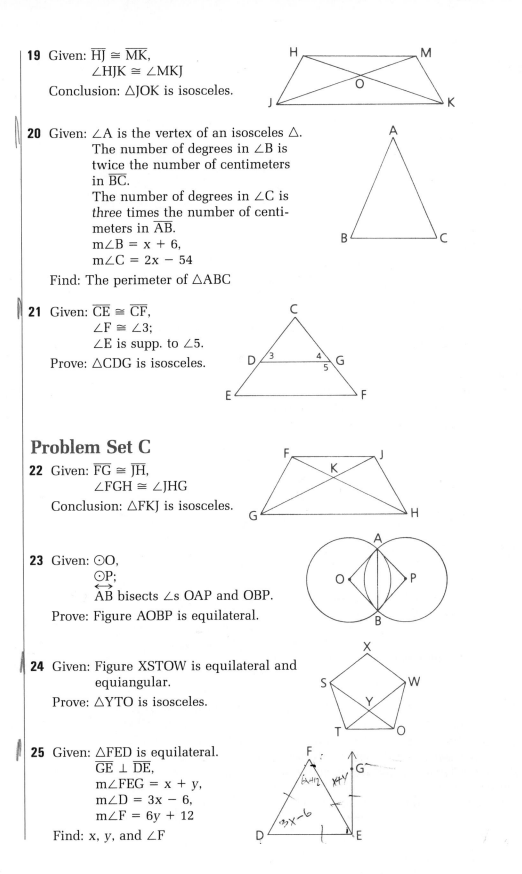

3.8 | THE HL POSTULATE

Objective

After studying this section, you will be able to
- Use the HL postulate to prove right triangles congruent

Part One: Introduction

The two right triangles below, △ABC and △DEF, can be shown to be congruent by a method that we shall call HL. Although HL congruence can be proved, we shall treat it as a postulate.

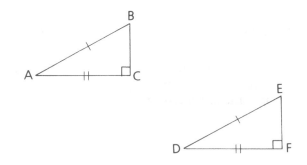

Postulate   ***If there exists a correspondence between the vertices of two right triangles such that the hypotenuse and a leg of one triangle are congruent to the corresponding parts of the other triangle, the two right triangles are congruent. (HL)***

It is important to note that the HL postulate applies only to right triangles. When we use it in proofs, therefore, we must establish that the triangles that we are dealing with are right triangles. We do this by inserting steps showing that each triangle contains a right angle. Clearly, any triangle containing a right angle is a right triangle.

Did you notice that once again three conditions are involved in proving that two triangles are congruent?

Part Two: Sample Problems

Problem 1

Given: $\overline{BC} \perp \overline{AC}$,
$\overline{BD} \perp \overline{AD}$,
$\overline{AC} \cong \overline{AD}$

Prove: $\overrightarrow{AB}$ bisects $\angle CAD$.

Proof

Statements	Reasons
1 $\overline{BC} \perp \overline{AC}$	1 Given
2 $\angle ACB$ is a right $\angle$.	2 If two segments are $\perp$, they form right $\angle$s.
3 $\overline{BD} \perp \overline{AD}$	3 Given
4 $\angle BDA$ is a right $\angle$.	4 Same as 2
5 $\overline{AC} \cong \overline{AD}$	5 Given
6 $\overline{AB} \cong \overline{AB}$	6 Reflexive Property
7 $\triangle ACB \cong \triangle ADB$	7 HL (2, 4, 6, 5)
8 $\angle CAB \cong \angle DAB$	8 CPCTC
9 $\overrightarrow{AB}$ bisects $\angle CAD$.	9 A ray that divides an $\angle$ into two $\cong$ $\angle$s bisects the $\angle$.

Problem 2

Prove: *Corresponding angle bisectors of congruent triangles are congruent.*

Proof

Once again we must set up the proof and draw the figure. (Although this may look like a simple two-step proof based on CPCTC, it isn't. *Corresponding parts of congruent triangles* refers only to corresponding sides and angles.)

Given: $\triangle KPR \cong \triangle SAW$;
$\overrightarrow{RM}$ bisects $\angle KRP$.
$\overrightarrow{WT}$ bisects $\angle SWA$.

Prove: $\overline{RM} \cong \overline{WT}$

Statements	Reasons
1 $\triangle KPR \cong \triangle SAW$	1 Given
2 $\overline{KR} \cong \overline{SW}$	2 CPCTC
3 $\angle K \cong \angle S$	3 CPCTC
4 $\angle KRP \cong \angle SWA$	4 CPCTC
5 $\overrightarrow{RM}$ bisects $\angle KRP$.	5 Given
6 $\overrightarrow{WT}$ bisects $\angle SWA$.	6 Given
7 $\angle KRM \cong \angle SWT$	7 Division Property
8 $\triangle KRM \cong \triangle SWT$	8 ASA (3, 2, 7)
9 $\overline{RM} \cong \overline{WT}$	9 CPCTC

Problem 3 Given: $\overline{OF}$ is an altitude.
ㅤㅤㅤㅤㅤㅤ⊙O
ㅤㅤㅤㅤConclusion: $\overline{EF} \cong \overline{FG}$

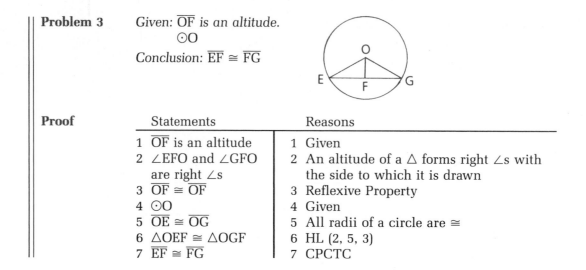

Proof

Statements	Reasons
1 $\overline{OF}$ is an altitude	1 Given
2 ∠EFO and ∠GFO are right ∠s	2 An altitude of a △ forms right ∠s with the side to which it is drawn
3 $\overline{OF} \cong \overline{OF}$	3 Reflexive Property
4 ⊙O	4 Given
5 $\overline{OE} \cong \overline{OG}$	5 All radii of a circle are ≅
6 △OEF ≅ △OGF	6 HL (2, 5, 3)
7 $\overline{EF} \cong \overline{FG}$	7 CPCTC

Part Three: Problem Sets

Problem Set A

1 Given: $\overline{GJ}$ is the altitude to $\overline{HK}$.
ㅤㅤㅤㅤ$\overline{HG} \cong \overline{KG}$

ㅤㅤProve: △HGJ ≅ △KGJ

2 Given: $\overline{MO} \perp \overline{OP}$,
ㅤㅤㅤㅤ$\overline{RP} \perp \overline{OP}$,
ㅤㅤㅤㅤ$\overline{MP} \cong \overline{RO}$

ㅤㅤProve: △MOP ≅ △RPO

3 Given: ⊙O,
ㅤㅤㅤㅤ$\overline{YO} \perp \overline{YX}$,
ㅤㅤㅤㅤ$\overline{ZO} \perp \overline{ZX}$

ㅤㅤConclusion: $\overline{YX} \cong \overline{ZX}$

4 Given: $\overline{AE} \cong \overline{CF}$,
ㅤㅤㅤㅤ$\overline{AB} \cong \overline{CD}$;
ㅤㅤㅤㅤ∠BFA is a right angle.
ㅤㅤㅤㅤ∠DEC is a right angle.

ㅤㅤProve: ∠CDE ≅ ∠ABF

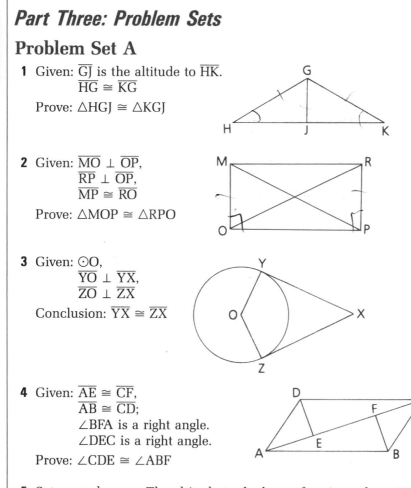

5 Set up and prove: The altitude to the base of an isosceles triangle divides the triangle into two congruent triangles.

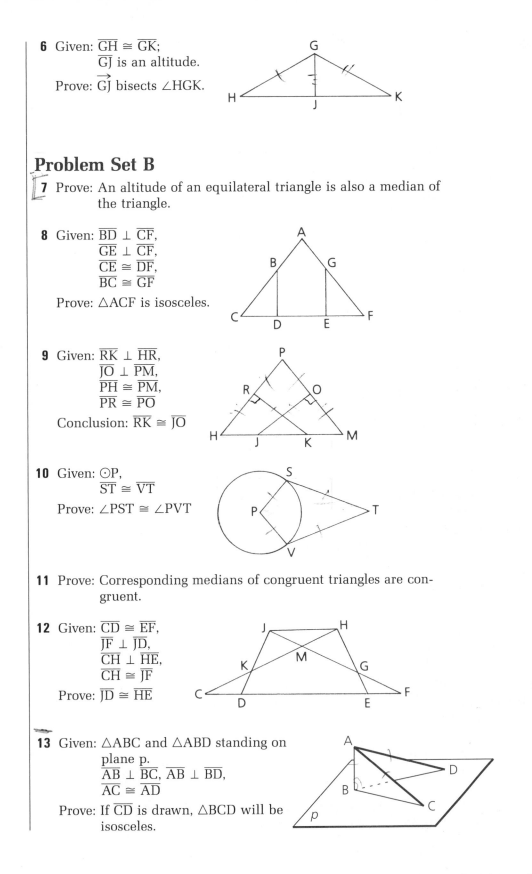

6 Given: $\overline{GH} \cong \overline{GK}$;
$\overline{GJ}$ is an altitude.

Prove: $\overrightarrow{GJ}$ bisects $\angle HGK$.

Problem Set B

7 Prove: An altitude of an equilateral triangle is also a median of the triangle.

8 Given: $\overline{BD} \perp \overline{CF}$,
$\overline{GE} \perp \overline{CF}$,
$\overline{CE} \cong \overline{DF}$,
$\overline{BC} \cong \overline{GF}$

Prove: $\triangle ACF$ is isosceles.

9 Given: $\overline{RK} \perp \overline{HR}$,
$\overline{JO} \perp \overline{PM}$,
$\overline{PH} \cong \overline{PM}$,
$\overline{PR} \cong \overline{PO}$

Conclusion: $\overline{RK} \cong \overline{JO}$

10 Given: $\odot P$,
$\overline{ST} \cong \overline{VT}$

Prove: $\angle PST \cong \angle PVT$

11 Prove: Corresponding medians of congruent triangles are congruent.

12 Given: $\overline{CD} \cong \overline{EF}$,
$\overline{JF} \perp \overline{JD}$,
$\overline{CH} \perp \overline{HE}$,
$\overline{CH} \cong \overline{JF}$

Prove: $\overline{JD} \cong \overline{HE}$

13 Given: $\triangle ABC$ and $\triangle ABD$ standing on plane p.
$\overline{AB} \perp \overline{BC}$, $\overline{AB} \perp \overline{BD}$,
$\overline{AC} \cong \overline{AD}$

Prove: If $\overline{CD}$ is drawn, $\triangle BCD$ will be isosceles.

Problem Set B, *continued*

14 Given: m∠A > m∠C

Find the restrictions on the value of x.

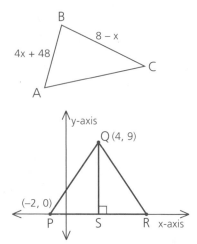

15 In the diagram, $\overline{PQ}$ is congruent to $\overline{QR}$.

a Find the coordinates of S.

b Explain why PS = SR.

c Find the coordinates of R.

d Find the area of △PQR.

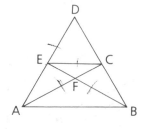

Problem Set C

16 Given: $\overline{BE} \perp \overline{AD}$, $\overline{AC} \perp \overline{BD}$,
$\overline{AC} \cong \overline{BE}$, $\overline{DE} \cong \overline{EC}$

Prove: △DEC is equilateral.

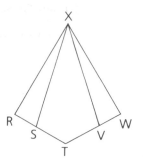

17 Given: ∠R and ∠W are right ∠s.
$\overline{RX} \cong \overline{WX}$;
S is $\frac{3}{7}$ of the way from R to T.
V is $\frac{4}{7}$ of the way from T to W.
Prove: $\overline{ST} \cong \overline{TV}$

Problem Set D

18 a Which of the triangles below are congruent?

b If two of the triangles are selected at random, what is the probability that they are congruent?

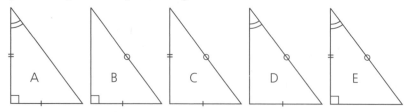

CHAPTER SUMMARY

CONCEPTS AND PROCEDURES

After studying this chapter, you should be able to
- Understand the concept of congruent figures (3.1)
- Accurately identify the corresponding parts of figures (3.1)
- Identify included angles and included sides (3.2)
- Apply the SSS postulate (3.2)
- Apply the SAS postulate (3.2)
- Apply the ASA postulate (3.2)
- Apply the principle of CPCTC (3.3)
- Recognize some basic properties of circles (3.3)
- Apply the formulas for the area and the circumference of a circle (3.3)
- Identify medians of triangles (3.4)
- Identify altitudes of triangles (3.4)
- Understand why auxiliary lines are used in some proofs (3.4)
- Write proofs involving steps beyond CPCTC (3.4)
- Use overlapping triangles in proofs (3.5)
- Name the various types of triangles and their parts (3.6)
- Apply theorems relating the angle measures and side lengths of triangles (3.7)
- Use the HL postulate to prove right triangles congruent (3.8)

VOCABULARY

acute triangle (3.6)
altitude (3.4)
auxiliary line (3.4)
base (3.6)
base angles (3.6)
congruent polygons (3.1)
congruent triangles (3.1)
equiangular triangle (3.6)
equilateral triangle (3.6)
hypotenuse (3.6)
included (3.2)

isosceles triangle (3.6)
leg (3.6)
median (3.4)
obtuse triangle (3.6)
reflection (3.1)
Reflexive Property (3.1)
right triangle (3.6)
rotate (3.1)
scalene triangle (3.6)
slide (3.1)
vertex angle (3.6)

REVIEW PROBLEMS

Problem Set A

1 For each of the following statements, write
A if the statement is always true
S if the statement is sometimes true
N if the statement is never true

a Two triangles are congruent if two sides and an angle of one are congruent to the corresponding parts of the other.

b If two sides of a right triangle are congruent to the corresponding parts of another right triangle, the triangles are congruent.

c All three altitudes of a triangle fall outside the triangle.

d A median of a triangle does not contain the midpoint of the side to which it is drawn.

e A right triangle is congruent to an obtuse triangle.

2 Given: $\overline{AB} \perp \overline{BC}$,
$\overline{DC} \perp \overline{BC}$,
$\angle 1 \cong \angle 2$
Conclusion: $\overline{AC} \cong \overline{DB}$

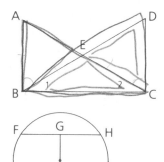

3 Given: $\odot O$,
$\overline{OG} \perp \overline{FH}$
Conclusion: $\overline{FG} \cong \overline{GH}$

4 Given: $\overline{PK}$ and $\overline{JM}$ bisect each other at R.
Prove: $\overline{PJ} \cong \overline{MK}$

5 Given: $\odot P$;
$\overrightarrow{PR}$ bisects $\angle KPM$.
Conclusion: $\overline{PR}$ is a median.

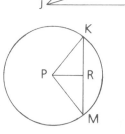

6 Given: $\overline{DG} \cong \overline{JF}$,
$\overline{DE} \cong \overline{JH}$,
$\overline{EG} \cong \overline{HF}$

Prove: $\triangle HCE$ is isosceles.

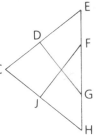

7 $\triangle HGF$ is equilateral.

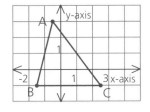

  a If $\angle F = (x + 32)°$ and $\angle H = (2x + 4)°$, solve for x and find m$\angle G$.

  b If the perimeter of $\triangle HGF = 6y + 24$ and $HG = 3y - 7$, find the perimeter of $\triangle HGF$.

8 Given: $\triangle RST \cong \triangle DFE$, $\angle R = 50°$, $\angle T = 40°$, $\angle E = (y + 10)°$, $\angle S = 90°$, $\angle D = (x + 20)°$, $\angle F = (z - 30)°$

Find: The values of x, y, and z (Draw your own diagram for this problem.)

9 Find the area of $\triangle ABC$.

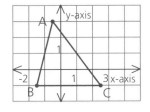

10 Find the area and the circumference of ⊙C to the nearest tenth.

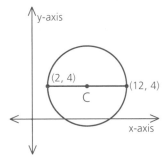

Problem Set B

11 Kate and Jaclyn wished to find the distance from N on one side of a lake to P on the other side. They put stakes at N, P, and T, then extended $\overline{PT}$ to S, making sure that $\overline{PT}$ was congruent to $\overline{TS}$. They followed a similar process in extending $\overline{NT}$ to R. They then measured $\overline{SR}$ and found it to be 70 m long. They concluded that NP was 70 m. Prove that they were correct.

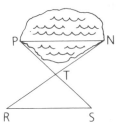

12 Given: $\overline{AD} \cong \overline{BC}$,
  $\angle DAB \cong \angle CBA$
  Prove: △ABE is isosceles.

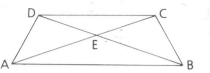

13 Given: $\overline{FJ}$ is the base of an isosceles △.
  $\overline{FG} \cong \overline{JH}$;
  O is the midpt. of $\overline{MF}$.
  K is the midpt. of $\overline{MJ}$.
  Conclusion: $\overline{OH} \cong \overline{KG}$

14 Given: $\overline{VX} \cong \overline{VZ}$;
  Y is the midpt of $\overline{XZ}$.
  Prove: $\overline{WY} \cong \overline{YA}$

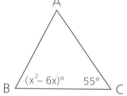

15 In the diagram, $\overline{AB} \cong \overline{AC}$. Solve for x.

16 Given: △NEW ≅ △CAR, EN = 11, AR = 2x − 4y, NW = x + y,
  CA = 4x + y, EW = 10
  Draw the triangles and find CR.

Problem Set C

17 Given: △FJH is isosceles, with base $\overline{JH}$.
  K and G are midpoints.
  FK = 2x + 3,
  GH = 5x − 9,
  JH = 4x
  Find: The perimeter of △FHJ

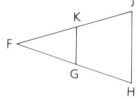

18 Given: $\overline{AC} \cong \overline{BC}$,
  $\angle 1 \cong \angle 3$
  Prove: △DFE is isosceles.

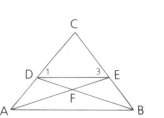

CUMULATIVE REVIEW
CHAPTERS 1–3

Problem Set A

1 a $\overline{BC} \cap \overline{CD} = $ _____.

b $\overline{BG} \cap \overline{EJ} = $ _____.

c $\overrightarrow{AF} \cup \overrightarrow{AB} = $ _____.

d $\overleftrightarrow{BC} \cap \overleftrightarrow{ED} = $ _____.

e $\overline{BC} \cap \overline{ED} = $ _____.

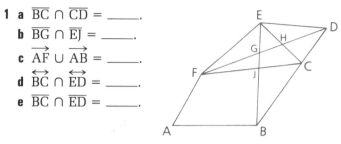

2 Three fifths of a degree is equivalent to how many minutes?

3 Find the complement of 43°17′51″.

4 How large is the angle formed by the hands of a clock at 11:20?

5 One of two supplementary angles is 8 degrees larger than the other. Find the measure of the larger angle.

6 Given: AB = 2r + 7,
CD = 3r − 1,
BC = 6;
C is the midpt. of $\overline{AD}$.

Find: AC

7 Given: ∠A is comp. to ∠BCA.
∠D is comp. to ∠DBC.
∠D ≅ ∠BCA

Prove: ∠A ≅ ∠DBC

8 Given: ⊙Q,
$\overline{RP} \cong \overline{PS}$

Conclusion: $\overrightarrow{PQ}$ bisects ∠RPS.

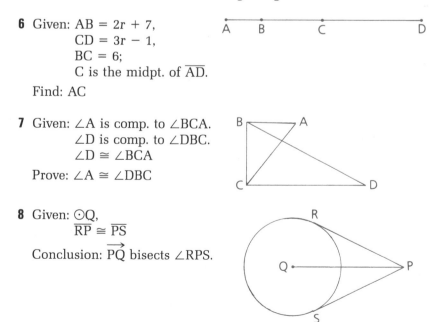

Cumulative Review Problem Set A, *continued*

9 Given: $\overline{PS} \perp \overline{SR}$;
∠QRP is comp. to ∠PRS.

Prove: ∠S ≅ ∠QRS

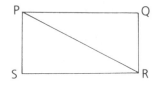

10 Given: ∠1 ≅ ∠2,
∠1 ≅ ∠3

Conclusion: $\overrightarrow{FH}$ bisects ∠EFG.

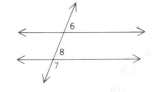

11 Given: Diagram as shown, with ∠6 supp.
to ∠7

Conclusion: ∠6 ≅ ∠8

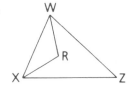

Problem Set B

12 Given: ∠T ≅ ∠W,
∠TSW ≅ ∠XSV,
$\overline{ST} \cong \overline{SW}$

Conclusion: $\overline{SX} \cong \overline{SV}$

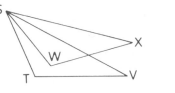

13 Given: $\overline{CE} \cong \overline{DF}$, $\overline{BD} \cong \overline{GE}$,
$\overline{BD} \perp \overline{CF}$,
$\overline{GE} \perp \overline{CF}$

Conclusion: △ACF is isosceles.

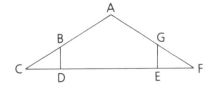

14 Given: △ZWX is isosceles, with base $\overline{WX}$.
$\overrightarrow{WR}$ bisects ∠XWZ.
$\overrightarrow{XR}$ bisects ∠ZXW.

Prove: ∠XWR ≅ ∠RXW

15 If angles 1, 2, and 3 are in the ratio 6:5:4,
find their measures.

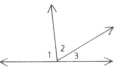

16 Prove: The segments drawn from the midpoint of the base of an
isosceles triangle to the midpoints of the legs are congruent.

17 Q is the midpoint of $\overline{PR}$. The ratio of PQ to QS is 2:5. What are the locations of P and S?

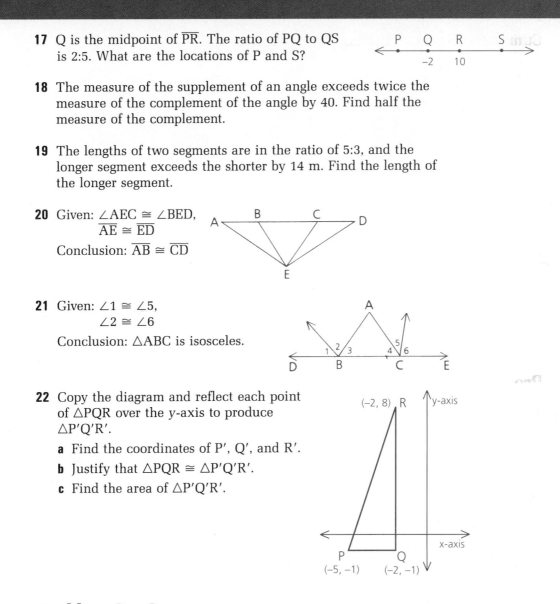

18 The measure of the supplement of an angle exceeds twice the measure of the complement of the angle by 40. Find half the measure of the complement.

19 The lengths of two segments are in the ratio of 5:3, and the longer segment exceeds the shorter by 14 m. Find the length of the longer segment.

20 Given: $\angle AEC \cong \angle BED$,
$\overline{AE} \cong \overline{ED}$
Conclusion: $\overline{AB} \cong \overline{CD}$

21 Given: $\angle 1 \cong \angle 5$,
$\angle 2 \cong \angle 6$
Conclusion: $\triangle ABC$ is isosceles.

22 Copy the diagram and reflect each point of $\triangle PQR$ over the y-axis to produce $\triangle P'Q'R'$.
  a Find the coordinates of P', Q', and R'.
  b Justify that $\triangle PQR \cong \triangle P'Q'R'$.
  c Find the area of $\triangle P'Q'R'$.

Problem Set C

23 Given: $\odot O$,
$\overline{OD} \cong \overline{OE}$,
$\angle DOB \cong \angle EOA$
Conclusion: $\overline{CD} \cong \overline{CE}$

24 Given: $\angle NOT \cong \angle POV$,
O is a midpoint.
$\angle N \cong \angle P$
Prove: $\overline{ST} \cong \overline{RV}$

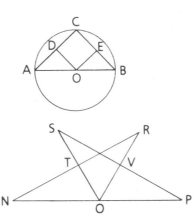

CHAPTER

4 | LINES IN THE PLANE

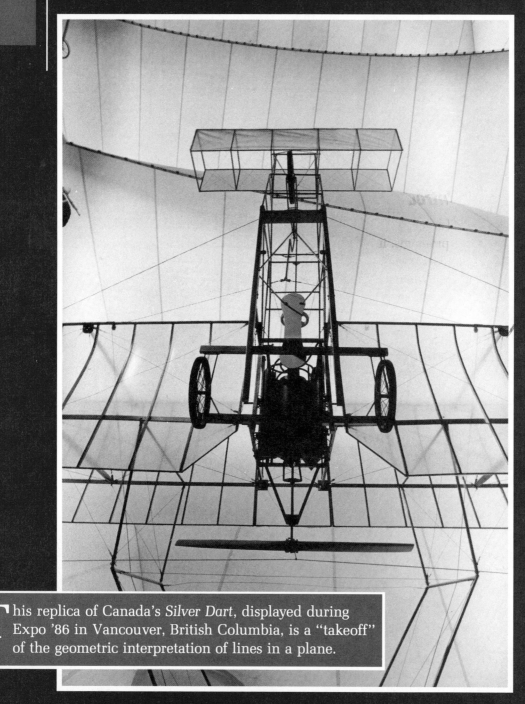

This replica of Canada's *Silver Dart*, displayed during Expo '86 in Vancouver, British Columbia, is a "takeoff" of the geometric interpretation of lines in a plane.

4.1   DETOURS AND MIDPOINTS

Objectives

After studying this section, you will be able to
- Use detours in proofs
- Apply the midpoint formula

Part One: Introduction

Detour Proofs

To solve some problems, it is necessary to prove more than one pair of triangles congruent. We call the proofs we use in such cases ***detour proofs***.

Analyze carefully the following example.

Example

Given: $\overline{AB} \cong \overline{AD}$,
$\quad\quad\;\;\; \overline{BC} \cong \overline{CD}$

Prove: $\triangle ABE \cong \triangle ADE$

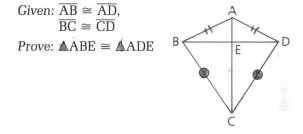

Notice that of the given information only $\overline{AB} \cong \overline{AD}$ seems to be usable. There does not seem to be enough information to prove that $\triangle ABE \cong \triangle ADE$. We must therefore prove something else first, taking a little detour to pick up the congruent parts we need.

	Statements	Reasons
1	$\overline{AB} \cong \overline{AD}$	1 Given
2	$\overline{BC} \cong \overline{CD}$	2 Given
3	$\overline{AC} \cong \overline{AC}$	3 Reflexive Property
4	$\triangle ABC \cong \triangle ADC$	4 SSS (1, 2, 3)
5	$\angle BAE \cong \angle DAE$	5 CPCTC
6	$\overline{AE} \cong \overline{AE}$	6 Reflexive Property
7	$\triangle ABE \cong \triangle ADE$	7 SAS (1, 5, 6)

Whenever you are asked to prove that triangles or parts of triangles are congruent and you suspect that a detour may be needed, use the following procedure.

1 Determine which triangles you must prove to be congruent to reach the required conclusion. (In the preceding example, these are △ABE and △ADE.)

2 Attempt to prove that these triangles are congruent. If you cannot do so for lack of enough given information, take a detour (steps 3–5 below).

3 Identify the parts that you must prove to be congruent to establish the congruence of the triangles. (Remember that there are many ways to prove that triangles are congruent. Consider them all.)

4 Find a pair of triangles that
  (a) You can readily prove to be congruent
  (b) Contain a pair of parts needed for the main proof (parts identified in step 3)

5 Prove that the triangles found in step 4 are congruent.

6 Use CPCTC and complete the proof planned in step 1.

The Midpoint Formula

In some coordinate-geometry problems, you will need to locate the midpoint of a line segment. A method of doing so is suggested by the following example.

Example *On the number line below, the coordinate of A is 2 and the coordinate of B is 14. Find the coordinate of M, the midpoint of $\overline{AB}$.*

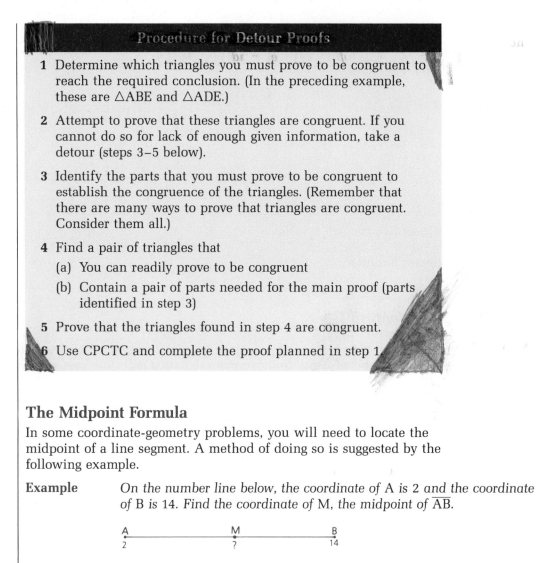

There are several ways of solving this problem. One of these is the *averaging* process (the average of two numbers is equal to half their sum). We will use x_m (read "x sub *m*") to represent the coordinate of M.

$$x_m = \frac{2 + 14}{2}$$

$$= \frac{16}{2} = 8$$

Check: AM = 8 − 2 = 6
        MB = 14 − 8 = 6

Therefore, 8 is the coordinate of M.

We can apply the averaging process to develop a formula, called the **_midpoint formula_**, that can be used to find the coordinates of the midpoint of any segment in the coordinate plane. The proof of this theorem is left to you.

Theorem 22

If A = (x_1, y_1) and B = (x_2, y_2), then the midpoint M = (x_m, y_m) of $\overline{AB}$ can be found by using the midpoint formula:

$$M = (x_m, y_m) = \left(\frac{x_1 + x_2}{2}, \frac{y_1 + y_2}{2}\right)$$

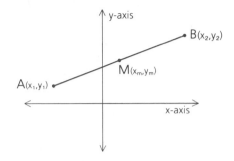

Part Two: Sample Problems

Problem 1

Given: $\overleftrightarrow{PQ}$ bisects $\overline{YZ}$.
Q is the midpt. of $\overline{WX}$.
$\angle Y \cong \angle Z$, $\overline{WZ} \cong \overline{XY}$

Conclusion: $\angle WQP \cong \angle XQP$

Proof

To reach the required conclusion, we must prove that $\triangle WQP \cong \triangle XQP$, but the given information is not sufficient to prove these triangles congruent. Therefore, we must detour through another pair of triangles. Can you see which pair of triangles we should use? Check your choice against the following proof.

Statements	Reasons
1 $\overleftrightarrow{PQ}$ bisects $\overline{YZ}$.	1 Given
2 $\overline{ZP} \cong \overline{PY}$	2 If a line bisects a segment, then it divides the segment into two $\cong$ segments.
3 $\angle Z \cong \angle Y$	3 Given
4 $\overline{WZ} \cong \overline{XY}$	4 Given
5 $\triangle ZWP \cong \triangle YXP$	5 SAS (2, 3, 4)
6 $\overline{WP} \cong \overline{PX}$	6 CPCTC
7 Q is the midpt. of $\overline{WX}$.	7 Given
8 $\overline{WQ} \cong \overline{QX}$	8 The midpoint of a segment divides the segment into two $\cong$ segments.
9 $\overline{PQ} \cong \overline{PQ}$	9 Reflexive Property
10 $\triangle WQP \cong \triangle XQP$	10 SSS (6, 8, 9)
11 $\angle WQP \cong \angle XQP$	11 CPCTC

DETOUR

Problem 2   *Find the coordinates of M, the mid-point of $\overline{AB}$.*

Solution   Use the midpoint formula.

$$x_m = \frac{x_1 + x_2}{2} \qquad y_m = \frac{y_1 + y_2}{2}$$

$$= \frac{-1 + 7}{2} \qquad\qquad = \frac{3 + 6}{2}$$

$$= 3 \qquad\qquad\qquad = 4\frac{1}{2}$$

Thus, $M = (x_m, y_m) = \left(3, 4\frac{1}{2}\right)$.

Problem 3   *In $\triangle ABC$, find the coordinates of the point at which the median from A intersects $\overline{BC}$.*

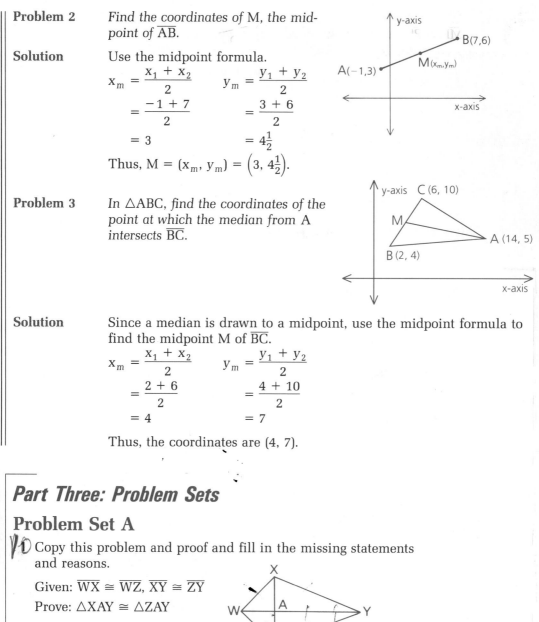

Solution   Since a median is drawn to a midpoint, use the midpoint formula to find the midpoint M of $\overline{BC}$.

$$x_m = \frac{x_1 + x_2}{2} \qquad y_m = \frac{y_1 + y_2}{2}$$

$$= \frac{2 + 6}{2} \qquad\qquad = \frac{4 + 10}{2}$$

$$= 4 \qquad\qquad\qquad = 7$$

Thus, the coordinates are (4, 7).

Part Three: Problem Sets

Problem Set A

1 Copy this problem and proof and fill in the missing statements and reasons.

Given: $\overline{WX} \cong \overline{WZ}$, $\overline{XY} \cong \overline{ZY}$
Prove: $\triangle XAY \cong \triangle ZAY$

Statements	Reasons
1 $\overline{WX} \cong \overline{WZ}$	1 Given
2 $\overline{XY} \cong \overline{ZY}$	2 Given
3 _____	3 Reflexive Property
4 $\triangle WXY \cong \triangle WZY$	4 _____
5 $\angle XYW \cong \angle ZYW$	5 _____
6 _____	6 Reflexive Property
7 $\triangle XAY \cong \triangle ZAY$	7 _____

2 Given: $\overline{MN} \cong \overline{NS}$,
$\overline{MP} \cong \overline{PS}$

Prove: $\angle MQP \cong \angle SQP$

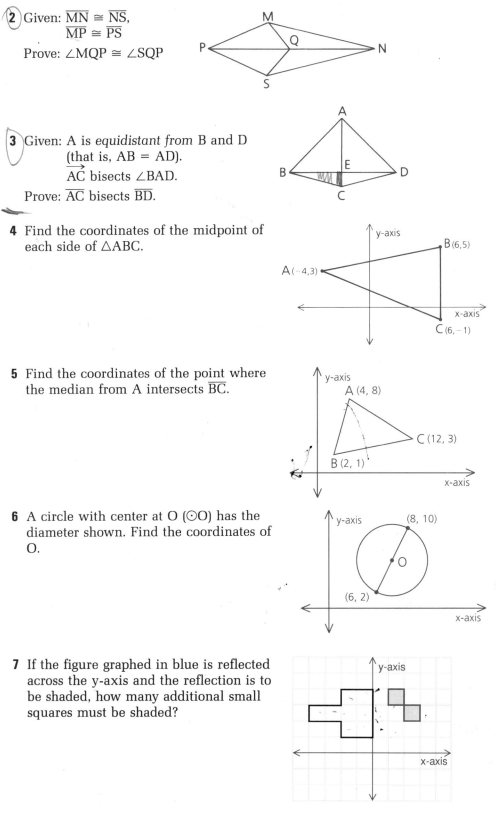

3 Given: A is *equidistant from* B and D
(that is, AB = AD).
$\overrightarrow{AC}$ bisects $\angle BAD$.

Prove: $\overline{AC}$ bisects $\overline{BD}$.

4 Find the coordinates of the midpoint of each side of $\triangle ABC$.

5 Find the coordinates of the point where the median from A intersects $\overline{BC}$.

6 A circle with center at O ($\odot O$) has the diameter shown. Find the coordinates of O.

7 If the figure graphed in blue is reflected across the y-axis and the reflection is to be shaded, how many additional small squares must be shaded?

Problem Set A, *continued*

8 If the shaded square has center at C and an area of $A_\square$, find C and $A_\square$.

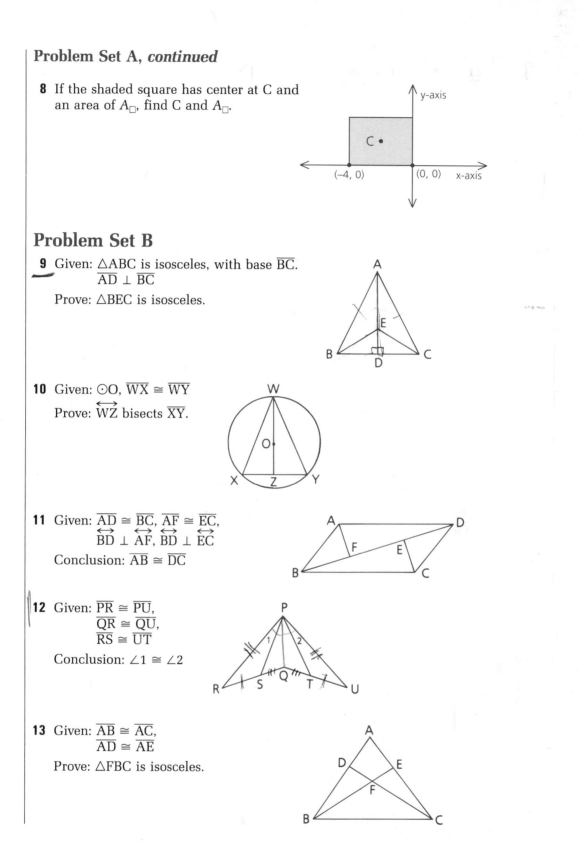

Problem Set B

9 Given: $\triangle ABC$ is isosceles, with base $\overline{BC}$.
$\overline{AD} \perp \overline{BC}$

Prove: $\triangle BEC$ is isosceles.

10 Given: $\odot O$, $\overline{WX} \cong \overline{WY}$
Prove: $\overleftrightarrow{WZ}$ bisects $\overline{XY}$.

11 Given: $\overline{AD} \cong \overline{BC}$, $\overline{AF} \cong \overline{EC}$,
$\overleftrightarrow{BD} \perp \overleftrightarrow{AF}$, $\overleftrightarrow{BD} \perp \overleftrightarrow{EC}$

Conclusion: $\overline{AB} \cong \overline{DC}$

12 Given: $\overline{PR} \cong \overline{PU}$,
$\overline{QR} \cong \overline{QU}$,
$\overline{RS} \cong \overline{UT}$

Conclusion: $\angle 1 \cong \angle 2$

13 Given: $\overline{AB} \cong \overline{AC}$,
$\overline{AD} \cong \overline{AE}$

Prove: $\triangle FBC$ is isosceles.

14 Given: T is the midpt. of $\overline{MN}$.
∠PMT and ∠QNT are right ∠s.
$\overline{MR} \cong \overline{SN}$, ∠1 ≅ ∠2

Conclusion: ∠P ≅ ∠Q

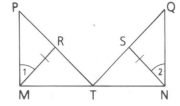

15 Given: ⊙O, ∠B ≅ ∠C
Prove: $\overline{AO}$ bisects $\overline{BC}$.

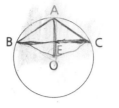

Problem Set C

16 Given: $\overline{AB} \cong \overline{AC}$;
$\overrightarrow{BD}$ bisects ∠ABE.
$\overrightarrow{CD}$ bisects ∠ACE.

Conclusion: $\overline{AE}$ bisects $\overline{BC}$.

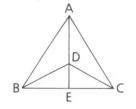

17 Given: $\overline{PT} \cong \overline{PU}$,
$\overline{PR} \cong \overline{PS}$

Prove: $\overrightarrow{PQ}$ bisects ∠RPS.

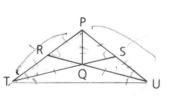

18 Given: $\overline{AD} \cong \overline{DB}$,
$\overline{AE} \cong \overline{BC}$,
$\overline{CD} \cong \overline{ED}$

Prove: △AFB is isosceles.

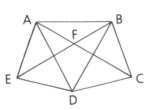

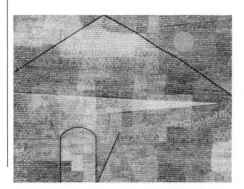

THE CASE OF THE MISSING DIAGRAM

Objective

After studying this section, you will be able to
- Organize the information in, and draw diagrams for, problems presented in words

Part One: Introduction

Some of the geometry problems you encounter will not be accompanied by diagrams. When you are faced with such a problem, it is important for you to be able to "set up" the problem—that is, to draw a diagram that accurately represents the problem and to express the given information and the conclusion you must reach in terms of that diagram. The following examples show some useful techniques for setting up problems.

Example 1   *Set up a proof of the statement, "If two altitudes of a triangle are congruent, then the triangle is isosceles."*

The statement in this problem is in "If . . ., then . . ." form; it is a conditional statement. In such statements the given information is usually to be found in the hypothesis (the *if* clause) and what we are to prove is stated in the conclusion (the *then* clause).

The diagram we draw should represent the given information but otherwise should be as general as possible. For instance, in the setup below we have not drawn the altitudes so that they bisect the sides, because bisections were not given. To draw bisectors would *overdetermine* the problem.

Setup for Example 1:

Given: $\overline{BD}$ and $\overline{CE}$ are altitudes to $\overline{AC}$ and $\overline{AD}$ of $\triangle ACD$.
$\overline{BD} \cong \overline{CE}$

Prove: $\triangle ACD$ is isosceles.

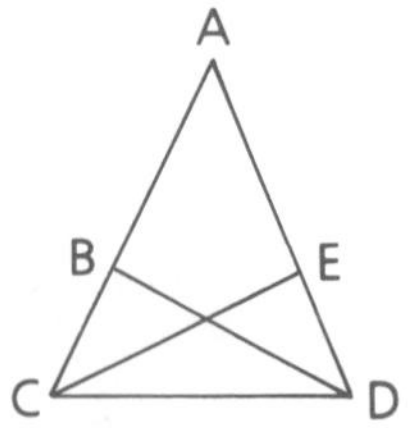

Sometimes the word *then* is left out of a conditional statement or the conclusion comes before the hypothesis. But the hypothesis always follows the word *if* and always contains given conditions. Occasionally, however, some of the given conditions appear in the conclusion, as in the next example.

Example 2 *Set up a proof of the statement, "The medians of a triangle are congruent if the triangle is equilateral."*

In the *if* clause, we are given an equilateral triangle, so we draw one. The conclusion tells us that we are to prove something about the medians, so the medians are also given. We draw them. We letter our diagram any way we wish and write our "Given:" and "Prove:" statements in terms of the diagram.

Setup for Example 2:

Given: △XYZ is equilateral.
$\overline{PZ}$, $\overline{RY}$, and $\overline{QX}$ are medians.
Prove: $\overline{PZ} \cong \overline{RY} \cong \overline{QX}$

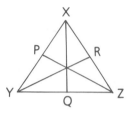

Example 3 *Set up a proof of the statement, "The altitude to the base of an isosceles triangle bisects the vertex angle."*

The statement in this example is a conditional statement with *if* and *then* left out. The main clue is that the sentence begins with given information and ends with a conclusion.

First, we are given an altitude to a base. Then we are given an isosceles triangle. We must prove that the altitude bisects the vertex angle of the triangle.

Setup for Example 3:

Given: △PQR is isosceles, with base $\overline{QR}$.
$\overline{PM}$ is an altitude.
Prove: $\overline{PM}$ bisects ∠QPR.

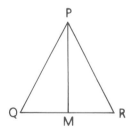

Why was it necessary to specify in the "Given:" statement that $\overline{QR}$ is the base of △PQR? Why was it not necessary to specify that ∠QPR is the vertex angle?

Part Two: Sample Problem

Problem   *Set up a proof of the statement, "If two angles of one triangle are congruent to two angles of another triangle, the remaining pair of angles are also congruent."*

Solution   We draw scalene triangles, since we are not told that the triangles are isosceles or equilateral. Also, we draw triangles of different sizes, since the triangles do not need to be congruent for the angles to be congruent.

Given: $\angle A \cong \angle D$,
          $\angle B \cong \angle E$
Prove: $\angle C \cong \angle F$

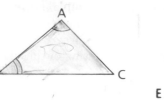 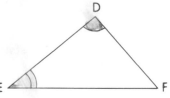

Part Three: Problem Sets

Problem Set A

In problems 1–4, draw your own diagram and write "Given:" and "Prove:" statements in terms of your diagram. Do *not* write a proof.

1 Given: An isosceles triangle and the median to the base

     Prove: The median is the *perpendicular bisector* of the base. (This sentence contains *two* conclusions—"the median is perpendicular to the base" and "the median bisects the base.")

2 Given: A four-sided polygon with all four sides congruent (This figure is called a *rhombus*.)

     Conclusion: The lines joining opposite vertices are perpendicular.

3 Given: Segments drawn perpendicular to each side of an angle from a point on the bisector of the angle

     Conclusion: These two segments are congruent.

4 The bisector of the vertex angle of an isosceles triangle is perpendicular to the base.

In problems 5–7, set up each problem and supply a proof of the statement.

5 The altitude to a side of a scalene triangle forms two congruent angles with that side of the triangle.

6 The median to the base of an isosceles triangle divides the triangle into two congruent triangles.

7 If the base of an isosceles triangle is extended in both directions, then the exterior angles formed are congruent.

Problem Set

In problems 8–12, set up and complete a proof of each statement.

8 If the median to a side of a triangle is also an altitude to that side, then the triangle is isosceles.

9 The line segments joining the vertex angle of an isosceles triangle to the trisection points of the base are congruent.

10 If the line joining a pair of opposite vertices of a four-sided polygon bisects both angles, then the remaining two angles are congruent.

11 If two triangles are congruent, then any pair of corresponding medians are congruent.

12 If a triangle is isosceles, the triangle formed by its base and the angle bisectors of its base angles is also isosceles.

Problem Set C

In problems 13–15, set up and complete a proof of each statement.

13 If each pair of opposite sides of a four-sided figure are congruent, then the segments joining opposite vertices bisect each other.

14 If a point on the base of an isosceles triangle is equidistant from the midpoints of the legs, then that point is the midpoint of the base.

15 If a point in the interior of an angle (between the sides) is equidistant from the sides of the angle, then the ray joining the vertex of the angle to this point bisects the angle. (Hint: The distance from a point to a line is defined as the length of the *perpendicular* segment from the point to the line.)

A RIGHT-ANGLE THEOREM

Objective

After studying this section, you will be able to
- Apply one way of proving that two angles are right angles

Part One: Introduction

Proving that lines are perpendicular depends on proving that they form right angles. For this reason, it is useful to know some ways of proving that angles are right angles. The following theorem will provide you with one such way.

Theorem 23   *If two angles are both supplementary and congruent, then they are right angles.*

Given: ∠1 ≅ ∠2
Prove: ∠1 and ∠2 are right angles.

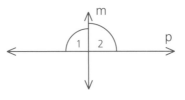

Proof: Since ∠1 and ∠2 form a straight angle (line p), they are supplementary. Therefore, m∠1 + m∠2 = 180. Since ∠1 ≅ ∠2, we can use substitution to get the equation m∠1 + m∠1 = 180, or m∠1 = 90. Thus, ∠1 is a right angle, and so is ∠2.

In the rest of this book, we shall assume that whenever two angles (such as ∠1 and ∠2 in the diagram for Theorem 23) form a straight angle, the two angles are supplementary. No formal statement of this fact will be necessary.

Part Two: Sample Problems

By this time, you should be familiar with the format used in two-column proofs. Therefore, we shall no longer include the headings "Statements" and "Reasons" in such proofs.

Problem 1   *Given:* $\overline{AB} \cong \overline{AC}$,
$\qquad\qquad\quad \overline{BD} \cong \overline{CD}$

Conclusion: $\overline{AD}$ *is an altitude.*

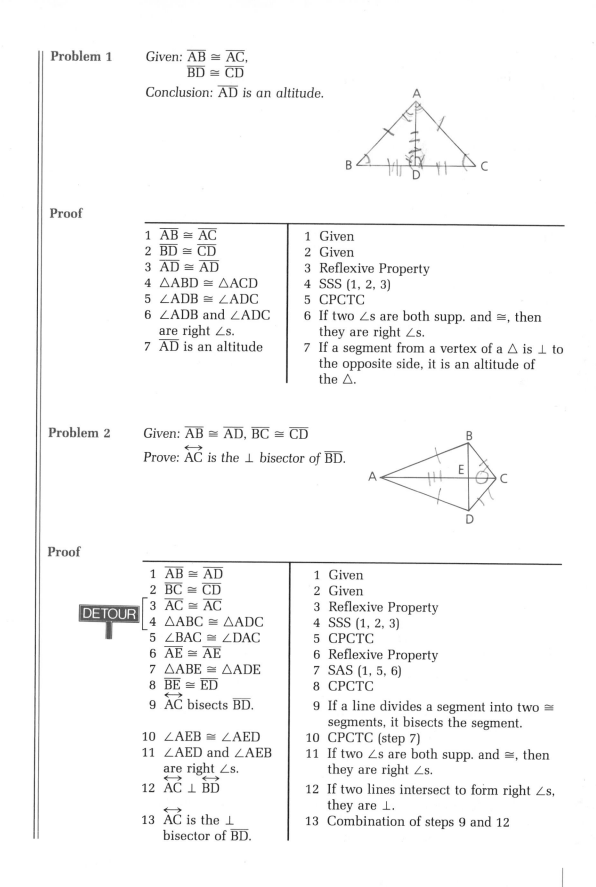

Proof

1 $\overline{AB} \cong \overline{AC}$	1 Given
2 $\overline{BD} \cong \overline{CD}$	2 Given
3 $\overline{AD} \cong \overline{AD}$	3 Reflexive Property
4 $\triangle ABD \cong \triangle ACD$	4 SSS (1, 2, 3)
5 $\angle ADB \cong \angle ADC$	5 CPCTC
6 $\angle ADB$ and $\angle ADC$ are right $\angle$s.	6 If two $\angle$s are both supp. and $\cong$, then they are right $\angle$s.
7 $\overline{AD}$ is an altitude	7 If a segment from a vertex of a $\triangle$ is $\perp$ to the opposite side, it is an altitude of the $\triangle$.

Problem 2   *Given:* $\overline{AB} \cong \overline{AD}$, $\overline{BC} \cong \overline{CD}$

Prove: $\overleftrightarrow{AC}$ *is the* $\perp$ *bisector of* $\overline{BD}$.

Proof

DETOUR

1 $\overline{AB} \cong \overline{AD}$	1 Given
2 $\overline{BC} \cong \overline{CD}$	2 Given
3 $\overline{AC} \cong \overline{AC}$	3 Reflexive Property
4 $\triangle ABC \cong \triangle ADC$	4 SSS (1, 2, 3)
5 $\angle BAC \cong \angle DAC$	5 CPCTC
6 $\overline{AE} \cong \overline{AE}$	6 Reflexive Property
7 $\triangle ABE \cong \triangle ADE$	7 SAS (1, 5, 6)
8 $\overline{BE} \cong \overline{ED}$	8 CPCTC
9 $\overleftrightarrow{AC}$ bisects $\overline{BD}$.	9 If a line divides a segment into two $\cong$ segments, it bisects the segment.
10 $\angle AEB \cong \angle AED$	10 CPCTC (step 7)
11 $\angle AED$ and $\angle AEB$ are right $\angle$s.	11 If two $\angle$s are both supp. and $\cong$, then they are right $\angle$s.
12 $\overleftrightarrow{AC} \perp \overleftrightarrow{BD}$	12 If two lines intersect to form right $\angle$s, they are $\perp$.
13 $\overleftrightarrow{AC}$ is the $\perp$ bisector of $\overline{BD}$.	13 Combination of steps 9 and 12

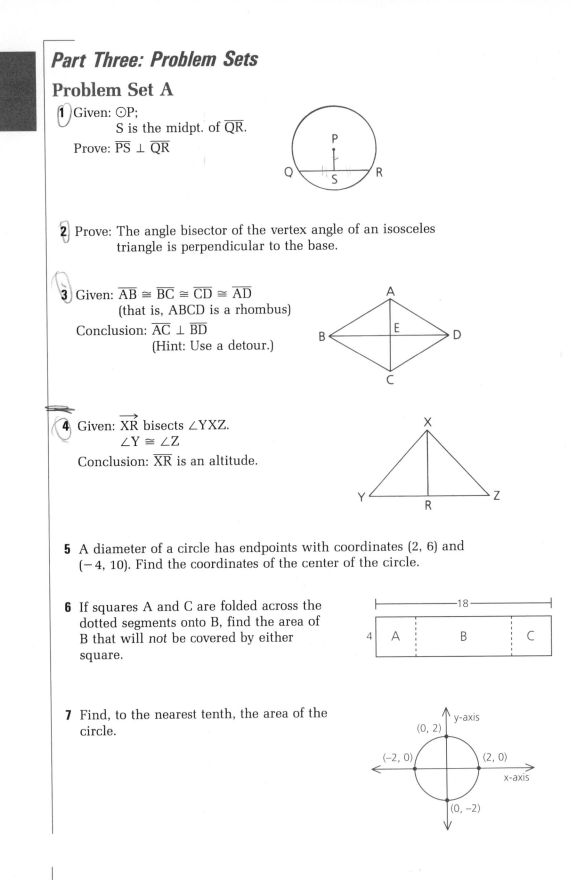

Part Three: Problem Sets

Problem Set A

1 Given: ⊙P;
  S is the midpt. of $\overline{QR}$.
  Prove: $\overline{PS} \perp \overline{QR}$

2 Prove: The angle bisector of the vertex angle of an isosceles triangle is perpendicular to the base.

3 Given: $\overline{AB} \cong \overline{BC} \cong \overline{CD} \cong \overline{AD}$
  (that is, ABCD is a rhombus)
  Conclusion: $\overline{AC} \perp \overline{BD}$
  (Hint: Use a detour.)

4 Given: $\overrightarrow{XR}$ bisects $\angle YXZ$.
  $\angle Y \cong \angle Z$
  Conclusion: $\overline{XR}$ is an altitude.

5 A diameter of a circle has endpoints with coordinates (2, 6) and (−4, 10). Find the coordinates of the center of the circle.

6 If squares A and C are folded across the dotted segments onto B, find the area of B that will *not* be covered by either square.

7 Find, to the nearest tenth, the area of the circle.

Problem Set B

8 If $\overline{CD}$ is the hypotenuse of a right triangle CAD and A has integral coordinates, find all possible values of the coordinates of A.

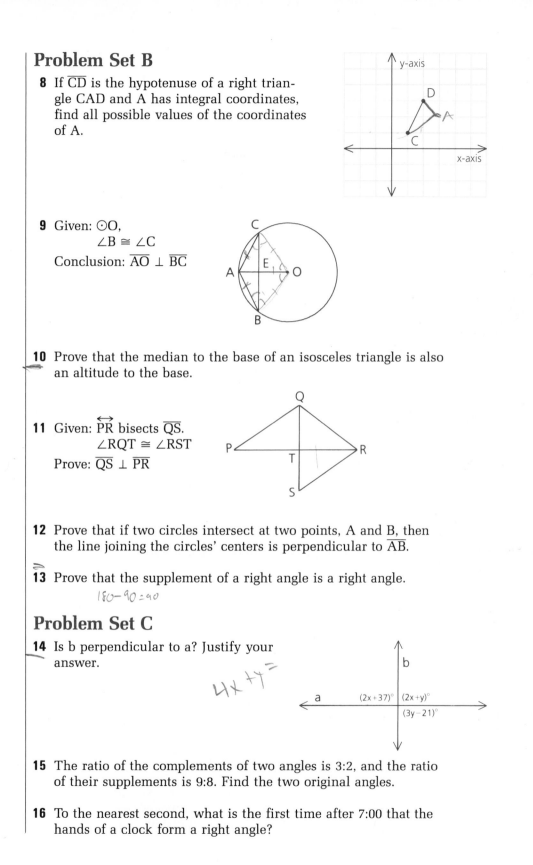

9 Given: $\odot O$,
      $\angle B \cong \angle C$
   Conclusion: $\overline{AO} \perp \overline{BC}$

10 Prove that the median to the base of an isosceles triangle is also an altitude to the base.

11 Given: $\overleftrightarrow{PR}$ bisects $\overline{QS}$.
       $\angle RQT \cong \angle RST$
    Prove: $\overline{QS} \perp \overline{PR}$

12 Prove that if two circles intersect at two points, A and B, then the line joining the circles' centers is perpendicular to $\overline{AB}$.

13 Prove that the supplement of a right angle is a right angle.

$180 - 90 = 90$

Problem Set C

14 Is b perpendicular to a? Justify your answer.

$4x + y =$

$(2x + 37)°$ $(2x + y)°$
            $(3y - 21)°$

15 The ratio of the complements of two angles is 3:2, and the ratio of their supplements is 9:8. Find the two original angles.

16 To the nearest second, what is the first time after 7:00 that the hands of a clock form a right angle?

THE EQUIDISTANCE THEOREMS

Objective

After studying this section, you will be able to
■ Recognize the relationship between equidistance and perpendicular bisection

Part One: Introduction

In geometry, the term *distance* has a special meaning.

Definition   The ***distance*** between two objects is the length of the shortest path joining them.

Postulate   ***A line segment is the shortest path between two points.***

The distance between points R and S is the length of $\overline{RS}$, or RS.

R •————————————• S

    If two points P and Q are the same distance from a third point X, then X is said to be ***equidistant*** from P and Q.

$$\overline{PX} \cong \overline{XQ}$$
means that
X is equidistant from P and Q.

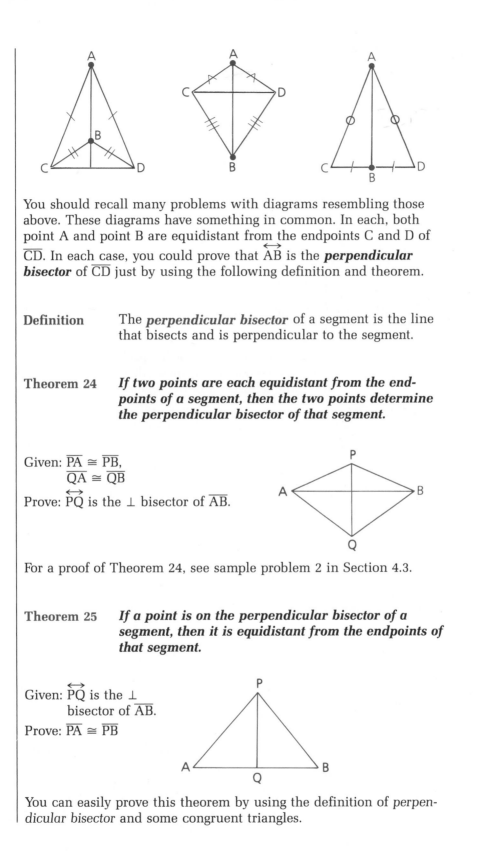

You should recall many problems with diagrams resembling those above. These diagrams have something in common. In each, both point A and point B are equidistant from the endpoints C and D of $\overline{CD}$. In each case, you could prove that $\overleftrightarrow{AB}$ is the ***perpendicular bisector*** of $\overline{CD}$ just by using the following definition and theorem.

Definition   The ***perpendicular bisector*** of a segment is the line that bisects and is perpendicular to the segment.

Theorem 24   *If two points are each equidistant from the endpoints of a segment, then the two points determine the perpendicular bisector of that segment.*

Given: $\overline{PA} \cong \overline{PB}$,
$\quad\quad\quad \overline{QA} \cong \overline{QB}$
Prove: $\overleftrightarrow{PQ}$ is the $\perp$ bisector of $\overline{AB}$.

For a proof of Theorem 24, see sample problem 2 in Section 4.3.

Theorem 25   *If a point is on the perpendicular bisector of a segment, then it is equidistant from the endpoints of that segment.*

Given: $\overleftrightarrow{PQ}$ is the $\perp$
$\quad\quad\quad$ bisector of $\overline{AB}$.
Prove: $\overline{PA} \cong \overline{PB}$

You can easily prove this theorem by using the definition of *perpendicular bisector* and some congruent triangles.

Part Two: Sample Problems

Problem 1 Given: $\angle 1 \cong \angle 2$,
$\qquad \angle 3 \cong \angle 4$

Prove: $\overset{\leftrightarrow}{AE} \perp$ bis. $\overline{BD}$

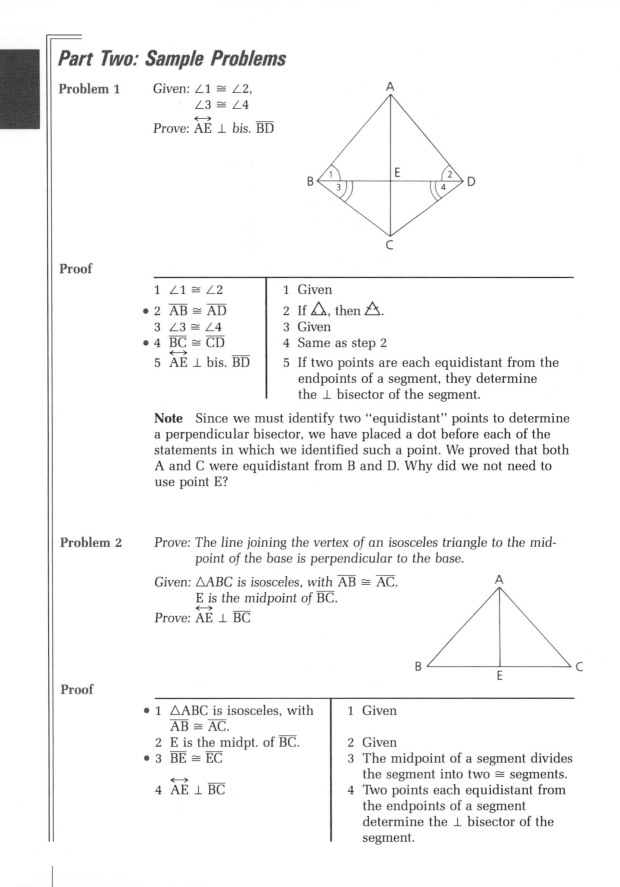

Proof

1 $\angle 1 \cong \angle 2$	1 Given
• 2 $\overline{AB} \cong \overline{AD}$	2 If △, then △.
3 $\angle 3 \cong \angle 4$	3 Given
• 4 $\overline{BC} \cong \overline{CD}$	4 Same as step 2
5 $\overset{\leftrightarrow}{AE} \perp$ bis. $\overline{BD}$	5 If two points are each equidistant from the endpoints of a segment, they determine the $\perp$ bisector of the segment.

Note Since we must identify two "equidistant" points to determine a perpendicular bisector, we have placed a dot before each of the statements in which we identified such a point. We proved that both A and C were equidistant from B and D. Why did we not need to use point E?

Problem 2 Prove: *The line joining the vertex of an isosceles triangle to the midpoint of the base is perpendicular to the base.*

Given: *$\triangle ABC$ is isosceles, with $\overline{AB} \cong \overline{AC}$.*
$\qquad$ *E is the midpoint of $\overline{BC}$.*
Prove: *$\overset{\leftrightarrow}{AE} \perp \overline{BC}$*

Proof

• 1 $\triangle ABC$ is isosceles, with $\overline{AB} \cong \overline{AC}$.	1 Given
2 E is the midpt. of $\overline{BC}$.	2 Given
• 3 $\overline{BE} \cong \overline{EC}$	3 The midpoint of a segment divides the segment into two $\cong$ segments.
4 $\overset{\leftrightarrow}{AE} \perp \overline{BC}$	4 Two points each equidistant from the endpoints of a segment determine the $\perp$ bisector of the segment.

Problem 3   Given: $\overline{AB} \cong \overline{AD}$,
 $\overline{BC} \cong \overline{CD}$
 Conclusion: $\overline{BE} \cong \overline{ED}$

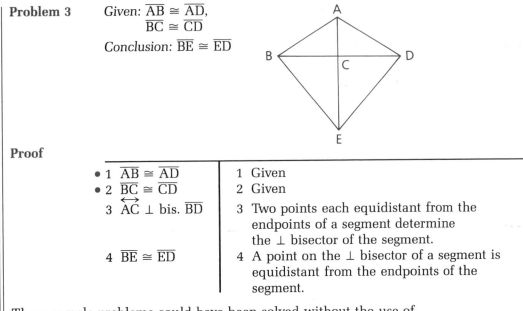

Proof

• 1 $\overline{AB} \cong \overline{AD}$	1 Given
• 2 $\overline{BC} \cong \overline{CD}$	2 Given
3 $\overleftrightarrow{AC} \perp$ bis. $\overline{BD}$	3 Two points each equidistant from the endpoints of a segment determine the $\perp$ bisector of the segment.
4 $\overline{BE} \cong \overline{ED}$	4 A point on the $\perp$ bisector of a segment is equidistant from the endpoints of the segment.

These sample problems could have been solved without the use of Theorems 24 and 25, but the proofs would have been harder and longer.

Part Three: Problem Sets

Problem Set A

As you work on these proofs, see if the equidistance theorems apply; they can save you a lot of work.

1 Given: $\odot O$; M is the midpt. of $\overline{AB}$.
 Conclusion: $\overline{OM} \perp \overline{AB}$ (Hint: Draw two
 auxiliary lines.)

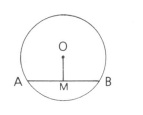

2 Given: $\overleftrightarrow{WZ} \perp$ bis. $\overline{XY}$
 Prove: $\triangle WXY$ is isosceles. (Hint: This
 proof can be written in three
 steps by using Theorem 25.)

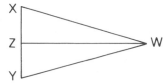

3 Given: $\odot O$, $\overline{AB} \cong \overline{AC}$
 Conclusion: $\overleftrightarrow{AD} \perp$ bis. $\overline{BC}$ (Hint: Show
 that A and O are each equi-
 distant from B and C.)

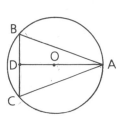

Problem Set A, *continued*

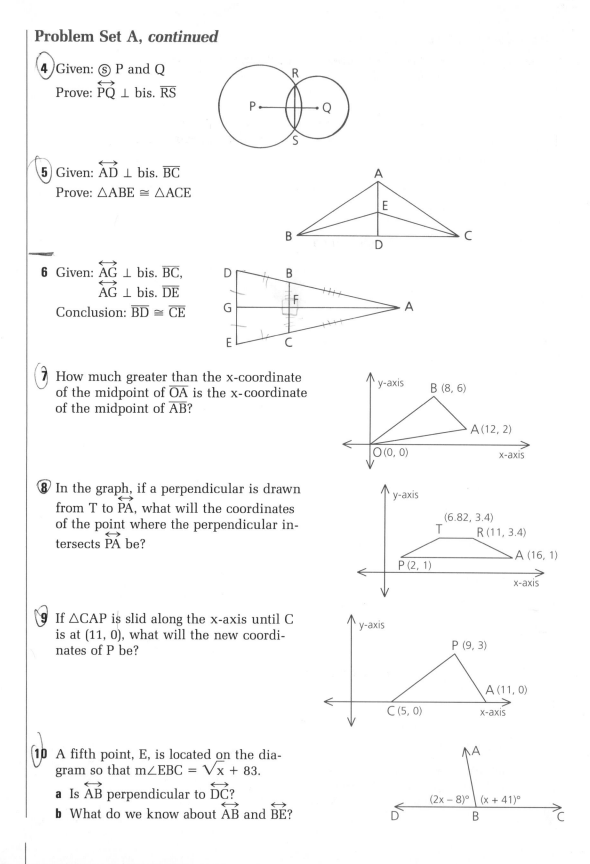

4 Given: ⓢ P and Q
Prove: $\overleftrightarrow{PQ}$ ⊥ bis. $\overline{RS}$

5 Given: $\overleftrightarrow{AD}$ ⊥ bis. $\overline{BC}$
Prove: △ABE ≅ △ACE

6 Given: $\overleftrightarrow{AG}$ ⊥ bis. $\overline{BC}$,
$\overleftrightarrow{AG}$ ⊥ bis. $\overline{DE}$
Conclusion: $\overline{BD}$ ≅ $\overline{CE}$

7 How much greater than the x-coordinate of the midpoint of $\overline{OA}$ is the x-coordinate of the midpoint of $\overline{AB}$?

8 In the graph, if a perpendicular is drawn from T to $\overleftrightarrow{PA}$, what will the coordinates of the point where the perpendicular intersects $\overleftrightarrow{PA}$ be?

9 If △CAP is slid along the x-axis until C is at (11, 0), what will the new coordinates of P be?

10 A fifth point, E, is located on the diagram so that m∠EBC = $\sqrt{x}$ + 83.

a Is $\overleftrightarrow{AB}$ perpendicular to $\overleftrightarrow{DC}$?
b What do we know about $\overleftrightarrow{AB}$ and $\overleftrightarrow{BE}$?

Problem Set B

Remember, the equidistance theorems will help you write a concise proof.

11 Draw isosceles $\triangle PQR$, with P the vertex. Draw the bisectors of the base angles and label their point of intersection S. Prove that $\overleftrightarrow{PS} \perp \overleftrightarrow{QR}$. (Hint: Use Theorem 24.)

12 Given: $\overline{AB} \cong \overline{BC}$,
$\overline{AE} \cong \overline{EC}$
Prove: $\overline{AD} \cong \overline{DC}$ (Hint: This can be done in four steps.)

13 Given: $\overline{WY}$ and $\overline{XZ} \perp$ bis. each other.
Prove: $\overline{WX} \cong \overline{XY} \cong \overline{YZ} \cong \overline{ZW}$ (that is, WXYZ is a rhombus)

14 Given: $\overline{WX} \cong \overline{WZ}$, $\overline{XY} \cong \overline{YZ}$ (WXYZ is a *kite*.)
Prove: $\triangle WPZ$ is a right $\triangle$.

15 Given: $\angle ADC$ and $\angle ABC$ are right $\angle$s.
$\overline{AB} \cong \overline{AD}$
Conclusion: $\overleftrightarrow{AC} \perp$ bis. $\overline{BD}$

16 Prove: The median to the base of an isosceles triangle is also an altitude. (Prove this without using congruent triangles.)

17 Given: F is the midpt. of $\overline{BC}$.
$\overline{DB} \cong \overline{EC}$,
$\overline{DB} \perp \overline{DF}$,
$\overline{EC} \perp \overline{EF}$
Conclusion: $\overleftrightarrow{AF} \perp \overleftrightarrow{BC}$

Problem Set B, *continued*

18 Given: $\overline{PS} \cong \overline{SR}$,
  $\overline{PQ} \cong \overline{QR}$

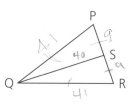

  a Prove that $\overline{QS}$ is an altitude.

  b If RS = 9, QS = 40, and QR = 41, find the area of triangle PQR.

  c What relationship exists among the numbers 9, 40, and 41, the lengths of the sides of right triangle QRS?

19 **a** On the rectangle shown, how much farther is the trip from P to T to R to E than the trip from P to C to E?

  b If rectangle RECT is rotated 90° clockwise about point R, what will the coordinates of the new location of P be?

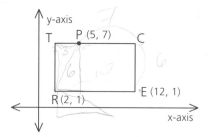

Problem Set C

20 Given: $\overline{AB} \cong \overline{BC}$,
  $\overline{AE} \cong \overline{EC}$
  Conclusion: $\overline{AD} \cong \overline{DC}$

21 Given: ABCDE is equilateral and equiangular.
  F is the midpt. of $\overline{AE}$.
  Prove: $\overleftrightarrow{FC} \perp$ bis. $\overline{BD}$

22 A four-sided figure with two disjoint pairs of consecutive sides congruent is called a *kite*. The two segments joining opposite vertices are its diagonals. Prove that one of these diagonals is the perpendicular bisector of the other diagonal.

23 Prove that if each of the three altitudes of a triangle bisects the side to which it is drawn, then the triangle is equilateral.

190 Chapter 4 Lines in the Plane

24 a If two of the points A, B, C, D, E, and M are chosen at random, what is the probability that the two points determine the perpendicular bisector of $\overline{AB}$?

b If three of the six points are chosen at random, what is the probability that the three points are collinear?

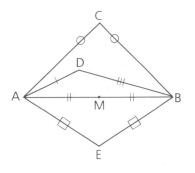

PLOTTING THE STRUCTURE OF A MOLECULE
Elizabeth Getzoff deduces the locations of atoms

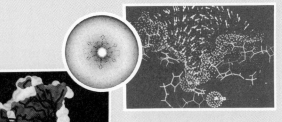

If you sight along the plane of a phonograph record toward a source of light, you'll notice a *diffraction spectrum*, a rainbow created by the separation of the light into its component colors by the parallel grooves. Crystallographers exploit a similar, though far more complex, phenomenon to create *X-ray diffraction* patterns, a powerful tool for determining the atomic structure of molecules.

Crystallographer Elizabeth Getzoff specializes in decoding the structures of protein molecules. She begins by growing crystals made of the protein she wishes to map. Then she bombards the crystals with X-rays. "The X-rays are diffracted by the parallel planes of atoms within the crystal," she explains. "The diffracted rays interfere with each other, producing an array of spots on a photographic film. I can measure the angles and spacings of the diffraction spots and deduce the arrangement and packing of molecules in the crystal." Once she understands the structure of the crystal, she can analyze the structure of the protein molecule from the intensities of the diffraction spots. "My goal is to find the x-, y-, and z-coordinates of the atoms that make up the protein. Then I can plot them in a three-dimensional coordinate system." Computer graphics, another field in which Getzoff has made a series of important contributions, help simplify the task of plotting.

As a high school student in Whippany, New Jersey, Getzoff participated in a National Science Foundation summer program in inorganic chemistry and computer science. She attended Duke University, where she earned a bachelor's degree in chemistry and a doctorate in X-ray crystallography. Since 1985 she has been an assistant member of the molecular biology department at Scripps Clinic in La Jolla, California. There, she runs a research group in molecular structure. Her work, she says, could not proceed without the use of mathematics, especially geometry. For example, to aid in her analysis of the effect of protein upon its function, she is currently developing computer graphic visualizations based on fractal geometry. However difficult the challenge, her reason for taking it on is simple: "I'm finding out how molecules work," she says. "How they work is how life works."

INTRODUCTION TO PARALLEL LINES

Objectives

After studying this section, you will be able to
- Recognize planes
- Recognize transversals
- Identify the pairs of angles formed by a transversal
- Recognize parallel lines

Part One: Introduction

Planes

In order to explain parallel lines adequately, we must first acquaint you with the meaning of **plane**.

Definition   A *plane* is a surface such that if any two points on the surface are connected by a line, all points of the line are also on the surface.

A plane has only two dimensions—length and width. Both the length and the width are infinite. A plane has no thickness.

Definition   If points, lines, segments, and so forth, lie in the same plane, we call them *coplanar*. Points, lines, segments, and so forth, that do not lie in the same plane are called *noncoplanar*.

Planes are discussed more fully in Chapter 6.

Transversals

In the figure, line t is a **transversal** of lines a and b.

Definition   A *transversal* is a line that intersects two coplanar lines in two distinct points.

The region between lines d and e is the *interior* of the figure. The rest of the plane is the *exterior*.

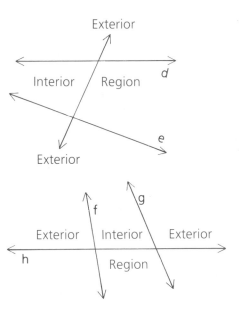

The diagram of lines f and g cut by transversal h provides another illustration of the regions formed by two lines and a transversal.

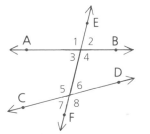

Angle Pairs Formed by Transversals

$\overleftrightarrow{AB}$ and $\overleftrightarrow{CD}$ are cut by transversal $\overleftrightarrow{EF}$.

The two pairs of *alternate interior angles* are 3 and 6, 4 and 5.
The two pairs of *alternate exterior angles* are 1 and 8, 2 and 7.
The four pairs of *corresponding angles* are 1 and 5, 2 and 6, 3 and 7, 4 and 8.

$\overleftrightarrow{GH}$ and $\overleftrightarrow{JK}$ are cut by transversal $\overleftrightarrow{MO}$.

The alternate interior angles are b and g, f and c.
The alternate exterior angles are a and h, e and d.
The corresponding angles are a and c, b and d, e and g, f and h.

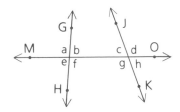

Definition   *Alternate interior angles* are a pair of angles formed by two lines and a transversal. The angles must both lie in the interior of the figure, must lie on alternate sides of the transversal, and must have different vertices.

Look for an N or Z shape.

Definition   ***Alternate exterior angles*** are a pair of angles formed by two lines and a transversal. The angles must both lie in the exterior of the figure, must lie on alternate sides of the transversal, and must have different vertices.

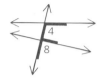

Definition   ***Corresponding angles*** are a pair of angles formed by two lines and a transversal. One angle must lie in the interior of the figure, and the other must lie in the exterior. The angles must lie on the same side of the transversal but have different vertices.

Look for an F shape.

It is important to be able to recognize these pairs of angles when they appear in figures made up of a number of segments. In each of the following examples, the segment corresponding to the transversal is shown in red, and the segments corresponding to the lines it cuts are shown in blue.

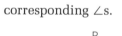

∠1 and ∠2 are corresponding ∠s.

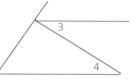

∠3 and ∠4 are alternate interior ∠s.

∠5 and ∠6 are alternate exterior ∠s.

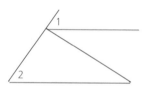

∠BCA and ∠DFE are alternate interior ∠s.

∠BCD and ∠EFA are alternate exterior ∠s.

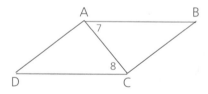

∠7 and ∠8 are alternate interior ∠s.

Can you find a pair of alternate interior ∠s formed by $\overleftrightarrow{AD}$ and $\overleftrightarrow{BC}$ with transversal $\overleftrightarrow{AC}$?

Parallel Lines

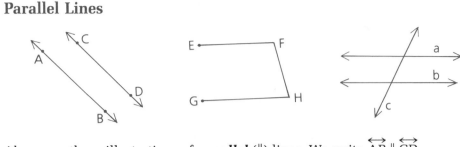

Above are three illustrations of ***parallel*** (∥) lines. We write $\overleftrightarrow{AB} \parallel \overleftrightarrow{CD}$, $\overleftrightarrow{EF} \parallel \overleftrightarrow{GH}$, and a ∥ b.

Definition   *Parallel lines* are two coplanar lines that do not intersect.

We shall also call segments or rays parallel if they are parts of parallel lines. For example, we can say that in the preceding diagrams $\overline{AB} \parallel \overline{CD}$ and $\overline{EF} \parallel \overline{GH}$.

There are many lines that do not intersect yet are not parallel. *To be parallel, lines must be coplanar.* In Chapter 6, lines that are noncoplanar and nonintersecting are defined as *skew* lines.

Part Two: Sample Problem

Problem

  a *Which of the lines in the figure at the right is the transversal?*

  b *Name all pairs of alternate interior angles.*

  c *Name all pairs of alternate exterior angles.*

  d *Name all pairs of corresponding angles.*

  e *Name all pairs of interior angles on the same side of the transversal.*

  f *Name all pairs of exterior angles on the same side of the transversal.*

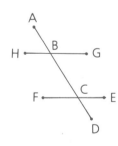

Answers

  a $\overleftrightarrow{AD}$

  b ∠GBC and ∠FCB, ∠HBC and ∠ECB

  c ∠ABG and ∠DCF, ∠ABH and ∠DCE

  d ∠ABG and ∠BCE, ∠GBC and ∠ECD, ∠ABH and ∠BCF, ∠HBC and ∠FCD

  e ∠GBC and ∠ECB, ∠HBC and ∠FCB

  f ∠ABG and ∠DCE, ∠ABH and ∠DCF

Part Three: Problem Set

1 **a** Name all pairs of alternate interior angles.

    b Name all pairs of alternate exterior angles.

    c Name all pairs of corresponding angles.

    d Name all pairs of interior angles on the same side of the transversal.

    e Name all pairs of exterior angles on the same side of the transversal.

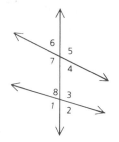

2 **a** What name is given to ∠1 and ∠2 for $\overleftrightarrow{AB}$ and $\overleftrightarrow{CD}$? What is the transversal?

    b What type of angles are 3 and 4? Which lines and transversal form them?

    c What type of angles are 4 and 5? Which lines and transversal form them?

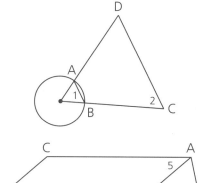

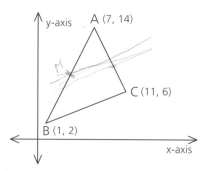

3 Copy the diagram.

    a Find the coordinates of M, the midpoint of $\overline{AB}$.

    b Find the coordinates of N, the midpoint of $\overline{AC}$.

    c Draw $\overleftrightarrow{MN}$. What *appears* to be true about $\overleftrightarrow{MN}$ and $\overleftrightarrow{BC}$?

    d What *appears* to be true about ∠AMN and ∠ABC?

    e Name a pair of corresponding angles formed by $\overleftrightarrow{MN}$ and $\overleftrightarrow{BC}$ with transversal $\overleftrightarrow{AC}$.

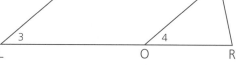

4 **a** For which pair of lines are angles 1 and 4 a pair of alternate interior angles?

b For which pair of lines are angles 2 and 3 a pair of alternate interior angles?

c How many transversals of $\overleftrightarrow{JO}$ and $\overleftrightarrow{KM}$ are shown?

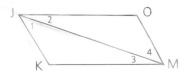

5 Locate the following points on a graph: $(x_1, y_1) = (0, 0)$, $(x_2, y_2) = (4, 5)$, $(x_3, y_3) = (0, 3)$ and $(x_4, y_4) = (4, 8)$.

a Find $\frac{y_2 - y_1}{x_2 - x_1}$.

b Find $\frac{y_4 - y_3}{x_4 - x_3}$.

c Draw a line through the first two points and a line through the second two points. What *appears* to be true about these lines?

FROM MUD TO THE STARS
The reach of geometry

Since before recorded history, human beings have used basic geometric principles in building and surveying. But with the rise of civilization, people came gradually to recognize the power of geometry as a means of controlling and explaining the world around them. As the encyclopedist Isidore of Seville (A.D. 560–636) tells us,

The science of geometry is said to have been discovered by the Egyptians, for after the Nile would flood, covering all their property with mud, they would mark off their landholdings with boundaries and measurements, thus giving geometry its name [from Greek gē, "earth," and metra, "measurements"]. Later, when this study had been further perfected by the ingenuity of the wise, it was also used to measure the expanses of sea and stars and air. For after investigating the dimensions of the earth by geometry, people began to investigate even the extent of the heavens—how far the moon is from the earth, and the sun from the moon, all the way to the limits of the universe.

The development of geometric thought from its beginnings to the present day, when it guides scientists' explorations of realms of space stretching from the subatomic to the intergalactic, makes for a fascinating story. The Historical Snapshots in this book will give you a few brief glimpses into that story. If you find them interesting, you may wish to look further into the history of geometry.

SLOPE

Objectives

After studying this section, you will be able to
- Understand the concept of slope
- Relate the slope of a line to its orientation in the coordinate plane
- Recognize the relationships between the slopes of parallel and perpendicular lines

Part One: Introduction

Definition of *Slope*

To understand how the principles of coordinate geometry can be applied to the study of parallelism and perpendicularity, you need to be familiar with the concept of *slope*.

Definition   The *slope* m of a nonvertical line, segment, or ray containing (x_1, y_1) and (x_2, y_2) is defined by the formula

$$m = \frac{y_2 - y_1}{x_2 - x_1} \text{ or } m = \frac{y_1 - y_2}{x_1 - x_2} \text{ or } m = \frac{\Delta y}{\Delta x}$$

Note   In more-advanced mathematics classes, it is common to use Δy (read "delta y") instead of $y_2 - y_1$ and Δx ("delta x") instead of $x_2 - x_1$. The symbol Δ is used to indicate change, so that Δy, for example, means "the change in y-coordinates between two points."

Example   *Find the slope of the segment joining* $(-2, 3)$ *and* $(6, 5)$.

$$m = \frac{y_2 - y_1}{x_2 - x_1} \text{ or } m = \frac{y_1 - y_2}{x_1 - x_2}$$

$$= \frac{5 - 3}{6 - (-2)} \qquad = \frac{3 - 5}{-2 - 6}$$

$$= \frac{2}{8} = \frac{1}{4} \qquad = \frac{-2}{-8} = \frac{1}{4}$$

Notice that it does not matter which point is chosen as (x_1, y_1).

When the slope formula is applied to a vertical line, such as $\overleftrightarrow{CD}$, the denominator is zero. Division by zero is undefined, so a vertical line has no slope.

$$m = \frac{y_2 - y_1}{x_2 - x_1}$$

$$= \frac{12 - 2}{6 - 6}$$

$$= \frac{10}{0} \text{ (An undefined expression)}$$

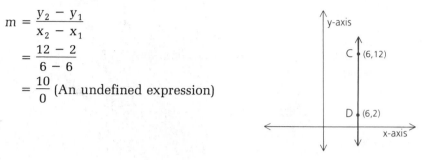

Do not confuse no slope with a slope of zero. On a horizontal line, $y_2 = y_1$, but $x_2 \neq x_1$. Therefore, the numerator is zero, while the denominator is not. Hence, a horizontal line has zero slope.

Visual Interpretation of Slope

The numerical value of a slope gives us a clue to the direction a line is taking. The following diagrams illustrate this notion.

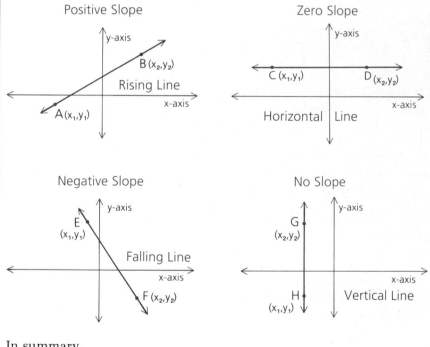

In summary,
- Rising line $\Longleftrightarrow$ positive slope
- Horizontal line $\Longleftrightarrow$ zero slope
- Falling line $\Longleftrightarrow$ negative slope
- Vertical line $\Longleftrightarrow$ no slope

Slopes of Parallel and Perpendicular Lines

The proofs of the following four theorems require a knowledge of the properties of similar triangles and will be omitted here.

Theorem 26   *If two nonvertical lines are parallel, then their slopes are equal.*

Given: $\overleftrightarrow{AB} \parallel \overleftrightarrow{CD}$

Prove: Slope $\overleftrightarrow{AB}$ = slope $\overleftrightarrow{CD}$

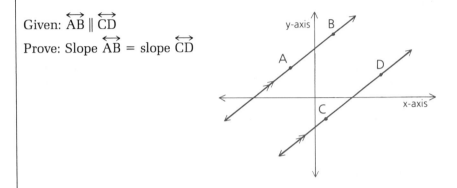

The next theorem is the converse of Theorem 26, with the statements in the *if* clause and the *then* clause reversed.

Theorem 27   *If the slopes of two nonvertical lines are equal, then the lines are parallel.*

It can also be shown that there is a relationship between the slopes of two perpendicular lines—they are ***opposite reciprocals*** of each other. For example, if the slope of a line is $\frac{2}{5}$, the slope of any line perpendicular to it is $-\frac{5}{2}$. As with parallel lines, we can develop two converse theorems.

Theorem 28   *If two lines are perpendicular and neither is vertical, each line's slope is the opposite reciprocal of the other's.*

Theorem 29   *If a line's slope is the opposite reciprocal of another line's slope, the two lines are perpendicular.*

Part Two: Sample Problems

Problem 1 If $A = (4, -6)$ and $B = (-2, -8)$, find the slope of $\overleftrightarrow{AB}$.

Solution By the slope formula,

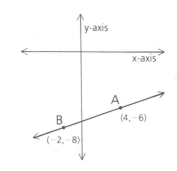

$$m = \frac{y_2 - y_1}{x_2 - x_1}$$
$$= \frac{-8 - (-6)}{-2 - 4}$$
$$= \frac{-8 + 6}{-6} = \frac{1}{3}$$

Note The line is rising, so the slope is positive. Drawing a diagram helps prevent careless errors.

Problem 2 *Show that CEF is a right triangle.*

Solution Find the slopes of the sides.

Slope of $\overleftrightarrow{CE} = \frac{\Delta y}{\Delta x} = \frac{4 - 3}{8 - 1} = \frac{1}{7}$

Slope of $\overleftrightarrow{FE} = \frac{\Delta y}{\Delta x} = \frac{7 - 4}{4 - 8} = \frac{3}{-4} = -\frac{3}{4}$

Slope of $\overleftrightarrow{FC} = \frac{\Delta y}{\Delta x} = \frac{3 - 7}{1 - 4} = \frac{-4}{-3} = \frac{4}{3}$

Since the slopes of $\overleftrightarrow{FE}$ and $\overleftrightarrow{FC}$ are opposite reciprocals, $\angle F$ is a right angle. Therefore, $\triangle CEF$ is a right triangle.

Problem 3 *Given: $\triangle ABE$ as shown*

*Find: **a** The slope of altitude $\overline{AC}$*
***b** The slope of median $\overline{AD}$*

Solution **a** Slope of $\overleftrightarrow{BE} = \frac{\Delta y}{\Delta x} = \frac{5 - 3}{6 - (-4)} = \frac{1}{5}$

Since the slope of the altitude to $\overline{BE}$ is the opposite reciprocal of the slope of $\overleftrightarrow{BE}$, the slope of $\overleftrightarrow{AC} = -5$.

b By the midpoint formula, $D = (1, 4)$. Since $A = (-2, 10)$, the slope of $\overleftrightarrow{AD} = \frac{\Delta y}{\Delta x} = \frac{4 - 10}{1 - (-2)} = -2.$

Problem 4 Find the slope of $\overleftrightarrow{AB}$ to the nearest hundredth.

Solution By the slope formula,

$$m = \frac{y_2 - y_1}{x_2 - x_1}$$

$$= \frac{2\sqrt{5} - \sqrt{5}}{6 - 3}$$

$$= \frac{\sqrt{5}}{3}$$

To approximate, use a calculator.

$$\frac{\sqrt{5}}{3} \approx \frac{2.236067977}{3}$$

$$\approx 0.75$$

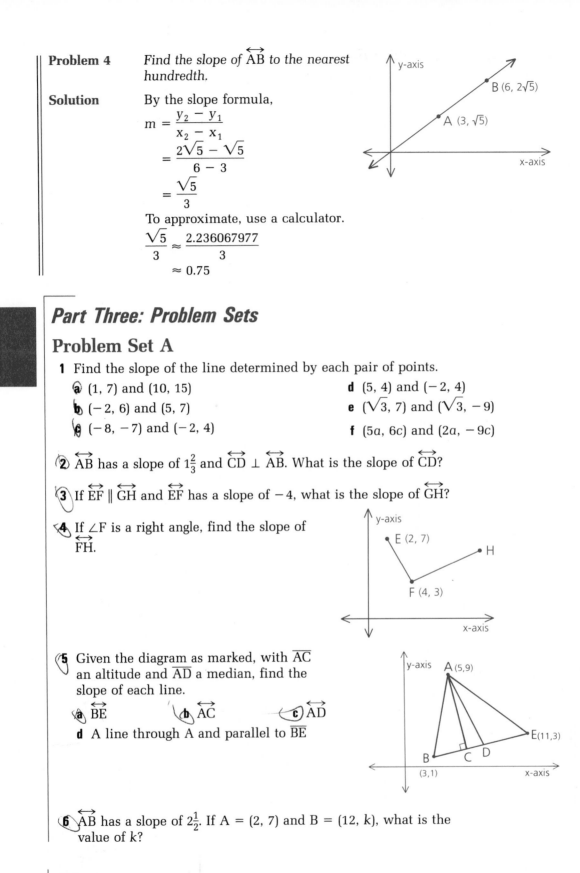

Part Three: Problem Sets

Problem Set A

1 Find the slope of the line determined by each pair of points.

   a (1, 7) and (10, 15)

   b (−2, 6) and (5, 7)

   c (−8, −7) and (−2, 4)

   d (5, 4) and (−2, 4)

   e $(\sqrt{3}, 7)$ and $(\sqrt{3}, -9)$

   f $(5a, 6c)$ and $(2a, -9c)$

2 $\overleftrightarrow{AB}$ has a slope of $1\frac{2}{3}$ and $\overleftrightarrow{CD} \perp \overleftrightarrow{AB}$. What is the slope of $\overleftrightarrow{CD}$?

3 If $\overleftrightarrow{EF} \parallel \overleftrightarrow{GH}$ and $\overleftrightarrow{EF}$ has a slope of -4, what is the slope of $\overleftrightarrow{GH}$?

4 If $\angle F$ is a right angle, find the slope of $\overleftrightarrow{FH}$.

5 Given the diagram as marked, with $\overline{AC}$ an altitude and $\overline{AD}$ a median, find the slope of each line.

   a $\overleftrightarrow{BE}$ **b** $\overleftrightarrow{AC}$ **c** $\overleftrightarrow{AD}$

   d A line through A and parallel to $\overline{BE}$

6 $\overleftrightarrow{AB}$ has a slope of $2\frac{1}{2}$. If A = (2, 7) and B = (12, k), what is the value of k?

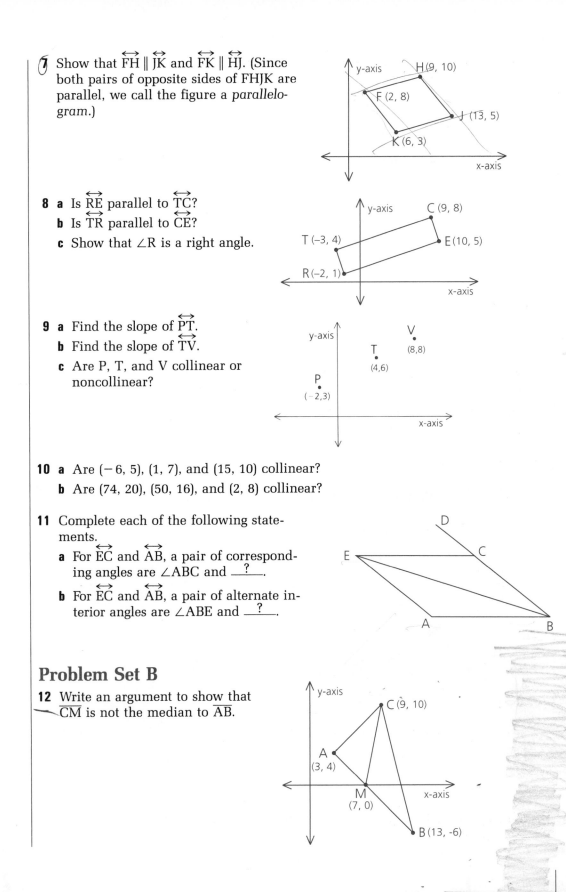

7 Show that $\overleftrightarrow{FH} \parallel \overleftrightarrow{JK}$ and $\overleftrightarrow{FK} \parallel \overleftrightarrow{HJ}$. (Since both pairs of opposite sides of FHJK are parallel, we call the figure a *parallelogram*.)

8 a Is $\overleftrightarrow{RE}$ parallel to $\overleftrightarrow{TC}$?
  b Is $\overleftrightarrow{TR}$ parallel to $\overleftrightarrow{CE}$?
  c Show that $\angle R$ is a right angle.

9 a Find the slope of $\overleftrightarrow{PT}$.
  b Find the slope of $\overleftrightarrow{TV}$.
  c Are P, T, and V collinear or noncollinear?

10 a Are $(-6, 5)$, $(1, 7)$, and $(15, 10)$ collinear?
   b Are $(74, 20)$, $(50, 16)$, and $(2, 8)$ collinear?

11 Complete each of the following statements.
  a For $\overleftrightarrow{EC}$ and $\overleftrightarrow{AB}$, a pair of corresponding angles are $\angle ABC$ and ___?___.
  b For $\overleftrightarrow{EC}$ and $\overleftrightarrow{AB}$, a pair of alternate interior angles are $\angle ABE$ and ___?___.

Problem Set B

12 Write an argument to show that $\overline{CM}$ is not the median to $\overline{AB}$.

13 If A = (6, 11), B = (1, 5), and C = (7, 0), show by means of slopes that △ABC is a right triangle. Name the hypotenuse.

14 Suppose that point H is rotated 90° in a clockwise direction about the origin to point J.

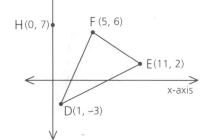

 a Does J lie on $\overleftrightarrow{DE}$? Show why or why not.
 b Write an argument to show that $\overline{FJ}$ is not the altitude to $\overline{DE}$.

15 If square OABC is rotated 180° clockwise about its center, what will the new coordinates of O be?

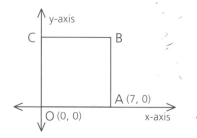

16 Goofy Guff wanted to reflect the outline figure (the figure to the right of the y-axis) across the dashed line. Goofy shaded what he thought was the reflected figure as shown, but Goofy had goofed.

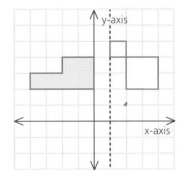

 a How many 1-unit squares did Goofy shade that he shouldn't have?
 b How many additional 1-unit squares should Goofy have shaded?

Problem Set C

17 △ABC has vertices at A = (2, 1), B = (12, 3), and C = (6, 7). Write an argument to show that the median from C to $\overline{AB}$ is not longer than the altitude from C to $\overline{AB}$.

18 In any right triangle, if a and b are the lengths of the legs and c is the length of the hypotenuse, $a^2 + b^2 = c^2$. Given △CAT as shown, find $(CA)^2 + (AT)^2$.

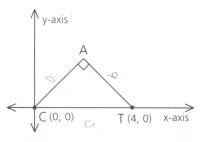

CHAPTER SUMMARY

CONCEPTS AND PROCEDURES

After studying this chapter, you should be able to
- Use detours in proofs (4.1)
- Apply the midpoint formula (4.1)
- Organize the information in, and draw diagrams for, problems presented in words (4.2)
- Apply one way of proving that two angles are right angles (4.3)
- Recognize the relationship between equidistance and perpendicular bisection (4.4)
- Recognize planes (4.5)
- Recognize transversals (4.5)
- Identify the pairs of angles formed by a transversal (4.5)
- Recognize parallel lines (4.5)
- Understand the concept of slope (4.6)
- Relate the slope of a line to its orientation in the coordinate plane (4.6)
- Recognize the relationships between the slopes of parallel and perpendicular lines (4.6)

VOCABULARY

alternate exterior angles (4.5)
alternate interior angles (4.5)
coplanar (4.5)
corresponding angles (4.5)
detour proof (4.1)
distance (4.4)
equidistant (4.4)
exterior (4.5)
interior (4.5)

midpoint formula (4.1)
noncoplaner (4.5)
opposite reciprocal (4.6)
parallel lines (4.5)
perpendicular bisector (4.4)
plane (4.5)
slope (4.6)
transversal (4.5)

REVIEW PROBLEMS

Problem Set A

1 Copy the problem and proof, filling in the blanks with the correct statements and reasons.

Given: P is the midpt. of $\overline{XZ}$.
$\qquad \angle 1 \cong \angle 2$

Conclusion: $\overline{XY} \cong \overline{YZ}$

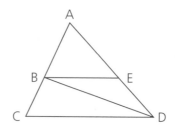

1 P is the midpt. of $\overline{XZ}$.	1 Given
2 _____	2 _____
3 $\angle 1 \cong \angle 2$	3 Given
4 _____	4 _____
5 $\overleftrightarrow{WY} \perp$ bis. $\overline{XZ}$	5 _____
6 $\overline{XY} \cong \overline{YZ}$	6 _____

2 a Identify a pair of corresponding angles formed by $\overleftrightarrow{BE}$ and $\overleftrightarrow{CD}$ with transversal $\overleftrightarrow{BC}$.

b Identify a pair of alternate interior angles formed by $\overleftrightarrow{BE}$ and $\overleftrightarrow{CD}$ with transversal $\overleftrightarrow{BD}$.

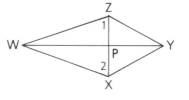

3 Given: $\angle ADB \cong \angle CDB$,
$\qquad \overline{AD} \cong \overline{DB}$
Prove: $\overline{BD}$ is an altitude.

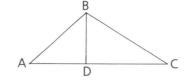

4 Given: $\angle 1 \cong \angle 4$;
$\qquad \overrightarrow{FC}$ bisects $\angle BFD$.
Conclusion: $\overleftrightarrow{CF} \perp \overleftrightarrow{AE}$

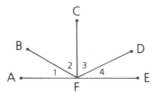

5 Set up a proof for the following information. Then complete the proof.

Given: Two isosceles triangles with the same base

Prove: The line joining the vertices of the vertex ∠s of the △ is the ⊥ bisector of the base.

6 Given: △ABC is isosceles, with base $\overline{AC}$.
∠1 ≅ ∠2

Conclusion: $\overleftrightarrow{BD} \perp \overleftrightarrow{AC}$

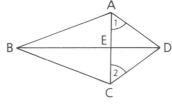

7 Given: ⊙O;
M is the midpt. of $\overline{AB}$.

Conclusion: $\overline{OM} \perp \overline{AB}$

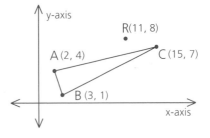

8 Set up a proof of, but do not prove, the statement, "If two chords of a circle are congruent, then the segments joining the midpoints of the chords to the center of the circle are congruent." (A *chord* is a segment whose endpoints are on the circle.)

9 a If the median from A intersects $\overline{BC}$ at M, what are the coordinates of M?

b Find the slope of $\overleftrightarrow{BC}$.

c Is $\overleftrightarrow{AR}$ parallel to $\overleftrightarrow{BC}$? Why or why not?

d Find the slope of the altitude from A to $\overline{BC}$.

e If Rhonda Right walked from A to M, how far did she walk?

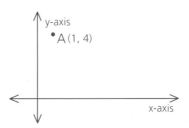

Problem Set B

10 a Point A = (1, 4) is reflected across the y-axis to point B. Find the coordinates of B.

b Point A is rotated, with respect to the origin, 90° clockwise to point C. Find the coordinates of C.

c If A is slid two units up and then seven units to the right to point D, what are the coordinates of D? (This "sliding" procedure is called a *translation*.)

11 Given: ⊙O,
∠1 ≅ ∠2
Conclusion: $\overline{OY} \perp \overline{WX}$

12 Given: ∠1 ≅ ∠2 ≅ ∠3 ≅ ∠4,
$\overline{BE} \cong \overline{BF}$
Conclusion: △ABE ≅ △CBF

13 Given: ⊙O,
$\overline{DX} \cong \overline{DY}$
Conclusion: $\overleftrightarrow{DZ}$ bisects $\overline{XY}$.

14 Given: ∠WXY ≅ ∠ZYX,
$\overline{WX} \cong \overline{ZY}$
Conclusion: $\overline{WR} \cong \overline{RZ}$

15 Given: $\overline{AB} \cong \overline{AF}$,
$\overline{BD} \cong \overline{DF}$,
∠1 ≅ ∠2
Conclusion: $\overline{AD} \perp \overline{CE}$

16 Given: $\overleftrightarrow{AD} \perp$ bis. $\overline{BC}$
Conclusion: ∠1 ≅ ∠2

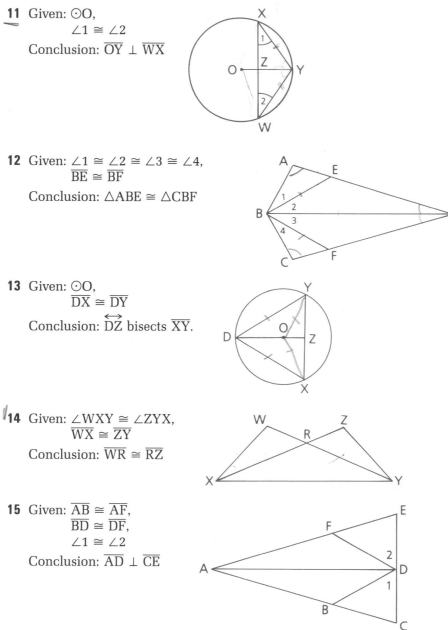

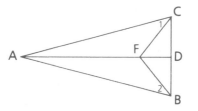

17 Use slopes to show that EFHJ is a parallelogram.

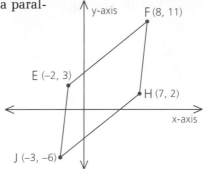

Problem Set C

18 ∠F is a right angle. Explain why (9, 6) could not be the coordinates of H.

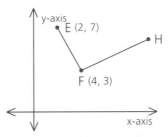

19 Given △PQR, with P = (3, 6), Q = (4, 1), and R = (14, 3), find the measure of the largest angle of △PQR. Explain your reasoning.

20 Given: $\overline{AB} \cong \overline{AF}$,
    $\overline{BC} \cong \overline{FE}$
    Conclusion: $\overline{CD} \cong \overline{DE}$

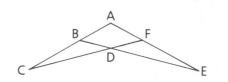

21 Prove: If the bisector of an angle whose vertex lies on a circle passes through the center of the circle, then it is the perpendicular bisector of the segment joining the points where the sides of the angle intersect the circle.

22 Given: $\overline{AB} \cong \overline{AC}$,
    $\overline{BF} \cong \overline{FC}$,
    ∠BAE ≅ ∠CAD
    Prove: $\overleftrightarrow{AF} \perp \overleftrightarrow{DE}$

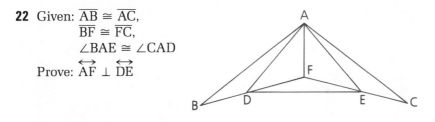

PARALLEL LINES AND RELATED FIGURES

The Piazza di Spagna in Rome, a masterpiece of early eighteenth-century architecture, is a study in parallelism.

5.1 INDIRECT PROOF

Objective

After studying this section, you will be able to
- Write indirect proofs

Part One: Introduction

At the beginning of this book, we mentioned that mathematicians believe that today's students should be familiar with a variety of proof styles. This is why we have provided you with several alternatives to the two-column proof. To give you an efficient way to work certain problems, we now introduce the concept of ***indirect proof.***

An indirect proof may be useful in a problem where a direct proof would be difficult to apply. Study the following example of an indirect proof.

Example

Given: $\angle A \cong \angle D$, $\overline{AB} \cong \overline{DE}$, $\overline{AC} \not\cong \overline{DF}$

Prove: $\angle B \not\cong \angle E$

Proof: Either $\angle B \cong \angle E$ or $\angle B \not\cong \angle E$.
Assume $\angle B \cong \angle E$.
From the given information, $\angle A \cong \angle D$ and $\overline{AB} \cong \overline{DE}$.
Thus, $\triangle ABC \cong \triangle DEF$ by ASA.
$\therefore \overline{AC} \cong \overline{DF}$

But this is impossible, since $\overline{AC} \not\cong \overline{DF}$ is given.
Thus, our assumption was false and $\angle B \not\cong \angle E$, because this is the only other possibility.

The following procedure will help you to write indirect proofs.

Indirect-Proof Procedure

1 List the possibilities for the conclusion.
2 Assume that the *negation* of the desired conclusion is correct.
3 Write a chain of reasons until you reach an impossibility.
   This will be a contradiction of either
   (a) given information or
   (b) a theorem, definition, or other known fact.
4 State the remaining possibility as the desired conclusion.

Part Two: Sample Problems

Note   Remember to start by looking at the conclusion.

Problem 1   *Given:* $\overline{RS} \perp \overline{PQ}$,
$\overline{PR} \not\cong \overline{QR}$
Prove: $\overrightarrow{RS}$ *does not bisect* $\angle PRQ$.

Proof   Either $\overrightarrow{RS}$ bisects $\angle PRQ$ or $\overrightarrow{RS}$ does not bisect $\angle PRQ$.
Assume $\overrightarrow{RS}$ bisects $\angle PRQ$.
Then we can say that $\angle PRS \cong \angle QRS$.
Since $\overline{RS} \perp \overline{PQ}$, we know that $\angle PSR \cong \angle QSR$.
Thus, $\triangle PSR \cong \triangle QSR$ by ASA ($\overline{SR} \cong \overline{SR}$).
Hence, $\overline{PR} \cong \overline{QR}$ by CPCTC.

But this is impossible because it contradicts the given fact that
$\overline{PR} \not\cong \overline{QR}$. Consequently, the assumption must be false. $\therefore$ $\overrightarrow{RS}$ does
not bisect $\angle PRQ$, the only other possibility.

Problem 2   *Given:* $\odot O$, $\overline{AB} \not\cong \overline{BC}$
Prove: $\angle AOB \not\cong \angle COB$

Proof   Either $\angle AOB \cong \angle COB$ or $\angle AOB \not\cong \angle COB$. We will assume that
$\angle AOB \cong \angle COB$. Since O is the center of the circle, $\overline{AO} \cong \overline{CO}$. By
the Reflexive Property, $\overline{BO} \cong \overline{BO}$. Thus, $\triangle AOB \cong \triangle COB$ by SAS,
which means that $\overline{AB} \cong \overline{CB}$ by CPCTC.
    This is impossible because it contradicts the given fact that
$\overline{AB} \not\cong \overline{BC}$. Consequently, our assumption ($\angle AOB \cong \angle COB$) is false.
$\therefore$ $\angle AOB \not\cong \angle COB$, because that is the only other possibility.

Part Three: Problem Sets

Problem Set A

1 Given: $\overline{AB} \cong \overline{AD}$, $\angle BAC \not\cong \angle DAC$
Prove: $\overline{BC} \not\cong \overline{DC}$

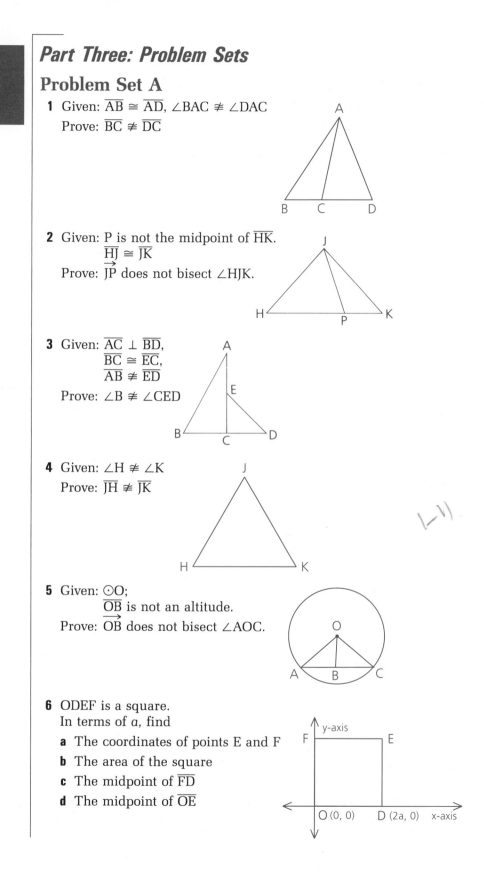

2 Given: P is not the midpoint of $\overline{HK}$.
$\overline{HJ} \cong \overline{JK}$
Prove: $\overrightarrow{JP}$ does not bisect $\angle HJK$.

3 Given: $\overline{AC} \perp \overline{BD}$,
$\overline{BC} \cong \overline{EC}$,
$\overline{AB} \not\cong \overline{ED}$
Prove: $\angle B \not\cong \angle CED$

4 Given: $\angle H \not\cong \angle K$
Prove: $\overline{JH} \not\cong \overline{JK}$

5 Given: $\odot O$;
$\overline{OB}$ is not an altitude.
Prove: $\overrightarrow{OB}$ does not bisect $\angle AOC$.

6 ODEF is a square.
In terms of a, find
  a The coordinates of points E and F
  b The area of the square
  c The midpoint of $\overline{FD}$
  d The midpoint of $\overline{OE}$

Problem Set A, *continued*

7 RECT is a rectangle.

    a In terms of a and b, find the coordinates of C.

    b Does $\overline{RC}$ appear to be congruent to $\overline{ET}$?

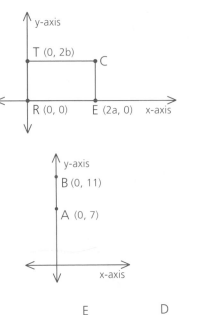

8 With respect to the origin, point A is rotated 90° clockwise to point C, and point B is rotated 180° clockwise to point D. Find the slope of $\overleftrightarrow{CD}$.

9 Identify each of the following pairs of angles as alternate interior, alternate exterior, or corresponding.

    a For $\overleftrightarrow{BE}$ and $\overleftrightarrow{CD}$ with transversal $\overleftrightarrow{BC}$, $\angle 1$ and $\angle C$

    b For $\overleftrightarrow{AE}$ and $\overleftrightarrow{BD}$ with transversal $\overleftrightarrow{BE}$, $\angle 2$ and $\angle 4$

Problem Set B

10 Given: $\overline{PA} \perp \overline{AB}$,
          $\overline{PA} \perp \overline{AC}$,
          $\angle B \not\cong \angle C$
   Prove: $\overline{AB} \not\cong \overline{AC}$

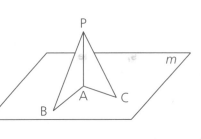

11 Given: $\overrightarrow{BD}$ bisects $\angle ABC$.
          $\angle ADB$ is acute.
   Prove: $\overline{AB} \not\cong \overline{BC}$

12 Given: $\odot O$; $\overline{HE}$ is not the perpendicular bisector of $\overline{DF}$.

   Prove: $\overline{DE} \not\cong \overline{EF}$

13 Prove that if △ABC is isosceles, with base $\overline{BC}$, and if P is a point on $\overline{BC}$ that is not the midpoint, then $\overrightarrow{AP}$ does not bisect ∠BAC.

Problem Set C

14 Prove that if no two medians of a triangle are congruent, then the triangle is scalene.

15 a Show that the diagonals, $\overline{CS}$ and $\overline{OI}$, of the given isosceles trapezoid do not bisect each other.

  b Are the diagonals of this isosceles trapezoid perpendicular?

  c Do you think that the diagonals of every isosceles trapezoid are perpendicular?

  d Can you figure out what to draw so that you could use the formula $a^2 + b^2 = c^2$ (see Section 4.6, problem 18) to find that OS ≈ 8.25?

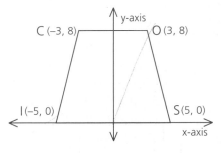

A LINE TO THE STARS
Geometry guides navigator Paul Wotherspoon

Perhaps the primary task of a navigator is to fix, or identify exactly, the ship's position. To appreciate the problem this presents, imagine yourself on the ocean with no land in sight. How do you tell where you are? The most reliable way, says Senior Chief Quartermaster Paul Wotherspoon—an assistant navigator in the United States Coast Guard—is to get out your sextant.

A sextant is a hand-held instrument used to measure the angle between a star and the horizon. Its effectiveness is based on the fact that all lines of sight to a star from anywhere on earth are parallel. Because of the earth's curvature, the angle between the lines of sight to the star and to the horizon changes as your position on earth changes.

"With the sextant," explains Wotherspoon, "we find the position of a known star in the sky by measuring its angle above the horizon.

Horizon

EP
Earthly position of star

Next, [based on the time of night, charts, and a complicated procedure called sight reduction] we identify the point on the earth that is directly beneath the star. Using this information we can draw a *line of position*, an arc the ship must lie on." The navigator repeats the process for a second star. "Your location is the point where the two lines of position intersect. Since there are two such places on the earth's surface, it's best to take a third sighting to confirm your position."

Wotherspoon attended high school in Vernon, Connecticut. Following graduation he joined the Coast Guard. He attended quartermaster school. During his nineteen years in the Coast Guard, he has served on five ships. Today he is stationed in Boston. His many duties as an assistant navigator include planning trips, giving directions on the bridge, securing tide and current information, steering the ship in close quarters, and taking official deck logs.

Line of position 2

Line of position 1

PROVING THAT LINES ARE PARALLEL

Objectives

After studying this section, you will be able to
- Apply the Exterior Angle Inequality Theorem
- Use various methods to prove lines parallel

Part One: Introduction

The Exterior Angle Inequality Theorem

An exterior angle of a triangle is formed whenever a side of the triangle is extended to form an angle supplementary to the adjacent interior angle.

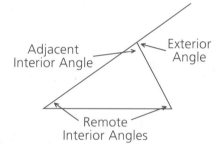

Theorem 30   *The measure of an exterior angle of a triangle is greater than the measure of either remote interior angle.*

Given: Exterior angle BCD

Prove: m∠BCD > m∠B,
        m∠BCD > m∠BAC

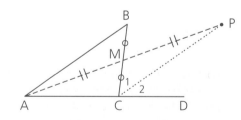

Proof: Locate the midpoint, M, of $\overline{BC}$. Draw $\overline{AP}$ so that AM = MP. Draw $\overline{CP}$. $\overline{MB} \cong \overline{MC}$, $\overline{AM} \cong \overline{MP}$, and vertical angles are congruent. Thus, △ABM ≅ △PCM and∠1 ≅ ∠B. Since m∠BCD > m∠1, we know that m∠BCD > m∠B. The second part of the theorem is proved by extending $\overline{BC}$ to form the other exterior angle, a vertical angle to ∠BCD. The result follows.

Identifying Parallel Lines

When two lines are cut by a transversal, eight angles are formed. You can use several pairs of angles to prove that the lines are parallel.

Theorem 31 *If two lines are cut by a transversal such that two alternate interior angles are congruent, the lines are parallel. (Short form: Alt. int. ∠s ≅ ⇒ ∥ lines)*

Given: ∠3 ≅ ∠6
Prove: a ∥ b

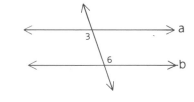

Proof: (Indirect proof) *Assume that the lines are not parallel.* Then a and b must intersect at some point P. ∠3 is an exterior angle of the triangle formed, so by the Exterior Angle Inequality Theorem, m∠3 > m∠6. But this contradicts the given: ∠3 ≅ ∠6. Thus, our assumption was false; the lines *are* parallel.

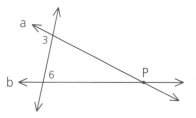

Theorem 32 *If two lines are cut by a transversal such that two alternate exterior angles are congruent, the lines are parallel. (Alt. ext. ∠s ≅ ⇒ ∥ lines.)*

Given: ∠1 ≅ ∠8
Prove: a ∥ b

This can be proved by use of alt. int. ∠s ≅ ⇒ ∥ lines.

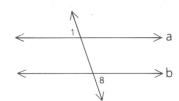

Theorem 33 *If two lines are cut by a transversal such that two corresponding angles are congruent, the lines are parallel. (Corr. ∠s ≅ ⇒ ∥ lines)*

Given: ∠2 ≅ ∠6
Prove: a ∥ b

This can be proved by use of alt. int. ∠s ≅ ⇒ ∥ lines.

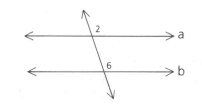

Theorem 34   *If two lines are cut by a transversal such that two interior angles on the same side of the transversal are supplementary, the lines are parallel.*

Given: ∠3 supp. ∠5
Prove: a ∥ b
This can be proved by use of alt. int. ∠s ≅ ⇒ ∥ lines.

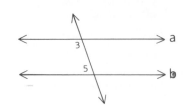

Theorem 35   *If two lines are cut by a transversal such that two exterior angles on the same side of the transversal are supplementary, the lines are parallel.*

Given: ∠1 supp. ∠7
Prove: a ∥ b
This can be proved by use of alt. int. ∠s ≅ ⇒ ∥ lines.

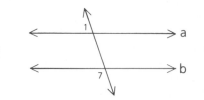

Theorem 36   *If two coplanar lines are perpendicular to a third line, they are parallel.*

Given: a ⊥ c and b ⊥ c
Prove: a ∥ b
This can be proved by use of corr. ∠s ≅ ⇒ ∥ lines.

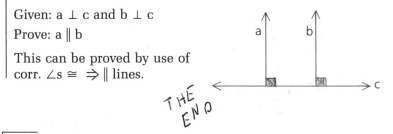

THE END

Part Two: Sample Problems

Problem 1   Prove Theorem 36.
Given: $\overleftrightarrow{AB} \perp \overleftrightarrow{BD}$ and $\overleftrightarrow{CD} \perp \overleftrightarrow{BD}$
Prove: $\overleftrightarrow{AB} \parallel \overleftrightarrow{CD}$

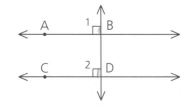

Proof

1 $\overleftrightarrow{BD} \perp \overleftrightarrow{AB}$	1 Given
2 ∠1 is a right ∠.	2 ⊥ lines form right ∠s.
3 $\overleftrightarrow{BD} \perp \overleftrightarrow{CD}$	3 Given
4 ∠2 is a right ∠.	4 Same as 2
5 ∠1 ≅ ∠2	5 Right ∠s are ≅.
6 $\overleftrightarrow{AB} \parallel \overleftrightarrow{CD}$	6 Corr. ∠s ≅ ⇒ ∥ lines

Problem 2   *A parallelogram is a four-sided figure with both pairs of opposite sides parallel.*

Given: ∠1 ≅ ∠2,
           ∠PQR ≅ ∠RSP
Prove: PQRS is a parallelogram.

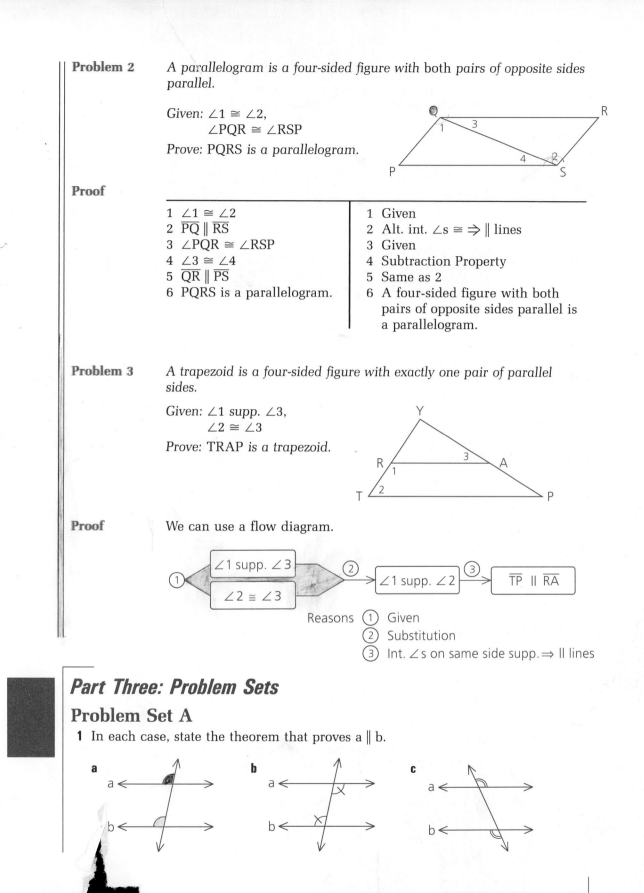

Proof

1 ∠1 ≅ ∠2	1 Given
2 $\overline{PQ} \parallel \overline{RS}$	2 Alt. int. ∠s ≅ ⟹ ∥ lines
3 ∠PQR ≅ ∠RSP	3 Given
4 ∠3 ≅ ∠4	4 Subtraction Property
5 $\overline{QR} \parallel \overline{PS}$	5 Same as 2
6 PQRS is a parallelogram.	6 A four-sided figure with both pairs of opposite sides parallel is a parallelogram.

Problem 3   *A trapezoid is a four-sided figure with exactly one pair of parallel sides.*

Given: ∠1 supp. ∠3,
           ∠2 ≅ ∠3
Prove: TRAP is a trapezoid.

Proof   We can use a flow diagram.

Reasons ① Given
          ② Substitution
          ③ Int. ∠s on same side supp. ⟹ ∥ lines

Part Three: Problem Sets

Problem Set A

1 In each case, state the theorem that proves a ∥ b.

a

b

c

2 In each case, state the theorem that proves c ∥ d.

a

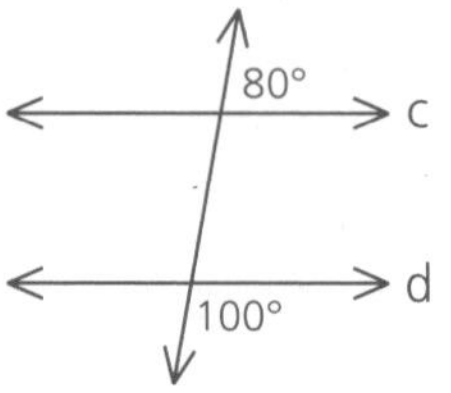

80°

100°

b

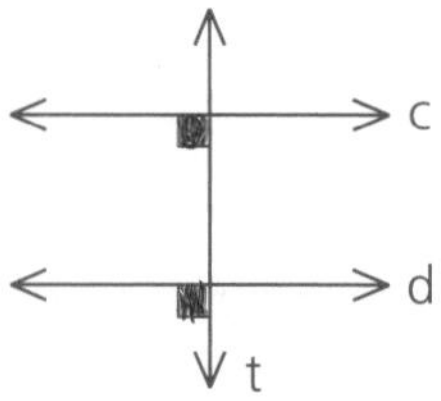

t

c

1

2

∠1 supp. ∠2

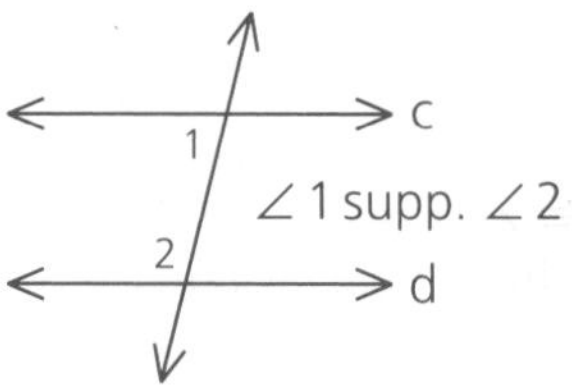

3 If certain pairs of angles in the diagram
are given to be congruent, we can prove
that a ∥ b. List all such pairs.

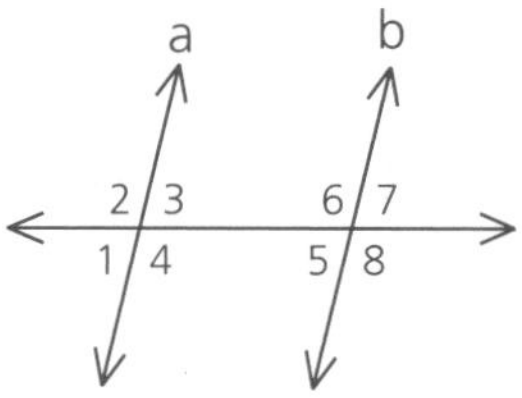

a   b

2 3   6 7

1 4   5 8

4 If ∠1 ≅ ∠2, which lines are parallel?
Write the theorem that justifies your
answer.

Q   R

1

2

P   S

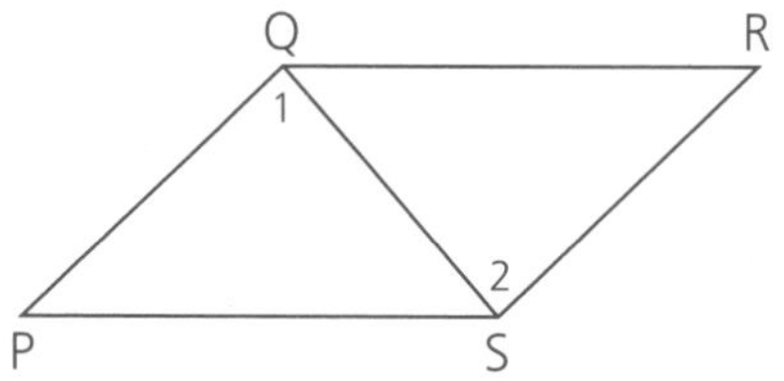

5 If ∠3 ≅ ∠4, which lines are parallel?
Write the theorem that justifies your
answer.

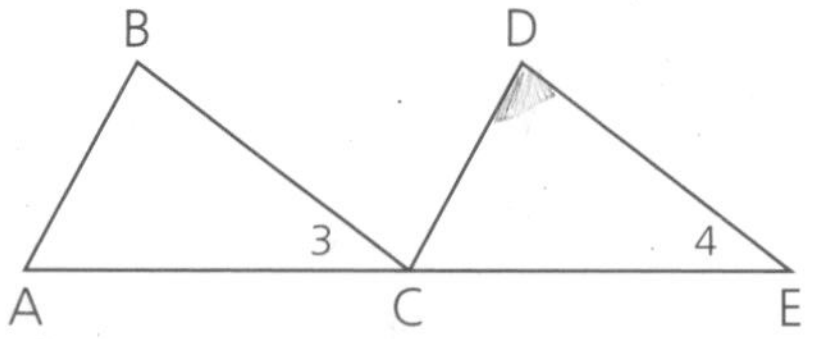

B   D

3   4

A   C   E

6 Given: $\overleftrightarrow{QD} \nparallel \overleftrightarrow{UA}$
Prove: ∠1 ≇ ∠2

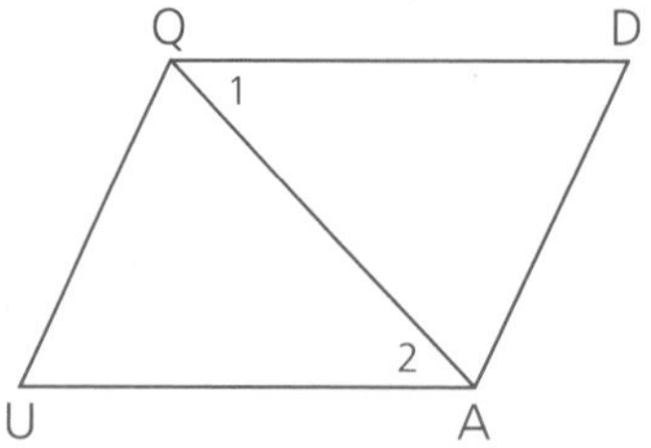

Q   D

1

2

U   A

7 Find the slope of $\overleftrightarrow{RS}$ to the nearest tenth.

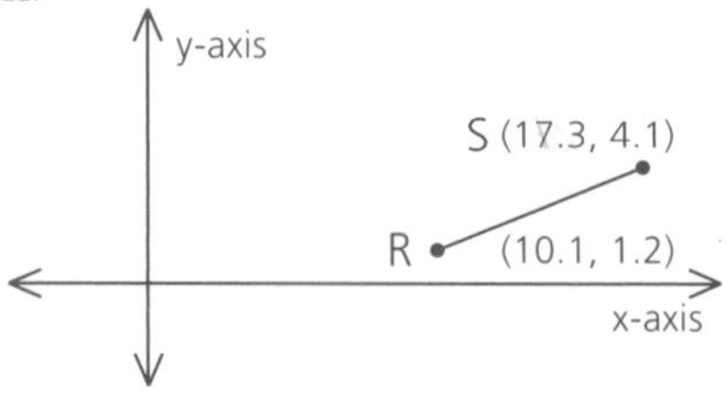

y-axis

S (17.3, 4.1)

R • (10.1, 1.2)

x-axis

8 Which two lines are parallel? Write the theorem that justifies your answer.

9 If ∠1 ≅ ∠2, which two lines are parallel? Write the theorem that justifies your answer.

10 If exactly two of the three labeled angles are congruent, what is the probability that one can prove that c ∥ d?

11 Complete the inequality that shows the restrictions on x.

$$\underline{\quad?\quad} < x < \underline{\quad?\quad}$$

12 Given: ⊙O,
   ∠1 ≅ ∠2
Prove: $\overline{PS} \parallel \overline{QR}$

13 Given: ∠FAT ≅ ∠HOG
Prove: $\overline{AT} \parallel \overline{GO}$

14 Given: $\overline{AB} \cong \overline{CD}$,
   $\overline{BC} \cong \overline{AD}$
Prove: $\overline{AB} \parallel \overline{CD}$

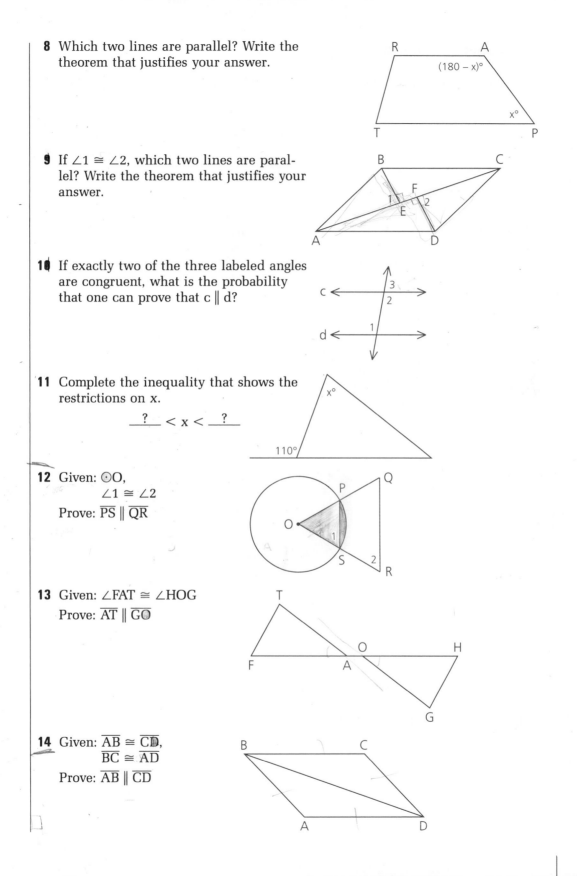

Problem Set A, *continued*

15 If P = (−3, 1), Q = (2, 4), R = (1, −2), and S = (7, 2), are $\overline{PQ}$ and $\overline{RS}$ parallel? Explain your answer.

16 Solve for x and justify that m ∥ n.

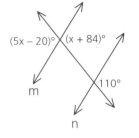

17 Write a valid inequality and find the restrictions on x.

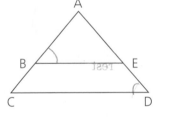

18 If x is 14.5, are p and q parallel? Explain.

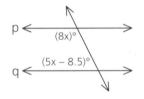

Problem Set B

19 Given: ∠D ≅ ∠ABE,
    $\overline{BE} \not\parallel \overline{CD}$
    Prove: $\overline{AC} \neq \overline{AD}$

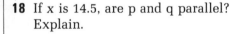

20 Given: ∠1 comp. ∠2,
    ∠3 comp. ∠2
    Prove: $\overline{QT} \parallel \overline{RS}$

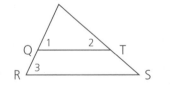

21 Given: ∠MOP is a right angle.
    $\overline{RP} \perp \overline{OP}$
    Prove: $\overline{MO} \parallel \overline{RP}$

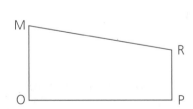

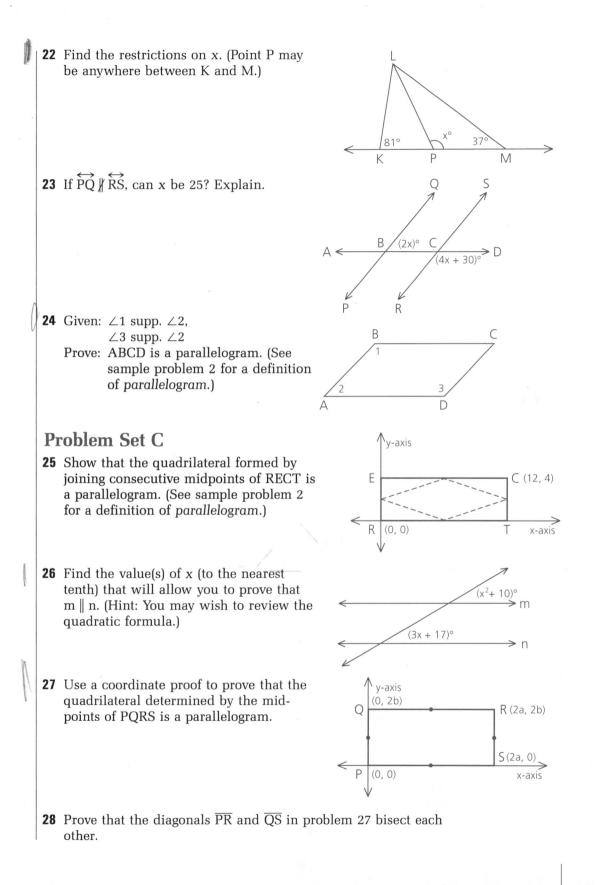

22 Find the restrictions on x. (Point P may be anywhere between K and M.)

23 If $\overleftrightarrow{PQ} \parallel \overleftrightarrow{RS}$, can x be 25? Explain.

24 Given: ∠1 supp. ∠2,
ㅤㅤㅤ∠3 supp. ∠2
ㅤProve: ABCD is a parallelogram. (See sample problem 2 for a definition of *parallelogram*.)

Problem Set C

25 Show that the quadrilateral formed by joining consecutive midpoints of RECT is a parallelogram. (See sample problem 2 for a definition of *parallelogram*.)

26 Find the value(s) of x (to the nearest tenth) that will allow you to prove that m ∥ n. (Hint: You may wish to review the quadratic formula.)

27 Use a coordinate proof to prove that the quadrilateral determined by the midpoints of PQRS is a parallelogram.

28 Prove that the diagonals $\overline{PR}$ and $\overline{QS}$ in problem 27 bisect each other.

CONGRUENT ANGLES ASSOCIATED WITH PARALLEL LINES

Objectives

After studying this section, you will be able to
- Apply the Parallel Postulate
- Identify the pairs of angles formed by a transversal cutting parallel lines
- Apply six theorems about parallel lines

Part One: Introduction

The Parallel Postulate

In this section we shall see that the converses of many of the theorems in Section 5.2 are also true.

A fundamental postulate for parallel lines in the plane is the *Parallel Postulate.*

Postulate	***Through a point not on a line there is exactly one parallel to the given line.***

Although this idea may seem reasonable, mathematicians argued for centuries over the truth of the Parallel Postulate. Some even created their own geometries based on the assumptions that there may be *more than one parallel* to a given line at a given point or *no parallels* to the given line (a geometry in which *any* two lines intersect at some point). If you are interested in learning more about these *non-Euclidean* geometries, see your teacher for a list of sources. We, however, will assume that the Parallel Postulate is true.

Angles Formed When Parallel Lines Are Cut by a Transversal

In Section 5.2 we saw that when alternate interior angles are congruent, lines are parallel. In this section you will learn that the converse is true—that is, if we start with parallel lines, then we can conclude that alternate interior angles are congruent. In fact, many pairs of congruent angles are determined by parallel lines cut by a transversal.

Theorem 37   *If two parallel lines are cut by a transversal, each pair of alternate interior angles are congruent. (Short form: ‖ lines ⇒ alt. int. ∠s ≅)*

Given: Lines a and b are parallel.

Prove: ∠1 ≅ ∠2

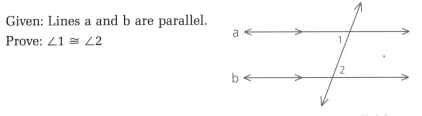

Notice the special tick marks (⇉) used to designate parallel lines.

Proof: This theorem can be verified by indirect proof.

We are given a ‖ b. Assume that ∠1 is not congruent to ∠2. Then there must be another line, c, that intersects the transversal at P to form an angle, ∠3, that is congruent to ∠2. But in Section 5.2 we observed that congruent alternate interior angles lead to parallel lines. Thus, c ‖ b.

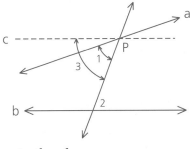

This means that line b is parallel to *two* lines in the plane at point P. This violates the Parallel Postulate. So we can conclude that our assumption is false. Therefore, ∠1 ≅ ∠2.

You may be surprised to learn the following.

Theorem 38   *If two parallel lines are cut by a transversal, then any pair of the angles formed are either congruent or supplementary.*

The proof of this may be developed algebraically by letting x be the measure of any one of the angles. Follow the steps below. In each diagram, a ‖ b.

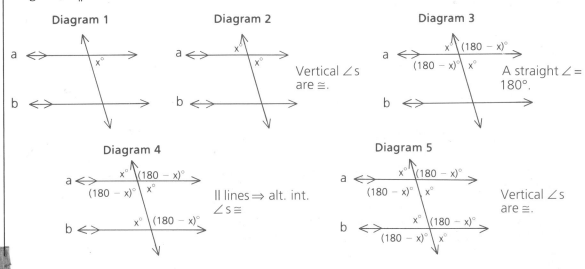

Six Theorems About Parallel Lines

Diagram 5 on the preceding page is the basis for each of the following five theorems.

Theorem 39 *If two parallel lines are cut by a transversal, each pair of alternate exterior angles are congruent.*
(∥ lines ⇒ alt. ext. ∠s ≅)

Given: a ∥ b
Prove: ∠1 ≅ ∠8
Proof: See Diagram 5.

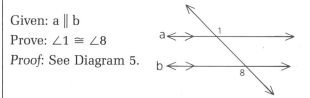

Theorem 40 *If two parallel lines are cut by a transversal, each pair of corresponding angles are congruent.*
(∥ lines ⇒ corr. ∠s ≅)

Given: a ∥ b
Prove: ∠1 ≅ ∠5
Proof: See Diagram 5.

Theorem 41 *If two parallel lines are cut by a transversal, each pair of interior angles on the same side of the transversal are supplementary.*

Given: a ∥ b
Prove: ∠3 supp. ∠5
Proof: See Diagram 5.

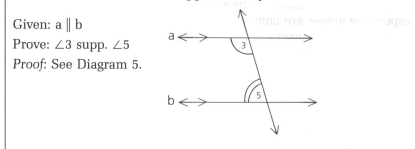

Theorem 42 *If two parallel lines are cut by a transversal, each pair of exterior angles on the same side of the transversal are supplementary.*

Given: a ∥ b
Prove: ∠1 supp. ∠7
Proof: See Diagram 5.

Theorem 43 *In a plane, if a line is perpendicular to one of two parallel lines, it is perpendicular to the other.*

Given: a ∥ b,
      c ⊥ a

Prove: c ⊥ b

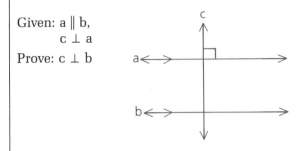

Proof: See Diagram 5 and let x = 90.

The following is another useful theorem about parallel lines.

Theorem 44 *If two lines are parallel to a third line, they are parallel to each other. (**Transitive Property of Parallel Lines**)*

Given: a ∥ b, b ∥ c

Prove: a ∥ c

    a ⟵⟶
    c ⟵⟶
    b ⟵⟶

By using "∥ lines ⟹ alt. int. ∠s ≅" and "alt. int. ∠s ≅ ⟹ ∥ lines," you can prove that Theorem 44 is true when all three lines lie in the same plane. It also can be shown that the theorem holds for lines in three-dimensional space.

In summary, if two parallel lines are cut by a transversal, then
- Each pair of alternate interior angles are congruent
- Each pair of alternate exterior angles are congruent
- Each pair of corresponding angles are congruent
- Each pair of interior angles on the same side of the transversal are supplementary
- Each pair of exterior angles on the same side of the transversal are supplementary

Part Two: Sample Problems

Problem 1 If c ∥ d, find m∠1.

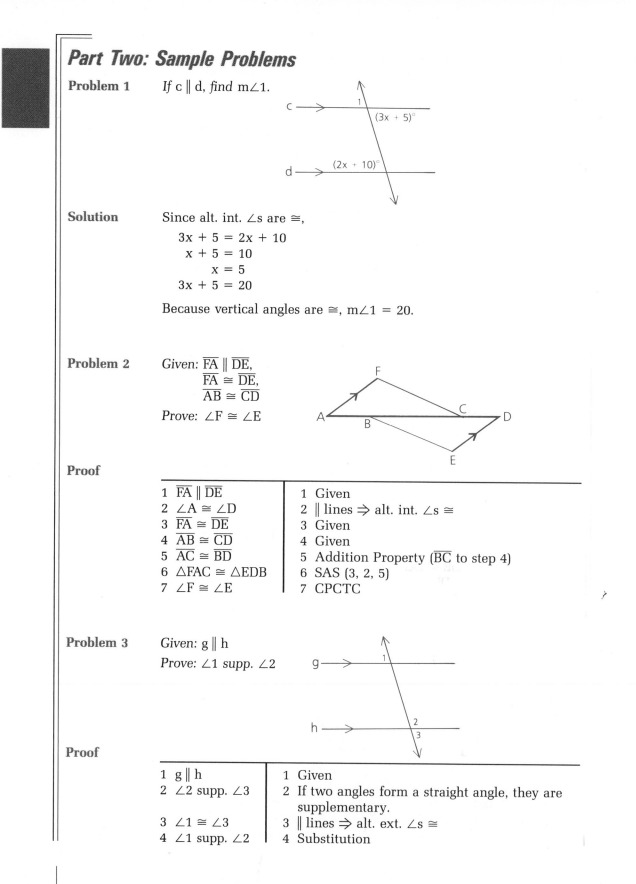

Solution Since alt. int. ∠s are ≅,

$$3x + 5 = 2x + 10$$
$$x + 5 = 10$$
$$x = 5$$
$$3x + 5 = 20$$

Because vertical angles are ≅, m∠1 = 20.

Problem 2 Given: $\overline{FA} \parallel \overline{DE}$,
$\overline{FA} \cong \overline{DE}$,
$\overline{AB} \cong \overline{CD}$
Prove: ∠F ≅ ∠E

Proof

1 $\overline{FA} \parallel \overline{DE}$	1 Given
2 ∠A ≅ ∠D	2 ∥ lines ⇒ alt. int. ∠s ≅
3 $\overline{FA} \cong \overline{DE}$	3 Given
4 $\overline{AB} \cong \overline{CD}$	4 Given
5 $\overline{AC} \cong \overline{BD}$	5 Addition Property ($\overline{BC}$ to step 4)
6 △FAC ≅ △EDB	6 SAS (3, 2, 5)
7 ∠F ≅ ∠E	7 CPCTC

Problem 3 Given: g ∥ h
Prove: ∠1 supp. ∠2

Proof

1 g ∥ h	1 Given
2 ∠2 supp. ∠3	2 If two angles form a straight angle, they are supplementary.
3 ∠1 ≅ ∠3	3 ∥ lines ⇒ alt. ext. ∠s ≅
4 ∠1 supp. ∠2	4 Substitution

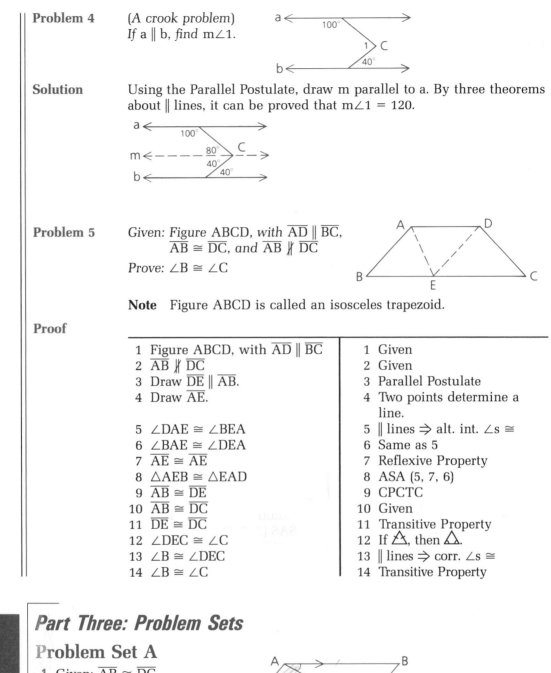

Problem 4   (*A crook problem*)
If a ∥ b, find m∠1.

Solution   Using the Parallel Postulate, draw m parallel to a. By three theorems about ∥ lines, it can be proved that m∠1 = 120.

Problem 5   *Given: Figure ABCD, with* $\overline{AD} \parallel \overline{BC}$,
$\overline{AB} \cong \overline{DC}$, *and* $\overline{AB} \nparallel \overline{DC}$

Prove: ∠B ≅ ∠C

Note   Figure ABCD is called an isosceles trapezoid.

Proof

1 Figure ABCD, with $\overline{AD} \parallel \overline{BC}$	1 Given
2 $\overline{AB} \nparallel \overline{DC}$	2 Given
3 Draw $\overline{DE} \parallel \overline{AB}$.	3 Parallel Postulate
4 Draw $\overline{AE}$.	4 Two points determine a line.
5 ∠DAE ≅ ∠BEA	5 ∥ lines ⇒ alt. int. ∠s ≅
6 ∠BAE ≅ ∠DEA	6 Same as 5
7 $\overline{AE} \cong \overline{AE}$	7 Reflexive Property
8 △AEB ≅ △EAD	8 ASA (5, 7, 6)
9 $\overline{AB} \cong \overline{DE}$	9 CPCTC
10 $\overline{AB} \cong \overline{DC}$	10 Given
11 $\overline{DE} \cong \overline{DC}$	11 Transitive Property
12 ∠DEC ≅ ∠C	12 If △, then △.
13 ∠B ≅ ∠DEC	13 ∥ lines ⇒ corr. ∠s ≅
14 ∠B ≅ ∠C	14 Transitive Property

Part Three: Problem Sets

Problem Set A

1 Given: $\overline{AB} \cong \overline{DC}$,
$\overline{AB} \parallel \overline{DC}$

Conclusion: $\overline{AD} \cong \overline{BC}$

2 Given: $\overline{EF} \parallel \overline{GH}$,
$\overline{EF} \cong \overline{GH}$

Conclusion: $\overline{EJ} \cong \overline{JH}$

Problem Set A, *continued*

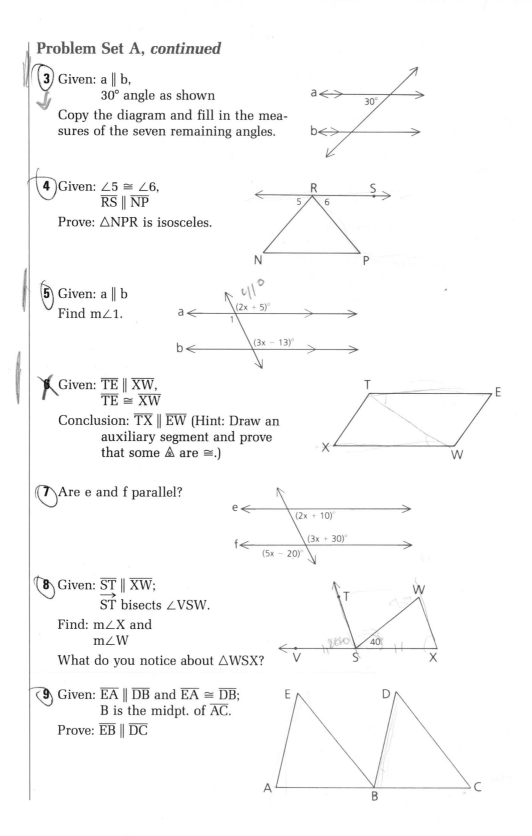

3 Given: a ∥ b,
   30° angle as shown
Copy the diagram and fill in the measures of the seven remaining angles.

4 Given: ∠5 ≅ ∠6,
   $\overline{RS}$ ∥ $\overline{NP}$
   Prove: △NPR is isosceles.

5 Given: a ∥ b
   Find m∠1.

6 Given: $\overline{TE}$ ∥ $\overline{XW}$,
   $\overline{TE}$ ≅ $\overline{XW}$
   Conclusion: $\overline{TX}$ ∥ $\overline{EW}$ (Hint: Draw an
      auxiliary segment and prove
      that some ⊿ are ≅.)

7 Are e and f parallel?

8 Given: $\overrightarrow{ST}$ ∥ $\overline{XW}$;
   $\overrightarrow{ST}$ bisects ∠VSW.
   Find: m∠X and
      m∠W
   What do you notice about △WSX?

9 Given: $\overline{EA}$ ∥ $\overline{DB}$ and $\overline{EA}$ ≅ $\overline{DB}$;
      B is the midpt. of $\overline{AC}$.
   Prove: $\overline{EB}$ ∥ $\overline{DC}$

10 (*A crook problem*)
If f ∥ g, find m∠8.

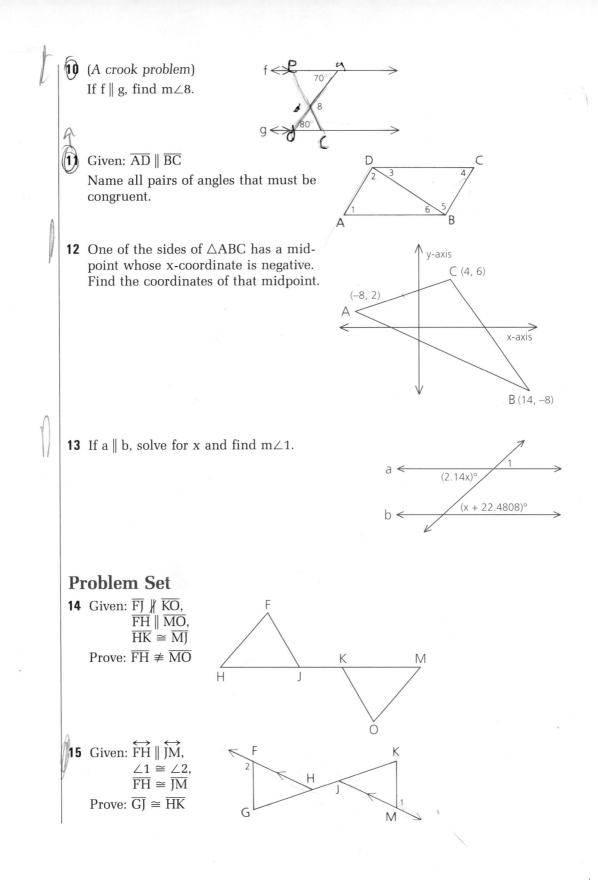

11 Given: $\overline{AD} \parallel \overline{BC}$
Name all pairs of angles that must be congruent.

12 One of the sides of △ABC has a midpoint whose x-coordinate is negative. Find the coordinates of that midpoint.

13 If a ∥ b, solve for x and find m∠1.

Problem Set

14 Given: $\overline{FJ} \parallel\!\!\!/ \ \overline{KO}$,
$\overline{FH} \parallel \overline{MO}$,
$\overline{HK} \cong \overline{MJ}$
Prove: $\overline{FH} \not\cong \overline{MO}$

15 Given: $\overleftrightarrow{FH} \parallel \overleftrightarrow{JM}$,
∠1 ≅ ∠2,
$\overline{FH} \cong \overline{JM}$
Prove: $\overline{GJ} \cong \overline{HK}$

Problem Set B, *continued*

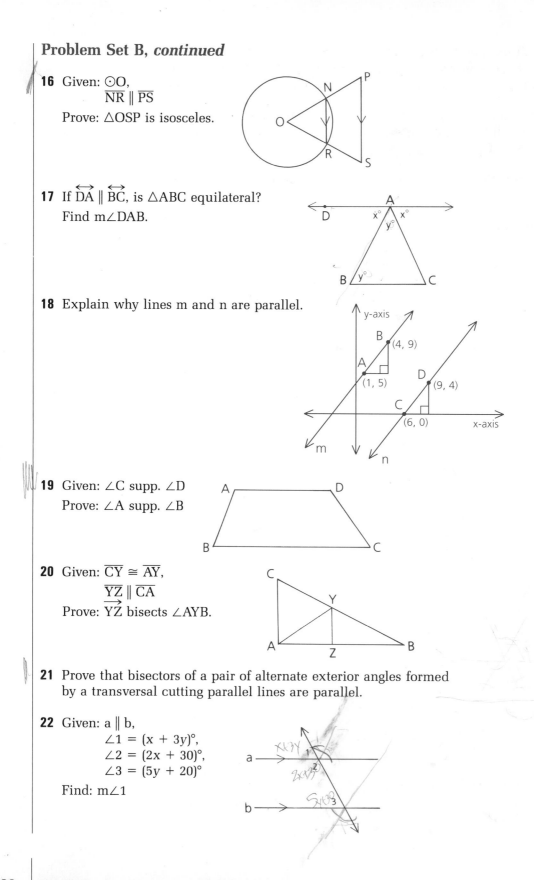

16 Given: ⊙O,
$\overline{NR} \parallel \overline{PS}$
Prove: △OSP is isosceles.

17 If $\overleftrightarrow{DA} \parallel \overleftrightarrow{BC}$, is △ABC equilateral?
Find m∠DAB.

18 Explain why lines m and n are parallel.

19 Given: ∠C supp. ∠D
Prove: ∠A supp. ∠B

20 Given: $\overline{CY} \cong \overline{AY}$,
$\overline{YZ} \parallel \overline{CA}$
Prove: $\overrightarrow{YZ}$ bisects ∠AYB.

21 Prove that bisectors of a pair of alternate exterior angles formed
by a transversal cutting parallel lines are parallel.

22 Given: a ∥ b,
∠1 = (x + 3y)°,
∠2 = (2x + 30)°,
∠3 = (5y + 20)°
Find: m∠1

23 A line is described by the equation $y = 5x - 7$. Points (x, y) that solve the equation must lie on the line. Which of the points $(3, 8)$, $(-2, -17)$, $(0, -7)$, $(4, 11)$ and $(1, -2)$ are on the line?

24 Prove that the opposite sides of a parallelogram are congruent. (Recall that a parallelogram is a four-sided figure in which both pairs of opposite sides are parallel.)

25 Prove that the opposite angles of a parallelogram are congruent.

Problem Set C

26 If two parallel lines are cut by a transversal, eight angles are formed (not counting the straight angles).

   a How many pairs of angles are formed?
   b If one of these pairs is chosen at random, what is the probability that the angles will be alternate interior angles *or* alternate exterior angles *or* corresponding angles?
   c If one of the pairs is chosen at random, what is the probability that the angles are supplementary?

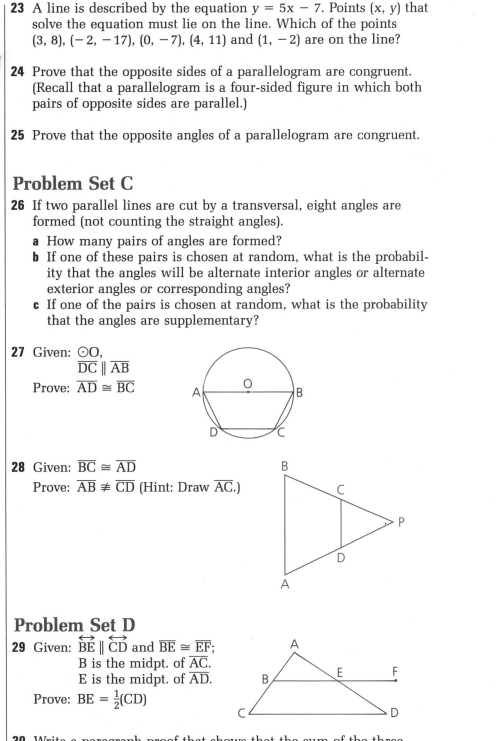

27 Given: $\odot O$,
          $\overline{DC} \parallel \overline{AB}$
   Prove: $\overline{AD} \cong \overline{BC}$

28 Given: $\overline{BC} \cong \overline{AD}$
   Prove: $\overline{AB} \not\cong \overline{CD}$ (Hint: Draw $\overline{AC}$.)

Problem Set D

29 Given: $\overleftrightarrow{BE} \parallel \overleftrightarrow{CD}$ and $\overline{BE} \cong \overline{EF}$;
          B is the midpt. of $\overline{AC}$.
          E is the midpt. of $\overline{AD}$.
   Prove: $BE = \frac{1}{2}(CD)$

30 Write a paragraph proof that shows that the sum of the three angles of a triangle is 180°. (Hint: Draw a triangle and use the Parallel Postulate.)

5.4 | FOUR-SIDED POLYGONS

Objectives

After studying this section, you will be able to
- Recognize polygons
- Understand how polygons are named
- Recognize convex polygons
- Recognize diagonals of polygons
- Identify special types of quadrilaterals

Part One: Introduction

Polygons

Polygons are plane figures. The following are examples of polygons.

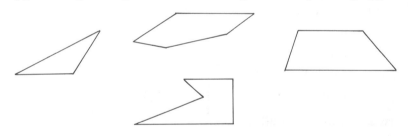

The following are examples of figures that are not polygons.

EFGH is not a polygon, because a polygon consists entirely of segments.

ABCDE is not a polygon. In a polygon, consecutive sides intersect only at endpoints. Nonconsecutive sides do not intersect.

PKMO, PKMOR, and POR are polygons, but PKMOPRO is not, because each vertex must belong to exactly two sides. (Vertex P belongs to three sides in PKMOPRO.)

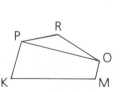

SVTY is a polygon, but SVTXY is not, because consecutive sides must be noncollinear.

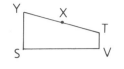

Why is PLAN not a polygon?

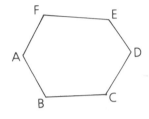

Naming Polygons

We name a polygon by starting at any vertex and then proceeding either clockwise or couterclockwise. If we start at A, we can call this polygon ABCDEF or AFEDCB. Can you start at B and name the polygon in two different ways?

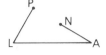

Convex Polygons

Many of the polygons you encounter in your geometry studies will be *convex.*

Definition   A *convex polygon* is a polygon in which each interior angle has a measure less than 180.

Polygon ABCDE is not convex because the angle that lies in the interior of the polygon at E has a measure greater than 180.

In the rest of this book, unless it is expressly stated otherwise, assume that all polygons are convex.

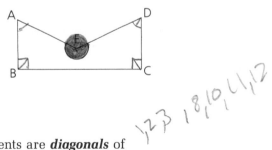

Diagonals of Polygons

In the two following figures, the dashed segments are *diagonals* of the polygons.

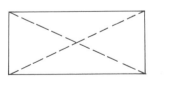

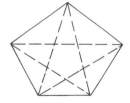

Definition   A *diagonal* of a polygon is any segment that connects two nonconsecutive (nonadjacent) vertices of the polygon.

Quadrilaterals

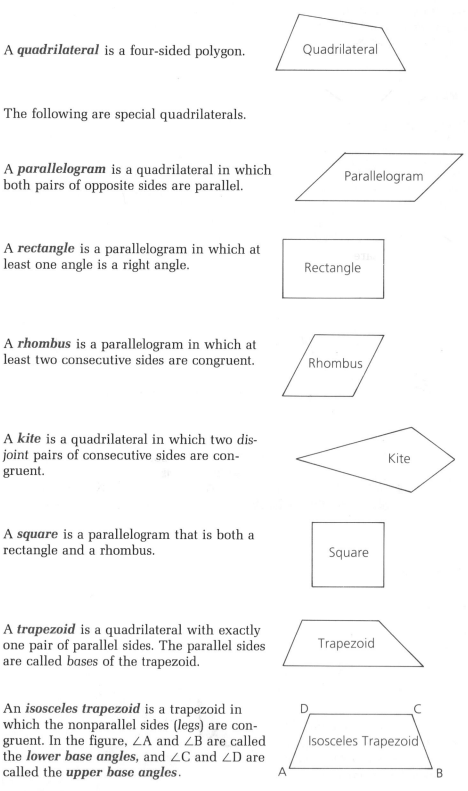

A **quadrilateral** is a four-sided polygon.

The following are special quadrilaterals.

A **parallelogram** is a quadrilateral in which both pairs of opposite sides are parallel.

A **rectangle** is a parallelogram in which at least one angle is a right angle.

A **rhombus** is a parallelogram in which at least two consecutive sides are congruent.

A **kite** is a quadrilateral in which two *disjoint* pairs of consecutive sides are congruent.

A **square** is a parallelogram that is both a rectangle and a rhombus.

A **trapezoid** is a quadrilateral with exactly one pair of parallel sides. The parallel sides are called *bases* of the trapezoid.

An **isosceles trapezoid** is a trapezoid in which the nonparallel sides (*legs*) are congruent. In the figure, ∠A and ∠B are called the **lower base angles,** and ∠C and ∠D are called the **upper base angles**.

We have given the meaning (definition) of each of the previous figures in as simple a manner as possible. Each special quadrilateral will have further properties associated with it. Those properties are discussed in the next section.

Part Two: Sample Problem

Solve the Quadrilateral Mystery!

No solution is provided for the following problem. It is intended to help you understand how mathematicians go about testing ideas that they *think* are true but which they have not yet *proved*. As you work through the problem, think carefully about the ideas you formulate and the ways you test them. (A computer with exploratory geometry software—such as *The Geometric Supposer*, by Sunburst—is an excellent tool for testing ideas. If you do not have access to such resources, try making careful drawings and using a ruler and a protractor to test your ideas.)

Problem   *What truths can you discover about a parallelogram and a rectangle?*

a *Draw a parallelogram ABCD.*
  i *What true statements do you think you might be able to make about the parallelogram? Test your ideas and discuss your results in class.*
  ii *Draw diagonals $\overline{AC}$ and $\overline{BD}$. What true statements can be made about the diagonals? Again, test your ideas and discuss your results in class.*

b *Draw a rectangle PQRS.*
  i *What true statements can be made about the rectangle? Test your ideas and discuss your results in class.*
  ii *Draw diagonals $\overline{PR}$ and $\overline{QS}$. What true statements can be made about the diagonals? Again, test your ideas and discuss your results in class.*

Part Three: Problem Sets

Problem Set A

A computer and exploratory geometry software may be used for problems 1–5.

1 Examine the rhombus. Which of the following statements appear to be true?

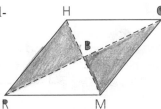

  a All four sides are congruent.
  b The diagonals are perpendicular.
  c The diagonals bisect the angles.
  d The diagonals bisect each other.
  e The diagonals are congruent.

Problem Set A, *continued*

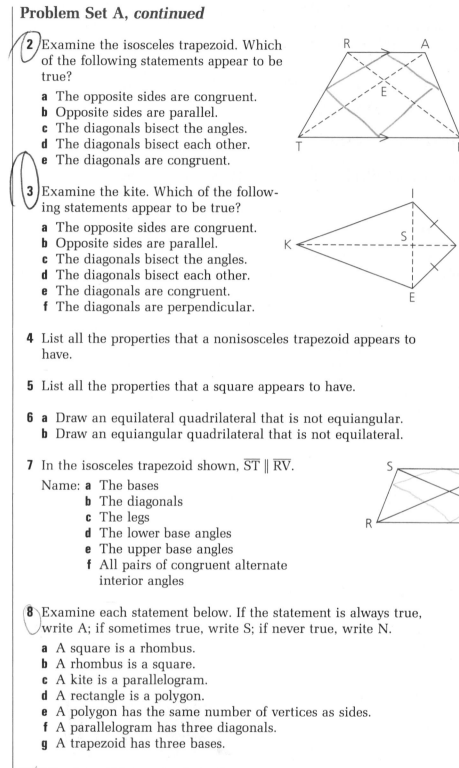

2 Examine the isosceles trapezoid. Which of the following statements appear to be true?

  a The opposite sides are congruent.
  b Opposite sides are parallel.
  c The diagonals bisect the angles.
  d The diagonals bisect each other.
  e The diagonals are congruent.

3 Examine the kite. Which of the following statements appear to be true?

  a The opposite sides are congruent.
  b Opposite sides are parallel.
  c The diagonals bisect the angles.
  d The diagonals bisect each other.
  e The diagonals are congruent.
  f The diagonals are perpendicular.

4 List all the properties that a nonisosceles trapezoid appears to have.

5 List all the properties that a square appears to have.

6 a Draw an equilateral quadrilateral that is not equiangular.
  b Draw an equiangular quadrilateral that is not equilateral.

7 In the isosceles trapezoid shown, $\overline{ST} \parallel \overline{RV}$.

  Name: **a** The bases
         b The diagonals
         c The legs
         d The lower base angles
         e The upper base angles
         f All pairs of congruent alternate
           interior angles

8 Examine each statement below. If the statement is always true, write A; if sometimes true, write S; if never true, write N.

  a A square is a rhombus.
  b A rhombus is a square.
  c A kite is a parallelogram.
  d A rectangle is a polygon.
  e A polygon has the same number of vertices as sides.
  f A parallelogram has three diagonals.
  g A trapezoid has three bases.

9 Why is a circle not a polygon?

10 Using the diagram, explain how the formula for the area of a parallelogram can be the same as that for the area of a rectangle.

11 If the sum of the measures of the angles of a triangle is 180, what is the sum of the measures of the angles in

    a A quadrilateral?
    b A pentagon (five-sided polygon)?

12 Find the area of a square whose perimeter is 65 feet.

Problem Set B

13 Prove that in a parallelogram each pair of consecutive angles are supplementary.

14 Prove that in a parallelogram each pair of opposite sides are congruent.

15 Prove that the diagonals of a rectangle are congruent.

16 Given: ABCD is a kite.
       AB = x + 3,
       BC = x + 4,
       CD = 2x − 1,
       AD = 3x − y

    a Solve for x and y.
    b What is the perimeter of the kite?
    c Is it possible for $\overline{AC}$ to be 19 units long? Why or why not?

17 **a** PQRS is a kite and also a rectangle. What else do we know about PQRS?
    b Draw a quadrilateral that is not convex and still satisfies the definition of a kite.

18 What is the area of a triangle whose vertices are (−4, −3), (8, 7), and (8, −3)?

19 The trapezoidal region is actually the union of two triangles and a rectangle. Find the area of the trapezoid.

Problem Set B, *continued*

20 How many rectangles are shown in the figure at the right, in which all of the angles are right angles?

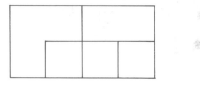

Problem Set C

21 a How many diagonals does a triangle have?
  b How many diagonals does a quadrilateral have?
  c How many diagonals does a five-sided polygon have?
  d How many diagonals does a six-sided polygon have?
  e How many diagonals meet at one vertex of a polygon with n sides?
  f How many vertices does an n-sided polygon have?
  g How many diagonals does an n-sided polygon have?

22 Refer to the seven special quadrilaterals on page 236. What is the probability that if two are picked at random, each will have a pair of congruent opposite sides?

HISTORICAL SNAPSHOT

A NEW KIND OF PROOF
The computer and the four-color conjecture

How many colors does it take to color any map so that no two adjacent regions will be the same color? (Regions that touch only at a single point are not considered to be adjacent.) In 1852 it was suggested that four colors are enough for any possible map. Although no one ever succeeded in constructing a map that needed more than four colors, for over 100 years no one was able to furnish a satisfactory proof that such a map could not exist.

Then, in 1976, it was announced that a group of mathematicians led by Kenneth Appel and Wolfgang Haken at the University of Illinois had proved the four-color conjecture. Having determined that all possible maps could be represented by a set of 1936 particular configurations of regions, they programmed a computer to test each of these cases for four-colorability.

The computer found no instance in which more than four colors were required.

Traditionally, however, a proof has been considered a way of presenting mathematical reasoning that can be understood and verified by other people. The four-color proof is so complex that it would take lifetimes to verify it by hand. It is one of the first examples of a proof that can be produced and checked only using a computer.

5.5 PROPERTIES OF QUADRILATERAL

Objectives

After studying this section, you will be able to
- Identify some properties of parallelograms
- Identify some properties of rectangles
- Identify some properties of kites
- Identify some properties of rhombuses
- Identify some properties of squares
- Identify some properties of isosceles trapezoids

Part One: Introduction

Properties of Parallelograms

In this section, we will list some of the properties of special quadri-laterals, beginning with parallelograms. (You should be able to prove many of these properties.) Read the properties carefully and learn them. They will be used often in the sections to follow.

Learning so many properties may seem overwhelming at first, but most are concepts that you already know or that you discovered in Section 5.4. With some effort you will soon learn them all.

In a parallelogram,

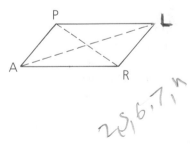

1. The opposite sides are parallel by definition ($\overline{PL} \parallel \overline{AR}$, $\overline{AP} \parallel \overline{RL}$)
2. The opposite sides are congruent ($\overline{PL} \cong \overline{AR}$, $\overline{AP} \cong \overline{RL}$)
3. The opposite angles are congruent (∠PAR ≅ ∠PLR, ∠ARL ≅ ∠APL)
4. The diagonals bisect each other ($\overline{AL}$ bis. $\overline{PR}$, $\overline{PR}$ bis. $\overline{AL}$)
5. Any pair of consecutive angles are supplementary (∠PAR supp. ∠ARL, etc.)

Properties of Rectangles

In a rectangle,

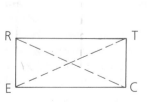

1. All the properties of a parallelogram apply by definition
2. All angles are right angles (∠REC is a right angle, etc.)
3. The diagonals are congruent ($\overline{ET} \cong \overline{RC}$)

Properties of Kites

In a kite,

1 Two disjoint pairs of consecutive sides are congruent by definition ($\overline{IT} \cong \overline{ET}$, $\overline{IK} \cong \overline{EK}$)
2 The diagonals are perpendicular ($\overline{TK} \perp \overline{IE}$)
3 One diagonal is the perpendicular bisector of the other ($\overline{TK} \perp$ bis. $\overline{IE}$)
4 One of the diagonals bisects a pair of opposite angles ($\overrightarrow{TK}$ bis. $\angle ITE$, $\overrightarrow{TK}$ bis. $\angle IKE$)
5 One pair of opposite angles are congruent ($\angle TIK \cong \angle TEK$)

Properties 3–5 are sometimes called the *half properties* of kites.

Properties of Rhombuses

In a rhombus,

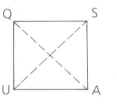

1 All the properties of a parallelogram apply by definition
2 All the properties of a kite apply (In fact, the half properties become full properties)
3 All sides are congruent—that is, a rhombus is equilateral ($\overline{RH} \cong \overline{HO} \cong \overline{OM} \cong \overline{MR}$)
4 The diagonals bisect the angles ($\overrightarrow{RO}$ bis. $\angle MRH$, $\overrightarrow{RO}$ bis. $\angle MOH$, etc.)
5 The diagonals are perpendicular bisectors of each other ($\overline{RO} \perp$ bis. $\overline{MH}$, $\overline{MH} \perp$ bis. $\overline{RO}$)
6 The diagonals divide the rhombus into four congruent right triangles

Properties of Squares

In a square,

1 All the properties of a rectangle apply by definition
2 All the properties of a rhombus apply by definition
3 The diagonals form four isosceles right triangles (45°-45°-90° triangles)

Properties of Isosceles Trapezoids

In an isosceles trapezoid,

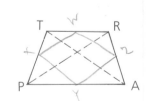

1 The legs are congruent by definition ($\overline{TP} \cong \overline{RA}$)
2 The bases are parallel (by definition of *trapezoid*) ($\overline{TR} \parallel \overline{PA}$)
3 The lower base angles are congruent ($\angle RAP \cong \angle TPA$)
4 The upper base angles are congruent ($\angle PTR \cong \angle ART$)
5 The diagonals are congruent ($\overline{PR} \cong \overline{AT}$)
6 Any lower base angle is supplementary to any upper base angle ($\angle PAR$ supp. $\angle PTR$, etc.)

In the problems that follow, you will be asked to prove some of these properties. You may use any prior property to help in the proof of a later property. For example, if you are asked to prove property 5 of parallelograms, you may use properties 1–4 to help you in the proof.

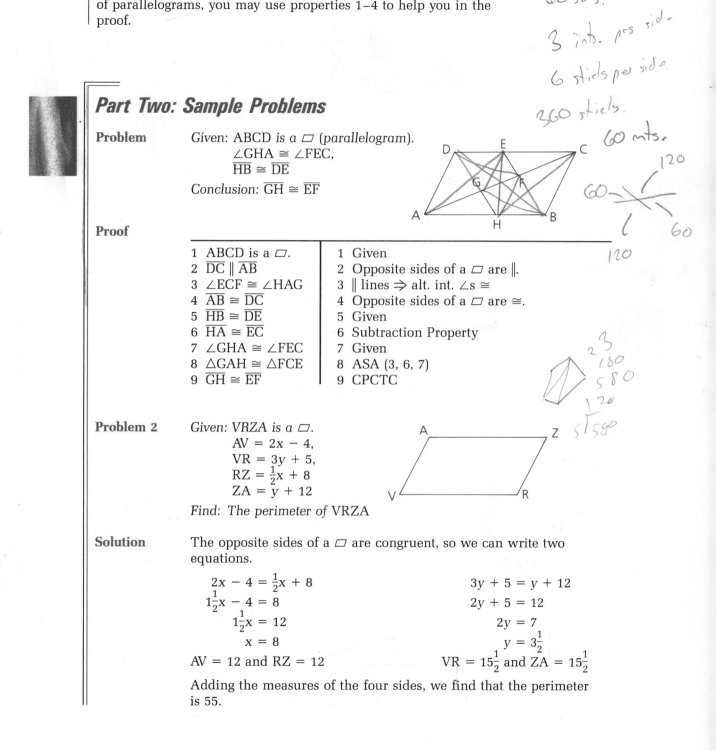

Part Two: Sample Problems

Problem

Given: ABCD is a $\square$ (parallelogram).
$\angle GHA \cong \angle FEC$,
$\overline{HB} \cong \overline{DE}$

Conclusion: $\overline{GH} \cong \overline{EF}$

Proof

1 ABCD is a $\square$.	1 Given
2 $\overline{DC} \parallel \overline{AB}$	2 Opposite sides of a $\square$ are $\parallel$.
3 $\angle ECF \cong \angle HAG$	3 $\parallel$ lines $\Rightarrow$ alt. int. $\angle$s $\cong$
4 $\overline{AB} \cong \overline{DC}$	4 Opposite sides of a $\square$ are $\cong$.
5 $\overline{HB} \cong \overline{DE}$	5 Given
6 $\overline{HA} \cong \overline{EC}$	6 Subtraction Property
7 $\angle GHA \cong \angle FEC$	7 Given
8 $\triangle GAH \cong \triangle FCE$	8 ASA (3, 6, 7)
9 $\overline{GH} \cong \overline{EF}$	9 CPCTC

Problem 2

Given: VRZA is a $\square$.
AV = 2x − 4,
VR = 3y + 5,
RZ = $\frac{1}{2}$x + 8
ZA = y + 12

Find: The perimeter of VRZA

Solution

The opposite sides of a $\square$ are congruent, so we can write two equations.

$$2x - 4 = \tfrac{1}{2}x + 8$$
$$1\tfrac{1}{2}x - 4 = 8$$
$$1\tfrac{1}{2}x = 12$$
$$x = 8$$

AV = 12 and RZ = 12

$$3y + 5 = y + 12$$
$$2y + 5 = 12$$
$$2y = 7$$
$$y = 3\tfrac{1}{2}$$

VR = $15\tfrac{1}{2}$ and ZA = $15\tfrac{1}{2}$

Adding the measures of the four sides, we find that the perimeter is 55.

Problem   Prove property 4 of parallelograms.
Given: ▱ ABCD
Prove: $\overline{AC}$ and $\overline{BD}$ bisect each other.

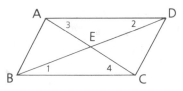

Proof

1 ▱ ABCD	1 Given
2 $\overline{AD} \parallel \overline{BC}$	2 Opposite sides of a ▱ are $\parallel$.
3 $\angle 1 \cong \angle 2$	3 $\parallel$ lines $\Rightarrow$ alt. int. $\angle$s $\cong$
4 $\angle 3 \cong \angle 4$	4 $\parallel$ lines $\Rightarrow$ alt. int. $\angle$s $\cong$
5 $\overline{AD} \cong \overline{BC}$	5 Opposite sides of a ▱ are $\cong$.
6 $\triangle BEC \cong \triangle DEA$	6 ASA (3, 5, 4)
7 $\overline{BE} \cong \overline{DE}$	7 CPCTC
8 $\overline{AE} \cong \overline{EC}$	8 CPCTC
9 $\overline{AC}$ and $\overline{BD}$ bisect each other.	9 If two segments divide each other into $\cong$ segments, they bisect each other.

Part Three: Problem Sets

Problem Set

1 Given: ▱ ABCD (ABCD is a ▱.)
Conclusion: $\triangle ABC \cong \triangle CDA$

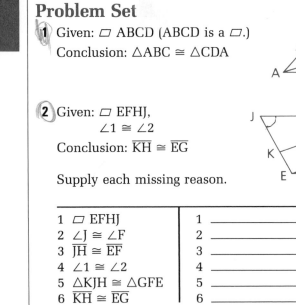

2 Given: ▱ EFHJ,
$\angle 1 \cong \angle 2$
Conclusion: $\overline{KH} \cong \overline{EG}$

Supply each missing reason.

1 ▱ EFHJ	1 _____
2 $\angle J \cong \angle F$	2 _____
3 $\overline{JH} \cong \overline{EF}$	3 _____
4 $\angle 1 \cong \angle 2$	4 _____
5 $\triangle KJH \cong \triangle GFE$	5 _____
6 $\overline{KH} \cong \overline{EG}$	6 _____

3 Given: Rectangle MPRS,
$\overline{MO} \cong \overline{PO}$
Prove: $\triangle ROS$ is isosceles.

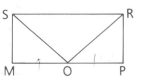

Given: ▱ABCD,
$\overline{AE} \cong \overline{CF}$

Conclusion: $\overline{DE} \cong \overline{BF}$

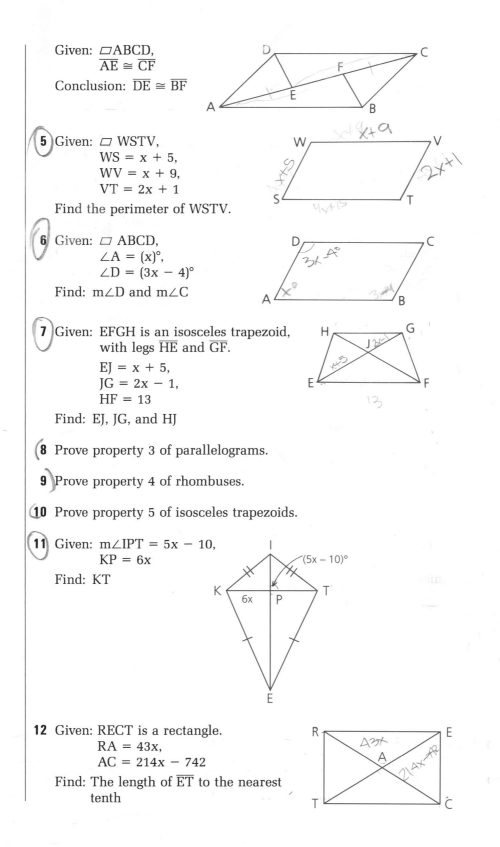

(5) Given: ▱ WSTV,
WS = x + 5,
WV = x + 9,
VT = 2x + 1

Find the perimeter of WSTV.

(6) Given: ▱ ABCD,
∠A = (x)°,
∠D = (3x − 4)°

Find: m∠D and m∠C

(7) Given: EFGH is an isosceles trapezoid,
with legs $\overline{HE}$ and $\overline{GF}$.

EJ = x + 5,
JG = 2x − 1,
HF = 13

Find: EJ, JG, and HJ

(8) Prove property 3 of parallelograms.

(9) Prove property 4 of rhombuses.

(10) Prove property 5 of isosceles trapezoids.

(11) Given: m∠IPT = 5x − 10,
KP = 6x

Find: KT

12 Given: RECT is a rectangle.
RA = 43x,
AC = 214x − 742

Find: The length of $\overline{ET}$ to the nearest tenth

13 Which of the dotted lines represent an *axis of symmetry* of the figure? (One side of a figure is a reflection of the other side over an axis of symmetry.)

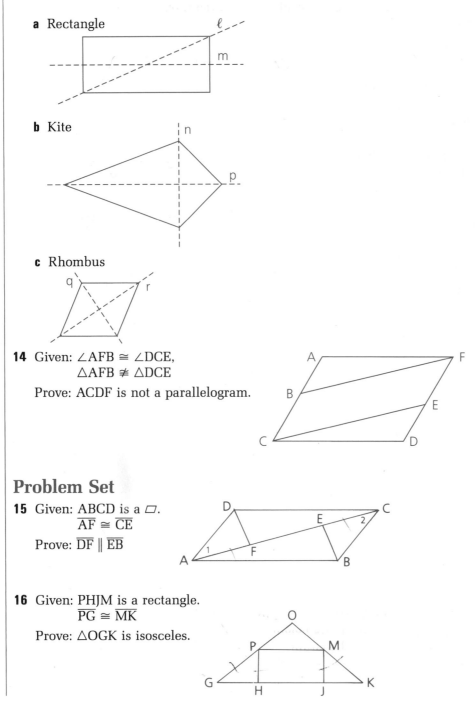

a Rectangle

b Kite

c Rhombus

14 Given: ∠AFB ≅ ∠DCE,
△AFB ≇ △DCE

Prove: ACDF is not a parallelogram.

Problem Set

15 Given: ABCD is a ▱.
$\overline{AF} \cong \overline{CE}$

Prove: $\overline{DF} \parallel \overline{EB}$

16 Given: PHJM is a rectangle.
$\overline{PG} \cong \overline{MK}$

Prove: △OGK is isosceles.

17 Given: VRST is an isosceles trapezoid,
with legs $\overline{VR}$ and $\overline{TS}$.

Prove: $\triangle ARS$ is isosceles.

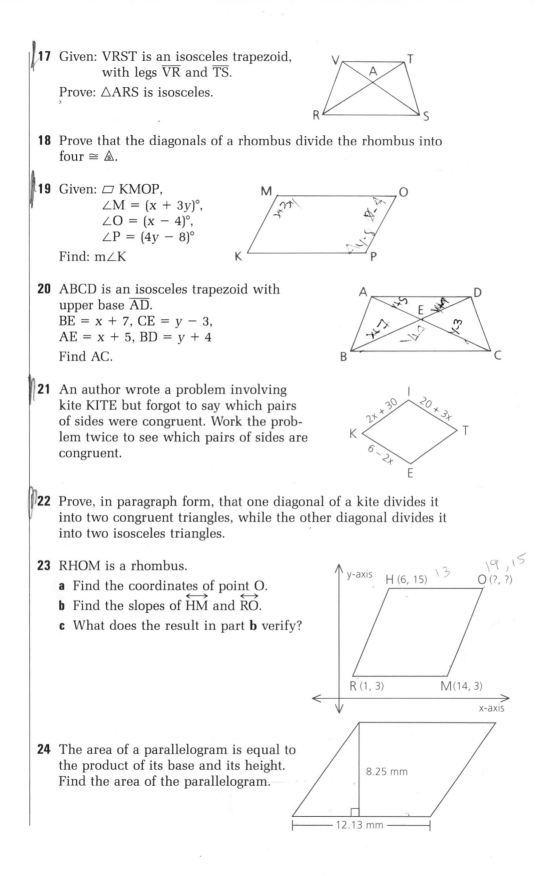

18 Prove that the diagonals of a rhombus divide the rhombus into four $\cong$ $\triangle$.

19 Given: $\square$ KMOP,
$\angle M = (x + 3y)°$,
$\angle O = (x - 4)°$,
$\angle P = (4y - 8)°$

Find: m$\angle K$

20 ABCD is an isosceles trapezoid with upper base $\overline{AD}$.
$BE = x + 7$, $CE = y - 3$,
$AE = x + 5$, $BD = y + 4$

Find AC.

21 An author wrote a problem involving kite KITE but forgot to say which pairs of sides were congruent. Work the problem twice to see which pairs of sides are congruent.

22 Prove, in paragraph form, that one diagonal of a kite divides it into two congruent triangles, while the other diagonal divides it into two isosceles triangles.

23 RHOM is a rhombus.

a Find the coordinates of point O.

b Find the slopes of $\overleftrightarrow{HM}$ and $\overleftrightarrow{RO}$.

c What does the result in part **b** verify?

24 The area of a parallelogram is equal to the product of its base and its height. Find the area of the parallelogram.

Problem Set B, *continued*

25 SQUA is a square. If one of the triangles shown in the figure is chosen at random, what is the probability that it is isosceles?

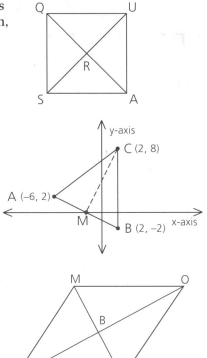

26 $\overline{CM}$ is a median.

   a Find the coordinates of M.
   b Is $\overline{CM}$ an altitude?
   c What type of triangle is △ABC?

27 RHOM is a rhombus.
m∠MBR = 21x + 13,
MR = 6.2x

Find the length of $\overline{RH}$ to the nearest tenth.

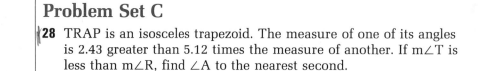

Problem Set C

28 TRAP is an isosceles trapezoid. The measure of one of its angles is 2.43 greater than 5.12 times the measure of another. If m∠T is less than m∠R, find ∠A to the nearest second.

29 Given: m ∥ n

   a Solve for a in terms of x and y.
   b If a > 90, what must be true of y − x?

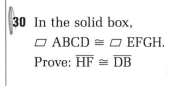

30 In the solid box,
   ▱ ABCD ≅ ▱ EFGH.
   Prove: $\overline{HF} \cong \overline{DB}$

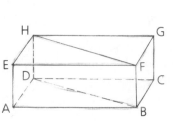

$(180 - x - y)$

$180 - (180 - x - y) = a$

$x + y =$

5.6 | PROVING THAT A QUADRILATERAL IS A PARALLELOGRAM

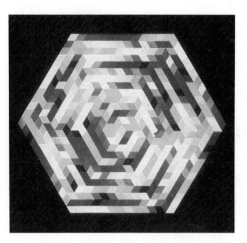

Objective

After studying this section, you will be able to
- Prove that a quadrilateral is a parallelogram

Part One: Introduction

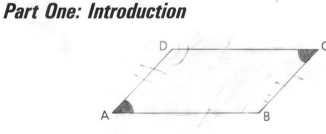

Any one of the following methods might be used to prove that quadrilateral ABCD is a parallelogram.

1 If both pairs of opposite sides of a quadrilateral are parallel, then the quadrilateral is a parallelogram (reverse of the definition).

2 If both pairs of opposite sides of a quadrilateral are congruent, then the quadrilateral is a parallelogram (converse of a property).

3 If one pair of opposite sides of a quadrilateral are both parallel and congruent, then the quadrilateral is a parallelogram.

4 If the diagonals of a quadrilateral bisect each other, then the quadrilateral is a parallelogram (converse of a property).

5 If both pairs of opposite angles of a quadrilateral are congruent, then the quadrilateral is a parallelogram (converse of a property).

Part Two: Sample Problems

Problem 1 *Given:* ACDF is a ▱.
$\angle AFB \cong \angle ECD$

Prove: FBCE is a ▱.

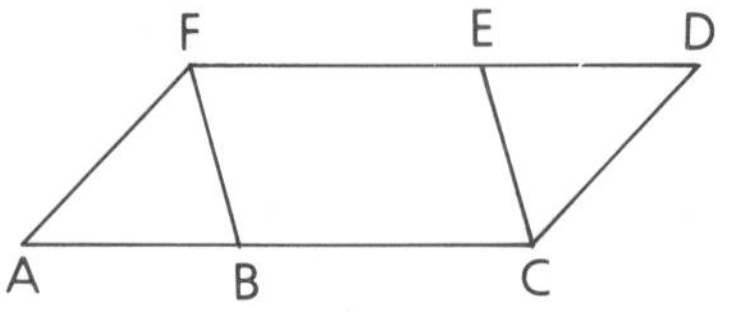

Proof

1 ACDF is a ▱.	1 Given
2 $\angle A \cong \angle D$	2 Opposite $\angle$s of a ▱ are $\cong$.
3 $\overline{AF} \cong \overline{DC}$	3 Opposite sides of a ▱ are $\cong$.
4 $\angle AFB \cong \angle ECD$	4 Given
5 $\triangle AFB \cong \triangle DCE$	5 ASA (2, 3, 4)
6 $\overline{FB} \cong \overline{EC}$	6 CPCTC
7 $\overline{AB} \cong \overline{ED}$	7 CPCTC
8 $\overline{AC} \cong \overline{FD}$	8 Same as 3
9 $\overline{BC} \cong \overline{FE}$	9 Subtraction Property
10 FBCE is a ▱.	10 If both pairs of opposite sides of a quadrilateral are $\cong$, it is a ▱.

Problem 2 *Given:* $\triangle$CAR *is isosceles, with base* $\overline{CR}$.
$\overline{AC} \cong \overline{BK}$,
$\angle C \cong \angle K$

Prove: BARK is a ▱.

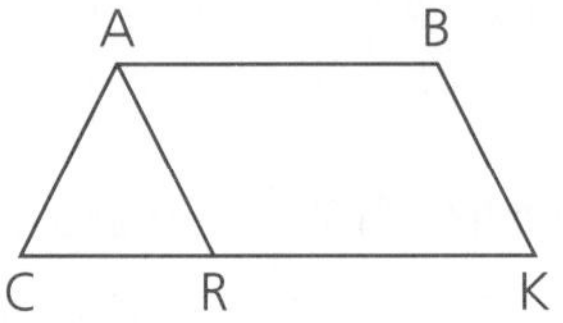

Proof

1 $\triangle$CAR is isos., with base $\overline{CR}$.	1 Given
2 $\overline{AC} \cong \overline{AR}$	2 Legs of an isos. $\triangle$ are $\cong$.
3 $\overline{AC} \cong \overline{BK}$	3 Given
4 $\overline{AR} \cong \overline{BK}$	4 Transitive Property
5 $\angle C \cong \angle ARC$	5 Base $\angle$s of an isos. $\triangle$ are $\cong$.
6 $\angle C \cong \angle K$	6 Given
7 $\angle ARC \cong \angle K$	7 Transitive Property
8 $\overleftrightarrow{AR} \parallel \overleftrightarrow{BK}$	8 Corr. $\angle$s $\cong \Rightarrow \parallel$ lines
9 BARK is a ▱.	9 If one pair of opposite sides of a quadrilateral are both $\parallel$ and $\cong$, it is a ▱.

Problem 3 *Given: Quadrilateral* QUAD, *with angles as shown*

Show that QUAD *is a* ▱.

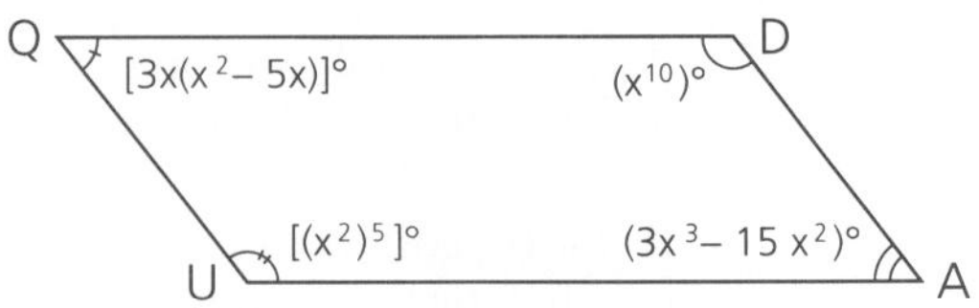

Solution By the Distributive Property of Multiplication over Subtraction, $3x(x^2 - 5x) = 3x^3 - 15x^2$; and $(x^2)^5 = x^{10}$ by the rules of exponents. This means that $\angle Q \cong \angle A$ and $\angle U \cong \angle D$. Thus, QUAD is a parallelogram, since both pairs of opposite angles are congruent.

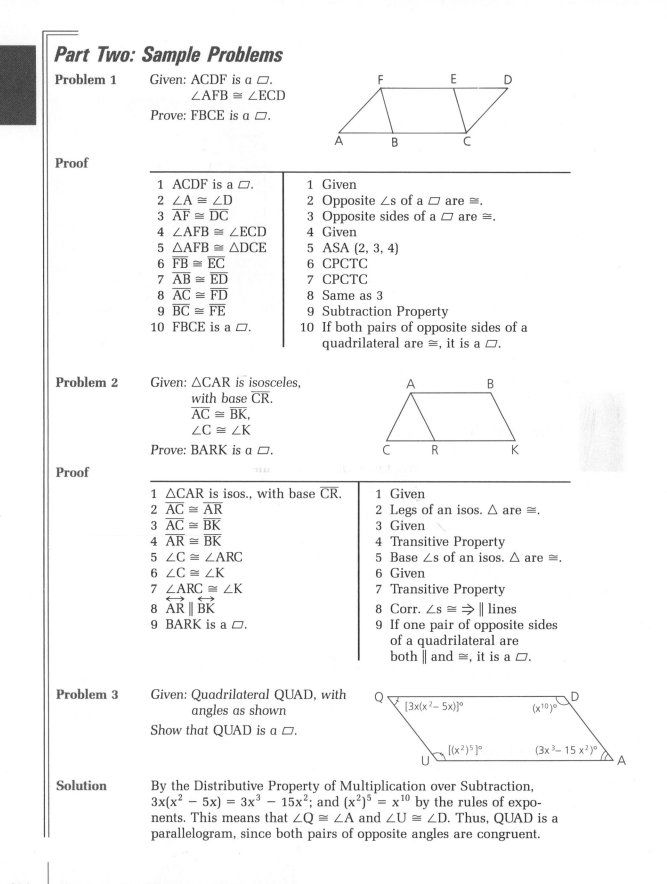

Problem

Given: NRTW is a ▱.
$\overline{NX} \cong \overline{TS}$,
$\overline{WV} \cong \overline{PR}$

Prove: XPSV is a ▱.

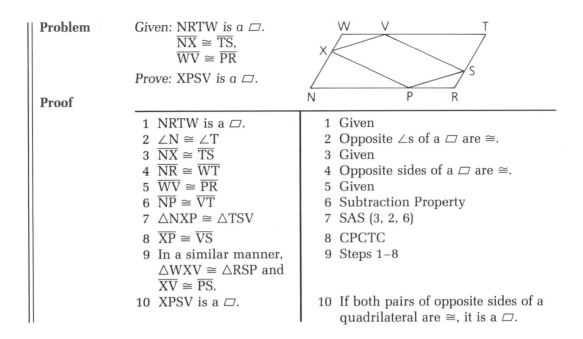

Proof

1 NRTW is a ▱.	1 Given
2 $\angle N \cong \angle T$	2 Opposite $\angle$s of a ▱ are $\cong$.
3 $\overline{NX} \cong \overline{TS}$	3 Given
4 $\overline{NR} \cong \overline{WT}$	4 Opposite sides of a ▱ are $\cong$.
5 $\overline{WV} \cong \overline{PR}$	5 Given
6 $\overline{NP} \cong \overline{VT}$	6 Subtraction Property
7 $\triangle NXP \cong \triangle TSV$	7 SAS (3, 2, 6)
8 $\overline{XP} \cong \overline{VS}$	8 CPCTC
9 In a similar manner, $\triangle WXV \cong \triangle RSP$ and $\overline{XV} \cong \overline{PS}$.	9 Steps 1–8
10 XPSV is a ▱.	10 If both pairs of opposite sides of a quadrilateral are $\cong$, it is a ▱.

Part Three: Problem Sets

Problem Set A

1 For each quadrilateral QUAD, state the property or definition (if there is one) that proves that QUAD is a parallelogram.

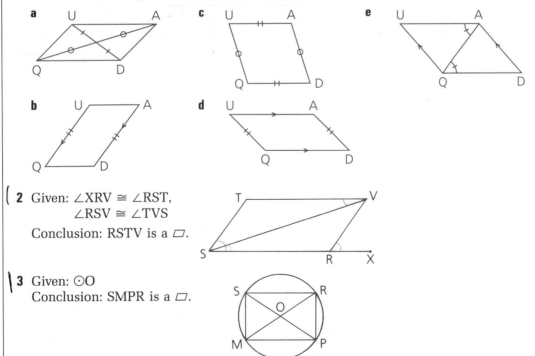

2 Given: $\angle XRV \cong \angle RST$,
$\angle RSV \cong \angle TVS$
Conclusion: RSTV is a ▱.

3 Given: ⊙O
Conclusion: SMPR is a ▱.

4 Given: RKMP is a ▱.
   ∠JRK ≅ ∠PMO
Prove: RJMO is a ▱.
Supply each missing reason.

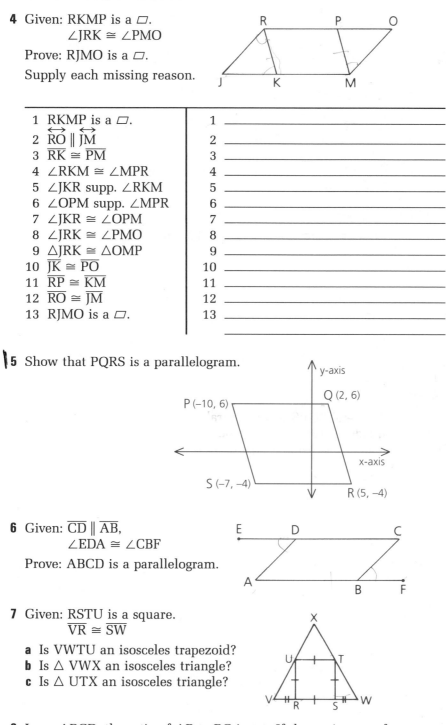

1 RKMP is a ▱.	1 _____
2 ↔RO ∥ ↔JM	2 _____
3 $\overline{RK}$ ≅ $\overline{PM}$	3 _____
4 ∠RKM ≅ ∠MPR	4 _____
5 ∠JKR supp. ∠RKM	5 _____
6 ∠OPM supp. ∠MPR	6 _____
7 ∠JKR ≅ ∠OPM	7 _____
8 ∠JRK ≅ ∠PMO	8 _____
9 △JRK ≅ △OMP	9 _____
10 $\overline{JK}$ ≅ $\overline{PO}$	10 _____
11 $\overline{RP}$ ≅ $\overline{KM}$	11 _____
12 $\overline{RO}$ ≅ $\overline{JM}$	12 _____
13 RJMO is a ▱.	13 _____

5 Show that PQRS is a parallelogram.

P (−10, 6)   Q (2, 6)   y-axis   x-axis   S (−7, −4)   R (5, −4)

6 Given: $\overline{CD}$ ∥ $\overline{AB}$,
   ∠EDA ≅ ∠CBF
Prove: ABCD is a parallelogram.

E   D   C   A   B   F

7 Given: RSTU is a square.
   $\overline{VR}$ ≅ $\overline{SW}$

 a Is VWTU an isosceles trapezoid?
 b Is △ VWX an isosceles triangle?
 c Is △ UTX an isosceles triangle?

X   U   T   V   R   S   W

8 In ▱ ABCD, the ratio of AB to BC is 5:3. If the perimeter of ABCD is 32, find AB.

9 JKMO is a $\square$.

$\overleftrightarrow{JM}$ bisects $\angle OJK$ and $\angle OMK$.

OJ = $x + 5$, KM = $y - 3$,

JK = $2x - 4$

a Solve for x.

b Solve for y.

c Find the perimeter of OJKM.

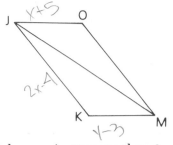

10 The measure of one angle of a parallelogram is 40 more than 3 times another. Find the measure of each angle.

Problem Set B

11 Answer Always, Sometimes, or Never: A quadrilateral is a parallelogram if

a Diagonals are congruent

b One pair of opposite sides are congruent and one pair of opposite sides are parallel

c Each pair of consecutive angles are supplementary

d All angles are right angles

12 Given: Quadrilateral PQRS,

P = $(-10, 7)$, Q = $(4, 3)$,

R = $(-2, -5)$, S = $(-16, 1)$

a Prove that quadrilateral PQRS is not a parallelogram.

b Prove that the quadrilateral formed by joining consecutive midpoints of the sides of PQRS is a parallelogram.

13 Prove that the quadrilateral is a parallelogram.

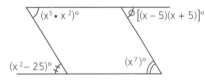

14 Given: RSOT is a $\square$.

$\overline{MS} \cong \overline{TP}$

Conclusion: MOPR is a $\square$.

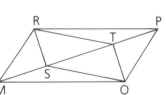

15 Prove: If both pairs of opposite sides of a quadrilateral are $\cong$, the quadrilateral is a $\square$ (method 2 of proving that a quadrilateral is a $\square$). (Hint: Use method 1.)

16 Prove: If two sides of a quadrilateral are both $\parallel$ and $\cong$, the quadrilateral is a $\square$ (method 3 of proving that a quadrilateral is a $\square$).

Problem Set B, *continued*

17 Find the value of x.

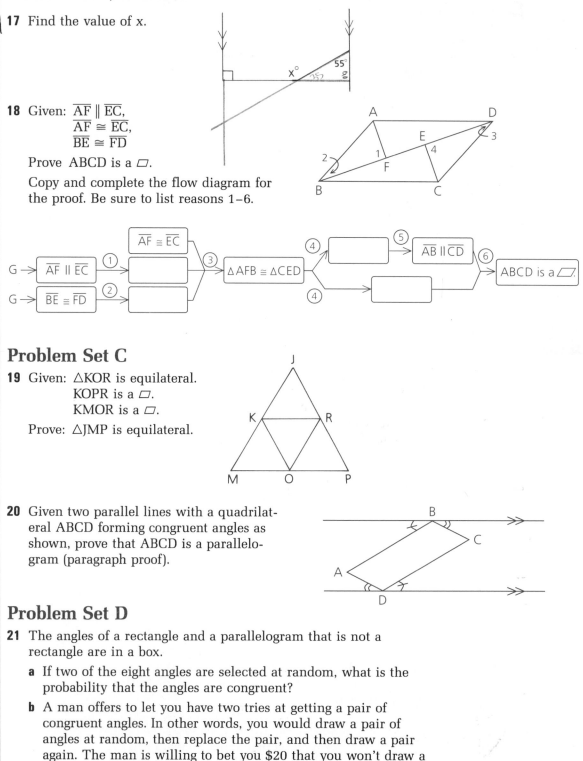

18 Given: $\overline{AF} \parallel \overline{EC}$,
   $\overline{AF} \cong \overline{EC}$,
   $\overline{BE} \cong \overline{FD}$

Prove ABCD is a ▱.

Copy and complete the flow diagram for the proof. Be sure to list reasons 1–6.

Problem Set C

19 Given: △KOR is equilateral.
   KOPR is a ▱.
   KMOR is a ▱.

Prove: △JMP is equilateral.

20 Given two parallel lines with a quadrilateral ABCD forming congruent angles as shown, prove that ABCD is a parallelogram (paragraph proof).

Problem Set D

21 The angles of a rectangle and a parallelogram that is not a rectangle are in a box.

a If two of the eight angles are selected at random, what is the probability that the angles are congruent?

b A man offers to let you have two tries at getting a pair of congruent angles. In other words, you would draw a pair of angles at random, then replace the pair, and then draw a pair again. The man is willing to bet you $20 that you won't draw a congruent pair either time. Should you take the bet?

PROVING THAT FIGURES ARE SPECIAL QUADRILATERALS

Objectives

After studying this section, you will be able to
- Prove that a quadrilateral is a rectangle
- Prove that a quadrilateral is a kite
- Prove that a quadrilateral is a rhombus
- Prove that a quadrilateral is a square
- Prove that a quadrilateral is an isosceles trapezoid

Part One: Introduction

Proving That a Quadrilateral Is a Rectangle

When you want to prove that a figure is one of the special quadrilaterals, you must be sure that you prove sufficient properties to establish the quadrilateral's identity.

You can prove that quadrilateral EFGH is a rectangle by first showing that the quadrilateral is a parallelogram and then using either of the following methods to complete the proof.

2;3;5

1 If a parallelogram contains at least one right angle, then it is a rectangle (reverse of the definition).

2 If the diagonals of a parallelogram are congruent, then the parallelogram is a rectangle.

You can also prove that a quadrilateral is a rectangle without first showing that it is a parallelogram.

3 If all four angles of a quadrilateral are right angles, then it is a rectangle.

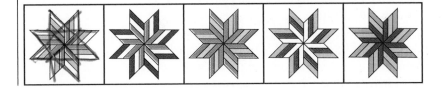

Proving That a Quadrilateral Is a Kite

To prove that a quadrilateral is a kite, either
of the following methods can be used.

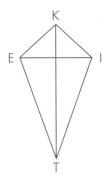

1 If two disjoint pairs of consecutive sides of a quadrilateral are
   congruent, then it is a kite (reverse of the definition).

2 If one of the diagonals of a quadrilateral is the perpendicular
   bisector of the other diagonal, then the quadrilateral is a kite.

Proving That a Quadrilateral Is a Rhombus

To prove that quadrilateral KMOJ is a rhombus, you may first show
that it is a parallelogram and then apply either of the following
methods.

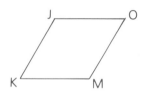

1 If a parallelogram contains a pair of consecutive sides that are
   congruent, then it is a rhombus (reverse of the definition).

2 If either diagonal of a parallelogram bisects two angles of the
   parallelogram, then it is a rhombus.

You can also prove that a quadrilateral is a rhombus without first
showing that it is a parallelogram.

3 If the diagonals of a quadrilateral are perpendicular bisectors of
   each other, then the quadrilateral is a rhombus.

Proving That a Quadrilateral is a Square

The following method can be used to prove that NPRS is a square:

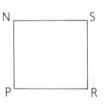

■ If a quadrilateral is both a rectangle and a rhombus, then it is a
  square (reverse of the definition).

Proving That a Trapezoid Is Isosceles

Any one of the following methods can be used to prove that a
trapezoid is isosceles.

1 If the nonparallel sides of a trapezoid are congruent, then it is
   isosceles (reverse of the definition).

2 If the lower or the upper base angles of a trapezoid are congruent,
   then it is isosceles.

3 If the diagonals of a trapezoid are congruent, then it is isosceles.

Part Two: Sample Problems

Problem 1   *What is the most descriptive name for quadrilateral ABCD with vertices A = (−3, −7), B = (−9, 1), C = (3, 9), and D = (9, 1)?*

Solution   We must check every detail to see if sides are parallel or perpendicular, and we must also check diagonals. We must be careful to identify what we are finding with each calculation. A graph may prove helpful in directing our work.

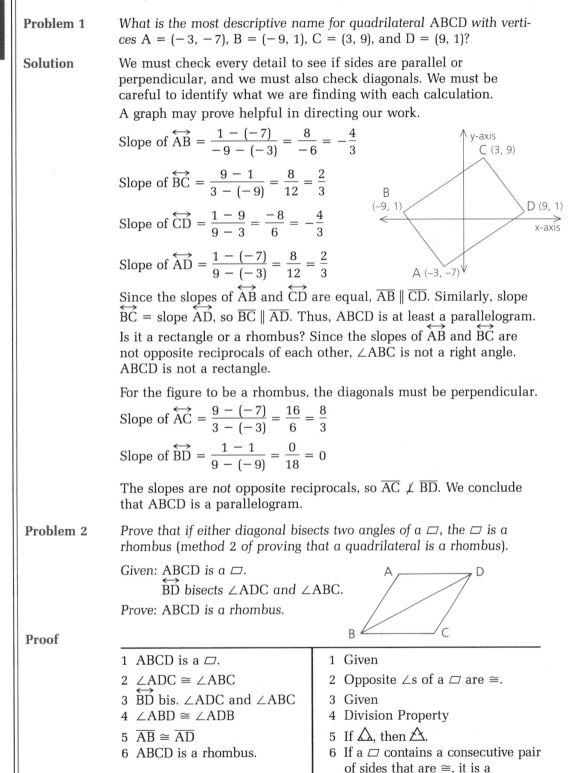

$$\text{Slope of } \overleftrightarrow{AB} = \frac{1 - (-7)}{-9 - (-3)} = \frac{8}{-6} = -\frac{4}{3}$$

$$\text{Slope of } \overleftrightarrow{BC} = \frac{9 - 1}{3 - (-9)} = \frac{8}{12} = \frac{2}{3}$$

$$\text{Slope of } \overleftrightarrow{CD} = \frac{1 - 9}{9 - 3} = \frac{-8}{6} = -\frac{4}{3}$$

$$\text{Slope of } \overleftrightarrow{AD} = \frac{1 - (-7)}{9 - (-3)} = \frac{8}{12} = \frac{2}{3}$$

Since the slopes of $\overleftrightarrow{AB}$ and $\overleftrightarrow{CD}$ are equal, $\overline{AB} \parallel \overline{CD}$. Similarly, slope $\overleftrightarrow{BC}$ = slope $\overleftrightarrow{AD}$, so $\overline{BC} \parallel \overline{AD}$. Thus, ABCD is at least a parallelogram.

Is it a rectangle or a rhombus? Since the slopes of $\overleftrightarrow{AB}$ and $\overleftrightarrow{BC}$ are not opposite reciprocals of each other, $\angle ABC$ is not a right angle. ABCD is not a rectangle.

For the figure to be a rhombus, the diagonals must be perpendicular.

$$\text{Slope of } \overleftrightarrow{AC} = \frac{9 - (-7)}{3 - (-3)} = \frac{16}{6} = \frac{8}{3}$$

$$\text{Slope of } \overleftrightarrow{BD} = \frac{1 - 1}{9 - (-9)} = \frac{0}{18} = 0$$

The slopes are *not* opposite reciprocals, so $\overline{AC} \not\perp \overline{BD}$. We conclude that ABCD is a parallelogram.

Problem 2   *Prove that if either diagonal bisects two angles of a $\square$, the $\square$ is a rhombus (method 2 of proving that a quadrilateral is a rhombus).*

Given: ABCD is a $\square$.
      $\overleftrightarrow{BD}$ bisects $\angle ADC$ and $\angle ABC$.

Prove: ABCD is a rhombus.

Proof

1 ABCD is a $\square$.	1 Given
2 $\angle ADC \cong \angle ABC$	2 Opposite $\angle$s of a $\square$ are $\cong$.
3 $\overleftrightarrow{BD}$ bis. $\angle ADC$ and $\angle ABC$	3 Given
4 $\angle ABD \cong \angle ADB$	4 Division Property
5 $\overline{AB} \cong \overline{AD}$	5 If $\triangle$, then $\triangle$.
6 ABCD is a rhombus.	6 If a $\square$ contains a consecutive pair of sides that are $\cong$, it is a rhombus.

Problem 3   Given: GJMO is a ▱.
$\overline{OH} \perp \overline{GK}$;
$\overline{MK}$ is an altitude of △MKJ.

Prove: OHKM is a rectangle.

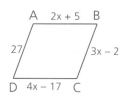

Proof

1 GJMO is a ▱.	1 Given
2 $\overleftrightarrow{OM} \parallel \overleftrightarrow{GK}$	2 Opposite sides of a ▱ are ∥.
3 $\overline{OH} \perp \overline{GK}$	3 Given
4 $\overline{MK}$ is an alt. of △MKJ.	4 Given
5 $\overline{MK} \perp \overline{GK}$	5 An altitude of a △ is ⊥ to the side to which it is drawn.
6 $\overline{OH} \parallel \overline{MK}$	6 If two coplanar lines are ⊥ to a third line, they are ∥.
7 OHKM is a ▱.	7 If both pairs of opposite sides of a quadrilateral are ∥, it is a ▱.
8 ∠OHK is a right ∠.	8 ⊥ segments form a right ∠.
9 OHKM is a rectangle.	9 If a ▱ contains at least one right ∠, it is a rectangle.

Part Three: Problem Sets

Problem Set A

1 Locate points Q = (2, 4), U = (2, 7), A = (10, 7), and D = (10, 4) on a graph. Then give the most descriptive name for QUAD.

2 If $\overline{AB} \cong \overline{DC}$, show that ABCD is not a rhombus.

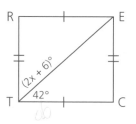

3 In order for RECT to be a rectangle, what must the value of x be?

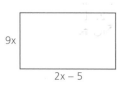

4 What is the most descriptive name for a quadrilateral with vertices (−11, 5), (7, 5), (7, −13), and (−11, −13)?

5 a Write an expression for the area of the rectangle.
   b Write an expression for the perimeter of the rectangle.
   c Evaluate each when x is 4.2.

6 Give the most descriptive name for

a A quadrilateral with diagonals that are perpendicular bisectors of each other

b A rectangle that is also a kite

c A quadrilateral with opposite angles supplementary and consecutive angles supplementary

d A quadrilateral with one pair of opposite sides congruent and the other pair of opposite sides parallel

7 Given: $\overrightarrow{AC}$ bisects ∠BAD.
  $\overline{AB} \cong \overline{BC}$,
  $\overline{AB} \not\parallel \overline{CD}$

  Prove: ABCD is a trapezoid.

8 Given: YTWX is a ▱.
  $\overline{YP} \perp \overline{TW}$,
  $\overline{ZW} \perp \overline{TY}$,
  $\overline{TP} \cong \overline{TZ}$

  Conclusion: TWXY is a rhombus.

9 Given: Right △PQR, with hypotenuse $\overline{PR}$. M is the midpoint of $\overline{PR}$. Through M, lines are drawn parallel to the legs.

  Prove: The quadrilateral formed is a rectangle.

10 Given: $\overline{ID}$ bisects $\overline{RB}$,
  $\overline{BI} \cong \overline{IR}$

  Prove: BIRD is a kite.

Problem Set B

11 Given: ABDE is a ▱.
  $\overline{BC}$ is the base of isosceles △BCD.

  Prove: ACDE is an isosceles trapezoid.

12 ABCD is a parallelogram with perimeter 52. The perimeter of ABNM is 36, and $\overline{NC} \cong \overline{AM}$. Find NM.

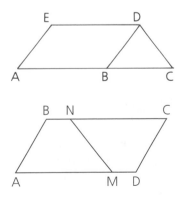

13 What is the most descriptive name for each quadrilateral below?

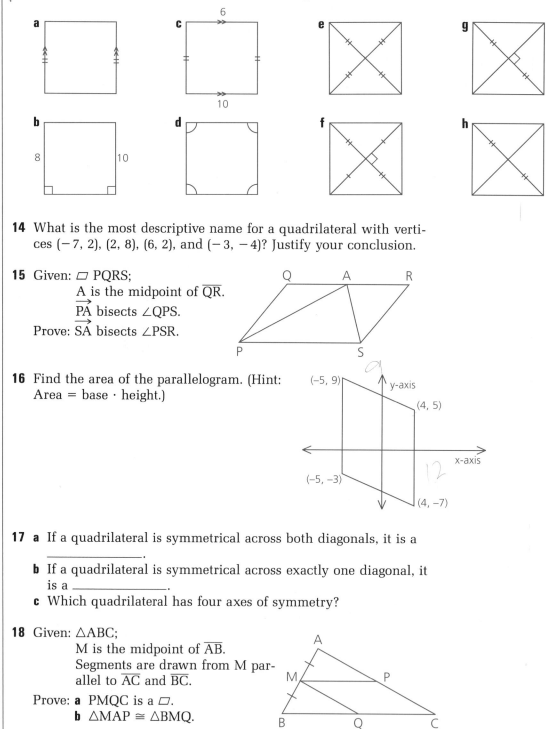

14 What is the most descriptive name for a quadrilateral with vertices $(-7, 2)$, $(2, 8)$, $(6, 2)$, and $(-3, -4)$? Justify your conclusion.

15 Given: ▱ PQRS;
A is the midpoint of $\overline{QR}$.
$\overrightarrow{PA}$ bisects $\angle QPS$.
Prove: $\overrightarrow{SA}$ bisects $\angle PSR$.

16 Find the area of the parallelogram. (Hint: Area = base · height.)

17 a If a quadrilateral is symmetrical across both diagonals, it is a _____.

  b If a quadrilateral is symmetrical across exactly one diagonal, it is a _____.

  c Which quadrilateral has four axes of symmetry?

18 Given: △ABC;
M is the midpoint of $\overline{AB}$.
Segments are drawn from M parallel to $\overline{AC}$ and $\overline{BC}$.
Prove: **a** PMQC is a ▱.
  b △MAP ≅ △BMQ.

19 Write a quadratic equation to represent the area of the rectangle. If the area is 160 square meters, find the perimeter.

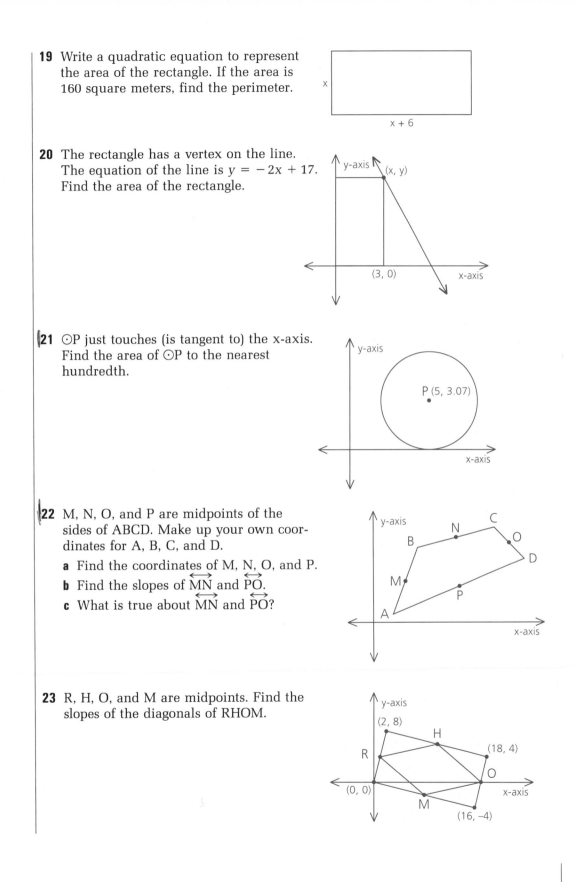

x

x + 6

20 The rectangle has a vertex on the line. The equation of the line is $y = -2x + 17$. Find the area of the rectangle.

y-axis

(x, y)

(3, 0)

x-axis

21 ⊙P just touches (is tangent to) the x-axis. Find the area of ⊙P to the nearest hundredth.

y-axis

P (5, 3.07)

x-axis

22 M, N, O, and P are midpoints of the sides of ABCD. Make up your own coordinates for A, B, C, and D.

a Find the coordinates of M, N, O, and P.
b Find the slopes of $\overleftrightarrow{MN}$ and $\overleftrightarrow{PO}$.
c What is true about $\overleftrightarrow{MN}$ and $\overleftrightarrow{PO}$?

y-axis

C

N

B

O

D

M

P

A

x-axis

23 R, H, O, and M are midpoints. Find the slopes of the diagonals of RHOM.

y-axis

(2, 8)

H

R

(18, 4)

O

(0, 0)

x-axis

M

(16, –4)

Problem Set B, *continued*

24 D is the reflection of E = (x, 14) across the y-axis. If $\overleftrightarrow{CD} \parallel \overleftrightarrow{AB}$, solve for x.

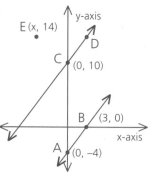

25 ABCD is a parallelogram. If two of the following conclusions are selected at random, what is the probability that both conclusions are true?

a $\overline{AB} \cong \overline{DC}$

b E is the midpoint of $\overline{AC}$.

c ∠ADC is supplementary to ∠DAB.

d $\overrightarrow{AC}$ bisects ∠DAB.

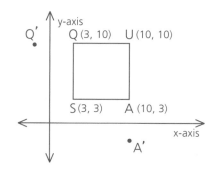

Problem Set C

26 What is the most descriptive name for the quadrilaterals SQUA and Q′QAA′, where Q′ is the reflection of Q over the y-axis and A′ is the reflection of A over the x-axis? Justify your conclusions.

27 The diagonals of a quadrilateral are congruent. Exactly one pair of opposite sides are congruent. Prove that two of the triangles formed are isosceles.

28 What is the most descriptive name for the quadrilateral with vertices (3, 2), (8, 1), (7, 6), and (2, 7)?

29 a Write an expression to represent the shaded area.

b Write an inequality that gives the limits of the area of the square.

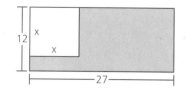

CHAPTER SUMMARY

CONCEPTS AND PROCEDURES

After studying this chapter, you should be able to
- Write indirect proofs (5.1)
- Apply the Exterior Angle Inequality Theorem (5.2)
- Use various methods to prove lines parallel (5.2)
- Apply the Parallel Postulate (5.3)
- Identify the pairs of angles formed by a transversal cutting parallel lines (5.3)
- Apply six theorems about parallel lines (5.3)
- Solve crook problems (5.3)
- Recognize polygons (5.4)
- Understand how polygons are named (5.4)
- Recognize convex polygons (5.4)
- Recognize diagonals of polygons (5.4)
- Identify special types of quadrilaterals (5.4)
- Identify some properties of parallelograms, rectangles, kites, rhombuses, squares, and isosceles trapezoids (5.5)
- Prove that a quadrilateral is a parallelogram (5.6)
- Prove that a quadrilateral is a rectangle (5.7)
- Prove that a quadrilateral is a kite (5.7)
- Prove that a quadrilateral is a rhombus (5.7)
- Prove that a quadrilateral is a square (5.7)
- Prove that a quadrilateral is an isosceles trapezoid (5.7)

VOCABULARY

convex polygon (5.4)
diagonal (5.4)
indirect proof (5.1)
isosceles trapezoid (5.4)
kite (5.4)
lower base angles (5.4)
parallelogram (5.4)
Parallel Postulate (5.3)

polygon (5.4)
quadrilateral (5.4)
rectangle (5.4)
rhombus (5.4)
square (5.4)
trapezoid (5.4)
upper base angles (5.4)

REVIEW PROBLEMS

Problem Set A

1 Give the most descriptive name for

a A quadrilateral whose consecutive sides measure 15, 18, 15, and 18

b A quadrilateral whose consecutive sides measure 15, 18, 18, and 15

c A quadrilateral with consecutive angles of 30°, 150°, 110°, and 70°

d A quadrilateral whose diagonals are perpendicular and congruent and bisect each other

e A quadrilateral whose congruent diagonals bisect each other and bisect the angles

2 ABCD is a ▱.
AB = 2x + 6,
BC = 8,
CD = x + 8
Find the perimeter of ABCD.

3 Write an inequality stating the restrictions on x.

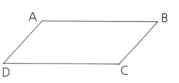

4 JKMP is a rectangle.
PK = 0.2x,
JM = x − 12
Find PK.

5 Given: ∠1 ≅ ∠2;
         ABCD is not a ▱.
Prove: ∠3 ≇ ∠4

6 In a parallelogram, the measure of one of the angles is twice that of another. Are these opposite angles or consecutive angles? Find the measure of each angle of the parallelogram.

7 In each of these diagrams, is m ∥ p?

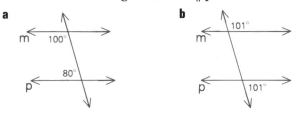

a

m 100°

80°

p

b

101°

m

p 101°

c

120°

m (x + 40)°

(3x)°

p

8 Name five properties of a parallelogram.

9 Given: $\overline{AB} \cong \overline{CD}$, $\overline{AG} \cong \overline{BE}$,
$\overline{AG} \parallel \overline{BE}$
Conclusion: $\overline{GC} \parallel \overline{ED}$

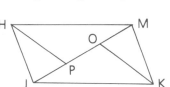

10 Given: HJKM is a ▱.
∠JHP ≅ ∠MKO
Conclusion: $\overline{MP} \cong \overline{JO}$

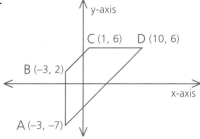

11 Show that ABCD is an isosceles trapezoid.

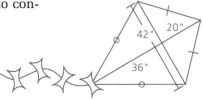

12 Find the area of the paper used to construct the kite.

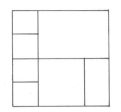

13 Two polygons are selected at random from a group consisting of a nonisosceles trapezoid, an isosceles trapezoid, and a parallelogram. Find the probability that both polygons have two pairs of congruent angles.

14 a How many squares appear to be in the figure at the right?
b How many rectangles?

15 Given: $\overline{KR}$ is a median to $\overline{JO}$.
  $\overline{RP} \cong \overline{KM}$,
  $\overline{RM} \cong \overline{KM}$

  Prove: JMOP is a $\square$.

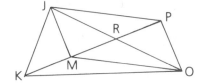

16 In $\square$ ABCD, $\angle A = (2x + 6)°$ and $\angle B = (x + 24)°$. Find m$\angle C$.

17 $\overline{TP}$ (a diameter) passes through the center of $\odot O$. Find the area of the circle to three decimal places.

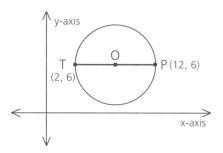

Problem Set B

18 Given: $\overleftrightarrow{AD} \parallel \overleftrightarrow{BC}$,
  m$\angle 1 = 5.63x + 2.42$,
  m$\angle 2 = 2.1x$,
  m$\angle 3 = 6x - 5.1$,
  m$\angle 4 = 42$

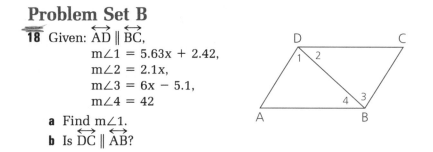

  a Find m$\angle 1$.
  b Is $\overleftrightarrow{DC} \parallel \overleftrightarrow{AB}$?

19 If the statement is always true, write A; if sometimes true, write S; if never true, write N.

  a If the diagonals of a quadrilateral are congruent, the quadrilateral is an isosceles trapezoid.
  b If the diagonals of a quadrilateral divide each angle into two 45-degree angles, the quadrilateral is a square.
  c If a parallelogram is equilateral, it is equiangular.
  d If two of the angles of a trapezoid are congruent, the trapezoid is isosceles.

20 Prove: The figure produced by joining the consecutive midpoints of a parallelogram is a parallelogram.

21 Prove: If the bisector of an exterior angle formed by extending one of the sides of a triangle is parallel to a side of the triangle, the triangle is isosceles.

22 What is the most descriptive name for the quadrilateral with vertices $(0, -6)$, $(-4, 2)$, $(4, 6)$, and $(8, -2)$? Justify your conclusion.

23 Given: EFGH is a ▱.
$\overline{AE} \cong \overline{BF} \cong \overline{CG} \cong \overline{DH}$

Prove: ABCD is a ▱.

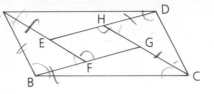

24 Given: P is the midpt. of $\overline{RO}$.
K is the midpt. of $\overline{JM}$.
$\angle 1 \cong \angle 2$,
$\overline{PS} \cong \overline{KS}$

Prove: RJMO is a ▱.

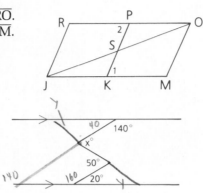

25 Find the value of x.

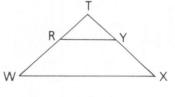

26 Given: △TWX is isosceles, with base $\overline{WX}$.
$\overline{RY} \parallel \overline{WX}$

Prove: RWXY is an isosceles trapezoid.

27 If two of the five labeled angles are chosen at random, what is the probability that they are supplementary?

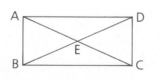

Problem Set C

28 Given: $\overline{AB} \cong \overline{DC}$,
$\overline{AB} \perp \overline{BC}$, $\overline{DC} \perp \overline{BC}$

Prove: △DEC is isosceles.

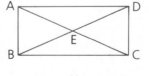

29 Given: △AED and △BEC are isosceles,
with congruent bases $\overline{AD}$ and $\overline{BC}$.

Prove: ABCD is a rectangle.

30 Given: Kite KITE

Find: The three possible values of the perimeter of KITE

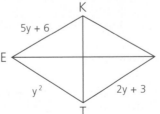

LINES AND PLANES IN SPACE

I n this model, the Ruck-A-Chucky Bridge in
Auburn, California, appears suspended in space.

RELATING LINES TO PLANES

Objectives

After studying this chapter, you will be able to
- Understand basic concepts relating to planes
- Identify four methods of determining a plane
- Apply two postulates concerning lines and planes

Part One: Introduction

Preliminary Concepts

Recall the definition of *plane* from Section 4.5: *A plane is a surface such that if any two points on the surface are connected by a line, all points of the line are also on the surface.* Because a surface has no thickness, a plane must be "flat" if it is to contain the straight lines determined by all pairs of points on it. It must also be infinitely long and wide. Thus, a plane has only two dimensions, length and width.

A surface that is not a plane   Plane surface

A plane is frequently drawn as shown in the right-hand diagram above. In this case, the diagram represents part of a horizontal plane, with the edges nearest to you darkened. A plane can be named by placing a single lowercase letter in one of the corners.

It is important to understand that although our picture of a plane has edges and corners, an actual plane has neither and should be thought of as infinite in length and width.

You may recall the following definitions from Section 4.5: *If points, lines, segments, and so forth, lie in the same plane, we call them coplanar. Points, lines, segments, and so forth, that do not lie in the same plane are called noncoplanar.* In the diagram on the next page, $\overleftrightarrow{AB}$ and $\overleftrightarrow{ST}$ lie in plane m. $\overleftrightarrow{RP}$ does not lie in the plane but intersects m at V.

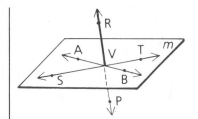

A, B, S, T, and V are *coplanar* points.
$\overleftrightarrow{AB}$ and $\overleftrightarrow{ST}$ are *coplanar* lines.
$\overline{AB}$ and $\overline{ST}$ are *coplanar* segments.

A, B, S, T, and R are *noncoplanar* points.
$\overleftrightarrow{AB}$, $\overleftrightarrow{ST}$, and $\overleftrightarrow{RP}$ are *noncoplanar* lines.
$\overline{AB}$, $\overline{ST}$, and $\overline{RP}$ are *noncoplanar* segments.

Definition   The point of intersection of a line and a plane is called the *foot* of the line.

In the preceding diagram, V is the foot of $\overleftrightarrow{RP}$ in plane m.

Four Ways to Determine a Plane

In Chapter 3, you learned that two points determine a line. We would now like to find conditions under which a plane is determined.

One point obviously does not determine a plane, since infinitely many planes pass through a single point.

The diagram at the right shows that two points also do not determine a unique plane. It shows two different planes, m and n, each of which contains both point A and point B. The same diagram shows that three points—A, B, and C—do not determine a plane if the three points are collinear.

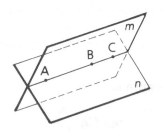

If the three points are noncollinear, however, they do determine a plane.

There is one and only one plane that contains the three noncollinear points A, B, and C. This plane can be called either plane ABC or plane k.

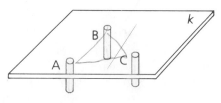

The preceding observations suggest an important postulate.

Postulate   ***Three noncollinear points determine a plane.***

There are other ways of determining a plane. The following three are stated as theorems.

Theorem	*A line and a point not on the line determine a plane.*	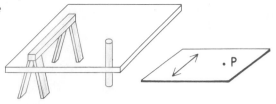

Theorem 46   *Two intersecting lines determine a plane.*

The proofs of Theorems 45 and 46 are asked for in Problem Set B.

Theorem 47   *Two parallel lines determine a plane.*

Proof: If $\overleftrightarrow{AB}$ and $\overleftrightarrow{CD}$ are parallel, then according to the definition of
parallel lines, they lie in a plane. We need to show that they
lie in *only one* plane. If P is any point on $\overleftrightarrow{AB}$, then according
to Theorem 45, there is only one plane containing P and $\overleftrightarrow{CD}$.
Thus, there is only one plane that contains $\overleftrightarrow{AB}$ and $\overleftrightarrow{CD}$,
because every plane containing $\overleftrightarrow{AB}$ contains P.

Two Postulates Concerning Lines and Planes

We shall assume the following two statements.

Postulate   *If a line intersects a plane not containing it, then the intersection is exactly one point.*

Postulate   *If two planes intersect, their intersection is exactly one line.*

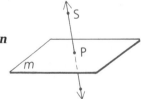

Part Two: Sample Problems

Problem 1   **a** $m \cap n =$ ___?___

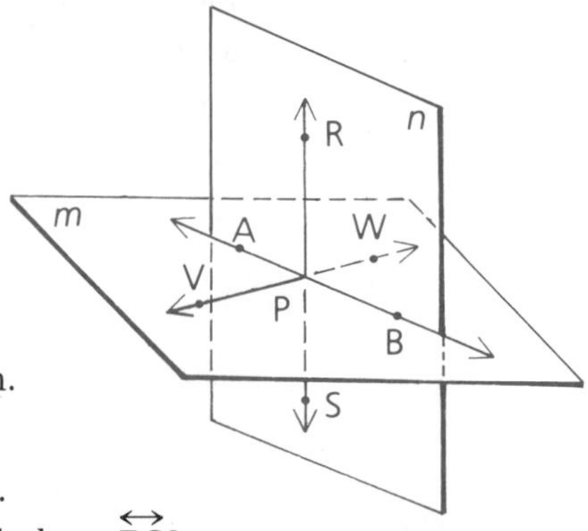

b A, B, and V determine plane ___?___.

c Name the foot of $\overleftrightarrow{RS}$ in m.

d $\overleftrightarrow{AB}$ and $\overleftrightarrow{RS}$ determine plane ___?___.

e $\overleftrightarrow{AB}$ and point ___?___ determine plane n.

f Does W lie in plane n?

g Line AB and line ___?___ determine plane m.

h A, B, V, and ___?___ are coplanar points.

i A, B, V, and ___?___ are noncoplanar points.

j If R and S lie in plane n, what can be said about $\overleftrightarrow{RS}$?

Answers   **a** $\overleftrightarrow{AB}$ **d** n   **g** VW   **j** $\overleftrightarrow{RS}$ lies in

b m   **e** R or s   **h** W or P   plane n.

c P   **f** No   **i** R or S

Note   In this problem, other planes are determined besides the two shown in the diagram. For example, the noncollinear points R, P, and V determine a plane.

Problem 2   Given: A, B, and C lie in plane m.

$\overline{PB} \perp \overline{AB}$,

$\overline{PB} \perp \overline{BC}$,

$\overline{AB} \cong \overline{BC}$

Prove: $\angle APB \cong \angle CPB$

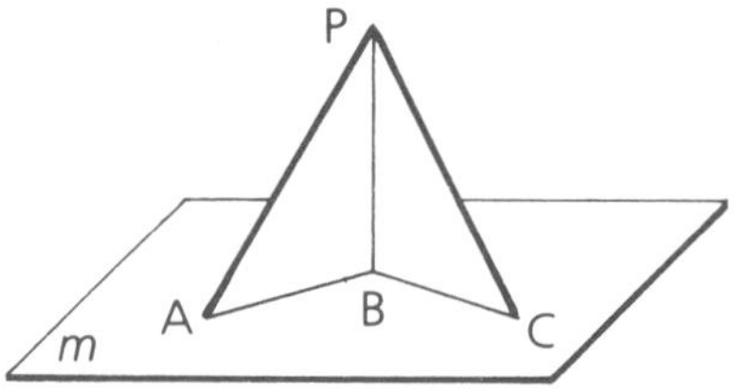

Proof

1 $\overline{PB} \perp \overline{AB}$, $\overline{PB} \perp \overline{BC}$	1 Given
2 $\angle PBA$ and $\angle PBC$ are right $\angle$s.	2 $\perp$ lines form right $\angle$s.
3 $\angle PBA \cong \angle PBC$	3 Right $\angle$s are $\cong$.
4 $\overline{AB} \cong \overline{BC}$	4 Given
5 $\overline{PB} \cong \overline{PB}$	5 Reflexive Property
6 $\triangle PBA \cong \triangle PBC$	6 SAS (4, 3, 5)
7 $\angle APB \cong \angle CPB$	7 CPCTC

Part Three: Problem Sets

Problem Set A

1 Consider a spherical object, such as an orange or a globe. If two points are marked on it and a straight line is drawn through the two points, does the line lie on the surface? Is it possible to draw a straight line that will lie entirely on the surface?

2 a $r \cap s =$ ___?___

b $\overleftrightarrow{AB} \cap s =$ ___?___

c Name three collinear points.

d Name four noncoplanar points.

e What plane do points A, B, and E determine?

f What plane do $\overleftrightarrow{AB}$ and $\overleftrightarrow{ED}$ determine?

g Name the foot of $\overleftrightarrow{TC}$ in plane s.

h Name the foot of $\overleftrightarrow{TC}$ in plane r.

i Do $\overleftrightarrow{CD}$ and $\overleftrightarrow{ED}$ determine a plane?

j If $\overleftrightarrow{CD} \perp \overleftrightarrow{AB}$, name the right angles formed.

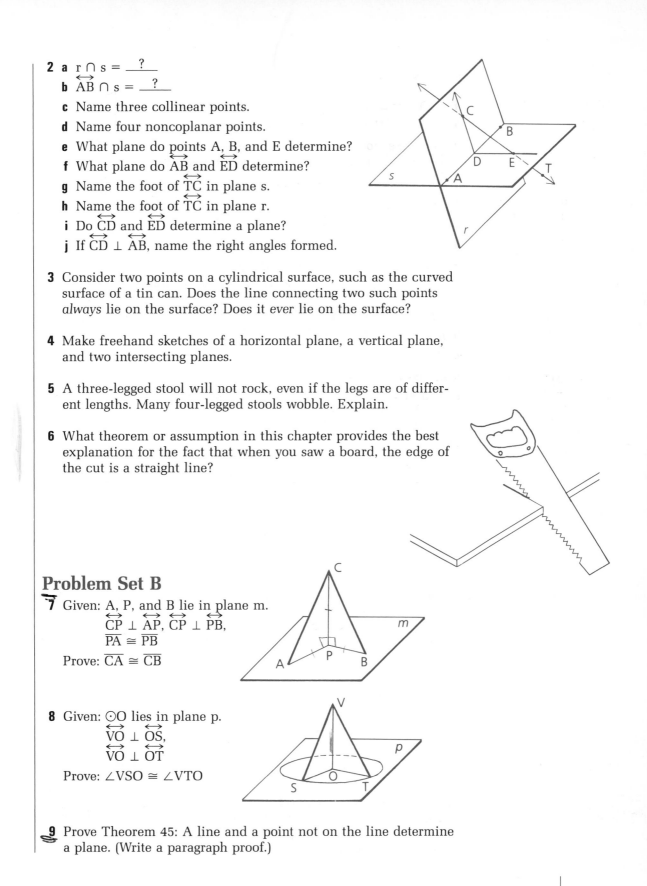

3 Consider two points on a cylindrical surface, such as the curved surface of a tin can. Does the line connecting two such points *always* lie on the surface? Does it *ever* lie on the surface?

4 Make freehand sketches of a horizontal plane, a vertical plane, and two intersecting planes.

5 A three-legged stool will not rock, even if the legs are of different lengths. Many four-legged stools wobble. Explain.

6 What theorem or assumption in this chapter provides the best explanation for the fact that when you saw a board, the edge of the cut is a straight line?

Problem Set B

7 Given: A, P, and B lie in plane m.
$\overleftrightarrow{CP} \perp \overleftrightarrow{AP}$, $\overleftrightarrow{CP} \perp \overleftrightarrow{PB}$,
$\overline{PA} \cong \overline{PB}$

Prove: $\overline{CA} \cong \overline{CB}$

8 Given: $\odot O$ lies in plane p.
$\overleftrightarrow{VO} \perp \overleftrightarrow{OS}$,
$\overleftrightarrow{VO} \perp \overleftrightarrow{OT}$

Prove: $\angle VSO \cong \angle VTO$

9 Prove Theorem 45: A line and a point not on the line determine a plane. (Write a paragraph proof.)

Problem Set B, *continued*

10 Prove Theorem 46: Two intersecting lines determine a plane. (Write a paragraph proof.)

11 Can you hold two pencils so that they do not intersect and are not parallel? Are they coplanar? (Lines that do not intersect and that are not coplanar are called *skew* lines.)

12 Cut a quadrilateral out of paper and fold it along a diagonal as shown in the figure. Is every four-sided figure a plane figure?

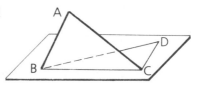

13 If two points in space are equidistant from the endpoints of a segment, will the line joining them be the perpendicular bisector of the segment? Explain.

14 Given: Planes m and n
   intersect in $\overleftrightarrow{RS}$.
   m contains R, S, and V.
   n contains R, S, and T.
   $\overline{TS} \cong \overline{VR}$,
   $\overline{TR} \perp \overline{RS}$,
   $\overline{VS} \perp \overline{RS}$
   Prove: $\overline{TR} \cong \overline{VS}$

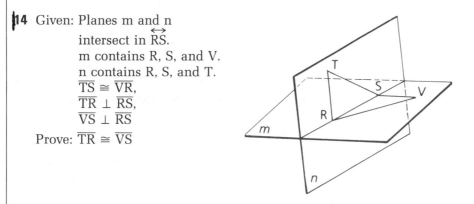

Problem Set C

15 The figure at the right is a square pyramid. How many planes are determined by its vertices? (There are more than five.) Name them.

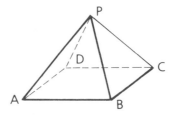

16 Given: A, B, C, and D lie in plane m.
   $\overleftrightarrow{ST}$ intersects m at B.
   D is any point on $\overline{AC}$.
   $\overleftrightarrow{ST} \perp \overleftrightarrow{AB}$, $\overleftrightarrow{ST} \perp \overleftrightarrow{BC}$,
   $\overline{SB} \cong \overline{TB}$
   Prove: $\overleftrightarrow{ST} \perp \overleftrightarrow{BD}$

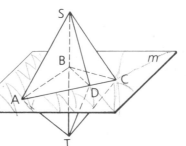

17 Given: A, B, and X lie in plane m.
X is on $\overline{AB}$. P and Q are above m.
B is equidistant from P and Q.
A is equidistant from P and Q.

Prove: X is equidistant from P and Q.

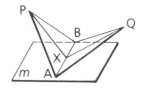

18 Given: △ABC ≅ △DBC

Prove: △AXD is isosceles.

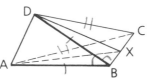

THE GEOMETRY OF ARCHITECTURE
Thalia and Steve Lubin organize space

The geometry of a building can express itself in a multitude of ways. On a technical level there are the angles and dimensions of the hallways and rooms that compose the building. At the creative level the architect who designs the building must be able to see it in abstract geometrical terms. Explains architect Steve Lubin: "When we look at an empty lot we envision volumes of space where there are none now. It's all geometry, imagining a progression of interlocking spaces that will ultimately become a building."

Then there is the geometry of scale. According to architect Thalia Lubin: "When you enter a space you relate it to yourself. That's why a house cannot be restful and orderly unless everything in it relates to people and their sense of proportion and scale."

In designing a building, an architect must take into consideration the client's wishes, legal requirements, and environmental constraints dictated by the building site. The purest expression of geometry in a building is one of logic. "The final design is a bundle of compromises," says Thalia Lubin. "The architect's job is to impose a sense of logic on all of the competing forces, to find the natural order of things."

Both members of this unusual husband-and-wife team of architects took five-year degrees in architecture from the University of Oregon at Eugene. After working briefly for others, they decided to go into business together in Woodside, California. In designing a building, Thalia works with the client, while Steve oversees the technical aspects of the project. The system works, though Thalia admits, "We take a lot of chaos wherever we go." Steve says, "Every job is completely different. You need incredible patience to be an architect, but you dream of achieving poetry in the end."

Computer-generated renderings courtesy of Skidmore, Owings & Merrill.

PERPENDICULARITY OF A LINE AND A PLANE

Objectives

After studying this section, you will be able to
- Recognize when a line is perpendicular to a plane
- Apply the basic theorem concerning the perpendicularity of a line and a plane

Part One: Introduction

A Line Perpendicular to a Plane

What does it mean to say that a line is perpendicular to a plane? Think about that for a moment and then read the following formal definition.

Definition   A line is perpendicular to a plane if it is perpendicular to *every* one of the lines in the plane that pass through its foot.

Observe that we now have two kinds of perpendicularity:

1 Between two lines ($\overleftrightarrow{AB} \perp \overleftrightarrow{BD}$)
2 Between a line and a plane ($\overleftrightarrow{AB} \perp m$)

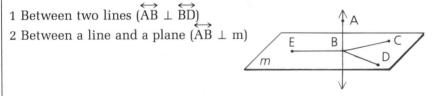

The definition above is a very powerful statement because of the words *every one*. If we are given that $\overleftrightarrow{AB} \perp m$ (in the diagram above), we can draw *three* conclusions:

$$\overleftrightarrow{AB} \perp \overleftrightarrow{BC} \qquad \overleftrightarrow{AB} \perp \overleftrightarrow{BD} \qquad \overleftrightarrow{AB} \perp \overleftrightarrow{BE}$$

The Basic Theorem Concerning the Perpendicularity of a Line and a Plane

You have just seen that a number of conclusions can be drawn from the information that a line is perpendicular to a plane. What about the reverse situation? How can we prove that a given line is perpendicular to a plane? To apply the preceding definition in reverse, we would have to show that the line is perpendicular to *every* line that passes through its foot. Considering the infinite number of lines one by one would be an endless process.

If a line is perpendicular to only one line that lies in the plane and passes through its foot, is it perpendicular to the plane? Or must it be perpendicular to two, three, or four lines in order to be perpendicular to the plane? The following theorem answers that question.

Theorem 48   *If a line is perpendicular to two distinct lines that lie in a plane and that pass through its foot, then it is perpendicular to the plane.*

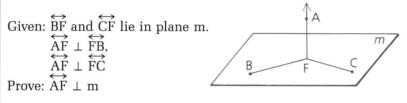

Given: $\overleftrightarrow{BF}$ and $\overleftrightarrow{CF}$ lie in plane m.
$\overleftrightarrow{AF} \perp \overleftrightarrow{FB}$,
$\overleftrightarrow{AF} \perp \overleftrightarrow{FC}$
Prove: $\overleftrightarrow{AF} \perp$ m

The proof is left as a challenge. (You may already have written part of the proof in Section 6.1, problem 16.)

Part Two: Sample Problems

Problem 1   If ∠STR is a right angle, can we conclude that $\overleftrightarrow{ST} \perp$ m? Why or why not?

Solution   No. To be perpendicular to plane m, $\overleftrightarrow{ST}$ must be perpendicular to at least *two* lines that lie in m and pass through T, the foot of $\overleftrightarrow{ST}$.

Problem 2   Given: $\overline{PF} \perp$ k,
$\overline{PG} \cong \overline{PH}$

Prove: ∠G ≅ ∠H

Proof

1 $\overline{PF} \perp$ k	1 Given
2 $\overline{PF} \perp \overline{FG}$, $\overline{PF} \perp \overline{FH}$	2 If a line is ⊥ to a plane, it is ⊥ to every line in the plane that passes through its foot.
3 ∠PFG is a right ∠. ∠PFH is a right ∠.	3 ⊥ lines form right ∠s.
4 $\overline{PG} \cong \overline{PH}$	4 Given
5 $\overline{PF} \cong \overline{PF}$	5 Reflexive Property
6 △PFG ≅ △PFH	6 HL (3, 4, 5)
7 ∠G ≅ ∠H	7 CPCTC

Problem 3   *Given:* B, C, D, *and* E *lie in plane* n.

$\overline{AB} \perp$ n,

$\overleftrightarrow{BE} \perp$ *bis.* $\overline{CD}$

Prove: △ADC *is isosceles.*

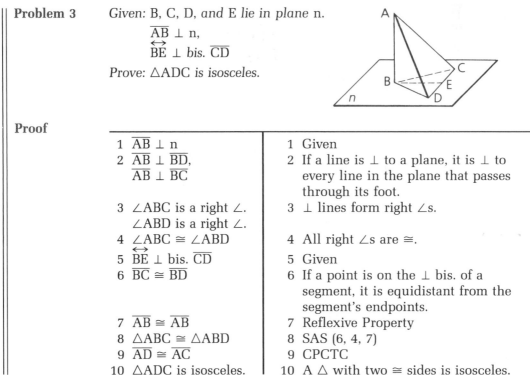

Proof

1 $\overline{AB} \perp$ n	1 Given
2 $\overline{AB} \perp \overline{BD}$, $\overline{AB} \perp \overline{BC}$	2 If a line is $\perp$ to a plane, it is $\perp$ to every line in the plane that passes through its foot.
3 $\angle ABC$ is a right $\angle$. $\angle ABD$ is a right $\angle$.	3 $\perp$ lines form right $\angle$s.
4 $\angle ABC \cong \angle ABD$	4 All right $\angle$s are $\cong$.
5 $\overleftrightarrow{BE} \perp$ bis. $\overline{CD}$	5 Given
6 $\overline{BC} \cong \overline{BD}$	6 If a point is on the $\perp$ bis. of a segment, it is equidistant from the segment's endpoints.
7 $\overline{AB} \cong \overline{AB}$	7 Reflexive Property
8 $\triangle ABC \cong \triangle ABD$	8 SAS (6, 4, 7)
9 $\overline{AD} \cong \overline{AC}$	9 CPCTC
10 $\triangle ADC$ is isosceles.	10 A $\triangle$ with two $\cong$ sides is isosceles.

Part Three: Problem Sets

Problem Set A

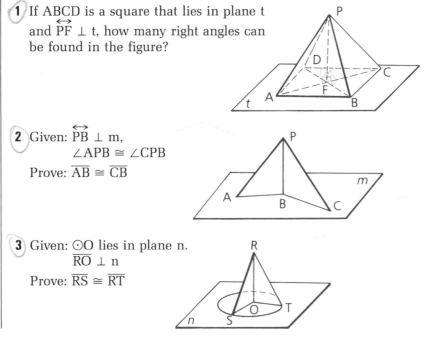

1 If ABCD is a square that lies in plane t and $\overleftrightarrow{PF} \perp$ t, how many right angles can be found in the figure?

2 *Given:* $\overleftrightarrow{PB} \perp$ m,
$\angle APB \cong \angle CPB$
Prove: $\overline{AB} \cong \overline{CB}$

3 *Given:* ⊙O *lies in plane* n.
$\overline{RO} \perp$ n
Prove: $\overline{RS} \cong \overline{RT}$

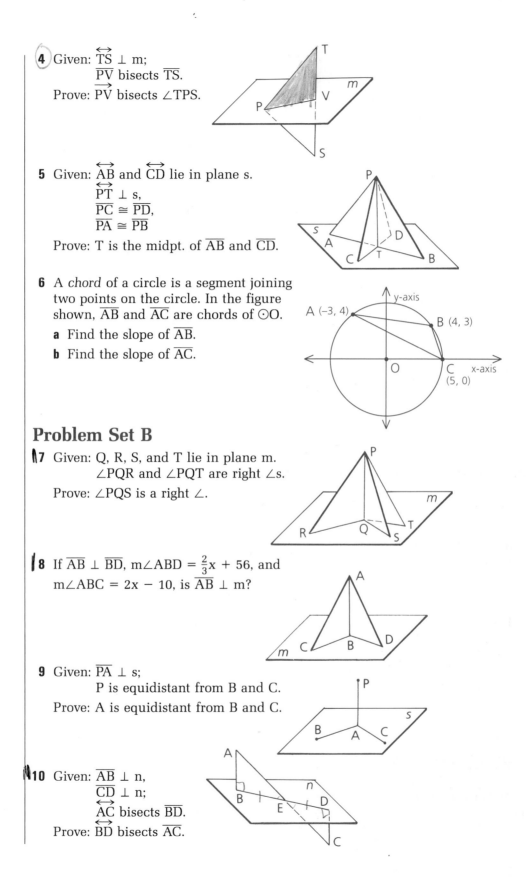

4 Given: $\overleftrightarrow{TS} \perp m$;
  $\overline{PV}$ bisects $\overline{TS}$.
  Prove: $\overrightarrow{PV}$ bisects $\angle TPS$.

5 Given: $\overleftrightarrow{AB}$ and $\overleftrightarrow{CD}$ lie in plane s.
  $\overleftrightarrow{PT} \perp s$,
  $\overline{PC} \cong \overline{PD}$,
  $\overline{PA} \cong \overline{PB}$
  Prove: T is the midpt. of $\overline{AB}$ and $\overline{CD}$.

6 A *chord* of a circle is a segment joining two points on the circle. In the figure shown, $\overline{AB}$ and $\overline{AC}$ are chords of $\odot O$.
  a Find the slope of $\overline{AB}$.
  b Find the slope of $\overline{AC}$.

Problem Set B

7 Given: Q, R, S, and T lie in plane m.
  $\angle PQR$ and $\angle PQT$ are right $\angle$s.
  Prove: $\angle PQS$ is a right $\angle$.

8 If $\overline{AB} \perp \overline{BD}$, m$\angle ABD = \frac{2}{3}x + 56$, and m$\angle ABC = 2x - 10$, is $\overline{AB} \perp m$?

9 Given: $\overline{PA} \perp s$;
  P is equidistant from B and C.
  Prove: A is equidistant from B and C.

10 Given: $\overline{AB} \perp n$,
  $\overline{CD} \perp n$;
  $\overleftrightarrow{AC}$ bisects $\overline{BD}$.
  Prove: $\overleftrightarrow{BD}$ bisects $\overline{AC}$.

Problem Set B, *continued*

11 Given: $\overline{AB} \perp m$;
  equilateral $\triangle DBC$ lies in plane m.
Prove: $\triangle ACD$ is isosceles.

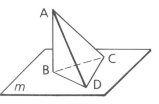

12 Given: $\overleftrightarrow{PB} \perp m$;
  D is the midpt. of $\overline{AC}$.
  $\triangle PAC$ is isosceles, with base $\overline{AC}$.
Prove: $\overleftrightarrow{BD} \perp$ bis. $\overline{AC}$

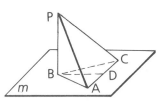

13 From any point on a line perpendicular to a plane, two lines are drawn oblique to the plane. If the foot of the perpendicular is equidistant from the feet of the oblique lines, prove that the oblique segments are congruent.

Problem Set C

14 Given: $\overline{EF} \perp \overline{CF}$,
  $\overline{CE} \cong \overline{DE}$,
  $\angle FCD \cong \angle FDC$
Prove: $\overline{EF} \perp m$

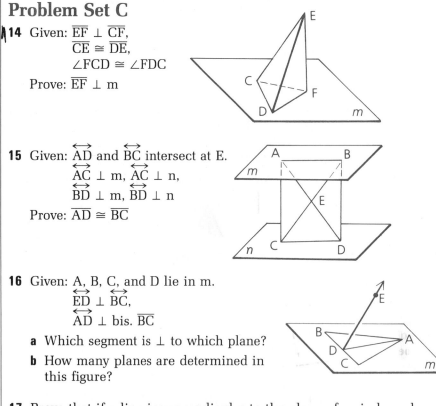

15 Given: $\overleftrightarrow{AD}$ and $\overleftrightarrow{BC}$ intersect at E.
  $\overleftrightarrow{AC} \perp m$, $\overleftrightarrow{AC} \perp n$,
  $\overleftrightarrow{BD} \perp m$, $\overleftrightarrow{BD} \perp n$
Prove: $\overline{AD} \cong \overline{BC}$

16 Given: A, B, C, and D lie in m.
  $\overleftrightarrow{ED} \perp \overleftrightarrow{BC}$,
  $\overleftrightarrow{AD} \perp$ bis. $\overline{BC}$

  a Which segment is $\perp$ to which plane?

  b How many planes are determined in this figure?

17 Prove that if a line is perpendicular to the plane of a circle and passes through the circle's center, any point on the line is equidistant from any two points of the circle.

280 | Chapter 6 Lines and Planes in Space

18 Given: ABCD is an isosceles trapezoid in
plane t.
$\overline{BC} \parallel \overline{AD}$,
$\overline{PF} \perp$ t;
$\overline{PF}$ bisects $\overline{AD}$.

Prove: $\triangle PAB \cong \triangle PDC$

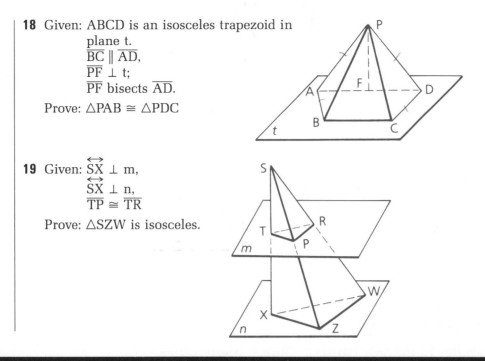

19 Given: $\overleftrightarrow{SX} \perp$ m,
$\overleftrightarrow{SX} \perp$ n,
$\overline{TP} \cong \overline{TR}$

Prove: $\triangle SZW$ is isosceles.

PROBABILITY AND PI
The ubiquity of a geometric constant

Georges-Louis Leclerc, comte de Buffon (1707–1788), one of the most celebrated naturalists of all time and a pioneer in such fields as ecology and paleontology, was also extremely interested in mathematics. Besides translating Isaac Newton's work on the calculus into French, he was among the first to deal with probability in a geometrical fashion.

Imagine a tabletop ruled with equally spaced parallel lines. If you toss a needle at random onto the table, what is the probability that it will land across one of the ruled lines? Buffon found that if the length of the needle is less than or equal to the distance between the lines, this probability can be expressed as $\frac{2\ell}{\pi d}$, where ℓ is the needle's length and d is the distance between the lines.

It is somewhat surprising that the answer to a probability problem that does not involve circles should involve π, the ratio between a cir-

cle's circumference and its diameter. But π has a habit of popping up in unlikely places, even ones entirely unconnected with geometry, as in these amazing infinite sums:

$$\frac{1}{1} - \frac{1}{3} + \frac{1}{5} - \frac{1}{7} + \frac{1}{9} - \frac{1}{11} + \ldots = \frac{\pi}{4}$$

$$\frac{1}{1^2} + \frac{1}{2^2} + \frac{1}{3^2} + \frac{1}{4^2} + \frac{1}{5^2} + \ldots = \frac{\pi^2}{6}$$

BASIC FACTS ABOUT PARALLEL PLANES

Objectives

After studying this section, you will be able to
- Recognize lines parallel to planes, parallel planes, and skew lines
- Use properties relating parallel lines and planes

Part One: Introduction

Lines Parallel to Planes, Parallel Planes, Skew Lines

Since we examined the concept of parallel lines in Chapter 4, it seems logical now to investigate the possibilities of a line being parallel to a plane and of two planes being parallel to each other.

Definition   A line and a plane are parallel if they do not intersect.

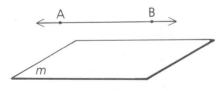

Definition   Two planes are parallel if they do not intersect.

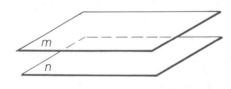

   The diagram at the right shows two lines located in two parallel planes. Although the planes are parallel, the lines are not parallel, because A, B, C, and D do not determine a plane. Such lines are said to be *skew.*

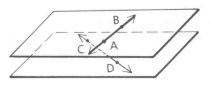

Definition   Two lines are *skew* if they are not coplanar.

You will see that parallelism in space is very similar to parallelism in a plane. There are, however, a few notable differences. For example, there are no skew planes. Planes are either intersecting or parallel.

The following theorem is basic to the understanding of parallelism in space.

Theorem 49   *If a plane intersects two parallel planes, the lines of intersection are parallel.*

Given: m ∥ n;
    s intersects
    m and n in lines
    $\overleftrightarrow{AB}$ and $\overleftrightarrow{CD}$.
Prove: $\overleftrightarrow{AB} \parallel \overleftrightarrow{CD}$

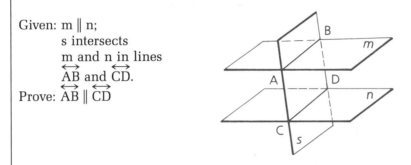

Proof: We know that $\overleftrightarrow{AB}$ and $\overleftrightarrow{CD}$ are coplanar, since they both lie in plane s. Also, they cannot intersect each other, because one lies in plane m and the other lies in plane n—two planes that, being parallel, have no intersection. Thus, $\overleftrightarrow{AB} \parallel \overleftrightarrow{CD}$ by the definition of *parallel lines.*

Properties Relating Parallel Lines and Planes

There are numerous properties relating lines and planes in space, many of which are similar to the theorems about parallel lines you have already seen. We will present some of these properties without their proofs.

Parallelism of Lines and Planes

1 If two planes are perpendicular to the same line, they are parallel to each other.
2 If a line is perpendicular to one of two parallel planes, it is perpendicular to the other plane as well.
3 If two planes are parallel to the same plane, they are parallel to each other.
4 If two lines are perpendicular to the same plane, they are parallel to each other.
5 If a plane is perpendicular to one of two parallel lines, it is perpendicular to the other line as well.

Part Two: Sample Problem

Problem

Given: m ∥ n;
$\overleftrightarrow{AB}$ lies in m.
$\overleftrightarrow{CD}$ lies in n.
$\overleftrightarrow{AC} \parallel \overleftrightarrow{BD}$

Prove: $\overline{AD}$ bisects $\overline{BC}$.

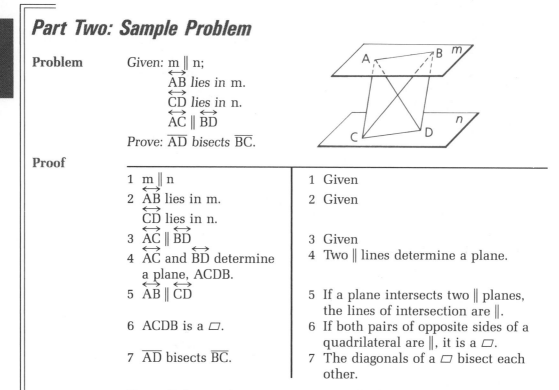

Proof

1 m ∥ n	1 Given
2 $\overleftrightarrow{AB}$ lies in m. $\overleftrightarrow{CD}$ lies in n.	2 Given
3 $\overleftrightarrow{AC} \parallel \overleftrightarrow{BD}$	3 Given
4 $\overleftrightarrow{AC}$ and $\overleftrightarrow{BD}$ determine a plane, ACDB.	4 Two ∥ lines determine a plane.
5 $\overleftrightarrow{AB} \parallel \overleftrightarrow{CD}$	5 If a plane intersects two ∥ planes, the lines of intersection are ∥.
6 ACDB is a ▱.	6 If both pairs of opposite sides of a quadrilateral are ∥, it is a ▱.
7 $\overline{AD}$ bisects $\overline{BC}$.	7 The diagonals of a ▱ bisect each other.

Note Before making statement 6, we had to show that ABDC is a plane figure. See Section 6.1, problem 12, for an example of a four-sided figure that is not a plane figure.

Part Three: Problem Sets

Problem Set A

1 Indicate whether each statement is True (T) or False (F).

a If a plane contains one of two skew lines, it contains the other.

b If a line and a plane never meet, they are parallel.

c If two parallel lines lie in different planes, the planes are parallel.

d If a line is perpendicular to two planes, the planes are parallel.

e If a plane and a line not in the plane are each perpendicular to the same line, then they are parallel to each other.

2 By substituting 3 for x and 4 for y, verify that point D is on the circle that is the graph of the equation $x^2 + y^2 = 25$.

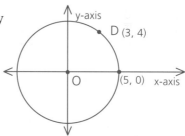

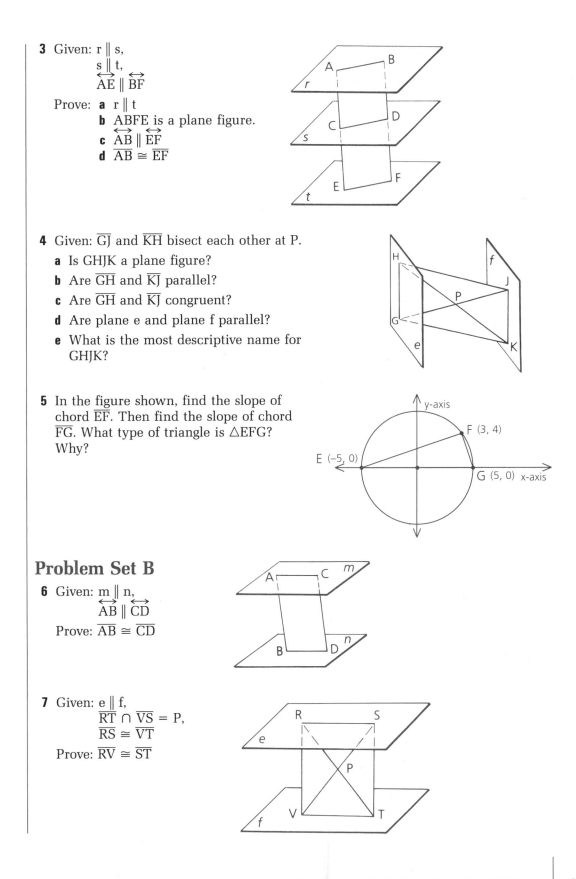

3 Given: $r \parallel s$,
$\qquad s \parallel t$,
$\qquad \overleftrightarrow{AE} \parallel \overleftrightarrow{BF}$

Prove: **a** $r \parallel t$
$\qquad$ **b** ABFE is a plane figure.
$\qquad$ **c** $\overleftrightarrow{AB} \parallel \overleftrightarrow{EF}$
$\qquad$ **d** $\overline{AB} \cong \overline{EF}$

4 Given: $\overline{GJ}$ and $\overline{KH}$ bisect each other at P.

a Is GHJK a plane figure?

b Are $\overline{GH}$ and $\overline{KJ}$ parallel?

c Are $\overline{GH}$ and $\overline{KJ}$ congruent?

d Are plane e and plane f parallel?

e What is the most descriptive name for GHJK?

5 In the figure shown, find the slope of chord $\overline{EF}$. Then find the slope of chord $\overline{FG}$. What type of triangle is $\triangle EFG$? Why?

Problem Set B

6 Given: $m \parallel n$,
$\qquad \overleftrightarrow{AB} \parallel \overleftrightarrow{CD}$
Prove: $\overline{AB} \cong \overline{CD}$

7 Given: $e \parallel f$,
$\qquad \overline{RT} \cap \overline{VS} = P$,
$\qquad \overline{RS} \cong \overline{VT}$
Prove: $\overline{RV} \cong \overline{ST}$

Problem Set B, *continued*

8 If a slide projector is set up so that the slide is parallel to the screen,

   a Prove that a segment on the slide is parallel to its image on the screen

   b Prove that the angles marked 1 and 2 in the diagram are congruent

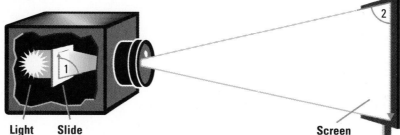

Light   Slide   Screen

9 Given: f ∥ g;
         RTW is an isosceles △,
         with base $\overline{TW}$.

   Prove: △RSV is isosceles.

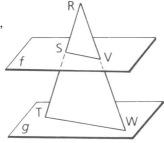

Problem Set C

10 Given: m ∥ n,
          $\overline{BD} \cong \overline{CE}$

    Prove: △ADE is isosceles.

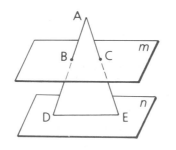

11 Given: p ∥ q,
          $\overleftrightarrow{AD} \parallel \overleftrightarrow{BE}$, $\overleftrightarrow{CF} \parallel \overleftrightarrow{BE}$

    Prove: ∠BAC ≅ ∠EDF

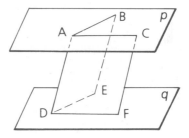

CHAPTER SUMMARY

CONCEPTS AND PROCEDURES

After studying this chapter, you should be able to
- Understand basic concepts relating to planes (6.1)
- Identify four methods of determining a plane (6.1)
- Apply two postulates concerning lines and planes (6.1)
- Recognize when a line is perpendicular to a plane (6.2)
- Apply the basic theorem concerning the perpendicularity of a line and a plane (6.2)
- Recognize lines parallel to planes, parallel planes, and skew lines (6.3)
- Use properties relating parallel lines and planes (6.3)

VOCABULARY

foot (6.1)
skew (6.3)

REVIEW PROBLEMS

Problem Set A

1 Indicate whether each statement is True or False. Be prepared to defend your choice.

   a Two lines must either intersect or be parallel.

   b In a plane, two lines perpendicular to the same line are parallel.

   c In space, two lines perpendicular to the same line are parallel.

   d If a line is perpendicular to a plane, it is perpendicular to every line in the plane.

   e It is possible for two planes to intersect at one point.

   f If a line is perpendicular to a line in a plane, it is perpendicular to the plane.

   g Two lines perpendicular to the same line are parallel.

   h A triangle is a plane figure.

   i A line that is perpendicular to a horizontal line is vertical.

   j Three parallel lines must be coplanar.

   k Every four-sided figure is a plane figure.

2 Given: $\overline{PB} \perp$ m,
      $\overline{PA} \cong \overline{PC}$

   Prove: △ABC is isosceles.

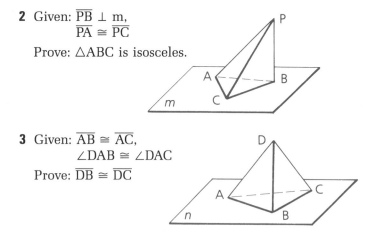

3 Given: $\overline{AB} \cong \overline{AC}$,
      ∠DAB ≅ ∠DAC

   Prove: $\overline{DB} \cong \overline{DC}$

Problem Set B

4 How many planes are determined by a set of four noncoplanar points if no three of the points are collinear?

5 From the top of a flagpole 48 ft in height, two 60-ft ropes reach two points on the ground, each of which is 36 ft from the pole. If the ground is level, is the pole perpendicular to the ground?

6 a At a given point on a line, how many lines can be drawn perpendicular to the given line?

b At a given point on a plane, how many lines can be drawn perpendicular to the plane?

7 Given: $\angle ADC = (x + 88)°$,
$\angle ADE = (74 - 8x)°$,
$\angle BDE = (2x + 94)°$

a Are $\overline{AD}$ and m perpendicular?
b Are $\overline{AD}$ and $\overline{CD}$ perpendicular?
c Are $\overline{AD}$ and $\overline{DE}$ perpendicular?

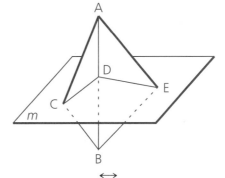

8 ⊙P lies in plane m. If A and B are points on ⊙P and if $\overleftrightarrow{QP} \perp m$, which of the following must be true?

a $\angle APQ \cong \angle BPQ$
b $\overline{AP} \cong \overline{PB}$
c $\overline{QP} \perp \overline{AB}$

9 $\overleftrightarrow{AB}$ is parallel to plane m and perpendicular to plane r. $\overleftrightarrow{CD}$ lies in r. Which of the following must be true?

a $r \perp m$ **c** $\overleftrightarrow{CD} \perp m$ **e** $\overleftrightarrow{AB}$ and $\overleftrightarrow{CD}$ are skew.
b $r \parallel m$ **d** $\overleftrightarrow{AB} \parallel \overleftrightarrow{CD}$

10 Given: △BDC is isosceles, with $\overline{BD} \cong \overline{CD}$.
$\angle ADB \cong \angle ADC$

Prove: △BAC is isosceles.

11 Given: $\overline{BP} \perp \overline{PQ}$,
$\overline{AP} \perp \overline{PQ}$;
A and B are equidistant from P.

Prove: $\angle ABQ \cong \angle BAQ$

12 A line is drawn perpendicular to the plane of a square at the point of intersection of the square's diagonals. Prove that any point on the perpendicular is equidistant from the vertices of the square.

Problem Set C

13 Given: $\overleftrightarrow{PR} \perp m$,
 $\angle PAB \cong \angle PBA$
 Prove: $\angle PAR \cong \angle PBR$

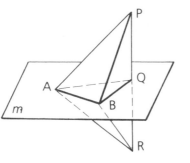

14 Given: $\triangle ABC$ lies in n.
 $\overline{PA} \cong \overline{PC}$,
 $\overline{AB} \cong \overline{BC}$;
 T and S are midpoints.
 Prove: $\overline{RT} \cong \overline{RS}$

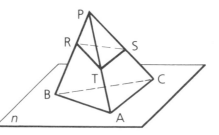

15 Given: $\overline{PC} \cong \overline{QC}$;
 A is the midpoint of $\overline{PQ}$.
 $\angle PCB \cong \angle QCB$
 Prove: $\overleftrightarrow{BA} \perp \overleftrightarrow{PQ}$

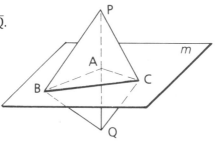

16 Given: m $\parallel$ n,
 p $\parallel$ n;
 $\overline{AD}$ bisects $\overline{BC}$.
 Prove: $\overline{BC}$ bisects $\overline{AD}$.

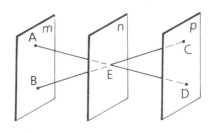

CUMULATIVE REVIEW
CHAPTERS 1–6

Problem Set A

1 Write the most descriptive name for each figure.

    a A four-sided figure in which the diagonals are perpendicular bisectors of each other

    b A four-sided figure in which the diagonals bisect each other

    c A triangle in which there is a hypotenuse

    d A four-sided figure in which the diagonals are congruent and all sides are congruent

2 Find the angle formed by the hands of a clock at 9:30.

3 If one of two supplementary angles is 16° smaller than three times the other, find the measure of the larger.

4 Given: ∠OMP ≅ ∠OPM,
            ∠PMR ≅ ∠MPR
   Prove: $\overleftrightarrow{OR}$ ⊥ bis. $\overline{PM}$

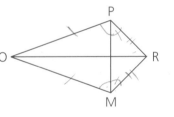

5 Given: TVAX is a rectangle.
   Conclusion: ∠TXV ≅ ∠VAT

6 Two consecutive angles of a parallelogram are in a ratio of 7 to 5. Find the measure of the larger.

7 Given: NPRS is a ▱, with diagonals $\overline{SP}$
        and $\overline{NR}$ intersecting at O.
        $\overline{TO}$ is perpendicular to the plane
        of ▱NPRS.
   Prove: △STP is isosceles.

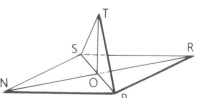

8 Find m∠1.

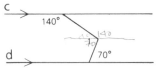

9 Given: ⊙P;
   M is the midpoint of $\overline{AB}$.
   Prove: $\overleftrightarrow{PQ} \perp \overleftrightarrow{AB}$

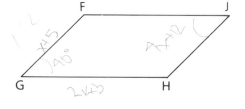

10 Indicate whether each statement is true Always, Sometimes, or Never (A, S, or N).

a If a triangle is obtuse, it is isosceles.

b The bisector of the vertex angle of a scalene triangle is perpendicular to the base.

c If one of the diagonals of a quadrilateral is the perpendicular bisector of the other, the quadrilateral is a kite.

d If A, B, C, and D are noncoplanar, $\overline{AB} \perp \overline{BC}$, and $\overline{AB} \perp \overline{BD}$, then $\overline{AB}$ is perpendicular to the plane determined by B, C, and D.

e Two parallel lines determine a plane.

f Planes that contain two skew lines are parallel.

g Supplements of complementary angles are congruent.

11 Given: FGHJ is a ▱.
   FG = x + 5, GH = 2x + 3,
   ∠G = 40°, ∠J = (4x + 12)°

Find: **a** m∠F
   b The perimeter of FGHJ

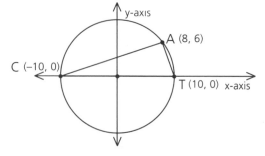

12 In the figure shown, find the slope of chord $\overline{AC}$. Then find the slope of chord $\overline{AT}$. What type of triangle is △CAT? Why?

Problem Set B

13 Given: $\overline{AB} \cong \overline{AC}$,
$\overline{BD} \cong \overline{DC}$

Conclusion: $\angle B \cong \angle C$

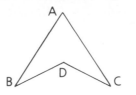

14 Given: $\overline{GH} \cong \overline{GK}$,
$\overline{HM} \cong \overline{KM}$

Conclusion: HMKJ is a kite.

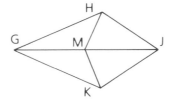

15 Given: ABCD is a $\square$.
$\angle A = (3x + y)°$,
$\angle D = (5x + 10)°$,
$\angle C = (5y + 20)°$

Find: $m\angle B$

16 Given: A, B, C, and D lie in m.
FBCE is a $\square$.
$\overline{FE} \parallel \overline{AD}$,
$\overline{AD} \cong \overline{BC}$

Prove: ABCD is a $\square$.

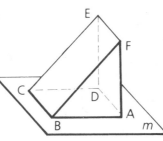

17 Prove: If segments drawn from the midpoint of one side of a triangle perpendicular to the other two sides are congruent, then the triangle is isosceles.

18 The measure of the supplement of an angle exceeds three times the measure of the complement of the angle by 12. Find the measure of half of the supplement.

Problem Set C

19 Given: $\overline{AC} \cong \overline{BD}$,
$\overline{AB} \cong \overline{CD}$

Prove: $\angle B \cong \angle C$

20 Given: $\odot A$ lies in m.
$\overline{PA} \perp m$,
$\overline{PD} \cong \overline{PE}$

Prove: $\overline{BE} \cong \overline{CD}$

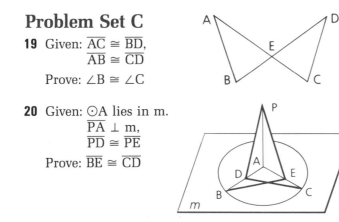

7 POLYGONS

Polygons of various shapes and sizes are interwoven to create this intricate ceiling design of inlaid wood in the Hall of the Blessing, the Alhambra, Granada, Spain.

TRIANGLE APPLICATION THEOREMS

Objective

After studying this section, you will be able to

- Apply theorems about the interior angles, the exterior angles, and the midlines of triangles.

Part One: Introduction

In elementary school you probably learned that the sum of the measures of the angles of a triangle is 180°. This property of triangles has a number of important applications.

Theorem   ***The sum of the measures of the three angles of a triangle is 180.***

Given: △ABC

Prove: m∠A + m∠B + m∠C = 180

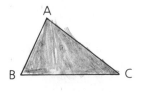

Proof: According to the Parallel Postulate, there exists exactly one line through point A parallel to $\overleftrightarrow{BC}$, so the figure at the right can be drawn.

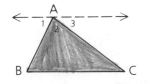

Because of the straight angle, we know that
∠1 + ∠2 + ∠3 = 180°. Since ∠1 ≅ ∠B and ∠3 ≅ ∠C (by ∥ lines ⇒ alt. int. ∠s ≅), we may substitute to obtain ∠B + ∠2 + ∠C = 180°. Hence, m∠A + m∠B + m∠C = 180.

Before proving the next theorem, we need to explain what an *exterior angle* of a polygon is. In each of the figures below, ∠1 is an exterior angle of a polygon.

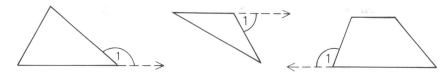

You can see that an exterior angle of a polygon is formed by extending one of the sides of the polygon. The following definition puts this idea in a form that is much more useful in proofs and problems.

Definition   An *exterior angle* of a polygon is an angle that is adjacent to and supplementary to an interior angle of the polygon.

The next theorem applies only to triangles.

Theorem 51   *The measure of an exterior angle of a triangle is equal to the sum of the measures of the remote interior angles.*

Given: △DEF, with exterior angle 1 at F

Prove: m∠1 = m∠D + m∠E

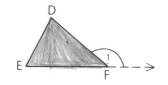

Do you see how Theorem 50 and the definition of *exterior angle* are the keys to a proof of Theorem 51?

The following theorem could have been presented in the chapter on parallelograms, but you may find it more useful now.

Theorem 52   *A segment joining the midpoints of two sides of a triangle is parallel to the third side, and its length is one-half the length of the third side. (Midline Theorem)*

Given: H is a midpoint.
        M is a midpoint.

Prove: **a** $\overline{HM} \parallel \overline{JK}$

        b $HM = \frac{1}{2}(JK)$

Proof: Extend $\overleftrightarrow{HM}$ through M to a point P so that $\overline{MP} \cong \overline{HM}$. P is now established, so P and K determine $\overleftrightarrow{PK}$.

We know that $\overline{GM} \cong \overline{KM}$ (by the definition of midpoint) and that $\angle GMH \cong \angle KMP$ (vertical $\angle$s are $\cong$). Thus, $\triangle GMH \cong \triangle KMP$ by SAS.

Since $\angle G = \angle PKM$ by CPCTC, $\overleftrightarrow{PK} \parallel \overleftrightarrow{HJ}$ by alt. int. $\angle$s $\Rightarrow \parallel$ lines. Also, $\overline{GH} \cong \overline{PK}$ by CPCTC, and $\overline{GH} \cong \overline{HJ}$ (by the definition of *midpoint*). By transitivity, then, $\overline{PK} \cong \overline{HJ}$.

Two sides, $\overline{PK}$ and $\overline{HJ}$, are parallel and congruent, so PKJH is a parallelogram. Therefore, $\overleftrightarrow{HP} \parallel \overleftrightarrow{JK}$.

Opposite sides of a parallelogram are congruent, so HP = JK.

Also, since we made MP = HM, HM = $\frac{1}{2}$(HP) and, by substitution, HM = $\frac{1}{2}$(JK).

Part Two: Sample Problems

Problem 1

Given: Diagram as marked

Find: x, y, and z

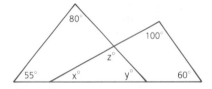

Solution

Since the sum of the measures of the angles of a triangle is 180,

x + 100 + 60 = 180	55 + 80 + y = 180	x + y + z = 180
x + 160 = 180	135 + y = 180	20 + 45 + z = 180
x = 20	y = 45	z = 115

Substitution

Substitution

Problem 2

The measures of the three angles of a triangle are in the ratio 3:4:5. Find the measure of the largest angle.

Solution

Let the measures of the three angles be 3x, 4x, and 5x. Since the sum of the measures of the three angles of a triangle is 180,

$$3x + 4x + 5x = 180$$
$$12x = 180$$
$$x = 15$$

Therefore, the measure of the largest angle is 5(15), or 75.

Problem 3   *If one of the angles of a triangle is 80°, find the measure of the angle formed by the bisectors of the other two angles.*

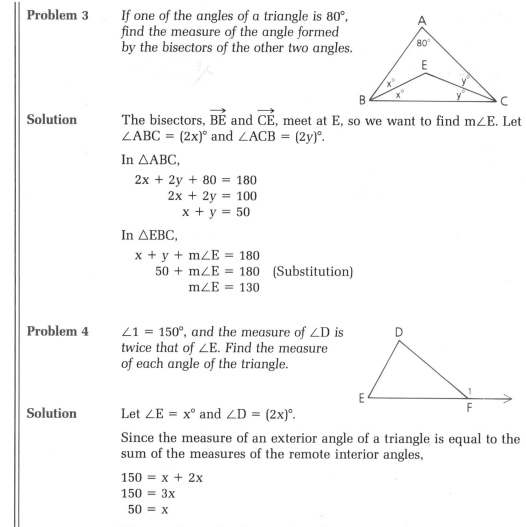

Solution   The bisectors, $\overrightarrow{BE}$ and $\overrightarrow{CE}$, meet at E, so we want to find m∠E. Let ∠ABC = $(2x)°$ and ∠ACB = $(2y)°$.

In △ABC,

$$2x + 2y + 80 = 180$$
$$2x + 2y = 100$$
$$x + y = 50$$

In △EBC,

$$x + y + m∠E = 180$$
$$50 + m∠E = 180 \quad \text{(Substitution)}$$
$$m∠E = 130$$

Problem 4   *∠1 = 150°, and the measure of ∠D is twice that of ∠E. Find the measure of each angle of the triangle.*

Solution   Let ∠E = $x°$ and ∠D = $(2x)°$.

Since the measure of an exterior angle of a triangle is equal to the sum of the measures of the remote interior angles,

$$150 = x + 2x$$
$$150 = 3x$$
$$50 = x$$

Hence, ∠E = 50°, ∠D = 100°, and ∠DFE = 30°.

Part Three: Problem Sets

Problem Set A

1 Given: Diagram as marked
   Find: m∠B

2 Given: ∠1 = 130°,
        ∠7 = 70°
   Find the measures of ∠2, ∠3, ∠4, ∠5, and ∠6.

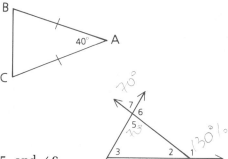

3 Given: ∠CAB = 80°,
　　　　∠CBA = 60°,
　　　　$\overline{AE}$ and $\overline{BD}$ are altitudes.
　Find: m∠C and m∠AFB

4 In the diagram as marked,
　if m∠G = 50, find m∠M.
　(Hint: See sample problem 3.)

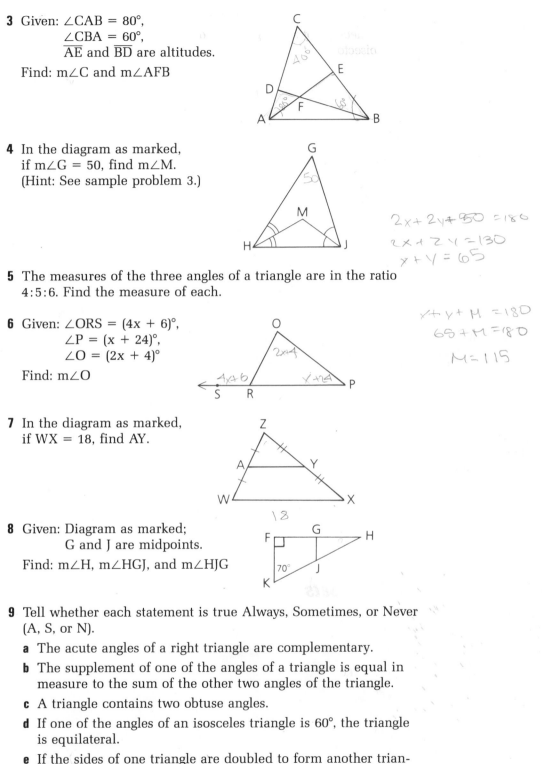

2x + 2y + 50 = 180
2x + 2y = 130
x + y = 65

5 The measures of the three angles of a triangle are in the ratio
　4:5:6. Find the measure of each.

x + y + M = 180
65 + M = 180
M = 115

6 Given: ∠ORS = (4x + 6)°,
　　　　∠P = (x + 24)°,
　　　　∠O = (2x + 4)°
　Find: m∠O

7 In the diagram as marked,
　if WX = 18, find AY.

8 Given: Diagram as marked;
　　　　G and J are midpoints.
　Find: m∠H, m∠HGJ, and m∠HJG

9 Tell whether each statement is true Always, Sometimes, or Never
　(A, S, or N).

　a The acute angles of a right triangle are complementary.

　b The supplement of one of the angles of a triangle is equal in
　　measure to the sum of the other two angles of the triangle.

　c A triangle contains two obtuse angles.

　d If one of the angles of an isosceles triangle is 60°, the triangle
　　is equilateral.

　e If the sides of one triangle are doubled to form another trian-
　　gle, each angle of the second triangle is twice as large as the
　　corresponding angle of the first triangle.

Problem Set A, *continued*

10 The vertex angle of an isosceles triangle is twice as large as one of the base angles. Find the measure of the vertex angle.

11 Given: ∠P = 10°;
$\overrightarrow{RO}$ bisects ∠MRP.
Find: m∠ORP and m∠MOR

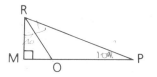

Problem Set B

12 In △DEF, the sum of the measures of ∠D and ∠E is 110. The sum of the measures of ∠E and ∠F is 150. Find the sum of the measures of ∠D and ∠F.

13 Prove, in paragraph form, that the acute angles of a right triangle are complementary.

14 Prove, in paragraph form, that if a right triangle is isosceles, it must be a 45°-45°-90° triangle.

15 The measures of two angles of a triangle are in the ratio 2:3. If the third angle is 4 degrees larger than the larger of the other two angles, find the measure of an exterior angle at the third vertex.

16 Given: ∠A = 30°, $\overline{AB} \cong \overline{AC}$;
$\overrightarrow{CD}$ bisects ∠ACB.
$\overrightarrow{BD}$ is one of the trisectors of ∠ABC.
Find: m∠D

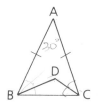

17 Given: EFGH is a rectangle.
FH = 20;
J, K, M, and O are midpoints.

a Find the perimeter of JKMO.

b What is the most descriptive name for JKMO?

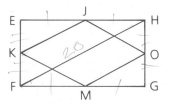

18 Given: ∠PST = (x + 3y)°,
∠P = 45°, ∠R = (2y)°,
∠PSR = (5x)°
Find: m∠PST

Problem Set C

19 Prove that the midpoint of the hypotenuse of a right triangle is equidistant from all three vertices. (Hint: See the method used to prove the Midline Theorem, page 296.)

20 Prove that if the midpoints of a quadrilateral are joined in order, the figure formed is a parallelogram.

21 Given: $\overline{AB} \cong \overline{AC}$,
$\overline{AE} \cong \overline{DE} \cong \overline{DB} \cong \overline{BC}$

Find: $m\angle A$

22 Given: $\angle E = 70°$;
$\overrightarrow{JH}$ and $\overrightarrow{FH}$ bisect the exterior angles of $\triangle JEF$ at J and F.

a Find $m\angle H$.

b Can you find a formula that expresses $m\angle H$ in terms of $m\angle E$?

23 Show that $a + e_1 + c_1 = d + e_2 + b_2$.

TWO PROOF–ORIENTED TRIANGLE THEOREMS

Objective

After studying this section, you will be able to
- Apply the No-Choice Theorem and the AAS theorem

Part One: Introduction

We shall refer to the following theorem as the No-Choice Theorem, since it shows that two angles "have no choice" but to be congruent.

Theorem 53   *If two angles of one triangle are congruent to two angles of a second triangle, then the third angles are congruent. (No-Choice Theorem)*

Given: $\angle A \cong \angle D$,
       $\angle B \cong \angle E$
Conclusion: $\angle C \cong \angle F$

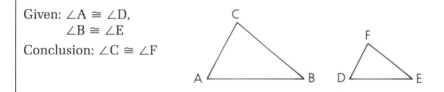

Proof: Since the sum of the angles in each triangle is 180°, the sums may be set equal. If we then apply the Subtraction Property, we see that $\angle C$ and $\angle F$ must be congruent.

Note   The two triangles need not be congruent for us to apply the No-Choice Theorem.

Theorem 54   *If there exists a correspondence between the vertices of two triangles such that two angles and a nonincluded side of one are congruent to the corresponding parts of the other, then the triangles are congruent. (AAS)*

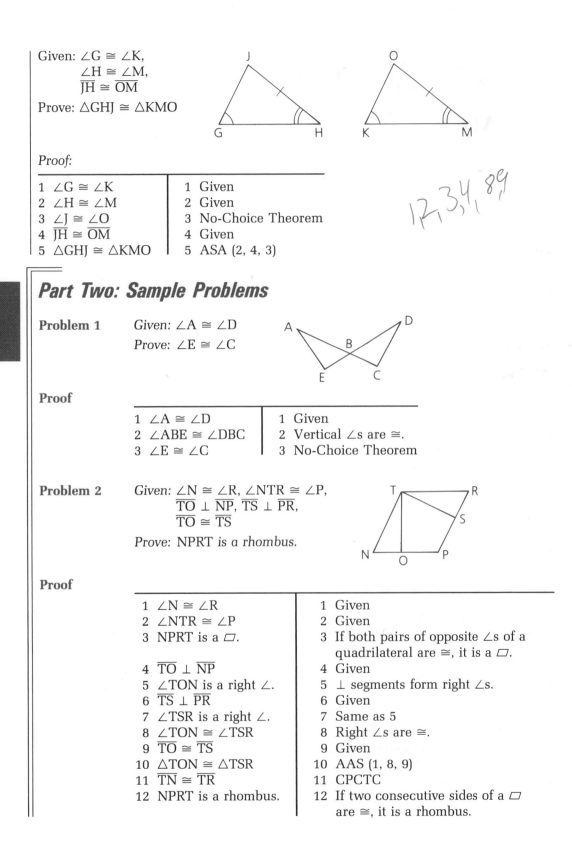

Given: ∠G ≅ ∠K,
       ∠H ≅ ∠M,
       $\overline{JH} ≅ \overline{OM}$
Prove: △GHJ ≅ △KMO

Proof:

1 ∠G ≅ ∠K	1 Given
2 ∠H ≅ ∠M	2 Given
3 ∠J ≅ ∠O	3 No-Choice Theorem
4 $\overline{JH} ≅ \overline{OM}$	4 Given
5 △GHJ ≅ △KMO	5 ASA (2, 4, 3)

1, 3, 4, 8 9

Part Two: Sample Problems

Problem 1   Given: ∠A ≅ ∠D
                 Prove: ∠E ≅ ∠C

Proof

1 ∠A ≅ ∠D	1 Given
2 ∠ABE ≅ ∠DBC	2 Vertical ∠s are ≅.
3 ∠E ≅ ∠C	3 No-Choice Theorem

Problem 2   Given: ∠N ≅ ∠R, ∠NTR ≅ ∠P,
                 $\overline{TO} ⊥ \overline{NP}$, $\overline{TS} ⊥ \overline{PR}$,
                 $\overline{TO} ≅ \overline{TS}$

                 Prove: NPRT *is a rhombus.*

Proof

1 ∠N ≅ ∠R	1 Given
2 ∠NTR ≅ ∠P	2 Given
3 NPRT is a ▱.	3 If both pairs of opposite ∠s of a quadrilateral are ≅, it is a ▱.
4 $\overline{TO} ⊥ \overline{NP}$	4 Given
5 ∠TON is a right ∠.	5 ⊥ segments form right ∠s.
6 $\overline{TS} ⊥ \overline{PR}$	6 Given
7 ∠TSR is a right ∠.	7 Same as 5
8 ∠TON ≅ ∠TSR	8 Right ∠s are ≅.
9 $\overline{TO} ≅ \overline{TS}$	9 Given
10 △TON ≅ △TSR	10 AAS (1, 8, 9)
11 $\overline{TN} ≅ \overline{TR}$	11 CPCTC
12 NPRT is a rhombus.	12 If two consecutive sides of a ▱ are ≅, it is a rhombus.

Part Three: Problem Sets

Problem Set A

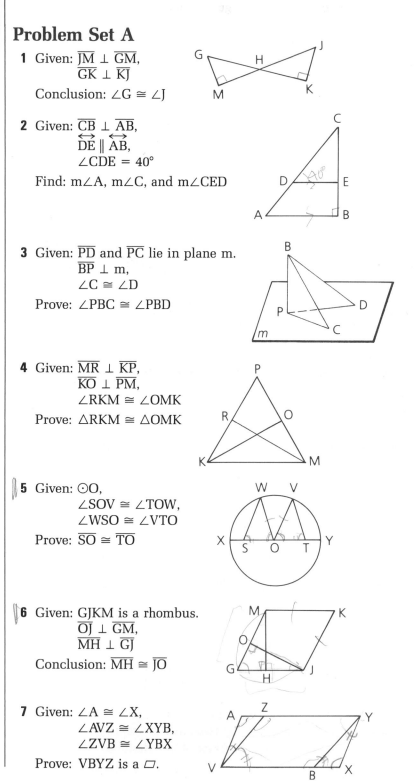

1 Given: $\overline{JM} \perp \overline{GM}$,
$\overline{GK} \perp \overline{KJ}$

Conclusion: $\angle G \cong \angle J$

2 Given: $\overline{CB} \perp \overline{AB}$,
$\overleftrightarrow{DE} \parallel \overleftrightarrow{AB}$,
$\angle CDE = 40°$

Find: m$\angle$A, m$\angle$C, and m$\angle$CED

3 Given: $\overline{PD}$ and $\overline{PC}$ lie in plane m.
$\overline{BP} \perp$ m,
$\angle C \cong \angle D$

Prove: $\angle PBC \cong \angle PBD$

4 Given: $\overline{MR} \perp \overline{KP}$,
$\overline{KO} \perp \overline{PM}$,
$\angle RKM \cong \angle OMK$

Prove: $\triangle RKM \cong \triangle OMK$

5 Given: $\odot O$,
$\angle SOV \cong \angle TOW$,
$\angle WSO \cong \angle VTO$

Prove: $\overline{SO} \cong \overline{TO}$

6 Given: GJKM is a rhombus.
$\overline{OJ} \perp \overline{GM}$,
$\overline{MH} \perp \overline{GJ}$

Conclusion: $\overline{MH} \cong \overline{JO}$

7 Given: $\angle A \cong \angle X$,
$\angle AVZ \cong \angle XYB$,
$\angle ZVB \cong \angle YBX$

Prove: VBYZ is a $\square$.

8 The measures of the angles of a triangle are in the ratio $3:4:8$. Find the measure of the supplement of the largest angle.

9 Given: Triangle as marked

    Find: m∠1

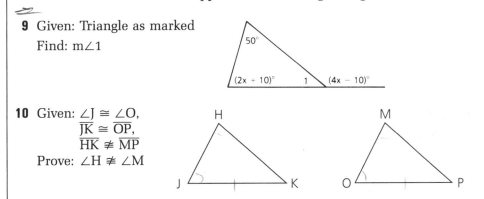

10 Given: ∠J ≅ ∠O,
         $\overline{JK} \cong \overline{OP}$,
         $\overline{HK} \not\cong \overline{MP}$
    Prove: ∠H ≇ ∠M

Problem Set B

11 Prove that the altitude to the base of an isosceles triangle is also a median to the base.

12 Prove that segments drawn from the midpoint of the base of an isosceles triangle and perpendicular to the legs are congruent if they terminate at the legs.

13 Given: OHJM is an isosceles trapezoid, with bases $\overline{HJ}$ and $\overline{OM}$.
        ∠HPJ ≅ ∠JKH

    Prove: **a** △HRJ is isosceles.

         b $\overline{HP} \cong \overline{JK}$

         c R is equidistant from O and M.

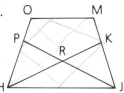

14 Given: $\overleftrightarrow{AC} \parallel \overleftrightarrow{XY}$,
         $\overleftrightarrow{AB} \parallel \overleftrightarrow{CY}$,
         ∠ZAC ≅ ∠XAB

    Prove: ∠X ≅ ∠Z

15 Prove the HL postulate.

    Given: $\overline{TW} \cong \overline{GR}$,
         $\overline{WE} \cong \overline{AR}$;
         ∠E and ∠A are rt. ∠s.

    Conclusion: △WET ≅ △RAG

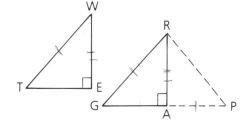

    (Hint: Extend $\overrightarrow{GA}$ to P so that $\overline{AP} \cong \overline{ET}$. Use SAS to prove that △WET ≅ △RAP. Prove that △RGP is isosceles. Use AAS to prove that △RAG ≅ △RAP. What does it mean that two triangles are congruent to △RAP?)

Problem Set B, *continued*

16 a If the perimeter of △DEF is 145, find the perimeter of △GHJ.

b Can you state a generalization based on your solution to part **a**?

Problem Set C

17 Give the most descriptive name to the figure formed by connecting consecutive midpoints of each of the following figures. Be prepared to defend your answer in each case.

a Rhombus   **c** Square   **e** Parallelogram   **g** Isosceles trapezoid

b Kite   **d** Rectangle   **f** Quadrilateral

18 Given: $\overline{EF}$ is the median to $\overline{AC}$.
         ∠CBD ≅ ∠ADB;
         $\overline{CD}$ is the base of isosceles △FDC.

Prove: ABCD is a rectangle.

19 Given: P, T, and R lie in plane f.
         ∠TNR ≅ ∠TSR, $\overline{NS} \perp$ f,
         ∠TNP ≅ ∠TSP

Conclusion: △NPR ≅ △SPR

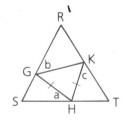

Problem Set D

20 Given: △RST is equiangular.
         $\overline{GH} \cong \overline{KH}$

Solve for *a* in terms of *b* and *c*.

EUCLIDEAN DOG

FORMULAS INVOLVING POLYGONS

1-12 / No Nine

Objective

After studying this section, you will be able to

■ Use some important formulas that apply to polygons

Part One: Introduction

A polygon with three sides can be called a 3-gon. Similarly, a polygon with seven sides can be called a 7-gon. Most of the polygons you will encounter have special names, like those given in the following chart.

No. of Sides (or Vertices)	Polygon	No. of Sides (or Vertices)	Polygon
3	Triangle	8	Octagon
4	Quadrilateral	9	Nonagon
5	Pentagon	10	Decagon
6	Hexagon	12	Dodecagon
7	Heptagon	15	Pentadecagon
		n	n-gon

What is the sum of the measures of the five angles in the figure? To answer that question, start at any vertex and draw diagonals. Three triangles are formed. By adding the measures of the angles of the three triangles, we can obtain the sum of the measures of the five original angles. In this case, the sum of the measures of the angles of pentagon ABCDE is 3(180), or 540.

We follow a similar process with the next figure.

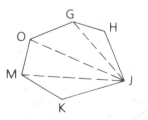

Since there are four triangles, the sum of the measures of the angles of figure GHJKMO is 4(180), or 720.

These two examples suggest the following theorem, which we present without formal proof.

Theorem 55   *The sum S_i of the measures of the angles of a polygon with n sides is given by the formula $S_i = (n - 2)180$.*

On occasion, we may refer to the angles of a polygon as the *interior angles* of the polygon.

In the following diagram, we have formed an exterior angle at each vertex by extending one of the sides of the polygon.

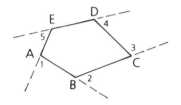

At vertex A, $m\angle 1 + m\angle EAB = 180$. In a similar manner, we can add each exterior angle to its adjacent interior angle, getting a sum of 180 at each vertex. Since there are five vertices, the total is 5(180), or 900.

According to Theorem 55, the sum of the measures of the angles of polygon ABCDE is 540. Since $900 - 540 = 360$, we may conclude that $m\angle 1 + m\angle 2 + m\angle 3 + m\angle 4 + m\angle 5 = 360$.

What is the sum of the measures of exterior angles 1, 2, 3, 4, 5, and 6 in this
figure?

Again, the sum of the interior and the
exterior angle is 180 at each of the six vertices, for a total measure of 6(180), or 1080.
Moreover, according to Theorem 55, the sum
of the measures of the angles of polygon
GHJKMO is 720.

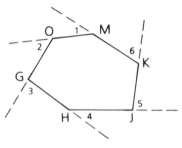

Because $1080 - 720 = 360$, we may conclude that in this figure, too, $m\angle 1 + m\angle 2 + m\angle 3 + m\angle 4 + m\angle 5 + m\angle 6 = 360$.

These two examples suggest the next theorem, which we present without formal proof.

Theorem 56   *If one exterior angle is taken at each vertex, the sum S_e of the measures of the exterior angles of a polygon is given by the formula $S_e = 360$.*

The following theorem is presented without proof. Problem 21 in Problem Set C asks you to explain this formula.

Theorem 57   *The number d of diagonals that can be drawn in a polygon of n sides is given by the formula*

$$d = \frac{n(n - 3)}{2}$$

Part Two: Sample Problems

Problem 1   Find the sum of the measures of the angles of the figure to the right.

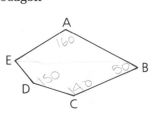

Solution   The figure has five sides and five vertices.
The formula is $S_i = (n - 2)180$.
By substituting 5 for n, we find that
$S_i = (5 - 2)180$, or 540.

Problem 2   Find the number of diagonals that can be drawn in a pentadecagon.

Solution   We use the formula in Theorem 57.

$$d = \frac{n(n - 3)}{2}$$
$$= \frac{15(15 - 3)}{2}$$
$$= 90$$

Problem 3   What is the name of a polygon if the sum of the measures of its angles is 1080?

Solution   We use the formula in Theorem 55.

$$S_i = (n - 2)180$$
$$1080 = (n - 2)180$$
$$1080 = 180n - 360$$
$$1440 = 180n$$
$$8 = n$$

Since it has eight sides, the polygon is an octagon.

Part Three: Problem Sets

Problem Set A

1 Find the sum of the measures of the angles of

a A quadrilateral   **c** An octagon   **e** A 93-gon

b A heptagon 900 **d** A dodecagon

2 Given: m∠A = 160, m∠B = 50,
m∠C = 140, m∠D = 150

Find: m∠E

3 How many diagonals can be drawn in each figure below?

Problem Set A, *continued*

4 Given: m∠F = 110,
m∠G = 80,
m∠H = 74

Find: m∠1

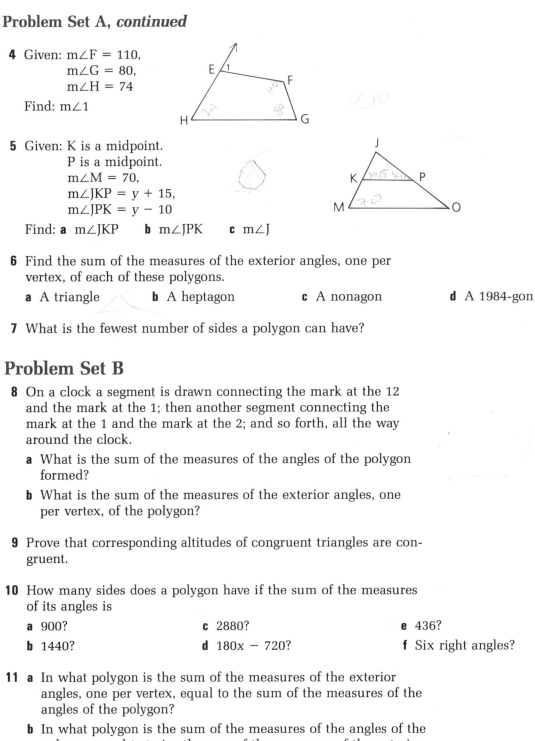

5 Given: K is a midpoint.
P is a midpoint.
m∠M = 70,
m∠JKP = y + 15,
m∠JPK = y − 10

Find: **a** m∠JKP　　**b** m∠JPK　　**c** m∠J

6 Find the sum of the measures of the exterior angles, one per vertex, of each of these polygons.

a A triangle　　**b** A heptagon　　**c** A nonagon　　**d** A 1984-gon

7 What is the fewest number of sides a polygon can have?

Problem Set B

8 On a clock a segment is drawn connecting the mark at the 12 and the mark at the 1; then another segment connecting the mark at the 1 and the mark at the 2; and so forth, all the way around the clock.

a What is the sum of the measures of the angles of the polygon formed?

b What is the sum of the measures of the exterior angles, one per vertex, of the polygon?

9 Prove that corresponding altitudes of congruent triangles are congruent.

10 How many sides does a polygon have if the sum of the measures of its angles is

a 900?　　　　　　**c** 2880?　　　　　　**e** 436?

b 1440?　　　　　　**d** 180x − 720?　　　　**f** Six right angles?

11 a In what polygon is the sum of the measures of the exterior angles, one per vertex, equal to the sum of the measures of the angles of the polygon?

b In what polygon is the sum of the measures of the angles of the polygon equal to twice the sum of the measures of the exterior angles, one per vertex?

12 If the sum of the measures of the angles of a polygon is increased by 900, how many sides will have been added to the polygon?

13 What are the names of the polygons that contain the following numbers of diagonals?

    a 14   **b** 35   **c** 209

14 Tell whether each statement is true Always, Sometimes, or Never (A, S, or N).

    a As the number of sides of a polygon increases, the number of exterior angles increases.

    b As the number of sides of a polygon increases, the sum of the measures of the exterior angles increases.

    c The sum of the lengths of the diagonals of a polygon is greater than the perimeter of the polygon.

    d The sum of the measures of the angles of a polygon formed by joining consecutive midpoints of a polygon's sides is equal to the sum of the measures of the angles of the original polygon.

15 Find the restrictions on x.

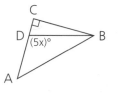

16 If AB > BC, find the restrictions on point B's

    a x-coordinate

    b y-coordinate

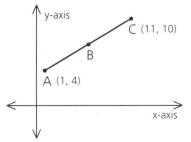

17 Find the area of a rectangle with vertices at $(-5, 2)$, $(3, 2)$, $(3, 8)$, and $(-5, 8)$.

18 Using the diagram, write a coordinate proof of the Midline Theorem.

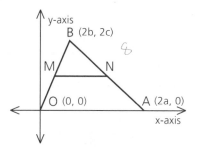

Problem Set B, *continued*

19 If three of the following four statements are chosen at random as given information, what is the probability that the fourth statement can be proved?

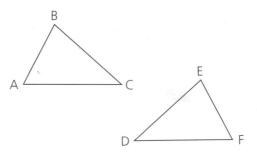

a ∠C ≅ ∠D   **c** ∠A ≅ ∠F
b $\overline{AC}$ ≅ $\overline{DF}$ **d** $\overline{AB}$ ≅ $\overline{EF}$

Problem Set C

20 In Chapter 5, we noted that one of the ways to show that a quadrilateral is a parallelogram is to prove that both pairs of opposite angles are congruent. Without the information presented in this chapter, the proof of that method would be extremely long and involved. Use your new knowledge to prove it now.

Given: ∠B ≅ ∠D,
        ∠A ≅ ∠C

Prove: ABCD is a ▱. (Hint: Let m∠B = x and m∠C = y.)

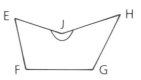

21 Explain why each of the three ingredients in the formula of Theorem 57 (the *n*, the *n* − 3, and the 2) is needed.

22 We have stated that in this text the word *polygon* will mean a *convex* polygon and that angles greater than 180° will not be considered. Ignore those rules for this problem.

a Consider the nonconvex polygon EFGHJ, whose interior angle at J is greater than 180°. Can you demonstrate that the sum of the measures of the angles of this nonconvex polygon is 540?

b Can you demonstrate that the sum of the measures of the angles of the nonconvex octagon at the right is 1080?

c Is the sum of the measures of the angles of a nonconvex polygon of *n* sides (*n* − 2)180?

d Is the sum of the measures of the exterior angles, one per vertex, of a nonconvex polygon equal to 360? Explain.

23 Seven of the angles of a decagon have measures whose sum is 1220. Of the remaining three angles, exactly two are complementary and exactly two are supplementary. Find the measures of these three angles.

Problem Set D

24 Find the set of polygons in which the number of diagonals is greater than the sum of the measures of the angles.

PRECISE ANGLES PAY OFF
John C. Buchholz cuts a solid with 58 facets

Make a mistake drawing a 34° angle with your pencil and protractor, and the consequences will probably be minimal. Make a similar mistake cutting a facet on a diamond, and the consequences may be disastrous. A flawless, beautifully colored 1 carat (200 milligram or $\frac{1}{142}$ ounce) diamond may be worth $25,000, according to Denver, Colorado, diamond cutter John C. Buchholz. That is the size Buchholz typically works on, and an error in cutting a diamond cannot be corrected.

Diamond is the hardest, and one of the rarest, naturally occurring substances. Diamond crystals often occur as octahedra. To turn a rough diamond into a brilliant gem requires precise and painstaking work. Buchholz describes the cutting of the fifty-eight *facets* (faces or planes) that characterize the familiar *round brilliant-cut* diamond: "Since only diamond can cut diamond, I use a 3000-rpm wheel impregnated with diamond powder. As I cut, I aim for maximum brilliance. I use gauges to cut the first

eight facets: four in the crown at $32\frac{1}{2}°$ and four in the pavilion at $40\frac{3}{4}°$ The other fifty facets I cut by eye." As he works on the tiny facets he must keep his eye on the overall proportions of the diamond. For example, the table, or top facet, must be uniform and centered, with a diameter 53 percent to 57 percent of the stone's diameter.

Buchholz was born in Iola, Wisconsin. Following his discharge from the army he undertook a three-year apprenticeship at a diamond-cutting school in Gardnerville, Nevada. Says Buchholz: "American cutters are the most skilled and the best paid in the world today." Unlike many cutters, he has refused to specialize, remaining proficient in all facets of cutting. He takes as his motto the words of Michelangelo: "Only human genius enlivens a rough stone into a masterpiece."

Describe the plane figures that form the facets of a round brilliant-cut diamond.

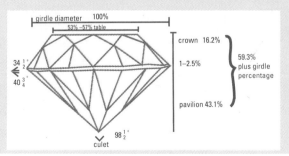

7.4 | REGULAR POLYGONS

Objectives

After studying this section, you will be able to
- Recognize regular polygons
- Use a formula to find the measure of an exterior angle of an equiangular polygon

Part One: Introduction

Regular Polygons

The figures below are examples of **regular polygons**.

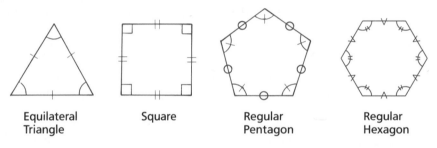

| Equilateral Triangle | Square | Regular Pentagon | Regular Hexagon |

Definition A **regular polygon** is a polygon that is both equilateral and equiangular.

A Special Formula for Equiangular Polygons

Can you find m∠1 in the equiangular pentagon below?

In Section 7.3, you learned that the sum of the measures of the exterior angles, one per vertex, of any polygon is 360. Since each of the five exterior angles has the same measure, we can find m∠1 by dividing 360 by 5.

$$m\angle 1 = \frac{360}{5} = 72$$

This result suggests the next theorem, which we present without formal proof.

314 Chapter 7 Polygons

Theorem 58   **The measure E of each exterior angle of an equiangular polygon of n sides is given by the formula**

$$E = \frac{360}{n}$$

You will see several applications of this theorem in the problems
that follow.

Part Two: Sample Problems

Problem 1   *How many degrees are there in each exterior angle of an equiangular heptagon?*

Solution   Using $E = \frac{360}{n}$, we find that $E = \frac{360}{7}$, or $51\frac{3}{7}$.

Problem 2   *If each exterior angle of a polygon is 18°, how many sides does the polygon have?*

Solution   We can use the formula $E = \frac{360}{n}$.

$$18 = \frac{360}{n}$$
$$18n = 360$$
$$n = 20$$

1-12, NO 8-9

Problem 3   *If each angle of a polygon is 108°, how many sides does the polygon have?*

Solution   First, we find the measure of an exterior angle. Since an angle of a polygon and its adjacent exterior angle are supplementary, an exterior angle of this polygon has a measure of 180 − 108, or 72. Now we can substitute 72 for E in the formula $E = \frac{360}{n}$.

$$72 = \frac{360}{n}$$
$$72n = 360$$
$$n = 5$$

Problem 4   *Find the measure of each angle of a regular octagon.*

Solution   We use the formula $E = \frac{360}{n}$, finding that $E = \frac{360}{8}$, or 45. Thus, the measure of each interior angle is 180 − 45, or 135.

Problem 5   *Find the measure of each exterior angle of an equilateral quadrilateral.*

Solution   An equilateral quadrilateral is not necessarily equiangular, so there is no answer.

Part Three: Problem Sets

Problem Set A

1 Find the measure of an exterior angle of each of the following equiangular polygons.

    a A triangle   **c** An octagon   **e** A 23-gon

    b A quadrilateral   **d** A pentadecagon

2 Find the measure of an angle of each of the following equiangular polygons.

    a A pentagon   **c** A nonagon   **e** A 21-gon

    b A hexagon   **d** A dodecagon

3 Find the number of sides an equiangular polygon has if each of its exterior angles is

    a 60°   **b** 40°   **c** 36°   **d** 2°   **e** $7\frac{1}{2}°$

4 Find the number of sides an equiangular polygon has if each of its angles is

    a 144°   **b** 120°   **c** 156°   **d** 162°   **e** $172\frac{4}{5}°$

5 Given: PENTA is a regular pentagon.

    Prove: △PNT is isosceles.

6 In the stop sign shown, is △NTE scalene, isosceles, equilateral, or undetermined?

7 In an equiangular polygon, the measure of each exterior angle is 25% of the measure of each interior angle. What is the name of the polygon?

Problem Set B

8 a Prove that the perpendicular bisector of a side of a regular pentagon passes through the opposite vertex.

    b Can you generalize about the perpendicular bisectors of the sides of regular polygons?

9 Given: $\overline{AB} \cong \overline{AD}$,
$\overline{FC} \perp \overline{BD}$

Conclusion: $\triangle AEF$ is isosceles.

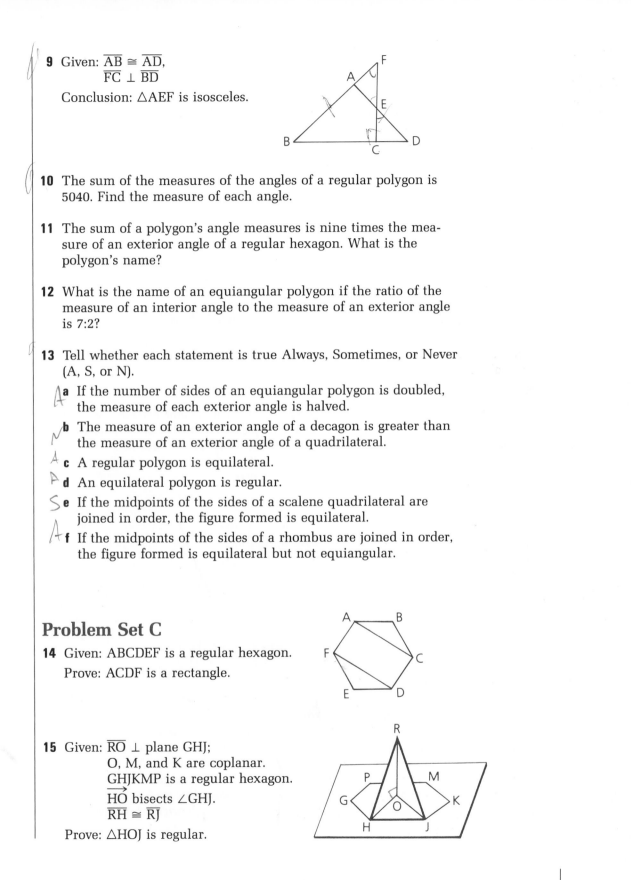

10 The sum of the measures of the angles of a regular polygon is 5040. Find the measure of each angle.

11 The sum of a polygon's angle measures is nine times the measure of an exterior angle of a regular hexagon. What is the polygon's name?

12 What is the name of an equiangular polygon if the ratio of the measure of an interior angle to the measure of an exterior angle is 7:2?

13 Tell whether each statement is true Always, Sometimes, or Never (A, S, or N).

a If the number of sides of an equiangular polygon is doubled, the measure of each exterior angle is halved.

b The measure of an exterior angle of a decagon is greater than the measure of an exterior angle of a quadrilateral.

c A regular polygon is equilateral.

d An equilateral polygon is regular.

e If the midpoints of the sides of a scalene quadrilateral are joined in order, the figure formed is equilateral.

f If the midpoints of the sides of a rhombus are joined in order, the figure formed is equilateral but not equiangular.

Problem Set C

14 Given: ABCDEF is a regular hexagon.
Prove: ACDF is a rectangle.

15 Given: $\overline{RO} \perp$ plane GHJ;
O, M, and K are coplanar.
GHJKMP is a regular hexagon.
$\overrightarrow{HO}$ bisects $\angle GHJ$.
$\overline{RH} \cong \overline{RJ}$
Prove: $\triangle HOJ$ is regular.

Problem Set C, *continued*

16 Given: 105 < m∠T < 145;
an equiangular polygon
can be drawn with ∠T
as one of the angles.

Find: The set of possible values of m∠V

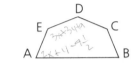

17 We shall call the figure to the right a
regular semioctagon. (What do you think
that means?)

If m∠E = 3x + 3y + 9 and m∠A = 2x + y − 4½,
what are the values of x and y?

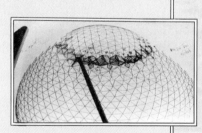

POLYGONS IN THE NORTH COUNTRY
The Vegreville Egg

Polygons can be tiled in three dimensions as well as two. One result: an aluminum sculpture of an egg—31 feet long, three and a half stories high, weighing 2.5 tons, and decorated in the intricate Ukrainian style—in the town of Vegreville, Alberta, Canada.

To make a long story short, the town had got a grant to build a huge Ukrainian-style egg to celebrate the centennial of the Royal Canadian Mounted Police. The project, however, was more than most architects and engineers were willing to take on. Their reluctance arose from the fact that the surface of an egg cannot be defined mathematically.

Fortunately, true to the spirit of the Mounties, there was one computer science professor from Utah who would not give up until he had cracked the problem and who finally hatched a plan. After much computer analysis of the structures of various birds' eggs, he designed an egg that could be built using very thin aluminum tiles.

He tiled the egg using more than two thousand congruent equilateral triangles and more than five hundred hexagons in the shapes of stars, as shown in the illustration. The tiles, ranging from $\frac{1}{16}$ inch to $\frac{1}{8}$ inch thick, are joined at angles ranging from less than 1° near the middle of the egg to about 7° at its tip. They are held together by an internal structure consisting of a central shaft from which radiate spokes that connect it with the egg's "shell."

How can flat tiles be used to simulate a curved surface such as an egg's? Are the stars equilateral hexagons? Are they regular hexagons? Why or why not?

CHAPTER SUMMARY

CONCEPTS AND PROCEDURES

After studying this chapter, you should be able to
- Apply theorems about the interior angles, the exterior angles, and the midlines of triangles. (7.1)
- Apply the No-Choice Theorem and the AAS theorem (7.2)
- Use some important formulas that apply to polygons (7.3)
- Recognize regular polygons (7.4)
- Use a formula to find the measure of an exterior angle of an equiangular polygon (7.4)

VOCABULARY

decagon (7.3)
dodecagon (7.3)
exterior angle (7.1)
heptagon (7.3)
hexagon (7.3)
interior angle (7.3)

octagon (7.3)
pentadecagon (7.3)
pentagon (7.3)
nonagon (7.3)
regular polygon (7.4)

REVIEW PROBLEMS

Problem Set A

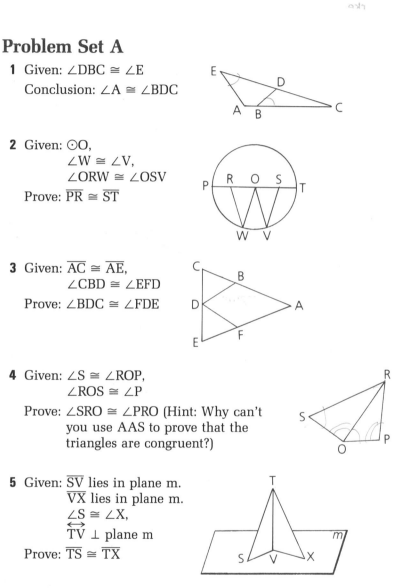

1 Given: ∠DBC ≅ ∠E
   Conclusion: ∠A ≅ ∠BDC

2 Given: ⊙O,
   ∠W ≅ ∠V,
   ∠ORW ≅ ∠OSV
   Prove: $\overline{PR}$ ≅ $\overline{ST}$

3 Given: $\overline{AC}$ ≅ $\overline{AE}$,
   ∠CBD ≅ ∠EFD
   Prove: ∠BDC ≅ ∠FDE

4 Given: ∠S ≅ ∠ROP,
   ∠ROS ≅ ∠P
   Prove: ∠SRO ≅ ∠PRO (Hint: Why can't
   you use AAS to prove that the
   triangles are congruent?)

5 Given: $\overline{SV}$ lies in plane m.
   $\overline{VX}$ lies in plane m.
   ∠S ≅ ∠X,
   $\overleftrightarrow{TV}$ ⊥ plane m
   Prove: $\overline{TS}$ ≅ $\overline{TX}$

6 The measures of three of the angles of a quadrilateral are 40, 70, and 130. What is the measure of the fourth angle?

7 The measures of the angles of a triangle are in the ratio 1:2:3. Find half the measure of the largest angle.

8 Given: Diagram as marked
Find: m∠1 and m∠2

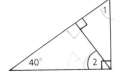

9 Given: Diagram as marked
Find: m∠YZA

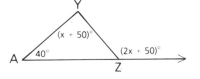

10 Given: C is the midpt. of $\overline{BD}$.
E is the midpt. of $\overline{BF}$.
DF = 12,
m∠D = 80, m∠B = 60
Find: CE, m∠BCE, and m∠BEC

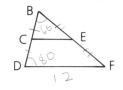

11 Find m∠3 in the diagram as marked.

$= \dfrac{360}{n}$

12 If the measure of an exterior angle of a regular polygon is 15, how many sides does the polygon have?

13 If a polygon has 33 sides, what is

a The sum of the measures of the angles of the polygon?

b The sum of the measures of the exterior angles, one per vertex, of the polygon?

14 The sum of the measures of the angles of a polygon is 1620. Find the number of sides of the polygon.

15 Find the number of diagonals that can be drawn in a pentadecagon.

16 The measure of an exterior angle of an equiangular polygon is twice that of an interior angle. What is the name of the polygon?

Problem Set B

17 Prove that any two diagonals of a regular pentagon are congruent. Are any two diagonals congruent in any regular polygon?

18 The measure of one of the angles of a right triangle is five times the measure of another angle of the triangle. What are the possible values of the measure of the second largest angle?

19 Given: △ABC is isosceles, with base $\overline{BC}$.
$\overrightarrow{BE}$ bisects ∠ABC.
$\overrightarrow{CE}$ bisects ∠FCD.
∠A = 50°

Find: **a** m∠ABF   **b** m∠BCE   **c** m∠E

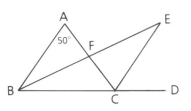

20 Given: $\overline{AB} \cong \overline{AC}$,
∠DBC ≅ ∠DCA,
m∠A = 50

Find: m∠BDC

21 Tell whether each statement is true Always, Sometimes, or Never (A, S, or N).

a An equiangular triangle is isosceles.

b The number of diagonals in a polygon is the same as the number of sides.

c An exterior angle of a triangle is larger in measure than any angle of a triangle.

d One of the base angles of an isosceles triangle has a measure greater than that of one of the exterior angles of the triangle.

22 The sum of the measures of five of the angles of an "octagon" is 540. What conclusion can you draw about the "octagon"?

23 An *arithmetic progression* is a sequence of terms in which the difference between any two consecutive terms is always the same. (For example, 1, 5, 9, 13 is an arithmetic progression because the difference between any two consecutive terms is 4.) Do the numbers of diagonals in a triangle, a quadrilateral, a pentagon, and a hexagon form an arithmetic progression?

24 The measure of an angle of an equiangular polygon exceeds four times the measure of one of the polygon's exterior angles by 30. What is the name of the polygon?

Problem Set C

25 Given: $\overline{BC} \cong \overline{FE}$,
   $\angle C \cong \angle E$
   Prove: $\triangle ABF$ is isosceles.

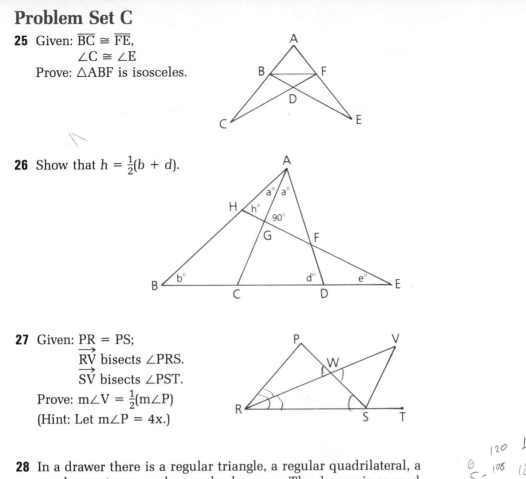

26 Show that $h = \frac{1}{2}(b + d)$.

27 Given: $PR = PS$;
   $\overrightarrow{RV}$ bisects $\angle PRS$.
   $\overrightarrow{SV}$ bisects $\angle PST$.
   Prove: $m\angle V = \frac{1}{2}(m\angle P)$
   (Hint: Let $m\angle P = 4x$.)

28 In a drawer there is a regular triangle, a regular quadrilateral, a regular pentagon, and a regular hexagon. The drawer is opened, and an angle from one of the polygons is selected at random. What is the probability that the measure of the angle is an integral multiple of 30?

29 A square has vertices $A = (-4, 0)$, $B = (-4, 4)$, $C = (0, 4)$, and $O = (0, 0)$. When the square is rotated $90°$ counterclockwise about the origin, points A, B, and C are rotated to points E, F, and G respectively. Find the area of the polygon with vertices at A, B, F, and G.

Problem Set D

30 Show that the number of diagonals in a polygon is never the same as the sum of the measures of the exterior angles, one per vertex, of the polygon.

SIMILAR POLYGONS

L inda MacDonald used similar
polygons to create a geometric design
in her quilt, *Titus Canyon*.

8.1 | RATIO and PROPORTION

Objectives

After studying this section, you will be able to
- Recognize and work with ratios
- Recognize and work with proportions
- Apply the product and ratio theorems
- Calculate geometric means

Part One: Introduction

Ratio

You may recall the following definition from your previous mathematics studies.

Definition   A *ratio* is a quotient of two numbers.

The ratio of 5 meters to 3 meters can be written in any of the following ways:

$$\frac{5}{3} \qquad 5:3 \qquad 5 \text{ to } 3 \qquad 5 \div 3$$

Notice that the first number, 5, is the numerator and the second number, 3, is the denominator.

Unless otherwise specified, a ratio is given in lowest terms. For example, the ratio of 15 to 6, or $\frac{15}{6}$, when reduced to lowest terms is $\frac{5}{2}$.

The slope of a line is the ratio of the *rise* between any two points on the line to the *run* between the two points.

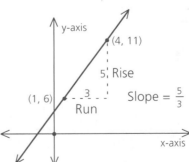

On a map, the scale gives the ratio of the map distance to the actual distance. The distance from A-ville to B-ville on the map is 2.5 centimeters. The scale indicates that 1 centimeter represents 30 miles. We can conclude that the distance from A-ville to B-ville is 2.5(30), or 75, miles.

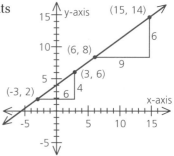

A-ville

B-ville

Scale: 1 cm : 30 miles

cm 0   1   2

mi 0   30   60

Proportion

Proportions are related to ratios.

Definition   A **proportion** is an equation stating that two or more ratios are equal. Here are three examples of proportions.

$$\frac{1}{2} = \frac{5}{10} \qquad 5:15 = 15:45 \qquad \frac{4}{6} = \frac{10}{15} = \frac{x}{y} = \frac{2}{3}$$

Most proportions you encounter, however, will contain only two ratios and will be written in one of the following equivalent forms.

$$\frac{a}{b} = \frac{c}{d} \qquad a:b = c:d$$

In both of these forms,

a is called the first term c is called the third term

b is called the second term d is called the fourth term

The equation $y = \frac{2}{3}x + 4$ relates the x- and y-coordinates of points on the graph of the equation.

If $x = -3$, then $y = \frac{2}{3}(-3) + 4 = 2$, so $(-3, 2)$ is on the line.

If $x = 3$, then $y = \frac{2}{3}(3) + 4 = 6$, so $(3, 6)$ is on the line.

If $x = 6$, then $y = 8$, so $(6, 8)$ is on the line.

If $x = 15$, then $y = 14$, so $(15, 14)$ is on the line.

The slope of the segment joining $(-3, 2)$ and $(3, 6)$ is the ratio

$$\frac{6 - 2}{3 - (-3)} = \frac{4}{6}$$

The slope of the segment joining $(6, 8)$ and $(15, 14)$ is the ratio

$$\frac{14 - 8}{15 - 6} = \frac{6}{9}$$

No matter what pair of points on the line we choose, the slope should be the same. The proportion $\frac{4}{6} = \frac{6}{9}$ is a true statement, since both ratios reduce to $\frac{2}{3}$.

The Product and Ratio Theorems

In a proportion containing four terms,
- The first and fourth terms are called the *extremes*
- The second and third terms are called the *means*

Theorem 59   *In a proportion, the product of the means is equal to the product of the extremes. (Means-Extremes Products Theorem)*

This theorem allows us to "multiply out" a proportion.

$$\text{If } \frac{a}{b} = \frac{c}{d}, \text{ then } ad = bc.$$

Theorem 60   *If the product of a pair of nonzero numbers is equal to the product of another pair of nonzero numbers, then either pair of numbers may be made the extremes, and the other pair the means, of a proportion. (Means-Extremes Ratio Theorem)*

This theorem is harder to state than to use. Given that $pq = rs$, we can create proportions such as $\frac{p}{r} = \frac{s}{q}$, $\frac{p}{s} = \frac{r}{q}$, and $\frac{r}{p} = \frac{q}{s}$. All these proportions are equivalent forms, since multiplying them out yields equivalent equations.

The Geometric Mean

In a *mean proportion,* the means are the same.

$$\frac{1}{4} = \frac{4}{16} \qquad \frac{a}{x} = \frac{x}{r}$$

Definition   If the means in a proportion are equal, either mean is called a *geometric mean,* or *mean proportional,* between the extremes.

In the first example above, 4 is a geometric mean between 1 and 16. What is the mean proportional (geometric mean) in the second example?

In other mathematics classes, you have probably had to calculate averages. The average of two numbers is another kind of mean between the numbers, called the **arithmetic mean**.

Example   *Find the geometric and arithmetic means between 3 and 27.*

Arithmetic Mean:

$$\text{Average} = \frac{3 + 27}{2}$$
$$= 15$$

Geometric Mean:

Write a proportion, using 3 and 27 as the extremes and x as both means.

$$\frac{3}{x} = \frac{x}{27}$$
$$x^2 = 81$$
$$x = \pm 9$$

The arithmetic mean is 15. There are two possible values of the geometric mean. The geometric mean is either 9 or -9.

Part Two: Sample Problems

Problem 1   If $\frac{3}{x} = \frac{7}{14}$, solve for x.

Solution

$$\frac{3}{x} = \frac{7}{14}$$
$$\frac{3}{x} = \frac{1}{2} \qquad \tfrac{7}{14} \text{ reduces to } \tfrac{1}{2}.$$
$$1 \cdot x = 3 \cdot 2 \qquad \text{Means-Extremes Products Theorem}$$
$$x = 6$$

Problem 2   Find the fourth term (sometimes called the fourth proportional) of a proportion if the first three terms are 2, 3, and 4.

Solution

$$\frac{2}{3} = \frac{4}{x}$$
$$\frac{2}{x} = 3 \cdot 4$$
$$x = 6$$

Problem 3   Find the mean proportional(s) between 4 and 16.

Solution

$$\frac{4}{x} = \frac{x}{16}$$
$$x \cdot x = 4 \cdot 16$$
$$x^2 = 64$$
$$x = \pm 8 \text{ (Two answers)}$$

Note   There are two mean proportionals (or geometric means) between the numbers. In certain geometry problems, we reject one of these algebraic answers. For example, a segment cannot have a length of -8.

Problem 4 If $3x = 4y$, *find the ratio of x to y.*

Solution Use Theorem 60 to write a proportion, making x and 3 the extremes and y and 4 the means.

$$3x = 4y$$
$$\frac{x}{y} = \frac{4}{3}$$

Problem 5 Is $\frac{x}{y} = \frac{a}{b}$ equivalent to $\frac{x-2y}{y} = \frac{a-2b}{b}$?

Solution

$$\frac{x}{y} = \frac{a}{b} \qquad \frac{x-2y}{y} = \frac{a-2b}{b}$$
$$xb = ya \qquad (x-2y)b = (a-2b)y$$
$$xb = ay \qquad xb - 2by = ay - 2by$$
$$xb = ay$$

The answer is yes. The Means-Extremes Products Theorem reveals that the two proportions are equivalent forms.

Problem 6 *Show that* $\frac{a}{b} = \frac{c}{d}$ *and* $\frac{a+b}{b} = \frac{c+d}{d}$ *are equivalent proportions.*

Solution Start with the first proportion and add 1 to each side.

$$\frac{a}{b} = \frac{c}{d}$$

$$\frac{a}{b} + 1 = \frac{c}{d} + 1$$

$$\frac{a}{b} + \frac{b}{b} = \frac{c}{d} + \frac{d}{d} \qquad \text{Substitute fractions equal to 1.}$$

$$\frac{a+b}{b} = \frac{c+d}{d}$$

Part Three: Problem Sets

Problem Set A

1 a In $\frac{3}{4} = \frac{9}{12}$, what is the third term?
  b Name the means and the extremes of the proportion in part **a**.

2 Is $\frac{p}{q} = \frac{r}{s}$ equivalent to $\frac{r}{p} = \frac{s}{q}$?

3 Solve each proportion for x.

  a $\frac{3}{x} = \frac{12}{16}$ **b** $\frac{x}{18} = \frac{3}{7}$ **c** $\frac{7}{x-4} = \frac{3}{5}$

4 Find the fourth proportional for each set of three terms.
  a 1, 2, 3 **b** $\frac{1}{2}$, 3, 4 **c** a, b, 5

Problem Set A, *continued*

5 a Use the coordinates of points A and B to find the slope of $\overleftrightarrow{AC}$.

b Use the coordinates of points B and C to find the slope of $\overleftrightarrow{AC}$.

c Should your answers in parts **a** and **b** be the same?

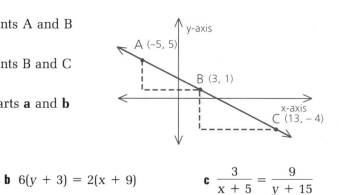

6 Find the ratio of x to y if

a $2x = 3y$

b $6(y + 3) = 2(x + 9)$

c $\dfrac{3}{x + 5} = \dfrac{9}{y + 15}$

7 What is the ratio of the number of diagonals in a pentagon to the measure of each exterior angle of a regular decagon?

8 Given two squares with sides 5 and 7,

a What is the ratio of their perimeters?

b What is the ratio of their areas?

9 If the ratio of the measures of a pair of sides of a parallelogram is 2:3 and the ratio of the measures of the diagonals is 1:1, what is the most descriptive name of the parallelogram?

10 a What is the ratio of AB to BC?

b What is AB:AC?

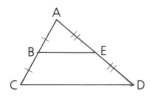

11 Find the geometric mean(s) between each pair of extremes.

a 4 and 25

b 3 and 5

c a and b

12 A 60-m steel pole is cut into two parts in the ratio of 11 to 4. How much longer is the longer part than the shorter?

13 The ratio of the measures of the sides of a quadrilateral is 2:3:5:7. If the figure's perimeter is 68, find the length of each side.

Problem Set B

14 Find the positive arithmetic and geometric means between each pair of numbers. Note which mean is greater in each case.

a 8 and 50

b 6 and 12

15 If 4 is a mean proportional between 6 and a number, what is the number?

Copy the number line and locate the
arithmetic mean and the positive geometric mean between the two numbers.

17 The ratio of the measure of the supplement of an angle to the
measure of the complement of the angle is 5:2. Find the measure
of the supplement.

18 Is $\frac{x-5}{4} = \frac{c}{3}$ equivalent to $\frac{x-1}{4} = \frac{c+3}{3}$? (Hint: Use what was
proved in sample problem 6 as a theorem.)

19 If $x(a + b) = y(c + d)$, find the ratio of x to y.

20 If $ex - fy = gx + hy$, find the ratio of x to y.

21 Reduce the ratio $\frac{x^2 - 7x + 12}{x^2 - 16}$ to lowest terms.

22 The length of a model plane is $10\frac{1}{2}$ in. The scale of the model is
1:72.

    a What is the length of the real plane?

    b If the real plane has a wingspan of $43\frac{1}{2}$ ft, find the wingspan of
the model.

    c If another model of the same plane has a scale of 1:48, find the
length of that model.

Problem Set

23 Show that no polygon exists in which the ratio of the number of
diagonals to the sum of the measures of the polygon's angles is 1
to 18.

24 If $\frac{a}{b} = \frac{c}{d}$, show that $\frac{a-b}{b} = \frac{c-d}{d}$.

25 In the figure, P is said to *divide* $\overline{AB}$
externally into two segments, $\overline{AP}$ and $\overline{PB}$.
If AB = 30 and $\frac{AP}{AB} = \frac{5}{2}$, find AP.

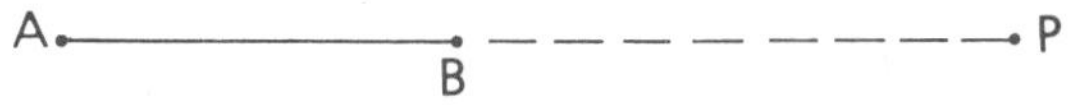

26 The equation $y = \frac{5}{2}x - 3$ relates the x- and y-coordinates of
points on a line. Find the points on the line whose x-coordinates
are 6 and 10. Then use these points to find the slope of the line.

Problem Set D

27 If two ratios are formed at random from the four numbers 1, 2,
4, and 8, what is the probability that the ratios are equal?

8.2 | SIMILARITY

Objective

After studying this section, you will be able to
- Identify the characteristics of similar figures

Part One: Introduction

Below are three pairs of *similar* figures—figures that have the same shape but not necessarily the same size.

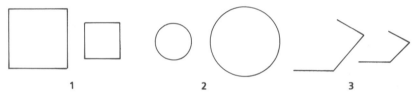

You need only look around you to find examples of similar figures. Whenever you use a pair of binoculars, look at a photograph, or read a map, you are dealing with similar figures. A knowledge of similarity and proportion is also useful in the building of model planes and automobiles and in the construction of electric-train layouts.

One way in which a figure similar to another figure can be produced is called *dilation*, or enlargement. The opposite of dilation, called *reduction*, also produces similar figures.

Example 1   *A pinhole camera produces a reduced image of a candle. The size of the image is proportional to the distance of the candle from the camera. Given the measurements shown in the diagram, find the height of the candle.*

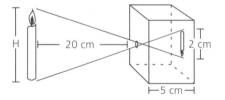

To find the height, we write and solve a proportion.

$$\frac{H}{2} = \frac{20}{5}$$

$$H = 8$$

The candle is 8 cm tall.

In this book, except for a few problems, we shall limit our study of similar figures to similar polygons.

Definition   *Similar polygons* are polygons in which

1 The ratios of the measures of corresponding sides are equal

2 Corresponding angles are congruent

The triangles below are similar triangles. They have the same shape, although they differ in size.

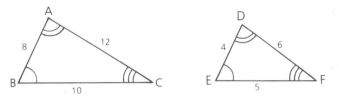

We write △ABC ~ △DEF ("triangle ABC is similar to triangle DEF"), which means that A corresponds to D, B corresponds to E, and C corresponds to F.

As you can see,

1 The ratios of the measures of all pairs of corresponding sides are equal

$$\frac{AB}{DE} = \frac{2}{1} \qquad \frac{AC}{DF} = \frac{2}{1} \qquad \frac{BC}{EF} = \frac{2}{1}$$

2 Each pair of corresponding angles are congruent

$$\angle B \cong \angle E \qquad \angle A \cong \angle D \qquad \angle C \cong \angle F$$

Example 2   △MCN *is a dilation of* △MED, *with an enlargement ratio of 2:1 for each pair of corresponding sides. Find the lengths of the sides of* △MCN.

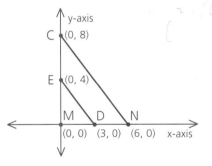

Since each side of △MCN is twice as long as the corresponding side of △MED, MC = 8 and MN = 6. To find the length of $\overline{CN}$, we can use the fact that in any right triangle with legs a and b and hypotenuse c, $a^2 + b^2 = c^2$.

$$(CN)^2 = 8^2 + 6^2$$
$$= 100$$
$$CN = 10$$

Example 3   Given: ABCD ~ EFGH, *with measures as shown.*

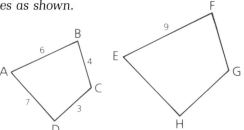

a *Find FG, GH, and EH.*

Since the quadrilaterals are similar, the ratios of the measures of their corresponding sides are equal. We begin with one ratio of measures of corresponding sides, preferably one we can simplify.

Thus, $\frac{AB}{EF} = \frac{6}{9} = \frac{2}{3}$.

$$\frac{AB}{EF} = \frac{BC}{FG} \qquad \frac{AB}{EF} = \frac{CD}{GH} \qquad AB{:}EF = AD{:}EH$$

$$\frac{2}{3} = \frac{4}{FG} \qquad\qquad \frac{2}{3} = \frac{3}{GH} \qquad\qquad 2{:}3 = 7{:}EH$$

$$2(FG) = 12 \qquad 2(GH) = 9 \qquad 2(EH) = 21$$
$$FG = 6 \qquad\quad GH = 4\tfrac{1}{2} \qquad\quad EH = 10\tfrac{1}{2}$$

b *Find the ratio of the perimeter of ABCD to the perimeter of EFGH.*

Perimeter of ABCD = 6 + 4 + 3 + 7 = 20

Perimeter of EFGH = 9 + 6 + $4\tfrac{1}{2}$ + $10\tfrac{1}{2}$ = 30

$$\frac{P_{ABCD}}{P_{EFGH}} = \frac{20}{30} = \frac{2}{3}$$

Notice that in the preceding example the ratio of perimeters was equal to the ratio of sides. This result suggests the following theorem.

Theorem 61   ***The ratio of the perimeters of two similar polygons equals the ratio of any pair of corresponding sides.***

Part Two: Sample Problems

Problem 1   Given that △JHK ~ △POM, ∠H = 90°, ∠J = 40°, m∠M = x + 5, *and* m∠O = $\frac{1}{2}$y, *find the values of x and y.*

Solution   First draw triangles JHK and POM so that ∠H = 90°, ∠J = 40°, and the corresponding angles are congruent.

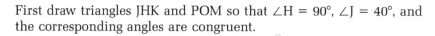

$$\left.\begin{array}{l}\angle J \text{ comp. } \angle K \\ \angle J = 40°\end{array}\right\} \Rightarrow$$

$$\angle K = 50°$$

$$\angle K \cong \angle M \qquad \angle H \cong \angle O$$

$$50 = x + 5 \qquad 90 = \tfrac{1}{2}y$$

$$45 = x \qquad 180 = y$$

Problem 2

Given: $\triangle BAT \sim \triangle DOT$,
OT = 15, BT = 12, TD = 9

Find the value of x (AO).

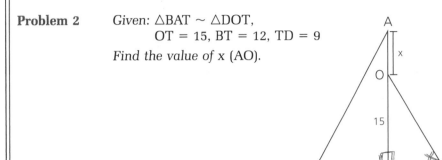

Solution

Since $\triangle BAT \sim \triangle DOT$, the ratios of the measures of corresponding sides are equal.

$$\frac{AT}{OT} = \frac{BT}{TD}$$

$$\frac{x + 15}{15} = \frac{12}{9}$$

$$\frac{x + 15}{15} = \frac{4}{3}$$

$$3(x + 15) = 4(15) \qquad \text{Means-Extremes Products Theorem}$$

$$3x + 45 = 60$$

$$3x = 15$$

$$x = 5$$

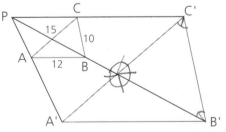

Problem 3

In the diagram, segments PA, PB, and PC are drawn to the vertices of $\triangle ABC$ from an external point P, then extended to three times their original lengths to points A′, B′, and C′. What are the lengths of the sides of $\triangle A'B'C'$?

Solution

It appears that $\triangle A'B'C' \sim \triangle ABC$. (In the next section we will develop some theorems that will allow you to prove that the triangles are similar.) In fact, $\triangle A'B'C'$ is a dilation of $\triangle ABC$, with a dilation ratio of 3:1 for each pair of corresponding sides.

$$A'B' = 3(AB) = 3(12) = 36$$
$$B'C' = 3(BC) = 3(10) = 30$$
$$A'C' = 3(AC) = 3(15) = 45$$

BOOTY

Part Three: Problem Sets

Problem Set A

1 Which pairs of figures *appear* to be similar?

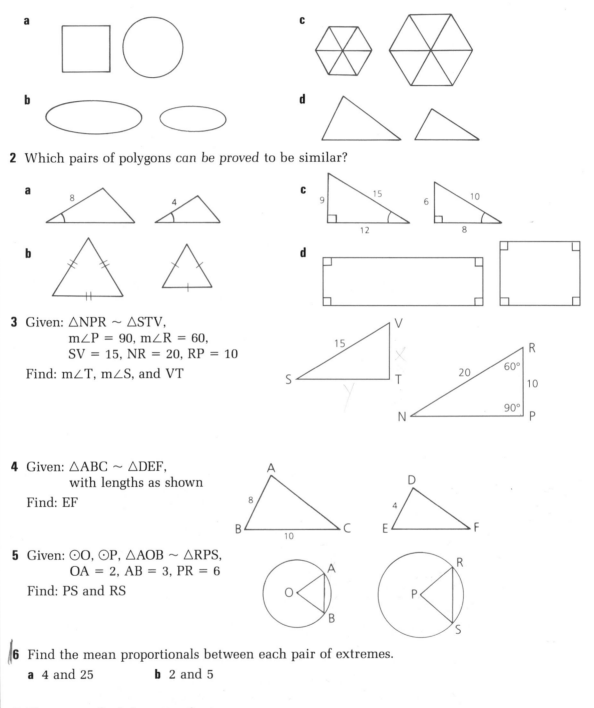

2 Which pairs of polygons *can be proved* to be similar?

3 Given: △NPR ~ △STV,
    m∠P = 90, m∠R = 60,
    SV = 15, NR = 20, RP = 10
  Find: m∠T, m∠S, and VT

4 Given: △ABC ~ △DEF,
    with lengths as shown
  Find: EF

5 Given: ⊙O, ⊙P, △AOB ~ △RPS,
    OA = 2, AB = 3, PR = 6
  Find: PS and RS

6 Find the mean proportionals between each pair of extremes.
  a 4 and 25   **b** 2 and 5

7 If 3x = 5y, find the ratio of x to y.

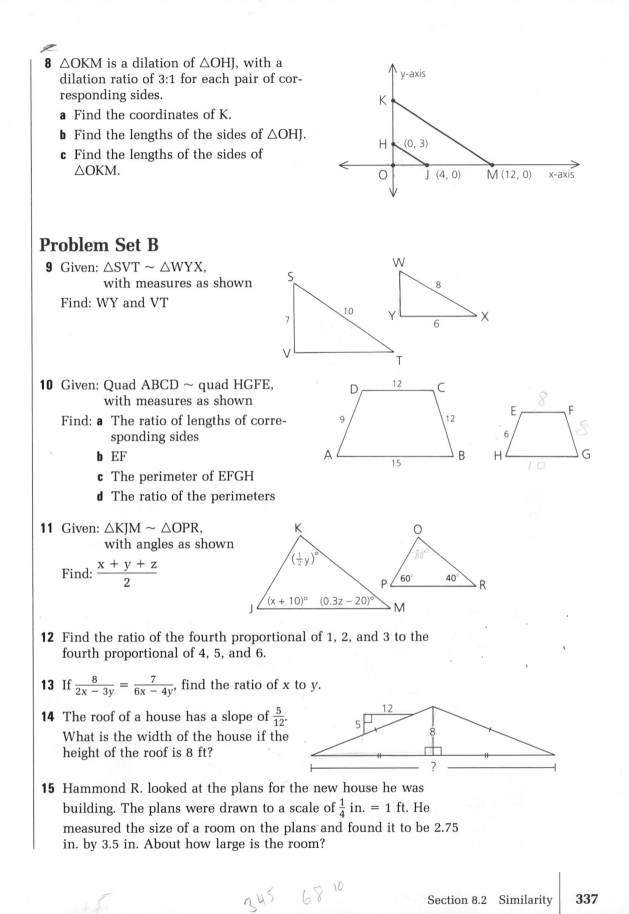

8 △OKM is a dilation of △OHJ, with a dilation ratio of 3:1 for each pair of corresponding sides.

   a Find the coordinates of K.

   b Find the lengths of the sides of △OHJ.

   c Find the lengths of the sides of △OKM.

Problem Set B

9 Given: △SVT ~ △WYX,
with measures as shown

   Find: WY and VT

10 Given: Quad ABCD ~ quad HGFE,
with measures as shown

   Find: **a** The ratio of lengths of corresponding sides

       b EF

       c The perimeter of EFGH

       d The ratio of the perimeters

11 Given: △KJM ~ △OPR,
with angles as shown

   Find: $\dfrac{x + y + z}{2}$

12 Find the ratio of the fourth proportional of 1, 2, and 3 to the fourth proportional of 4, 5, and 6.

13 If $\dfrac{8}{2x - 3y} = \dfrac{7}{6x - 4y}$, find the ratio of x to y.

14 The roof of a house has a slope of $\dfrac{5}{12}$. What is the width of the house if the height of the roof is 8 ft?

15 Hammond R. looked at the plans for the new house he was building. The plans were drawn to a scale of $\frac{1}{4}$ in. = 1 ft. He measured the size of a room on the plans and found it to be 2.75 in. by 3.5 in. About how large is the room?

Problem Set B, *continued*

16 Draw a triangle. Using some point P in the interior of the triangle as the point of dilation, draw a triangle twice the size of the original triangle.

17 The projector shown uses a slide in which the rectangular transparency measures 3 cm by 4 cm. The slide is 5 cm behind the lens. How large is the rectangular image on the screen?

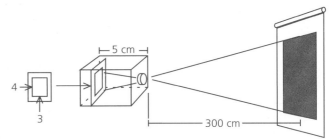

Problem Set C

18 Given: △ABC ~ △DEF,
   m∠A = 50, m∠D = 2x + 5y,
   m∠F = 5x + y, m∠B = 102 − x
   Find: m∠F

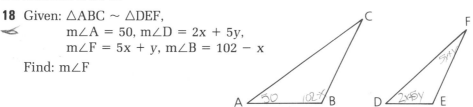

19 Look again at problem 3. Find the length of $\overline{NP}$ in simplified form. Then quickly find ST.

Methods of Proving Triangles Similar

Objective

After studying this section, you will be able to
- Use several methods to prove that triangles are similar

Part One: Introduction

In this section, we will present ways to prove that triangles are similar. We start by accepting one method as a postulate.

Postulate   ***If there exists a correspondence between the vertices of two triangles such that the three angles of one triangle are congruent to the corresponding angles of the other triangle, then the triangles are similar. (AAA)***

The following three theorems will be used in proofs much as SSS, SAS, ASA, HL, and AAS were used in proofs to establish congruency.

Theorem 62   ***If there exists a correspondence between the vertices of two triangles such that two angles of one triangle are congruent to the corresponding angles of the other, then the triangles are similar. (AA)***

Given: ∠A ≅ ∠D,
     ∠B ≅ ∠E
Conclusion: △ABC ∼ △DEF

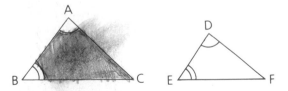

The proof of Theorem 62 follows from the No-Choice Theorem (p. 302).

We also present, without proof, two additional methods of proving that two triangles are similar. You will discover, however, that AA is the most frequently used of the three methods.

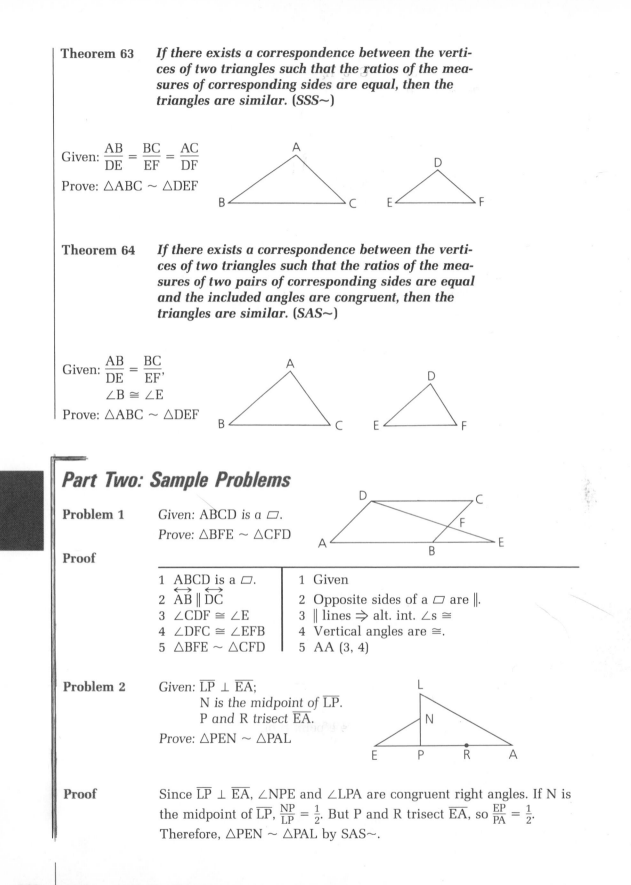

Theorem 63   *If there exists a correspondence between the vertices of two triangles such that the ratios of the measures of corresponding sides are equal, then the triangles are similar. (SSS~)*

Given: $\dfrac{AB}{DE} = \dfrac{BC}{EF} = \dfrac{AC}{DF}$

Prove: $\triangle ABC \sim \triangle DEF$

Theorem 64   *If there exists a correspondence between the vertices of two triangles such that the ratios of the measures of two pairs of corresponding sides are equal and the included angles are congruent, then the triangles are similar. (SAS~)*

Given: $\dfrac{AB}{DE} = \dfrac{BC}{EF}$,

$\quad\quad \angle B \cong \angle E$

Prove: $\triangle ABC \sim \triangle DEF$

Part Two: Sample Problems

Problem 1   Given: ABCD is a ▱.

Prove: $\triangle BFE \sim \triangle CFD$

Proof

1 ABCD is a ▱.	1 Given
2 $\overleftrightarrow{AB} \parallel \overleftrightarrow{DC}$	2 Opposite sides of a ▱ are ∥.
3 $\angle CDF \cong \angle E$	3 ∥ lines $\Rightarrow$ alt. int. $\angle$s $\cong$
4 $\angle DFC \cong \angle EFB$	4 Vertical angles are $\cong$.
5 $\triangle BFE \sim \triangle CFD$	5 AA (3, 4)

Problem 2   Given: $\overline{LP} \perp \overline{EA}$;

$\quad\quad$ N is the midpoint of $\overline{LP}$.

$\quad\quad$ P and R trisect $\overline{EA}$.

Prove: $\triangle PEN \sim \triangle PAL$

Proof   Since $\overline{LP} \perp \overline{EA}$, $\angle NPE$ and $\angle LPA$ are congruent right angles. If N is the midpoint of $\overline{LP}$, $\dfrac{NP}{LP} = \dfrac{1}{2}$. But P and R trisect $\overline{EA}$, so $\dfrac{EP}{PA} = \dfrac{1}{2}$. Therefore, $\triangle PEN \sim \triangle PAL$ by SAS~.

Problem 3 Given: $\overline{KH}$ is the altitude to hypotenuse $\overline{GJ}$ of right $\triangle GHJ$.

Prove: $\triangle KHJ \sim \triangle HGJ$

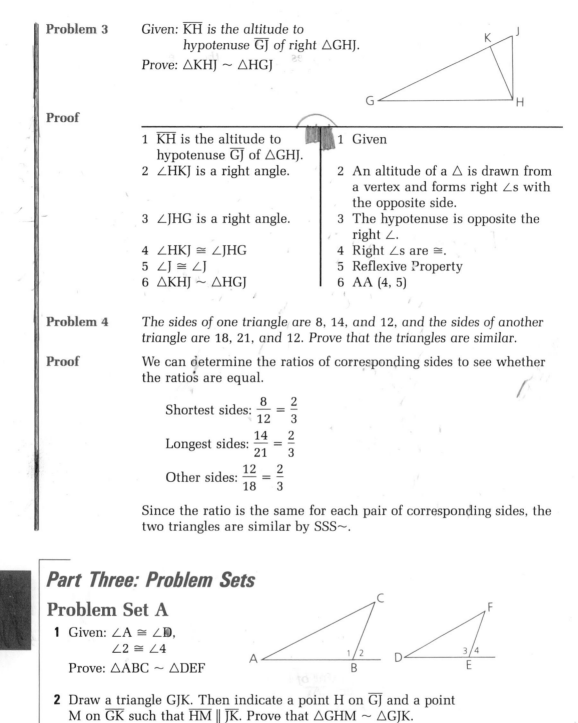

Proof

1 $\overline{KH}$ is the altitude to hypotenuse $\overline{GJ}$ of $\triangle GHJ$.	1 Given
2 $\angle HKJ$ is a right angle.	2 An altitude of a $\triangle$ is drawn from a vertex and forms right $\angle$s with the opposite side.
3 $\angle JHG$ is a right angle.	3 The hypotenuse is opposite the right $\angle$.
4 $\angle HKJ \cong \angle JHG$	4 Right $\angle$s are $\cong$.
5 $\angle J \cong \angle J$	5 Reflexive Property
6 $\triangle KHJ \sim \triangle HGJ$	6 AA (4, 5)

Problem 4 The sides of one triangle are 8, 14, and 12, and the sides of another triangle are 18, 21, and 12. Prove that the triangles are similar.

Proof We can determine the ratios of corresponding sides to see whether the ratios are equal.

Shortest sides: $\dfrac{8}{12} = \dfrac{2}{3}$

Longest sides: $\dfrac{14}{21} = \dfrac{2}{3}$

Other sides: $\dfrac{12}{18} = \dfrac{2}{3}$

Since the ratio is the same for each pair of corresponding sides, the two triangles are similar by SSS~.

Part Three: Problem Sets

Problem Set A

1 Given: $\angle A \cong \angle D$,
$\angle 2 \cong \angle 4$

Prove: $\triangle ABC \sim \triangle DEF$

2 Draw a triangle GJK. Then indicate a point H on $\overline{GJ}$ and a point M on $\overline{GK}$ such that $\overline{HM} \parallel \overline{JK}$. Prove that $\triangle GHM \sim \triangle GJK$.

3 Given: NPRV is a $\square$.

Conclusion: $\triangle NWO \sim \triangle SWT$

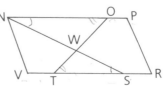

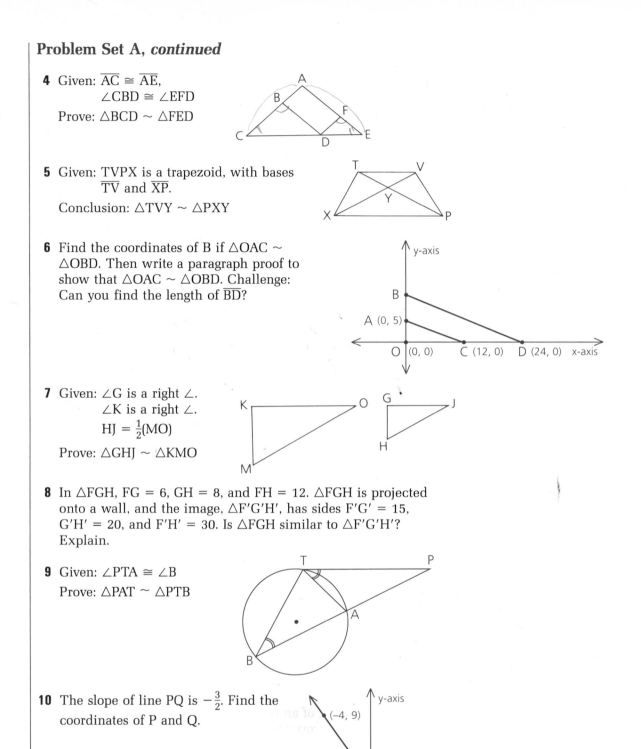

4 Given: $\overline{AC} \cong \overline{AE}$,
   $\angle CBD \cong \angle EFD$
   Prove: $\triangle BCD \sim \triangle FED$

5 Given: TVPX is a trapezoid, with bases
   $\overline{TV}$ and $\overline{XP}$.
   Conclusion: $\triangle TVY \sim \triangle PXY$

6 Find the coordinates of B if $\triangle OAC \sim \triangle OBD$. Then write a paragraph proof to show that $\triangle OAC \sim \triangle OBD$. Challenge: Can you find the length of $\overline{BD}$?

7 Given: $\angle G$ is a right $\angle$.
   $\angle K$ is a right $\angle$.
   $HJ = \frac{1}{2}(MO)$
   Prove: $\triangle GHJ \sim \triangle KMO$

8 In $\triangle FGH$, $FG = 6$, $GH = 8$, and $FH = 12$. $\triangle FGH$ is projected onto a wall, and the image, $\triangle F'G'H'$, has sides $F'G' = 15$, $G'H' = 20$, and $F'H' = 30$. Is $\triangle FGH$ similar to $\triangle F'G'H'$? Explain.

9 Given: $\angle PTA \cong \angle B$
   Prove: $\triangle PAT \sim \triangle PTB$

10 The slope of line PQ is $-\frac{3}{2}$. Find the coordinates of P and Q.

11 Given: $\triangle A'B'C'$ is not a dilation of $\triangle ABC$.

Prove: $A'C' \neq 12.3$

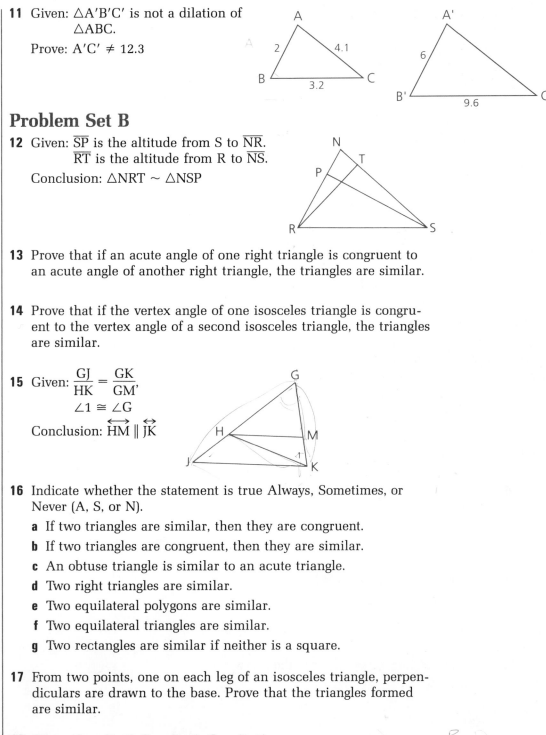

Problem Set B

12 Given: $\overline{SP}$ is the altitude from S to $\overline{NR}$.
$\overline{RT}$ is the altitude from R to $\overline{NS}$.

Conclusion: $\triangle NRT \sim \triangle NSP$

13 Prove that if an acute angle of one right triangle is congruent to an acute angle of another right triangle, the triangles are similar.

14 Prove that if the vertex angle of one isosceles triangle is congruent to the vertex angle of a second isosceles triangle, the triangles are similar.

15 Given: $\dfrac{GJ}{HK} = \dfrac{GK}{GM}$,

$\angle 1 \cong \angle G$

Conclusion: $\overleftrightarrow{HM} \parallel \overleftrightarrow{JK}$

16 Indicate whether the statement is true Always, Sometimes, or Never (A, S, or N).

a If two triangles are similar, then they are congruent.

b If two triangles are congruent, then they are similar.

c An obtuse triangle is similar to an acute triangle.

d Two right triangles are similar.

e Two equilateral polygons are similar.

f Two equilateral triangles are similar.

g Two rectangles are similar if neither is a square.

17 From two points, one on each leg of an isosceles triangle, perpendiculars are drawn to the base. Prove that the triangles formed are similar.

18 Given: A = (1, 2), B = (9, 8), C = (1, 8),
P = (5, −3), Q = (−7, 6), R = (−7, −3),
AB = 10, PQ = 15

By which theorem is $\triangle ABC \sim \triangle QPR$?

Problem Set B, *continued*

19 Given: Figure as shown

  a Is △PQT ~ △PRS? Justify your reasoning.

  b Is $\overline{QT}$ parallel to $\overline{RS}$? Justify your reasoning.

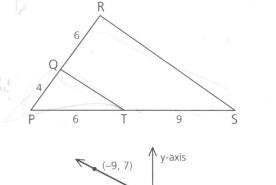

20 A line is graphed at the right.

  a What is the slope of the line?

  b As the x values of points on the line increase by 3, by how much do the y values increase or decrease?

Problem Set C

21 Prove that two triangles similar to a third triangle are similar to each other (the transitive property of similar triangles). Do you think the transitive property could be applied to other similar polygons?

22 If two of the six triangles below are selected at random, what is the probability that the two triangles are similar?

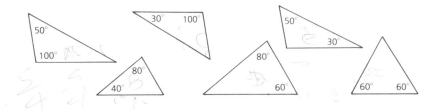

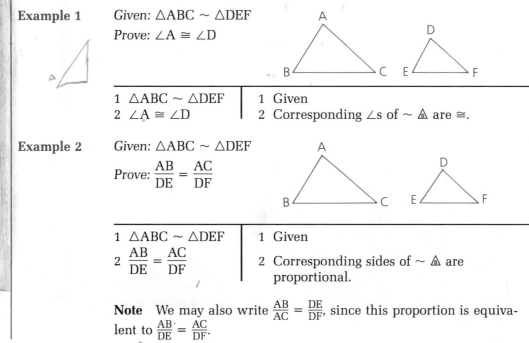

8.4 CONGRUENCES AND PROPORTIONS IN SIMILAR TRIANGLES

Objective

After studying this section, you will be able to
- Use the concept of similarity to establish the congruence of angles and the proportionality of segments

Part One: Introduction

As you have seen, if we know that two triangles are congruent, we can use the definition of *congruent triangles* (CPCTC) to prove that pairs of angles and sides are congruent. In like fashion, once we know that two triangles are similar, we can use the definition of *similar polygons* to prove that

    1 Corresponding sides of the triangles are proportional (The ratios of the measures of corresponding sides are equal.)
    2 Corresponding angles of the triangles are congruent

    If a problem asks you to prove that *products* of the measures of sides are equal, try using the Means-Extremes Products Theorem.

Example 1   Given: $\triangle ABC \sim \triangle DEF$
                 Prove: $\angle A \cong \angle D$

1 $\triangle ABC \sim \triangle DEF$	1 Given
2 $\angle A \cong \angle D$	2 Corresponding $\angle$s of $\sim$ ⧌ are $\cong$.

Example 2   Given: $\triangle ABC \sim \triangle DEF$
                 Prove: $\dfrac{AB}{DE} = \dfrac{AC}{DF}$

1 $\triangle ABC \sim \triangle DEF$	1 Given
2 $\dfrac{AB}{DE} = \dfrac{AC}{DF}$	2 Corresponding sides of $\sim$ ⧌ are proportional.

Note We may also write $\dfrac{AB}{AC} = \dfrac{DE}{DF}$, since this proportion is equivalent to $\dfrac{AB}{DE} = \dfrac{AC}{DF}$.

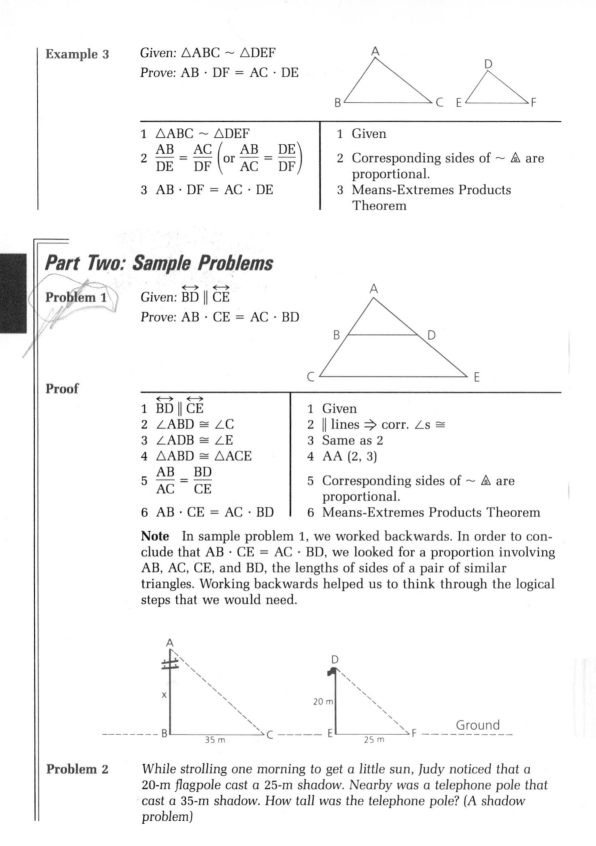

Example 3   Given: △ABC ~ △DEF
Prove: AB · DF = AC · DE

1 △ABC ~ △DEF	1 Given
2 $\dfrac{AB}{DE} = \dfrac{AC}{DF}$ $\left(\text{or } \dfrac{AB}{AC} = \dfrac{DE}{DF}\right)$	2 Corresponding sides of ~ △ are proportional.
3 AB · DF = AC · DE	3 Means-Extremes Products Theorem

Part Two: Sample Problems

Problem 1   Given: $\overleftrightarrow{BD} \parallel \overleftrightarrow{CE}$
Prove: AB · CE = AC · BD

Proof

1 $\overleftrightarrow{BD} \parallel \overleftrightarrow{CE}$	1 Given
2 ∠ABD ≅ ∠C	2 ∥ lines ⇒ corr. ∠s ≅
3 ∠ADB ≅ ∠E	3 Same as 2
4 △ABD ≅ △ACE	4 AA (2, 3)
5 $\dfrac{AB}{AC} = \dfrac{BD}{CE}$	5 Corresponding sides of ~ △ are proportional.
6 AB · CE = AC · BD	6 Means-Extremes Products Theorem

Note   In sample problem 1, we worked backwards. In order to conclude that AB · CE = AC · BD, we looked for a proportion involving AB, AC, CE, and BD, the lengths of sides of a pair of similar triangles. Working backwards helped us to think through the logical steps that we would need.

Problem 2   *While strolling one morning to get a little sun, Judy noticed that a 20-m flagpole cast a 25-m shadow. Nearby was a telephone pole that cast a 35-m shadow. How tall was the telephone pole? (A shadow problem)*

Solution Because the sun is very far from us, its rays are nearly parallel.
△ABC ~ △DEF by AA, so we can write a proportion.

$$\frac{x}{35} = \frac{20}{25}$$

$$\frac{x}{35} = \frac{4}{5}$$

$$5x = 140$$

$$x = 28$$

The pole was 28 m high.

Problem 3 Given: ▱YSTW,
$\overline{SX} \perp \overline{YW}$,
$\overline{SV} \perp \overline{WT}$

Prove: SX · YW = SV · WT

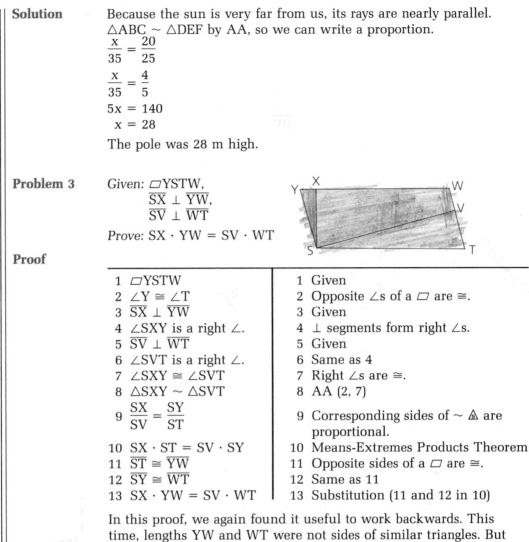

Proof

1 ▱YSTW	1 Given
2 ∠Y ≅ ∠T	2 Opposite ∠s of a ▱ are ≅.
3 $\overline{SX} \perp \overline{YW}$	3 Given
4 ∠SXY is a right ∠.	4 ⊥ segments form right ∠s.
5 $\overline{SV} \perp \overline{WT}$	5 Given
6 ∠SVT is a right ∠.	6 Same as 4
7 ∠SXY ≅ ∠SVT	7 Right ∠s are ≅.
8 △SXY ~ △SVT	8 AA (2, 7)
9 $\dfrac{SX}{SV} = \dfrac{SY}{ST}$	9 Corresponding sides of ~ △ are proportional.
10 SX · ST = SV · SY	10 Means-Extremes Products Theorem
11 $\overline{ST} \cong \overline{YW}$	11 Opposite sides of a ▱ are ≅.
12 $\overline{SY} \cong \overline{WT}$	12 Same as 11
13 SX · YW = SV · WT	13 Substitution (11 and 12 in 10)

In this proof, we again found it useful to work backwards. This
time, lengths YW and WT were not sides of similar triangles. But
since SYTW is a parallelogram, we were able to substitute these
lengths for the lengths of the opposite sides.

Part Three: Problem Sets

Problem Set A

1 Given: ∠C ≅ ∠F,
$\overline{AB} \perp \overline{BC}$,
$\overline{DE} \perp \overline{EF}$

Prove: $\dfrac{AB}{BC} = \dfrac{DE}{EF}$

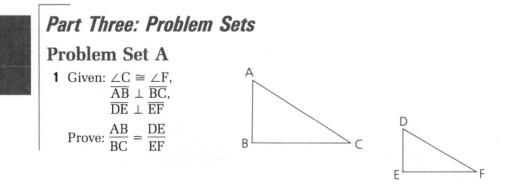

Problem Set A, *continued*

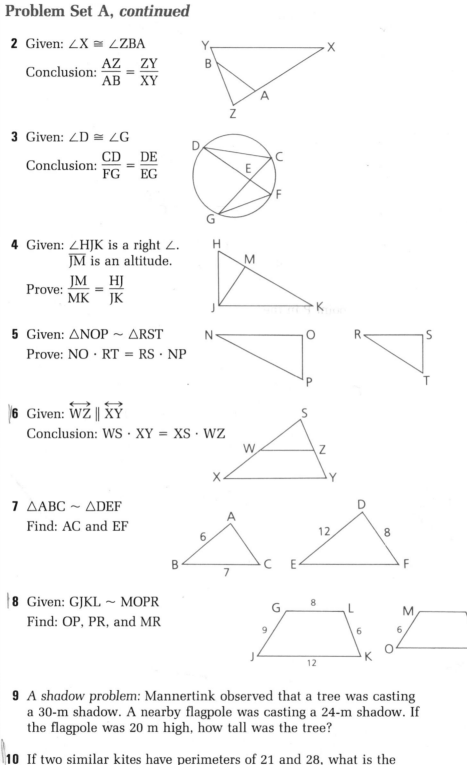

2 Given: $\angle X \cong \angle ZBA$

Conclusion: $\dfrac{AZ}{AB} = \dfrac{ZY}{XY}$

3 Given: $\angle D \cong \angle G$

Conclusion: $\dfrac{CD}{FG} = \dfrac{DE}{EG}$

4 Given: $\angle HJK$ is a right $\angle$.
$\overline{JM}$ is an altitude.

Prove: $\dfrac{JM}{MK} = \dfrac{HJ}{JK}$

5 Given: $\triangle NOP \sim \triangle RST$

Prove: $NO \cdot RT = RS \cdot NP$

6 Given: $\overleftrightarrow{WZ} \parallel \overleftrightarrow{XY}$

Conclusion: $WS \cdot XY = XS \cdot WZ$

7 $\triangle ABC \sim \triangle DEF$

Find: AC and EF

8 Given: $GJKL \sim MOPR$

Find: OP, PR, and MR

9 *A shadow problem:* Mannertink observed that a tree was casting a 30-m shadow. A nearby flagpole was casting a 24-m shadow. If the flagpole was 20 m high, how tall was the tree?

10 If two similar kites have perimeters of 21 and 28, what is the ratio of the measures of two corresponding sides?

11 Using the diagram at the right, show that $\overline{AB} \parallel \overline{DE}$.

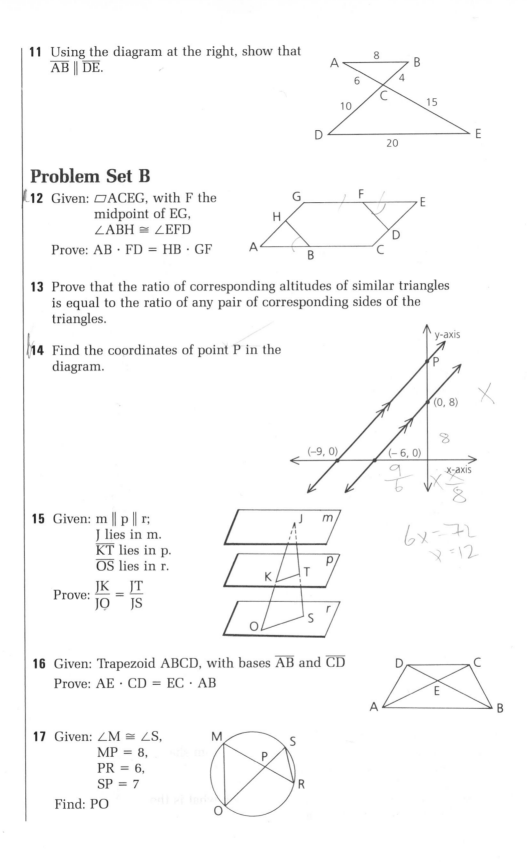

Problem Set B

12 Given: $\square ACEG$, with F the midpoint of EG,
$\angle ABH \cong \angle EFD$
Prove: $AB \cdot FD = HB \cdot GF$

13 Prove that the ratio of corresponding altitudes of similar triangles is equal to the ratio of any pair of corresponding sides of the triangles.

14 Find the coordinates of point P in the diagram.

15 Given: $m \parallel p \parallel r$;
J lies in m.
$\overline{KT}$ lies in p.
$\overline{OS}$ lies in r.
Prove: $\dfrac{JK}{JO} = \dfrac{JT}{JS}$

16 Given: Trapezoid ABCD, with bases $\overline{AB}$ and $\overline{CD}$
Prove: $AE \cdot CD = EC \cdot AB$

17 Given: $\angle M \cong \angle S$,
$MP = 8$,
$PR = 6$,
$SP = 7$
Find: PO

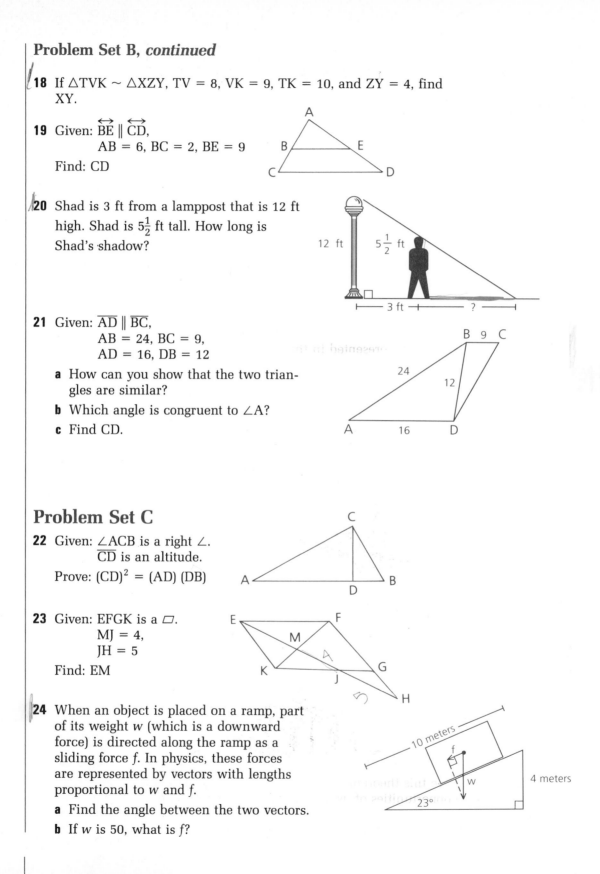

18 If △TVK ~ △XZY, TV = 8, VK = 9, TK = 10, and ZY = 4, find XY.

19 Given: $\overleftrightarrow{BE} \parallel \overleftrightarrow{CD}$,
   AB = 6, BC = 2, BE = 9
   Find: CD

20 Shad is 3 ft from a lamppost that is 12 ft high. Shad is $5\frac{1}{2}$ ft tall. How long is Shad's shadow?

21 Given: $\overline{AD} \parallel \overline{BC}$,
   AB = 24, BC = 9,
   AD = 16, DB = 12

   a How can you show that the two triangles are similar?
   b Which angle is congruent to ∠A?
   c Find CD.

Problem Set C

22 Given: ∠ACB is a right ∠.
   $\overline{CD}$ is an altitude.
   Prove: $(CD)^2 = (AD)(DB)$

23 Given: EFGK is a ▱.
   MJ = 4,
   JH = 5
   Find: EM

24 When an object is placed on a ramp, part of its weight *w* (which is a downward force) is directed along the ramp as a sliding force *f*. In physics, these forces are represented by vectors with lengths proportional to *w* and *f*.

   a Find the angle between the two vectors.
   b If *w* is 50, what is *f*?

THREE THEOREMS INVOLVING PROPORTIONS

Objective

After studying this section, you will be able to
- Apply three theorems frequently used to establish proportionality

Part One: Introduction

You will find the theorems presented in this section useful in a number of applications.

Theorem 65 *If a line is parallel to one side of a triangle and intersects the other two sides, it divides those two sides proportionally. (Side-Splitter Theorem)*

Given: $\overleftrightarrow{BE} \parallel \overleftrightarrow{CD}$

Prove: $\dfrac{AB}{BC} = \dfrac{AE}{ED}$

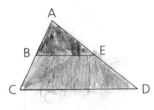

Theorem 66 *If three or more parallel lines are intersected by two transversals, the parallel lines divide the transversals proportionally.*

Given: $\overleftrightarrow{AB} \parallel \overleftrightarrow{CD} \parallel \overleftrightarrow{EF}$

Conclusion: $\dfrac{AC}{CE} = \dfrac{BD}{DF}$

If you wish to prove this theorem, draw auxiliary segment AF and think about two opportunities of using the Side-Splitter Theorem. You may also find it a challenge to prove Theorem 66 for transversals intersecting four parallel lines.

Another useful statement that can be made about parallel lines and their transversals is the following: *If parallel lines cut off (intercept) congruent segments on one transversal, they cut off congruent segments on any transversal.* Do you see how this statement is a consequence of Theorem 66? What is the ratio of lengths in such a case?

Theorem 67   *If a ray bisects an angle of a triangle, it divides the opposite side into segments that are proportional to the adjacent sides.* (**Angle Bisector Theorem**)

Given: $\triangle ABD$;
$\qquad \overrightarrow{AC}$ bisects $\angle BAD$.

Prove: $\dfrac{BC}{CD} = \dfrac{AB}{AD}$

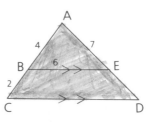

Proof:

1 $\triangle ABD$	1 Given
2 $\overrightarrow{AC}$ bisects $\angle BAD$.	2 Given
3 $\angle 1 \cong \angle 2$	3 If a ray bisects an $\angle$, it divides the $\angle$ into two $\cong \angle$s.
4 Draw through B the line that is $\parallel$ to $\overline{AC}$.	4 Parallel Postulate
5 Extend $\overleftrightarrow{DA}$ to intersect the $\parallel$ line at some point E.	5 A line can be extended as far as desired
6 $\dfrac{BC}{CD} = \dfrac{EA}{AD}$	6 Side-Splitter Theorem
7 $\angle 1 \cong \angle 3$	7 $\parallel$ lines $\Rightarrow$ alt. int. $\angle$s $\cong$
8 $\angle 2 \cong \angle 4$	8 $\parallel$ lines $\Rightarrow$ corr. $\angle$s $\cong$
9 $\angle 3 \cong \angle 4$	9 Transitive Property (3, 7, 8)
10 $\overline{EA} \cong \overline{AB}$	10 If $\triangle$, then $\triangle$.
11 $\dfrac{BC}{CD} = \dfrac{AB}{AD}$	11 Substitution (10 in 6)

Part Two: Sample Problems

Problem 1   Given: $\overleftrightarrow{BE} \parallel \overleftrightarrow{CD}$,
$\qquad\qquad$ lengths as shown

$\qquad$ Find: **a** ED
$\qquad\qquad$ **b** CD

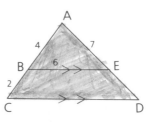

Solution Be alert. In problems involving this type of figure, you may need to use both the Side-Splitter Theorem and the properties of similar triangles.

a By the Side-Splitter Theorem,

$$\frac{AB}{BC} = \frac{AE}{ED}$$

$$\frac{4}{2} = \frac{7}{ED}$$

$$\frac{2}{1} = \frac{7}{ED}$$

$$2(ED) = 7$$

$$ED = 3\frac{1}{2}$$

b Since the parallel segments are involved, use the fact that $\triangle ABE \sim \triangle ACD$ to write a proportion.

$$\frac{AB}{AC} = \frac{BE}{CD}$$

$$\frac{4}{4+2} = \frac{6}{CD}$$

$$\frac{2}{3} = \frac{6}{CD}$$

$$2(CD) = 18$$

$$CD = 9$$

Problem 2 Given: a ∥ b ∥ c ∥ d,
lengths as shown,
KP = 24

Find: KM

Solution According to Theorem 66, the ratio KM:MO:OP is equal to 5:2:8. Therefore, we let KM = 5x, MO = 2x, and OP = 8x. Since KP = 24,

$$5x + 2x + 8x = 24$$

$$15x = 24$$

$$x = \frac{24}{15} = \frac{8}{5}$$

Thus, $KM = 5\left(\frac{8}{5}\right) = 8$

Problem 3 Given: $\angle RVS \cong \angle SVT$,
lengths as shown

Find: ST

Solution By Theorem 67,

$$\frac{VR}{VT} = \frac{RS}{ST}$$

$$\frac{8}{10} = \frac{4}{ST}$$

$$\frac{4}{5} = \frac{4}{ST}$$

$$4(ST) = 20$$

$$ST = 5$$

Problem 4   Given: $\overleftrightarrow{XA} \parallel \overleftrightarrow{YZ}$,
$\angle XAY \cong \angle XYA$

Conclusion: $\dfrac{WX}{XA} = \dfrac{WA}{AZ}$

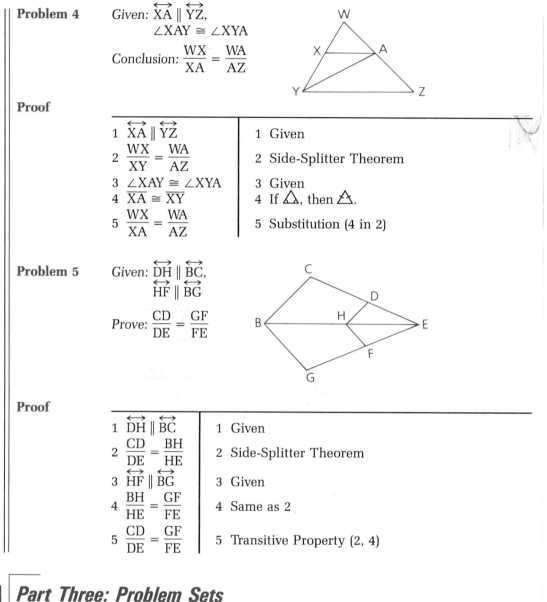

Proof

1 $\overleftrightarrow{XA} \parallel \overleftrightarrow{YZ}$	1 Given
2 $\dfrac{WX}{XY} = \dfrac{WA}{AZ}$	2 Side-Splitter Theorem
3 $\angle XAY \cong \angle XYA$	3 Given
4 $\overline{XA} \cong \overline{XY}$	4 If △, then △.
5 $\dfrac{WX}{XA} = \dfrac{WA}{AZ}$	5 Substitution (4 in 2)

Problem 5   Given: $\overleftrightarrow{DH} \parallel \overleftrightarrow{BC}$,
$\overleftrightarrow{HF} \parallel \overleftrightarrow{BG}$

Prove: $\dfrac{CD}{DE} = \dfrac{GF}{FE}$

Proof

1 $\overleftrightarrow{DH} \parallel \overleftrightarrow{BC}$	1 Given
2 $\dfrac{CD}{DE} = \dfrac{BH}{HE}$	2 Side-Splitter Theorem
3 $\overleftrightarrow{HF} \parallel \overleftrightarrow{BG}$	3 Given
4 $\dfrac{BH}{HE} = \dfrac{GF}{FE}$	4 Same as 2
5 $\dfrac{CD}{DE} = \dfrac{GF}{FE}$	5 Transitive Property (2, 4)

Part Three: Problem Sets

Problem Set A

For problems 1–3, see sample problem 1.

1 Given: $\overline{BE} \parallel \overline{CD}$,
lengths as shown

Find: **a** ED
b CD

2 Solve for x and y in the figure shown.

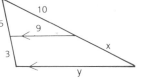

3 Solve for p and q in the figure shown.

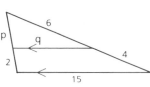

For problems 4 and 5, see sample problem 2.

4 Given: a ∥ b ∥ c ∥ d,
   lengths as shown,
   KP = 15

Find: KM, MO, and OP

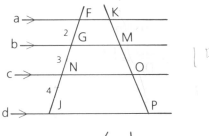

15

5 Solve for x in the diagram shown.

For problems 6 and 7, see sample problem 3.

6 Given: ∠RVS ≅ ∠SVT,
   lengths as shown

Find: ST

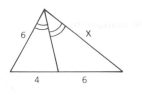

7 Given the diagram as marked, solve for x.

8 A 60-m tower casts a 50-m shadow, while one-half block away a telephone pole casts a 20-m shadow. How tall is the telephone pole?

9 Given: ∠J ≅ ∠MKO,
MK = 12, KO = 8,
MO = 10, JK = 3

Find: PO and JP

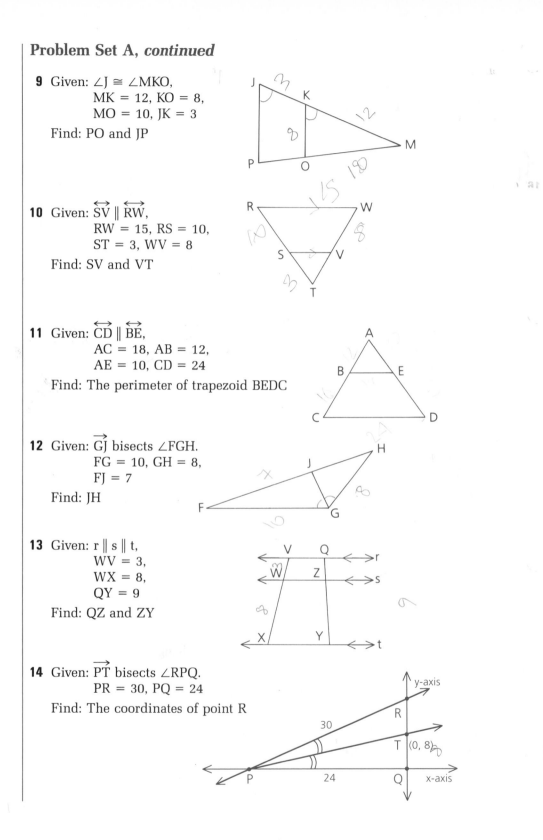

10 Given: $\overleftrightarrow{SV} \parallel \overleftrightarrow{RW}$,
RW = 15, RS = 10,
ST = 3, WV = 8

Find: SV and VT

11 Given: $\overleftrightarrow{CD} \parallel \overleftrightarrow{BE}$,
AC = 18, AB = 12,
AE = 10, CD = 24

Find: The perimeter of trapezoid BEDC

12 Given: $\overrightarrow{GJ}$ bisects ∠FGH.
FG = 10, GH = 8,
FJ = 7

Find: JH

13 Given: r ∥ s ∥ t,
WV = 3,
WX = 8,
QY = 9

Find: QZ and ZY

14 Given: $\overrightarrow{PT}$ bisects ∠RPQ.
PR = 30, PQ = 24

Find: The coordinates of point R

Problem Set B

15 Given: $\angle 1 \cong \angle 2$

Conclusion: $\dfrac{KM}{JK} = \dfrac{MO}{OP}$

16 Given: $\angle 3 \cong \angle 5$

Prove: $\dfrac{RV}{VT} = \dfrac{RS}{ST}$

17 Given: WYZB is a trapezoid with bases
$\overline{WB}$ and $\overline{YZ}$.
$\overleftrightarrow{XA} \parallel \overleftrightarrow{YZ}$

Prove: $\dfrac{WX}{XY} = \dfrac{WC}{CZ} = \dfrac{BA}{AZ}$

18 Given: $\overleftrightarrow{BE} \parallel \overleftrightarrow{CD}$,
AB = 4x, BC = x,
AD = 8x, BE = 5x

Find: AE and CD (in terms of x)

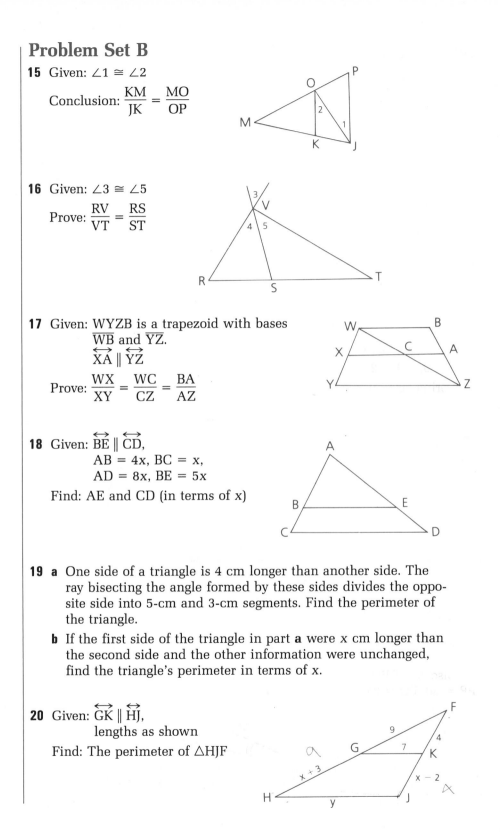

19 a One side of a triangle is 4 cm longer than another side. The ray bisecting the angle formed by these sides divides the opposite side into 5-cm and 3-cm segments. Find the perimeter of the triangle.

b If the first side of the triangle in part **a** were x cm longer than the second side and the other information were unchanged, find the triangle's perimeter in terms of x.

20 Given: $\overleftrightarrow{GK} \parallel \overleftrightarrow{HJ}$,
lengths as shown

Find: The perimeter of $\triangle HJF$

Problem Set B, *continued*

21 Sketch a triangle ABC, and locate a point P on $\overline{BC}$ such that $\overrightarrow{AP}$ bisects ∠BAC. If the perimeter of △ABC is 44, BP = 6, and PC = 10, find AB and AC.

22 Given: $\overleftrightarrow{VS} \parallel \overleftrightarrow{MR}$,
　　　　TV = 12, VM = 8, TS = 15,
　　　　SR = TW = TX
　　Find: XP

23 Given: $\overleftrightarrow{AC} \perp \overline{BE}$,
　　　　∠1 ≅ ∠4
　　Conclusion: $\dfrac{BD}{BF} = \dfrac{DE}{EF}$

24 Given: $\overleftrightarrow{GD} \parallel \overleftrightarrow{FE}$,
　　　　$\overleftrightarrow{BD} \parallel \overleftrightarrow{CE}$
　　Prove: $\dfrac{AB}{AC} = \dfrac{AG}{AF}$

25 Prove that if a line bisects one side of a triangle and is parallel to a second side, it bisects the third side.

Problem Set C

26 Given: $\overleftrightarrow{GK} \parallel \overleftrightarrow{HJ}$,
　　　　lengths as shown
　　Find: The perimeter of △HJF

27 If two flagpoles are 10 m and 70 m tall and are 100 m apart, find the height of the point where a line from the top of the first to the bottom of the second intersects a line from the bottom of the first to the top of the second.

28 Prove that a line that divides two sides of a triangle proportionally is parallel to the third side.

29 Given: $\overrightarrow{RW}$ bisects ∠SRT.
$\overrightarrow{TV}$ bisects ∠RTS.
RV = 4, SV = 5,
SW = 6, WT = 7

Show that the given information is impossible.

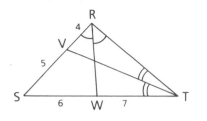

30 In the diagram, $\overline{BR}$ ∥ y-axis, $\overline{AR}$ ∥ x-axis, and point P divides $\overline{AB}$ in the ratio 2:3. Find the coordinates of points R and Q. (Hint: Find BQ and QR.)

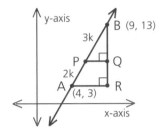

PUTTING QUILTS IN PERSPECTIVE
The patchwork world of Linda MacDonald, quilt maker

Quilt patterns traditionally have been based on two-dimensional geometric shapes. Linda MacDonald, a California artist, has taken this tradition and raised it to a new dimension.

"I'm interested in creating a three-dimensional space instead of a flat pattern," she explains, "a window you can move through—a fantasy landscape." Her quilt *Salmon Ladders*, for example, consists of hundreds of delicately colored polygons arranged in an intricate lattice of interlocking planes.

To create perspective, MacDonald designs a set of similar polygons and arranges them from largest to smallest moving toward a horizon. She designs these figures freehand, which gives her the artistic flexibility that precisely constructed figures might not allow. She hand-dyes her fabrics and stitches them by hand.

MacDonald received a bachelor of arts degree in painting from San Francisco State University. She began quilt making in 1974. "It's such a rich art form," she says. "Traditionally, quilt patterns have told the story of American history. With the themes that I choose, I'm trying to tell my own history."

Project: Use one or more sets of hand-drawn similar polygons to create a sense of space in a rectangular area.

CHAPTER SUMMARY

CONCEPTS AND PROCEDURES

After studying this chapter, you should be able to
- Recognize and work with ratios (8.1)
- Recognize and work with proportions (8.1)
- Apply the product and ratio theorems (8.1)
- Calculate geometric means (8.1)
- Identify the characteristics of similar figures (8.2)
- Use several methods to prove that triangles are similar (8.3)
- Use the concept of similarity to establish the congruence of angles and the proportionality of segments (8.4)
- Solve shadow problems (8.4)
- Apply three theorems frequently used to establish proportionality (8.5)

VOCABULARY

arithmetic mean (8.1)   proportion (8.1)
dilation (8.2)   ratio (8.1)
extremes (8.1)   reduction (8.2)
geometric mean (8.1)   rise (8.1)
mean proportion (8.1)   run (8.1)
mean proportional (8.1)   similar (8.2)
means (8.1)   similar polygons (8.2)

REVIEW PROBLEMS

Problem Set A

1 Identify the means and the extremes in the proportion $\frac{a}{b} = \frac{c}{d}$.

2 Find the fourth proportional to 4, 6, and 8.

3 Find the mean proportionals between 5 and 20.

4 Find the geometric means between 3 and 6.

5 If $9x = 4y$, find the ratio of x to y.

6 Given: $\triangle ABC \sim DEF$, with lengths as shown
   Find: DF and EF

7 Pentagon ABCDE is similar to pentagon A′B′C′D′E′. The pentagons' respective perimeters are 24 and 30. If AB = 6, find A′B′.

8 If $\frac{GH}{HJ} = \frac{3}{4}$ and GJ = 56, find HJ.

9 If $\frac{r}{3x} = \frac{a}{2b}$, what is the value of x in terms of a, b, and r?

10 A radio antenna that is 100 m tall casts an 80-m shadow. At the same time, a nearby telephone pole casts a 16-m shadow. Find the height of the telephone pole.

11 Given: $\overleftrightarrow{MR} \parallel \overleftrightarrow{OP}$,
   lengths as shown
   Find: RP and OP

12 Given: $\overleftrightarrow{TP} \parallel \overleftrightarrow{VW}$,
   lengths as shown
   Find: ST, TV, and PT

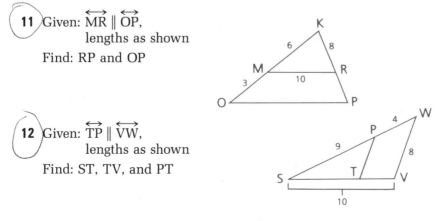

13 Given: $\overrightarrow{CD}$ bisects $\angle ACB$.
AC = 8, BC = 6, BD = 5
Find: AD

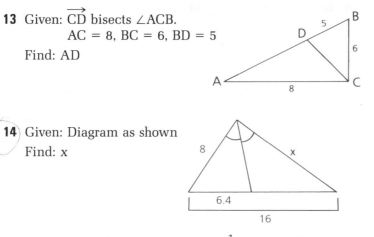

14 Given: Diagram as shown
Find: x

15 A scale model of the *Titanic* is $18\frac{1}{2}$ in. long. The scale is 1:570. To the nearest foot, how long was the *Titanic*?

16 Given: $\overleftrightarrow{EF} \parallel \overleftrightarrow{GO} \parallel \overleftrightarrow{HM} \parallel \overleftrightarrow{JK}$,
FG = 2, GH = 8,
HJ = 5, EM = 6
Find: EO and EK

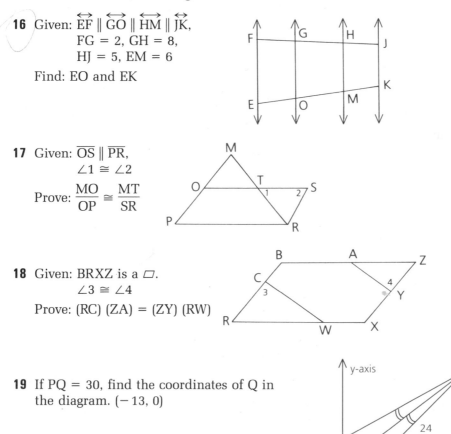

17 Given: $\overline{OS} \parallel \overline{PR}$,
$\angle 1 \cong \angle 2$
Prove: $\dfrac{MO}{OP} \cong \dfrac{MT}{SR}$

18 Given: BRXZ is a $\square$.
$\angle 3 \cong \angle 4$
Prove: (RC)(ZA) = (ZY)(RW)

19 If PQ = 30, find the coordinates of Q in the diagram. (−13, 0)

Problem Set B

20 Indicate whether the statement is true Always, Sometimes, or Never (A, S, or N)

   a Two isosceles triangles are similar if a base angle of one is congruent to a base angle of the other.

   b Two isosceles triangles are similar if the vertex angle of one is congruent to the vertex angle of the other.

   c An equilateral triangle is similar to a scalene triangle.

   d If two sides of one triangle are proportional to two sides of another triangle, the triangles are similar.

   e In $\triangle ABC$, $\angle A = 40°$, $AB = 6$, and $BC = 8$.
   In $\triangle RST$, $RS = 12$, $ST = 16$, and $\angle R = 80°$.
   Therefore, $\triangle ABC \sim \triangle RST$.

   f If a line intersects a side of a triangle at one of its trisection points and is parallel to a second side, then it intersects the third side at one of its trisection points.

   g Two right triangles are similar if the legs of one are proportional to the legs of the other.

   h If the ratio of the measures of a pair of corresponding sides of two polygons is 3:4, then the ratio of the polygons' perimeters is 5:6.

21 Given: ABDF is a $\square$.
   Conclusion: $\triangle CBD \sim \triangle DFE$

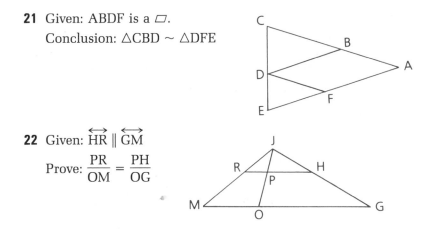

22 Given: $\overleftrightarrow{HR} \parallel \overleftrightarrow{GM}$

   Prove: $\dfrac{PR}{OM} = \dfrac{PH}{OG}$

23 Prove that diagonals of a trapezoid divide each other proportionally.

24 If 78 is divided into three parts in the ratio 3:5:7, what is the sum of the smallest and the largest part?

25 One side of a triangle is 4 cm shorter than a second side. The ray bisecting the angle formed by these sides divides the opposite side into 4-cm and 6-cm segments. Find the perimeter of the triangle.

26 If $\dfrac{7}{x + 4y} = \dfrac{9}{2x - y}$, find the ratio of x to y.

27 Given: $\overleftrightarrow{PT} \parallel \overleftrightarrow{RS}$,
      NP = 5x − 21, PR = 5,
      NT = x, TS = 8

   Find: NR + NS

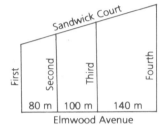

28 The diagram shows a part of the town of Oola, La. First, Second, Third, and Fourth streets are each perpendicular to Elmwood Avenue. If the total frontage on Sandwick Court is 400 m, find the length of each block of Sandwick Court.

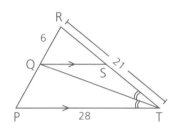

Problem Set C

29 Given: $\overrightarrow{TQ}$ bisects ∠RTP.
      $\overleftrightarrow{QS} \parallel \overleftrightarrow{PT}$

   Find: QP, RS, and QS

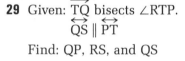

30 Llong is 5 ft tall and is standing in the light of a 15-ft lamppost. Her shadow is 4 ft long. If she walks 1 ft farther away from the lampost, by how much will her shadow lengthen?

31 The sum of four numbers is 771. The ratio of the first to the second is 2:3. The ratio of the second to the third is 5:4. The ratio of the third to the fourth is 5:6. Find the second number.

32 Given: $\overline{GB} \perp \overline{AC}$, $\overline{HD} \perp \overline{EC}$,
      $\overline{JF} \perp \overline{AE}$,
      AB = 8,
      BC = 12,
      EC = 15,
      AE = 10,
      GH = 5

   Find: GJ and HJ

33 Prove that if an altitude is drawn to the hypotenuse of a right triangle, then the product of the measures of the altitude and the hypotenuse is equal to the product of the measures of the legs of the right triangle.

34 Filbert knows that the two triangles ABC and XYZ are similar, but he cannot remember what the correct correspondence of vertices should be. He guesses that △ABC ~ △XYZ.

a What is the probability that his guess is correct?

b If Filbert finds out that the triangles are isosceles, what will the probability be then?

c If the triangles are equilateral, what are his chances of guessing a correct correspondence?

35 Given: CARD and GAME are parallelograms.
The perimeter of GAME is 48.
AD:DE = 2:1

Find: The perimeter of CARD

A MASTER TECHNOLOGIST
The sketchbook of Villard de Honnecourt

In the Middle Ages, master architects were much more than merely designers of buildings. Because they had to supervise every aspect of the planning and construction of many types of structures, they needed to be adept in all the arts and sciences of their times. The wide-ranging interests and expertise of these men are strikingly illustrated by the surviving sketchbook of one of them, the thirteenth-century French architect Villard de Honnecourt.

Villard seems to have used his sketchbook as a sort of technological diary and as a way of sharing his ideas and discoveries with his colleagues. In addition to drawings of interesting architectural features and procedures that Villard noticed in his travels, the book includes such diverse material as plans for a variety of mechanical devices, including a powerful catapult and a water-driven saw; notes on lion taming; recipes for medicines; and more than a hundred drawings of different animals.

Among the most curious pages, however, are those devoted to sketches of people, beasts, and birds on which Villard has superimposed various geometric figures. Some of these sketches may have been intended to demonstrate the proper proportions to use in drawing, but it is thought that their main purpose was to exemplify a method of reproducing drawings in any desired size. By associating a sketch with a geometric diagram and then drawing a dilation of the diagram on a wall or on a block of stone that was to be carved, an artist could create a basic framework that would serve as a guide for the accurate enlargement of the sketch itself.

THE PYTHAGOREAN THEOREM

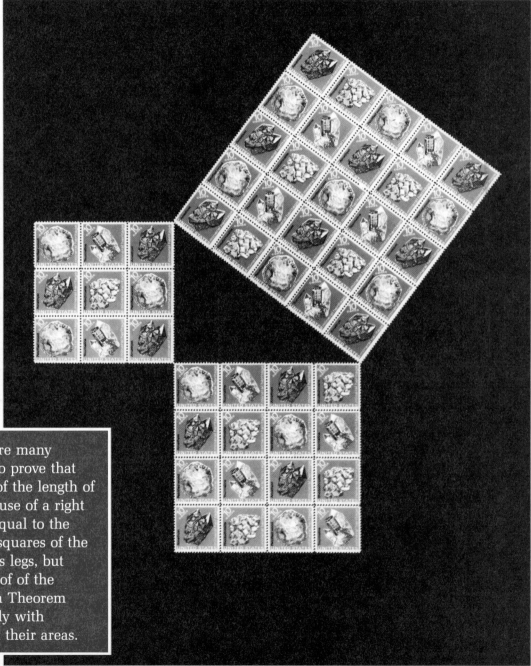

There are many ways to prove that the square of the length of the hypotenuse of a right triangle is equal to the sum of the squares of the lengths of its legs, but Euclid's proof of the Pythagorean Theorem deals directly with squares and their areas.

REVIEW OF RADICALS AND QUADRATIC EQUATIONS

Objective

After studying this section, you will be able to
- Simplify radical expressions and solve quadratic equations

Part One: Introduction

Some of the problems in the next three chapters will involve radicals and quadratic equations. Although you have already completed a course in algebra, you may have forgotten some algebraic techniques. Carefully read the following sample problems, which review these two concepts.

Part Two: Sample Problems

Problem 1   *Simplify* $\sqrt{48}$.

Solution
$$\sqrt{48} = \sqrt{16 \cdot 3} \quad \text{(16 is a perfect square.)}$$
$$= \sqrt{16} \cdot \sqrt{3}$$
$$= 4\sqrt{3}$$

Problem 2   *Simplify* $\sqrt{18} + \sqrt{32} + \sqrt{75}$.

Solution
$$\sqrt{18} + \sqrt{32} + \sqrt{75} = \sqrt{9 \cdot 2} + \sqrt{16 \cdot 2} + \sqrt{25 \cdot 3}$$
$$= 3\sqrt{2} + 4\sqrt{2} + 5\sqrt{3}$$
$$= 5\sqrt{3} + 7\sqrt{2}$$

Problem 3   *Simplify* $\sqrt{\frac{5}{3}}$.

Solution
$$\sqrt{\frac{5}{3}} = \frac{\sqrt{5}}{\sqrt{3}}$$
$$= \frac{\sqrt{5}}{\sqrt{3}} \cdot \frac{\sqrt{3}}{\sqrt{3}}$$
$$= \frac{\sqrt{15}}{3} \text{ or } \frac{1}{3}\sqrt{15} \quad \text{(The two answers are equivalent simplifications.)}$$

Problem 4   Solve $x^2 + 9 = 25$ for x.

Solution   Method 1:

$$x^2 + 9 = 25$$
$$x^2 = 16$$
$$x = \pm 4$$

Method 2 (factoring):

$$x^2 + 9 = 25$$
$$x^2 - 16 = 0$$
$$(x - 4)(x + 4) = 0$$
$$x - 4 = 0 \text{ or } x + 4 = 0$$
$$x = 4 \text{ or } x = -4$$

Problem 5   Solve $\left(3\sqrt{5}\right)^2 + \left(3\sqrt{2}\right)^2 = x^2$ for x.

Solution
$$\left(3\sqrt{5}\right)^2 + \left(3\sqrt{2}\right)^2 = x^2$$
$$9 \cdot 5 + 9 \cdot 2 = x^2$$
$$45 + 18 = x^2$$
$$63 = x^2$$
$$\pm\sqrt{63} = x$$
$$\pm\sqrt{9 \cdot 7} = x$$
$$\pm 3\sqrt{7} = x$$

Problem 6   Solve for x.   **a** $x^2 - 10x = -16$ **b** $x^2 + 5x = 0$

Solution   **a** $x^2 - 10x = -16$
$$x^2 - 10x + 16 = 0$$
$$(x - 8)(x - 2) = 0$$
$$x - 8 = 0 \text{ or } x - 2 = 0$$
$$x = 8 \text{ or } x = 2$$

b $x^2 + 5x = 0$
$$x(x + 5) = 0$$
$$x = 0 \text{ or } x + 5 = 0$$
$$x = 0 \text{ or } x = -5$$

Part Three: Problem Sets

Problem Set A

1 Simplify.

   a $\sqrt{4}$ **c** $\sqrt{72}$ **e** $\sqrt{98}$ **g** $\sqrt{20}$
   b $\sqrt{27}$ **d** $\sqrt{32}$ **f** $\sqrt{200}$ **h** $\sqrt{24}$

2 Simplify.

   a $5\sqrt{18}$ **c** $\sqrt{3^2 + 4^2}$ **e** $\frac{1}{6}\sqrt{48}$
   b $\sqrt{4 + 9}$ **d** $\sqrt{5^2 + 12^2}$ **f** $\sqrt{49 \cdot 3}$

3 Simplify.

   a $\frac{1}{\sqrt{2}}$ **b** $\frac{1}{\sqrt{5}}$ **c** $\frac{4}{\sqrt{2}}$ **d** $\frac{6}{\sqrt{3}}$

4 Simplify.

   a $4\sqrt{3} + 7\sqrt{3}$ **c** $\sqrt{12} + \sqrt{27}$
   b $7\sqrt{2} + \sqrt{3} + 6\sqrt{3} + \sqrt{2}$ **d** $\sqrt{72} + \sqrt{75} - \sqrt{48}$

5 Solve for x.

   a $x^2 = 25$ **c** $x^2 = 169$ **e** $x^2 = 12$

   b $x^2 = 144$ **d** $x^2 = \frac{1}{4}$ **f** $x^2 = 18$

6 Solve for x.

   a $x^2 + 16 = 25$ **c** $12^2 + x^2 = 13^2$ **e** $\left(\sqrt{5}\right)^2 + \left(\sqrt{11}\right)^2 = x^2$

   b $x^2 + 6^2 = 100$ **d** $x^2 + \left(3\sqrt{3}\right)^2 = 36$ **f** $x^2 = \left(5\sqrt{3}\right)^2 + \left(\sqrt{5}\right)^2$

7 Solve for x.

   a $x^2 - 5x - 6 = 0$ **c** $x^2 - 8x + 15 = 0$ **e** $x^2 - 36 = 9x$

   b $x^2 + 4x - 12 = 0$ **d** $x^2 - 18 - 3x = 0$ **f** $-x^2 + 5x + 36 = 0$

$(x+6)(x-2)=0$

8 Solve for x.

   a $x^2 - 4x = 0$ $x(x-4)=0$ **c** $x^2 - 2x = 11x$

   b $x^2 = 10x$ $x(x-10)=0$ **d** $5x = x^2 - 3x$

9 If, in the given figure, $x^2 + y^2 = r^2$,

   a Find x if y = 21 and r = 29

   b Find y, in simplified radical form, if
       x = 2 and r = 4

   c Find r to the nearest tenth if x = 4.1
       and y = 7.1

Problem Set B

10 Solve for x.

   a $3x^2 + 5x - 7 = x^2 + 8x + 28$ **c** $8x^2 - 7x + 9 = 2x^2 + 6x + 7$

   b $12x^2 - 15 = -11x$

11 Solve $\frac{7}{x+1} = \frac{2x+4}{3x-3}$ for x.

12 Find AB to the nearest tenth.

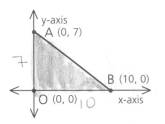

Problem Set C

13 Simplify.

   a $\sqrt{h^2}$, if h represents a negative number

   b $\sqrt{(x-3)^2}$, if x < 3

   c $\sqrt{p^2q^2}$, if p and q both represent negative numbers

   d $\sqrt{x^3y^2}$, if x > 0 and y < 0

21.21
3.6

9.2 | INTRODUCTION TO CIRCLES

Objective

After studying this section, you will be able to
- Begin solving problems involving circles

Part One: Introduction

Because of the unfamiliar terms and concepts involved, many students find working with circles the most difficult part of their geometry studies. To help you deal with circles more effectively, this section will informally introduce you to some of the basic concepts used in circle problems. If you study this section carefully and solve the circle problems presented in the problem sets of this chapter, you will be better prepared for the formal study of circles in Chapter 10.

You have already encountered some problems that have asked you to find the *circumferences* (perimeters) and the areas of circles, so you should be familiar with the relevant formulas.

Example 1   *Find the circumference and the area of ⊙O.*

The circumference is found with the formula $C = \pi d$, where d is the diameter of the circle.

$C = \pi d$
   $= 14\pi$

The area is found with the formula $A = \pi r^2$, where r is the circle's radius.

$A = \pi r^2$
   $= \pi(7^2)$
   $= 49\pi$

The circle's circumference is 14π, or about 43.98, inches and its area is 49π, or about 153.94, square inches.

An *arc* is made up of two points on a circle and all the points of the circle needed to connect those two points by a single path. The blue portion of the figure at the right is called arc CD (symbolized $\overset{\frown}{CD}$).

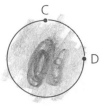

The *measure* of an arc is equivalent to the number of degrees it occupies. (A complete circle occupies 360°.) The *length* of an arc is a fraction of a circle's circumference, so it is expressed in linear units, such as feet, centimeters, or inches.

Example 2   *Find the measure and the length of* $\overset{\frown}{AB}$.

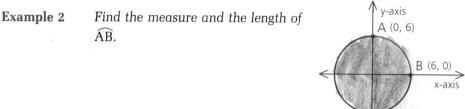

Since the arc is one fourth of the circle, its measure is $\frac{1}{4}(360)$, or 90. The arc's length (ℓ) can be expressed as a part of the circle's circumference.

$$\ell = \frac{90}{360}C$$
$$= \frac{1}{4}\pi d$$
$$= \frac{1}{4}(\pi \cdot 12)$$
$$= 3\pi, \text{ or} \approx 9.42$$

A *sector* of a circle is a region bounded by two radii and an arc of the circle. The figure at the right shows sector CAT of ⊙A.

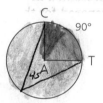

Since we know that $\overset{\frown}{CT}$ has a measure of 90, we can calculate the area of sector CAT as a fraction of the area of ⊙A.

$$\text{Area of sector CAT} = \frac{90}{360}(\text{area of } ⊙A)$$
$$= \frac{1}{4}(\pi \cdot 6^2)$$
$$= 9\pi, \text{ or} \approx 28.27$$

A *chord* is a line segment joining two points on a circle. (A diameter is a chord that passes through the center of its circle.) An *inscribed angle* is an angle whose vertex is on a circle and whose sides are determined by two chords of the circle.

In the figure at the right, $\overline{AB}$ and $\overline{AC}$ are chords, and ∠BAC is an inscribed angle. ∠BAC is said to *intercept* $\overset{\frown}{BC}$. (An intercepted arc is an arc whose endpoints are on the sides of an angle and whose other points all lie within the angle. Although ∠BAC intercepts only one arc, in Chapter 10 you will deal with some angles that intercept two arcs of a circle.)

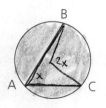

Part Two: Sample Problems

Problem 1   Find the circumference and the area of ⊙P.

Solution

$$C = \pi d \qquad\qquad A = \pi r^2$$
$$\quad= \pi(5.4) \qquad\qquad\quad = \pi(2.7^2)$$
$$\quad= 5.4\pi,\ \text{or} \approx 16.96 \qquad = 7.29\pi,\ \text{or} \approx 22.90$$

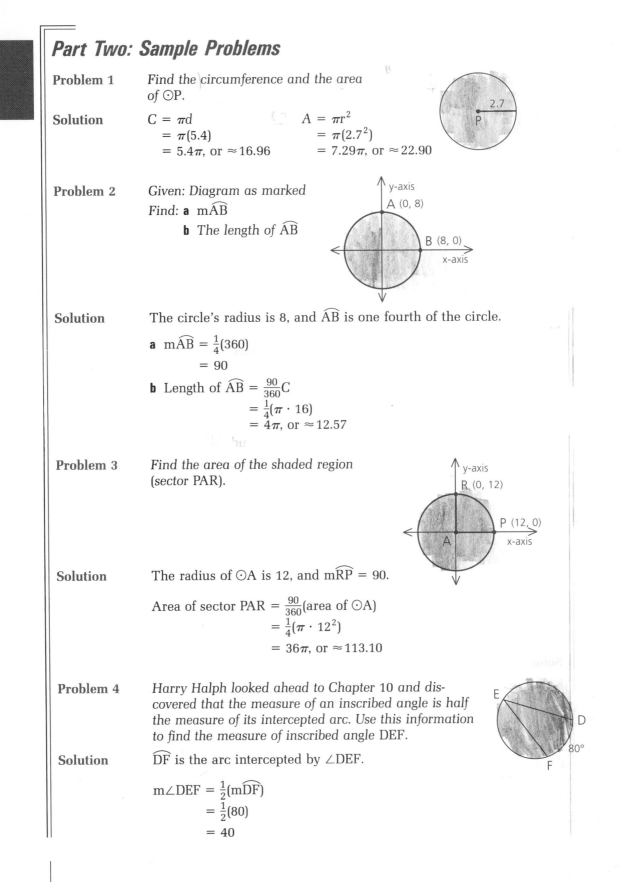

Problem 2   Given: Diagram as marked

Find: **a** m$\widehat{AB}$

      b The length of $\widehat{AB}$

Solution   The circle's radius is 8, and $\widehat{AB}$ is one fourth of the circle.

a m$\widehat{AB} = \frac{1}{4}(360)$
$$= 90$$

b Length of $\widehat{AB} = \frac{90}{360}C$
$$= \frac{1}{4}(\pi \cdot 16)$$
$$= 4\pi,\ \text{or} \approx 12.57$$

Problem 3   Find the area of the shaded region (sector PAR).

Solution   The radius of ⊙A is 12, and m$\widehat{RP}$ = 90.

Area of sector PAR $= \frac{90}{360}$(area of ⊙A)
$$= \frac{1}{4}(\pi \cdot 12^2)$$
$$= 36\pi,\ \text{or} \approx 113.10$$

Problem 4   Harry Halph looked ahead to Chapter 10 and discovered that the measure of an inscribed angle is half the measure of its intercepted arc. Use this information to find the measure of inscribed angle DEF.

Solution $\widehat{DF}$ is the arc intercepted by ∠DEF.

$$m\angle DEF = \frac{1}{2}(m\widehat{DF})$$
$$= \frac{1}{2}(80)$$
$$= 40$$

Problem 5 If $\overline{HJ}$ is a diameter of $\odot O$, what are the coordinates of point O?

Solution We can use the midpoint formula.

$$x_m = \frac{x_1 + x_2}{2} \qquad y_m = \frac{y_1 + y_2}{2}$$

$$= \frac{8 + (-4)}{2} \qquad\quad = \frac{5 + (-3)}{2}$$

$$= 2 \qquad\qquad\qquad = 1$$

The coordinates of point O are (2, 1).

Problem 6 Show that $\triangle$INS is a right triangle by
a Finding m$\angle$INS
b Finding the slopes of $\overleftrightarrow{IN}$ and $\overleftrightarrow{NS}$

Solution **a** $\overparen{ICS}$ is one-half the circle, so m$\overparen{ICS}$ = 180.

Since $\overparen{ICS}$ is intercepted by inscribed angle INS,

$$m\angle INS = \tfrac{1}{2}(m\overparen{ICS})$$
$$= \tfrac{1}{2}(180)$$
$$= 90$$

Therefore, $\angle$INS is a right angle, and $\triangle$INS is a right triangle.

b Recall that two lines are perpendicular if their slopes are opposite reciprocals.

$$\text{Slope of } \overleftrightarrow{IN} = \frac{8 - 0}{6 - (-10)} = \frac{1}{2}$$

$$\text{Slope of } \overleftrightarrow{NS} = \frac{0 - 8}{10 - 6} = -2$$

Since $\overleftrightarrow{IN} \perp \overleftrightarrow{NS}$, $\triangle$INS is a right triangle.

Problem 7 Reflect point H over the y-axis to H′. Then find the slope of $\overleftrightarrow{TH'}$.

Solution Since H is four units to the right of the y-axis, H′ must be four units to the left of the y-axis. Therefore, H′ = $(-4, 9)$.

$$\text{Slope of } \overleftrightarrow{TH'} = \frac{9 - 2}{-4 - 10}$$

$$= \frac{7}{-14}$$

$$= -\frac{1}{2}$$

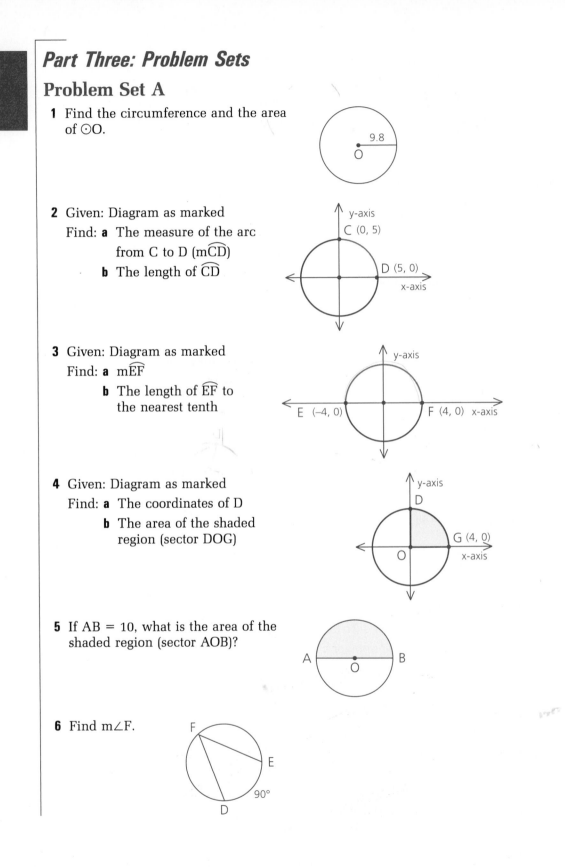

Part Three: Problem Sets

Problem Set A

1 Find the circumference and the area of ⊙O.

2 Given: Diagram as marked
   Find: **a** The measure of the arc
         from C to D (m$\widehat{CD}$)
      b The length of $\widehat{CD}$

3 Given: Diagram as marked
   Find: **a** m$\widehat{EF}$
      b The length of $\widehat{EF}$ to
         the nearest tenth

4 Given: Diagram as marked
   Find: **a** The coordinates of D
      b The area of the shaded
         region (sector DOG)

5 If AB = 10, what is the area of the
   shaded region (sector AOB)?

6 Find m∠F.

7 Given: Diagram as marked

  Find: **a** m∠A
  b m∠D

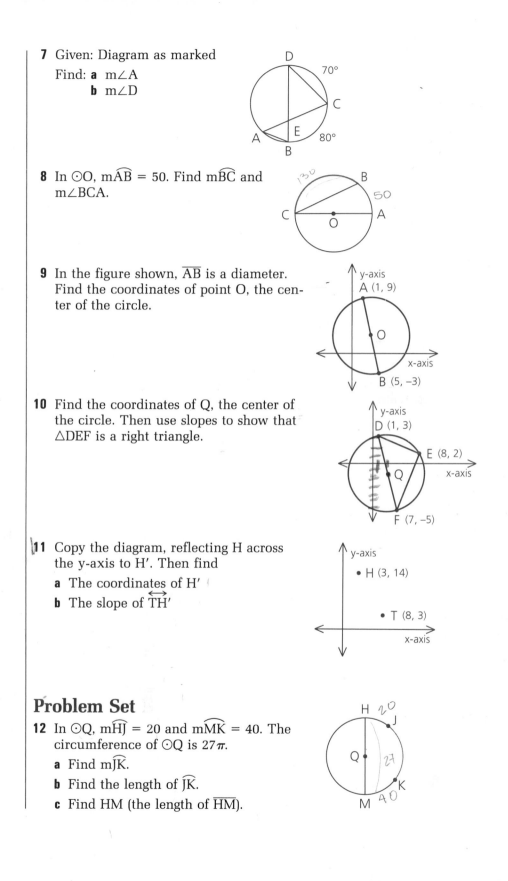

8 In ⊙O, mÂB = 50. Find mB̂C and m∠BCA.

9 In the figure shown, $\overline{AB}$ is a diameter. Find the coordinates of point O, the center of the circle.

10 Find the coordinates of Q, the center of the circle. Then use slopes to show that △DEF is a right triangle.

11 Copy the diagram, reflecting H across the y-axis to H'. Then find
  a The coordinates of H'
  b The slope of $\overset{\leftrightarrow}{TH'}$

Problem Set

12 In ⊙Q, mĤJ = 20 and mM̂K = 40. The circumference of ⊙Q is 27π.
  a Find mĴK.
  b Find the length of ĴK.
  c Find HM (the length of $\overline{HM}$).

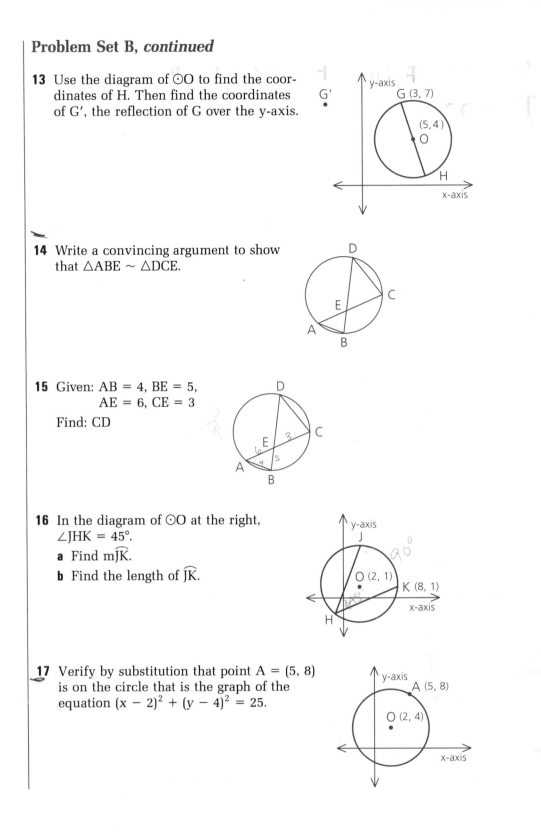

13 Use the diagram of ⊙O to find the coordinates of H. Then find the coordinates of G′, the reflection of G over the y-axis.

14 Write a convincing argument to show that △ABE ~ △DCE.

15 Given: AB = 4, BE = 5,
AE = 6, CE = 3

Find: CD

16 In the diagram of ⊙O at the right, ∠JHK = 45°.

a Find m$\overset{\frown}{JK}$.

b Find the length of $\overset{\frown}{JK}$.

17 Verify by substitution that point A = (5, 8) is on the circle that is the graph of the equation $(x - 2)^2 + (y - 4)^2 = 25$.

ALTITUDE-ON-HYPOTENUSE THEOREMS

Objective

After studying this section, you will be able to
- Identify the relationships between the parts of a right triangle when an altitude is drawn to the hypotenuse

Part One: Introduction

When altitude $\overline{CD}$ is drawn to the hypotenuse of $\triangle ABC$, three similar triangles are formed.

$$\triangle ABC \sim \triangle ACD \sim \triangle CBD$$

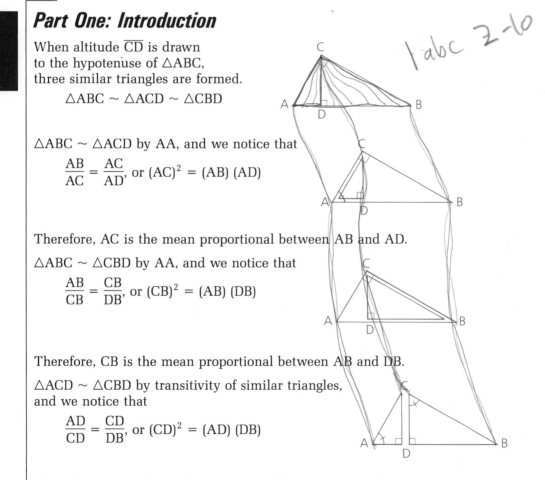

$\triangle ABC \sim \triangle ACD$ by AA, and we notice that

$$\frac{AB}{AC} = \frac{AC}{AD}, \text{ or } (AC)^2 = (AB)(AD)$$

Therefore, AC is the mean proportional between AB and AD.

$\triangle ABC \sim \triangle CBD$ by AA, and we notice that

$$\frac{AB}{CB} = \frac{CB}{DB}, \text{ or } (CB)^2 = (AB)(DB)$$

Therefore, CB is the mean proportional between AB and DB.

$\triangle ACD \sim \triangle CBD$ by transitivity of similar triangles, and we notice that

$$\frac{AD}{CD} = \frac{CD}{DB}, \text{ or } (CD)^2 = (AD)(DB)$$

Therefore, CD is the mean proportional between AD and DB.

These illustrations prove three closely related theorems, which we will present as one theorem.

Theorem 68   *If an altitude is drawn to the hypotenuse of a right triangle, then*

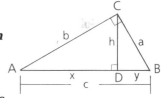

a *The two triangles formed are similar to the given right triangle and to each other*

$$\triangle ADC \sim \triangle ACB \sim \triangle CDB$$

b *The altitude to the hypotenuse is the mean proportional between the segments of the hypotenuse*

$$\frac{x}{h} = \frac{h}{y}, \text{ or } h^2 = xy$$

c *Either leg of the given right triangle is the mean proportional between the hypotenuse of the given right triangle and the segment of the hypotenuse adjacent to that leg (i.e., the projection of that leg on the hypotenuse)*

$$\frac{y}{a} = \frac{a}{c}, \text{ or } a^2 = yc; \text{ and } \frac{x}{b} = \frac{b}{c}, \text{ or } b^2 = xc$$

Parts **b** and **c** of Theorem 68 can be summarized as follows.

$$h^2 = x \cdot y$$
$$b^2 = x \cdot c$$
$$a^2 = y \cdot c$$

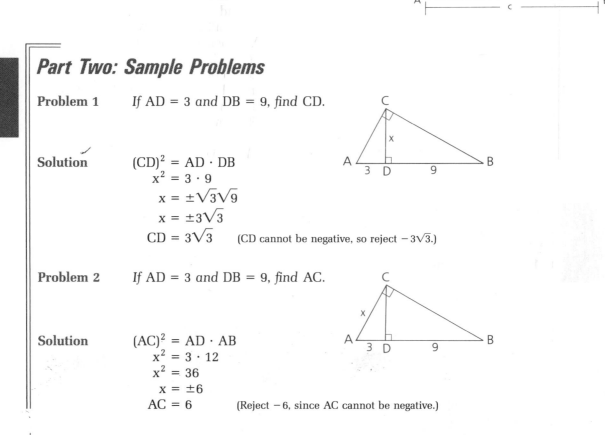

Part Two: Sample Problems

Problem 1   *If AD = 3 and DB = 9, find CD.*

Solution
$$(CD)^2 = AD \cdot DB$$
$$x^2 = 3 \cdot 9$$
$$x = \pm\sqrt{3}\sqrt{9}$$
$$x = \pm 3\sqrt{3}$$
$$CD = 3\sqrt{3} \qquad \text{(CD cannot be negative, so reject } -3\sqrt{3}.)$$

Problem 2   *If AD = 3 and DB = 9, find AC.*

Solution
$$(AC)^2 = AD \cdot AB$$
$$x^2 = 3 \cdot 12$$
$$x^2 = 36$$
$$x = \pm 6$$
$$AC = 6 \qquad \text{(Reject } -6, \text{ since AC cannot be negative.)}$$

Problem 3   If $DB = 21$ and $AC = 10$, find AD.

Solution

$$(AC)^2 = AD \cdot AB$$
$$10^2 = x(x + 21)$$
$$x(x + 21) = 10 \cdot 10$$
$$x^2 + 21x = 100$$
$$x^2 + 21x - 100 = 0$$
$$(x + 25)(x - 4) = 0$$
$$x + 25 = 0 \text{ or } x - 4 = 0$$
$$x = -25 \text{ or } x = 4$$

Since AD cannot be negative, $AD = 4$.

Problem 4   Given: $\overline{PK} \perp \overline{JM}$, $\overline{RK} \perp \overline{JP}$, $\overline{KO} \perp \overline{PM}$

Prove: $(PO)(PM) = (PR)(PJ)$

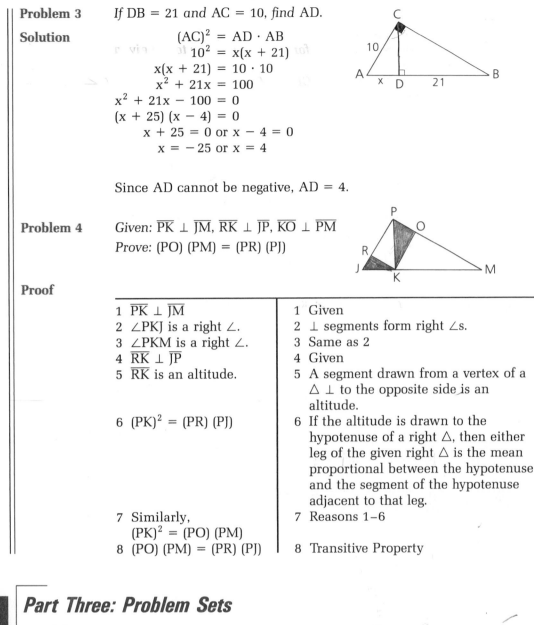

Proof

1 $\overline{PK} \perp \overline{JM}$	1 Given
2 $\angle PKJ$ is a right $\angle$.	2 $\perp$ segments form right $\angle$s.
3 $\angle PKM$ is a right $\angle$.	3 Same as 2
4 $\overline{RK} \perp \overline{JP}$	4 Given
5 $\overline{RK}$ is an altitude.	5 A segment drawn from a vertex of a $\triangle \perp$ to the opposite side is an altitude.
6 $(PK)^2 = (PR)(PJ)$	6 If the altitude is drawn to the hypotenuse of a right $\triangle$, then either leg of the given right $\triangle$ is the mean proportional between the hypotenuse and the segment of the hypotenuse adjacent to that leg.
7 Similarly, $(PK)^2 = (PO)(PM)$	7 Reasons 1–6
8 $(PO)(PM) = (PR)(PJ)$	8 Transitive Property

Part Three: Problem Sets

Problem Set A

1 a If $EH = 7$ and $HG = 3$, find HF.

b If $EH = 7$ and $HG = 4$, find EF.

c If $GF = 6$ and $EG = 9$, find HG.

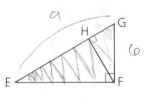

2 a Find $2x$.   **b** Find $\frac{1}{2}y$.   **c** Find $z + 8$.

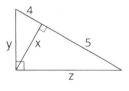

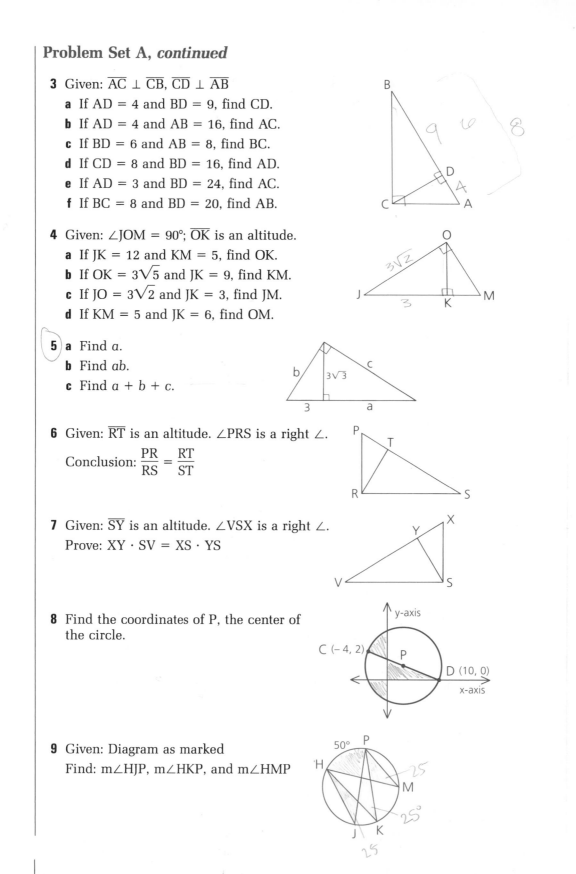

3 Given: $\overline{AC} \perp \overline{CB}$, $\overline{CD} \perp \overline{AB}$

  a If AD = 4 and BD = 9, find CD.

  b If AD = 4 and AB = 16, find AC.

  c If BD = 6 and AB = 8, find BC.

  d If CD = 8 and BD = 16, find AD.

  e If AD = 3 and BD = 24, find AC.

  f If BC = 8 and BD = 20, find AB.

4 Given: $\angle JOM = 90°$; $\overline{OK}$ is an altitude.

  a If JK = 12 and KM = 5, find OK.

  b If OK = $3\sqrt{5}$ and JK = 9, find KM.

  c If JO = $3\sqrt{2}$ and JK = 3, find JM.

  d If KM = 5 and JK = 6, find OM.

5 **a** Find a.

  b Find ab.

  c Find $a + b + c$.

6 Given: $\overline{RT}$ is an altitude. $\angle PRS$ is a right $\angle$.

  Conclusion: $\dfrac{PR}{RS} = \dfrac{RT}{ST}$

7 Given: $\overline{SY}$ is an altitude. $\angle VSX$ is a right $\angle$.

  Prove: $XY \cdot SV = XS \cdot YS$

8 Find the coordinates of P, the center of the circle.

9 Given: Diagram as marked

  Find: $m\angle HJP$, $m\angle HKP$, and $m\angle HMP$

10 Find the measure of $\overset{\frown}{\text{RH}}$.

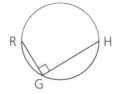

11 Find the area of sector MOG.

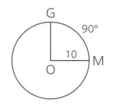

Problem Set B

12 a Find the coordinates of point C.
  b Find the measure of the arc from A to B to C ($m\overset{\frown}{\text{ABC}}$).
  c Find the length of $\overset{\frown}{\text{ABC}}$.

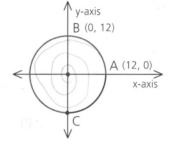

13 In $\odot$P, $m\overset{\frown}{\text{FG}} = 80$ and $m\overset{\frown}{\text{DE}} = 40$. Find $m\overset{\frown}{\text{EF}}$ and $m\angle\text{EDF}$.

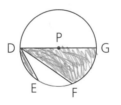

14 As Slarpy stood at B, the foot of a 6-m pole, he asked Carpy how far it was across the pond from B to C. Carpy got his carpenter's square and climbed the pole. Using his lines of sight, he set up the figure shown. When Slarpy found that AB = 3 m, Carpy knew the answer. What was it?

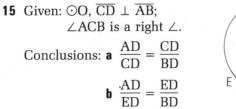

15 Given: $\odot$O, $\overline{\text{CD}} \perp \overline{\text{AB}}$;
       $\angle\text{ACB}$ is a right $\angle$.

  Conclusions: **a** $\dfrac{\text{AD}}{\text{CD}} = \dfrac{\text{CD}}{\text{BD}}$

       b $\dfrac{\text{AD}}{\text{ED}} = \dfrac{\text{ED}}{\text{BD}}$

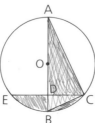

Problem Set B, *continued*

16 a If HG = 4 and EF = 3√5, find EH.
   b If GF = 6 and EH = 9, find EG.

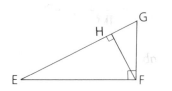

17 a If AD = 7 and AB = 11, find CD.
   b If CD = 8 and AD = 6, find AB.
   c If AB = 12 and AD = 4, find BC.
   d If AC = 7 and AB = 12, find BD.

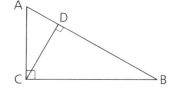

18 $\overline{CD}$ is the altitude to hypotenuse $\overline{AB}$. If the lengths AD, CD, CD, and BD are written down at random to form two ratios, what is the probability that the ratios are equal?

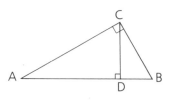

Problem Set C

19 If √5 ≈ 2.236, find DE to the nearest tenth. (The symbol ≈ means "approximately equals.")

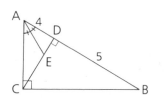

20 Prove: The product of the measures of the legs of a right triangle is equal to the product of the measures of the hypotenuse and the altitude to the hypotenuse.

21 Given: $\overline{AD} \perp \overline{CD}$,
       $\overline{BD} \perp \overline{AC}$,
       BC = 5, AD = 6
  Find: BD

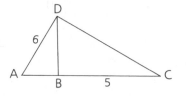

22 Given: $\overline{FG} \perp \overline{GH}$;
       ∠1 is comp. to ∠3.
  Prove: $\dfrac{JH}{GH} = \dfrac{GH}{HF}$

Problem Set D

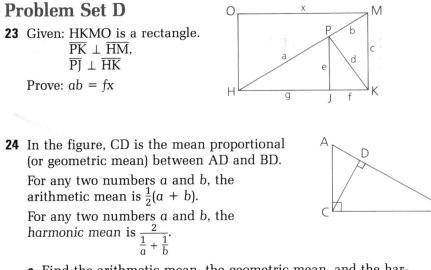

23 Given: HKMO is a rectangle.
$\overline{PK} \perp \overline{HM}$,
$\overline{PJ} \perp \overline{HK}$

Prove: $ab = fx$

24 In the figure, CD is the mean proportional (or geometric mean) between AD and BD.

For any two numbers a and b, the arithmetic mean is $\frac{1}{2}(a + b)$.

For any two numbers a and b, the harmonic mean is $\dfrac{2}{\frac{1}{a} + \frac{1}{b}}$.

a Find the arithmetic mean, the geometric mean, and the harmonic mean between each pair of lengths.

  i AD = 2, BD = 8
 ii AD = 3, BD = 12
iii AD = 4, BD = 25

b Given two positive numbers a and b, prove that their arithmetic mean, $\frac{1}{2}(a + b)$, is always greater than or equal to their positive geometric mean, $\sqrt{ab}$.

MATHEMATICAL EXCURSION

THE PYTHAGOREAN THEOREM AND TRIGONOMETRIC RATIOS

The magnifying properties of gravity

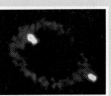

Using sophisticated technology, astronomers have recently observed a phenomenon called *Einstein rings*, which occur when three objects, such as a galaxy, a quasar, and the earth, are collinear. Einstein rings are multiple images of the farther object—for example, the quasar—as its light or energy curves around the intervening object—the galaxy. In this case, the galaxy acts as a gravitational lens. It helps astronomers see more of the distant object than they could by observing a single image.

Astronomers can calculate a distance to a flaring quasar by applying the Pythagorean The-

orem and trigonometric ratios to data that include: the difference in arrival times of the light from the flare by different paths it takes around the galaxy, the angles separating the images, the red-shift velocities of light from the quasar and from the galaxy, and the mass of the galaxy.

GEOMETRY'S MOST ELEGANT THEOREM

Objective

After studying this section, you will be able to

- Use the Pythagorean Theorem and its converse

Part One: Introduction

As the plays of Shakespeare are to literature, as the Constitution is to the United States, so is the **Pythagorean Theorem** to geometry. First, it is basic, for it is the rule for solving right triangles. Second, it is widely applied, because every polygon can be divided into right triangles by diagonals and altitudes. Third, it enables many ideas (and objects) to fit together very simply. Indeed, it is elegant in concept and extremely powerful.

Theorem 69   ***The square of the measure of the hypotenuse of a right triangle is equal to the sum of the squares of the measures of the legs. (Pythagorean Theorem)***

Given: $\triangle ACB$ is a right $\triangle$
      with right $\angle ACB$.

Prove: $a^2 + b^2 = c^2$

Proof:

1 $\angle ACB$ is a right $\angle$.	1 Given
2 Draw $\overline{CD} \perp$ to $\overline{AB}$.	2 From a point outside a line, only one $\perp$ can be drawn to the line.
3 $\overline{CD}$ is an altitude.	3 A segment drawn from a vertex of a $\triangle \perp$ to the opposite side is an altitude.
4 $a^2 = (c - x)c$	4 In a right $\triangle$ with an altitude drawn to the hypotenuse, $(\text{leg})^2 = (\text{adjacent seg.})(\text{hypot.})$.
5 $a^2 = c^2 - cx$	5 Distributive Property
6 $b^2 = xc$	6 Same as 4
7 $a^2 + b^2 = c^2 - cx + cx$	7 Addition Property
8 $a^2 + b^2 = c^2$	8 Algebra

The Pythagorean Theorem was known to the ancient Egyptians and Greeks. The first proof is attributed to Pythagoras, a Greek mathematician who lived about 500 B.C. There are now more than 300 proofs of the theorem, and a book has been published consisting solely of such proofs. (Different sets of postulates and theorems lead to different proofs.)

One of the simplest ways to know that two lines are perpendicular is to find out if they form a right angle in a triangle. To use this method, we need the converse of the Pythagorean Theorem, given next.

Theorem 70 *If the square of the measure of one side of a triangle equals the sum of the squares of the measures of the other two sides, then the angle opposite the longest side is a right angle.*

If $a^2 + b^2 = c^2$,
then $\triangle ACB$ is a right $\triangle$
and $\angle C$ is the right $\angle$.

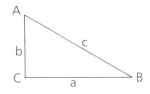

If, in the diagram above, we increased c while keeping a and b the same, $\angle C$ would become larger. Try it. Thus, a valuable extension of Theorem 70 can be stated:

If c is the length of the longest side of a triangle, and
- $a^2 + b^2 > c^2$, then the triangle is acute
- $a^2 + b^2 = c^2$, then the triangle is right
- $a^2 + b^2 < c^2$, then the triangle is obtuse

Part Two: Sample Problems

Problem 1 *Solve for x.*

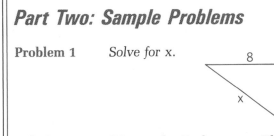

Solution We use the Pythagorean Theorem.
$$6^2 + 8^2 = x^2$$
$$36 + 64 = x^2$$
$$100 = x^2$$
$$\pm 10 = x \quad \text{(Reject } -10.\text{)}$$
$$x = 10$$

Problem 2   Find the perimeter of the rectangle shown.

Solution   We use the Pythagorean Theorem.

$$x^2 + 5^2 = 13^2$$
$$x^2 + 25 = 169$$
$$x^2 = 144$$
$$x = \pm 12 \quad \text{(Reject } -12.)$$

Perimeter = $5 + 12 + 5 + 12 = 34$

Problem 3   Find the perimeter of a rhombus with diagonals of 6 and 10.

Solution   Remember that the diagonals of a rhombus are perpendicular bisectors of each other.

$$3^2 + 5^2 = x^2$$
$$9 + 25 = x^2$$
$$34 = x^2$$
$$\pm\sqrt{34} = x \quad \text{(Reject } -\sqrt{34}.)$$

Since all sides of a rhombus are congruent, the perimeter is $4\sqrt{34}$.

Problem 4   Nadia skipped 3 m north, 2 m east, 4 m north, 13 m east, and 1 m north. How far is Nadia from where she started?

Solution   Since Nadia started at S and ended at E, we are looking for the hypotenuse of △SAE. She has gone a total of 8 m north and 15 m east.

$$8^2 + 15^2 = x^2$$
$$64 + 225 = x^2$$
$$289 = x^2$$
$$\pm 17 = x \quad \text{(Reject } -17.)$$
$$SE = 17 \text{ m}$$

Problem 5   Find the altitude of an isosceles trapezoid whose sides have lengths of 10, 30, 10, and 20.

Solution   An altitude of a trapezoid is a segment, such as $\overline{AE}$, perpendicular to both bases. We often draw two altitudes, such as $\overline{AE}$ and $\overline{BD}$, to obtain a rectangle, AEDB. Thus, ED = 20, right △AEF is congruent to right △BDC, and FE = DC = $\frac{1}{2}(30 - 20) = 5$.

In △AEF, $x^2 + 5^2 = 10^2$
$$x^2 + 25 = 100$$
$$x^2 = 75$$
$$x = \pm\sqrt{75}$$
$$= \pm\sqrt{25 \cdot 3}$$
$$= \pm 5\sqrt{3} \quad \text{(Reject } -5\sqrt{3}.)$$

Altitude = $5\sqrt{3}$

Problem 6 Classify the triangle shown.

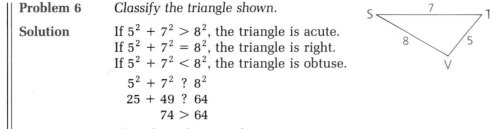

Solution

If $5^2 + 7^2 > 8^2$, the triangle is acute.
If $5^2 + 7^2 = 8^2$, the triangle is right.
If $5^2 + 7^2 < 8^2$, the triangle is obtuse.

$$5^2 + 7^2 \; ? \; 8^2$$
$$25 + 49 \; ? \; 64$$
$$74 > 64$$

Therefore, the triangle is acute.

Part Three: Problem Sets

Problem Set A

1 Solve for the third side.

a $x = 4, y = 5$

b $x = 15, r = 17$

c $y = 9, r = 15$

d $x = 12, r = 13$

e $x = 5, y = 5\sqrt{3}$

f $x = 5, r = \sqrt{29}$

g $x = 2\sqrt{5}, r = \sqrt{38}$

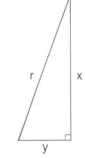

2 Find the length of the diagonal of a square with perimeter 12 cm.

3 Find the perimeter of a rhombus with diagonals 12 km and 16 km.

4 Find the perimeter of a rectangle whose diagonal is 17 mm long and whose base is 15 mm long.

1,2,1,0.

5 Given: $\overline{JG}$ is the altitude to base $\overline{FH}$ of isosceles triangle JFH.
FJ = 15, FH = 24
Find: JG

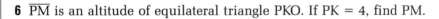

6 $\overline{PM}$ is an altitude of equilateral triangle PKO. If PK = 4, find PM.

7 Find the missing length in the trapezoid.

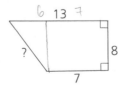

Problem Set A, *continued*

8 How far is the foot of the ladder from the wall?

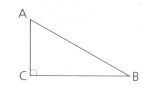

50dm

48dm

?

9 $\overline{AC} \parallel$ y-axis and $\overline{CB} \parallel$ x-axis.

  a Find the coordinates of C.

  b Find AC and CB.

  c Find AB.

  d Is $AB = \sqrt{(8-2)^2 + (11-3)^2}$?

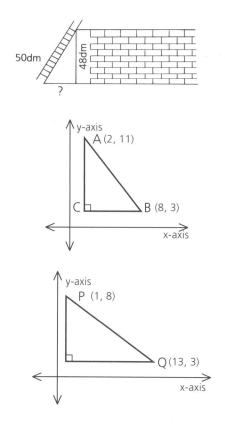

y-axis

A (2, 11)

C

B (8, 3)

x-axis

10 Use the method suggested by part **d** of problem 9 to find PQ.

y-axis

P (1, 8)

Q (13, 3)

x-axis

Problem Set B

11 Find the missing length in terms of the variable(s) provided.

  a AC = x, BC = y, AB = ___?___

  b AC = 2, BC = x, AB = ___?___

  c AC = 3a, BC = 4a, AB = ___?___

  d AB = 13c, AC = 5c, BC = ___?___

A

C

B

12 ∠ACB is a right angle and $\overline{CD} \perp \overline{AB}$.

  a If AD = 7 and BD = 4, find CD.

  b If CD = 8 and DB = 6, find CB.

  c If BC = 8 and BD = 2, find AB.

  d If AC = 21 and AB = 29, find CB.

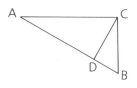

A

C

D

B

13 Al Capone walked 2 km north, 6 km west, 4 km north, and 2 km west. If Big Al decides to "go straight," how far must he walk across the fields to his starting point?

14 Find the altitude (length of a segment perpendicular to both bases) of the isosceles trapezoid shown.

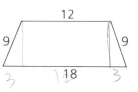

12

9

9

3

18

3

15 A piece broke off rectangle ABDF, leaving trapezoid ACDF. If BD = 16, BC = 7, FD = 24, and E is the midpoint of $\overline{FD}$, what is the perimeter of $\triangle$ACE?

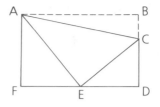

16 Given: Diagram as shown

Find: CD

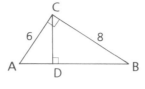

17 Solve for x in the partial spiral to the right.

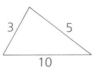

18 If the perimeter of a rhombus is $8\sqrt{5}$ and one diagonal has a length of $4\sqrt{2}$, find the length of the other diagonal.

19 Woody Woodpecker pecked at a 17-m wooden pole until it cracked and the upper part fell, with the top hitting the ground 10 m from the foot of the pole. Since the upper part had not completely broken off, Woody pecked away where the pole had cracked. How far was Woody above the ground?

20 Find the perimeter of an isosceles right triangle with a 6-cm hypotenuse.

21 The lengths of the diagonals of a rhombus are in the ratio 2:1. If the perimeter of the rhombus is 20, find the sum of the lengths of the diagonals.

22 Classify the triangles.

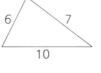

23 George and Diane bought a plot of land along Richard Road with the dimensions shown.

a Find the area of the plot.

b Find, to the nearest meter, the length of frontage on Richard Road.

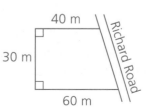

Problem Set C

24 Find the perimeter of △DBC.

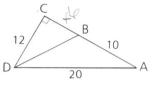

25 a Find HF.

   b Is △EHF similar to △HGF?

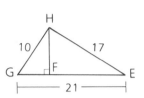

26 The perimeter of an isosceles triangle is 32, and the length of the altitude to its base is 8. Find the length of a leg.

27 A ladder 25 ft long (JO) is leaning against a wall, reaching a point 20 ft above the ground (MO). The ladder is then moved so that JK = 2(PO). Find KM.

28 The medians of a right triangle that are drawn from the vertices of the acute angles have lengths of $2\sqrt{13}$ and $\sqrt{73}$. Find the length of the hypotenuse.

29 The diagonals of an isosceles trapezoid are each 17, the altitude is 8, and the upper base is 9. Find the perimeter of the trapezoid.

30 a Show that if the lengths of one leg of a right triangle and the hypotenuse are consecutive integers, then the square of the length of the second leg is equal to the sum of the lengths of the first leg and the hypotenuse.

   b Show by counterexample that the converse of the statement in part **a** is not necessarily true. (The converse is, "If the square of the length of one of the legs of a right triangle is equal to the sum of the lengths of the other leg and the hypotenuse, then the lengths of the second leg and the hypotenuse are consecutive integers.")

31 Quadrilateral QUAD has vertices at Q = (−7, 1), U = (1, 16), A = (9, 10), and D = (1, −5).

   a Plot the figure and indicate what type of quadrilateral QUAD is.

   b Find the perimeter of QUAD.

Problem Set D

32 The legs of a right triangle have lengths of 3 m and 4 m. A point on the hypotenuse is 2 m from the intersection of the hypotenuse with the longer leg. How far is the point from the vertex of the right angle?

33 RSTV is an isosceles trapezoid with RS = 9, RV = 12, and ST = 18.

Find the length of the perpendicular segment from T to $\overline{SW}$.

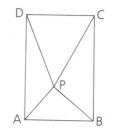

34 Given: $\overline{PR} \perp \overline{RT}$, PT = 25, PR = 15,
   PS = ST + 12

Find: SR

35 Abigail Adventuresome took a shortcut along the diagonal of a rectangular field and saved a distance equal to $\frac{1}{3}$ the length of the longer side. Find the ratio of the length of the shorter side of the rectangle to that of the longer side.

36 a Given: P is any point in the interior of rectangle ABCD.
   Show: $(BP)^2 + (PD)^2 = (AP)^2 + (CP)^2$

   b Is the result the same when P is in the exterior of the rectangle?

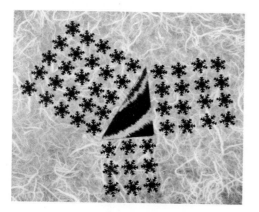

THE DISTANCE FORMULA

Objective

After studying this section, you will be able to
- Use the distance formula to compute lengths of segments in the coordinate plane

Part One: Introduction

In $\triangle AOB$, $AO = 4$, since we can count the 4 spaces from O to A. $OB = 3$, since we can count the 3 spaces from O to B.

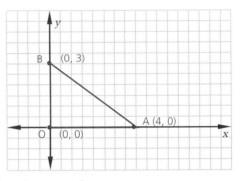

When a segment in the coordinate plane is either horizontal or vertical, its length is easily computed. To compute the length of $\overline{AB}$, we must find a new method. Since $\triangle AOB$ is a right triangle, we can apply the Pythagorean Theorem.

$$(OA)^2 + (OB)^2 = (BA)^2$$
$$3^2 + 4^2 = (BA)^2$$
$$25 = (BA)^2$$
$$5 = BA$$

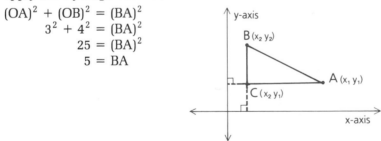

To compute any nonvertical, nonhorizontal length, we could draw a right triangle and use the Pythagorean Theorem.

$$(AB)^2 = (CA)^2 + (BC)^2$$
$$(AB)^2 = (x_2 - x_1)^2 + (y_2 - y_1)^2$$
$$AB = \sqrt{(x_2 - x_1)^2 + (y_2 - y_1)^2}$$
$$\text{or } AB = \sqrt{(\Delta x)^2 + (\Delta y)^2}$$

However, it is easier to use the ***distance formula,*** which is derived from the Pythagorean Theorem.

Theorem 71 *If P = (x_1, y_1) and Q = (x_2, y_2) are any two points, then the distance between them can be found with the formula*

$$PQ = \sqrt{(x_2 - x_1)^2 + (y_2 - y_1)^2} \text{ or}$$
$$PQ = \sqrt{(\Delta x)^2 + (\Delta y)^2}$$

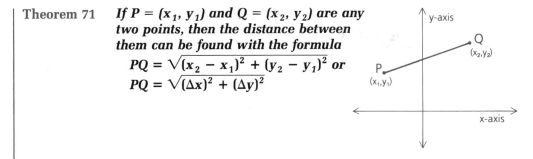

When doing coordinate proofs (sometimes called analytic proofs), you may select any convenient position in the coordinate plane for the figure *as long as complete generality is preserved.* Here are some convenient locations for a right triangle, an isosceles triangle, and a parallelogram.

Right Triangle	Isosceles Triangle	Parallelogram

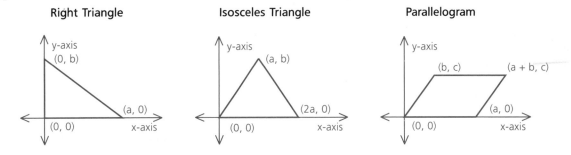

When midpoints are involved in a problem, it is helpful to use coordinates that make computations easier. For example, you could locate a rectangle as shown at the right.

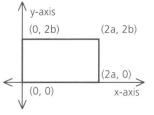

Part Two: Sample Problems

Problem 1   If A = (2, 3) and B = (7, 15), find AB.

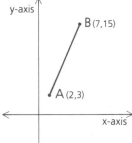

Solution   By the distance formula,

$$AB = \sqrt{(\Delta x)^2 + (\Delta y)^2}$$
$$= \sqrt{(7 - 2)^2 + (15 - 3)^2}$$
$$= \sqrt{5^2 + 12^2}$$
$$= \sqrt{169}$$
$$= 13$$

Problem 2   If D = (7, 1), E = (9, −5), and F = (6, −4), find the length of the median from F to $\overline{DE}$.

Solution   By the midpoint formula, the midpoint M of $\overline{DE}$ is (8, −2).

By the distance formula,

$$FM = \sqrt{(\Delta x)^2 + (\Delta y)^2}$$
$$= \sqrt{(6 - 8)^2 + [-4 - (-2)]^2}$$
$$= \sqrt{(-2)^2 + (-2)^2}$$
$$= \sqrt{8} = 2\sqrt{2}$$

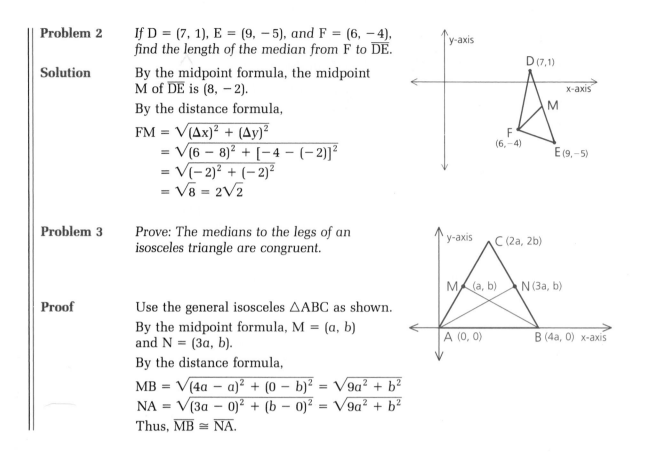

Problem 3   Prove: The medians to the legs of an isosceles triangle are congruent.

Proof   Use the general isosceles △ABC as shown.

By the midpoint formula, M = (a, b) and N = (3a, b).

By the distance formula,

$$MB = \sqrt{(4a - a)^2 + (0 - b)^2} = \sqrt{9a^2 + b^2}$$
$$NA = \sqrt{(3a - 0)^2 + (b - 0)^2} = \sqrt{9a^2 + b^2}$$

Thus, $\overline{MB} \cong \overline{NA}$.

Part Three: Problem Sets

Problem Set A

1 Find the distance between each pair of points.

a (4, 0) and (6, 0)

b (2, 3) and (2, −1)

c (4, 1) and (7, 5)

d (−2, −4) and (−8, 4)

e The origin and (2, 5)

f (2, 1) and (6, 3)

2 Find, to the nearest tenth, the perimeter of △ABC if A = (2, 6), B = (5, 10), and C = (0, 13).

3 Show that the triangle with vertices at (8, 4), (3, 5), and (4, 10) is a right triangle by using
a The distance formula   **b** Slopes

4 Use the distance formula to show that △DOG is equilateral if D = (6, 0), O = (0, 0), and G = (3, 3$\sqrt{3}$).

5 Find the area of the circle that passes through (9, −4) and whose center is (−3, 5).

6 Given: △RTV as shown

Find: **a** The length of the median from T

b The length of the segment joining the midpoints of $\overline{RT}$ and $\overline{TV}$

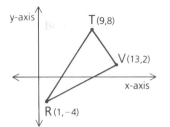

7 Find AD and BC.

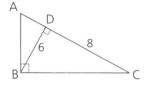

8 Given: Rectangle ABCO

a Find the coordinates of A, B, C, and O.

b Find the coordinates of M, N, P, and Q, the midpoints of the sides.

c Find the slopes of $\overline{MN}$, $\overline{QP}$, $\overline{MQ}$, and $\overline{NP}$. What can we conclude about MNPQ?

d Find the lengths of $\overline{MN}$, $\overline{QP}$, $\overline{MQ}$, and $\overline{NP}$. What can we now conclude about MNPQ?

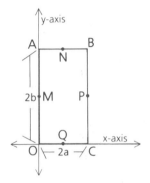

9 Given: Trapezoid PQRS

a Find PQ and SR and verify that PQRS is an isosceles trapezoid.

b Prove that the diagonals $\overline{PR}$ and $\overline{QS}$ are congruent.

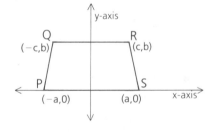

10 In the figure at the right, RECT is a rectangle. Is $\overline{RC}$ a diameter? Why or why not?

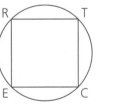

11 In rectangle RECT, RE = 5 and EC = 12.

a Find the circumference of the circle.

b Find the area of the circle to the nearest tenth.

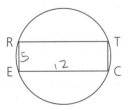

Problem Set A, *continued*

12 Prove that the diagonals of a square are congruent and perpendicular.

Problem Set B

13 Given: $\odot$R, m$\widehat{VW}$ = 120,
RW = 9

Find: **a** The area of sector TRV to the nearest tenth

b The difference, to the nearest tenth, between the length of $\overline{TW}$ and the length of $\widehat{VW}$

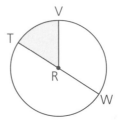

14 Show that (7, 11), (7, −13), and (14, 4) lie on a circle with its center at (2, −1).

15 Find, to the nearest tenth, the perimeter of a quadrilateral with vertices A = (2, 1), B = (7, 3), C = (12, 1), and D = (7, −4), and give the figure's most descriptive name.

16 Show that the parallelogram whose vertices are (−1, −3), (2, 1), (3, −2), and (−2, 0) is not a rhombus.

17 Show that the triangle with vertices (−2, 1), (5, 5), and (−1, −7) is isosceles.

18 The vertices of a rectangle are (0, 0) (8, 0), (0, 6), and (8, 6). Find the sum of the lengths of the two diagonals.

19 Show that (1, 2) (4, 6), and (10, 14) are collinear by using

a The distance formula (Hint: What is true about the lengths of the three segments joining three collinear points?)

b Slopes

20 The point (5, y) is equidistant from (1, 4) and (10, −3). Find y.

21 Find the altitude of a trapezoid with sides having the respective lengths 2, 41, 20, and 41.

22 A model rocket shot up to a point 20 m above the ground, hitting a smokestack, and then dropped straight down to a point 11 m from its launch site. Find, to the nearest meter, the total distance traveled from launch to touchdown.

23 Prove that the midpoint of the hypotenuse of a right triangle is equidistant from the three vertices.

24 Prove that the sum of the squares of the sides of a parallelogram is equal to the sum of the squares of the diagonals.

Problem Set C

25 Prove that in any quadrilateral the sum of the squares of the sides is equal to the sum of the squares of the diagonals plus four times the square of the segment joining the midpoints of the diagonals.

26 In isosceles trapezoid ABCD, A = $(-2a, 0)$ and B = $(2a, 0)$, where $a > 0$. The altitude of the trapezoid is $2h$, and the upper base, $\overline{CD}$, has a length of $4p$.

Find: **a** The coordinates of C and D

   b The length of the lower base

   c The length of the segment joining the midpoints of $\overline{AD}$ and $\overline{BC}$

   d The length of the segment joining the midpoints of the diagonals of the trapezoid

27 Two of the vertices of an equilateral triangle are (2, 1) and (6, 5). Find the possible coordinates of the remaining vertex.

FINDING DISTANCE WITH LASERS
Don Milligan draws the contours of the land

Don Milligan, whose work as a surveyor is heavily dependent on mathematics, admits that he hated geometry in high school. "But I enjoyed trigonometry," he says. "Then I found that trigonometric identities are related to SAS similarity. That changed my mind about geometry."

A surveyor's job is to determine the exact size, shape, and location of a plot of land. A survey can help establish boundary lines and compute the areas of irregularly shaped lots.

Angles are measured using a tool called a *transit*, a small telescope on a tripod. Transits in use today often employ lasers. Surveyors apply trigonometry, triangle proportions, and triangle similarity in their work.

Born in Salt Lake City, Utah, Milligan ob-

tained a bachelor's degree in forestry and wildlife management at Utah State University. After doing some survey work during the summer, he was hired by the Utah State Fish and Game Department. He left the department to work for a private surveying company, which he bought three years later.

FAMILIES OF RIGHT TRIANGLES

Objectives

After studying this section, you will be able to
- Recognize groups of whole numbers known as Pythagorean triples
- Apply the Principle of the Reduced Triangle

Part One: Introduction

Pythagorean Triples

In this section we consider some combinations of whole numbers that satisfy the Pythagorean Theorem. Knowing these combinations is not essential, but knowing some of them can save you appreciable time and effort.

Definition   Any three whole numbers that satisfy the equation $a^2 + b^2 = c^2$ form a ***Pythagorean triple.***

Below is a set of right triangles you have encountered many times in this chapter. Do you see how the triangles are related?

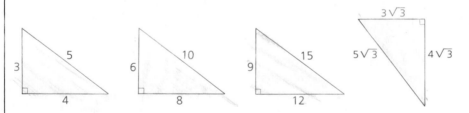

These four triangles are all members of the (3, 4, 5) family. For example, the triple (6, 8, 10) is $(3 \cdot 2, 4 \cdot 2, 5 \cdot 2)$.

Even though the last triangle, $(3\sqrt{3}, 4\sqrt{3}, 5\sqrt{3})$, is a member of the (3, 4, 5) family, the measures of its sides are not a Pythagorean triple because they are not whole numbers.

Other common families are

(5, 12, 13), of which (15, 36, 39) is another member

(7, 24, 25), of which (14, 48, 50) is another member

(8, 15, 17), of which $\left(4, 7\frac{1}{2}, 8\frac{1}{2}\right)$ is another member

There are infinitely many families, including (9, 40, 41), (11, 60, 61), (20, 21, 29), and (12, 35, 37), but most are not used very often.

The Principle of the Reduced Triangle

The following problem shows how a knowledge of Pythagorean triples can be useful even in situations where their applicability is not immediately apparent.

Example 1 *Given: The right triangle shown*
Find: x

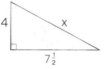

The fraction may complicate our work, and we may not wish to complete a long calculation to solve $4^2 + \left(7\frac{1}{2}\right)^2 = x^2$.

An alternative is to find a more easily recognized member of the same family. We multiply each side by the denominator of the fraction, 2. Clearly, the family is (8, 15, 17). Thus, $2x = 17$ and $x = 8\frac{1}{2}$ (in the original triangle).

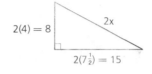

Principle of the Reduced Triangle

1 Reduce the difficulty of the problem by multiplying or dividing the three lengths by the same number to obtain a similar, but simpler, triangle in the same family.
2 Solve for the missing side of this easier triangle.
3 Convert back to the original problem.

The next example shows that the method may save time even if the sides of the "reduced" triangle are not a proper Pythagorean triple.

Example 2 *Find the value of x.*

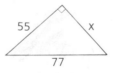

First, notice that both 55 and 77 are multiples of 11. Then reduce the problem to an easier problem as shown below.

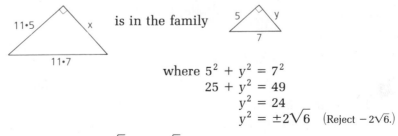

is in the family

where $5^2 + y^2 = 7^2$
$25 + y^2 = 49$
$y^2 = 24$
$y^2 = \pm 2\sqrt{6}$ (Reject $-2\sqrt{6}$.)

Thus, $x = 11 \cdot 2\sqrt{6} = 22\sqrt{6}$.

Part Two: Sample Problems

Problem 1   Find AB.

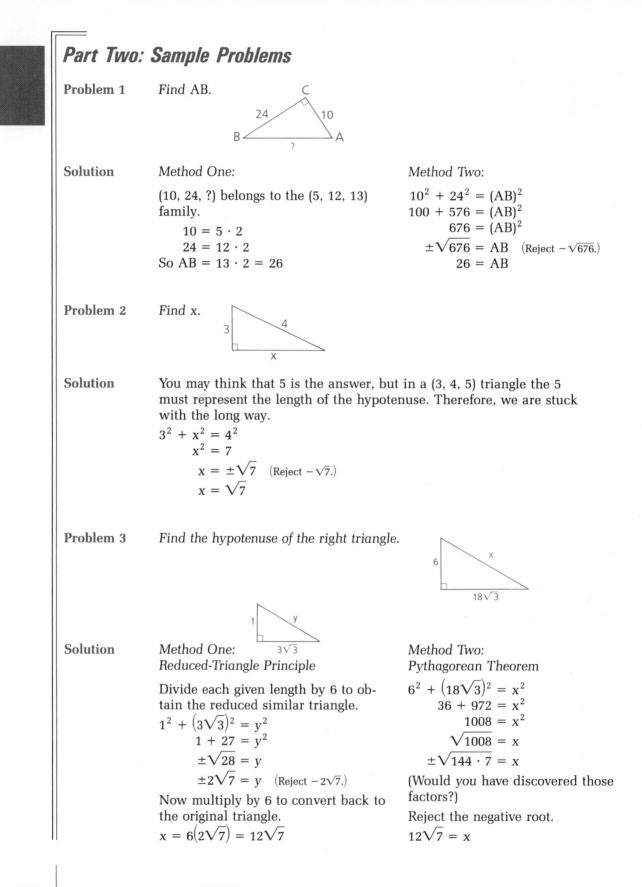

Solution

Method One:

(10, 24, ?) belongs to the (5, 12, 13) family.

$$10 = 5 \cdot 2$$
$$24 = 12 \cdot 2$$
So AB $= 13 \cdot 2 = 26$

Method Two:

$$10^2 + 24^2 = (AB)^2$$
$$100 + 576 = (AB)^2$$
$$676 = (AB)^2$$
$$\pm\sqrt{676} = AB \quad \text{(Reject } -\sqrt{676}.\text{)}$$
$$26 = AB$$

Problem 2   Find x.

Solution   You may think that 5 is the answer, but in a (3, 4, 5) triangle the 5 must represent the length of the hypotenuse. Therefore, we are stuck with the long way.

$$3^2 + x^2 = 4^2$$
$$x^2 = 7$$
$$x = \pm\sqrt{7} \quad \text{(Reject } -\sqrt{7}.\text{)}$$
$$x = \sqrt{7}$$

Problem 3   Find the hypotenuse of the right triangle.

Solution

Method One:
Reduced-Triangle Principle

Divide each given length by 6 to obtain the reduced similar triangle.

$$1^2 + (3\sqrt{3})^2 = y^2$$
$$1 + 27 = y^2$$
$$\pm\sqrt{28} = y$$
$$\pm2\sqrt{7} = y \quad \text{(Reject } -2\sqrt{7}.\text{)}$$

Now multiply by 6 to convert back to the original triangle.

$$x = 6(2\sqrt{7}) = 12\sqrt{7}$$

Method Two:
Pythagorean Theorem

$$6^2 + (18\sqrt{3})^2 = x^2$$
$$36 + 972 = x^2$$
$$1008 = x^2$$
$$\sqrt{1008} = x$$
$$\pm\sqrt{144 \cdot 7} = x$$

(Would you have discovered those factors?)

Reject the negative root.

$$12\sqrt{7} = x$$

Part Three: Problem Sets

Problem Set A
In problems 1–5, find the missing side in each triangle.

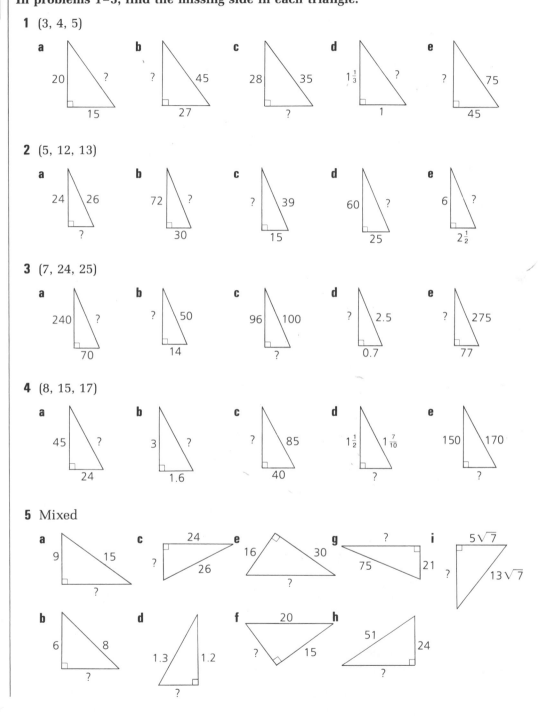

1 (3, 4, 5)

a   20   ?   15

b   ?   45   27

c   28   35   ?

d $1\frac{1}{3}$?   1

e   ?   75   45

2 (5, 12, 13)

a   24   26   ?

b   72   ?   30

c   ?   39   15

d   60   ?   25

e   6   ? $2\frac{1}{2}$

3 (7, 24, 25)

a   240   ?   70

b   ?   50   14

c   96   100   ?

d   ?   2.5   0.7

e   ?   275   77

4 (8, 15, 17)

a   45   ?   24

b   3   ?   1.6

c   ?   85   40

d $1\frac{1}{2}$ $1\frac{7}{10}$?

e   150   170   ?

5 Mixed

a   9   15   ?

b   6   8   ?

c   24   ?   26

d   1.3   1.2   ?

e   16   30   ?

f   20   ?   15

g   ?   75   21

h   51   24   ?

i $5\sqrt{7}$? $13\sqrt{7}$

Problem Set A, *continued*

6 Find the diagonal of a rectangle whose sides are 20 and 48.

7 Find the perimeter of an isosceles triangle whose base is 16 dm and whose height is 15 dm.

8 Find the length of the upper base of the isosceles trapezoid.

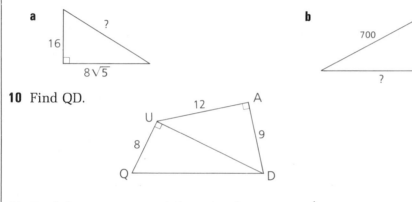

9 Use the reduced-triangle principle to find each missing side.

a

b

10 Find QD.

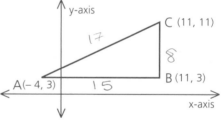

11 Find the perimeter and the area of △ABC.

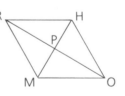

12 RHOM is a rhombus with diagonals RO = 48 and HM = 14. Find the perimeter of the rhombus.

Problem Set B

13 Mary and Larry left the riding stable at 10 A.M. Mary trotted south at 10 kph while Larry galloped east at 16 kph. To the nearest kilometer, how far apart were they at 11:30?

14 Write a coordinate proof to show that the diagonals of a rectangle are congruent.

15 Find the missing side of each triangle.

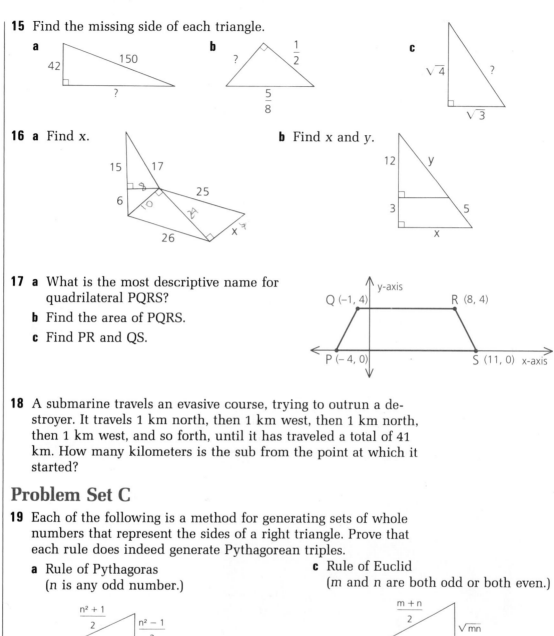

a

42 — 150 — ?

b

? — $\frac{1}{2}$ — $\frac{5}{8}$

c

$\sqrt{4}$ — ? — $\sqrt{3}$

16 a Find x.

15 — 17 — 6 — 25 — 26 — x

b Find x and y.

12 — y — 3 — 5 — x

17 a What is the most descriptive name for quadrilateral PQRS?

b Find the area of PQRS.

c Find PR and QS.

y-axis

Q (–1, 4)   R (8, 4)

P (–4, 0)   S (11, 0)   x-axis

18 A submarine travels an evasive course, trying to outrun a destroyer. It travels 1 km north, then 1 km west, then 1 km north, then 1 km west, and so forth, until it has traveled a total of 41 km. How many kilometers is the sub from the point at which it started?

Problem Set C

19 Each of the following is a method for generating sets of whole numbers that represent the sides of a right triangle. Prove that each rule does indeed generate Pythagorean triples.

a Rule of Pythagoras
(*n* is any odd number.)

$\frac{n^2 + 1}{2}$ $\frac{n^2 - 1}{2}$ n

c Rule of Euclid
(*m* and *n* are both odd or both even.)

$\frac{m + n}{2}$ $\sqrt{mn}$ $\frac{m - n}{2}$

b Rule of Plato
(*m* is any even number.)

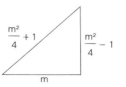

$\frac{m^2}{4} + 1$ $\frac{m^2}{4} - 1$ m

d Rule of Masères
(*m* and *n* are any two integers.)

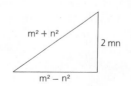

$m^2 + n^2$ $2mn$ $m^2 - n^2$

20 Show that the only right triangle in which the lengths of the sides are consecutive integers is the (3, 4, 5) triangle.

21 If a 650-cm ladder is placed against a building at a certain angle, it just reaches a point on the building that is 520 cm above the ground. If the ladder is moved to reach a point 80 cm higher up, how much closer will the foot of the ladder be to the building?

22 The lengths of the legs of a right triangle are x and 3x + y. The length of the hypotenuse is 4x − y. Find the ratio of x to y.

23 Six slips of paper, each containing a different one of the numbers 3, 4, 5, 6, 8, and 10, are placed in a hat. Then two of the slips are drawn at random.
   a What is the probability that the numbers drawn are the lengths of two of the sides of a triangle of the (3, 4, 5) family?
   b What is the probability that the numbers drawn are lengths of a leg and hypotenuse of a triangle of the (3, 4, 5) family?

Problem Set D

24 Find the length of the hypotenuse of the largest Pythagorean-triple triangle in which 16 is the measure of a leg.

25 Find all right triangles in which one side is 20 and other sides are integral.

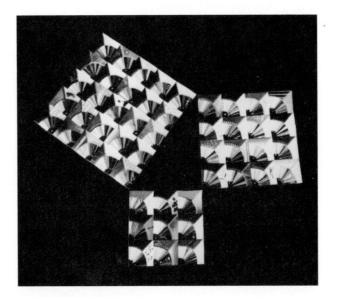

SPECIAL RIGHT TRIANGLES

Objectives

After studying this section, you will be able to
- Identify the ratio of side lengths in a 30°-60°-90° triangle
- Identify the ratio of side lengths in a 45°-45°-90° triangle

Part One: Introduction

30°-60°-90° Triangles

You will find it useful to know the ratio of the sides of a triangle with angles of 30°, 60°, and 90°.

Theorem 72   ***In a triangle whose angles have the measures 30, 60, and 90, the lengths of the sides opposite these angles can be represented by x, $x\sqrt{3}$, and 2x respectively. (30°-60°-90°-Triangle Theorem)***

Given: △ABC is equilateral.
$\overrightarrow{CD}$ bisects ∠ACB.
Prove: AD:DC:AC = $x:x\sqrt{3}:2x$

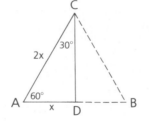

Proof: Since △ABC is equilateral, ∠ACD = 30°, ∠A = 60°, ∠ADC = 90°, and AD = $\frac{1}{2}$(AC).
By the Pythagorean Theorem, in △ADC,

$$x^2 + (DC)^2 = (2x)^2$$
$$x^2 + (DC)^2 = 4x^2$$
$$(DC)^2 = 3x^2$$
$$DC = x\sqrt{3}$$

Thus, AD:DC:AC = $x:x\sqrt{3}:2x$

45°-45°-90° Triangles

The sides of a triangle with angles of 45°, 45°, and 90° are also in an easily remembered ratio.

Theorem 73 *In a triangle whose angles have the measures 45, 45, and 90, the lengths of the sides opposite these angles can be represented by x, x, and x$\sqrt{2}$, respectively. (45°-45°-90°-Triangle Theorem)*

Given: △ACB, with ∠A = 45° and ∠B = 45°.

Prove: AC:CB:AB = x:x:x$\sqrt{2}$

The proof of this theorem is left to you.

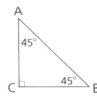

You will see 30°-60°-90° and 45°-45°-90° triangles frequently in this book and in other mathematics courses. Their ratios are worth memorizing now.

Six Common Families of Right Triangles		
30°-60°-90° ⟺ (x, x$\sqrt{3}$, 2x)	(5, 12, 13)	
45°-45°-90° ⟺ (x, x, x$\sqrt{2}$)	(7, 24, 25)	
(3, 4, 5)	(8, 15, 17)	

Part Two: Sample Problems

Problems 1 and 2 involve 30°-60°-90° triangles. In each, start by placing x on the side opposite (across from) the 30° angle, x$\sqrt{3}$ on the side opposite the 60° angle, and 2x on the hypotenuse.

Problem 1 *Type: Hypotenuse (2x) known*

Find BC and AC.

Solution Place x, x$\sqrt{3}$, and 2x on a copy of the diagram.

$$2x = 10$$
$$x = 5$$

Hence, BC = 5, and
$$AC = 5\sqrt{3}$$

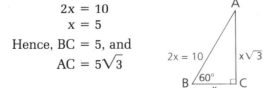

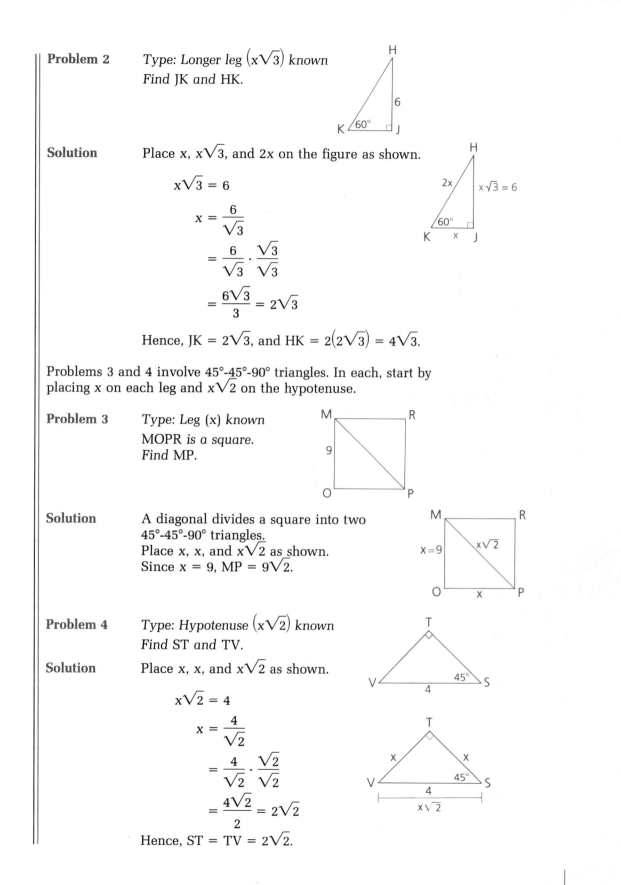

Problem 2

Type: Longer leg $\left(x\sqrt{3}\right)$ known
Find JK and HK.

Solution

Place x, $x\sqrt{3}$, and 2x on the figure as shown.

$$x\sqrt{3} = 6$$

$$x = \frac{6}{\sqrt{3}}$$

$$= \frac{6}{\sqrt{3}} \cdot \frac{\sqrt{3}}{\sqrt{3}}$$

$$= \frac{6\sqrt{3}}{3} = 2\sqrt{3}$$

Hence, JK = $2\sqrt{3}$, and HK = $2\left(2\sqrt{3}\right) = 4\sqrt{3}$.

Problems 3 and 4 involve 45°-45°-90° triangles. In each, start by placing x on each leg and $x\sqrt{2}$ on the hypotenuse.

Problem 3

Type: Leg (x) known
MOPR is a square.
Find MP.

Solution

A diagonal divides a square into two 45°-45°-90° triangles.
Place x, x, and $x\sqrt{2}$ as shown.
Since x = 9, MP = $9\sqrt{2}$.

Problem 4

Type: Hypotenuse $\left(x\sqrt{2}\right)$ known
Find ST and TV.

Solution

Place x, x, and $x\sqrt{2}$ as shown.

$$x\sqrt{2} = 4$$

$$x = \frac{4}{\sqrt{2}}$$

$$= \frac{4}{\sqrt{2}} \cdot \frac{\sqrt{2}}{\sqrt{2}}$$

$$= \frac{4\sqrt{2}}{2} = 2\sqrt{2}$$

Hence, ST = TV = $2\sqrt{2}$.

Part Three: Problem Sets

Problem Set A

1 Find the two missing sides in each 30°-60°-90° triangle. Try to do the calculations in your head.

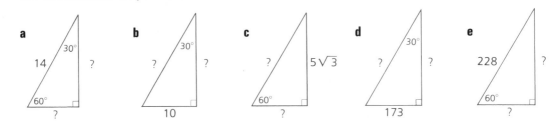

2 Find the two missing sides of each triangle. (Hint: These are a bit harder, and you may want to put x, x√3, and 2x on the proper sides as shown in the sample problems.)

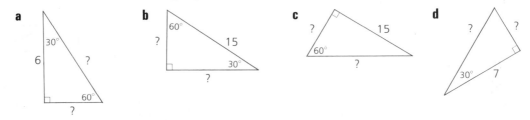

3 Solve for the variable in each of these equilateral triangles.

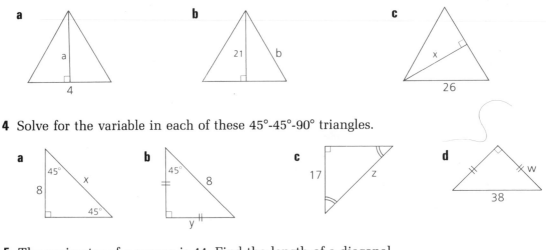

4 Solve for the variable in each of these 45°-45°-90° triangles.

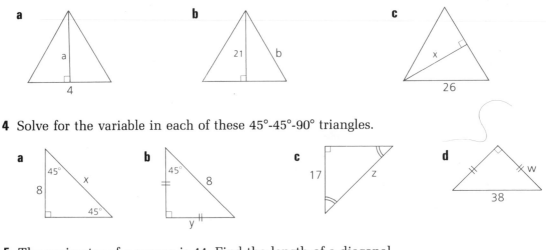

5 The perimeter of a square is 44. Find the length of a diagonal.

6 Find the length of the diagonal of the rectangle.

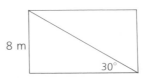

7 Find the altitude of an equilateral triangle if a side is 6 mm long.

8 Given: $\overline{AC} \perp \overline{BC}$, $\overline{CD} \perp \overline{AB}$, $\angle B = 30°$, $BC = 8\sqrt{3}$

Find: CD

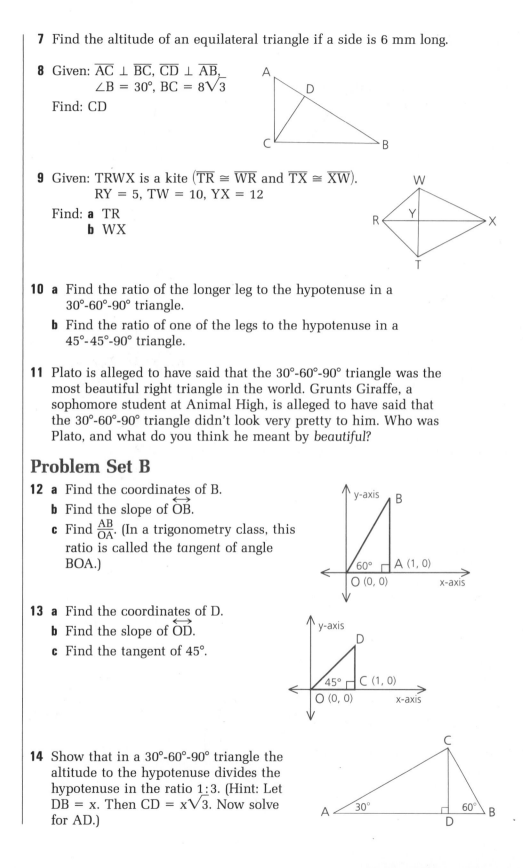

9 Given: TRWX is a kite ($\overline{TR} \cong \overline{WR}$ and $\overline{TX} \cong \overline{XW}$). RY = 5, TW = 10, YX = 12

Find: **a** TR
     b WX

10 a Find the ratio of the longer leg to the hypotenuse in a 30°-60°-90° triangle.

  b Find the ratio of one of the legs to the hypotenuse in a 45°-45°-90° triangle.

11 Plato is alleged to have said that the 30°-60°-90° triangle was the most beautiful right triangle in the world. Grunts Giraffe, a sophomore student at Animal High, is alleged to have said that the 30°-60°-90° triangle didn't look very pretty to him. Who was Plato, and what do you think he meant by *beautiful*?

Problem Set B

12 a Find the coordinates of B.

  b Find the slope of $\overleftrightarrow{OB}$.

  c Find $\frac{AB}{OA}$. (In a trigonometry class, this ratio is called the *tangent* of angle BOA.)

13 a Find the coordinates of D.

  b Find the slope of $\overleftrightarrow{OD}$.

  c Find the tangent of 45°.

14 Show that in a 30°-60°-90° triangle the altitude to the hypotenuse divides the hypotenuse in the ratio 1:3. (Hint: Let DB = x. Then CD = $x\sqrt{3}$. Now solve for AD.)

Problem Set B, *continued*

15 Find the perimeter of the isosceles trapezoid EFGH. (Hint: Drop altitudes of the trapezoid from E and H.)

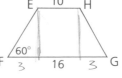

16 Given: $\overline{PK}$ is an altitude of isosceles trapezoid JMOP.
PK = 6, PO = 8, ∠J = 45°

Find: The perimeter of JMOP

17 Using the figure, find

  a VS

  b ST

  c VT

  d The ratio of the perimeter of △VSR to the perimeter of △VRT

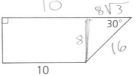

18 One of the angles of a rhombus has a measure of 120. If the perimeter of the rhombus is 24, find the length of each diagonal.

19 Find, to the nearest tenth, the perimeter of the trapezoid.

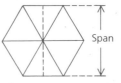

20 Any regular hexagon can be divided into six equilateral triangles by drawing the three diagonals shown. Find the span of a regular hexagon with sides 12 dm long.

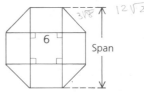

21 Any regular octagon can be divided into rectangles and right triangles. Here, a side of the central square is 6 units long.

  a Find the perimeter of the octagon.

  b Find the span of the octagon.

22 Find the altitude to the base of the isosceles triangle shown.

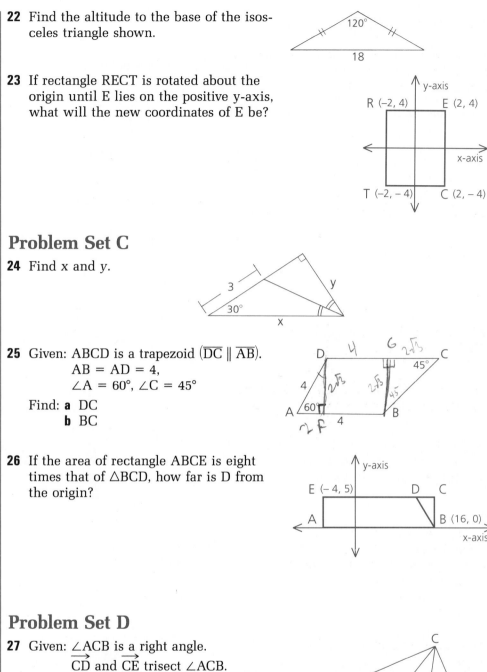

23 If rectangle RECT is rotated about the origin until E lies on the positive y-axis, what will the new coordinates of E be?

Problem Set C

24 Find x and y.

25 Given: ABCD is a trapezoid ($\overline{DC} \parallel \overline{AB}$).
 AB = AD = 4,
 ∠A = 60°, ∠C = 45°

Find: **a** DC
 b BC

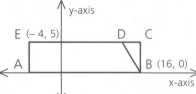

26 If the area of rectangle ABCE is eight times that of △BCD, how far is D from the origin?

Problem Set D

27 Given: ∠ACB is a right angle.
 $\overrightarrow{CD}$ and $\overrightarrow{CE}$ trisect ∠ACB.
 AC = 5, BC = 12

Find: CE (Hint: Draw a perpendicular from E to $\overline{CB}$.)

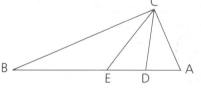

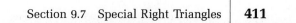

Problem Set D, *continued*

In solving probability problems, a tree diagram is sometimes helpful. Consider the following problem:

A bag contains seven red marbles, two blue marbles, and a white marble. A woman reaches into the bag and draws two marbles.

a What is the probability that she has drawn two red marbles?

b What is the probability that she has drawn one or more red marbles?

Solution:

a The tree diagram below shows that the probability of drawing a red marble and then another red marble is $\frac{7}{10} \cdot \frac{2}{3} = \frac{7}{15}$. So RR $= \frac{7}{15}$.

What are the probabilities of the other eight possible outcomes?

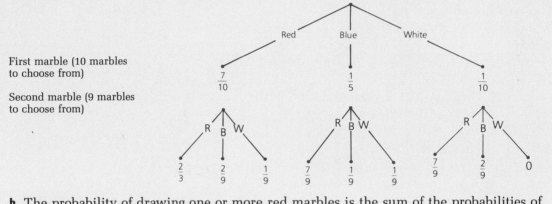

First marble (10 marbles to choose from)

Second marble (9 marbles to choose from)

b The probability of drawing one or more red marbles is the sum of the probabilities of RR, RB, RW, BR, and WR, or $\frac{14}{15}$.

---

28 Use a tree diagram to solve the following problem:

A bag contains eight right triangles. Five are members of the (3, 4, 5) family, and two are 30°-60°-90° triangles. A puppy falls over the bag, and two triangles fall out on the floor.

a What is the probability that both are members of the (3, 4, 5) family?

b What is the probability that at least one of the triangles is a member of the (3, 4, 5) family?

c What is the probability that one is a member of the (3, 4, 5) family and the other is a 30°-60°-90° triangle?

THE PYTHAGOREAN THEOREM AND SPACE FIGURES

Objective

After studying this section, you will be able to
- Apply the Pythagorean Theorem to solid figures

Part One: Introduction

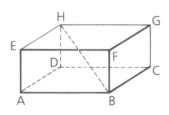

Rectangular Solid

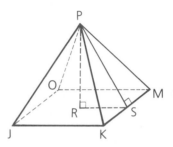

Regular Square Pyramid

Many of the problems in this section will involve the two figures shown above.

In the rectangular solid:

ABFE is one of the 6 rectangular *faces*

$\overline{AB}$ is one of the 12 *edges*

$\overline{HB}$ is one of the 4 *diagonals* of the solid. (The others are $\overline{AG}$, $\overline{CE}$, and $\overline{DF}$.)

In the regular square pyramid:

JKMO is a square, and it is called the *base*

P is the *vertex*

$\overline{PR}$ is the *altitude* of the pyramid and is perpendicular to the base at its center.

$\overline{PS}$ is called a *slant height* and is perpendicular to a side of the base.

Note   A *cube* is a rectangular solid in which all edges are congruent.

Part Two: Sample Problems

Problem 1   *The dimensions of a rectangular solid are 3, 5, and 7. Find the diagonal.*

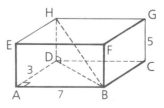

Solution It does not matter which edges are given the lengths 3, 5, and 7. Let AD = 3, AB = 7, and HD = 5, and use the Pythagorean Theorem twice.

In △ABD,
$$3^2 + 7^2 = (DB)^2$$
$$9 + 49 = (DB)^2$$
$$\sqrt{58} = DB$$

In △HDB,
$$5^2 + (\sqrt{58})^2 = (HB)^2$$
$$25 + 58 = (HB)^2$$
$$\sqrt{83} = HB$$

The measure of the diagonal is $\sqrt{83}$.

Problem 2 *Given: The regular square pyramid shown, with altitude $\overline{PR}$ and slant height $\overline{PS}$, perimeter of JKMO = 40, PK = 13*

Find: **a** JK   **b** PS   **c** PR

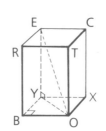

Solution **a** JK = $\frac{1}{4}(40)$ = 10

b The slant height of the pyramid is the ⊥ bis. of $\overline{MK}$, so PSK is a right △.
$$(SK)^2 + (PS)^2 = (PK)^2$$
$$5^2 + (PS)^2 = 13^2$$
$$PS = 12$$

c The altitude of a regular pyramid is perpendicular to the base at its center. Thus, RS = $\frac{1}{2}$(JK) = 5, and PRS is a right △.
$$(RS)^2 + (PR)^2 = (PS)^2$$
$$5^2 + (PR)^2 = 12^2$$
$$25 + (PR)^2 = 144$$
$$PR = \sqrt{119}$$

Part Three: Problem Sets

Problem Set A

1 Given: The rectangular solid shown, BY = 3, OB = 4, EY = 12

   Find: **a** YO, a diagonal of face BOXY

   b EO, a diagonal of the solid

2 Find the diagonal of a rectangular solid whose dimensions are 3, 4, and 5.

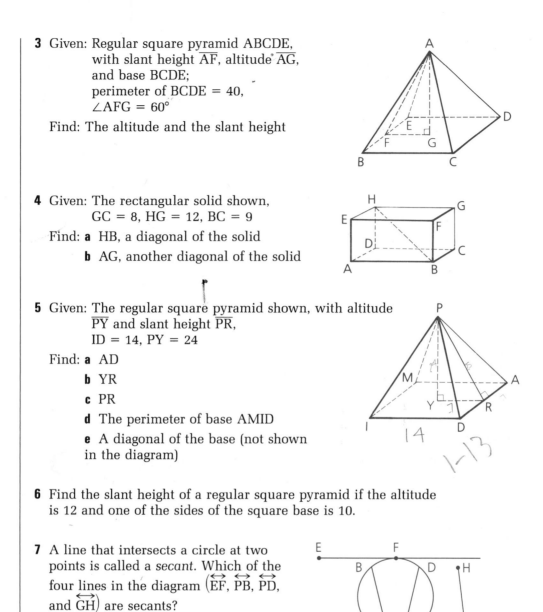

3 Given: Regular square pyramid ABCDE,
with slant height $\overline{AF}$, altitude $\overline{AG}$,
and base BCDE;
perimeter of BCDE = 40,
$\angle AFG = 60°$

Find: The altitude and the slant height

4 Given: The rectangular solid shown,
GC = 8, HG = 12, BC = 9

Find: **a** HB, a diagonal of the solid

b AG, another diagonal of the solid

5 Given: The regular square pyramid shown, with altitude
$\overline{PY}$ and slant height $\overline{PR}$,
ID = 14, PY = 24

Find: **a** AD

b YR

c PR

d The perimeter of base AMID

e A diagonal of the base (not shown
in the diagram)

6 Find the slant height of a regular square pyramid if the altitude
is 12 and one of the sides of the square base is 10.

7 A line that intersects a circle at two
points is called a *secant*. Which of the
four lines in the diagram ($\overleftrightarrow{EF}$, $\overleftrightarrow{PB}$, $\overleftrightarrow{PD}$,
and $\overleftrightarrow{GH}$) are secants?

8 Given: Diagram as marked
Find: m$\overparen{AC}$

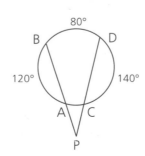

Problem Set A, *continued*

9 Daffy Difference looked ahead to Chapter 10 and found that the measure of a secant-secant angle (such as ∠BPD) is one-half the difference of its two intercepted arcs. Use this information to find m∠BPD.

10 Given: Diagram as marked
Find: m∠EJF

Problem Set B

11 Given: ⊙P as shown
Find: **a** The coordinates of point E
b The area of sector EPG to the nearest tenth
c The length of $\overparen{GE}$ to the nearest tenth

12 Given: Diagram as marked
Find: AB (the length of $\overline{AB}$)

13 ABCDEFGH is a rectangular solid.
a If face diagonal $\overline{CH}$ measures 17, edge $\overline{GH}$ measures 8, and edge $\overline{FG}$ measures 6, how long is diagonal $\overline{AG}$?
b If diagonal $\overline{AG}$ measures 50, edge $\overline{AE}$ measures 40, and edge $\overline{EF}$ measures 3, how long is edge $\overline{FG}$?

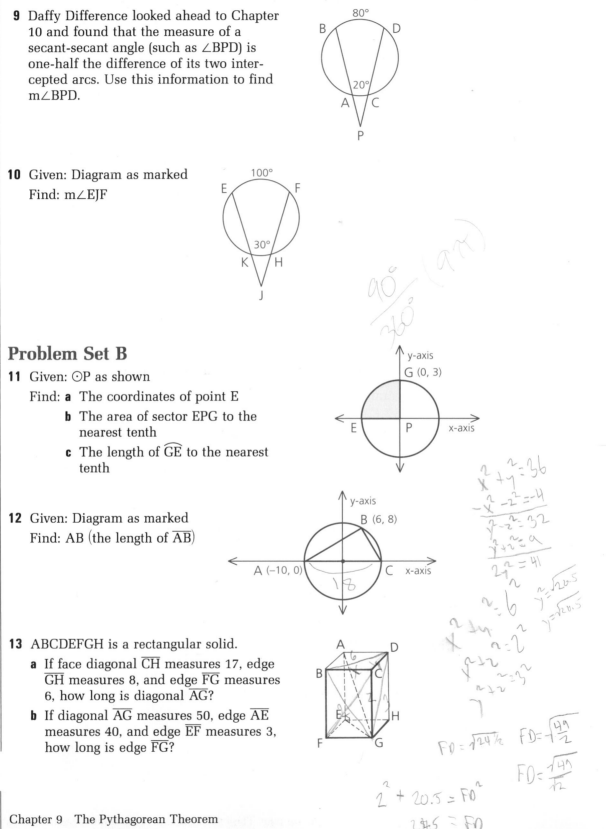

14 PADIM is a regular square pyramid. Slant height $\overline{PR}$ measures 10, and the base diagonals measure $12\sqrt{2}$.

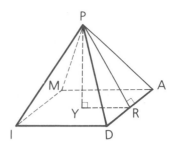

a Find ID.

b Find the altitude of the pyramid.

c Find RD.

d Find PD (length of a lateral edge).

15 Find the diagonal of a cube if each edge is 2.

16 Find the diagonal of a cube if the perimeter of a face is 20.

17 The perimeter of the base of a regular square pyramid is 24. If the slant height is 5, find the altitude.

Problem Set C

18 In the cube, find the measure of the diagonal in terms of x if

a AB = x   **b** AC = x

19 Find a formula for the length of a diagonal of a rectangular solid. (Use a, b, and c for the three dimensions.)

20 The dimensions of a rectangular solid are in the ratio 3:4:5. If the diagonal is $200\sqrt{2}$, find the three dimensions.

21 The face diagonals of a rectangular box are 2, 3, and 6. Find the diagonal of the box.

22 A pyramid is formed by assembling four equilateral triangles and a square having sides 6 cm long. Find the altitude and the slant height.

Problem Set D

23 The strongest rectangular beam that can be cut from a circular log is one having a cross section in which the diagonal joining two vertices is trisected by perpendicular segments dropped from the other vertices.

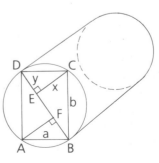

If AB = a, BC = b, CE = x, and DE = y, show that $\frac{b}{a} = \frac{\sqrt{2}}{1}$.

INTRODUCTION TO TRIGONOMETRY

Objective

After studying this section, you will be able to

■ Understand three basic trigonometric relationships

Part One: Introduction

This section presents the three basic trigonometric ratios **sine**, **cosine**, and **tangent**. The concept of similar triangles and the Pythagorean Theorem can be used to develop the *trigonometry of right triangles.*

Consider the following 30°-60°-90° triangles.

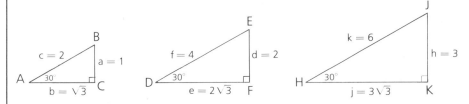

Compare the length of the leg opposite the 30° angle with the length of the hypotenuse in each triangle.

In $\triangle ABC$, $\frac{a}{c} = \frac{1}{2} = 0.5$.   In $\triangle DEF$, $\frac{d}{f} = \frac{2}{4} = 0.5$.   In $\triangle HJK$, $\frac{h}{k} = \frac{3}{6} = 0.5$.

If you think about similar triangles, you will see that in every 30°-60°-90° triangle,

$$\frac{\text{leg opposite } 30° \angle}{\text{hypotenuse}} = \frac{1}{2}$$

For each triangle shown, verify that $\dfrac{\text{leg adjacent to } 30° \angle}{\text{hypotenuse}} = \dfrac{\sqrt{3}}{2}$.

For each triangle shown, find the ratio $\dfrac{\text{leg opposite } 30° \angle}{\text{leg adjacent to } 30° \angle}$.

In △ABC and △DEF,

$$\frac{a}{c} = \frac{d}{f} = \frac{6}{10} = \frac{3}{5}$$

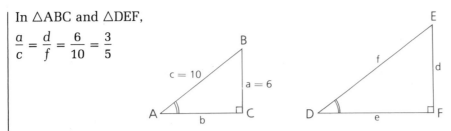

Engineers and scientists have found it convenient to formalize these relationships by naming the ratios of sides. You should memorize these three basic ratios.

Definition **Three Trigonometric Ratios**

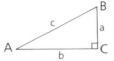

$$\textit{sine} \text{ of } \angle A = \sin \angle A = \frac{\text{opposite leg}}{\text{hypotenuse}}$$

$$\textit{cosine} \text{ of } \angle A = \cos \angle A = \frac{\text{adjacent leg}}{\text{hypotenuse}}$$

$$\textit{tangent} \text{ of } \angle A = \tan \angle A = \frac{\text{opposite leg}}{\text{adjacent leg}}$$

Part Two: Sample Problems

Problem 1   Find: **a** cos ∠A
              b tan ∠B

Solution   By the Pythagorean Theorem, $c = 13$.

$$\textbf{a } \cos \angle A = \frac{\text{leg adjacent to } \angle A}{\text{hypotenuse}} = \frac{12}{13}$$

$$\textbf{b } \tan \angle B = \frac{\text{leg opposite } \angle B}{\text{leg adjacent to } \angle B} = \frac{12}{5}$$

Problem 2   *Find the three trigonometric ratios for* ∠A *and* ∠B.

Solution
$$\sin \angle A = \frac{3}{5} \quad \sin \angle B = \frac{4}{5}$$

$$\cos \angle A = \frac{4}{5} \quad \cos \angle B = \frac{3}{5}$$

$$\tan \angle A = \frac{3}{4} \quad \tan \angle B = \frac{4}{3}$$

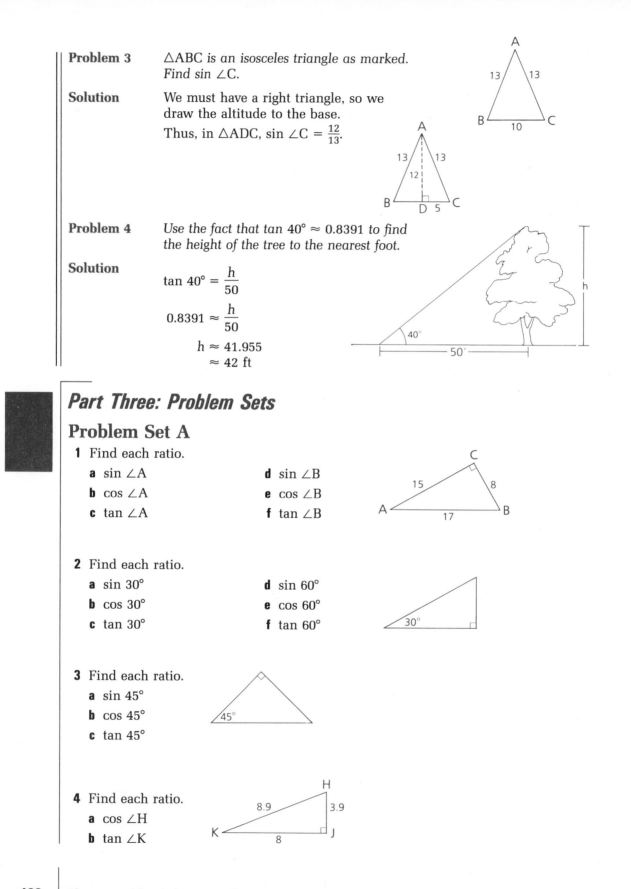

Problem 3   △ABC is an isosceles triangle as marked. Find sin ∠C.

Solution   We must have a right triangle, so we draw the altitude to the base.

Thus, in △ADC, sin ∠C = $\frac{12}{13}$.

Problem 4   Use the fact that tan 40° ≈ 0.8391 to find the height of the tree to the nearest foot.

Solution

$$\tan 40° = \frac{h}{50}$$

$$0.8391 \approx \frac{h}{50}$$

$$h \approx 41.955$$
$$\approx 42 \text{ ft}$$

Part Three: Problem Sets

Problem Set A

1 Find each ratio.

  a sin ∠A   **d** sin ∠B

  b cos ∠A   **e** cos ∠B

  c tan ∠A   **f** tan ∠B

2 Find each ratio.

  a sin 30°   **d** sin 60°

  b cos 30°   **e** cos 60°

  c tan 30°   **f** tan 60°

3 Find each ratio.

  a sin 45°

  b cos 45°

  c tan 45°

4 Find each ratio.

  a cos ∠H

  b tan ∠K

5 If $\tan \angle M = \frac{3}{4}$, find $\cos \angle M$. (Hint: Start by drawing the triangle.)

6 Using the figure as marked, name each missing angle.

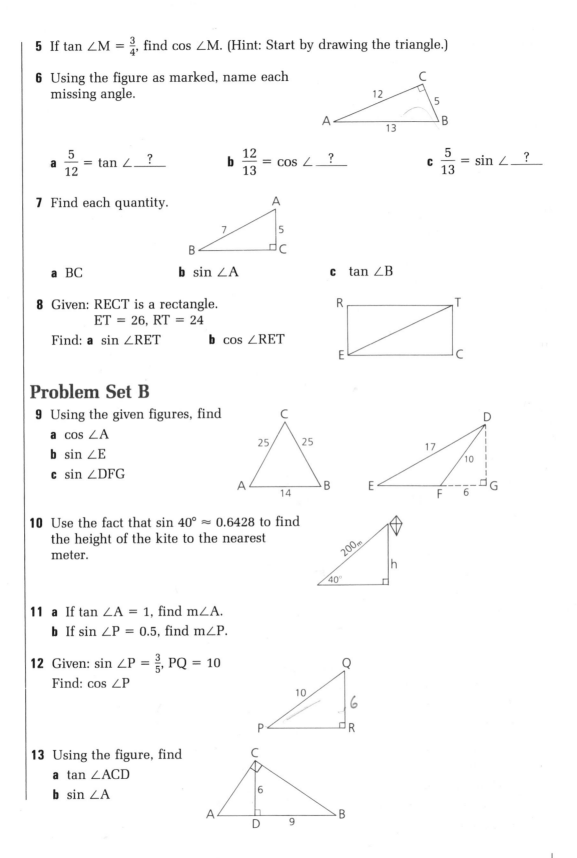

a $\dfrac{5}{12} = \tan \angle \underline{\quad ? \quad}$ **b** $\dfrac{12}{13} = \cos \angle \underline{\quad ? \quad}$ **c** $\dfrac{5}{13} = \sin \angle \underline{\quad ? \quad}$

7 Find each quantity.

a BC   **b** $\sin \angle A$ **c** $\tan \angle B$

8 Given: RECT is a rectangle.
ET = 26, RT = 24

Find: **a** $\sin \angle RET$ **b** $\cos \angle RET$

Problem Set B

9 Using the given figures, find
  a $\cos \angle A$
  b $\sin \angle E$
  c $\sin \angle DFG$

10 Use the fact that $\sin 40° \approx 0.6428$ to find the height of the kite to the nearest meter.

11 a If $\tan \angle A = 1$, find $m\angle A$.
    b If $\sin \angle P = 0.5$, find $m\angle P$.

12 Given: $\sin \angle P = \frac{3}{5}$, PQ = 10
Find: $\cos \angle P$

13 Using the figure, find
  a $\tan \angle ACD$
  b $\sin \angle A$

Problem Set B, *continued*

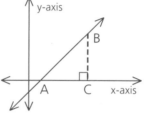

14 Given: RHOM is a rhombus.
RO = 18, HM = 24

Find: **a** cos ∠BRM   **b** tan ∠BHO

15 Given a trapezoid with sides 5, 10, 17, and 10, find the sine of one of the acute angles.

16 Given △ABC with ∠C = 90°, indicate whether each statement is true Always (A), Sometimes (S), or Never (N).

a sin ∠A = cos ∠B   **b** sin ∠A = tan ∠A   **c** sin ∠A = cos ∠A

17 If △EQU is equilateral and △RAT is a right triangle with RA = 2, RT = 1, and ∠T = 90°, show that sin ∠E = cos ∠A.

18 If the slope of $\overleftrightarrow{AB}$ is $\frac{5}{8}$, find the tangent of ∠BAC.

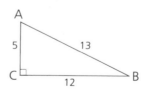

Problem Set C

19 Use the definitions of the trigonometric ratios to verify the following relationships, given △ABC in which ∠C = 90°.

a $(\sin ∠A)^2 + (\cos ∠A)^2 = 1$ **c** $\dfrac{\sin ∠A}{\cos ∠A} = \tan ∠A$

b $\dfrac{a}{\sin ∠A} = \dfrac{b}{\sin ∠B}$ **d** $\sin ∠A = \cos(90° − ∠A)$

20 Rhombus PQRS has a perimeter of 60 and one diagonal of 15. Find the two possible values of sin ∠PQS.

21 Two sides of the triangle shown are picked at random to form a ratio. What is the probability that the ratio is the tangent of ∠A?

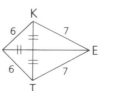

22 Given: KITE is a kite with sides as marked.

Find: tan ∠KEI

TRIGONOMETRIC RATIOS

1-6

Objective

After studying this section, you will be able to
- Use trigonometric ratios to solve right triangles

Part One: Introduction

Trigonometry is used to solve triangles other than 30°-60°-90° and 45°-45°-90° triangles. The Table of Trigonometric Ratios on the next page shows four-place decimal approximations of the ratios for other angles—for instance, sin 23° ≈ 0.3907, and the angle whose tangent is 1.5399 is approximately 57°.

Unless your teacher directs otherwise, we suggest you use a scientific calculator rather than the table to find trigonometric ratios.

For some applications of trigonometry, you need to know the meanings of ***angle of elevation*** and ***angle of depression***.

If an observer at a point P looks upward toward an object at A, the angle the line of sight $\overrightarrow{PA}$ makes with the horizontal $\overrightarrow{PH}$ is called the ***angle of elevation***.

If an observer at a point P looks downward toward an object at B, the angle the line of sight $\overrightarrow{PB}$ makes with the horizontal $\overrightarrow{PH}$ is called the ***angle of depression***.

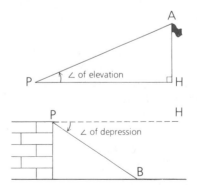

Note Do not forget that an angle of elevation or depression is an angle between a line of sight and the *horizontal*. Do not use the vertical.

Table of Trigonometric Ratios

∠A	sin ∠A	cos ∠A	tan ∠A	∠A	sin ∠A	cos ∠A	tan ∠A
1°	.0175	.9998	.0175	46°	.7193	.6947	1.0355
2°	.0349	.9994	.0349	47°	.7314	.6820	1.0724
3°	.0523	.9986	.0524	48°	.7431	.6691	1.1106
4°	.0698	.9976	.0699	49°	.7547	.6561	1.1504
5°	.0872	.9962	.0875	50°	.7660	.6428	1.1918
6°	.1045	.9945	.1051	51°	.7771	.6293	1.2349
7°	.1219	.9925	.1228	52°	.7880	.6157	1.2799
8°	.1392	.9903	.1405	53°	.7986	.6018	1.3270
9°	.1564	.9877	.1584	54°	.8090	.5878	1.3764
10°	.1736	.9848	.1763	55°	.8192	.5736	1.4281
11°	.1908	.9816	.1944	56°	.8290	.5592	1.4826
12°	.2079	.9781	.2126	57°	.8387	.5446	1.5399
13°	.2250	.9744	.2309	58°	.8480	.5299	1.6003
14°	.2419	.9703	.2493	59°	.8572	.5150	1.6643
15°	.2588	.9659	.2679	60°	.8660	.5000	1.7321
16°	.2756	.9613	.2867	61°	.8746	.4848	1.8040
17°	.2924	.9563	.3057	62°	.8829	.4695	1.8807
18°	.3090	.9511	.3249	63°	.8910	.4540	1.9626
19°	.3256	.9455	.3443	64°	.8988	.4384	2.0503
20°	.3420	.9397	.3640	65°	.9063	.4226	2.1445
21°	.3584	.9336	.3839	66°	.9135	.4067	2.2460
22°	.3746	.9272	.4040	67°	.9205	.3907	2.3559
23°	.3907	.9205	.4245	68°	.9272	.3746	2.4751
24°	.4067	.9135	.4452	69°	.9336	.3584	2.6051
25°	.4226	.9063	.4663	70°	.9397	.3420	2.7475
26°	.4384	.8988	.4877	71°	.9455	.3256	2.9042
27°	.4540	.8910	.5095	72°	.9511	.3090	3.0777
28°	.4695	.8829	.5317	73°	.9563	.2924	3.2709
29°	.4848	.8746	.5543	74°	.9613	.2756	3.4874
30°	.5000	.8660	.5774	75°	.9659	.2588	3.7321
31°	.5150	.8572	.6009	76°	.9703	.2419	4.0108
32°	.5299	.8480	.6249	77°	.9744	.2250	4.3315
33°	.5446	.8387	.6494	78°	.9781	.2079	4.7046
34°	.5592	.8290	.6745	79°	.9816	.1908	5.1446
35°	.5736	.8192	.7002	80°	.9848	.1736	5.6713
36°	.5878	.8090	.7265	81°	.9877	.1564	6.3138
37°	.6018	.7986	.7536	82°	.9903	.1392	7.1154
38°	.6157	.7880	.7813	83°	.9925	.1219	8.1443
39°	.6293	.7771	.8098	84°	.9945	.1045	9.5144
40°	.6428	.7660	.8391	85°	.9962	.0872	11.4301
41°	.6561	.7547	.8693	86°	.9976	.0698	14.3007
42°	.6691	.7431	.9004	87°	.9986	.0523	19.0811
43°	.6820	.7314	.9325	88°	.9994	.0349	28.6363
44°	.6947	.7193	.9657	89°	.9998	.0175	57.2900
45°	.7071	.7071	1.0000				

Part Two: Sample Problems

Problem 1   *Given: Right △DEF as shown*
    Find: **a** *m∠D to the nearest degree*
        b *e to the nearest tenth*

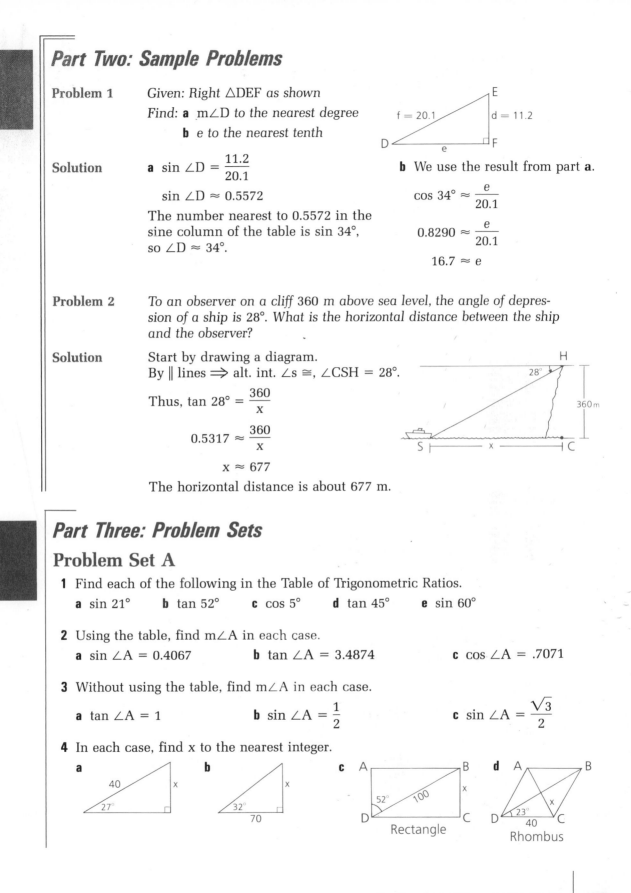

Solution   **a** $\sin \angle D = \dfrac{11.2}{20.1}$

    $\sin \angle D \approx 0.5572$

The number nearest to 0.5572 in the
sine column of the table is sin 34°,
so ∠D ≈ 34°.

b We use the result from part **a**.

$\cos 34° \approx \dfrac{e}{20.1}$

$0.8290 \approx \dfrac{e}{20.1}$

$16.7 \approx e$

Problem 2   *To an observer on a cliff 360 m above sea level, the angle of depression of a ship is 28°. What is the horizontal distance between the ship
and the observer?*

Solution   Start by drawing a diagram.
By ∥ lines ⟹ alt. int. ∠s ≅, ∠CSH = 28°.

Thus, $\tan 28° = \dfrac{360}{x}$

    $0.5317 \approx \dfrac{360}{x}$

        $x \approx 677$

The horizontal distance is about 677 m.

Part Three: Problem Sets

Problem Set A

1 Find each of the following in the Table of Trigonometric Ratios.
    a sin 21°   **b** tan 52°   **c** cos 5°   **d** tan 45°   **e** sin 60°

2 Using the table, find m∠A in each case.
    a sin ∠A = 0.4067   **b** tan ∠A = 3.4874   **c** cos ∠A = .7071

3 Without using the table, find m∠A in each case.

    a tan ∠A = 1   **b** sin ∠A = $\dfrac{1}{2}$ **c** sin ∠A = $\dfrac{\sqrt{3}}{2}$

4 In each case, find x to the nearest integer.

Problem Set A, *continued*

5 Find the height of isosceles trapezoid ABCD.

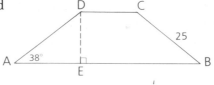

Problem Set B

6 Solve each equation for x to the nearest integer.

a $\sin 25° = \dfrac{x}{40}$ **b** $\cos 73° = \dfrac{35}{x}$ **c** $\sin x° = \dfrac{29}{30}$

7 A department-store escalator is 80 ft long. If it rises 32 ft vertically, find the angle it makes with the floor.

8 Given the regular pentagon shown, with center at O and EN = 12 cm,

  a Find m∠E

  b Find m∠NOM

  c Find OM to the nearest hundredth

  d Find the area of △NOT to the nearest hundredth

  e Explain how you could find the area of the pentagon

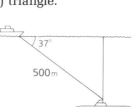

9 Find, to the nearest degree, the angles of a (3, 4, 5) triangle.

10 A sonar operator on a cruiser detects a submarine at a distance of 500 m and an angle of depression of 37°. How deep is the sub?

11 The legs of an isosceles triangle are each 18. The base is 14.

  a Find the base angles to the nearest degree.

  b Find the exact length of the altitude to the base.

12 One diagonal of a rhombus makes an angle of 27° with a side of the rhombus. If each side of the rhombus has a length of 6.2 in., find the length of each diagonal to the nearest tenth of an inch.

13 Find the perimeter of trapezoid ABCD, in which $\overline{CD} \parallel \overline{AB}$, $\cos \angle A = \frac{1}{2}$, and AD = DC = CB = 2.

14 Find the length of the apothem of a regular pentagon that has a perimeter of 50 cm.

15 Two buildings are 100 dm apart across a street. A sunbather at point P finds the angle of elevation of the roof of the taller building to be 25° and the angle of depression of its base to be 30°. Find the height of the taller building to the nearest decimeter.

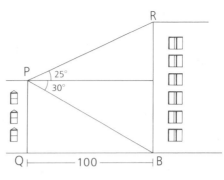

Problem Set C

16 An observer on a cliff 1000 dm above sea level sights two ships due east. The angles of depression of the ships are 47° and 32°. Find, to the nearest decimeter, the distance between the ships.

17 Each side of the base of a regular square pyramid is 20 and the altitude is 35.

   Find: **a** PT **b** BP **c** ∠PTF **d** ∠PBF

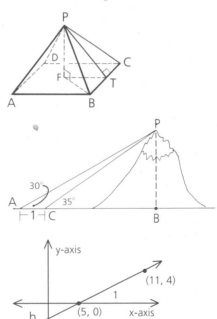

18 Find the height, PB, of a mountain whose base and peak are inaccessible. At point A the angle of elevation of the peak is 30°. One kilometer closer to the mountain, at point C, the angle of elevation is 35°.

19 a Find the slope of line h.

   b Find m∠1 to the nearest integer.

Problem Set D

20 Prove that $c^2 = a^2 + b^2 - 2ab(\cos \angle C)$ is true for any acute △ABC. (This formula is called the Law of Cosines.)

21 Given: Diagram as shown

   a Find ∠R to the nearest degree.

   b Find QR to the nearest integer.

   c Show that $\dfrac{PR}{\sin \angle Q} = \dfrac{PQ}{\sin \angle R}$.

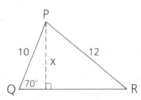

   d Generalize the result of part **c** for the sides and angles of any acute triangle. (The resulting formula is the Law of Sines.)

CHAPTER SUMMARY

CONCEPTS AND PROCEDURES

After studying this chapter, you should be able to

- Simplify radical expressions and solve quadratic equations (9.1)
- Begin solving problems involving circles (9.2)
- Identify the relationships between the parts of a right triangle when an altitude is drawn to the hypotenuse (9.3)
- Use the Pythagorean Theorem and its converse (9.4)
- Use the distance formula to compute lengths of segments in the coordinate plane (9.5)
- Recognize groups of whole numbers known as Pythagorean triples (9.6)
- Apply the Principle of the Reduced Triangle (9.6)
- Identify the ratio of side lengths in a 30°-60°-90° triangle (9.7)
- Identify the ratio of side lengths in a 45°-45°-90° triangle (9.7)
- Apply the Pythagorean Theorem to solid figures (9.8)
- Understand three basic trigonometric relationships (9.9)
- Use trigonometric ratios to solve right triangles (9.10)

VOCABULARY

altitude (9.8)
angle of depression (9.10)
angle of elevation (9.10)
base (9.8)
cosine (9.9)
cube (9.8)
diagonal (9.8)
distance formula (9.5)
edge (9.8)

face (9.8)
Pythagorean triple (9.6)
rectangular solid (9.8)
regular square pyramid (9.8)
sine (9.9)
slant height (9.8)
tangent (9.9)
trigonometry of right triangles (9.9)
vertex (9.8)

REVIEW PROBLEMS

Problem Set A

1 **a** Find GF if HG = 4 and EG = 6.
   b Find EH if GH = 4 and GF = 12.
   c Find HF if EF = $2\sqrt{5}$ and GF = 4.
   d Find HF if EH = 2 and EF = 3.

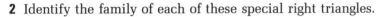

2 Identify the family of each of these special right triangles.

3 Find the missing lengths.

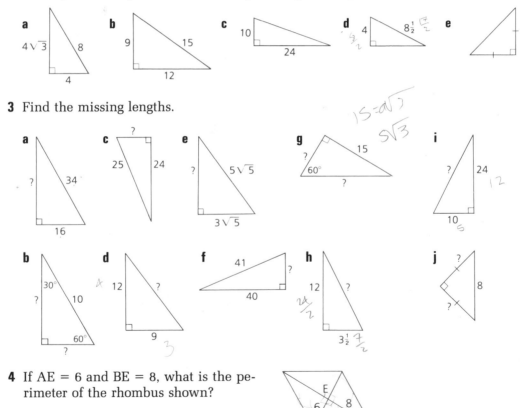

4 If AE = 6 and BE = 8, what is the perimeter of the rhombus shown?

5 Find the altitude of the triangle shown.

6 Vail skied 2 km north, 2 km west, 1 km north, and 2 km west. How far was she from her starting point?

7 A 25-ft ladder just reaches a point on a wall 24 ft above the ground. How far is the foot of the ladder from the wall?

8 Find, to the nearest tenth, the altitude to the base of an isosceles triangle whose sides have lengths of 8, 6, and 8.

9 If the altitude of an equilateral triangle is $8\sqrt{3}$, find the perimeter of the triangle.

10 What is the length of a diagonal of a 2-by-5 rectangle?

11 In the trapezoid shown, find RS.

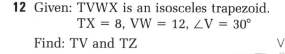

12 Given: TVWX is an isosceles trapezoid.
TX = 8, VW = 12, ∠V = 30°

Find: TV and TZ

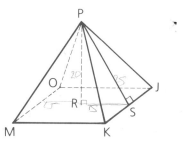

13 Find the diagonal of a rectangular solid whose dimensions are 4, 3, and 12.

14 Given: The regular square pyramid shown,
PR = 20, PS = 25

Find: The perimeter of base JKMO

15 In the rectangular solid shown, find AG to the nearest tenth if DC = 12, CG = 7, and AD = 4.

16 Given: $\overline{AC} \perp \overline{CB}$, $\overline{DE} \parallel \overline{CB}$,
AC = 15, AB = 17, DE = 4

Find: **a** CB   **c** AE   **e** DC
      b AD   **d** EB

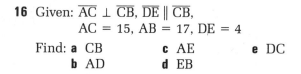

17 Find the distance from A to B if A = (1, 11) and B = (4, 15).

18 Given: Diagram as marked
Find: m∠M

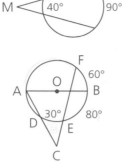

19 Given: ⊙O, mDE͡ = 30,
mEB͡ = 80, mBF͡ = 60
Find: **a** mAF͡
b m∠C
c m∠BAD

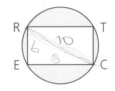

20 Given: RECT is a rectangle.
RE = 6, EC = 8
Find: **a** The measure of RTC͡
b The length of RTC͡
c The area of the shaded region to
the nearest tenth

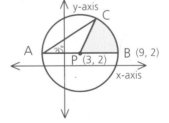

Problem Set B

21 a Find m∠DEF.
b Find mDEF͡.
c Find the length of DEF͡.

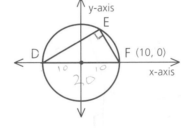

22 Given: ⊙P, ∠CAB = 30°
Find: **a** mBC͡
b mAC͡
c The length of BC͡
d The area of the shaded region

23 Two boats leave the harbor at 9:00 A.M. Boat A sails north at 20
km/hr. Boat B sails west at 15 km/hr. How far apart are the two
boats at noon?

24 a Find x.　　　　　　　**b** Find y.

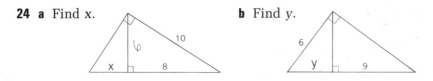

Review Problem Set B, *continued*

25 A boy standing on the shore of a lake 1 mi wide wants to reach the "Golden Arches" 3 mi down the shore on the opposite side of the lake. If he swims at 2 mph and walks at 4 mph, is it quicker for him to swim directly across the lake and then walk to the Golden Arches or to swim directly to the Golden Arches?

26 A boat is tied to a pier by a 25′ rope. The pier is 15′ above the boat. If 8′ of rope is pulled in, how many feet will the boat move forward?

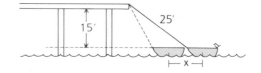

27 Find x.

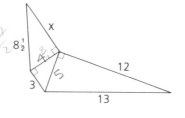

28 Follow the treasure map of Captain Zig Zag to see how far the treasure is from the old stump.

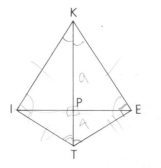

From the ol' pirate stump take ye 30 paces east, then 20 paces north, 6 paces west, and then another 25 paces north, and there ye find my treasure

29 Given: Kite KITE with right ∠s KIT and KET, KP = 9, TP = 4

Find: **a** IE

    b The perimeter of KITE

30 Given: RECT is a rectangle.
$\overline{CE} \parallel$ y-axis,
$\overline{RE} \parallel$ x-axis.

a Find the coordinates of E.

b Find the area of RECT.

c Find, to the nearest tenth, the length of $\overline{RC}$.

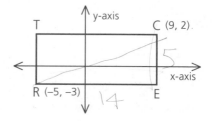

31 Show that quadrilateral QUAD, with Q = (−1, −4), U = (4, 11), A = (1, 12), and D = (−4, −3), is a rectangle.

Problem Set C

32 Given: ∠C is a right angle.
E is the midpoint of $\overline{AC}$.
F is the midpoint of $\overline{BC}$.
$AF = \sqrt{41}$, $BE = 2\sqrt{26}$
Find: AB

33 The altitude to the hypotenuse of a right triangle divides the hypotenuse in the ratio 4:1. What is the ratio of the legs of the triangle?

34 A 12-m rope is used to form a triangle the lengths of whose sides are integers. If one of the possible triangles is selected at random, what is the probability that the triangle is a right triangle?

35 Find the edge of a cube whose diagonal is $7\sqrt{3}$.

36 If △PQR is a right triangle, what is the probability that tan ∠R is not a trigonometric ratio?

37 Find the angle formed by
  a A diagonal of a cube and a diagonal of a face of the cube
  b Two face diagonals that intersect at a vertex of a cube

CUMULATIVE REVIEW

CHAPTERS 1–9

Problem Set A

1 A pair of consecutive angles of a parallelogram are in the ratio 5:3. Find the measure of the smaller angle.

2 Find x.

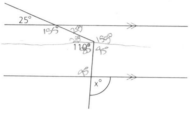

3 a Find the sum of the measures of the angles of a nonagon.

b If each angle of a regular polygon is a 168° angle, how many sides does the polygon have?

c How many diagonals does a heptagon have?

4 a Find x.

b Is △ABC isosceles?

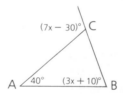

5 A boy 180 cm tall casts a 150-cm shadow. A nearby flagpole casts a shadow 12 m long. What is the length of the flagpole?

6 Given: ∠ABC = 60°, ∠ACB = 70°

Find: ∠BFC

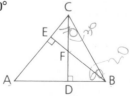

7 Find the perimeter of a rhombus whose diagonals are 10 and 24.

8 a Find BC.
  b Find AB.
  c Is △DEC acute, right, or obtuse?

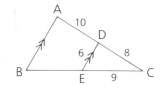

9 a Find the mean proportionals between $\frac{1}{4}$ and 49.
  b Solve $\frac{5}{5 - y} = \frac{10}{y - 10}$ for y.

10 Are lines a and b parallel?

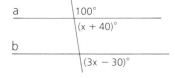

11 Given: $\overline{EB} \cong \overline{DF}$, $\overline{AG} \cong \overline{GC}$,
  $\angle EAG \cong \angle FCG$
  Prove: ABCD is a parallelogram.

12 Given: $\odot Q$ lies in plane m.
  $\overline{PQ} \perp m$
  Prove: $\angle R \cong \angle S$

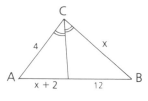

Problem Set B

13 Find the angle formed by the hands of a clock at each time.
  a 11:50   **b** 12:01

14 The sum of an angle and four times its complement is 20° greater than the supplement of the angle. Find the angle's complement.

15 The sum of the angles of an equiangular polygon is 3960°. Find the measure of each exterior angle.

16 Find AB.

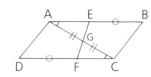

17 Points (1, 3), (−4, 7), and (−29, k) are collinear. Find k.

18 Given: ∠A = 120°;
$\overrightarrow{BD}$ and $\overrightarrow{BE}$ trisect ∠ABC.
$\overrightarrow{CD}$ and $\overrightarrow{CE}$ trisect ∠ACB.

a Find m∠D and m∠E.

b Do m∠A, m∠D, and m∠E form an arithmetic progression? (Hint: See Chapter 7, review problem 23.)

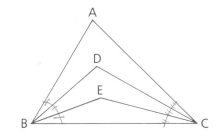

19 Given: $\overline{AB}$ lies in m, $\overline{CD}$ lies in n, and m ∥ n.
$\overline{AC}$ intersects $\overline{BD}$ at P.
$\overline{AD} \perp n, \overline{BC} \perp n$

Prove: $\overline{AC} \cong \overline{DB}$

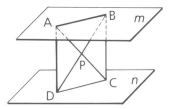

20 The shorter diagonal of a regular hexagon is 6. Find the length of the longer diagonal.

21 a Point A is rotated 127° clockwise about the origin to point B. Through how many degrees must B be rotated counterclockwise to be at (0, −4)?

b If A is reflected over a line parallel to the x-axis and 1 unit below the axis, find the coordinates of the point of reflection.

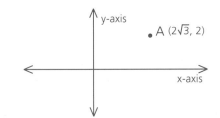

Problem Set C

22 Given: $\overrightarrow{BD}$ and $\overrightarrow{BE}$ trisect ∠ABC.
DE = 4, EC = 5, BD = 12

Find: **a** BC **b** BE **c** AD

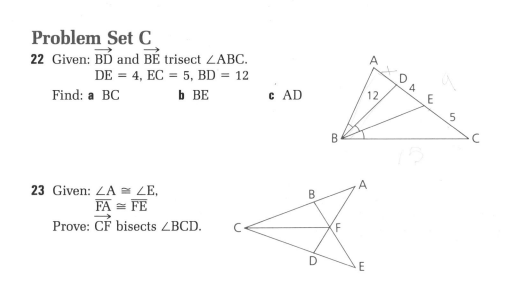

23 Given: ∠A ≅ ∠E,
$\overline{FA} \cong \overline{FE}$

Prove: $\overrightarrow{CF}$ bisects ∠BCD.

24 Given: A cube as shown, with
J the midpoint of $\overline{HF}$,
AB = 6

Find: AJ

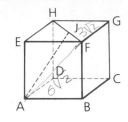

25 Given: $\overline{AD} \cong \overline{DC}$,
∠B + 50° = ∠DAB

Find: m∠CAB

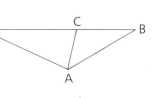

26 a Find the sum of the measures of angles A, B, C, D, and E.

b Does your answer depend on knowing whether any polygons are equilateral or equiangular?

27 What is the probability that a diagonal chosen at random in a regular decagon will be one of the shortest diagonals?

28 $\overline{GH} \cong \overline{GJ}$,
∠1 = (3x)°,
∠2 = x°

Find: m∠J

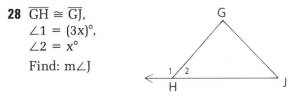

29 The consecutive sides of a quadrilateral measure (x − 17), (24 − x), (3x − 40), and (x + 1). The perimeter is 42. Is the figure a parallelogram? Explain.

30 Given: VRST is a ▱.
V is the midpt. of $\overline{NT}$.
R is the midpt. of $\overline{PS}$.

Prove: NPST is a ▱.

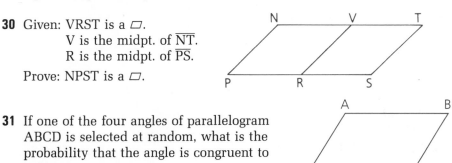

31 If one of the four angles of parallelogram ABCD is selected at random, what is the probability that the angle is congruent to ∠C?

10 CIRCLES

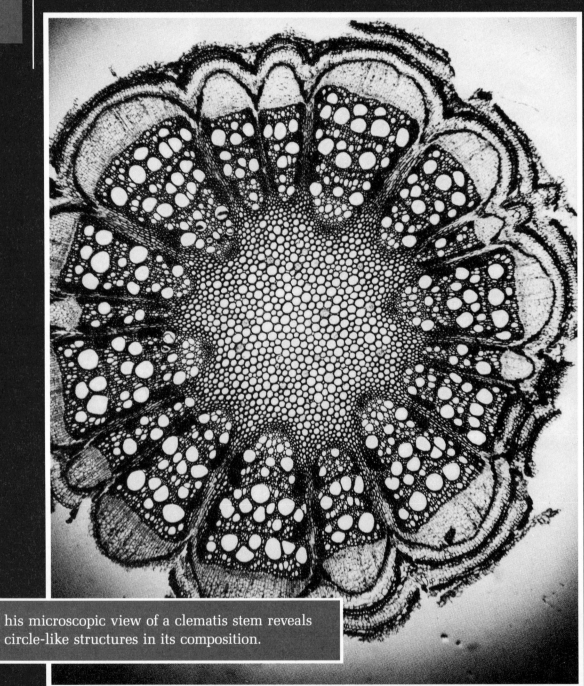

T his microscopic view of a clematis stem reveals
circle-like structures in its composition.

10.1 THE CIRCLE

Objectives

After studying this section, you will be able to
- Identify the characteristics of circles
- Recognize chords and diameters of circles
- Recognize special relationships between radii and chords

Part One: Introduction

Basic Properties and Definitions

The following definitions will help you extend and organize what you already know about circles.

Definition	A *circle* is the set of all points in a plane that are a given distance from a given point in the plane. The given point is the *center* of the circle, and the given distance is the *radius*. A segment that joins the center to a point on the circle is also called a radius. (The plural of *radius* is *radii*.)

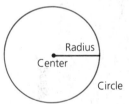

The definitions of *circle* and *radius* can be used to prove a theorem you saw in Chapter 3: *All radii of a circle are congruent* (Theorem 19).

Although all circles have the same shape, their sizes are determined by the measures of their radii.

Definition	Two or more coplanar circles with the same center are called *concentric* circles.

Definition	Two circles are congruent if they have congruent radii.

Definition	A point is inside (in the *interior* of) a circle if its distance from the center is less than the radius.

Points O and A are in the interior of ⊙O.

Definition   A point is outside (in the *exterior* of) a circle if its distance from the center is greater than the radius.

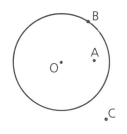

Point C is in the exterior of ⊙O.

Definition   A point is on a circle if its distance from the center is equal to the radius.

Point B is on ⊙O.

Chords and Diameters

Points on a circle can be connected by segments called **chords.**

Definition   A *chord* of a circle is a segment joining any two points on the circle.

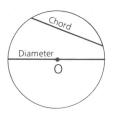

What is the longest chord of a circle? Is there a shortest chord?

Definition   A *diameter* of a circle is a chord that passes through the center of the circle.

The ideas of circumference and area of a circle are important in geometry. We now review two formulas presented in Chapter 3.

Circumference and Area of a Circle
The area of a circle can be found with the formula $$A = \pi r^2$$ and the circumference (perimeter) of a circle can be found with the formula $$C = \pi d$$ where r is the circle's radius, d is its diameter, and $\pi \approx 3.14$.

Radius-Chord Relationships

OP is the distance from O to chord $\overline{AB}$.

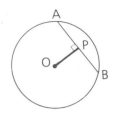

Definition   The distance from the center of a circle to a chord is the measure of the perpendicular segment from the center to the chord.

The following three theorems are useful in establishing special relationships between radii and chords.

Theorem 74   *If a radius is perpendicular to a chord, then it bisects the chord.*

Given: ⊙O,
       $\overline{OD} \perp \overline{AB}$
Prove: $\overline{OD}$ bisects $\overline{AB}$.

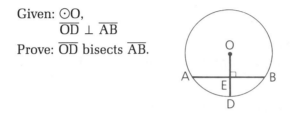

Theorem 75   *If a radius of a circle bisects a chord that is not a diameter, then it is perpendicular to that chord.*

Given: ⊙O;
       $\overline{OH}$ bisects $\overline{EF}$.
Prove: $\overline{OH} \perp \overline{EF}$

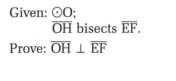

Theorem 76   *The perpendicular bisector of a chord passes through the center of the circle.*

Given: $\overleftrightarrow{PQ}$ is the ⊥ bisector
       of $\overline{CD}$.
Prove: $\overleftrightarrow{PQ}$ passes through O.

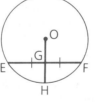

Part Two: Sample Problems

Problem 1

Given: ⊙Q,
$\overline{PR} \perp \overline{ST}$

Prove: $\overline{PS} \cong \overline{PT}$

Proof

1 ⊙Q, $\overline{PR} \perp \overline{ST}$	1 Given
2 $\overline{PR}$ bisects $\overline{ST}$.	2 If a radius is ⊥ to a chord, it bisects the chord. ($\overline{QR}$ is part of a radius.)
3 $\overline{PR} \perp$ bis. $\overline{ST}$	3 Combination of steps 1 and 2
4 $\overline{PS} \cong \overline{PT}$	4 If a point is on the ⊥ bis. of a segment, then it is equidistant from the endpoints.

Problem 2

The radius of circle O is 13 mm.
The length of chord $\overline{PQ}$ is 10 mm.
Find the distance from chord $\overline{PQ}$ to
the center, O.

Solution

Draw $\overline{OR}$ perpendicular to $\overline{PQ}$.
Draw radius $\overline{OP}$ to complete a
right △.
Since a radius perpendicular to a
chord bisects the chord,

$$PR = \tfrac{1}{2}(PQ) = \tfrac{1}{2}(10) = 5$$

By the Pythagorean Theorem,
$x^2 + 5^2 = 13^2$, so OR = 12.

Problem 3

Given: △ABC is isosceles ($\overline{AB} \cong \overline{AC}$).
Ⓢ P and Q,
$\overline{BC} \parallel \overline{PQ}$

Prove: ⊙P ≅ ⊙Q

Proof

1 △ABC is isosceles ($\overline{AB} \cong \overline{AC}$).	1 Given
2 Ⓢ P and Q, $\overline{BC} \parallel \overline{PQ}$	2 Given
3 ∠ABC ≅ ∠P, ∠ACB ≅ ∠Q	3 ∥ lines ⟹ corr. ∠s ≅
4 ∠ABC ≅ ∠ACB	4 If △, then △.
5 ∠P ≅ ∠Q	5 Transitive Property
6 $\overline{AP} \cong \overline{AQ}$	6 If △, then △.
7 $\overline{PB} \cong \overline{CQ}$	7 Subtraction (1 from 6)
8 ⊙P ≅ ⊙Q	8 Ⓢ with ≅ radii are ≅.

Part Three: Problem Sets

Problem Set A

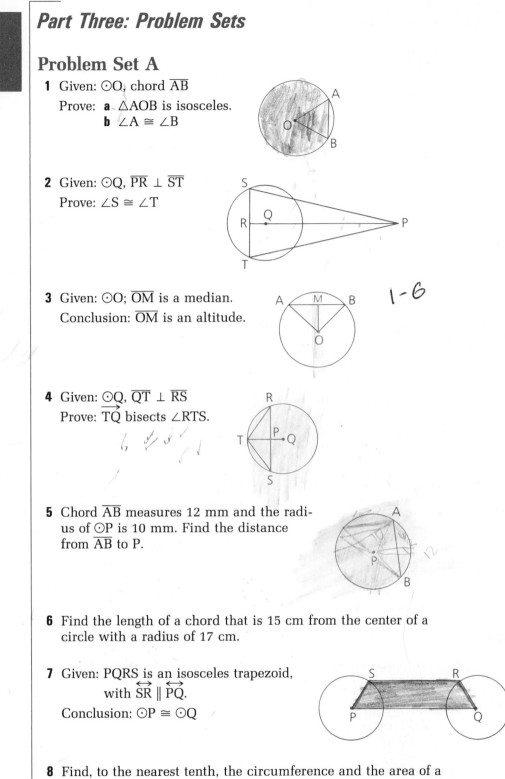

1 Given: ⊙O, chord $\overline{AB}$
   Prove: **a** △AOB is isosceles.
   b ∠A ≅ ∠B

2 Given: ⊙Q, $\overline{PR} \perp \overline{ST}$
   Prove: ∠S ≅ ∠T

3 Given: ⊙O; $\overline{OM}$ is a median.
   Conclusion: $\overline{OM}$ is an altitude.

1-6

4 Given: ⊙Q, $\overline{QT} \perp \overline{RS}$
   Prove: $\overrightarrow{TQ}$ bisects ∠RTS.

5 Chord $\overline{AB}$ measures 12 mm and the radius of ⊙P is 10 mm. Find the distance from $\overline{AB}$ to P.

6 Find the length of a chord that is 15 cm from the center of a circle with a radius of 17 cm.

7 Given: PQRS is an isosceles trapezoid, with $\overleftrightarrow{SR} \parallel \overleftrightarrow{PQ}$.
   Conclusion: ⊙P ≅ ⊙Q

8 Find, to the nearest tenth, the circumference and the area of a circle whose diameter is 7.8 cm.

9 Given: ⊙A ≅ ⊙B,
$\overleftrightarrow{AD} \parallel \overleftrightarrow{BC}$
Prove: ABCD is a ▱.

Problem Set B

10 Given: ⊙O;
$\overleftrightarrow{OR}$ bisects $\overline{PQ}$.
Prove: $\overrightarrow{RO}$ bisects ∠PRQ.

11 Find the distance from the center of a circle to a chord 30 m long if the diameter of the circle is 34 m.

12 Find the radius of a circle if a 24-cm chord is 9 cm from the center.

13 Given: ⓢ A and B intersect as shown.
$\overline{DE} \parallel \overline{FC}$, ∠ADE ≅ ∠FCB,
$\overline{DE} \cong \overline{FC}$
Prove: ⊙A ≅ ⊙B

14 Two circles intersect and have a common chord 24 cm long. The centers of the circles are 21 cm apart. The radius of one circle is 13 cm. Find the radius of the other circle.

15 Given: ⊙P,
$\overleftrightarrow{QT} \parallel \overleftrightarrow{RS}$
Conclusion: $\overline{QR} \cong \overline{TS}$

16 $\overline{PQ}$ is a diameter of ⊙O. P = (−3, 17) and Q = (5, 2). Find the center and the radius of ⊙O.

17 ⊙P just touches (is tangent to) the x-axis. P = (15, 13) and Q = (19, 16).
a Find the radius of ⊙P.
b Find PQ.
c Find the length of $\overline{AB}$.

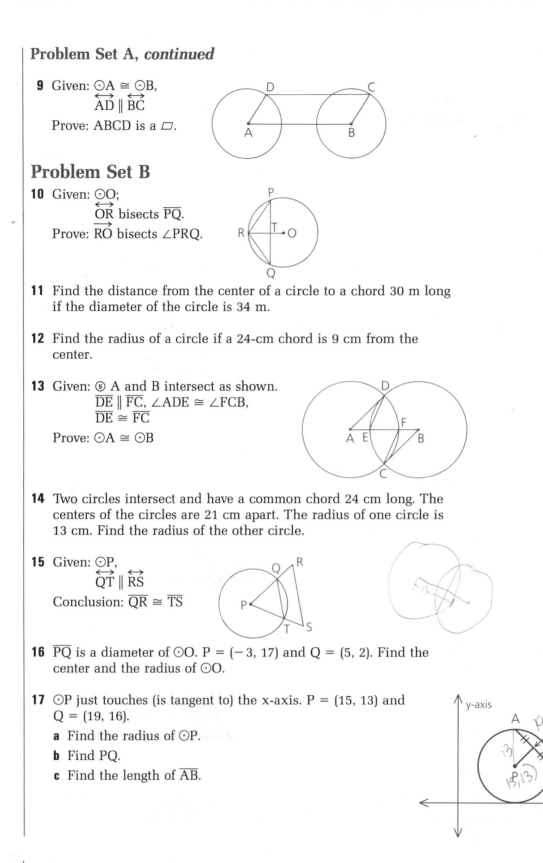

18 Given: ⊙P;
         Z is the midpt. of $\overline{WX}$.
         △WAX is isosceles, with
         base $\overline{WX}$.
    Prove: $\overrightarrow{AZ}$ passes through P.

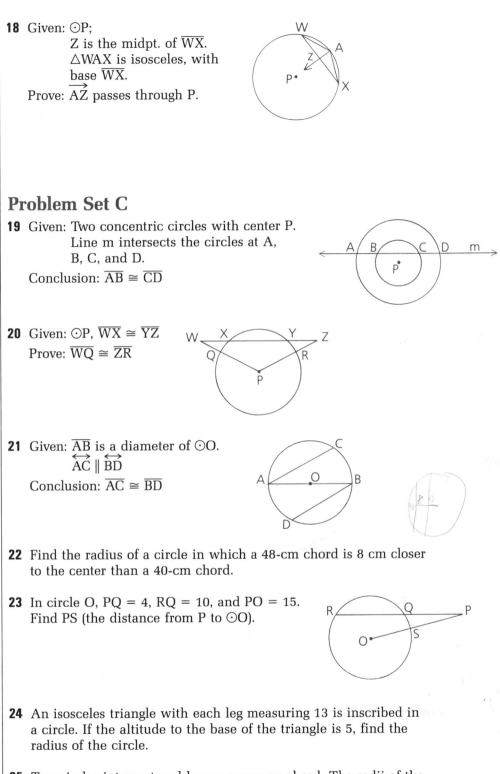

Problem Set C

19 Given: Two concentric circles with center P.
         Line m intersects the circles at A,
         B, C, and D.
    Conclusion: $\overline{AB} \cong \overline{CD}$

20 Given: ⊙P, $\overline{WX} \cong \overline{YZ}$
    Prove: $\overline{WQ} \cong \overline{ZR}$

21 Given: $\overline{AB}$ is a diameter of ⊙O.
         $\overleftrightarrow{AC} \parallel \overleftrightarrow{BD}$
    Conclusion: $\overline{AC} \cong \overline{BD}$

22 Find the radius of a circle in which a 48-cm chord is 8 cm closer
to the center than a 40-cm chord.

23 In circle O, PQ = 4, RQ = 10, and PO = 15.
Find PS (the distance from P to ⊙O).

24 An isosceles triangle with each leg measuring 13 is inscribed in
a circle. If the altitude to the base of the triangle is 5, find the
radius of the circle.

25 Two circles intersect and have a common chord. The radii of the
circles are 13 and 15. The distance between their centers is 14.
Find the length of their common chord.

CONGRUENT CHORDS

Objective

After studying this section, you will be able to
- Apply the relationship between congruent chords of a circle

Part One: Introduction

If two chords are the same distance from the center of a circle, what can we conclude?

Theorem 77   *If two chords of a circle are equidistant from the center, then they are congruent.*

Given: ⊙P, $\overline{PX} \perp \overline{AB}$, $\overline{PY} \perp \overline{CD}$, $\overline{PX} \cong \overline{PY}$
Prove: $\overline{AB} \cong \overline{CD}$

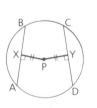

The proof of Theorem 77 is left for you to do. (Use four congruent triangles.) The converse of Theorem 77 can also be proved.

Theorem 78   *If two chords of a circle are congruent, then they are equidistant from the center of the circle.*

Given: ⊙O, $\overline{AB} \cong \overline{CD}$, $\overline{OE} \perp \overline{AB}$, $\overline{OF} \perp \overline{CD}$
Prove: $\overline{OE} \cong \overline{OF}$

Part Two: Sample Problems

Problem 1
Given: $\odot O$, $\overline{AB} \cong \overline{CD}$,
        $OP = 12x - 5$, $OQ = 4x + 19$
Find: OP

Solution
Since $\overline{AB} \cong \overline{CD}$, $OP = OQ$.

$$12x - 5 = 4x + 19$$
$$x = 3$$

Thus, $OP = 12(3) - 5 = 31$.

Problem 2
Given: $\triangle ABC$ is isosceles, with base $\overline{AC}$.
        $\odot P$, $\overline{PQ} \perp \overline{AB}$, $\overline{PR} \perp \overline{CB}$
Prove: $\triangle PQR$ is isosceles.

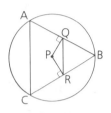

Proof

1 $\odot P$, $\overline{PQ} \perp \overline{AB}$, $\overline{PR} \perp \overline{CB}$	1 Given
2 $\triangle ABC$ is isosceles, with base $\overline{AC}$.	2 Given
3 $\overline{AB} \cong \overline{BC}$	3 An isosceles $\triangle$ has two $\cong$ sides.
4 $\overline{PQ} \cong \overline{PR}$	4 If two chords of a circle are $\cong$, then they are equidistant from the center.
5 $\triangle PQR$ is isosceles.	5 A $\triangle$ with two $\cong$ sides is isosceles.

Why do you think it was necessary to be given $\overline{PQ} \perp \overline{AB}$ and $\overline{PR} \perp \overline{CB}$, even though they did not seem to play an active role in the proof?

Part Three: Problem Sets

Problem Set A

1 In a circle, chord $\overline{AB}$ is 325 cm long and chord $\overline{CD}$ is $3\frac{1}{4}$ m long. Which is closer to the center?

2 Given: $\odot P$, $\overline{PQ} \cong \overline{PR}$,
      $AB = 6x + 14$,
      $CD = 4 - 4x$
Find: AB

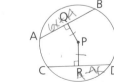

1-6 ; 11,13

Problem Set A, *continued*

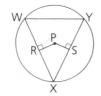

3 Given: ⊙P, $\overline{PR} \perp \overline{WX}$,
$\overline{PS} \perp \overline{XY}$, $\overline{PR} \cong \overline{PS}$
Conclusion: ∠W ≅ ∠Y

4 Given: Equilateral △ ABC is inscribed
in ⊙Q.
Conclusion: $\overline{AB}$, $\overline{BC}$, and $\overline{CA}$ are equidistant from the center.

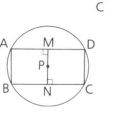

5 Given: ⊙P;
P is the midpoint of $\overline{MN}$.
$\overline{MN} \perp \overline{AD}$, $\overline{MN} \perp \overline{BC}$
Conclusion: ABCD is a ▱.

6 A fly is sitting at the midpoint of a
wooden chord of a circular wheel. The
wheel has a radius of 10 cm, and the
chord has a length of 12 cm.

a How far from the hub (center) is the fly?
b The wheel is spun. What is the path of the fly?

Problem Set B

7 To the nearest hundredth, find
a The area of the circle
b The circumference of the circle

19 mm

8 Given: ⊙Q, $\overline{PS} \perp \overline{RT}$,
$\overline{MQ} \perp \overline{RP}$, $\overline{NQ} \perp \overline{PT}$
Conclusion: $\overline{MQ} \cong \overline{QN}$

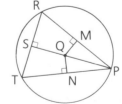

9 Given: ⊙F,
$\overline{FE} \perp \overline{BC}$, $\overline{FD} \perp \overline{AB}$;
$\overrightarrow{BF}$ bisects ∠ABC.
Prove: $\overline{BC} \cong \overline{BA}$

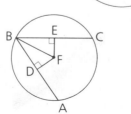

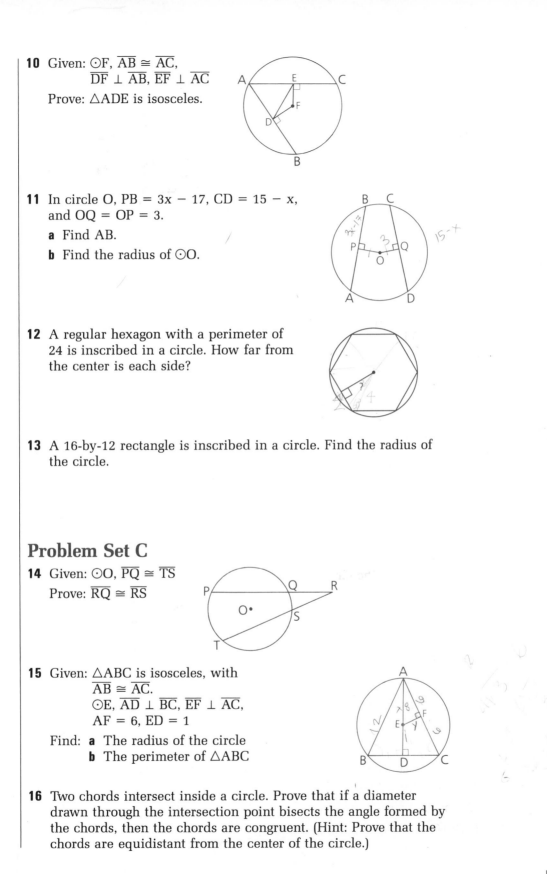

10 Given: ⊙F, $\overline{AB} \cong \overline{AC}$,
$\overline{DF} \perp \overline{AB}$, $\overline{EF} \perp \overline{AC}$
Prove: △ADE is isosceles.

11 In circle O, PB = 3x − 17, CD = 15 − x,
and OQ = OP = 3.
a Find AB.
b Find the radius of ⊙O.

12 A regular hexagon with a perimeter of
24 is inscribed in a circle. How far from
the center is each side?

13 A 16-by-12 rectangle is inscribed in a circle. Find the radius of
the circle.

Problem Set C

14 Given: ⊙O, $\overline{PQ} \cong \overline{TS}$
Prove: $\overline{RQ} \cong \overline{RS}$

15 Given: △ABC is isosceles, with
$\overline{AB} \cong \overline{AC}$.
⊙E, $\overline{AD} \perp \overline{BC}$, $\overline{EF} \perp \overline{AC}$,
AF = 6, ED = 1
Find: **a** The radius of the circle
b The perimeter of △ABC

16 Two chords intersect inside a circle. Prove that if a diameter
drawn through the intersection point bisects the angle formed by
the chords, then the chords are congruent. (Hint: Prove that the
chords are equidistant from the center of the circle.)

ARCS OF A CIRCLE

Objectives

After studying this section, you will be able to
- Identify the different types of arcs
- Determine the measure of an arc
- Recognize congruent arcs
- Apply the relationships between congruent arcs, chords, and central angles

Part One: Introduction

Types of Arcs

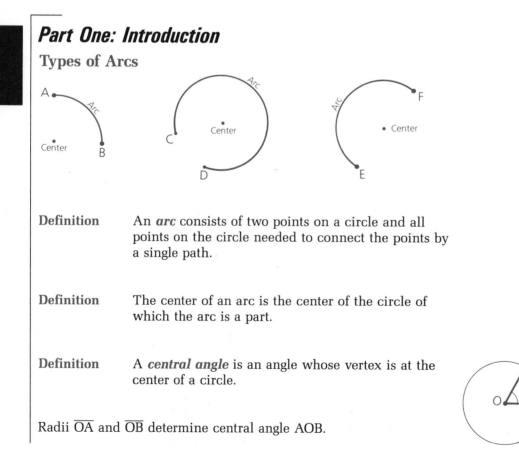

Definition	An *arc* consists of two points on a circle and all points on the circle needed to connect the points by a single path.

Definition	The center of an arc is the center of the circle of which the arc is a part.

Definition	A *central angle* is an angle whose vertex is at the center of a circle.

Radii $\overline{OA}$ and $\overline{OB}$ determine central angle AOB.

Definition	A *minor arc* is an arc whose points are on or be-tween the sides of a central angle.

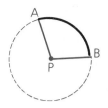

Central angle APB determines minor arc AB.

Definition	A *major arc* is an arc whose points are on or outside of a central angle.

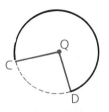

Central angle CQD determines major arc CD.

Definition	A *semicircle* is an arc whose endpoints are the end-points of a diameter.

Arc EF is a semicircle.

The symbol ⌒ is used to label arcs. The minor arc joining A and B is called $\overset{\frown}{AB}$. The major arc joining A and B is called $\overset{\frown}{AXB}$. (The extra point, X, is named to make it clear that we are referring to the arc from A to B *by way of* point X. This helps to avoid confusion when a major arc or a semicircle is being discussed.)

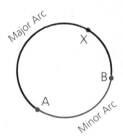

1-6

The Measure of an Arc

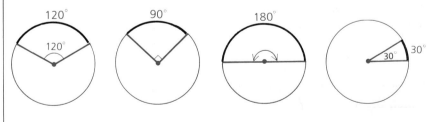

Definition	The measure of a minor arc or a semicircle is the same as the measure of the central angle that inter-cepts the arc.

Definition	The measure of a major arc is 360 minus the mea-sure of the minor arc with the same endpoints.

Example   **a** *Given:* m$\widehat{AB}$ = 20
                 Find: m$\widehat{ACB}$

b *Given:* m∠XQY = 110
       Find: m$\widehat{XDY}$

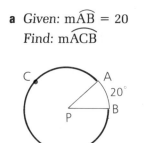

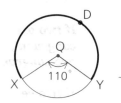

$$m\widehat{ACB} = 360 - 20$$
$$= 340$$

$$m\widehat{XY} = m∠XQY = 110$$
Therefore, m$\widehat{XDY}$ = 360 - 110
$$= 250$$

Congruent Arcs

Two arcs that have the same measure are not necessarily congruent arcs. In the concentric circles shown, m$\widehat{AB}$ = 65 and m$\widehat{CD}$ = 65, but $\widehat{AB}$ and $\widehat{CD}$ are *not* congruent. Under what conditions, do you think, will two arcs be congruent?

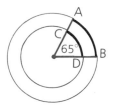

Definition   Two arcs are congruent whenever they have the same measure and are parts of the same circle or congruent circles.

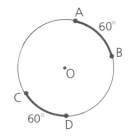

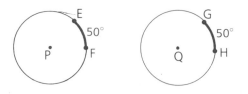

We may conclude that $\widehat{AB} \cong \widehat{CD}$.

If ⊙P ≅ ⊙Q, we may conclude that $\widehat{EF} \cong \widehat{GH}$.

Relating Congruent Arcs, Chords, and Central Angles

In the diagram, points A and B determine one central angle, one chord, and two arcs (one major and one minor).

   You can readily prove the following theorems.

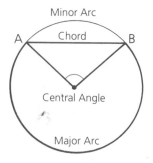

Theorem 79	*If two central angles of a circle (or of congruent circles) are congruent, then their intercepted arcs are congruent.*

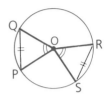

Theorem 80	*If two arcs of a circle (or of congruent circles) are congruent, then the corresponding central angles are congruent.*
Theorem 81	*If two central angles of a circle (or of congruent circles) are congruent, then the corresponding chords are congruent.*

Theorem 82	*If two chords of a circle (or of congruent circles) are congruent, then the corresponding central angles are congruent.*
Theorem 83	*If two arcs of a circle (or of congruent circles) are congruent, then the corresponding chords are congruent.*
Theorem 84	*If two chords of a circle (or of congruent circles) are congruent, then the corresponding arcs are congruent.*

To summarize, in the same circle or in congruent circles, congruent chords ⟺ congruent arcs ⟺ congruent central angles.

Part Two: Sample Problems

Problem 1   Given: ⊙B;
         D is the midpt. of $\widehat{AC}$.
      Conclusion: $\overrightarrow{BD}$ bisects ∠ABC.

Proof

1 ⊙B; D is the midpt. of $\widehat{AC}$.	1 Given
2 $\widehat{AD} \cong \widehat{DC}$	2 The midpoint of an arc divides the arc into two ≅ arcs.
3 ∠ABD ≅ ∠DBC	3 If two arcs of a circle are ≅, then the corresponding central ∠s are ≅.
4 $\overrightarrow{BD}$ bisects ∠ABC.	4 If a ray divides an ∠ into two ≅ ∠s, then the ray bisects the ∠.

Problem 2 If m$\widehat{AB}$ = 102 in ⊙O, find m∠A and m∠B in △AOB.

Solution $\widehat{AB}$ = 102°, so ∠AOB = 102°.
The sum of the measures of the angles of a triangle is 180, so

$$m\angle AOB + m\angle A + m\angle B = 180$$
$$102 + m\angle A + m\angle B = 180$$
$$m\angle A + m\angle B = 78$$

But $\overline{OA} \cong \overline{OB}$, so that ∠A ≅ ∠B.
Hence, m∠A = 39 and m∠B = 39.

Problem 3 **a** What fractional part of a circle is an arc of 36°? Of 200°?
b Find the measure of an arc that is $\frac{7}{12}$ of its circle.

Solution **a** 36° is $\frac{36}{360}$, or $\frac{1}{10}$, of a ⊙.
200° is $\frac{200}{360}$, or $\frac{5}{9}$, of a ⊙.

b There are 360° in a whole ⊙.
$\frac{7}{12}$ of 360 = $\frac{7}{12} \cdot \frac{360}{1}$ = 210

Problem 4 Given: ⊙ P and Q,
∠P ≅ ∠Q, $\overline{AR} \cong \overline{RD}$
Prove: $\widehat{AB} \cong \widehat{CD}$ (Hint: First prove
that ⊙P ≅ ⊙Q.)

Proof

1 ⊙ P and Q	1 Given
2 ∠P ≅ ∠Q	2 Given
3 $\overline{RP} \cong \overline{RQ}$	3 If △, then △.
4 $\overline{AR} \cong \overline{RD}$	4 Given
5 $\overline{AP} \cong \overline{DQ}$	5 Subtraction Property
6 ⊙P ≅ ⊙Q	6 ⊙ with ≅ radii are ≅.
7 $\widehat{AB} \cong \widehat{CD}$	7 If two central ∠s of ≅ ⊙ are ≅, then their intercepted arcs are ≅.

Part Three: Problem Sets

Problem Set A

1 Match each item in the left column with the correct term in the right column.

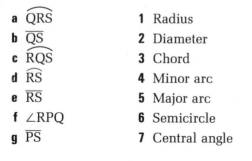

a	$\widehat{QRS}$	**1**	Radius
b	$\overline{QS}$	**2**	Diameter
c	$\widehat{RQS}$	**3**	Chord
d	$\widehat{RS}$	**4**	Minor arc
e	$\overline{RS}$	**5**	Major arc
f	∠RPQ	**6**	Semicircle
g	$\overline{PS}$	**7**	Central angle

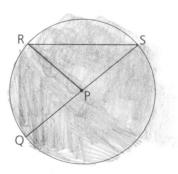

2 Given: Two concentric circles with center O;
∠BOC is acute.

a Name a major arc of the smaller circle.

b Name a minor arc of the larger circle.

c What is m$\widehat{BC}$ + m$\widehat{PQ}$?

d Which is greater, m$\widehat{BC}$ or m$\widehat{PQ}$?

e Is $\widehat{BC}$ congruent to $\widehat{QR}$?

3 In circle E, find each of the following.

  a m$\widehat{BC}$ **c** m$\widehat{ACD}$ **e** m$\widehat{ADC}$

  b m$\widehat{AD}$ **d** m$\widehat{BAD}$

4 Given: ⊙Q, ∠A = 25°
Find: m$\widehat{AB}$

5 Given: ⊙P,
$\widehat{WY} \cong \widehat{XZ}$
Conclusion: $\overline{WX} \cong \overline{YZ}$

6 Given: ⊙D, ∠B ≅ ∠C
Conclusion: $\widehat{AB} \cong \widehat{AC}$

7 Given: $\overline{AB} \cong \overline{CD}$
Conclusion: $\widehat{AC} \cong \widehat{BD}$

8 Given: ⊙E,
$\overline{AB} \cong \overline{CD}$
Prove: $\overline{BD} \cong \overline{AC}$

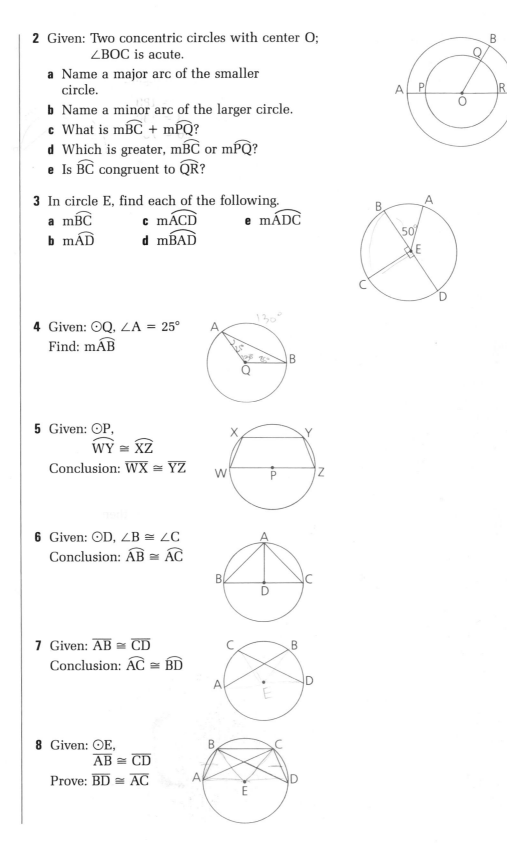

Problem Set A, *continued*

9 What fractional part of a circle is an arc that measures

   a 8   **c** 144

   b 240   **d** 315

10 Find the measure of an arc that is

   a $\frac{3}{5}$ of its circle   **b** $\frac{5}{9}$ of its circle   **c** 70% of its circle

Problem Set B

11 Given: $\overline{AD}$ is a diameter of $\odot E$.

          C is the midpoint of $\overparen{BD}$.

          $m\overparen{AB} = 9x + 30$,

          $m\overparen{CD} = 54 - x$

   Find: $m\angle AEC$

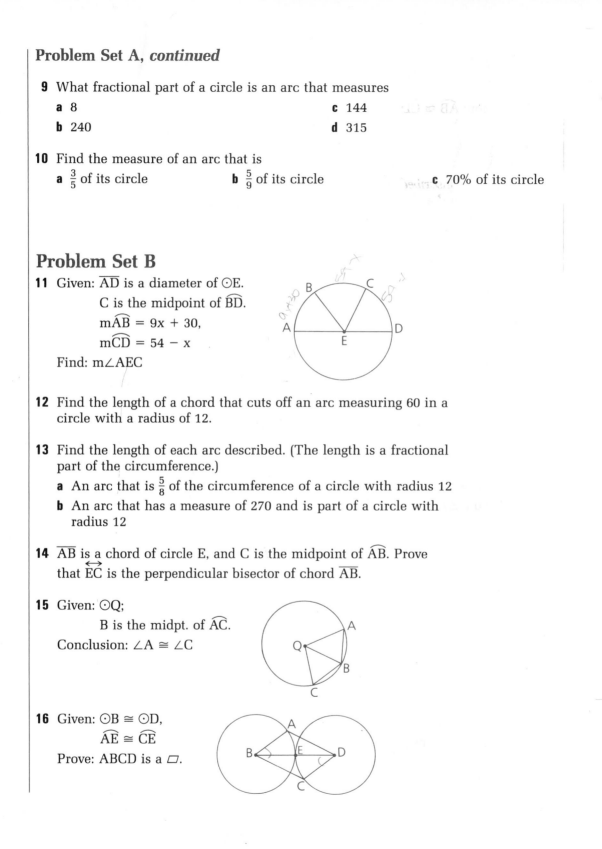

12 Find the length of a chord that cuts off an arc measuring 60 in a circle with a radius of 12.

13 Find the length of each arc described. (The length is a fractional part of the circumference.)

   a An arc that is $\frac{5}{8}$ of the circumference of a circle with radius 12

   b An arc that has a measure of 270 and is part of a circle with radius 12

14 $\overline{AB}$ is a chord of circle E, and C is the midpoint of $\overparen{AB}$. Prove that $\overleftrightarrow{EC}$ is the perpendicular bisector of chord $\overline{AB}$.

15 Given: $\odot Q$;

          B is the midpt. of $\overparen{AC}$.

   Conclusion: $\angle A \cong \angle C$

16 Given: $\odot B \cong \odot D$,

          $\overparen{AE} \cong \overparen{CE}$

   Prove: ABCD is a $\square$.

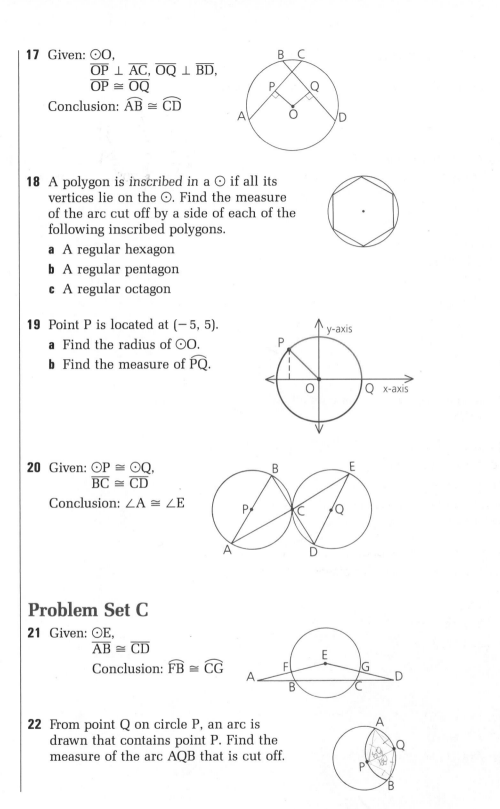

17 Given: ⊙O,
  $\overline{OP} \perp \overline{AC}$, $\overline{OQ} \perp \overline{BD}$,
  $\overline{OP} \cong \overline{OQ}$
  Conclusion: $\overparen{AB} \cong \overparen{CD}$

18 A polygon is *inscribed* in a ⊙ if all its
  vertices lie on the ⊙. Find the measure
  of the arc cut off by a side of each of the
  following inscribed polygons.
  a A regular hexagon
  b A regular pentagon
  c A regular octagon

19 Point P is located at $(-5, 5)$.
  a Find the radius of ⊙O.
  b Find the measure of $\overparen{PQ}$.

20 Given: ⊙P ≅ ⊙Q,
  $\overline{BC} \cong \overline{CD}$
  Conclusion: $\angle A \cong \angle E$

Problem Set C

21 Given: ⊙E,
  $\overline{AB} \cong \overline{CD}$
  Conclusion: $\overparen{FB} \cong \overparen{CG}$

22 From point Q on circle P, an arc is
  drawn that contains point P. Find the
  measure of the arc AQB that is cut off.

23 If *n* points are selected on a given circle, find a formula

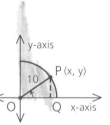

  a For the number of chords that can be drawn between pairs of these points

  b For the number of arcs formed—including major and minor arcs and semicircles (Hint: Draw circles and count arcs for *n* = 1, 2, 3, . . . until you see a number pattern.)

  c For the measure of an arc formed by a side of a regular *n*-gon inscribed in the circle

24 Given: ⊙P ≅ ⊙Q,
XY = 8,
RP = QS = 1
Find: PQ

25 Prove that if an equilateral polygon is inscribed in a circle, then it is equiangular.

26 Find, to the nearest tenth, the coordinates of point P on the circle with center O and radius 10, given that m$\overarc{PQ}$ = 40. (Hint: Use trigonometry.)

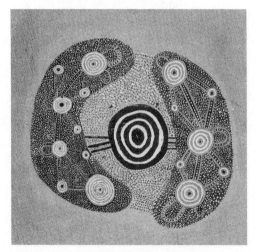

SECANTS AND TANGENTS

Objectives

After studying this section, you will be able to
- Identify secant and tangent lines
- Identify secant and tangent segments
- Distinguish between two types of tangent circles
- Recognize common internal and common external tangents

Part One: Introduction

Secant and Tangent Lines

Some lines and circles have special relationships.

Definition   A *secant* is a line that intersects a circle at
exactly two points. (Every secant contains
a chord of the circle.)

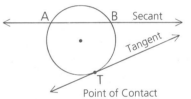

Definition   A *tangent* is a line that intersects a circle at exactly
one point. This point is called the *point of tangency*
or *point of contact*.

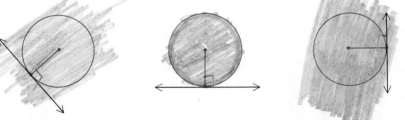

The diagrams above suggest the following postulates about tangents.

Postulate   ***A tangent line is perpendicular to the radius drawn
to the point of contact.***

Postulate   ***If a line is perpendicular to a radius at its outer
endpoint, then it is tangent to the circle.***

Secant and Tangent Segments

Some segments are related to circles in similar ways.

Definition   A *tangent segment* is the part of a tangent line between the point of contact and a point outside the
circle.

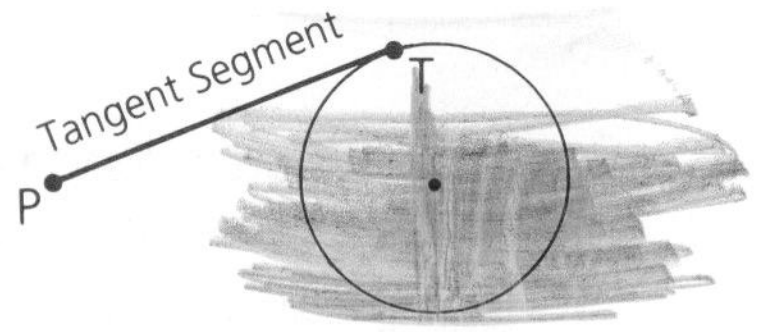

Definition   A *secant segment* is the part of a secant line
that joins a point outside the circle to the
farther intersection point of the secant
and the circle.

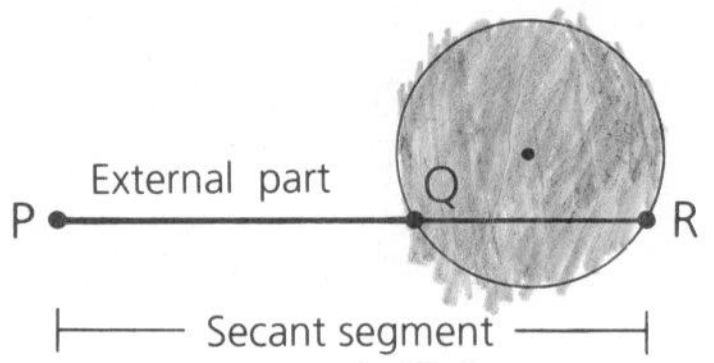

Definition   The *external part* of a secant segment is the part of
a secant line that joins the outside point to the
nearer intersection point.

Theorem 85   *If two tangent segments are drawn to a circle from
an external point, then those segments are congru-
ent. (Two-Tangent Theorem)*

Given: $\odot O$;
$\quad\quad$ $\overline{PX}$ and $\overline{PY}$ are tangent segments.
Prove: $\overline{PX} \cong \overline{PY}$

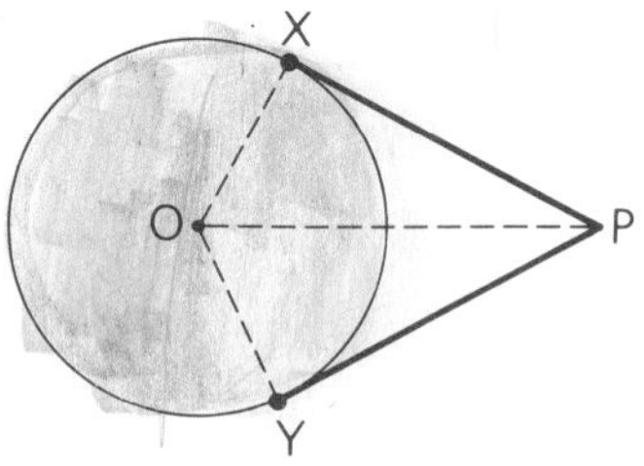

The Two-Tangent Theorem is easily
proved with congruent triangles.
More theorems relating to secant segments
and tangent segments are presented
in Section 10.8.

Tangent Circles

Definition   *Tangent circles* are circles that intersect each other
at exactly one point.

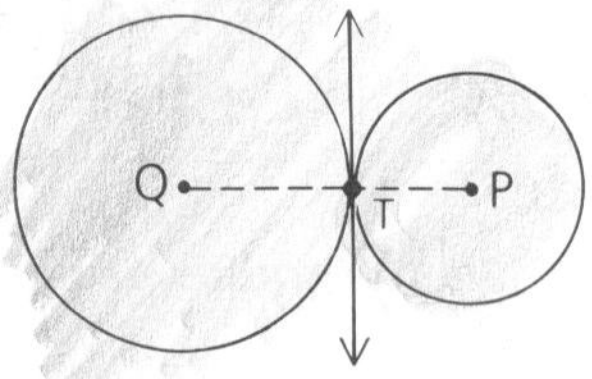

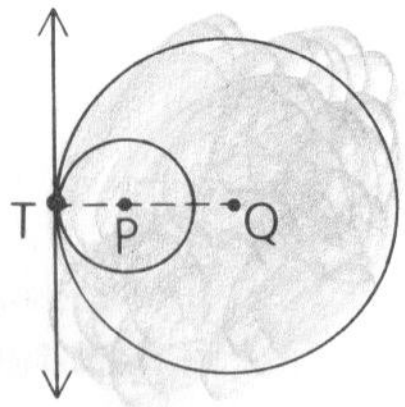

Definition   Two circles are *externally tangent* if each of the
tangent circles lies outside the other. (See the left-
hand figure above.)

Definition   Two circles are *internally tangent* if one of the tangent circles lies inside the other. (See the right-hand figure on the preceding page.)

Notice that in each case the tangent circles have one common tangent at their point of contact. Also, the point of contact lies on the *line of centers,* $\overleftrightarrow{PQ}$.

Common Tangents

$\overleftrightarrow{PQ}$ is the line of centers.
$\overleftrightarrow{XY}$ is a *common internal tangent.*
$\overleftrightarrow{AB}$ is a *common external tangent.*

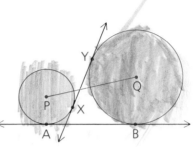

Definition   A *common tangent* is a line tangent to two circles (not necessarily at the same point). Such a tangent is a *common internal tangent* if it lies between the circles (intersects the segment joining the centers) or a *common external tangent* if it is not between the circles (does not intersect the segment joining the centers).

In practice, we will frequently refer to a *segment* as a common tangent if it lies on a common tangent and its endpoints are the tangent's points of contact. In the preceding diagram, for example, $\overline{XY}$ can be called a common internal tangent and $\overline{AB}$ can be called a common external tangent.

Part Two: Sample Problems

Problem 1   Given: $\overline{XY}$ *is a common internal tangent to* ⊚ *P and Q at X and Y.*
$\overline{XS}$ *is tangent to* ⊙P *at S.*
$\overline{YT}$ *is tangent to* ⊙Q *at T.*

Conclusion: $\overline{XS} \cong \overline{YT}$

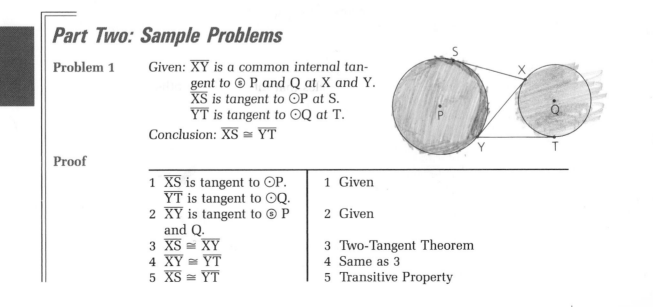

Proof

1 $\overline{XS}$ is tangent to ⊙P. $\overline{YT}$ is tangent to ⊙Q.	1 Given
2 $\overline{XY}$ is tangent to ⊚ P and Q.	2 Given
3 $\overline{XS} \cong \overline{XY}$	3 Two-Tangent Theorem
4 $\overline{XY} \cong \overline{YT}$	4 Same as 3
5 $\overline{XS} \cong \overline{YT}$	5 Transitive Property

Problem 2

$\overleftrightarrow{TP}$ is tangent to circle O at T.
The radius of circle O is 8 mm.
Tangent segment $\overline{TP}$ is 6 mm long.
Find the length of $\overline{OP}$.

Solution

Draw radius $\overline{OT}$ to form right triangle OTP.

$$(TP)^2 + (TO)^2 = (OP)^2$$
$$6^2 + 8^2 = (OP)^2$$
$$\pm 10 = OP \qquad \text{(Reject } -10.)$$

Thus, OP = 10 mm.

Problem 3

A circle with a radius of 8 cm is externally tangent to a circle with a radius of 18 cm. Find the length of a common external tangent.

Solution

There is a standard procedure for solving a problem involving a common tangent (either internal or external).

Common-Tangent Procedure

1 Draw the segment joining the centers.

2 Draw the radii to the points of contact.

3 Through the center of the smaller circle, draw a line parallel to the common tangent.

4 Observe that this line will intersect the radius of the larger circle (extended if necessary) to form a rectangle and a right triangle.

5 Use the Pythagorean Theorem and properties of a rectangle.

In $\triangle RPQ$,
$$(QR)^2 + (RP)^2 = (PQ)^2$$
$$10^2 + (RP)^2 = 26^2$$
$$RP = \pm 24$$
Thus, AB = 24 cm.

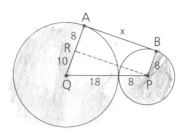

Problem 4
A walk-around problem:
Given: Each side of quadrilateral
ABCD is tangent to the circle.
AB = 10, BC = 15, AD = 18
Find: CD

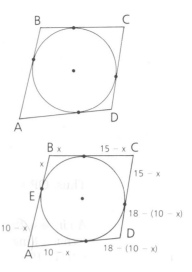

Solution
Let BE = x and "walk around" the
figure, using the given information
and the Two-Tangent Theorem.

$$CD = 15 - x + 18 - (10 - x)$$
$$= 15 - x + 18 - 10 + x$$
$$= 23$$

See problems 16, 21, 22, and 29 for other types of
walk-around problems.

1, 2, 6 7 , 10, 13, 6

Part Three: Problem Sets

Problem Set A

1 The radius of ⊙A is 8 cm.
Tangent segment $\overline{BC}$ is 15 cm long.
Find the length of $\overline{AC}$.

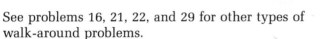

2 Concentric circles with radii 8 and 10
have center P.
$\overline{XY}$ is a tangent to the inner circle and is
a chord of the outer circle.
Find $\overline{XY}$. (Hint: Draw $\overline{PX}$ and $\overline{PY}$.)

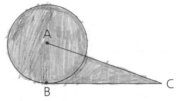

3 Given: $\overline{PR}$ and $\overline{PQ}$ are tangents to ⊙O at
R and Q.
Prove: $\overrightarrow{PO}$ bisects ∠RPQ. (Hint: Draw $\overline{RO}$
and $\overline{OQ}$.)

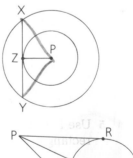

4 Given: $\overline{AC}$ is a diameter of ⊙B.
Lines s and m are tangents to the
⊙ at A and C.
Conclusion: s ∥ m

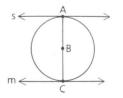

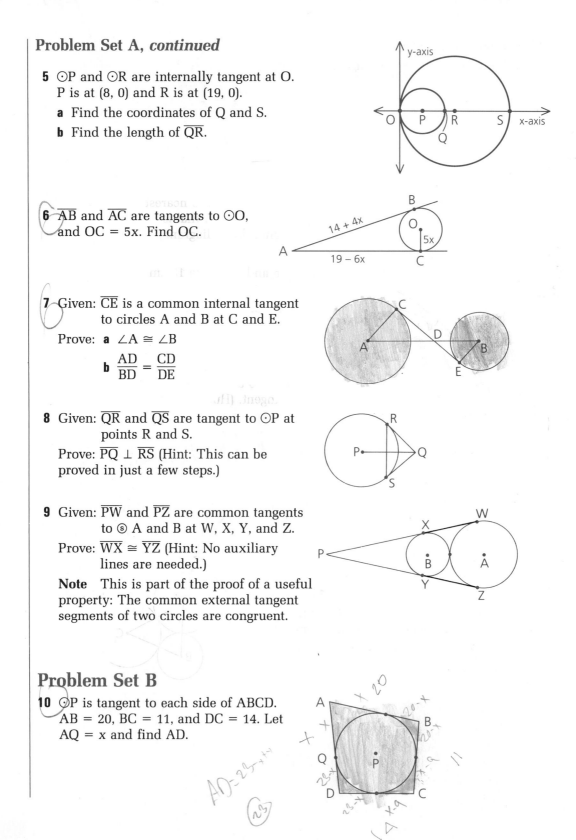

5 ⊙P and ⊙R are internally tangent at O.
P is at (8, 0) and R is at (19, 0).

   a Find the coordinates of Q and S.

   b Find the length of $\overline{QR}$.

6 $\overline{AB}$ and $\overline{AC}$ are tangents to ⊙O,
and OC = 5x. Find OC.

7 Given: $\overline{CE}$ is a common internal tangent
       to circles A and B at C and E.

   Prove: **a** $\angle A \cong \angle B$

       b $\dfrac{AD}{BD} = \dfrac{CD}{DE}$

8 Given: $\overline{QR}$ and $\overline{QS}$ are tangent to ⊙P at
       points R and S.

   Prove: $\overline{PQ} \perp \overline{RS}$ (Hint: This can be
proved in just a few steps.)

9 Given: $\overline{PW}$ and $\overline{PZ}$ are common tangents
       to ⊙ A and B at W, X, Y, and Z.

   Prove: $\overline{WX} \cong \overline{YZ}$ (Hint: No auxiliary
lines are needed.)

   Note This is part of the proof of a useful
property: The common external tangent
segments of two circles are congruent.

Problem Set B

10 ⊙P is tangent to each side of ABCD.
AB = 20, BC = 11, and DC = 14. Let
AQ = x and find AD.

11 a Find the radius of ⊙P.

b Find the slope of the tangent to ⊙P at point Q.

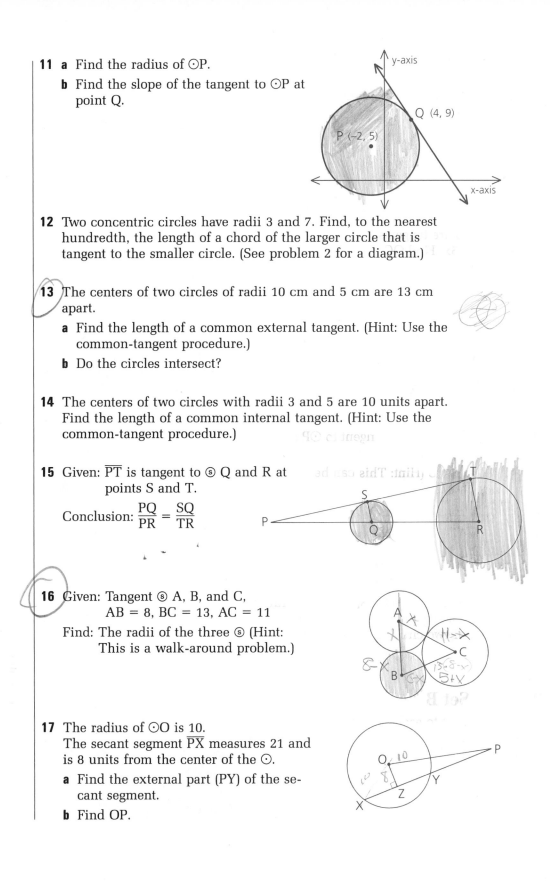

12 Two concentric circles have radii 3 and 7. Find, to the nearest hundredth, the length of a chord of the larger circle that is tangent to the smaller circle. (See problem 2 for a diagram.)

13 The centers of two circles of radii 10 cm and 5 cm are 13 cm apart.

a Find the length of a common external tangent. (Hint: Use the common-tangent procedure.)

b Do the circles intersect?

14 The centers of two circles with radii 3 and 5 are 10 units apart. Find the length of a common internal tangent. (Hint: Use the common-tangent procedure.)

15 Given: $\overline{PT}$ is tangent to ⊙ Q and R at points S and T.

Conclusion: $\dfrac{PQ}{PR} = \dfrac{SQ}{TR}$

16 Given: Tangent ⊙ A, B, and C,
AB = 8, BC = 13, AC = 11

Find: The radii of the three ⊙ (Hint: This is a walk-around problem.)

17 The radius of ⊙O is 10.
The secant segment $\overline{PX}$ measures 21 and is 8 units from the center of the ⊙.

a Find the external part (PY) of the secant segment.

b Find OP.

Problem Set B, *continued*

18 Given: △ABC is isosceles, with base $\overline{BC}$.
Conclusion: $\overline{BR} \cong \overline{RC}$

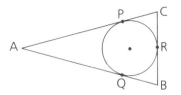

19 If two of the seven circles are chosen at random, what is the probability that the chosen pair are

   a Internally tangent?

   b Externally tangent?

   c Not tangent?

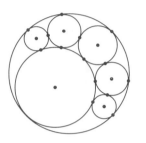

20 Find, to the nearest tenth, the distance between two circles if their radii are 1 and 4 and the length of a common external tangent is $7\frac{1}{2}$.

Problem Set C

21 Given: Quadrilateral WXYZ is *circum-scribed about* ⊙O (that is, its sides are tangent to the ⊙).

   Prove: XY + WZ = WX + YZ

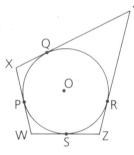

22 Find the perimeter of right triangle WXY if the radius of the circle is 4 and WY = 20.

23 B is 34 mm from the center of circle O, which has radius 16 mm. $\overline{BP}$ and $\overline{BR}$ are tangent segments. $\overleftrightarrow{AC}$ is tangent to ⊙O at point Q. Find the perimeter of △ABC.

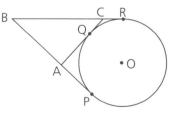

24 Find the coordinates of the center of a circle that is tangent to the y-axis and intersects the x-axis at (8, 0) and (18, 0).

25 Given: Two concentric circles with center E, AB = 40, CD = 24, $\overline{CD} \perp \overline{AE}$; $\overline{AB}$ is tangent at C.

Find: AF

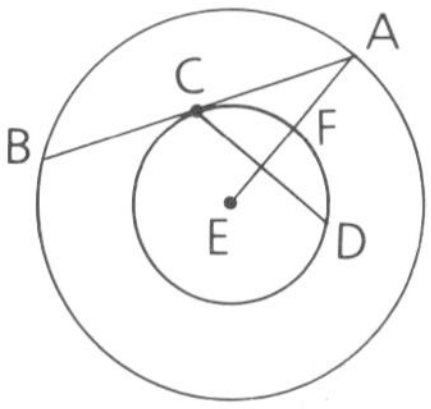

26 $\overline{BC}$ is tangent to $\odot A$ at B, and $\overline{BD} \cong \overline{BA}$. Explain why $\overline{BD}$ bisects $\overline{AC}$.

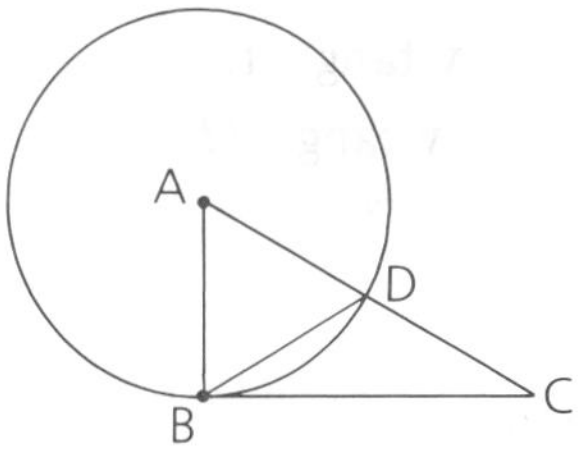

27 Given: $\circledS$ E and F, with $\overline{AC}$ tangent at B and C, DE = 10, FB = 4

Find: AB

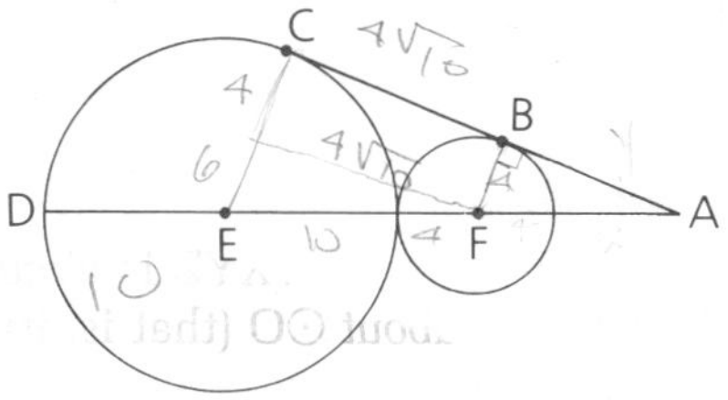

28 Circles P and Q are tangent to each other and to the axes as shown. PQ = 26 and AB = 24. Find the coordinates of P and Q.

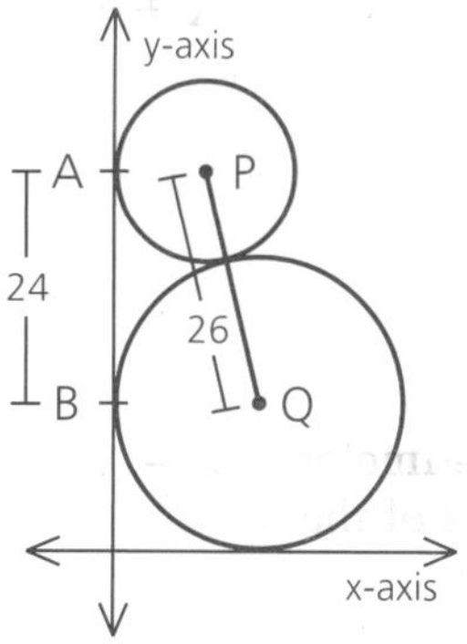

29 Given: Three tangent $\circledS$, A, B, and C, BC = a, AC = b, AB = c

Find: The radius of $\odot A$ in terms of a, b, and c

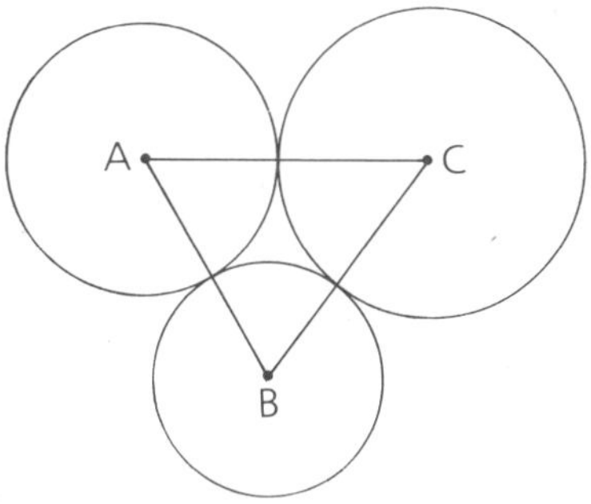

ANGLES RELATED TO A CIRCLE

Objectives

After studying this section, you will be able to
- Determine the measures of central angles
- Determine the measures of inscribed and tangent-chord angles
- Determine the measures of chord-chord angles
- Determine the measures of secant-secant, secant-tangent, and tangent-tangent angles

Part One: Introduction

Angles with Vertices at the Center of a Circle

The measure of an angle whose sides intersect a circle is determined by the measure of its intercepted arcs. The location of the vertex of each angle is the key to remembering how to compute the measure of the angle.

An angle with its vertex at the center of a circle is a central angle, already defined to be equal in measure to its intercepted arc (Section 10.3).

In $\odot$O, $\overparen{AB}$ = 50°, so m∠AOB = 50.

Angles with Vertices on a Circle

Two important types of angles whose vertices are on a circle are shown below.

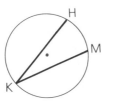

∠HKM is an ***inscribed angle.***

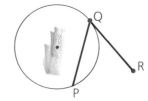

∠PQR is a ***tangent-chord angle.***

Definition	An *inscribed angle* is an angle whose vertex is on a circle and whose sides are determined by two chords.

Definition	A *tangent-chord angle* is an angle whose vertex is on a circle and whose sides are determined by a tangent and a chord that intersect at the tangent's point of contact.

Theorem 86	***The measure of an inscribed angle or a tangent-chord angle (vertex on a circle) is one-half the measure of its intercepted arc.***

The proof of Theorem 86 for inscribed angles is unusual because three cases must be considered. Shown below are some key steps for each case in the proof that $m\angle BAC = \frac{1}{2}(m\widehat{BC})$.

Case 1:
The center lies on a side of the angle.
1 $m\angle BOC = m\widehat{BC}$
2 $\angle BOC = \angle BAC + \angle ABO$, so $m\angle BOC = 2(m\angle BAC)$

Case 2:
The center lies inside the angle.
1 Use case 1 twice.
2 Add $\angle$s and arcs.

Case 3:
The center lies outside the angle.
1 Use case 1 twice.
2 Subtract $\angle$s and arcs.

Example 1 Given: $m\widehat{AC} = 112$
Find: $m\angle B$

$m\angle B = \frac{1}{2}(m\widehat{AC})$

$\qquad = \frac{1}{2} \cdot 112$

$\qquad = 56$

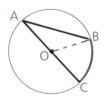

Example 2 Given: $\overline{FE}$ *is tangent at E.*
$m\widehat{DE} = 80$
Find: $m\angle DEF$

$m\angle DEF = \frac{1}{2}(m\widehat{DE})$

$\qquad\quad = \frac{1}{2} \cdot 80$

$\qquad\quad = 40$

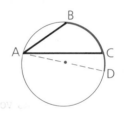

Angles with Vertices Inside, but Not at the Center of, a Circle

One type of angle other than a central angle has a vertex inside a circle.

Definition   A *chord-chord angle* is an angle formed by two chords that intersect inside a circle but not at the center.

∠CPD is one of four chord-chord angles formed by chords $\overline{CF}$ and $\overline{DE}$ in circle O.

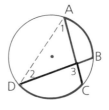

Theorem 87   *The measure of a chord-chord angle is one-half the sum of the measures of the arcs intercepted by the chord-chord angle and its vertical angle.*

Notice that one-half the sum of the arc measures is the same as the *average* of the arc measures.

Given: ∠3 is a chord-chord angle.
Prove: $m\angle 3 = \frac{1}{2}(m\widehat{AB} + m\widehat{CD})$

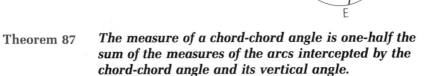

Here are two key steps in a proof of Theorem 87.
1 $m\angle 3 = m\angle 1 + m\angle 2$
2 $m\angle 3 = \frac{1}{2}(m\widehat{CD}) + \frac{1}{2}(m\widehat{AB})$

Angles with Vertices Outside a Circle

There are three types of angles having a vertex outside a circle and both sides intersecting the circle.

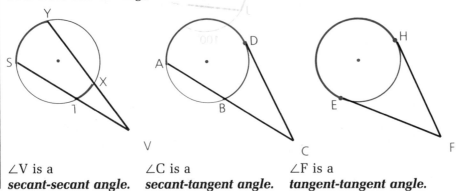

∠V is a
secant-secant angle.

∠C is a
secant-tangent angle.

∠F is a
tangent-tangent angle.

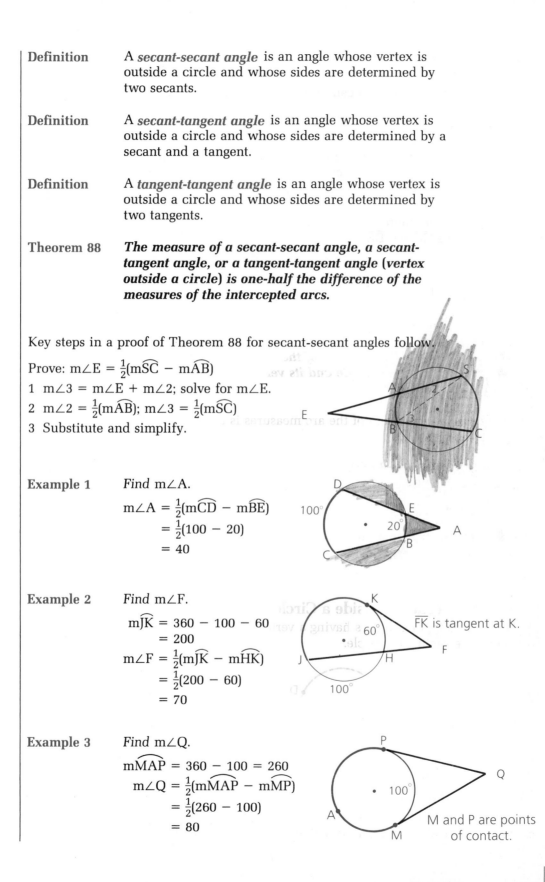

Definition	A *secant-secant angle* is an angle whose vertex is outside a circle and whose sides are determined by two secants.
Definition	A *secant-tangent angle* is an angle whose vertex is outside a circle and whose sides are determined by a secant and a tangent.
Definition	A *tangent-tangent angle* is an angle whose vertex is outside a circle and whose sides are determined by two tangents.
Theorem 88	**The measure of a secant-secant angle, a secant-tangent angle, or a tangent-tangent angle (vertex outside a circle) is one-half the difference of the measures of the intercepted arcs.**

Key steps in a proof of Theorem 88 for secant-secant angles follow.

Prove: $m\angle E = \frac{1}{2}(m\overset{\frown}{SC} - m\overset{\frown}{AB})$

1 $m\angle 3 = m\angle E + m\angle 2$; solve for $m\angle E$.
2 $m\angle 2 = \frac{1}{2}(m\overset{\frown}{AB})$; $m\angle 3 = \frac{1}{2}(m\overset{\frown}{SC})$
3 Substitute and simplify.

Example 1 *Find* $m\angle A$.

$m\angle A = \frac{1}{2}(m\overset{\frown}{CD} - m\overset{\frown}{BE})$
$ = \frac{1}{2}(100 - 20)$
$ = 40$

Example 2 *Find* $m\angle F$.

$m\overset{\frown}{JK} = 360 - 100 - 60$
$\phantom{m\overset{\frown}{JK}} = 200$
$m\angle F = \frac{1}{2}(m\overset{\frown}{JK} - m\overset{\frown}{HK})$
$ = \frac{1}{2}(200 - 60)$
$ = 70$

$\overline{FK}$ is tangent at K.

Example 3 *Find* $m\angle Q$.

$m\overset{\frown}{MAP} = 360 - 100 = 260$
$m\angle Q = \frac{1}{2}(m\overset{\frown}{MAP} - m\overset{\frown}{MP})$
$ = \frac{1}{2}(260 - 100)$
$ = 80$

M and P are points of contact.

Angle-Arc Summary

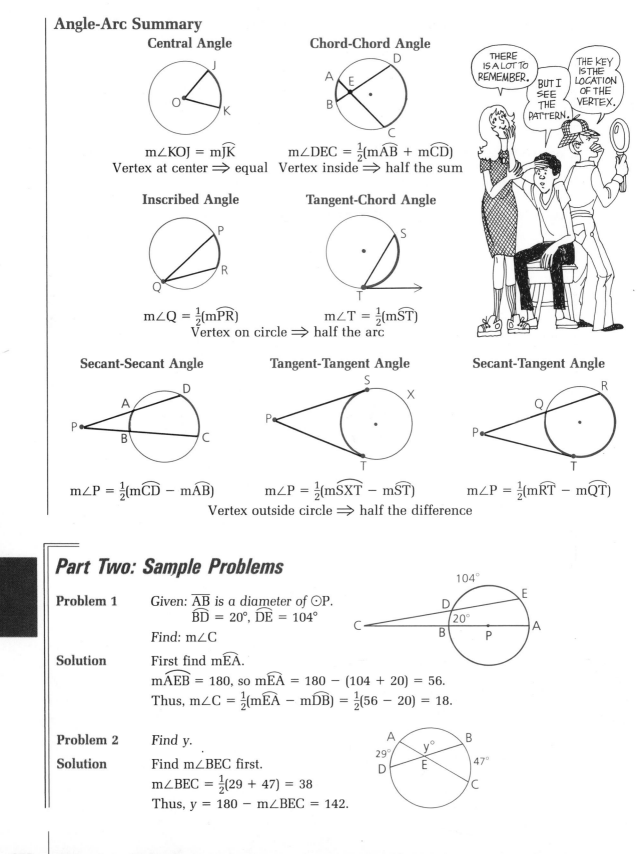

Central Angle

$m\angle KOJ = m\widehat{JK}$

Vertex at center $\Rightarrow$ equal

Chord-Chord Angle

$m\angle DEC = \frac{1}{2}(m\widehat{AB} + m\widehat{CD})$

Vertex inside $\Rightarrow$ half the sum

Inscribed Angle

$m\angle Q = \frac{1}{2}(m\widehat{PR})$

Tangent-Chord Angle

$m\angle T = \frac{1}{2}(m\widehat{ST})$

Vertex on circle $\Rightarrow$ half the arc

Secant-Secant Angle

$m\angle P = \frac{1}{2}(m\widehat{CD} - m\widehat{AB})$

Tangent-Tangent Angle

$m\angle P = \frac{1}{2}(m\widehat{SXT} - m\widehat{ST})$

Secant-Tangent Angle

$m\angle P = \frac{1}{2}(m\widehat{RT} - m\widehat{QT})$

Vertex outside circle $\Rightarrow$ half the difference

THERE IS A LOT TO REMEMBER.

BUT I SEE THE PATTERN.

THE KEY IS THE LOCATION OF THE VERTEX.

Part Two: Sample Problems

Problem 1   *Given:* $\overline{AB}$ *is a diameter of* $\odot P$.

$\widehat{BD} = 20°$, $\widehat{DE} = 104°$

Find: $m\angle C$

Solution   First find $m\widehat{EA}$.

$m\widehat{AEB} = 180$, so $m\widehat{EA} = 180 - (104 + 20) = 56$.

Thus, $m\angle C = \frac{1}{2}(m\widehat{EA} - m\widehat{DB}) = \frac{1}{2}(56 - 20) = 18$.

Problem 2   *Find y.*

Solution   Find $m\angle BEC$ first.

$m\angle BEC = \frac{1}{2}(29 + 47) = 38$

Thus, $y = 180 - m\angle BEC = 142$.

Problem 3   **a** *Find x.*   **b** *Find y.*   **c** *Find z.*

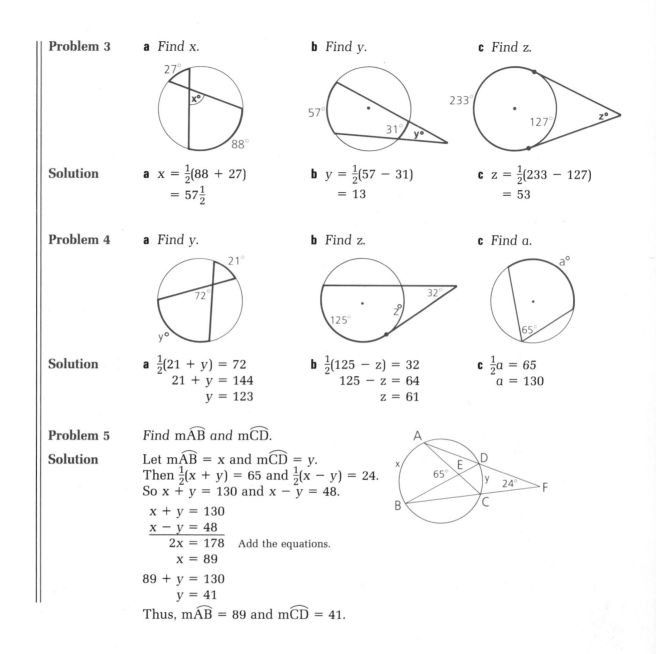

Solution   **a** $x = \frac{1}{2}(88 + 27)$ **b** $y = \frac{1}{2}(57 - 31)$ **c** $z = \frac{1}{2}(233 - 127)$

$= 57\frac{1}{2}$ $= 13$ $= 53$

Problem 4   **a** *Find y.*   **b** *Find z.*   **c** *Find a.*

Solution   **a** $\frac{1}{2}(21 + y) = 72$ **b** $\frac{1}{2}(125 - z) = 32$ **c** $\frac{1}{2}a = 65$

$21 + y = 144$ $125 - z = 64$ $a = 130$

$y = 123$ $z = 61$

Problem 5   *Find m$\widehat{AB}$ and m$\widehat{CD}$.*

Solution   Let m$\widehat{AB}$ = x and m$\widehat{CD}$ = y.
Then $\frac{1}{2}(x + y) = 65$ and $\frac{1}{2}(x - y) = 24$.
So $x + y = 130$ and $x - y = 48$.

$x + y = 130$
$\underline{x - y = 48}$
$2x = 178$ Add the equations.
$x = 89$

$89 + y = 130$
$y = 41$

Thus, m$\widehat{AB}$ = 89 and m$\widehat{CD}$ = 41.

Part Three: Problem Sets

Problem Set A

1 *Vertex at center:*
Given: $\widehat{AB} = 62°$
Find: m∠O

Problem Set A, *continued*

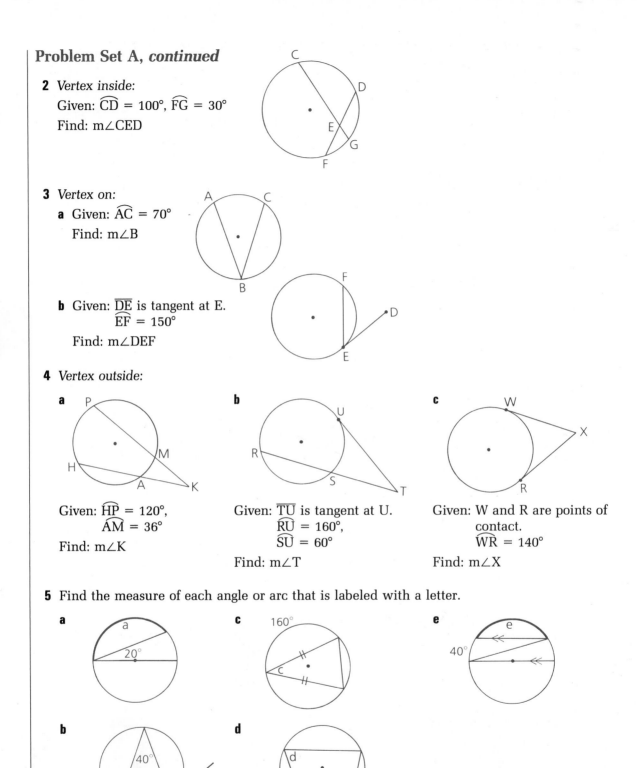

2 Vertex inside:
Given: $\overset{\frown}{CD} = 100°$, $\overset{\frown}{FG} = 30°$
Find: m∠CED

3 Vertex on:
  a Given: $\overset{\frown}{AC} = 70°$
    Find: m∠B

  b Given: $\overline{DE}$ is tangent at E.
      $\overset{\frown}{EF} = 150°$
    Find: m∠DEF

4 Vertex outside:

  a
  Given: $\overset{\frown}{HP} = 120°$,
      $\overset{\frown}{AM} = 36°$
  Find: m∠K

  b
  Given: $\overline{TU}$ is tangent at U.
      $\overset{\frown}{RU} = 160°$,
      $\overset{\frown}{SU} = 60°$
  Find: m∠T

  c
  Given: W and R are points of
      contact.
      $\overset{\frown}{WR} = 140°$
  Find: m∠X

5 Find the measure of each angle or arc that is labeled with a letter.

  a

  c 160°

  e

  b 120° 40°

  d 81° 82°

6 Find the measure of each angle or arc that is labeled with a letter.

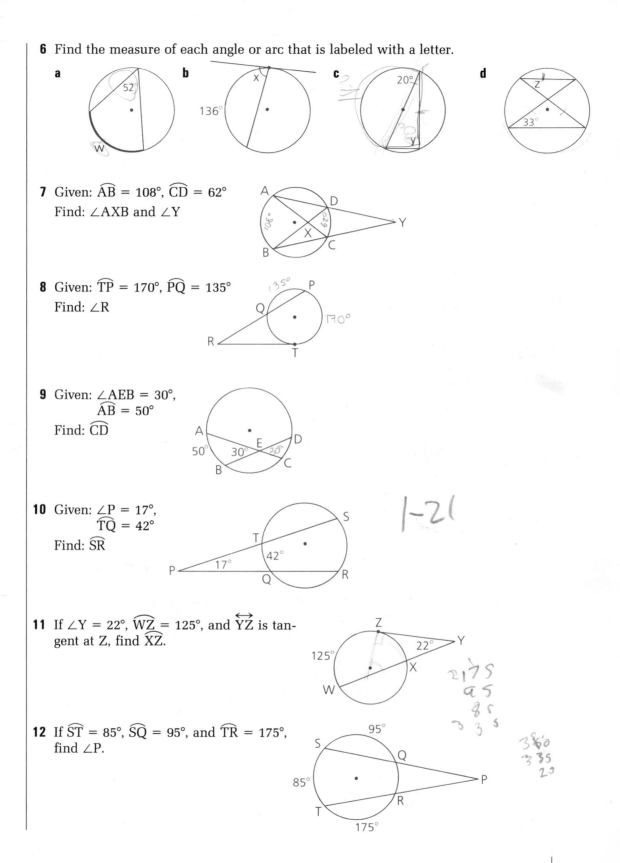

a 52° w

b 136° x

c 20°

d z 33°

7 Given: $\overarc{AB} = 108°$, $\overarc{CD} = 62°$
Find: ∠AXB and ∠Y

8 Given: $\overarc{TP} = 170°$, $\overarc{PQ} = 135°$
Find: ∠R

9 Given: ∠AEB = 30°,
$\overarc{AB} = 50°$
Find: $\overarc{CD}$

10 Given: ∠P = 17°,
$\overarc{TQ} = 42°$
Find: $\overarc{SR}$

11 If ∠Y = 22°, $\overarc{WZ} = 125°$, and $\overleftrightarrow{YZ}$ is tangent at Z, find $\overarc{XZ}$.

12 If $\overarc{ST} = 85°$, $\overarc{SQ} = 95°$, and $\overarc{TR} = 175°$,
find ∠P.

Problem Set A, *continued*

13 Given: $\overparen{AB} = 85°$,
$\overparen{CD} = 25°$

Find: $\angle AED$

14 Given: $\overline{WY}$ is a diameter of $\odot E$.
$\overparen{WX} = 50°$, $\angle XPY = 120°$
Find: $\overparen{WZ}$

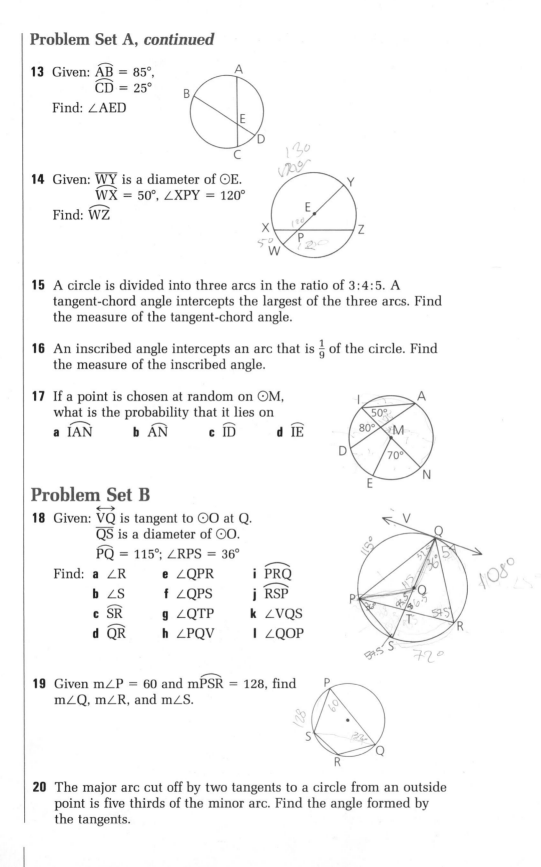

15 A circle is divided into three arcs in the ratio of $3:4:5$. A tangent-chord angle intercepts the largest of the three arcs. Find the measure of the tangent-chord angle.

16 An inscribed angle intercepts an arc that is $\frac{1}{9}$ of the circle. Find the measure of the inscribed angle.

17 If a point is chosen at random on $\odot M$, what is the probability that it lies on
a $\overparen{IAN}$ **b** $\overparen{AN}$ **c** $\overparen{ID}$ **d** $\overparen{IE}$

Problem Set B

18 Given: $\overleftrightarrow{VQ}$ is tangent to $\odot O$ at Q.
$\overline{QS}$ is a diameter of $\odot O$.
$\overparen{PQ} = 115°$; $\angle RPS = 36°$

Find: **a** $\angle R$ **e** $\angle QPR$ **i** $\overparen{PRQ}$
       b $\angle S$ **f** $\angle QPS$ **j** $\overparen{RSP}$
       c $\overparen{SR}$ **g** $\angle QTP$ **k** $\angle VQS$
       d $\overparen{QR}$ **h** $\angle PQV$ **l** $\angle QOP$

19 Given $m\angle P = 60$ and $m\overparen{PSR} = 128$, find $m\angle Q$, $m\angle R$, and $m\angle S$.

20 The major arc cut off by two tangents to a circle from an outside point is five thirds of the minor arc. Find the angle formed by the tangents.

21 Find the measure of each arc or angle labeled with a letter.

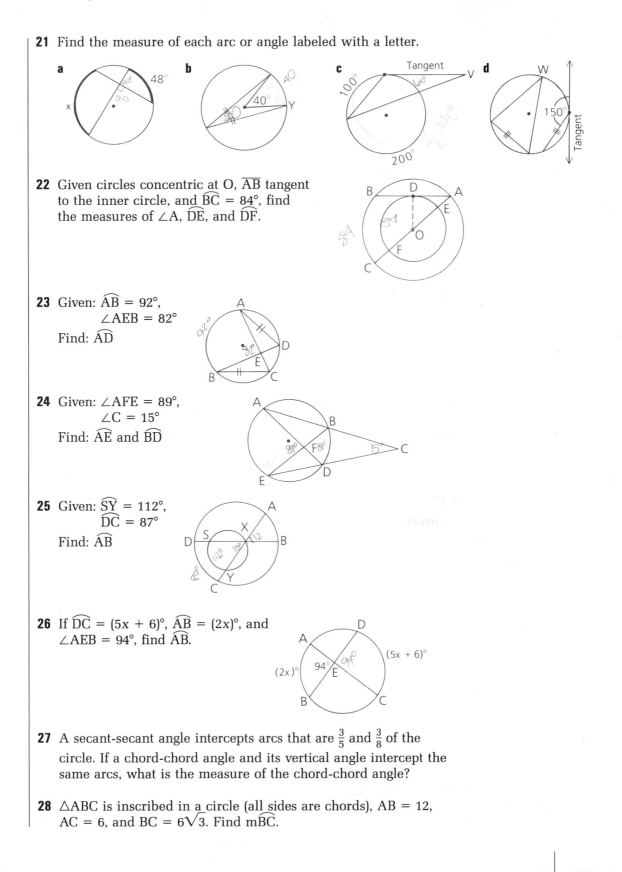

a
48°
x

b
40°
40°
Y

c Tangent
V
100°
200°

d
W
150°
Tangent

22 Given circles concentric at O, $\overline{AB}$ tangent to the inner circle, and $\widehat{BC} = 84°$, find the measures of $\angle A$, $\widehat{DE}$, and $\widehat{DF}$.

B D A
E
O
F
C

23 Given: $\widehat{AB} = 92°$,
$\angle AEB = 82°$
Find: $\widehat{AD}$

A
D
E
B C

24 Given: $\angle AFE = 89°$,
$\angle C = 15°$
Find: $\widehat{AE}$ and $\widehat{BD}$

A
B
89° F
15° C
E D

25 Given: $\widehat{SY} = 112°$,
$\widehat{DC} = 87°$
Find: $\widehat{AB}$

A
S X
D 112 B
Y
C

26 If $\widehat{DC} = (5x + 6)°$, $\widehat{AB} = (2x)°$, and $\angle AEB = 94°$, find $\widehat{AB}$.

D
A
(5x + 6)°
(2x)° 94° E
B C

27 A secant-secant angle intercepts arcs that are $\frac{3}{5}$ and $\frac{3}{8}$ of the circle. If a chord-chord angle and its vertical angle intercept the same arcs, what is the measure of the chord-chord angle?

28 $\triangle ABC$ is inscribed in a circle (all sides are chords), $AB = 12$, $AC = 6$, and $BC = 6\sqrt{3}$. Find $m\widehat{BC}$.

29 a An angle is inscribed in a circle and intercepts an arc of 140°. Find the measure of the angle.

b An angle is inscribed in a 140° arc (the vertex is on the arc and the sides contain the endpoints of the arc). Find the measure of the angle.

30 a Find the area and the circumference of ⊙Q to the nearest tenth.

b Find the area of the shaded region to the nearest tenth.

c Find the length of $\overparen{PR}$ to the nearest tenth.

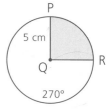

Problem Set C

31 Given: $\overleftrightarrow{AB} \parallel \overleftrightarrow{CD}$;
$\overleftrightarrow{DC}$ is tangent to ⊙O at T.
Conclusion: $\overparen{AT} \cong \overparen{BT}$

32 A quadrilateral ABCD is inscribed in a circle. Its diagonals intersect at X. If $\overparen{AB}$ = 100°, $\overparen{BC}$ = 50°, and $\overline{AD} \cong \overline{BD}$, find m∠DXC.

33 Given: $\overline{WZ} \cong \overline{XY}$,
$\overparen{WXY}$ = 200°
Find: ∠P

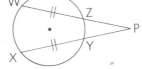

34 A secant and a tangent to a circle intersect to form an angle of 38°. If the measures of the arcs intercepted by this angle are in a ratio of 2:1, find the measure of the third arc.

35 Given: ⓢ P and Q are internally tangent at T.
Diameter $\overline{NS}$ of ⊙Q is tangent to ⊙P at A.
$m\overparen{MR}$ = 42; $\overline{TM}$ passes through A.
Find: $m\overparen{NM}$

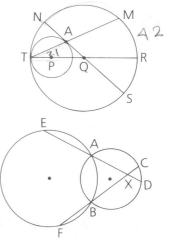

36 The two circles shown intersect at A and B. If ∠AXB = 70°, $\overparen{CD}$ = 20°, and $\overparen{EF}$ = 160°, find the difference between the measures of $\overparen{AB}$ of the smaller circle and $\overparen{AB}$ of the larger circle.

MORE ANGLE–ARC THEOREMS

Objectives

After studying this section, you will be able to
- Recognize congruent inscribed and tangent-chord angles
- Determine the measure of an angle inscribed in a semicircle
- Apply the relationship between the measures of a tangent-tangent angle and its minor arc

Part One: Introduction

Congruent Inscribed and Tangent-Chord Angles

Our knowledge of the relationships between angles and their intercepted arcs leads easily to the next two theorems.

Theorem 89   *If two inscribed or tangent-chord angles intercept the same arc, then they are congruent.*

Given: X and Y are inscribed angles intercepting arc AB.

Conclusion: $\angle X \cong \angle Y$

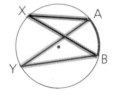

Theorem 90   *If two inscribed or tangent-chord angles intercept congruent arcs, then they are congruent.*

If $\overleftrightarrow{ED}$ is the tangent at D and $\overset{\frown}{AB} \cong \overset{\frown}{CD}$, we may conclude that $\angle P \cong \angle CDE$.

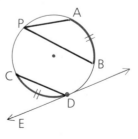

Angles Inscribed in Semicircles

All angles inscribed in semicircles have the same measure. What do you think that measure might be?

Theorem 91 *An angle inscribed in a semicircle is a right angle.*

Given: $\overline{AB}$ is a diameter of $\odot O$.
Prove: $\angle C$ is a right angle.

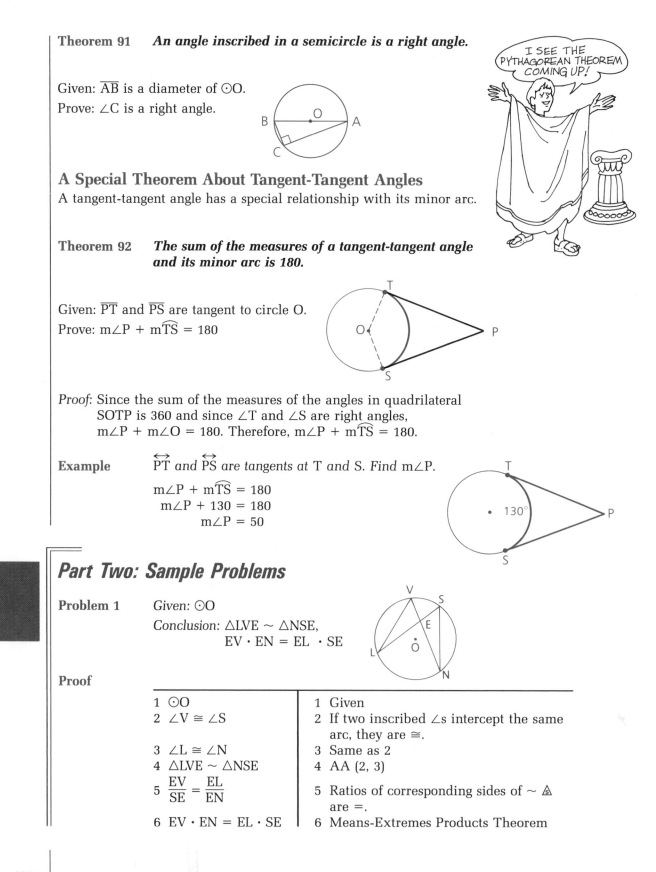

I SEE THE PYTHAGOREAN THEOREM COMING UP!

A Special Theorem About Tangent-Tangent Angles

A tangent-tangent angle has a special relationship with its minor arc.

Theorem 92 *The sum of the measures of a tangent-tangent angle and its minor arc is 180.*

Given: $\overline{PT}$ and $\overline{PS}$ are tangent to circle O.
Prove: $m\angle P + m\widehat{TS} = 180$

Proof: Since the sum of the measures of the angles in quadrilateral SOTP is 360 and since $\angle T$ and $\angle S$ are right angles, $m\angle P + m\angle O = 180$. Therefore, $m\angle P + m\widehat{TS} = 180$.

Example $\overleftrightarrow{PT}$ and $\overleftrightarrow{PS}$ are tangents at T and S. Find $m\angle P$.

$$m\angle P + m\widehat{TS} = 180$$
$$m\angle P + 130 = 180$$
$$m\angle P = 50$$

Part Two: Sample Problems

Problem 1   Given: $\odot O$
Conclusion: $\triangle LVE \sim \triangle NSE$,
$EV \cdot EN = EL \cdot SE$

Proof

1 $\odot O$	1 Given
2 $\angle V \cong \angle S$	2 If two inscribed $\angle$s intercept the same arc, they are $\cong$.
3 $\angle L \cong \angle N$	3 Same as 2
4 $\triangle LVE \sim \triangle NSE$	4 AA (2, 3)
5 $\dfrac{EV}{SE} = \dfrac{EL}{EN}$	5 Ratios of corresponding sides of $\sim \triangle$ are =.
6 $EV \cdot EN = EL \cdot SE$	6 Means-Extremes Products Theorem

Chapter 10   Circles

Problem 2 In circle O, $\overline{BC}$ is a diameter and the radius of the circle is 20.5 mm.
Chord $\overline{AC}$ has a length of 40 mm. Find AB.

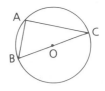

Solution Since $\angle A$ is inscribed in a semicircle, it is a right angle. By the Pythagorean Theorem,

$$(AB)^2 + (AC)^2 = (BC)^2$$
$$(AB)^2 + 40^2 = 41^2$$
$$AB = 9 \text{ mm}$$

Problem 3 Given: $\odot O$ with $\overleftrightarrow{AB}$ tangent at B, $\overleftrightarrow{AB} \parallel \overleftrightarrow{CD}$
Prove: $\angle C \cong \angle BDC$

Proof

1 $\overleftrightarrow{AB}$ is tangent to $\odot O$.	1 Given
2 $\overleftrightarrow{AB} \parallel \overleftrightarrow{CD}$	2 Given
3 $\angle ABD \cong \angle BDC$	3 $\parallel$ lines $\Rightarrow$ alt. int. $\angle$s $\cong$
4 $\angle C \cong \angle ABD$	4 If an inscribed $\angle$ and a tangent-chord $\angle$ intercept the same arc, they are $\cong$.
5 $\angle C \cong \angle BDC$	5 Transitive Property

Part Three: Problem Sets

Problem Set A

1 Given: X is the midpt. of $\overset{\frown}{WY}$.
   Prove: $\overrightarrow{ZX}$ bisects $\angle WZY$.

1 -7

2 Given: $\odot E$ with diameter $\overline{AC}$, $\overline{BC} \cong \overline{CD}$
   Conclusion: $\triangle ABC \cong \triangle ADC$

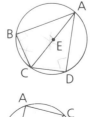

3 In $\odot P$, $\overline{BC}$ is a diameter, AC = 12 mm, and BA = 16 mm. Find the radius of the circle.

4 Given: $\overline{PQ}$ and $\overline{PR}$ are tangent segments.
$\overset{\frown}{QR} = 163°$

Find: **a** ∠P
b ∠PQR

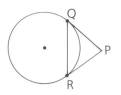

5 Given: A, B, and C are points of contact.
$\overset{\frown}{AB} = 145°$, ∠Y = 48°

Find: ∠Z

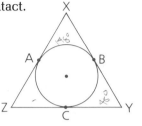

6 Given: $\overset{\frown}{BC} \cong \overset{\frown}{ED}$, AB = 8,
BC = 4, CD = 9

a Are $\overline{BE}$ and $\overline{CD}$ parallel?
b Find BE.
c Is △ACD scalene?

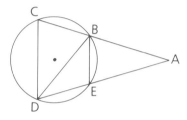

7 Given: $\overleftrightarrow{PY}$ and $\overleftrightarrow{QW}$ are tangents.
$\overset{\frown}{WZ} = 126°$, $\overset{\frown}{XY} = 40°$

Find: $\overset{\frown}{PQ}$

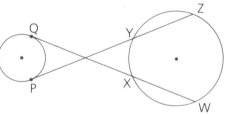

8 If △ABC is inscribed in a circle and
$\overset{\frown}{AC} \cong \overset{\frown}{AB}$, tell whether each of the following must be true, could be true, or cannot be true.

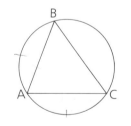

a $\overline{AB} \cong \overline{AC}$
b $\overline{AC} \cong \overline{BC}$
c $\overline{AB}$ and $\overline{AC}$ are equidistant from the center of the circle.

d ∠B ≅ ∠C
e ∠BAC is a right angle.
f ∠ABC is a right angle.

9 In the figure shown, find m∠P.

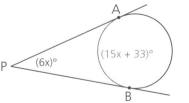

10 If $\overline{AB}$ is a diameter of $\odot P$, CB = 1.5 m, and CA = 2 m, find the radius of $\odot P$.

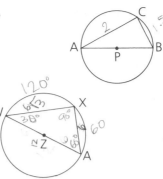

11 The radius of $\odot Z$ is 6 cm and $\overset{\frown}{WX} = 120°$.

Find: **a** AX
　　　 b The perimeter of $\triangle WAX$

12 M is the midpoint of $\overset{\frown}{AB}$. Find $m\overset{\frown}{CD}$.

Problem Set B

13 A rectangle with dimensions 18 by 24 is inscribed in a circle. Find the radius of the circle.

14 A square is inscribed in a circle with a radius of 10. Find the length of a side of the square.

15 Quadrilateral ABCD is inscribed in circle O. AB = 12, BC = 16, CD = 10, and $\angle ABC$ is a right angle. Find the measure of $\overline{AD}$ in simplified radical form.

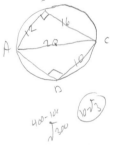

16 Circles O and P are tangent at F. $\overline{AC}$ and $\overline{CE}$ are tangent to $\odot P$ at B and D. If $\overset{\frown}{DFB} = 223°$, find $\overset{\frown}{AE}$.

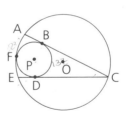

17 Given: $\angle S = 88°$, $\overset{\frown}{QT} = 104°$, $\overset{\frown}{ST} = 94°$, tangent $\overline{PQ}$

Find: **a** $\angle P$
　　　 b $\angle STQ$

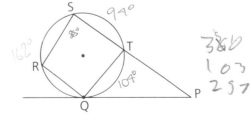

18 Given: $\overset{\frown}{BC} \cong \overset{\frown}{CD}$
Conclusion: $\triangle ABC \sim \triangle AED$

Problem Set B, *continued*

19 Given: $\overleftrightarrow{AC}$ is tangent at A. ∠APR and
∠AQR are right ∠s. R is the mid-
point of $\overparen{AB}$.

Conclusion: $\overline{PR} \cong \overline{RQ}$ (Hint: Draw $\overline{AR}$.)

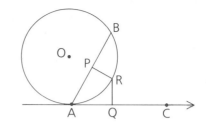

20 Given: △WXZ is isosceles, with $\overline{WX} \cong \overline{WZ}$.
$\overline{WZ}$ is a diameter of ⊙O.

Prove: Y is the midpoint of $\overline{XZ}$.
(Hint: Draw $\overline{WY}$.)

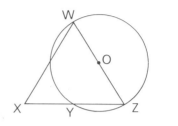

21 Given: $\overline{AC}$ is tangent to ⊙O at A.
Conclusion: △ADC ~ △BDA

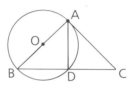

Problem Set C

22 Given: ⊙O, with chords $\overline{AC}$ and $\overline{BD}$ intersecting at E

Prove: **a** m$\overparen{AB}$ + m$\overparen{CD}$ = 2(m∠CED)
b AE · EC = BE · ED

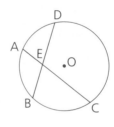

23 Given: $\overline{AB}$ is a diameter of ⊙P.
QR = 6, AB = 13, $\overline{QR} \perp \overline{AB}$
Find: RB.

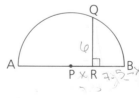

24 RHOM is a rhombus. $\overline{RH}$ and $\overline{RM}$ are
tangents. Find m$\overparen{HM}$.

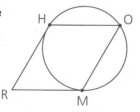

25 Given: △ABC is inscribed in ⊙P.
$\overline{AE}$ and $\overline{CD}$ are chords such that $\overline{AE} \perp \overline{BC}$ and $\overline{CD} \perp \overline{AB}$.

Prove: $\overparen{BD} \cong \overparen{BE}$

26 Two circles are internally tangent, and the center of the larger circle is on the smaller circle. Prove that any chord that has one endpoint at the point of tangency is bisected by the smaller circle.

27 Given: ⊙A is tangent to ⊙B at R.
$\overline{PT}$ is a common external tangent at P and T.
∠Q = 43°
Find: ∠S

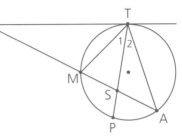

28 Given: $\overline{IT}$ is tangent to the circle.
$\overrightarrow{TS}$ bisects ∠ATM.
Prove: △SIT is isosceles.

10.7 INSCRIBED AND CIRCUMSCRIBED POLYGONS

Objectives

After studying this section, you will be able to
- Recognize inscribed and circumscribed polygons
- Apply the relationship between opposite angles of an inscribed quadrilateral
- Identify the characteristics of an inscribed parallelogram

Part One: Introduction

Inscribed and Circumscribed Polygons

Triangle ABC is ***inscribed in*** circle O.

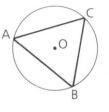

Definition A polygon is ***inscribed in*** a circle if all of its vertices lie on the circle.

Polygon PQRST is ***circumscribed about*** circle F.

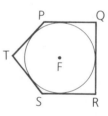

Definition A polygon is ***circumscribed about*** a circle if each of its sides is tangent to the circle.

We can also speak of a circle being circumscribed about a polygon or inscribed in a polygon.

The diagram shows that the statements "quadrilateral ABCD is inscribed in ⊙O" and "⊙O is circumscribed about quadrilateral ABCD" have the same meaning.

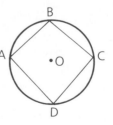

Definition The center of a circle circumscribed about a polygon is the ***circumcenter*** of the polygon.

In the preceding diagram, O is the circumcenter of ABCD. Hexagon PQRSTU is circumscribed about circle F. Circle F is inscribed in hexagon PQRSTU.

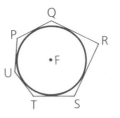

Definition   The center of a circle inscribed in a polygon is the *incenter* of the polygon.

F is the incenter of hexagon PQRSTU.

A Theorem About Inscribed Quadrilaterals

The following theorem can easily be proved by using the relationship between an inscribed angle and its intercepted arc.

Theorem 93   *If a quadrilateral is inscribed in a circle, its opposite angles are supplementary.*

Given: Quadrilateral ABCD is inscribed in circle O.
Prove: ∠A supp. ∠C, ∠B supp. ∠D
Proof: ∠A, ∠B, ∠C, and ∠D are inscribed angles, so

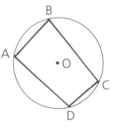

$m\angle A = \frac{1}{2}(m\overparen{BCD})$ and $m\angle C = \frac{1}{2}(m\overparen{BAD})$.

$m\angle A + m\angle C = \frac{1}{2}(m\overparen{BCD}) + \frac{1}{2}(m\overparen{BAD})$

$= \frac{1}{2}(m\overparen{BCD} + m\overparen{BAD})$

$= \frac{1}{2}(360)$ ($\overparen{BCD} \cup \overparen{BAD}$ = whole ⊙)

$= 180$

Thus, ∠A is supplementary to ∠C. Similarly, ∠B is supplementary to ∠D.

The Story of the Plain Old Parallelogram

Once there was a plain old parallelogram named Rex Tangle. Rex was always trying to fit in—into a circle, that is. One day when he awoke, he found that he had straightened out and was finally able to inscribe himself. What had the plain old parallelogram turned into?

The following theorem shows the moral of our story.

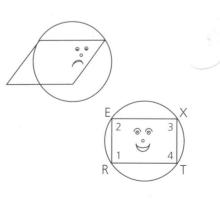

Theorem 94   *If a parallelogram is inscribed in a circle, it must be a rectangle.*

Here are some of the conclusions that follow from Theorem 94.

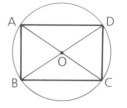

If ABCD is an inscribed parallelogram, then
1 $\overline{BD}$ and $\overline{AC}$ are diameters
2 O is the center of the circle
3 $\overline{OA}$, $\overline{OB}$, $\overline{OC}$, and $\overline{OD}$ are radii
4 $(AB)^2 + (BC)^2 = (AC)^2$, and so forth

Part Two: Sample Problems

Problem 1   Given: Quadrilateral ABCD is inscribed in ⊙O.
Prove: ∠B ≅ ∠ADE

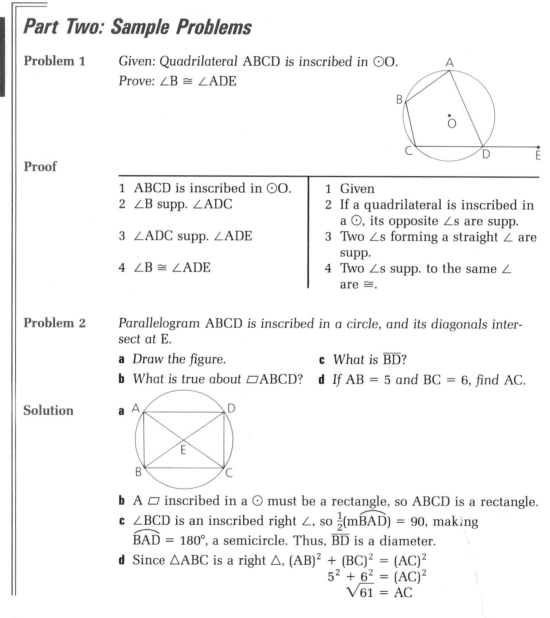

Proof

1 ABCD is inscribed in ⊙O.	1 Given
2 ∠B supp. ∠ADC	2 If a quadrilateral is inscribed in a ⊙, its opposite ∠s are supp.
3 ∠ADC supp. ∠ADE	3 Two ∠s forming a straight ∠ are supp.
4 ∠B ≅ ∠ADE	4 Two ∠s supp. to the same ∠ are ≅.

Problem 2   *Parallelogram ABCD is inscribed in a circle, and its diagonals intersect at E.*

a *Draw the figure.*   **c** *What is $\overline{BD}$?*

b *What is true about □ABCD?*   **d** *If AB = 5 and BC = 6, find AC.*

Solution   **a**

b A □ inscribed in a ⊙ must be a rectangle, so ABCD is a rectangle.
c ∠BCD is an inscribed right ∠, so $\frac{1}{2}(m\widehat{BAD}) = 90$, making $\widehat{BAD} = 180°$, a semicircle. Thus, $\overline{BD}$ is a diameter.
d Since △ABC is a right △, $(AB)^2 + (BC)^2 = (AC)^2$
$$5^2 + 6^2 = (AC)^2$$
$$\sqrt{61} = AC$$

Part Three: Problem Sets

Problem Set A

1 Given: ∠A = 104°, ∠B = 67°
Find: ∠D and ∠C

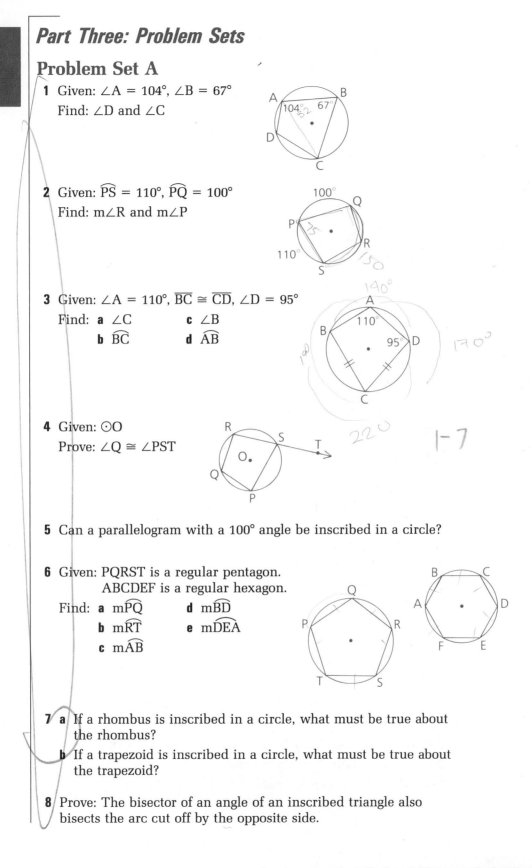

2 Given: $\overparen{PS}$ = 110°, $\overparen{PQ}$ = 100°
Find: m∠R and m∠P

3 Given: ∠A = 110°, $\overline{BC} \cong \overline{CD}$, ∠D = 95°
Find: **a** ∠C   **c** ∠B
        b $\overparen{BC}$ **d** $\overparen{AB}$

4 Given: ⊙O
Prove: ∠Q ≅ ∠PST

5 Can a parallelogram with a 100° angle be inscribed in a circle?

6 Given: PQRST is a regular pentagon.
       ABCDEF is a regular hexagon.
Find: **a** m$\overparen{PQ}$ **d** m$\overparen{BD}$
       b m$\overparen{RT}$ **e** m$\overparen{DEA}$
       c m$\overparen{AB}$

7 a If a rhombus is inscribed in a circle, what must be true about the rhombus?

  b If a trapezoid is inscribed in a circle, what must be true about the trapezoid?

8 Prove: The bisector of an angle of an inscribed triangle also bisects the arc cut off by the opposite side.

Problem Set B

9 Given: $\angle B = 115°$, $\overset{\frown}{AD} = 60°$, $\overline{BC} \parallel \overline{EF}$

  Find: **a** $\angle ADC$ **c** $\angle C$
          b $\angle CDF$ **d** $\angle A$

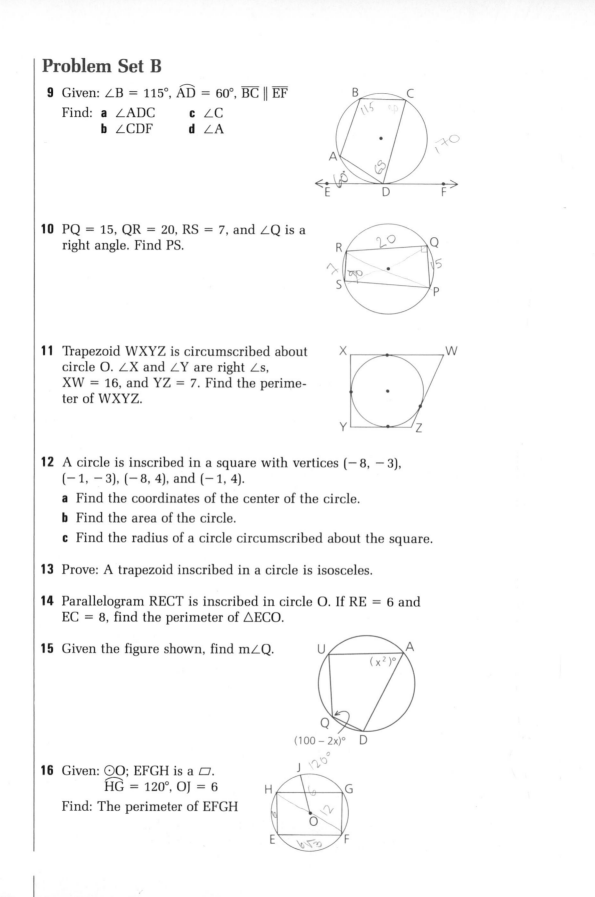

10 PQ = 15, QR = 20, RS = 7, and $\angle Q$ is a right angle. Find PS.

11 Trapezoid WXYZ is circumscribed about circle O. $\angle X$ and $\angle Y$ are right $\angle$s, XW = 16, and YZ = 7. Find the perimeter of WXYZ.

12 A circle is inscribed in a square with vertices $(-8, -3)$, $(-1, -3)$, $(-8, 4)$, and $(-1, 4)$.

  a Find the coordinates of the center of the circle.
  b Find the area of the circle.
  c Find the radius of a circle circumscribed about the square.

13 Prove: A trapezoid inscribed in a circle is isosceles.

14 Parallelogram RECT is inscribed in circle O. If RE = 6 and EC = 8, find the perimeter of $\triangle$ECO.

15 Given the figure shown, find m$\angle$Q.

16 Given: $\odot$O; EFGH is a $\square$.
  $\overset{\frown}{HG} = 120°$, OJ = 6
  Find: The perimeter of EFGH

17 A quadrilateral can be inscribed in a circle only if a pair of opposite angles are supplementary. Which of the following quadrilaterals can be inscribed in a circle?

a

b

c

18 Prove: Any isosceles trapezoid can be inscribed in a circle. (Hint: See problem 17.)

19 Equilateral triangle PQR is inscribed in one circle and circumscribed about another circle. The circles are concentric.

   a If the radius of the smaller circle is 10, find the radius of the larger circle.

   b In general, for an equilateral triangle, what is the ratio of the radius of the inscribed circle to the radius of the circumscribed circle?

20 ABCD is a kite, with $\overline{AB} \cong \overline{BC}$, $\overline{AD} \cong \overline{CD}$, and m∠B = 120. The radius of the circle is 3. Find the perimeter of ABCD.

Problem Set C

21 Discuss the location of the center of a circle circumscribed about each of the following types of triangles.

   a Right   **b** Acute   **c** Obtuse

22 A set of points are *concyclic* if they all lie on the same circle. Prove that the vertices of any triangle are concyclic.

23 Are the vertices of each figure concyclic Always, Sometimes, or Never?

   a A rectangle   **d** A nonisosceles trapezoid

   b A parallelogram   **e** An equilateral polygon

   c A rhombus   **f** An equiangular polygon

24 A right triangle has legs measuring 5 and 12. Find the ratio of the area of the inscribed circle to the area of the circumscribed circle.

25 Given: ⊙P is inscribed in trapezoid WXYZ.
   ∠W and ∠X are right ∠s.
   The radius of ⊙P is 5.
   YZ = 14

   Find: The perimeter of WXYZ

26 A circle is inscribed in a triangle with sides 8, 10, and 12. The point of tangency of the 8-unit side divides that side in the ratio $x:y$, where $x < y$. Find that ratio.

27 Determine the conditions under which an equiangular polygon inscribed in a circle will be equilateral. Prove your conjecture.

MATHEMATICAL EXCURSION

TANGENT, SLOPE, AND LOOPS
The geometry of coasting upside down

You are on a roller coaster going 70 miles per hour. Suddenly you find yourself doing a complete loop. For an instant, you are upside-down. Why doesn't the car fall downwards from the track?

The path of a roller coaster is a series of arcs of constantly varying radii. The speed of the car at any instant is related to the slope of the tangent to the arc at that point.

A roller coaster somersault is made possible through what is called a clothoid loop, first explained by the eighteenth-century mathematician Leonhard Euler. Its name comes from that of Clotho, one of the three Fates from Greek mythology. Clotho was the spinner of the thread of human life. A clothoid loop would result from trying to draw a circle whose radius was constantly decreasing, up to a point. Because the radius near the top of the clothoid loop is relatively small, our roller coaster spends less time traveling through that part of the loop and leaves the loop before gravity can take over. The cars speed up coming out of the loop. This is similar to the "slingshot" effect observed when a comet approaches the sun, speeds up, and seems to shoot out on the other side.

THE POWER THEOREMS

Objective

After studying this section, you will be able to

- Apply the power theorems

Part One: Introduction

The following theorems involve products of the measures of segments.

Theorem 95   *If two chords of a circle intersect inside the circle, then the product of the measures of the segments of one chord is equal to the product of the measures of the segments of the other chord.* (**Chord-Chord Power Theorem**)

Given: Chords $\overline{VN}$ and $\overline{LS}$ intersect at point E inside circle O.

Prove: $EV \cdot EN = EL \cdot SE$

Theorem 95 was proved in Section 10.6, sample problem 1.

Theorem 96   *If a tangent segment and a secant segment are drawn from an external point to a circle, then the square of the measure of the tangent segment is equal to the product of the measures of the entire secant segment and its external part.* (**Tangent-Secant Power Theorem**)

Given: $\overline{PR}$ is a secant segment.
$\overline{PT}$ is a tangent segment.

Prove: $(TP)^2 = (PR)(PQ)$

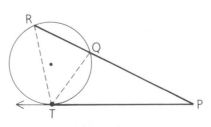

Proof: Similar triangles are formed by drawing $\overline{TQ}$ and $\overline{TR}$.
$\angle PTQ \cong \angle R$ (why?) and $\angle P \cong \angle P$, so $\triangle PTR \sim \triangle PQT$.

Thus, $\frac{TP}{PR} = \frac{PQ}{TP}$ and $(TP)^2 = (PQ)(PR)$.

Theorem 97 *If two secant segments are drawn from an external point to a circle, then the product of the measures of one secant segment and its external part is equal to the product of the measures of the other secant segment and its external part. (Secant-Secant Power Theorem)*

Given: Secant segments $\overline{PB}$ and $\overline{PD}$

Prove: $PB \cdot PA = PD \cdot PC$

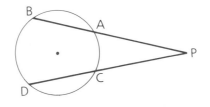

Part Two: Sample Problems

Problem 1   Find x, y, and z.

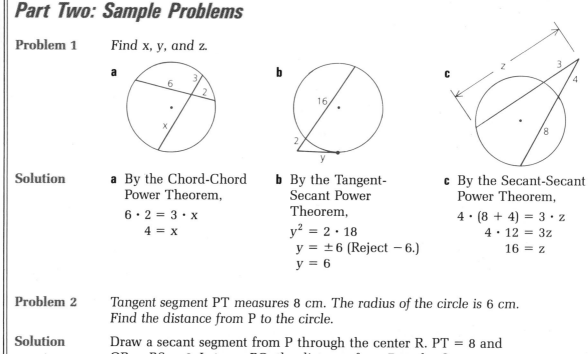

a   **b**   **c**

Solution

a By the Chord-Chord Power Theorem,

$$6 \cdot 2 = 3 \cdot x$$
$$4 = x$$

b By the Tangent-Secant Power Theorem,

$$y^2 = 2 \cdot 18$$
$$y = \pm 6 \text{ (Reject } -6.)$$
$$y = 6$$

c By the Secant-Secant Power Theorem,

$$4 \cdot (8 + 4) = 3 \cdot z$$
$$4 \cdot 12 = 3z$$
$$16 = z$$

Problem 2   *Tangent segment PT measures 8 cm. The radius of the circle is 6 cm. Find the distance from P to the circle.*

Solution   Draw a secant segment from P through the center R. PT = 8 and QR = RS = 6. Let x = PQ, the distance from P to the ⊙.

By the Tangent-Secant Power Theorem,

$$(PQ)(PS) = (PT)^2$$
$$x(x + 12) = 8^2$$
$$x^2 + 12x = 64$$
$$x^2 + 12x - 64 = 0$$
$$(x - 4)(x + 16) = 0$$
$$x - 4 = 0 \text{ or } x + 16 = 0$$
$$x = 4 \text{ or } x = -16$$

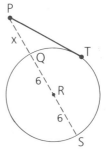

We reject the negative value, so PQ = 4 cm.

Part Three: Problem Sets

Problem Set A

1 Solve for x, y, and z.

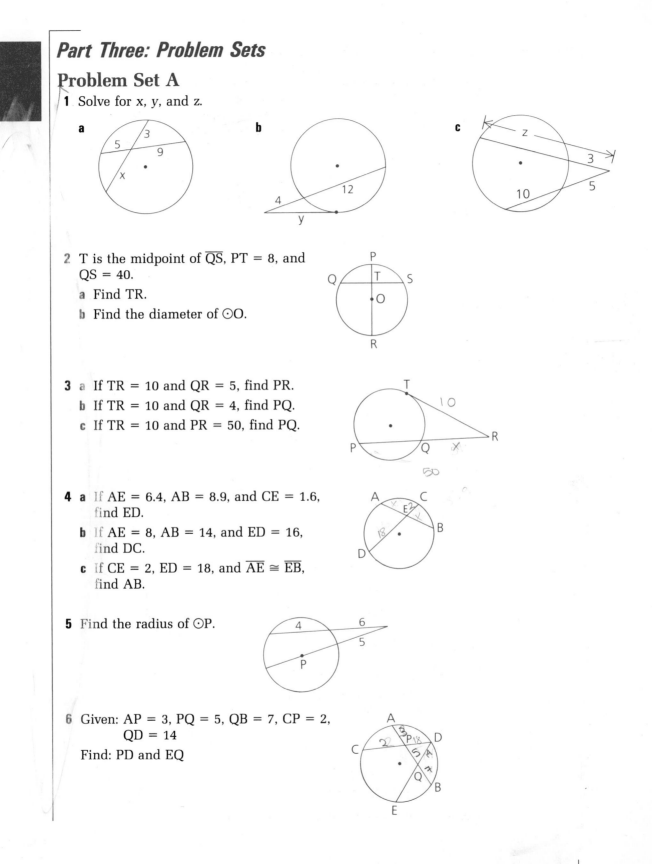

a

b

c

2 T is the midpoint of $\overline{QS}$, PT = 8, and QS = 40.

 a Find TR.

 b Find the diameter of ⊙O.

3 **a** If TR = 10 and QR = 5, find PR.

 b If TR = 10 and QR = 4, find PQ.

 c If TR = 10 and PR = 50, find PQ.

4 **a** If AE = 6.4, AB = 8.9, and CE = 1.6, find ED.

 b If AE = 8, AB = 14, and ED = 16, find DC.

 c If CE = 2, ED = 18, and $\overline{AE} \cong \overline{EB}$, find AB.

5 Find the radius of ⊙P.

6 Given: AP = 3, PQ = 5, QB = 7, CP = 2, QD = 14

 Find: PD and EQ

Problem Set A, *continued*

7 Given: TZ = 6, YZ = 4, SX = 3, WX = 1
Find: XT (Hint: Find SZ.)

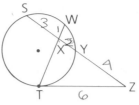

Problem Set B

8 a Find y.

   b Is the triangle acute, right, or obtuse?

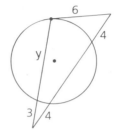

9 Given: AB = 7, CD = 5, ED = 2
Find: AE

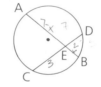

10 Given: PT = 3, QR = 8
Find: PQ

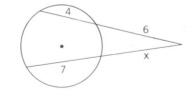

11 Solve for x.

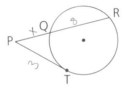

12 Find PQ.

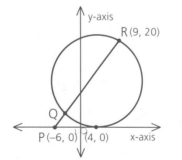

13 $\overline{AB}$ is a diameter of $\odot$O. $\overline{CD}$ is tangent at D, CD = 6, and BC = 4. Find the radius of the circle.

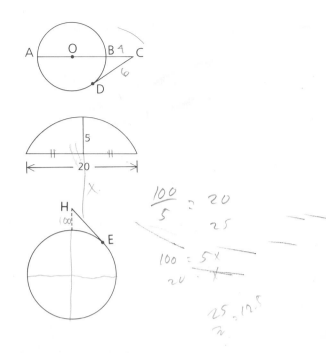

14 An arch supports a pipeline across a river 20 m wide. Midway, the suspending cable is 5 m long. Find the radius of the arch.

15 The diameter of the earth is approximately 8000 mi. Heavenly Helen, in a spaceship 100 mi above the earth, sights Earthy Ernest coming over the horizon. Approximately how far apart are Helen and Ernest?

16 Solve for x.

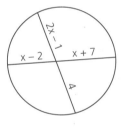

Problem Set C

17 Given concentric circles as shown, find DE and DC.

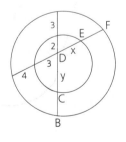

18 The radius of each circle is 3. Triangle WXY is equilateral.

  a Find WY.

  b Find the ratio of the perimeters of $\triangle$ABC, $\triangle$PQR, and $\triangle$WXY.

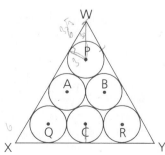

Problem Set C, *continued*

19 a Find x.

b What restrictions must be placed on *y* in this problem?

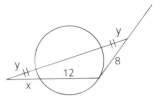

20 Tangent $\overline{AT}$ measures 12, AB = 8, and $\overline{AT} \perp \overline{AB}$.

a Find the diameter of the circle.

b How far is the circle from point A?

FROM ASTEROIDS TO DUST
Mathematics in space research

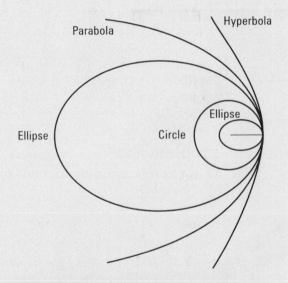

How does someone choose a life's profession? For physicist A.A. Jackson, it was a painting on the cover of a magazine. "It was 16 years before the first moon landing." he recalls. "*Collier's* magazine published a fantastic futuristic painting, the artist's conception of a lunar landing. It combined scientific precision with the romance and drama of space travel. From that moment I knew exactly what I wanted to do."

Pursuing his goal, Jackson majored in mathematics at North Texas State University, received a master's degree in physics from the same school, then went on to the University of Texas at Austin, where he earned his doctorate in relativistic physics. Today he is principal scientist in the solar-system exploration division of Lockheed Engineering in Houston.

Explaining the relevance of geometry to his work, Jackson refers to conic sections, the curves that result when a plane intersects a cone. "Planets move in ellipses around the sun. Satellites orbit the earth in ellipses. Some comets move in parabolic orbits. In my current research, I'm studying the motion of dust particles as they come off comets and asteroids. They move along conic sections."

Jackson's field is evolving constantly in unexpected directions. For example, recent studies of the way three bodies interact in a plane have turned up connections with the geometry of fractals. "Every time you look at something old," says Jackson, "you see something new."

One of the things that Jackson discovered as a teenager was science fiction. He reads it avidly to this day. The best science fiction, he says, brings together provocative ideas and "super science" in a landscape that feels not fantastic, but real—"lived in." He recommends the works of Robert Heinlein especially *Starman Jones*.

10.9 | CIRCUMFERENCE AND ARC LENGTH

Objectives

After studying this section, you will be able to
- Determine the circumference of a circle
- Determine the length of an arc

Part One: Introduction

Circumference

You should already know the meaning of *circumference*.

Definition   The *circumference* of a circle is its perimeter.

The formula for the circumference C of a circle of diameter d is based on the fact that, regardless of a circle's size, the ratio of its circumference to its diameter always has the same value. This value is given the special symbol π (the Greek letter pi). Its approximate value is 3.14159265.

Postulate $C = \pi d$

Example   *Find, to the nearest hundredth, the circumference of a circle whose radius is 5.37.*

The diameter is twice the radius, so $d = 2(5.37) = 10.74$.

$C = \pi d$
   $= \pi(10.74) = 10.74\pi \approx 33.74$

When you are asked to find a circumference, leave the answer in terms of π unless you are asked to approximate the answer. To find an approximation, use a calculator.

Length of an Arc

$\frac{\widehat{m}}{360}\pi d$

Arc length is a linear measurement similar to the length of a line segment. Arc lengths are therefore expressed in terms of such units as feet, meters, and centimeters. The length of an arc depends both on the arc's measure and on the circumference of its circle.

Example   *Find the length of a 40° arc of a circle with an 18-cm radius.*

The circumference is 36π, and the 40° arc is $\frac{40}{360}$, or $\frac{1}{9}$, of the circle.

$$\text{Length of } \overset{\frown}{AB} = \tfrac{1}{9}(\text{circumference})$$
$$= \tfrac{1}{9}(36\pi)$$
$$= 4\pi$$

Theorem 98   ***The length of an arc is equal to the circumference of its circle times the fractional part of the circle determined by the arc.***

$$\textbf{Length of } \overset{\frown}{PQ} = \left(\frac{m\overset{\frown}{PQ}}{360}\right)\pi d$$

where d is the diameter and $\overset{\frown}{PQ}$ ***is measured in degrees.***

Part Two: Sample Problems

Problem 1   *Find the radius of a circle whose circumference is 50π.*

Solution
$$C = \pi d$$
$$50\pi = \pi d$$
$$50 = d$$
$$25 = r$$

Problem 2   *Find the length of each arc of a circle with a 12-cm radius.*

a A 30° arc   **b** A 105° arc

Solution   **a** Length of arc $= \frac{30}{360}(24\pi)$ **b** Length of arc $= \frac{105}{360}(24\pi)$
$= 2\pi$ cm $= 7\pi$ cm

Problem 3   *The diameter of a bicycle wheel (including the tire) is 70 cm.*

a *How far will the bicycle travel if the wheel rotates 1000 times? (Approximate the answer in meters.)*

b *How many revolutions will the wheel make if the bicycle travels 15 m? (Approximate to the nearest tenth of a revolution.)*

Solution   The distance covered during one revolution is equal to the circumference of the wheel. Thus, the bicycle travels 70π, or about 220, centimeters per revolution.

a Distance = (number of rev.)(distance per rev.)
$\approx 1000(220)$
$\approx 220,000$

The bicycle will travel about 220,000 cm, or 2200 m.

b The bicycle travels approximately 2.2 m per revolution. Let x be the number of revolutions.

Distance = (number of rev.)(distance per rev.)

$$15 \approx x(2.2)$$
$$6.8 \approx x$$

The wheel will revolve approximately 6.8 times.

Part Three: Problem Sets

Problem Set A

1 Find the circumference of the circle. Then approximate the circumference to the nearest hundredth.

   a A circle whose diameter is 21 mm

   b A circle whose radius is 6 mm

2 Find, to the nearest hundredth, the radius of a circle whose circumference is

   a 56π **b** 314   **c** 17π **d** 88

3 Find the length of each arc of a circle with a radius of 10.

   a A 72° arc   **b** A 90° arc   **c** A 60° arc   **d** A semicircle

4 A bicycle has wheels 30 cm in diameter. Find, to the nearest tenth of a centimeter, the distance that the bicycle moves forward during

   a 1 revolution   **b** 10 revolutions   **c** 1000 revolutions

5 Find the complete perimeter of each figure. Leave your answers in terms of π and whole numbers.

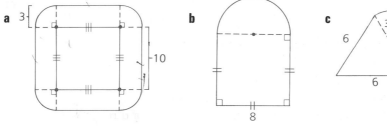

6 a Find the length of $\overarc{AB}$.

   b Find the perimeter of sector AOB. (The shaded region is a sector.)

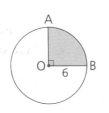

Problem Set A, *continued*

7 Find, to the nearest meter, the length of fencing needed to surround the racetrack.

12 m

50 m

8 The radius of ⊙O is 10 mm and the length of $\widehat{AB}$ is 4π mm.

A

O

B

a Find the circumference of ⊙O.

b Find m$\widehat{AB}$.

Problem Set B

9 Given arcs mounted on equilateral triangles as shown, find the length of each arc. In each case $\overline{OA}$ is a radius of $\widehat{AB}$.

a

A

18

O

B

b

A

18

O

B

c

A

18

O

B

10 There are 100 turns of thread on a spool with a diameter of 4 cm. Find the length of the thread to the nearest centimeter.

11 Awful Kanaufil plans to ride his cycle on a single-loop track. There is 100 m of straight track before the loop and 20 m after. The loop has a radius of 15 m. To the nearest meter, what is the total length of the track he must ride?

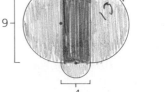

100 m

20 m

12 Find the outer perimeter of the figure, which is composed of semicircles mounted on the sides of a rectangle.

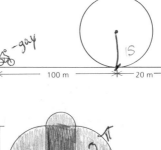

9

4

13 Sandy skated on the rink shown. To the nearest tenth of a meter, how far did she travel going once around in the outside lane? In the inside lane?

5 m

9 m

20 m

14 A belt wrapped tightly around circle O forms a right angle at P, a point outside the circle. Find the length of the belt if circle O has a radius of 6.

15 Find the distance traveled in one back-and-forth swing by the weight of a 12-in. pendulum that swings through a 75° angle.

75°

Problem Set C

16 A circular garbage can is wedged into a rectangular corner. The can has a diameter of 48 cm.

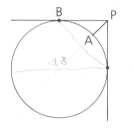

a Find the distance from the corner point to the can (PA).

b Find the distance from the corner point to the point of contact of the can with the wall (PB).

17 Two pulleys are connected by a belt. The radii of the pulleys are 3 cm and 15 cm, and the distance between their centers is 24 cm. Find the total length of belt needed to connect the pulleys.

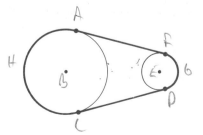

CHAPTER SUMMARY

CONCEPTS AND PROCEDURES

After studying this chapter, you should be able to

- Identify the characteristics of circles, chords, and diameters (10.1)
- Recognize special relationships between radii and chords (10.1)
- Apply the relationship between congruent chords of a circle (10.2)
- Identify different types of arcs, determine the measure of an arc, and recognize congruent arcs (10.3)
- Relate congruent arcs, chords, and central angles (10.3)
- Identify secant and tangent lines and segments (10.4)
- Distinguish between two types of tangent circles (10.4)
- Recognize common internal and common external tangents (10.4)
- Determine the measures of central, inscribed, tangent-chord, chord-chord, secant-secant, secant-tangent, and tangent-tangent angles (10.5)
- Recognize congruent inscribed and tangent-chord angles (10.6)
- Determine the measure of an angle inscribed in a semicircle (10.6)
- Apply the relationship between the measures of a tangent-tangent angle and its minor arc (10.6)
- Recognize inscribed and circumscribed polygons (10.7)
- Apply the relationship between opposite angles of an inscribed quadrilateral (10.7)
- Identify the characteristics of an inscribed parallelogram (10.7)
- Apply the three power theorems (10.8)
- Determine circle circumference and arc length (10.9)

VOCABULARY

arc (10.3)
center (10.1)
central angle (10.3)
chord (10.1)
chord-chord angle (10.5)
circle (10.1)
circumcenter (10.7)
circumference (10.9)
circumscribed polygon (10.7)
common external tangent (10.4)
common internal tangent (10.4)
common tangent (10.4)
concentric (10.1)

diameter (10.1)
exterior (10.1)
externally tangent (10.4)
external part (10.4)
incenter (10.7)
inscribed angle (10.5)
inscribed polygon (10.7)
interior (10.1)
internally tangent (10.4)
line of centers (10.4)
major arc (10.3)
minor arc (10.3)
point of contact (10.4)

point of tangency (10.4)
radius (10.1)
secant (10.4)
secant-secant angle (10.5)
secant segment (10.4)
secant-tangent angle (10.5)
semicircle (10.3)
tangent (10.4)
tangent-chord angle (10.5)
tangent circles (10.4)
tangent segment (10.4)
tangent-tangent angle (10.5)

REVIEW PROBLEMS

Problem Set A

1 Find x in each case.

a

b

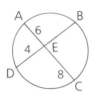

c

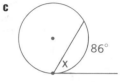

2 If $\overarc{AB} = 98°$ and $\overarc{CD} = 34°$, find x and y.

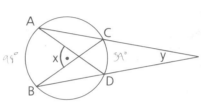

3 a Find BD.

b Find PT.

c Find WX.

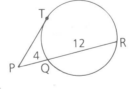

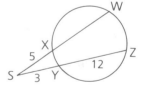

4 Find the radius of each circle.

a

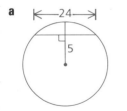

b

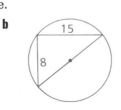

c

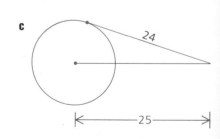

5 The circles shown are concentric at O. $\overline{PZ}$ and $\overline{PY}$ are tangent to the inner circle at W and X. If $\overarc{YZ} = 110°$, find the measure of $\overarc{WX}$.

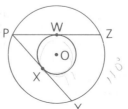

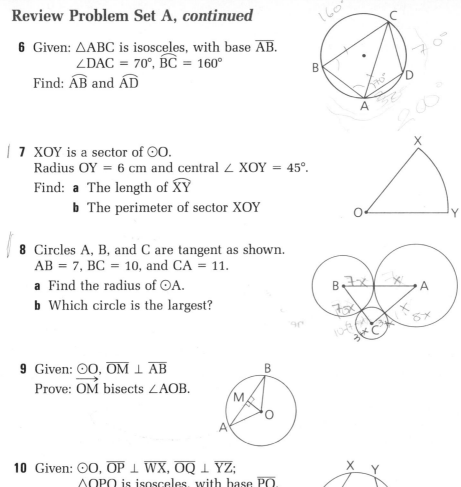

6 Given: △ABC is isosceles, with base $\overline{AB}$.
∠DAC = 70°, $\widehat{BC}$ = 160°
Find: $\widehat{AB}$ and $\widehat{AD}$

7 XOY is a sector of ⊙O.
Radius OY = 6 cm and central ∠ XOY = 45°.
Find: **a** The length of $\widehat{XY}$
b The perimeter of sector XOY

8 Circles A, B, and C are tangent as shown.
AB = 7, BC = 10, and CA = 11.
a Find the radius of ⊙A.
b Which circle is the largest?

9 Given: ⊙O, $\overline{OM} \perp \overline{AB}$
Prove: $\overrightarrow{OM}$ bisects ∠AOB.

10 Given: ⊙O, $\overline{OP} \perp \overline{WX}$, $\overline{OQ} \perp \overline{YZ}$;
△OPQ is isosceles, with base $\overline{PQ}$.
Conclusion: $\widehat{WX} \cong \widehat{YZ}$

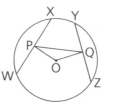

11 Given: $\overline{ZX}$ and $\overline{ZY}$ are tangent at X and Y.
Prove: $\overline{WZ}$ bisects $\widehat{XY}$.

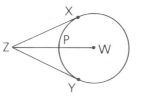

12 A parallelogram with sides 4 and 7.5 is inscribed in a circle.
Find the radius of the circle.

13 Given: TP = 8, PQ = 6
Find: RQ

14 Given: ⊙ O and P are externally tangent.
OA = 8, PB = 2

Find: The length of common external
tangent $\widehat{AB}$

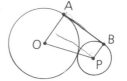

Problem Set B

15 If a point is chosen at random on ⊙P,
what is the probability that it lies on

a $\widehat{BA}$ **b** $\widehat{TUB}$

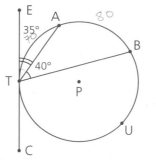

16 Jim knows that ⊙O is inscribed in isos-
celes △ ABC. He forgets which sides of
△ABC are congruent but remembers that
AB = 14 and the perimeter is 38.

a Find XC.

b What are the three possible lengths
of $\overline{BX}$?

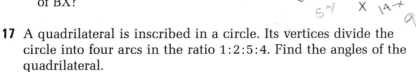

17 A quadrilateral is inscribed in a circle. Its vertices divide the
circle into four arcs in the ratio 1:2:5:4. Find the angles of the
quadrilateral.

18 Given: $\widehat{AB}$ = 30°, $\widehat{BC}$ = 40°, $\widehat{CD}$ = 50°

Find: **a** ∠X

       b ∠Y

       c ∠Z

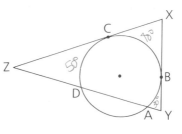

19 $\overline{TP}$ is a tangent segment, TP = 15, and
PQ = 5. Find the radius of ⊙O.

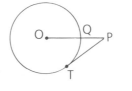

20 Given: m$\widehat{AD}$ + m$\widehat{BC}$ = 200,
m∠P = 30

Find: m$\widehat{AB}$ and m$\widehat{CD}$

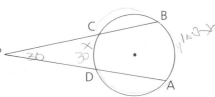

21 Given: ⊙F, $\overline{EG} \perp \overline{AB}$,
$\overline{EC} \cong \overline{ED}$

Prove: $\overline{AD}$ and $\overline{BC}$ are equidistant
from F.

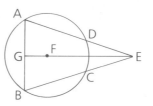

22 WXYZ is a parallelogram.
$\overline{WZ}$ and $\overline{YZ}$ are tangent segments.

a Show that WXYZ is a rhombus.

b Find m∠Z.

c If WY = 15, find the perimeter of
WXYZ.

d If WY = 15, find XZ.

23 Find x and y.

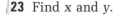

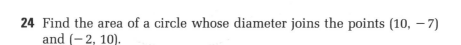

24 Find the area of a circle whose diameter joins the points (10, −7)
and (−2, 10).

25 Find, to the nearest centimeter, the circumference of a circle in
which an 80-cm chord is 9 cm from the center.

Problem Set C

26 Each circle below is inscribed in a regular polygon and is circumscribed about another regular polygon.

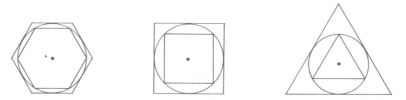

a If the length of a side of each outer polygon is 12, find the
length of a side of each inner polygon.

b In each case, find the ratio of the sides of the smaller polygon
to the sides of the larger polygon.

27 Given: $\overline{WZ}$ is a diameter of the $\odot$.

Show: $m\angle P = \dfrac{m\widehat{WX} + m\widehat{YZ}}{2}$

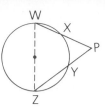

28 Given: $\odot$ P and Q are internally tangent at T.

Prove: AC:CT = BD:DT

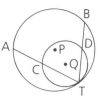

29 Given: $\widehat{AQ} \cong \widehat{RB}$; $\overline{PR}$ divides major and minor arcs AB in ratios of $\widehat{AQ}:\widehat{QB} = 4:3$ and $\widehat{AR}:\widehat{RB} = 7:5$.

Find: $\angle APQ:\angle BPQ$

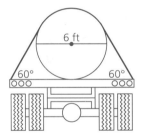

30 Three of the segments $\overline{PA}$, $\overline{PB}$, $\overline{PC}$, $\overline{PD}$, and $\overline{PE}$ are secant segments to circle O; the remaining two are tangent segments to circle O. If two of the segments are selected at random, what is the probability that a secant-tangent angle is formed?

31 A flatbed truck is hauling a cylindrical container with a diameter of 6 ft. Find, to the nearest hundredth, the length of cable needed to hold down the container.

AREA

The his painting by Sonia Delaunay
incorporates the areas of geometric shapes.

11.1 | UNDERSTANDING AREA

Objectives

After studying this section, you will be able to
- Understand the concept of area
- Find the areas of rectangles and squares
- Use the basic properties of area

Part One: Introduction

The Concept of Area

When we measure lengths of line segments, we use such standard units as meters, yards, miles, centimeters, and kilometers. These are often called *linear units* because they are measures of length.

The standard units of *area* are *square units* such as square meters, square yards, and square miles. A square meter, for example, is the space enclosed by a square whose sides are each one meter in length.

One Linear Unit — = — One Square Unit

Definition   The area of a closed region is the number of square units of space within the boundary of the region.

We can estimate the area of a region by determining the approximate number of square units it would take to fill the region.

Estimated Area = 10 sq units

Estimated Area = 18 sq units

Estimated Area = 19 sq units

Counting squares, however, is neither the easiest nor the best way to find the area of a region. We will develop formulas for computing the areas of regions bounded by the common geometrical figures. Such regions are usually named by their boundaries, as when we speak of "the area of a rectangle."

The Areas of Rectangles and Squares

In the figures to the right, there are two ways to find the areas:

1 The numbers of square units can be counted individually.
2 The areas can be computed by multiplying the number of columns (the measure of the base) by the number of rows (the height).

The second method suggests the following formula, which may be used to compute areas even when the lengths are fractions or irrational numbers.

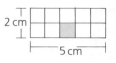

Area = 10 sq cm

Area = 16 sq cm

Postulate *The area of a rectangle is equal to the product of the base and the height for that base.*

$$A_{rect} = bh$$

where b is the length of the base and h is the height.

In a square, the base and the height are equal, so the following formula is used.

Theorem 99 *The area of a square is equal to the square of a side.*

$$A_{sq} = s^2$$

where s is the length of a side.

Basic Properties of Area

We make three basic assumptions about area:

Postulate *Every closed region has an area.*

Postulate *If two closed figures are congruent, then their areas are equal.*

If ABCDEF ≅ PQRSTU, then the area of region I = the area of region II.

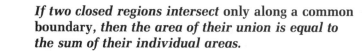

Postulate *If two closed regions intersect only along a common boundary, then the area of their union is equal to the sum of their individual areas.*

Part Two: Sample Problems

Problem 1   Find the area of the rectangle.

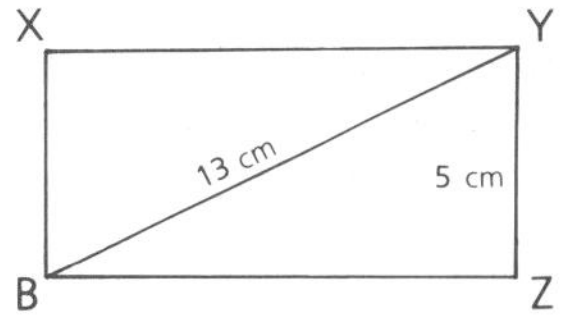

Solution $A_{rect} = bh$
We need to find base BZ.
$\triangle BZY$ is a right $\triangle$ of the (5, 12, 13) family, so BZ = 12.

$A_{rect} = 12(5) = 60$ sq cm

Problem 2   Given that the area of a rectangle is 20 sq dm and the altitude is 5 dm, find the base.

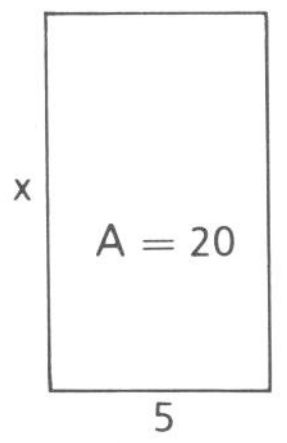

Solution   Let x be the number of decimeters in the base.

$A_{rect} = bh$
$\phantom{A_{rect}}20 = x(5)$
$\phantom{A_{rect}20}4 = x$
Base = 4 dm

Problem 3   Find the area of the shaded region.

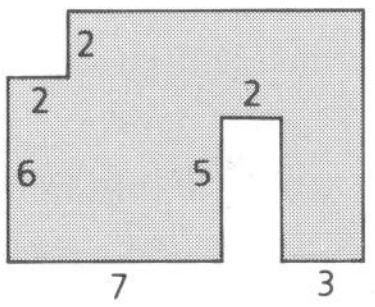

Solution   There are two methods of finding the area. One uses subtraction, and the other uses addition.

Method One:

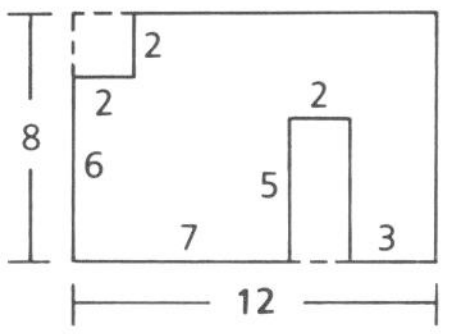

Area of large rectangle = $12 \cdot 8 = 96$
Area of square = $2^2 = 4$
Area of small rectangle = $2 \cdot 5 = 10$
Shaded area = $96 - 4 - 10 = 82$

Method Two ("Divide and Conquer"):

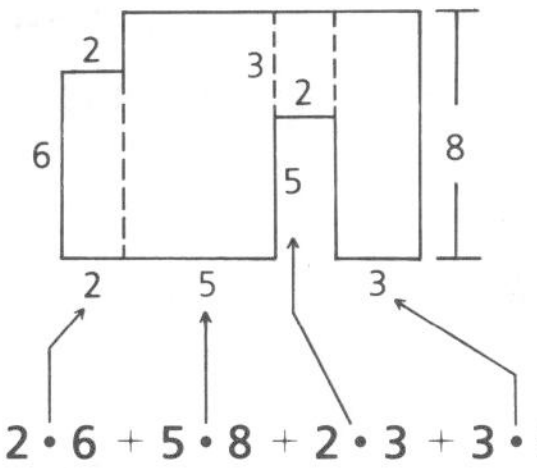

$A = 2 \cdot 6 + 5 \cdot 8 + 2 \cdot 3 + 3 \cdot 8$
Shaded area = 82

Part Three: Problem Sets

Problem Set A

1 Find the area of each figure below. (Assume right angles.)

a

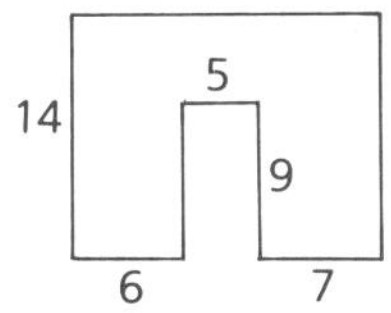

b

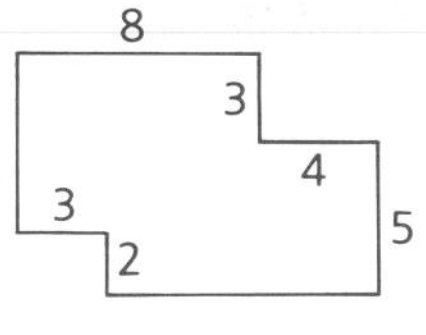

c

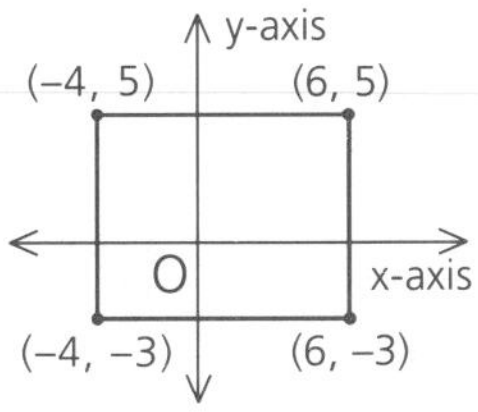

Problem Set A, *continued*

2 Find the area of a rectangle whose length and width are 12.5 cm and 6 cm respectively.

3 Find the area of each rectangle.

a

b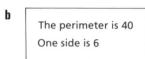

The perimeter is 40
One side is 6

4 The area of a rectangle is 48 sq mm, and the altitude is 6 mm.
  a Find the length of the base.
  b Find the length of a diagonal of the rectangle.

5 a Find the area of a square whose side is 12.
  b Find the area of a square whose diagonal is 10.
  c Find the side of a square whose area is 49.
  d Find the perimeter of a square whose area is 81.
  e Find the area of a square whose perimeter is 36.

6 Find the area of each shaded region. (Assume right angles.)

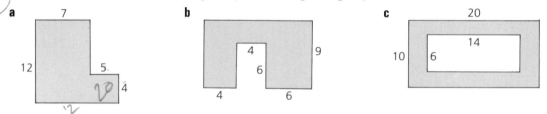

7 The diagonal of a rectangle is $\sqrt{29}$, and the rectangle's base is 2.
  a Find the area of the rectangle.
  b Find its semiperimeter.

Problem Set B

8 Each rectangular garden below has an area of 100.

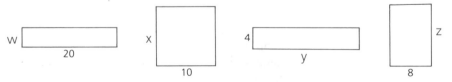

  a Find the missing dimension of each.
  b What length of fencing is needed to surround each?
  c Which figure has the shortest perimeter?
  d What do you think must be true about a rectangle that encloses the maximum possible area with the shortest possible perimeter?

9 A cross section of a steel I-beam is shown. Assume right angles and symmetry from appearances. Find the area of the cross section.

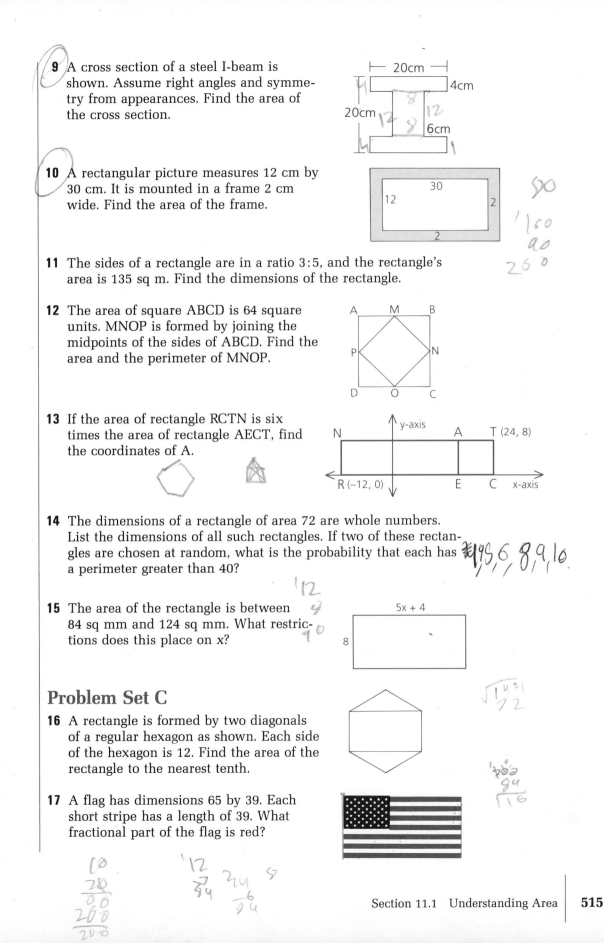

20cm

4cm

20cm

6cm

10 A rectangular picture measures 12 cm by 30 cm. It is mounted in a frame 2 cm wide. Find the area of the frame.

30

12

2

2

11 The sides of a rectangle are in a ratio 3:5, and the rectangle's area is 135 sq m. Find the dimensions of the rectangle.

12 The area of square ABCD is 64 square units. MNOP is formed by joining the midpoints of the sides of ABCD. Find the area and the perimeter of MNOP.

A   M   B

P   N

D   O   C

13 If the area of rectangle RCTN is six times the area of rectangle AECT, find the coordinates of A.

y-axis

N   A   T (24, 8)

R (−12, 0)   E   C   x-axis

14 The dimensions of a rectangle of area 72 are whole numbers. List the dimensions of all such rectangles. If two of these rectangles are chosen at random, what is the probability that each has a perimeter greater than 40?

15 The area of the rectangle is between 84 sq mm and 124 sq mm. What restrictions does this place on x?

5x + 4

8

Problem Set C

16 A rectangle is formed by two diagonals of a regular hexagon as shown. Each side of the hexagon is 12. Find the area of the rectangle to the nearest tenth.

17 A flag has dimensions 65 by 39. Each short stripe has a length of 39. What fractional part of the flag is red?

Areas of Parallelograms and Triangles

Objectives

After studying this section, you will be able to
- Find the areas of parallelograms
- Find the areas of triangles

Part One: Introduction

The Area of a Parallelogram

Many areas can be found by a "cut and paste" method. For example, to find the area of a parallelogram with base *b* and altitude *h*, we may do this:

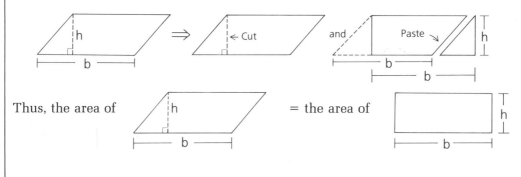

Thus, the area of [parallelogram with base *b*, height *h*] = the area of [rectangle with base *b*, height *h*]

Theorem 100   **The area of a parallelogram is equal to the product of the base and the height.**

$$A = bh$$

where *b* is the length of the base and *h* is the height.

Formal area proofs are often based on the cut-and-paste method. For instance, the key steps in a proof of Theorem 100 could be those below.

Given: PACT is a $\square$.
 $\overline{RT}$ is an altitude to $\overline{PA}$.

Prove: $A_{PACT} = (PA)(RT)$

Key Steps:

1 Extend $\overleftrightarrow{PA}$ and draw altitude $\overline{CE}$ to $\overleftrightarrow{PA}$; RECT is a rectangle.
2 $A_{PRT} = A_{AEC}$ because $\triangle PRT \cong \triangle AEC$ by HL.
3 $A_{PACT} = A_{RECT}$, since $A_{CART} + A_{PRT} = A_{CART} + A_{AEC}$.
4 $A_{RECT} = (TC)(RT)$ (Why?)
5 $A_{PACT} = (PA)(RT)$, because PA = TC.

The Area of a Triangle

The area of any triangle can be shown to be one half of the area of a parallelogram with the same base and height.

Area of 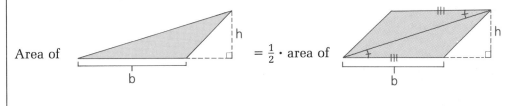 $= \frac{1}{2} \cdot$ area of

Theorem 101 ***The area of a triangle is equal to one-half the product of a base and the height (or altitude) for that base.***

$$A_{\triangle} = \tfrac{1}{2}bh$$

where b is the length of the base and h is the altitude.

Part Two: Sample Problems

Problem 1   *Find the area of each triangle.*

a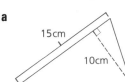

b

Solution

a $A_{\triangle} = \frac{1}{2}bh$
  $= \frac{1}{2}(15)(10)$
  $= 75$ sq cm

Note The base of a triangle is not always on the bottom. The 10-cm altitude is the altitude associated with the 15-cm base.

b $A_{\triangle} = \frac{1}{2}bh$
  $= \frac{1}{2}(7)(8)$
  $= 28$ sq mm

Note The altitude of a triangle is not always inside the triangle.

Problem 2   *Find the base of a triangle with altitude 15 and area 60.*

Solution   Let x be the base.

$$A_\triangle = \tfrac{1}{2}bh$$

$$60 = \tfrac{1}{2}x(15)$$

$$8 = x$$

Problem 3   *Find the area of a parallelogram whose sides are 14 and 6 and whose acute angle is 60°.*

Solution   We can use 14 as the base, but we must first find the height for that base. When altitude $\overline{BE}$ is drawn, a 30°-60°-90° triangle is formed, so $h = 3\sqrt{3}$.

$$A_\square = bh$$

$$= 14\left(3\sqrt{3}\right) = 42\sqrt{3}$$

Problem 4   *Find the area of a trapezoid WXYZ.*

Solution   Copy the diagram. Use the divide-and-conquer method. By drawing another altitude, $\overline{XB}$, you can divide the trapezoid into two right triangles and a rectangle.

Find the areas of these figures and add them.

The sides of $\triangle WBX$ form a Pythagorean triple, so WB = 5. Similarly, in $\triangle YAZ$, AZ = 9.

$$A_{\triangle WBX} = \tfrac{1}{2}bh \qquad A_{rect} = bh \qquad A_{\triangle YAZ} = \tfrac{1}{2}bh$$

$$= \tfrac{1}{2}(5)(12) \qquad\quad = 18(12) \qquad\qquad = \tfrac{1}{2}(9)(12)$$

$$= 30 \qquad\qquad\qquad = 216 \qquad\qquad\qquad = 54$$

The sum of the three areas, 300, is the area of the trapezoid.

Part Three: Problem Sets

Problem Set A

1 Find the area of each triangle.

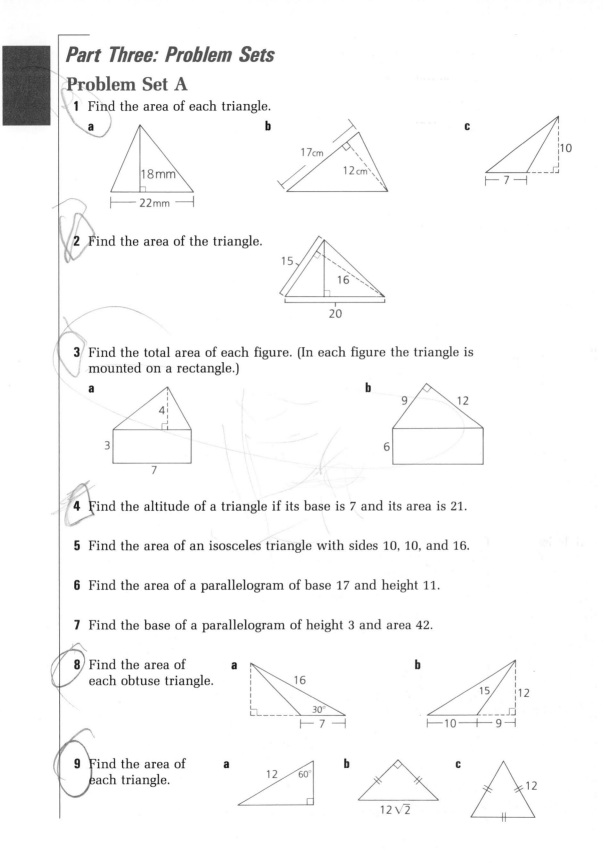

a

18mm
22mm

b

17cm
12cm

c

10
7

2 Find the area of the triangle.

15
16
20

3 Find the total area of each figure. (In each figure the triangle is mounted on a rectangle.)

a

4
3
7

b

9   12
6

4 Find the altitude of a triangle if its base is 7 and its area is 21.

5 Find the area of an isosceles triangle with sides 10, 10, and 16.

6 Find the area of a parallelogram of base 17 and height 11.

7 Find the base of a parallelogram of height 3 and area 42.

8 Find the area of each obtuse triangle.

a

16
30°
7

b

15   12
10   9

9 Find the area of each triangle.

a

12   60°

b

$12\sqrt{2}$

c

12

Problem Set A, *continued*

10 Find the area of each parallelogram to the nearest tenth.

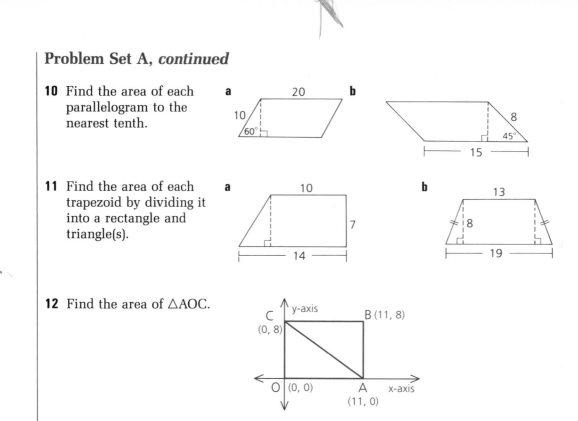

11 Find the area of each trapezoid by dividing it into a rectangle and triangle(s).

12 Find the area of △AOC.

Problem Set B

13 A triangle has the same area as a 6-by-8 rectangle. The base of the triangle is 8. Find the altitude of the triangle.

14 Lines $\overleftrightarrow{CF}$ and $\overleftrightarrow{AB}$ are parallel and 10 mm apart. Several triangles with base $\overline{AB}$ and a vertex on $\overleftrightarrow{CF}$ have been drawn below. Which triangle has the largest area? Explain.

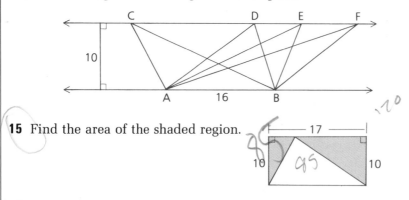

15 Find the area of the shaded region.

16 In a triangle, a base and its altitude are in a ratio of 3:2. The triangle's area is 48. Find the base and the altitude.

17 Find the area of the
shaded triangular region.

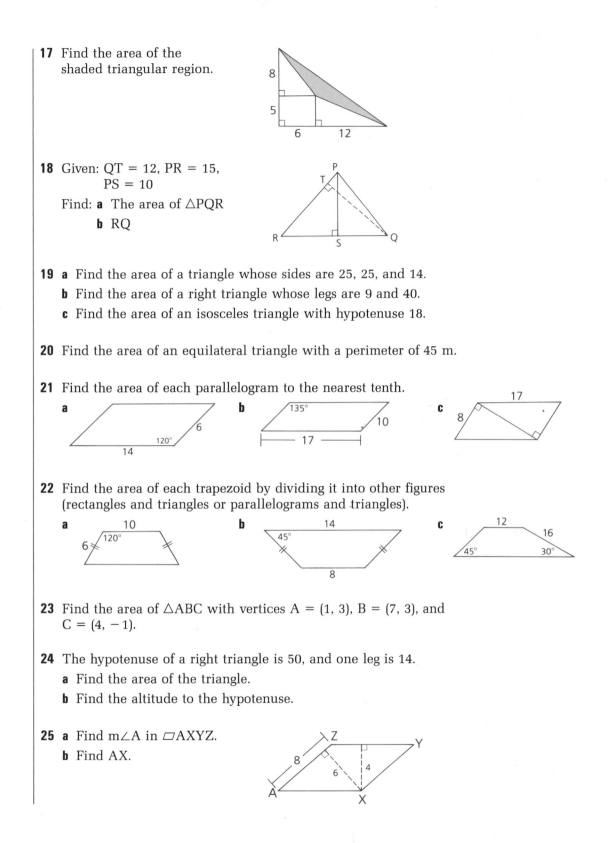

18 Given: QT = 12, PR = 15,
        PS = 10
  Find: **a** The area of △PQR
       b RQ

19 a Find the area of a triangle whose sides are 25, 25, and 14.
  b Find the area of a right triangle whose legs are 9 and 40.
  c Find the area of an isosceles triangle with hypotenuse 18.

20 Find the area of an equilateral triangle with a perimeter of 45 m.

21 Find the area of each parallelogram to the nearest tenth.

22 Find the area of each trapezoid by dividing it into other figures
(rectangles and triangles or parallelograms and triangles).

23 Find the area of △ABC with vertices A = (1, 3), B = (7, 3), and
C = (4, −1).

24 The hypotenuse of a right triangle is 50, and one leg is 14.
  a Find the area of the triangle.
  b Find the altitude to the hypotenuse.

25 a Find m∠A in ▱AXYZ.
  b Find AX.

Problem Set C

26 If the diagonals of a rhombus are 10 and 24, find the area and the perimeter of the rhombus.

27 a The area of an equilateral triangle is $9\sqrt{3}$. Find the length of one side.

    b Find a formula for the area of an equilateral triangle with sides s units long.

28 Find the area of the triangle.

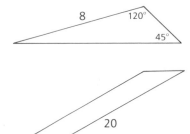

29 Find the area of the parallelogram.

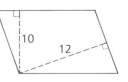

30 What is the name of the parallelogram having the greatest area for a given perimeter?

31 The diagonals of a kite are 10 and 24. Find the kite's area.

32 The perimeter of the parallelogram is 154. Find the parallelogram's area.

33 Let P be any point in the interior of rectangle ABCD. Four triangles are formed by joining P to each vertex.

    a Demonstrate that $A_{\triangle APD} + A_{\triangle BPC} = A_{\triangle APB} + A_{\triangle PCD}$.

    b Is this equation valid if ABCD is a parallelogram?

    c Is the equation valid if ABCD is a trapezoid?

$DOG^2 =$

THE AREA OF A TRAPEZOID

Objectives

After studying this section, you will be able to
- Find the areas of trapezoids
- Use the measure of a trapezoid's median to find its area

Part One: Introduction

The Area of a Trapezoid

You have seen that the area of a trapezoid can be found by dividing the trapezoid into simpler shapes, such as triangles, rectangles, and parallelograms ("divide and conquer"). There is, however, a formula that can be used to find the area of a trapezoid.

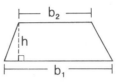

Theorem 102 **The area of a trapezoid equals one-half the product of the height and the sum of the bases.**

$$A_{trap} = \tfrac{1}{2}h(b_1 + b_2)$$

where b_1 is the length of one base, b_2 is the length of the other base, and h is the height.

The Median of a Trapezoid

We can use the Midline Theorem to find out what happens when the midpoints of the nonparallel sides of a trapezoid are joined.

Definition The line segment joining the midpoints of the nonparallel sides of a trapezoid is called the *median* of the trapezoid.

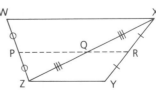

    In trapezoid WXYZ, P, Q, and R are midpoints of sides of $\triangle$WXZ and $\triangle$XYZ. P, Q, and R are collinear, because $\overline{PQ}$ and $\overline{QR}$ share Q, and each segment is parallel to $\overline{WX}$ and $\overline{ZY}$. $\overline{PR}$ is the median of trapezoid WXYZ. By the Midline Theorem, PQ = $\tfrac{1}{2}$(WX) and QR = $\tfrac{1}{2}$(YZ). Thus, PR = PQ + QR = $\tfrac{1}{2}$(WX) + $\tfrac{1}{2}$(YZ) = $\tfrac{1}{2}$(WX + YZ).

Theorem 103 *The measure of the median of a trapezoid equals the average of the measures of the bases.*

$$M = \tfrac{1}{2}(b_1 + b_2)$$

where b_1 is the length of one base and b_2 is the length of the other base.

You can now easily prove a shorter form of Theorem 102.

Theorem 104 *The area of a trapezoid is the product of the median and the height.*

$$A_{trap} = Mh$$

where M is the length of the median and h is the height.

Part Two: Sample Problems

Problem 1   Given: Trapezoid WXYZ, with height 7, lower base 18, and upper base 12

Find: The area of WXYZ

Solution $A_{trap} = \tfrac{1}{2}h(b_1 + b_2)$

$\qquad\quad = \tfrac{1}{2}(7)(18 + 12) = 105$

Problem 2   Find the shorter base of a trapezoid if the trapezoid's area is 52, its altitude is 8, and its longer base is 10.

Solution   Let x be the length of the shorter base.

$A_{trap} = \tfrac{1}{2}h(b_1 + b_2)$

$\quad 52 = \tfrac{1}{2}(8)(10 + x)$

$\quad 52 = 4(10 + x)$

$\qquad 3 = x$

Problem 3   The height of a trapezoid is 12. The bases are 6 and 14.

a Find the median.   **b** Find the area.

Solution   **a** $M = \tfrac{1}{2}(b_1 + b_2)$ **b** $A_{trap} = Mh$

$\qquad\qquad = \tfrac{1}{2}(14 + 6)$ $= 10(12)$

$\qquad\qquad = 10$ $= 120$

Part Three: Problem Sets

Problem Set A

1 A trapezoid has bases 15 and 11 and height 8.
  a Find the area.
  b Find the median.

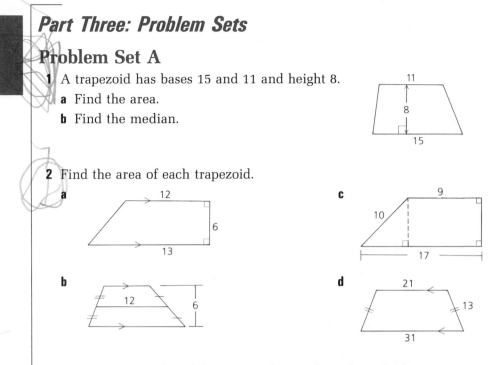

2 Find the area of each trapezoid.

  a

  c

  b

  d

3 Given a trapezoid with bases 6 and 15 and height 7, find the median and the area.

4 The bases of a trapezoid are 8 and 22, and the trapezoid's area is 135. Find the height.

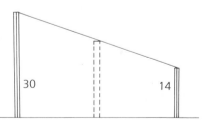

5 The height of a trapezoid is 10, and the trapezoid's area is 130. If one base is 15, find the other base.

6 A straight wire stretches between the tops of two poles whose heights are 30 ft and 14 ft. Find the height of a pole that is to be placed halfway between the original poles to support the wire. Assume that the poles are perpendicular to the ground. (Hint: Do you see a trapezoid and its median?)

Problem Set B

7 Find the total area of each figure.

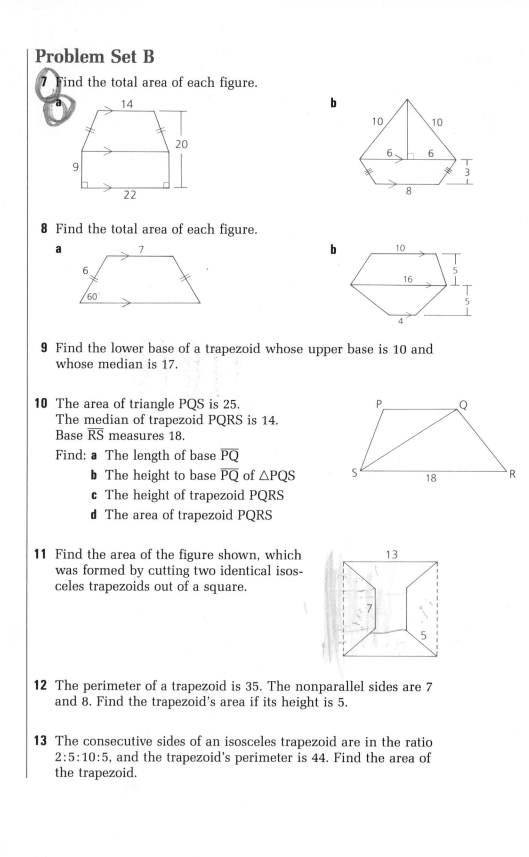

a

14

20

9

22

b

10   10

6   6

8

3

8 Find the total area of each figure.

a

7

6

60°

b

10

16

5

5

4

9 Find the lower base of a trapezoid whose upper base is 10 and whose median is 17.

10 The area of triangle PQS is 25. The median of trapezoid PQRS is 14. Base $\overline{RS}$ measures 18.

Find: **a** The length of base $\overline{PQ}$

 b The height to base $\overline{PQ}$ of △PQS

 c The height of trapezoid PQRS

 d The area of trapezoid PQRS

P   Q

S   18   R

11 Find the area of the figure shown, which was formed by cutting two identical isosceles trapezoids out of a square.

13

7

5

12 The perimeter of a trapezoid is 35. The nonparallel sides are 7 and 8. Find the trapezoid's area if its height is 5.

13 The consecutive sides of an isosceles trapezoid are in the ratio 2:5:10:5, and the trapezoid's perimeter is 44. Find the area of the trapezoid.

Problem Set C

14 The figure shown is composed of four regions of equal height. The triangle and the trapezoid are isosceles, and each side of the trapezoid is parallel to a side of the triangle. Find the total area of the figure.

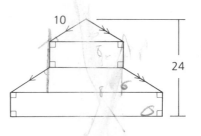

15 When an isosceles triangle is folded so that its vertex is on the midpoint of the base, a trapezoid with an area of 12 square units is formed. Find the area of the original triangle.

16 The sides of a trapezoid are in the ratio $2:5:8:5$. The trapezoid's area is 245. Find the height and the perimeter of the trapezoid.

17 Find the area of each trapezoid.

a

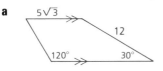

b

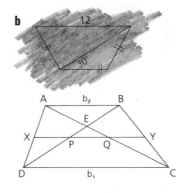

18 In trapezoid ABCD, X and Y are midpoints of sides, and P and Q are midpoints of diagonals. Develop a formula that can be used to find PQ. (Hint: See the proof of Theorem 103.)

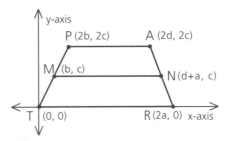

19 Prove that the area of a trapezoid is $\frac{1}{2}h(b_1 + b_2)$ by each of the following methods.

a Draw a diagonal and use the two triangles formed.

b Draw altitudes and use the rectangle and the triangles formed.

20 Write a coordinate proof that the median of a trapezoid is parallel to the bases and is equal to one-half their sum.

AREAS OF KITES AND RELATED FIGURES

Objective

After studying this section, you will be able to
■ Find the areas of kites

Part One: Introduction

Remember that in a kite the diagonals are perpendicular.
Also a kite can be divided into two isosceles triangles with a common base, so its area will equal the sum of the areas of these triangles.

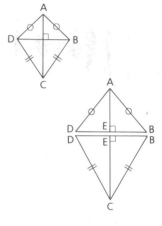

$$A_{\text{kite}} = A_{\triangle ABD} + A_{\triangle DBC}$$
$$= \tfrac{1}{2}(BD)(AE) + \tfrac{1}{2}(BD)(EC)$$
$$= \tfrac{1}{2}(BD)(AE + EC)$$
$$= \tfrac{1}{2}(BD)(AC)$$

Notice that $\overline{BD}$ and $\overline{AC}$ are the diagonals of the kite. We have just proved the following formula.

Theorem 105 **The area of a kite equals half the product of its diagonals.**
$$A_{kite} = \tfrac{1}{2}d_1 d_2$$
where d_1 is the length of one diagonal and d_2 is the length of the other diagonal.

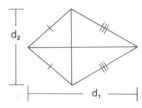

This formula can be applied to any kite, including the special cases of a rhombus and a square.

Part Two: Sample Problems

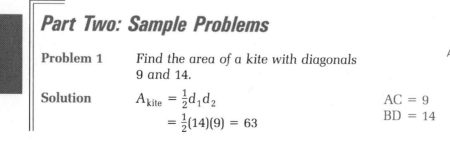

Problem 1 Find the area of a kite with diagonals 9 and 14.

Solution $A_{\text{kite}} = \tfrac{1}{2}d_1 d_2$
$$= \tfrac{1}{2}(14)(9) = 63$$

$AC = 9$
$BD = 14$

Problem 2   Find the area of a rhombus whose perimeter is 20 and whose longer diagonal is 8.

Solution   A rhombus is a $\square$, so its diagonals bisect each other. It is also a kite, so its diagonals are $\perp$ to each other. Thus, XZ = 8 and XP = 4.

The perimeter is 20, so XB = 5. (Why?)

$\triangle$BPX is a right triangle. Thus, BP = 3 and BY = 6.

$$A_{kite} = \tfrac{1}{2}d_1 d_2$$
$$= \tfrac{1}{2}(6)(8) = 24$$

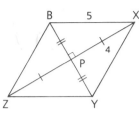

Part Three: Problem Sets

Problem Set A

1 Find the area of a kite with diagonals 6 and 20.

2 Find the area of each kite.

a

b

c

3 The area of a kite is 20. The longer diagonal is 8. Find the shorter diagonal.

Problem Set B

4 Find the area of the kite shown.

5 Find the area of each rhombus.

a

b

6 Given: ABCD is a kite.
     $\angle$BAD is a right $\angle$.
     BD = 10, BC = 13

Find: The area of ABCD

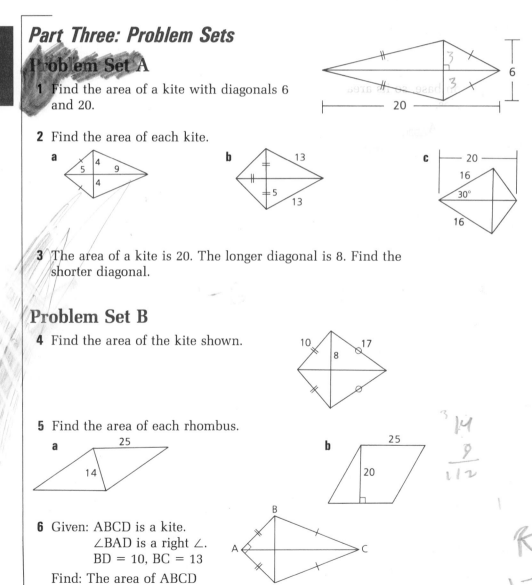

7 Find the area of the kite shown.

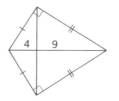

8 Find the area of a rhombus with a perimeter of 40 and one angle of 60°.

9 a Find the areas of region I, region II, and region III.

b Find the area of △OBD.

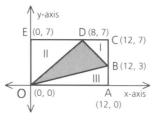

Problem Set C

10 Given a rhombus with diagonals 18 and 24, find the height.

11 The formula for the area of a kite applies to *any* quadrilateral whose diagonals are perpendicular.

Prove that the area of any quadrilateral with perpendicular diagonals equals half the product of the diagonals. (Hint: Use w, x, y, and z as marked to show that $A = \frac{1}{2}[w + x][y + z]$.)

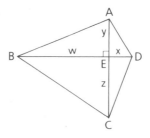

12 Observe the figure at the right. It resembles a kite, but it is not convex (it is "dented in"). Does the kite formula still hold? (That is, can it be shown that $A = \frac{1}{2}xy$?)

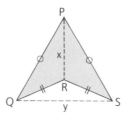

13 In rectangle ABCD, X and Y are midpoints of $\overline{AB}$ and $\overline{CD}$, and $\overline{PD} \cong \overline{QC}$.

a Compare the area of quadrilateral XQYP with the area of ABCD.

b Prove your conjecture.

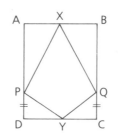

11.5 AREAS OF REGULAR POLYGONS

Objectives

After studying this section, you will be able to
- Find the areas of equilateral triangles
- Find the areas of other regular polygons

Part One: Introduction

The Area of an Equilateral Triangle

Equilateral triangles are encountered so frequently that a special formula for their areas will be useful.

Remember that the altitude of an equilateral triangle divides it into two 30°-60°-90° right triangles.

Thus, if $WY = s$, then $ZY = \frac{s}{2}$ and $WZ = \frac{s}{2}\sqrt{3}$.

Therefore, $A_{WXY} = \frac{1}{2}bh$

$$= \frac{1}{2}s\left(\frac{s}{2}\sqrt{3}\right) = \frac{s^2}{4}\sqrt{3}$$

Theorem 106 ***The area of an equilateral triangle equals the product of one-fourth the square of a side and the square root of 3.***

$$A_{eq. \triangle} = \frac{s^2}{4}\sqrt{3}$$

where s is the length of a side.

The Area of a Regular Polygon

Recall that in a regular polygon all interior angles are congruent and all sides are congruent.

In regular polygon PENTA,
- O is the center
- $\overline{OA}$ is a *radius*
- $\overline{OM}$ is an *apothem*

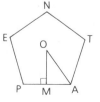

Definition	A *radius* of a regular polygon is a segment joining the center to any vertex.		

Definition	An *apothem* of a regular polygon is a segment joining the center to the midpoint of any side.		

Here are some important observations about apothems and radii:
- All apothems of a regular polygon are congruent.
- Only regular polygons have apothems.
- An apothem is a radius of a circle inscribed in the polygon.
- An apothem is the perpendicular bisector of a side.
- A radius of a regular polygon is a radius of a circle circumscribed about the polygon.
- A radius of a regular polygon bisects an angle of the polygon.

If all of the radii of a regular polygon are drawn, the polygon is divided into congruent isosceles triangles. (What is an altitude of each triangle?) If you write an expression for the sum of the areas of those isosceles triangles, you can derive the following formula.

Theorem 107	**The area of a regular polygon equals one-half the product of the apothem and the perimeter.**

$$A_{reg.\ poly.} = \tfrac{1}{2}ap$$

where a is the length of an apothem and p is the perimeter.

Part Two: Sample Problems

Problem 1   A regular polygon has a perimeter of 40 and an apothem of 5. Find the polygon's area.

Solution
$$A_{reg.\ poly.} = \tfrac{1}{2}ap$$
$$= \tfrac{1}{2}(5)(40) = 100$$

Problem 2   An equilateral triangle has a side 10 cm long. Find the triangle's area.

Solution
$$A_{eq.\ \triangle} = \tfrac{s^2}{4}\sqrt{3}$$
$$= \tfrac{10^2}{4}\sqrt{3}$$
$$= 25\sqrt{3} \text{ sq cm}$$

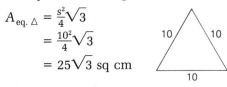

Problem 3 A circle with a radius of 6 is inscribed in an equilateral triangle. Find the area of the triangle.

Solution Notice that $\overline{OP}$ is an apothem 6 units long and that AOP is a 30°-60°-90° triangle. Thus, OA = 12, AP = $6\sqrt{3}$, and the perimeter of △ABC is $36\sqrt{3}$. An equilateral triangle is a regular polygon, so

$$A = \tfrac{1}{2}ap$$
$$= \tfrac{1}{2}(6)\left(36\sqrt{3}\right) = 108\sqrt{3}$$

Problem 4 Find the area of a regular hexagon with sides 18 units long.

Solution AF = 18, so AP = 9.

Observe that OPA is a 30°-60°-90° triangle, so that apothem OP = $9\sqrt{3}$.

Perimeter = 6(18) = 108
$$A = \tfrac{1}{2}ap$$
$$= \tfrac{1}{2}\left(9\sqrt{3}\right)(108) = 486\sqrt{3}$$

Part Three: Problem Sets

Problem Set A

1 The perimeter of a regular polygon is 24 and the apothem is 3. Find the polygon's area.

2 Find the areas of equilateral triangles with the following sides.

   a 6   **b** 7   **c** 8   **d** $2\sqrt{3}$

3 Find the areas of equilateral triangles with the following apothems.

   a 6   **b** 4   **c** 3   **d** $2\sqrt{3}$

4 Find, to the nearest tenth, the area of a regular hexagon whose

   a Side is 6   **c** Apothem is 6
   b Side is 8   **d** Apothem is 8

5 The radius of a regular hexagon is 12.
   Find: **a** The length of one side
            b The apothem
            c The area

Problem Set A, *continued*

6 Find the area of a square whose

   a Apothem is 5   **c** Side is 7   **e** Radius is 6

   b Apothem is 12   **d** Diagonal is 10   **f** Perimeter is 12

7 Find the apothem of a square whose area is 36 sq mm.

8 Find the side of an equilateral triangle whose area is $9\sqrt{3}$ sq km.

9 Find the area of a square if the radius of its inscribed circle is 9.

10 Find the area of an equilateral triangle if the radius of its inscribed circle is 3.

11 Find the area of a regular hexagon if the radius of its inscribed circle is 12.

Problem Set B

12 Find the area of

   a An equilateral triangle whose side is 9

   b A square whose apothem is $7\frac{1}{2}$

   c A regular hexagon whose side is 7

13 Find the length of one side and of the apothem of

   a A square whose area is 121

   b An equilateral triangle whose area is $36\sqrt{3}$ sq m

   c A regular hexagon whose perimeter is 24 cm

14 Find the perimeter of a regular polygon whose area is 64 and whose apothem is 4.

15 A circle of radius 12 is circumscribed about each regular polygon below. Find the area of each polygon.

   a   **b**   **c**

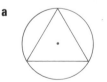 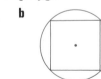

16 A circle is inscribed in one regular hexagon and circumscribed about another. If the circle has a radius of 6, find the ratio of the area of the smaller hexagon to the area of the larger hexagon.

17 Find the area of the shaded region in each polygon. (Assume regular polygons.)

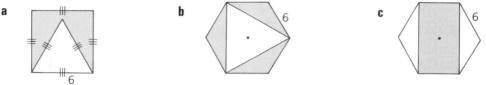

a

b 6

c 6

6

18 Suppose you are given a scalene triangle, an equilateral triangle, a kite, a square, a regular octagon, and a regular hexagon. If you choose two of the six figures at random, what is the probability that both have apothems?

Problem Set C

19 a The span s of a regular hexagon is 30. Find the hexagon's area.

b Find the span of a regular hexagon with an area of $32\sqrt{3}$.

c Find a formula for the area of a regular hexagon with a given span s.

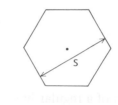

s

20 a Find the apothem of the regular octagon.

b Find the area of the octagon.

10

21 A square is formed by joining the midpoints of alternate sides of a regular octagon. A side of the octagon is 10.

a Find the area of the square.

b Find the area of the shaded region.

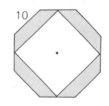

10

22 Given a set of four concentric regular hexagons, each with a radius 1 unit longer than that of the next smaller hexagon, find the total area of the shaded regions.

1 1

1 1

23 A square is inscribed in an equilateral triangle as shown. Find the area of the shaded region.

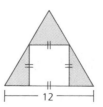

12

24 A square and a regular hexagon are inscribed in the same circle.
  a Find the ratio of a side of the square to a side of the hexagon.
  b Find the ratio of the area of the square to the area of the hexagon.

25 a Express the area of ABCD as the sum of the areas of the three triangles.
  b Express the area of ABCD as the area of a trapezoid with bases $\overline{AB}$ and $\overline{CD}$.
  c Equate your answers to parts **a** and **b** and simplify. Are you surprised? So was President James A. Garfield, who is said to have discovered this proof.

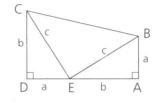

26 Find the area of △ABC.

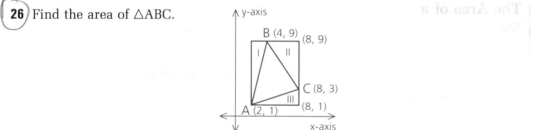

TILING AND AREA
Mathematics sheds light on chemistry problem

Finding the approximate area of a region by covering it with unit squares is one example of tiling. Tiling using squares is easy to imagine for anyone who has ever seen a checkerboard. Square tiling is an example of *periodic tiling* because the pattern repeats predictably throughout the region.

In the 1970's, Roger Penrose, a mathematical physicist at Oxford University in England, discovered tilings that could never be periodic. One such tiling consisted of kites and darts. Another consisted of fat diamonds and thin diamonds.

Penrose described specific rules governing which sides could come into contact with each other. These shapes, and portions of tilings using them, are shown here.

Penrose's tilings not only represented a mathematical breakthrough, they also have helped scientists better understand how molecules in certain complex crystal patterns "know" how to arrange themselves in such highly complicated ways.

If there were no restrictions regarding which sides could come into contact, how might the kites and darts be tiled periodically?

Kite Dart Thin diamond Fat diamond

AREAS OF CIRCLES, SECTORS, AND SEGMENTS

Objectives

After studying this section, you will be able to
- Find the areas of circles
- Find the areas of sectors
- Find the areas of segments

Part One: Introduction

The Area of a Circle

You may already know the formula for the area of a circle.

Postulate

The area of a circle is equal to the product of π and the square of the radius.

$$A_{\odot} = \pi r^2$$

where r is the radius.

The Area of a Sector

The region bounded by a circle may be divided into *sectors*.

Definition

A *sector* of a circle is a region bounded by two radii and an arc of the circle.

Sector HOP

Just as the length of an arc is a fractional part of the circumference of a circle, the area of a sector is a fractional part of the area of the circle.

Theorem 108

The area of a sector of a circle is equal to the area of the circle times the fractional part of the circle determined by the sector's arc.

$$A_{sector\ HOP} = \left(\frac{m\widehat{HP}}{360}\right)\pi r^2$$

where r is the radius and $\widehat{HP}$ is measured in degrees.

The Area of a Segment

Another way of dividing the interior of a circle produces a *segment*.

Definition	A *segment* of a circle is a region bounded by a chord of the circle and its corresponding arc.

By studying the diagram above, you may be able to see what to do to find the area of a segment. Sample problem 4 will illustrate the procedure in detail.

Part Two: Sample Problems

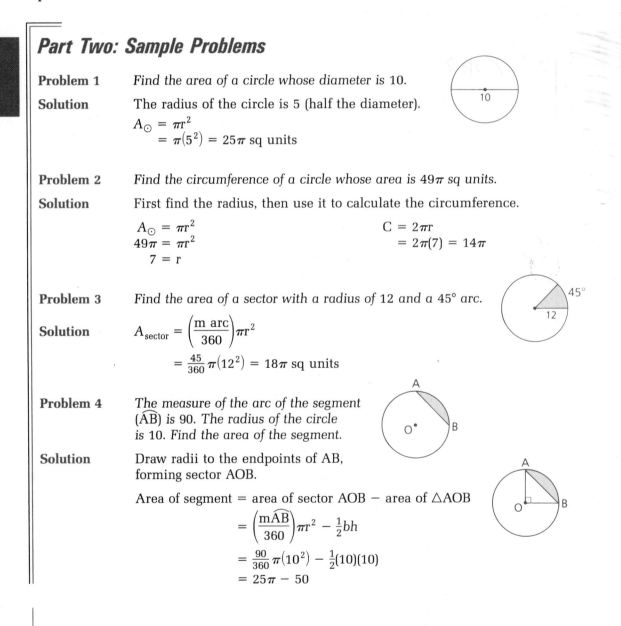

Problem 1   Find the area of a circle whose diameter is 10.

Solution   The radius of the circle is 5 (half the diameter).

$$A_\odot = \pi r^2$$
$$= \pi(5^2) = 25\pi \text{ sq units}$$

Problem 2   Find the circumference of a circle whose area is 49π sq units.

Solution   First find the radius, then use it to calculate the circumference.

$$A_\odot = \pi r^2 \qquad\qquad C = 2\pi r$$
$$49\pi = \pi r^2 \qquad\qquad\quad = 2\pi(7) = 14\pi$$
$$7 = r$$

Problem 3   Find the area of a sector with a radius of 12 and a 45° arc.

Solution
$$A_{\text{sector}} = \left(\frac{\text{m arc}}{360}\right)\pi r^2$$

$$= \frac{45}{360}\pi(12^2) = 18\pi \text{ sq units}$$

Problem 4   The measure of the arc of the segment ($\overset{\frown}{AB}$) is 90. The radius of the circle is 10. Find the area of the segment.

Solution   Draw radii to the endpoints of AB, forming sector AOB.

Area of segment = area of sector AOB − area of △AOB

$$= \left(\frac{m\overset{\frown}{AB}}{360}\right)\pi r^2 - \tfrac{1}{2}bh$$

$$= \frac{90}{360}\pi(10^2) - \tfrac{1}{2}(10)(10)$$

$$= 25\pi - 50$$

Part Three: Problem Sets

Problem Set A

1 Find the areas and circumferences of circles with the following radii.

   a 1   **b** 8   **c** 15

2 Find the radii of circles with the following areas.

   a 16π **b** 169π

3 Find the circumference of a circle whose area is 100π sq cm.

4 Find the area of a circle whose circumference is 18π dm.

5 Find the area of each shaded sector.

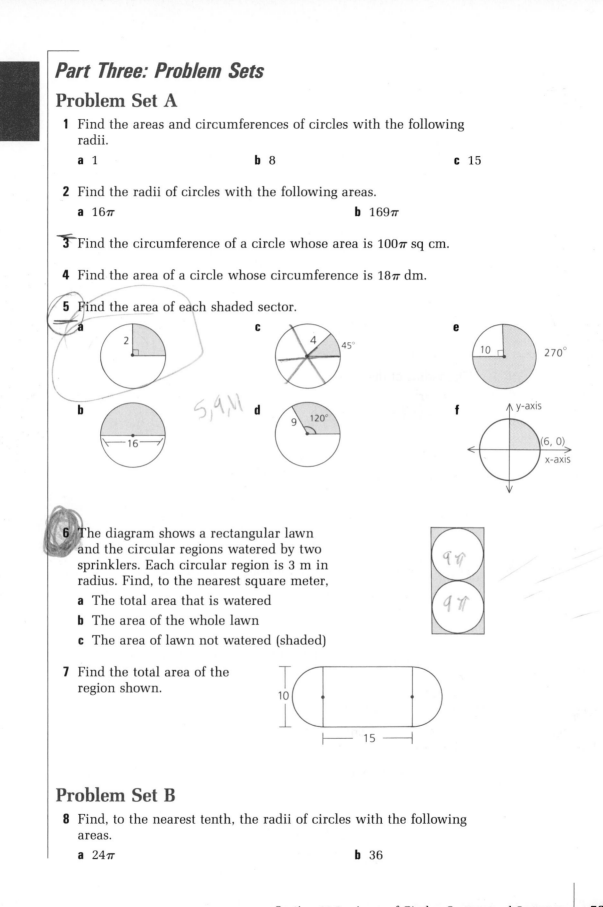

6 The diagram shows a rectangular lawn and the circular regions watered by two sprinklers. Each circular region is 3 m in radius. Find, to the nearest square meter,

   a The total area that is watered

   b The area of the whole lawn

   c The area of lawn not watered (shaded)

7 Find the total area of the region shown.

Problem Set B

8 Find, to the nearest tenth, the radii of circles with the following areas.

   a 24π **b** 36

9 Find the area of each sector.

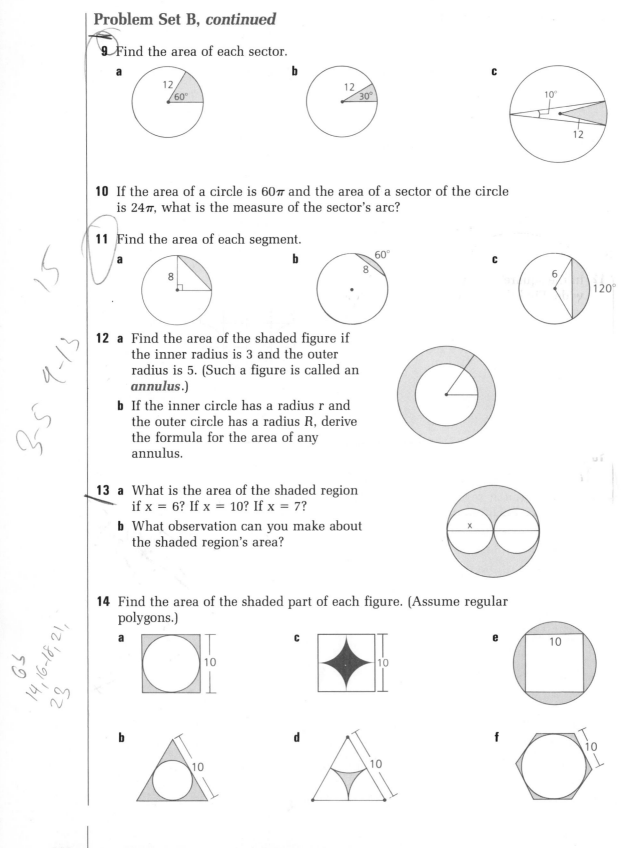

a

12
60°

b

12
30°

c

10°

12

10 If the area of a circle is 60π and the area of a sector of the circle is 24π, what is the measure of the sector's arc?

11 Find the area of each segment.

a

8

b

60°

8

c

6

120°

12 a Find the area of the shaded figure if the inner radius is 3 and the outer radius is 5. (Such a figure is called an *annulus*.)

b If the inner circle has a radius r and the outer circle has a radius R, derive the formula for the area of any annulus.

13 a What is the area of the shaded region if $x = 6$? If $x = 10$? If $x = 7$?

b What observation can you make about the shaded region's area?

x

14 Find the area of the shaded part of each figure. (Assume regular polygons.)

a

10

c

10

e

10

b

10

d

10

f

10

15 Find the area of the shaded region.

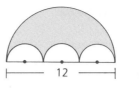

16 On the target, the radius of the bull's-eye is 5 cm, and each band is 5 cm wide.

a Find the total shaded area to the nearest square centimeter.

b Find the area of the unshaded bands to the nearest square centimeter.

c What is the probability that if you hit the target, you will get a bull's-eye? (Assume that no skill is involved.)

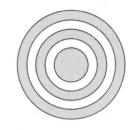

17 In the square grid, each square is 2 cm wide. Find the area of the region bounded by the circular arcs.

Problem Set C

18 Find the area of each shaded region.

a

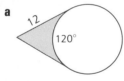

12

120°

b

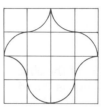

6   6

Diameter = 12

19 A rotor of a Wankel automotive engine has the geometric shape shown. The center of each arc is the opposite vertex of the equilateral triangle.

a Find the figure's area.

b Find the figure's perimeter.

10

20 Find the area of each shaded region.

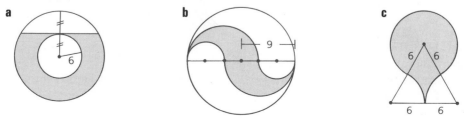

a

6

b

9

c

6   6

6   6

Problem Set C, *continued*

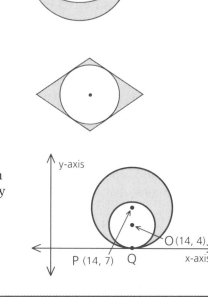

21 Three arcs are drawn, centered at the midpoints of the sides of a triangle and meeting at the vertices, as shown.

a Find the total area of the shaded regions (which are called the lunes of Hippocrates).

b Find the area of the triangle.

22 A circle is inscribed in a rhombus. Find the area of the shaded region if the diagonals of the rhombus are 30 and 40.

23 If ⊙O and ⊙P are tangent to the x-axis at Q and a point is selected at random in the interior of ⊙P, what is the probability that the point is in the shaded region?

RATIOS OF AREAS

Objectives

After studying this section, you will be able to
- Find ratios of areas by calculating and comparing the areas
- Find ratios of areas by applying properties of similar figures

Part One: Introduction

Computing the Areas

One way of determining the ratio of the areas of two figures is to calculate the quotient of the two areas.

Example 1 Find the ratio of the area of the parallelogram to the area of the triangle.

$$\frac{A_{\square}}{A_{\triangle}} = \frac{b_1 h_1}{\frac{1}{2} b_2 h_2} = \frac{9 \cdot 10}{\frac{1}{2} \cdot 12 \cdot 8} = \frac{90}{48} = \frac{15}{8}, \text{ or } 15:8$$

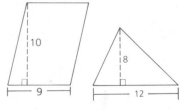

Example 2 In the diagram, AB = 5 and BC = 2. Find the ratio of the area of △ABD to that of △CBD.

Notice that the height of △ABD is the same as the height of △CBD and is labeled by the letter h.

$$\frac{A_{\triangle ABD}}{A_{\triangle CBD}} = \frac{\frac{1}{2} b_1 h}{\frac{1}{2} b_2 h} = \frac{b_1}{b_2} = \frac{5}{2}$$

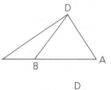

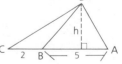

Similar Figures

As you know, if two triangles are similar, the ratio of any pair of their corresponding altitudes, medians, or angle bisectors equals the ratio of their corresponding sides. Application of this concept leads to an interesting formula.

Example 1   *Given that* △PQR ∼ △WXY, *find the ratio of their areas.*

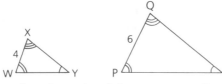

Notice that the ratio of the corresponding sides is $\frac{3}{2}$.
The ratio of the areas is

$$\frac{A_{\triangle PQR}}{A_{\triangle WXY}} = \frac{\frac{1}{2}b_1h_1}{\frac{1}{2}b_2h_2} = \frac{b_1}{b_2} \cdot \frac{h_1}{h_2}$$

But $\frac{b_1}{b_2} = \frac{3}{2}$ and $\frac{h_1}{h_2} = \frac{3}{2}$, so $\frac{A_{\triangle PQR}}{A_{\triangle WXY}} = \frac{3}{2} \cdot \frac{3}{2} = \left(\frac{3}{2}\right)^2 = \frac{9}{4}$.

Notice that $\frac{9}{4}$ is the square of $\frac{3}{2}$.

The preceding example shows the key steps that can be used to prove a theorem about the areas of similar triangles. Because convex polygons can be divided into triangles, you may suspect that the areas of similar polygons have the same relationship. They do.

Theorem 109   *If two figures are similar, then the ratio of their areas equals the square of the ratio of corresponding segments. (**Similar-Figures Theorem**)*

$$\frac{A_1}{A_2} = \left(\frac{s_1}{s_2}\right)^2$$

where A_1 and A_2 are areas and s_1 and s_2 are measures of corresponding segments.

Corresponding segments can be any segments associated with the figures, such as sides, altitudes, medians, diagonals, or radii.

Example 2   *Given the similar pentagons shown, find the ratio of their areas.*

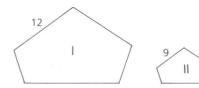

By the Similar-Figures Theorem,

$$\frac{A_I}{A_{II}} = \left(\frac{s_1}{s_2}\right)^2.$$

$$\frac{s_1}{s_2} = \frac{12}{9} = \frac{4}{3}$$

So $\dfrac{A_I}{A_{II}} = \left(\dfrac{4}{3}\right)^2 = \dfrac{16}{9}$, or 16:9.

Part Two: Sample Problems

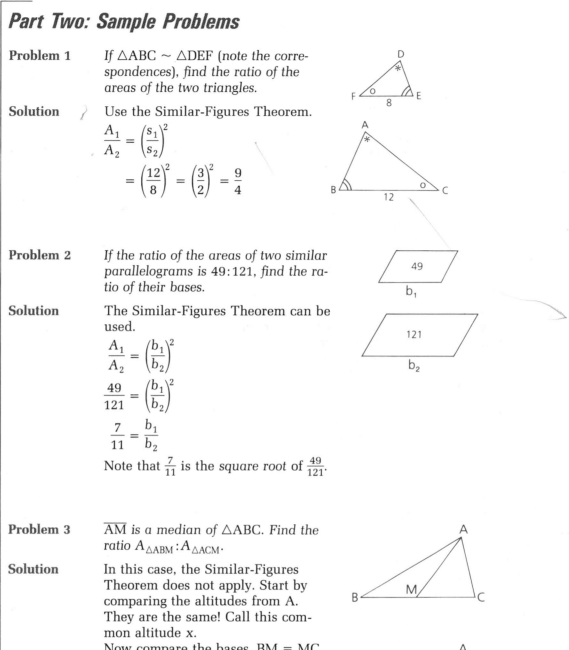

Problem 1   If $\triangle ABC \sim \triangle DEF$ (note the correspondences), find the ratio of the areas of the two triangles.

Solution   Use the Similar-Figures Theorem.

$$\frac{A_1}{A_2} = \left(\frac{s_1}{s_2}\right)^2$$

$$= \left(\frac{12}{8}\right)^2 = \left(\frac{3}{2}\right)^2 = \frac{9}{4}$$

Problem 2   If the ratio of the areas of two similar parallelograms is 49:121, find the ratio of their bases.

Solution   The Similar-Figures Theorem can be used.

$$\frac{A_1}{A_2} = \left(\frac{b_1}{b_2}\right)^2$$

$$\frac{49}{121} = \left(\frac{b_1}{b_2}\right)^2$$

$$\frac{7}{11} = \frac{b_1}{b_2}$$

Note that $\frac{7}{11}$ is the *square root* of $\frac{49}{121}$.

Problem 3 $\overline{AM}$ is a median of $\triangle ABC$. Find the ratio $A_{\triangle ABM} : A_{\triangle ACM}$.

Solution   In this case, the Similar-Figures Theorem does not apply. Start by comparing the altitudes from A. They are the same! Call this common altitude x.
Now compare the bases. BM = MC, because $\overline{AM}$ is a median. Let y represent BM and MC.

$$\frac{A_{\triangle ABM}}{A_{\triangle ACM}} = \frac{\frac{1}{2}b_1 h_1}{\frac{1}{2}b_2 h_2} = \frac{xy}{xy} = 1, \text{ or } 1:1$$

Since the triangles have equal bases and equal heights, their areas are equal.

The result of sample problem 3 may be stated as a theorem.

Theorem 110 *A median of a triangle divides the triangle into two triangles with equal areas.*

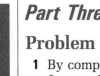

Part Three: Problem Sets

Problem Set A

1 By computing the areas, find the ratio of the areas of each pair of figures shown.

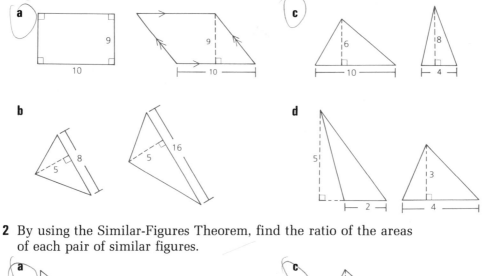

2 By using the Similar-Figures Theorem, find the ratio of the areas of each pair of similar figures.

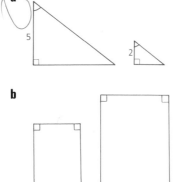

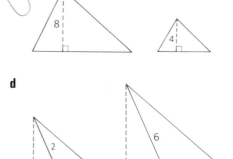

3 Given: $\overline{PM}$ is a median.

Find: **a** $A_{\triangle PQM}:A_{\triangle PRM}$
     b $A_{\triangle PQM}:A_{\triangle PQR}$
     c QR:MR

4 A pair of corresponding sides of two similar triangles are 4 and 9. Find the ratio of the triangles' areas.

5 If the ratio of the areas of two similar polygons is 9:16, find the ratio of a pair of corresponding altitudes.

6 Gladys Gardenia has a square garden, 3 m on a side. She wishes to make it exactly twice as large. Gladys decides to double the length and double the width. Does she succeed?

7 Find the ratio of the areas of the regular hexagons.

8 Find the ratio of the areas of the triangles.

Problem Set B

9 For each pair of figures, find the ratio of area I to area II.

a

c

b

d

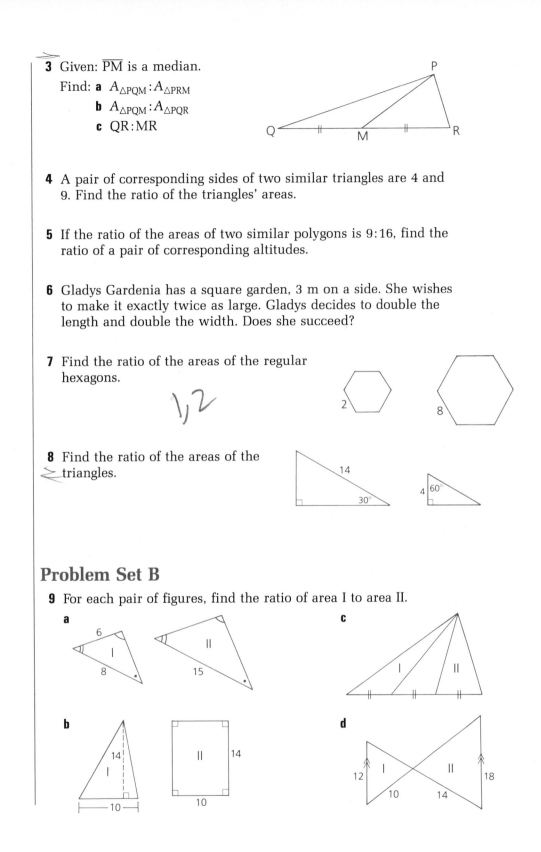

Problem Set B, *continued*

10 Find the ratio of the area of the shaded triangle to that of the whole triangle.

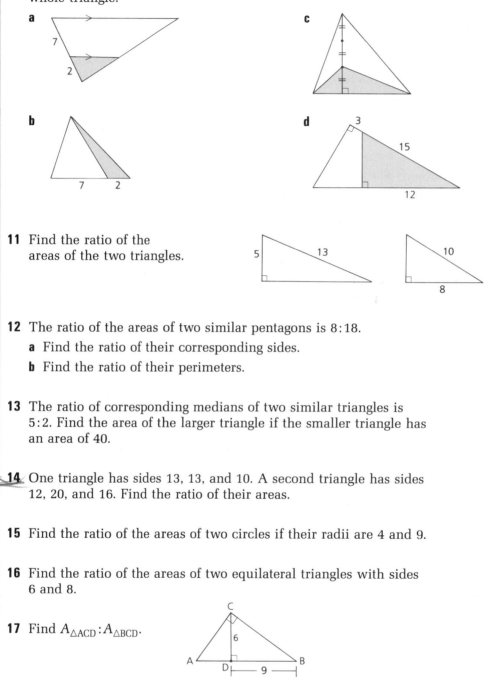

11 Find the ratio of the areas of the two triangles.

12 The ratio of the areas of two similar pentagons is 8:18.
  a Find the ratio of their corresponding sides.
  b Find the ratio of their perimeters.

13 The ratio of corresponding medians of two similar triangles is 5:2. Find the area of the larger triangle if the smaller triangle has an area of 40.

14 One triangle has sides 13, 13, and 10. A second triangle has sides 12, 20, and 16. Find the ratio of their areas.

15 Find the ratio of the areas of two circles if their radii are 4 and 9.

16 Find the ratio of the areas of two equilateral triangles with sides 6 and 8.

17 Find $A_{\triangle ACD} : A_{\triangle BCD}$.

Problem Set C

18 Given trapezoid WXYZ, find the ratio of
the areas of each pair of triangles.

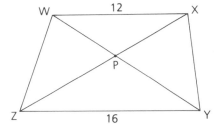

a △WYZ and △XYZ

b △WXZ and △WXY

c △WPZ and △XPY

d △WPX and △ZPY

e △WPX and △XPY

19 Given △ABC is a right △.
    E and F are midpoints.
    D, H, and G divide $\overline{AC}$ into
    four ≅ segments.

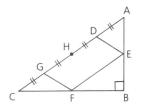

Find: **a** The ratio of the areas of △ABC and △EBF

     b The ratio of the areas of △ABC and △GFC

     c The ratio of the areas of △ADE and △GFC

     d The ratio of the areas of ▱DEFG and △ABC

     e The perimeter of ▱DEFG if AC = 20

20 If the midpoints of the sides of a quadrilateral are joined in
order, another quadrilateral is formed. Find the ratio of the area
of the larger quadrilateral to that of the smaller quadrilateral.

21 Given: Trapezoid ABCD
    Find: The ratio of areas I and II

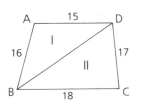

22 PQRS is a parallelogram.

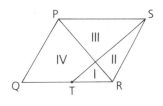

  a If T is a midpoint and the area of
    PQRS is 60, find the areas of regions I,
    II, III, and IV.

  b If T divides $\overline{QR}$ such that $\frac{QT}{TR} = \frac{x}{y}$, find
    the ratio of the area of region I to that
    of ▱PQRS.

HERO'S AND BRAHMAGUPTA'S FORMULAS

Objective

After studying this section, you will be able to
- Find the areas of figures by using Hero's formula and Brahmagupta's formula

Part One: Introduction

A useful formula for finding the area of a triangle was developed nearly 2000 years ago by the mathematician Hero of Alexandria.

Theorem 111 $A_\triangle = \sqrt{s(s-a)(s-b)(s-c)}$, *where a, b, and c are the lengths of the sides of the triangle and* $s = semiperimeter = \frac{a+b+c}{2}$. *(Hero's formula)*

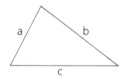

In about A.D. 628, a Hindu mathematician, Brahmagupta, recorded a formula for the area of an inscribed quadrilateral. This formula applies only to quadrilaterals that can be inscribed in circles (known as *cyclic quadrilaterals*).

Theorem 112 $A_{cyclic\ quad} = \sqrt{(s-a)(s-b)(s-c)(s-d)}$, *where a, b, c, and d are the sides of the quadrilateral and* $s = semiperimeter = \frac{a+b+c+d}{2}$. *(Brahmagupta's formula)*

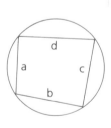

Part Two: Sample Problems

Problem 1   Find the area of a triangle with sides 3, 6, and 7.

Solution   First find the semiperimeter.

$$s = \frac{a+b+c}{2} = \frac{3+6+7}{2} = 8$$

Then use Hero's formula.

$$A_\triangle = \sqrt{s(s-a)(s-b)(s-c)}$$
$$= \sqrt{8(8-3)(8-6)(8-7)}$$
$$= \sqrt{8(5)(2)(1)} = \sqrt{16(5)} = 4\sqrt{5}$$

Problem 2   *Find the area of the inscribed quadrilateral with sides 2, 7, 6, and 9.*

Solution   First find the semiperimeter.

$$s = \frac{a + b + c + d}{2} = \frac{2 + 7 + 6 + 9}{2} = 12$$

Then use Brahmagupta's formula.

$$\begin{aligned} A_{\text{cyclic quad}} &= \sqrt{(s - a)(s - b)(s - c)(s - d)} \\ &= \sqrt{(12 - 2)(12 - 7)(12 - 6)(12 - 9)} \\ &= \sqrt{10(5)(6)(3)} = \sqrt{900} = 30 \end{aligned}$$

Part Three: Problem Sets

Problem Set A

1 Use Hero's formula to find the areas of triangles with sides of the following lengths.

a 3, 4, and 5   **c** 5, 6, and 9   **e** 8, 15, and 17
b 3, 3, and 4   **d** 3, 7 and 8   **f** 13, 14, and 15

2 Use Hero's formula to find the area of an equilateral triangle with a side 8 units long.

3 Use Brahmagupta's formula to find the areas of inscribed quadrilaterals with sides of the following lengths.

a 5, 7, 4, and 10   **c** 3, 5, 9, and 5
b 2, 4, 5, and 9   **d** 1, 5, 9, and 11

Problem Set B

4 a Use Hero's formula to find the area of a (2, 5, 7) triangle.

b Use Hero's formula to find the area of a (4, 6, 12) triangle.

c What explanation can you give for the results in parts **a** and **b?**

5 Find the area of the figure to the nearest hundredth.

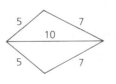

6 Find the area of each triangle.

a 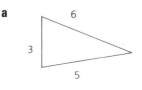   **b**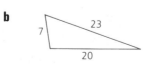

Problem Set B, *continued*

7 Verify that the area of the quadrilateral shown is $12\sqrt{21} + 54$.

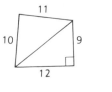

8 Find the measures of the three altitudes of the triangle at the right. (Hint: Use Hero's formula to find the area, and then use $A = \frac{1}{2}bh$ to find each altitude.)

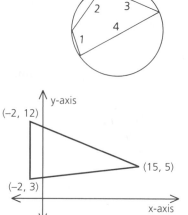

9 Find the area of the quadrilateral shown.

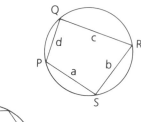

10 Find the area of the triangle.

Problem Set C

11 a As $\overline{PQ}$ gets smaller and smaller, what happens to quadrilateral PQRS?

  b What happens to Brahmagupta's formula if P and Q become the same point?

12 Find the area of the pentagon to the nearest tenth.

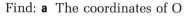

13 Given: $\odot$O, with C = (3, 8) and D = (9, 8), $m\overset{\frown}{CD} = 60$

Find: **a** The coordinates of O

  b The circumference of $\odot$O to the nearest tenth

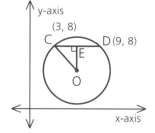

CHAPTER SUMMARY

CONCEPTS AND PROCEDURES

After studying this chapter, you should be able to
- Understand the concept of area (11.1)
- Find the areas of rectangles and squares (11.1)
- Use the basic properties of area (11.1)
- Find the areas of parallelograms (11.2)
- Find the areas of triangles (11.2)
- Find the areas of trapezoids (11.3)
- Use the measure of a trapezoid's median to find its area (11.3)
- Find the areas of kites (11.4)
- Find the areas of equilateral triangles (11.5)
- Find the areas of other regular polygons (11.5)
- Find the areas of circles (11.6)
- Find the areas of sectors (11.6)
- Find the areas of segments (11.6)
- Find ratios of areas by calculating and comparing the areas (11.7)
- Find ratios of areas by applying properties of similar figures (11.7)
- Find the areas of figures by using Hero's formula and Brahmagupta's formula (11.8)

VOCABULARY

annulus (11.6)

apothem (11.5)

area (11.1)

Brahmagupta's formula (11.8)

cyclic quadrilateral (11.8)

Hero's formula (11.8)

linear unit (11.1)

median (11.3)

radius (11.5)

sector (11.6)

segment (11.6)

square unit (11.1)

REVIEW PROBLEMS

Problem Set A

1 Find the areas of the following polygons.

    a A rectangle with base 12 and height 7

    b A triangle with base 12 and height 7

    c A parallelogram with base 15 and height 5

    d A trapezoid with bases 3 and 10 and height 8

    e A kite with diagonals 5 and 8

    f A trapezoid with median 4 and height 2

2 Find the areas of rhombuses with the following dimensions.

    a A base of 9 and a height of 7

    b Diagonals of 6 and 11

3 Find the area of each shaded region.

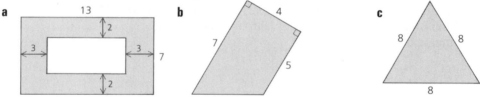

4 A rectangular driveway is to be paved. The driveway is 20 m long and 4 m wide. The cost will be $15 per square meter. What is the total cost of paving the driveway.

5 Find the area of a parallelogram with sides 12 and 8 and included angle 60°.

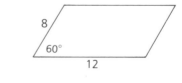

6 Find the area of an isosceles trapezoid with sides 8, 20, 40, and 20.

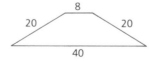

7 Find the area of the triangle shown at the right.

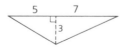

8 John has two sticks, 90 cm and 50 cm long, to use in making a paper kite. What will the cost of the kite be if the sticks and glue are gifts and the paper costs 3 cents per square decimeter?

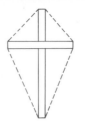

9 The apothem of a regular polygon is 7, and the polygon's perimeter is 56. Find the polygon's area.

10 Find the area of a circle if its circumference is 16π.

11 Find the area of a square whose semiperimeter is 18 m.

12 Find, to the nearest tenth, the area of a semicircle whose diameter is 14 mm.

13 Find the area of each shaded region.

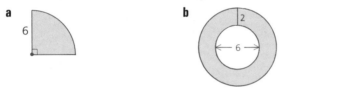

14 Find the area of each sector.

a

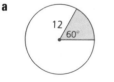

b

c

15 Find the ratio of the areas of each pair of figures.

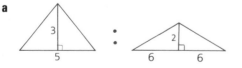

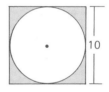

16 Find the coordinates of B so that $\triangle ABD$ will have the same area as $\triangle ACD$.

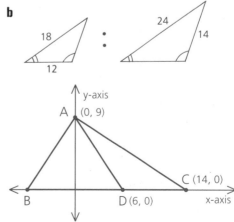

Problem Set B

17 Find the area of a triangle with sides 41, 41, and 18.

18 Find the area of a parallelogram with sides 6 and 7 and included angle 45°.

19 Find the area of a rhombus whose perimeter is 52 and longer diagonal is 24.

20 Find the area of an equilateral triangle with perimeter 21.

21 Find the area and the perimeter of an isosceles trapezoid with lower base 18, upper base 4, and upper base angle 120°.

22 Find, to the nearest tenth,
   a The circumference of the circle
   b The area of the circle

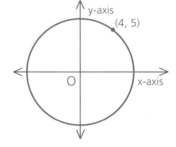

23 a The diagonal of a square is 26. Find the square's area.
   b Find the diagonal of a square whose area is 18.

24 Find the area of a regular hexagon whose span is 36.

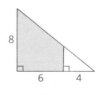

25 Find the area of the shaded region in each figure.

   a   **b**   **c**

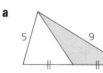

26 For each figure, find the ratio of the area of the whole figure to that of the shaded region.

   a   **b**   **c**

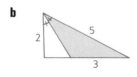   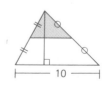

27 Find the area of each shaded segment.

a

6

b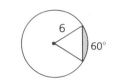

6

60°

28 For each figure, find the ratio of the area of region I to that of region II.

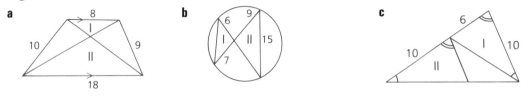

a

8

I

10

II

9

18

b

6   9

I   II   15

7

c

6

10

II

I   10

29 Which has a greater area, a circle with a circumference of 100 or a square with a perimeter of 100?

30 BRAT is a trapezoid, with M the midpoint of one of the legs. Show that the area of △CAT is equal to the area of BRAT.

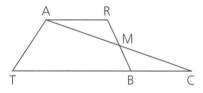

A   R

M

T   B   C

31 TRAP is an isosceles trapezoid.
  a Find the coordinates of R.
  b Find the area of TRAP.

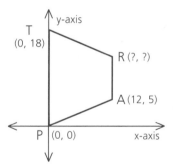

y-axis

T (0, 18)

R (?, ?)

A (12, 5)

P (0, 0)   x-axis

Problem Set C

32 In each figure, find the ratio of the area of region I to that of region II.

a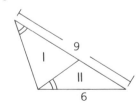

9

I

II

6

b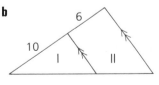

6

10

I   II

33 Given an isosceles trapezoid with a smaller base of 2, a perimeter of 70, and acute base angles of 60°, find the trapezoid's area.

34 The legs of one isosceles triangle are congruent to those of another isosceles triangle, and the triangles' vertex angles are supplementary. Prove that the triangles' areas are equal. (Write a paragraph proof.)

35 Five circles are tangent as shown. If each small circle has a radius of 3, find the shaded area.

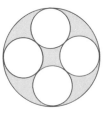

36 Find the shaded areas.

a

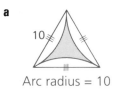

10

Arc radius = 10

b

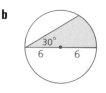

30°

6   6

37 Find the area of a trapezoid whose diagonals are each 30 and whose height is 18.

38 Given: AB:BC = 1:1 and FE:ED = 1:5

  a Find the ratio of the area of region I to the area of □ACDF.

  b What is the probability that a gnat landing in □ACDF would land in region II?

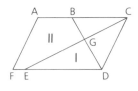

A   B   C

‖

G

I

F E   D

39 $\overline{AT}$ is tangent to ⊙P at T, and AB = 12. Find the shaded area.

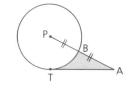

P

B

T

A

40 Archibold left his horse, Gremilda, tied to the corner of a barn by a 12-m rope. The barn measures 8 m by 10 m. Find the total grazing area for Gremilda.

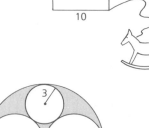

8

10

41 Find the area of the shaded region.

3

42 All 12 sides of the cross are congruent, each having a length of 4. All the angles are right angles. Find the area of the shaded region.

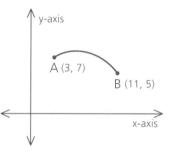

43 Find the area of a trapezoid with sides 12, 17, 40, and 25 if the bases are the sides measuring 12 and 40.

44 Buster Bee lives on a honeycomb. What percentage of the honeycomb is made of wax?

45 If m$\widehat{AB}$ = 90, find, to the nearest tenth, the area of the circle containing $\widehat{AB}$.

12 | SURFACE AREA AND VOLUME

The abstract concepts of surface area and volume become tangible in this solidscape by Pete Turner.

SURFACE AREAS OF PRISMS

Objective

After studying this section, you will be able to
- Find the surface areas of prisms

Part One: Introduction

Solids with flat faces are called ***polyhedra*** (meaning "many faces"). The faces are polygons, and the lines where they intersect are called edges.

One familiar type of polyhedron is the ***prism.*** Here are three examples:

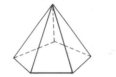 

Triangle   Rectangle   Pentagon

Triangular Prism   **Rectangular Prism**   **Pentagonal Prism**

Every prism has two congruent parallel faces (shaded in the examples) and a set of parallel edges that connect corresponding vertices of the two parallel faces.

The two parallel and congruent faces are called ***bases.*** The parallel edges joining the vertices of the bases are called ***lateral edges.*** The faces of the prism that are not bases are called ***lateral faces.*** The lateral faces of all prisms are parallelograms. Therefore, we name prisms by their bases—a prism with hexagonal bases, for example, is called a hexagonal prism.

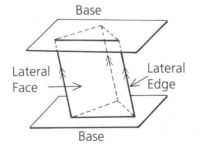

Base

Lateral Face →

Lateral Edge

Base

Definition   The *lateral surface area* of a prism is the sum of the areas of the lateral faces.

Definition   The *total surface area* of a prism is the sum of the prism's lateral area and the areas of the two bases.

If the lateral edges are perpendicular to the bases, then the lateral faces will be rectangles. (Why?) In such a case, we put the word *right* in front of the name of the prism. In this book, the word *box* will often be used to refer to a right prism.

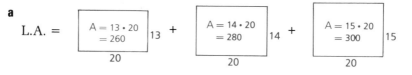

Right Triangular Prism   Right Pentagonal Prism

Note   The base of a right triangular prism is not necessarily a right triangle.

Part Two: Sample Problem

Problem   Given: The right triangular prism
                shown

    Find: **a** Its lateral area (L.A.)

          b Its total area (T.A.)

Solution   The right triangular prism can be divided into two triangles (the parallel bases) and three rectangles (the lateral faces).

a

L.A. =
$$\boxed{\begin{array}{c} A = 13 \cdot 20 \\ = 260 \end{array}}\;13 \quad + \quad \boxed{\begin{array}{c} A = 14 \cdot 20 \\ = 280 \end{array}}\;14 \quad + \quad \boxed{\begin{array}{c} A = 15 \cdot 20 \\ = 300 \end{array}}\;15$$
            20   20   20

Thus, L.A. = 260 + 280 + 300 = 840.

b T.A. = L.A. + 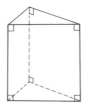   +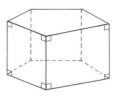

Since the area of each base is $\frac{1}{2}(12)(14)$, or 84,

T.A. = 840 + 84 + 84 = 1008.

Part Three: Problem Sets

Problem Set A

1 Find the total surface area of a right rectangular prism with the given dimensions.

   a $\ell = 15$ cm, $w = 5$ cm, $h = 10$ cm

   b $\ell = 12$ mm, $w = 7$ mm, $h = 3$ mm

   c $\ell = 18$ in., $w = 9$ in., $h = 9$ in.

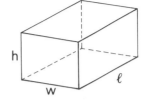

2 Find the lateral area of a right triangular prism with the given dimensions.

   a $\ell = 10$, $a = 3$, $b = 5$, $c = 7$

   b $\ell = 14$, $a = 2$, $b = 3$, $c = 4$

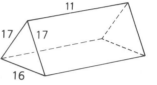

3 A right triangular prism has bases that are isosceles triangles. What is

   a The prism's lateral area?

   b The area of one base?

   c The prism's total area?

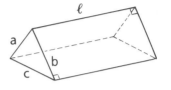

4 Find the total surface area of a right equilateral triangular prism with the given dimensions.

   a $s = 6$, $\ell = 5$

   b $s = 12$, $\ell = 10$

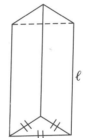

5 A cube is a rectangular prism in which each face is a square. What is the total surface area of a cube in which each edge has a measure of

   a 5?   **b** 7?

Problem Set B

6 Find the total area of the pieces of cardboard needed to construct each open box shown.

   a

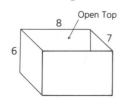

   b

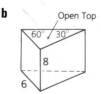

Problem Set B, *continued*

7 Find the lateral area and the total area of each prism.

a Right Square Prism

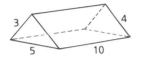

c Right Isosceles Triangular Prism

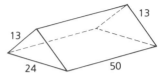

b Right Triangular Prism

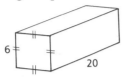

d Regular Hexagonal Prism

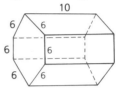

8 Find the total area of the right prism shown.

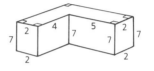

Problem Set C

9 Find the lateral area and the total area of the right prism shown.

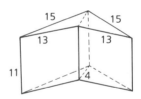

10 The perimeter of the scalene base of a pentagonal right prism is 17, and a lateral edge of the prism measures 10. Find the prism's lateral area.

11 A 6-inch cube is painted on the outside and cut into 27 smaller cubes.

a How many of the small cubes have six faces painted? Five faces painted? Four faces painted? Three faces painted? Two faces painted? One face painted? No face painted?

b If one of the small cubes is selected at random, what is the probability that it has at least two painted faces?

c What is the total area of the unpainted surfaces?

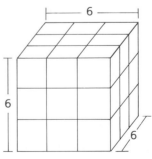

12.2 SURFACE AREAS OF PYRAMIDS

Objective

After studying this section, you will be able to
- Find the surface areas of pyramids

Part One: Introduction

 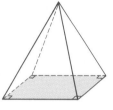 

Triangular Pyramid   **Rectangular Pyramid**   **Pentagonal Pyramid**

A ***pyramid*** has only one base. Its lateral edges are not parallel but meet at a single point called the vertex. The base may be any type of polygon, but the lateral faces will always be triangles. The diagrams above show three types of pyramids. Notice that each pyramid is named by its base.

A ***regular pyramid*** has a regular polygon as its base and also has congruent lateral edges. Thus, the lateral faces of a regular pyramid are congruent isosceles triangles.

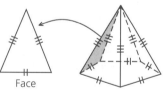

Face

Recall from Section 9.8 that the altitude of a regular pyramid is a perpendicular segment from the vertex to the base. (The foot of the altitude is the center of the base.) Also recall that a regular pyramid's slant height is the height of a lateral face.

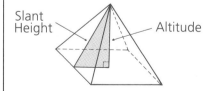   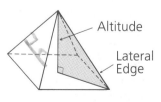

Slant Height — Altitude

Altitude

Lateral Edge

The altitude and a slant height determine a right triangle.

The altitude and a lateral edge determine a right triangle.

Part Two: Sample Problems

Problem 1   Given: *The regular pyramid shown at the right*

Find: **a** *Its lateral area (L.A.)*

      b *Its total area (T.A.)*

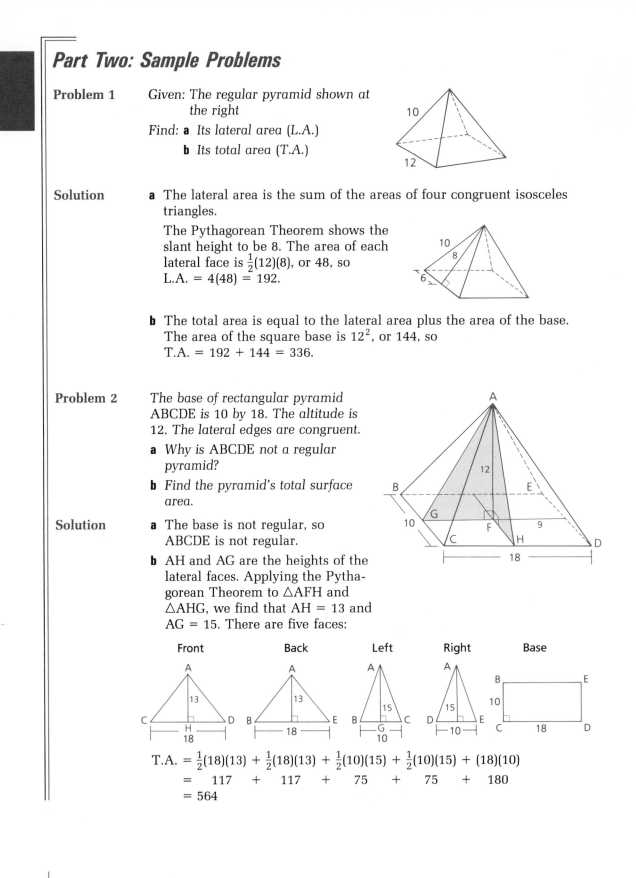

Solution   **a** The lateral area is the sum of the areas of four congruent isosceles triangles.

The Pythagorean Theorem shows the slant height to be 8. The area of each lateral face is $\frac{1}{2}(12)(8)$, or 48, so L.A. = 4(48) = 192.

b The total area is equal to the lateral area plus the area of the base. The area of the square base is 12^2, or 144, so T.A. = 192 + 144 = 336.

Problem 2   *The base of rectangular pyramid ABCDE is 10 by 18. The altitude is 12. The lateral edges are congruent.*

a *Why is ABCDE not a regular pyramid?*

b *Find the pyramid's total surface area.*

Solution   **a** The base is not regular, so ABCDE is not regular.

b AH and AG are the heights of the lateral faces. Applying the Pythagorean Theorem to △AFH and △AHG, we find that AH = 13 and AG = 15. There are five faces:

Front   Back   Left   Right   Base

T.A. = $\frac{1}{2}(18)(13) + \frac{1}{2}(18)(13) + \frac{1}{2}(10)(15) + \frac{1}{2}(10)(15) + (18)(10)$

    =   117   +   117   +   75   +   75   +   180

    = 564

Part Three: Problem Sets

Problem Set A

1 The pyramid shown is regular and has a square base.

   a Find the area of each lateral face.

   b Find the pyramid's lateral area.

   c Find the pyramid's total area.

2 The pyramid shown is regular and has a triangular base. What is

   a The area of each lateral face?

   b The area of the base?

   c The total area?

3 The pyramid shown has a rectangular base, and its lateral edges are congruent.

   a Why is this pyramid not regular?

   b What is its lateral area?

   c What is its total area?

4 The diagram shows a solid that is a combination of a prism and a regular pyramid.

   a Is ABCD a face of the solid?

   b How many faces does this solid have?

   c Find the total area.

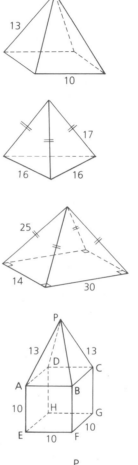

5 PRXYZ is a regular pyramid. The midpoints of its lateral edges are joined to form a square, ABCD. PR = 10 and RX = 12.

   a Find the lateral area of PRXYZ.

   b Find the lateral area of pyramid PABCD.

   c What is the area of square ABCD?

   d What is the area of square RXYZ?

   e Find the ratio of the area of ABCD to the area of RXYZ.

   f What is the area of trapezoid ABXR?

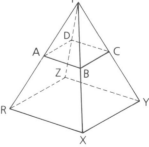

Problem Set B

6 A regular pyramid has a slant height of 8. The area of its square base is 25. Find its total area.

7 A regular pyramid has a slant height of 12 and a lateral edge of 15. What is

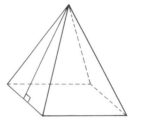

a The perimeter of the base?

b The pyramid's lateral area?

c The area of the base?

d The pyramid's total area?

8 PABCD is a regular square pyramid.

a If each side of the base has a length of 14 and the altitude (PQ) is 24, find the pyramid's lateral area and total area.

b If each slant height is 17 and the altitude is 15, find the pyramid's lateral area and total area.

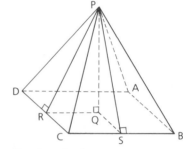

9 Suppose that the pyramid in problem 8 were not regular but had a rectangular base and congruent lateral edges.

a Given that PQ = 8, CD = 12, and BC = 30, find PR (the slant height of face PCD), PS (the slant height of face PBC), and the lateral area and the total area of the pyramid.

b If each lateral edge were 25 and the base were 24 by 30, what would the altitude (PQ) of the pyramid be?

Problem Set C

10 Each lateral edge of a regular square pyramid is 3, and the height of the pyramid is 1. What is

a The measure of a diagonal of the base?

b The pyramid's slant height?

c The area of the base?

d The pyramid's lateral area?

11 A regular *tetrahedron* ("four faces") is a pyramid with four equilateral triangular faces. If a regular tetrahedron has an edge of 6, what is

a Its total surface area?

b Its height?

12 A regular *octahedron* is a solid with eight faces, each of which is an equilateral triangle. If each edge of the regular octahedron shown is 6 mm long, what is

a The solid's total surface area?

b The distance from C to E?

c The distance from A to B?

d The shape of quadrilateral ACBE?

13 A regular *hexahedron* is a solid that does not have triangular faces. What is the common name for a regular hexahedron?

PACKAGING IDEAS
Jolene Randby engineers design

Each year American workers produce more than $1 trillion worth of manufactured products. Nearly all must be packaged in some kind of box, carton, bag, or can. Besides basic size considerations, economic, environmental, health, and safety factors also affect the design of a package. The task of harmonizing all these factors falls to packaging engineers, employed by all major manufacturers.

"My job is to write the specifications and packaging standards and to design the packages for all of the industrial tapes that we produce," explains Jolene Randby, a packaging engineer with the 3M Corporation in St. Paul, Minnesota. "Our tapes are manufactured in rolls varying from 60 yards to 1000 yards in length. When a new container is needed, I use basic geometric formulas to find the roll dimensions and then calculate the size of the primary container and the shipping container." Formulas for volume and surface area of rectangular prisms and cylinders are commonly used by packaging

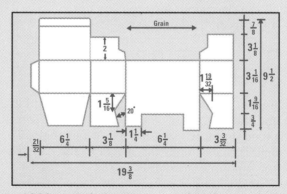

engineers. Randby also calculates the size of the pallet, the small platform on which shipping containers are stacked for storage and transportation.

Jolene Randby attended high school in her hometown of St. Paul. At the University of Wisconsin at Stout, where she earned her bachelor's degree, she majored in industrial technology, with a concentration in packaging engineering.

High on the list of benefits of her job is the necessary travel. "We have twelve converting plants where our packages are assembled," she explains. "I visit them all to oversee production." She also works closely with the marketing and purchasing departments at 3M.

Tape measuring 2 in. in width is manufactured in 250-foot rolls, each measuring $3\frac{3}{4}$ in. in diameter. A shipping container contains four stacks of tape arranged in a square array, with six rolls in each stack. How many shipping containers can fit in one layer on a pallet measuring 42 in. by 48 in.? The walls of each container are $\frac{1}{4}$ in. thick.

SURFACE AREAS OF CIRCULAR SOLIDS

Objective

After studying this section, you will be able to
- Find the surface areas of circular solids

Part One: Introduction

Consider the following three solids that are based on the circle.

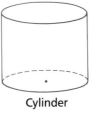

Cylinder

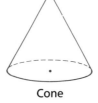

Cone

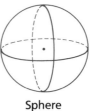

Sphere

A *cylinder* resembles a prism in having two congruent parallel bases. The bases of a cylinder, however, are circles. In this text, *cylinder* will mean a right circular cylinder—that is, one in which the line containing the centers of the bases is perpendicular to each base.

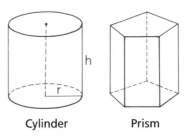

Cylinder   Prism

The lateral area of a cylinder can be visualized by thinking of a cylinder as a can, and the lateral area as the label on the can. If we cut the label and spread it out, we see that it is a rectangle. The height of the rectangle is the same as the height of the can. The base of the rectangle is the circumference of the can.

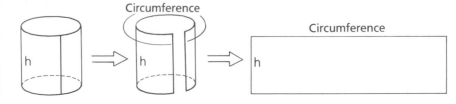

Theorem 113	***The lateral area of a cylinder is equal to the product of the height and the circumference of the base.***
	$$L.A._{cyl} = Ch = 2\pi rh$$
	where C is the circumference of the base, h is the height of the cylinder, and r is the radius of the base.

| **Definition** | The total area of a cylinder is the sum of the cylinder's lateral area and the areas of the two bases. |
| | $$T.A._{cyl} = L.A. + 2A_{base}$$ |

A *cone* resembles a pyramid, but its base is a circle. In a pyramid the slant height and the lateral edge are different; in a cone they are the same.

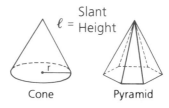

Cone   Pyramid

In this book, the word *cone* will mean a right circular cone—one in which the altitude passes through the center of the circular base.

Theorem 114	***The lateral area of a cone is equal to one-half the product of the slant height and the circumference of the base.***
	$$L.A._{cone} = \tfrac{1}{2}C\ell = \pi r\ell$$
	where C is the circumference of the base, ℓ is the slant height, and r is the radius of the base.

| **Definition** | The total area of a cone is the sum of the lateral area and the area of the base. |
| | $$T.A._{cone} = L.A. + A_{base}$$ |

A *sphere* is a special figure with a special surface-area formula. (A sphere has no lateral edges and no lateral area.) The proof of the formula requires the concept of limits and will not be given here.

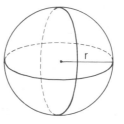

| **Postulate** | ***$T.A._{sphere} = 4\pi r^2$*** |
| | ***where r is the sphere's radius.*** |

Part Two: Sample Problem

Problem   *Find the total area of each figure.*

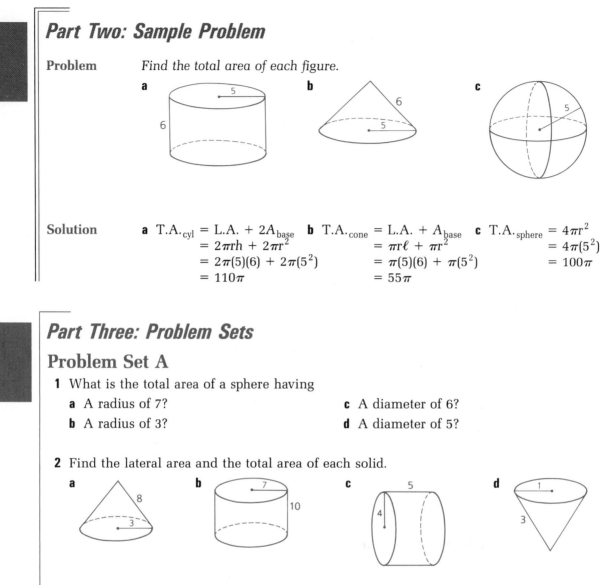

a   **b**   **c**

Solution

$$\text{a } \text{T.A.}_{\text{cyl}} = \text{L.A.} + 2A_{\text{base}} \quad \text{b } \text{T.A.}_{\text{cone}} = \text{L.A.} + A_{\text{base}} \quad \text{c } \text{T.A.}_{\text{sphere}} = 4\pi r^2$$
$$= 2\pi rh + 2\pi r^2 \qquad\qquad\quad = \pi r\ell + \pi r^2 \qquad\qquad = 4\pi(5^2)$$
$$= 2\pi(5)(6) + 2\pi(5^2) \qquad\quad = \pi(5)(6) + \pi(5^2) \qquad = 100\pi$$
$$= 110\pi \qquad\qquad\qquad\qquad = 55\pi$$

Part Three: Problem Sets

Problem Set A

1 What is the total area of a sphere having

   a A radius of 7?   **c** A diameter of 6?

   b A radius of 3?   **d** A diameter of 5?

2 Find the lateral area and the total area of each solid.

   a   **b**   **c**   **d**

3 Find the radius of a sphere whose surface area is 144π.

4 Find the total area of each solid. (Hint: Be sure that you include only outside surfaces and that you do not miss any.)

   a

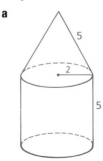

   b

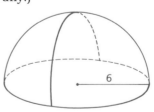

This is a *hemisphere* ("half sphere"). The T.A. includes the area of the circular base.

5 ABCD is a parallelogram, with A = (3, 6), B = (13, 6), C = (7, −2), and D = (−3, −2).

   a Find the slopes of the diagonals, $\overline{AC}$ and $\overline{BD}$.

   b Use your answers to part **a** to identify ⟁ABCD by its most specific name.

Problem Set B

6 Find the total (including the rectangular face) surface area of a half cylinder with a radius of 5 and a height of 2.

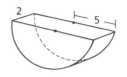

7 Find the total area of each solid.

  a 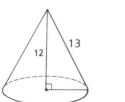   **b**   **c**

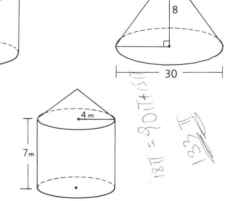

8 The total height of the tower shown is 10 m. If one liter of paint will cover an area of 10 sq m, how many 1-L cans of paint are needed to paint the entire tower? (Hint: First find the total area to be painted, using 3.14 for π.)

9 What size label (length and width) will just fit on a can 8 cm in diameter and 14 cm high?

10 Find the total area of the solid.

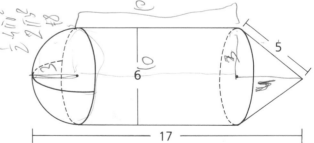

11 KITE is a kite.

   a Find the area of KITE.

   b Find the area of the rectangle formed when consecutive midpoints of the sides of KITE are connected.

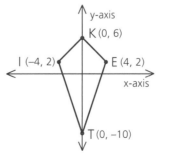

Problem Set C

12 Find the total surface area of the solid shown, including the surface inside the hole.

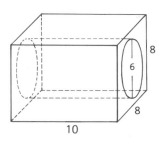

13 The solid at the right is called a *frustum* of a cone. Find its total area if the radii of the top and bottom bases are 4 and 8 respectively, and the slant height is 5.

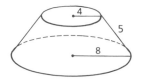

14 A *surface of rotation* is generated by revolving a shape about a fixed line, called the *axis of rotation*. For example, revolving a half circle about the line containing its endpoints produces a sphere.

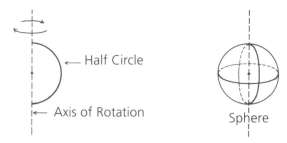

Identify the surface of rotation generated in each diagram below and compute the total area of each of these surfaces.

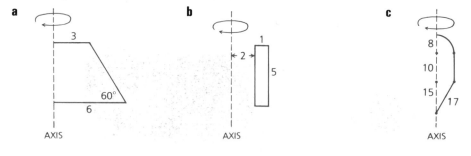

12.4 VOLUMES OF PRISMS AND CYLINDERS

Objectives

After studying this section, you will be able to

- Find the volumes of right rectangular prisms
- Find the volumes of other prisms
- Find the volumes of cylinders
- Use the area of a prism's or a cylinder's cross section to find the solid's volume

Part One: Introduction

Volume of a Right Rectangular Prism

The measure of the space enclosed by a solid is called the solid's **volume**. In a way, volume is to solids what area is to plane figures.

Definition	The **volume** of a solid is the number of cubic units of space contained by the solid.

A cubic unit is the volume of a cube with edges one unit long. A cube is a right rectangular prism with congruent edges, so all its faces are squares. In Section 12.1 we used the word *box* for a right prism. Thus, a right rectangular prism can also be called a rectangular box.

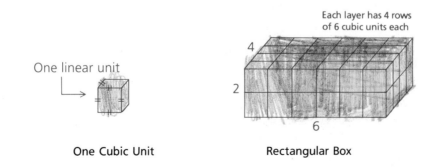

Each layer has 4 rows of 6 cubic units each

One linear unit

One Cubic Unit   Rectangular Box

The rectangular box above contains 48 cubic units. The formula that follows is not only a way of counting cubic units rapidly but also works with fractional dimensions.

Postulate *The volume of a right rectangular prism is equal to the product of its length, its width, and its height.*

$$V_{rect.\ box} = \ell wh$$

where ℓ is the length, w is the width, and h is the height.

Another way to think of the volume of a rectangular prism is to imagine the prism to be a stack of congruent rectangular sheets of paper. The area of each sheet is $\ell \cdot w$, and the height of the stack is h. Since the base of the prism is one of the congruent sheets, there is a second formula for the volume of a rectangular box.

$$V = \ell wh$$
$$= (\ell w)h$$
$$= (area\ of\ sheet) \cdot h$$

Theorem 115 *The volume of a right rectangular prism is equal to the product of the height and the area of the base.*

$$V_{rect.\ box} = \mathcal{B}h$$

where $\mathcal{B}$ is the area of the base and h is the height.

Volumes of Other Prisms

The formula in Theorem 115 can be used to compute the volume of any prism, since any prism can be viewed as a stack of sheets the same shape and size as the base.

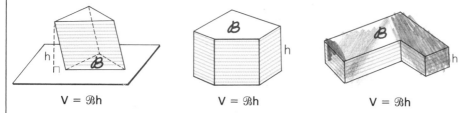

$$V = \mathcal{B}h \qquad V = \mathcal{B}h \qquad V = \mathcal{B}h$$

Theorem 116 *The volume of any prism is equal to the product of the height and the area of the base.*

$$V_{prism} = \mathcal{B}h$$

where $\mathcal{B}$ is the area of the base and h is the height.

Notice that the height of a right prism is equivalent to the measure of a lateral edge.

Volume of a Cylinder

The stacking property applies to a cylinder as well as to a prism, so the formula for a prism's volume can also be used to find a cylinder's. Furthermore, since the base of a cylinder is a circle, there is a second, more popular formula.

Theorem 117   *The volume of a cylinder is equal to the product of the height and the area of the base.*

$$V_{cyl} = \mathcal{B}h = \pi r^2 h$$

where $\mathcal{B}$ is the area of the base, h is the height, and r is the radius of the base.

Cross Section of a Prism or a Cylinder

When we visualize a prism or a cylinder as a stack of sheets, all the sheets are congruent, so the area of any one of them can be substituted for $\mathcal{B}$. Each of the sheets between the bases is an example of a ***cross section***.

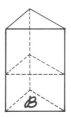

Definition   A ***cross section*** is the intersection of a solid with a plane.

In this book, unless otherwise noted, all references to cross sections will be to cross sections *parallel to the base*. We can now combine Theorems 116 and 117, using the symbol $\mathcal{C}$ to represent the area of a cross section parallel to the base.

Theorem 118   *The volume of a prism or a cylinder is equal to the product of the figure's cross-sectional area and its height.*

$$V_{prism\ or\ cyl} = \mathcal{C}h$$

where $\mathcal{C}$ is the area of a cross section and h is the height.

Part Two: Sample Problems

Problem 1 Find the volume of the rectangular prism.

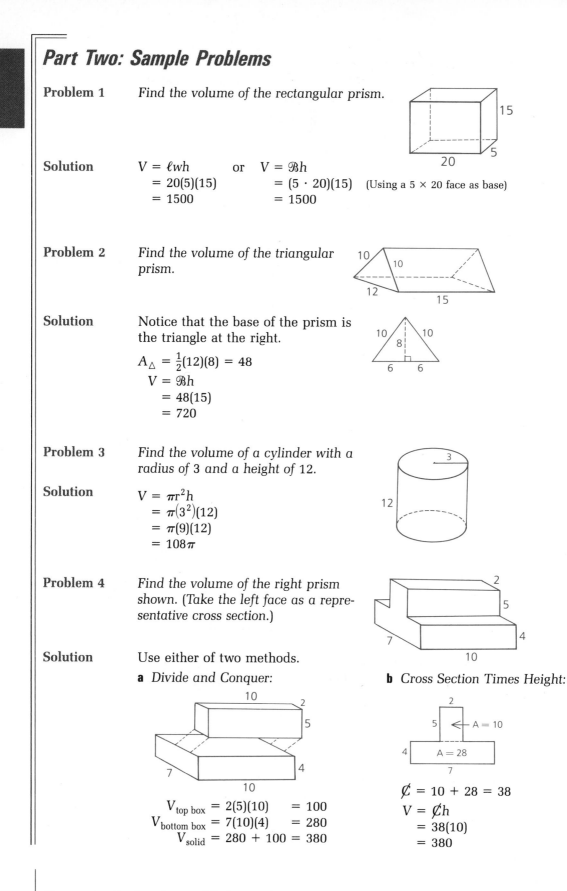

Solution

$$V = \ell w h \qquad \text{or} \quad V = \mathcal{B}h$$
$$ = 20(5)(15) \qquad = (5 \cdot 20)(15) \quad \text{(Using a } 5 \times 20 \text{ face as base)}$$
$$ = 1500 \qquad = 1500$$

Problem 2 Find the volume of the triangular prism.

Solution Notice that the base of the prism is the triangle at the right.

$$A_\triangle = \tfrac{1}{2}(12)(8) = 48$$
$$V = \mathcal{B}h$$
$$ = 48(15)$$
$$ = 720$$

Problem 3 Find the volume of a cylinder with a radius of 3 and a height of 12.

Solution

$$V = \pi r^2 h$$
$$ = \pi(3^2)(12)$$
$$ = \pi(9)(12)$$
$$ = 108\pi$$

Problem 4 Find the volume of the right prism shown. (Take the left face as a representative cross section.)

Solution Use either of two methods.

a Divide and Conquer:

$$V_{\text{top box}} = 2(5)(10) \quad = 100$$
$$V_{\text{bottom box}} = 7(10)(4) \quad = 280$$
$$V_{\text{solid}} = 280 + 100 = 380$$

b Cross Section Times Height:

$$A = 10$$
$$A = 28$$
$$\mathcal{C} = 10 + 28 = 38$$
$$V = \mathcal{C}h$$
$$ = 38(10)$$
$$ = 380$$

Problem 5   A box *(rectangular prism) is sitting in a corner of a room as shown.*

    a *Find the volume of the prism.*

    b *If the coordinates of point A in a three-dimensional coordinate system are (4, 5, 6), what are the coordinates of B?*

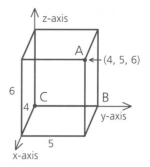

Solution   **a** $V = \mathcal{B}h$
        $= (4 \cdot 5)6$
        $= 120$

    b Point C = (0, 0, 0) is the corner. To get from C to B, you would travel 0 units in the x direction, 5 units in the y direction, and 0 units in the z direction. So the coordinates of B are (0, 5, 0).

Part Three: Problem Sets

Problem Set A

1 Find the volume of each solid.

    a

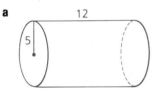

    b

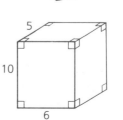

2 Find the volume of cement needed to form the concrete pedestal shown. (Leave your answer in π form.)

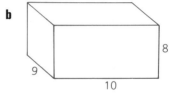

3 The area of the shaded face of the right pentagonal prism is 51. Find the prism's volume.

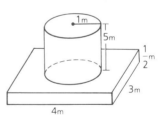

4 Find the volume and the total surface area of the rectangular box shown.

Problem Set A, *continued*

5 a Find the volume of a cube with an edge of 7.
b Find the volume of a cube with an edge of *e*.
c Find the edge of a cube with a volume of 125.

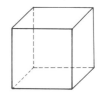

6 Find the length of a lateral edge of a right prism with a volume of 286 and a base area of 13.

Problem Set B

7 Traci's queen-size waterbed is 7 ft long, 5 ft wide, and 8 in. thick.

a Find the bed's volume to the nearest cubic foot.

b If 1 cu ft of water weighs 62.4 lb, what is the weight of the water in Traci's bed to the nearest pound?

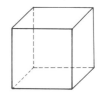

8 If point A's coordinates in the three-dimensional coordinate system are (2, 5, 8), what are the coordinates of B?

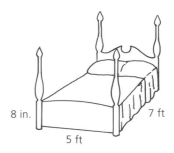

9 Find the volume and the total area of the prism.

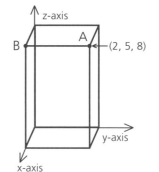

10 Find the volume and the total area of each right cylindrical solid shown.

a

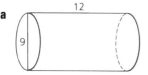

b

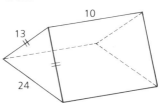

11 When Hilda computed the volume and the surface area of a cube, both answers had the same numerical value. Find the length of one side of the cube.

12 Find the volume and the surface area of the regular hexagonal right prism.

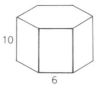

13 Find the volume of a cube in which a face diagonal is 10.

14 A rectangular cake pan has a base 10 cm by 12 cm and a height of 8 cm. If 810 cu cm of batter is poured into the pan, how far up the side will the batter come?

15 A rectangular container is to be formed by folding the cardboard along the dotted lines. Find the volume of this container.

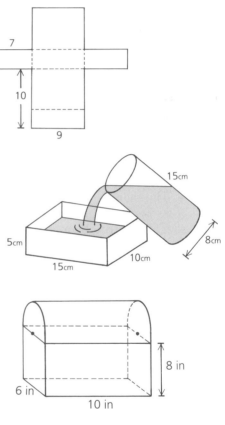

16 The cylindrical glass is full of water, which is poured into the rectangular pan. Will the pan overflow?

17 Jim's lunch box is in the shape of a half cylinder on a rectangular box. To the nearest whole unit, what is
   a The total volume it contains?
   b The total area of the sheet metal needed to manufacture it?

18 A cistern is to be built of cement. The walls and bottom will be 1 ft thick. The outer height will be 20 ft. The inner diameter will be 10 ft. To the nearest cubic foot, how much cement will be needed for the job?

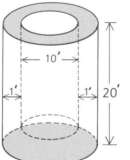

Problem Set C

19 A wedge of cheese is cut from a cylindrical block. Find the volume and the total surface area of this wedge.

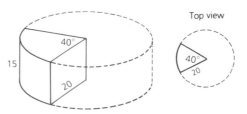

Top view

20 An ice-cube manufacturer makes ice cubes with holes in them. Each cube is 4 cm on a side and the hole is 2 cm in diameter.

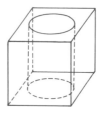

a To the nearest tenth, what is the volume of ice in each cube?

b To the nearest tenth, what will be the volume of the water left when ten cubes melt? (Water's volume decreases by 11% when it changes from a solid to a liquid.)

c To the nearest tenth, what is the total surface area (including the inside of the hole) of a single cube?

d The manufacturer claims that these cubes cool a drink twice as fast as regular cubes of the same size. Verify whether this claim is true by a comparison of surface areas. (Hint: The ratio of areas is equal to the ratio of cooling speeds.)

21 Find the volume of the solid at the right. (A representative cross section is shown.)

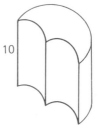

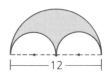

22 A cylinder is cut on a slant as shown. Find the solid's volume.

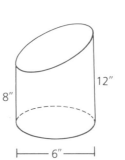

12.5 | VOLUMES OF PYRAMIDS AND CONES

Objectives

After studying this section, you will be able to
- Find the volumes of pyramids
- Find the volumes of cones
- Solve problems involving cross sections of pyramids and cones

Part One: Introduction

Volume of a Pyramid

The volume of a pyramid is related to the volume of a prism having the same base and height. At first glance, many people would guess that the volume of the pyramid is half that of the prism.

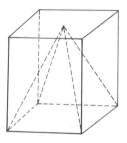

Such a guess would be wrong, though. The volume of a pyramid is actually *one third* of the volume of a prism with the same base and height.

Theorem 119 **The volume of a pyramid is equal to one third of the product of the height and the area of the base.**

$$V_{pyr} = \tfrac{1}{3}\mathscr{B}h$$

where $\mathscr{B}$ is the area of the base and h is the height.

The proof of this formula is complex and will not be shown here.

Volume of a Cone

Because a cone is a close relative of a pyramid, although its base is circular rather than polygonal, the formula for its volume is similar to the formula for a pyramid's volume.

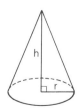

Theorem 120 *The volume of a cone is equal to one third of the product of the height and the area of the base.*

$$V_{cone} = \tfrac{1}{3}\mathscr{B}h = \tfrac{1}{3}\pi r^2 h$$

where $\mathscr{B}$ is the area of the base, h is the height, and r is the radius of the base.

Cross Section of a Pyramid or a Cone

Unlike a cross section of a prism or a cylinder, a cross section of a pyramid or a cone is not congruent to the figure's base. Observe that the cross section parallel to the base is *similar* to the base in each solid shown below.

Cross Section of a Cone

Cross Section of a Pyramid

The Similar-Figures Theorem (p. 544) suggests that in these solids the area of a cross section is related to the square of its distance from the vertex.

Theorem 121 *In a pyramid or a cone, the ratio of the area of a cross section to the area of the base equals the square of the ratio of the figures' respective distances from the vertex.*

$$\frac{\mathcal{C}}{\mathscr{B}} = \left(\frac{k}{h}\right)^2$$

where $\mathcal{C}$ is the area of the cross section, $\mathscr{B}$ is the area of the base, k is the distance from the vertex to the cross section, and h is the height of the pyramid or cone.

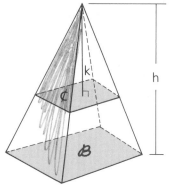

A proof of Theorem 121 is asked for in problem 15.

Part Two: Sample Problems

Problem 1 *If the height of a pyramid is 21 and the pyramid's base is an equilateral triangle with sides measuring 8, what is the pyramid's volume?*

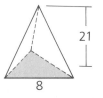

Solution $V_{pyr} = \tfrac{1}{3}\mathscr{B}h$

Since the base is an equilateral triangle, $\mathscr{B} = \tfrac{s^2}{4}\sqrt{3} = 16\sqrt{3}$.

So $V = \tfrac{1}{3}\left(16\sqrt{3}\right)(21) = 112\sqrt{3}$.

Problem 2   *Find the volume of a cone with a base radius of 6 and a slant height of 10.*

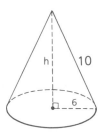

Solution   Using the right triangle shown, we find that the height of the cone is 8.

$$V_{cone} = \tfrac{1}{3}\pi r^2 h$$
$$= \tfrac{1}{3}\pi(6^2)(8) = 96\pi$$

Problem 3   *A pyramid has a base area of 24 sq cm and a height of 12 cm. A cross section is cut 3 cm from the base.*

a *Find the volume of the upper pyramid (the solid above the cross section).*

b *Find the volume of the **frustum** (the solid below the cross section).*

Solution   **a** Since the cross section is 3 cm from the base, its distance, k, from the peak is 9 cm.

$$\frac{\mathcal{C}}{\mathcal{B}} = \left(\frac{k}{h}\right)^2 \qquad\qquad V_{upper\ pyramid} = \tfrac{1}{3}\mathcal{C}k$$

$$\frac{\mathcal{C}}{24} = \left(\frac{9}{12}\right)^2 \qquad\qquad\qquad = \frac{1}{3}\cdot\frac{27}{2}\cdot 9$$

$$\mathcal{C} = \frac{27}{2} \qquad\qquad\qquad\qquad = 40.5 \text{ cu cm}$$

b To find the volume of the frustum, we subtract the volume of the upper pyramid from the volume of the whole pyramid.

$$V_{frustum} = V_{whole\ pyramid} - V_{upper\ pyramid}$$
$$= \tfrac{1}{3}(24)(12) - 40.5$$
$$= 96 - 40.5$$
$$= 55.5 \text{ cu cm}$$

Part Three: Problem Sets

Problem Set

1 Find the volume of a pyramid whose base is an equilateral triangle with sides measuring 14 and whose height is 30.

2 Find, to two decimal places, the volume of a cone with a slant height of 13 and a base radius of 5.

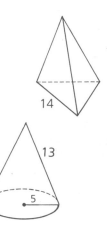

Problem Set A, *continued*

3 The pyramid shown has a square base and a height of 12.

a Find its volume.

b Find its total area.

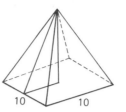

10   10

4 The volume of a pyramid is 42. If its base has an area of 14, what is the pyramid's height?

5 Given: The right circular cone shown

Find: **a** Its volume

    b Its lateral area

    c Its total area

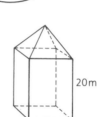

40   41

6 A tower has a total height of 24 m. The height of the wall is 20 m. The base is a rectangle with an area of 25 sq m. Find the total volume of the tower to the nearest cubic meter.

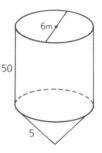

20m

7 A well has a cylindrical wall 50 m deep and a diameter of 6 m. The tapered bottom forms a cone with a slant height of 5 m. Find, to the nearest cubic foot, the volume of water the well could hold.

6m

50

5

Problem Set B

8 Find, to the nearest tenth, the volume of a cone with a 60° vertex angle and a slant height of 12.

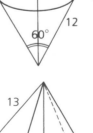

12

60°

9 A pyramid has a square base with a diagonal of 10. Each lateral edge measures 13. Find the volume of the pyramid.

13

10

10 PABCD is a regular square pyramid.

    a Find the coordinates of C.

    b Find the volume of the pyramid.

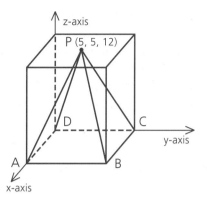

11 Find the volume remaining if the smaller cone is removed from the larger.

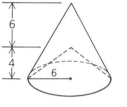

12 A rocket has the dimensions shown. If 60% of the space in the rocket is needed for fuel, what is the volume, to the nearest whole unit, of the portion of the rocket that is available for nonfuel items?

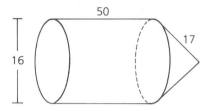

13 A gazebo (garden house) has a pentagonal base with an area of 60 sq m. The total height to the peak is 16 m. The height of the pyramidal roof is 6 m. Find the gazebo's total volume.

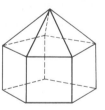

14 Use the diagram at the right to find

    a x

    b The radii of the circles

    c The volume of the smaller cone

    d The volume of the larger cone

    e The volume of the frustum

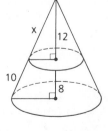

15 Set up and complete a proof of Theorem 121. (Hint: First prove that the ratio of corresponding segments of a cross section and a base equals the ratio of h to k.)

Problem Set B, *continued*

16 Find the volume of a cube whose total surface area is 150 sq in.

Problem Set C

17 A regular tetrahedron is shown. (Each of the four faces is an equilateral triangle.) Find the tetrahedron's total volume if each edge measures

   a 6   **b** s

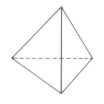

18 A regular octahedron (eight equilateral faces) has an edge of 6. Find the octahedron's volume.

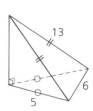

19 Find the volume of the pyramid shown.

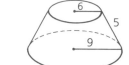

20 Find the volume of the frustum shown.

12.6 VOLUMES OF SPHERES

Objective

After studying this section, you will be able to
- Find the volumes of spheres

Part One: Introduction

The following theorem can be proved with the help of *Cavalieri's principle* (discussed in Problem Set D of this section), but we shall present it without proof.

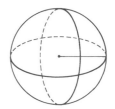

Theorem 122 **The volume of a sphere is equal to four thirds of the product of π and the cube of the radius.**

$$V_{sphere} = \tfrac{4}{3}\pi r^3$$

where r is the radius of the sphere.

Some of the problems in this section require you to find both the volumes and the surface areas of spheres. Recall from Section 12.3 that the total surface area of a sphere is equal to $4\pi r^2$.

Part Two: Sample Problem

Problem   *Find the volume of a hemisphere with a radius of 6.*

Solution   First we find the volume of a sphere with a radius of 6.

$$V_{sphere} = \tfrac{4}{3}\pi r^3$$
$$= \tfrac{4}{3}\pi(6)^3 = 288\pi$$

The hemisphere's volume is half that of the sphere. Thus,
$V_{hemisphere} = 144\pi$, or ≈ 452.39.

Part Three: Problem Sets

Problem Set A

1 Find the volume of a sphere with
  a A radius of 3   **b** A diameter of 18   **c** A radius of 5

2 Find the volume and the surface area of a sphere with a radius of 6.

3 Find the volume of the grain silo to the nearest cubic meter.

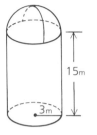

4 A plastic bowl is in the shape of a cylinder with a hemisphere cut out. The dimensions are shown.

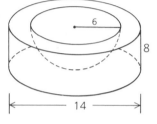

  a What is the volume of the cylinder?

  b What is the volume of the hemisphere?

  c What is the volume of plastic used to make the bowl?

5 What volume of gas, to the nearest cubic foot, is needed to inflate a spherical balloon to a diameter of 10 ft?

Problem Set B

6 A rubber ball is formed by a rubber shell filled with air. The shell's outer diameter is 48 mm, and its inner diameter is 42 mm. Find, to the nearest cubic centimeter, the volume of rubber used to make the ball.

7 Given: A cone and a hemisphere as marked

Find: **a** The total volume of the solid

  b The total surface area of the solid

8 A hemispherical dome has a height of 30 m.

  a Find, to the nearest cubic meter, the total volume enclosed.

  b Find, to the nearest square meter, the area of ground covered by the dome (the shaded area).

  c How much more paint is needed to paint the dome than to paint the floor?

  d Find, to the nearest meter, the radius of a dome that covers double the area of ground covered by this one.

9 A cold capsule is 11 mm long and 3 mm in diameter. Find, to the nearest cubic millimeter, the volume of medicine it contains.

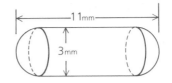

10 The radii of two spheres are in a ratio of 2:5.

    a Find the ratio of their volumes.

    b Find the ratio of their surface areas.

11 A minisubmarine has the dimensions shown.

    a What is the sub's total volume?

    b Knowing the sub's surface area is important in determining how much pressure it will withstand. What is the sub's total surface area?

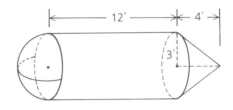

Problem Set C

12 An ice-cream cone is 9 cm deep and 4 cm across the top. A single scoop of ice cream, 4 cm in diameter, is placed on top. If the ice cream melts into the cone, will it overflow? (Assume that the ice cream's volume does not change as it melts.) Justify your answer.

13 The volume of a cube is 1000 cu m.

    a To the nearest cubic meter, what is the volume of the largest sphere that can be inscribed inside the cube?

    b To the nearest cubic meter, what is the volume of the smallest sphere that can be circumscribed about the cube?

14 Find the ratio of the volume of a sphere to the volume of the smallest right cylinder that can contain it.

15 In the diagram, ABGH is a rectangle and $\overline{AB} \cong \overline{BC} \cong \overline{CD}$. To the nearest whole number, what percentage of the area of ⊙O is the area of ABGH?

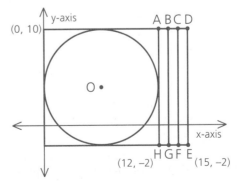

Problem Set C, *continued*

16 Compare the volumes of a hemisphere and a cone with congruent bases and equal heights.

Problem Set D

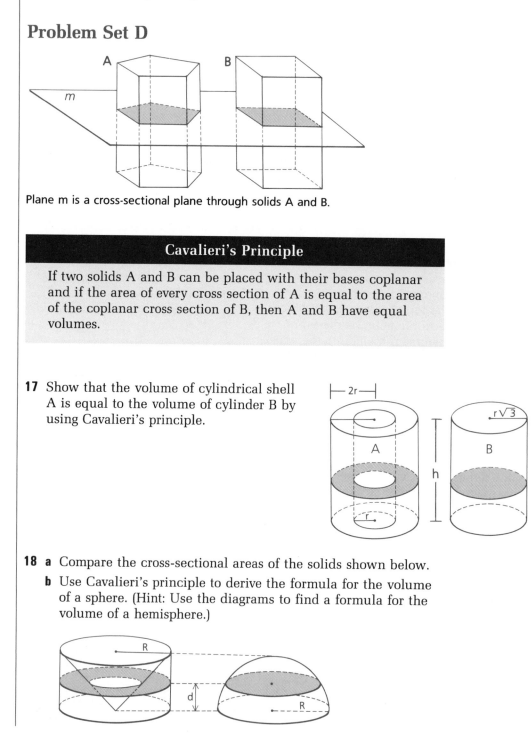

Plane m is a cross-sectional plane through solids A and B.

Cavalieri's Principle

If two solids A and B can be placed with their bases coplanar and if the area of every cross section of A is equal to the area of the coplanar cross section of B, then A and B have equal volumes.

17 Show that the volume of cylindrical shell A is equal to the volume of cylinder B by using Cavalieri's principle.

18 a Compare the cross-sectional areas of the solids shown below.

b Use Cavalieri's principle to derive the formula for the volume of a sphere. (Hint: Use the diagrams to find a formula for the volume of a hemisphere.)

CHAPTER SUMMARY

CONCEPTS AND PROCEDURES

After studying this chapter, you should be able to
- Find the surface areas of prisms (12.1)
- Find the surface areas of pyramids (12.2)
- Find the surface areas of circular solids (12.3)
- Find the volumes of right rectangular prisms (12.4)
- Find the volumes of other prisms (12.4)
- Find the volumes of cylinders (12.4)
- Use the area of a prism's or a cylinder's cross section to find the solid's volume (12.4)
- Find the volumes of pyramids (12.5)
- Find the volumes of cones (12.5)
- Solve problems involving cross sections of pyramids and cones (12.5)
- Find the volumes of spheres (12.6)

VOCABULARY

base (12.1)
Cavalieri's principle (12.6)
cone (12.3)
cross section (12.4)
cylinder (12.3)
frustum (12.5)
lateral edge (12.1)
lateral face (12.1)

lateral surface area (12.1)
polyhedron (12.1)
prism (12.1)
pyramid (12.2)
regular pyramid (12.2)
sphere (12.3)
total surface area (12.1)
volume (12.4)

REVIEW PROBLEMS

Problem Set A

1 Find the lateral area and the total area of the regular pyramid and the cylinder.

a
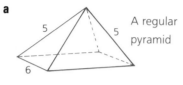
A regular pyramid

b

2 Find the volume of

   a A cube with a side of 8

   b A rectangular box that measures 3 by $4\frac{1}{2}$ by 8

   c A cylinder with a radius of 7 and a height of 2

   d A pyramid with a height of 5 and a base area of 12

   e A prism with a height of 5 and a base area of 12

   f A sphere with a radius of 2

3 Find the volume and the total surface area of each solid.

a
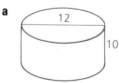

b
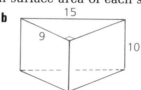

c

4 Find the volume of the solid that is formed when folds are made along the dotted lines.

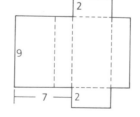

5 Find the height of

   a A box with a volume of 100, a length of 15, and a width of $1\frac{1}{3}$

   b A cube with a volume of 216

6 Find the volume of a cylindrical glass if its height is 15 cm and a 17-cm straw just fits inside it as shown.

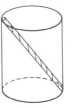

7 A concrete staircase is to be built. Each step is 15 cm high, 25 cm deep, and 1 m wide. The top platform is square. What volume of concrete is needed?

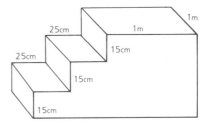

8 Given: A regular square pyramid with a slant height of 10 and a base measuring 16 by 16

Find: **a** The pyramid's lateral area

  b The pyramid's total area

  c The pyramid's volume

9 Find the volume of a sphere whose surface area is 36π.

Problem Set B

10 Find the lateral area and the total area of each solid.

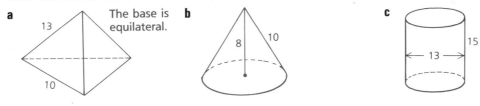

a The base is equilateral. **b** **c**

11 Find the total surface area of each solid. (Don't forget the flat faces.)

a

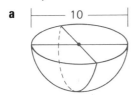

b

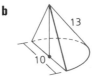

Review Problem Set B, *continued*

12 Find the volume of a cylinder formed from the pattern at the right. The area of each circle is 16π. The rectangle has an area of 24π.

13 A pyramid has a height of 5. Its base is a rhombus with diagonals measuring 7 and 6. Find the volume of the pyramid.

14 A cross section of a hatbox is a regular hexagon with a side 12 cm long. The height of the box is 20 cm. Find the box's surface area and volume.

15 Find the volume of the wedge.

16 Find the total volume of the castle, including the towers.

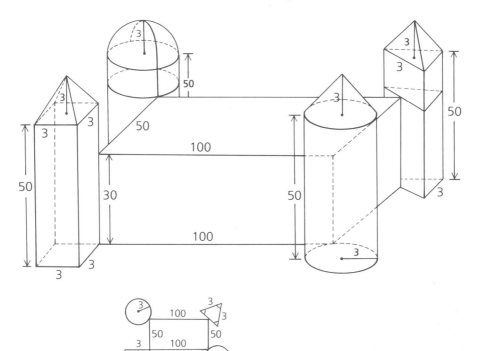

17 A hole with a diameter of 2 in. is drilled through a block as shown. Find the volume of the resulting solid to the nearest cubic inch.

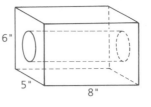

6"
5"
8"

18 Find the volume of the prism shown at the right. (Hint: If you solve this problem, you will be a Hero.)

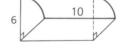

5
9
6
7

Problem Set C

19 A cylinder is cut into four equal parts. Find the total area of the part shown.

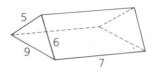

6
10

20 A right cylindrical log was cut parallel to the axis. Find the volume and the total surface area of the piece shown.

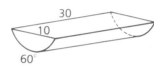

30
10
60°

21 A frustum of a cone is shown. Find the volume of this solid.

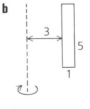

9
6
12

22 Find the volume of the surface of rotation generated by rotating each figure about the dashed line.

a

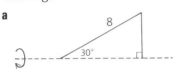

8
30°

b

3
5
1

CUMULATIVE REVIEW
CHAPTERS 1–12

Problem Set A

1 The measure of one of the acute angles of a right triangle is nine times the measure of the other acute angle. Find the measure of the larger acute angle.

2 The perimeter of △ABC is 28. If AB = 2x + 3, BC = 4x − 5, and CA = 8x − 19, is △ABC scalene, isosceles, or equilateral?

3 Given: $\overline{BD} \perp \overline{AD}$, $\overline{BD} \perp \overline{BC}$, $\overline{AB} \cong \overline{CD}$
Prove: ABCD is a ▱.

4 Given: $\overline{PQ} \parallel \overline{TR}$
Find: **a** PT
  b TR

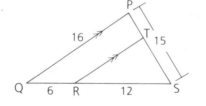

5 Find the value of x in each figure.

a

c

b

d

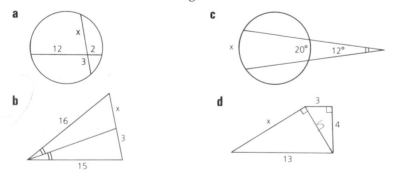

6 Two similar triangles have areas of 9 and 25.
  a What is the ratio of a pair of corresponding sides?
  b What is the ratio of the triangles' perimeters?

7 Given: Diagram as marked.

Find: **a** WY

     b YZ

     c XZ

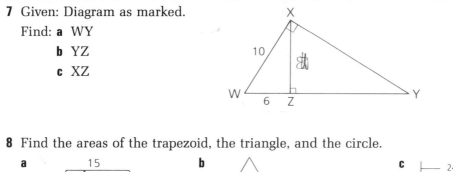

8 Find the areas of the trapezoid, the triangle, and the circle.

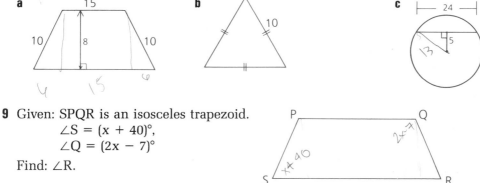

a

b

c

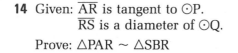

9 Given: SPQR is an isosceles trapezoid.

     $\angle S = (x + 40)°$,

     $\angle Q = (2x - 7)°$

Find: $\angle R$.

10 The numbers 3.14 and $3\frac{1}{7}$ are frequently used as approximations of π. Use your calculator to determine which of these approximations is the more accurate.

11 Find p, q, r, and s.

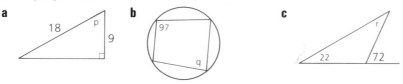

a

b

c

d

12 a Find the fourth proportional in a proportion whose first three terms are 5, 3, and 30.

    b Find the mean proportionals between 8 and 18.

13 Given: $\odot O$ with tangent $\overline{CD}$,

     CD = 15,

     BC = 9

Find: **a** AC 25

     b The diameter of $\odot O$

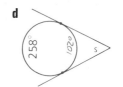

14 Given: $\overline{AR}$ is tangent to $\odot P$.

     $\overline{RS}$ is a diameter of $\odot Q$.

Prove: $\triangle PAR \sim \triangle SBR$

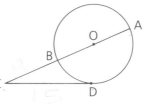

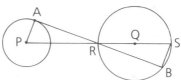

15 In △ABC, D and E are the midpoints of $\overline{AB}$ and $\overline{AC}$, DE = 4x, and BC = 2x + 48. Find BC.

16 Find the area of each polygon.

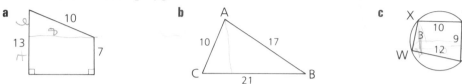

a
10
13
7

b
A
10   17
C   21   B

c
X   Y
10
3   9
W   12
Z

17 Find the number of sides of an equiangular polygon if each interior angle is 170°.

$$\frac{360}{S} = \text{?}$$

72

18 The perimeter of an isosceles triangle is 36. One side is 10. What are the possible lengths of the base?

19 Each polygon shown is regular.

  a Find the measure of ∠1.
  b Find the measure of ∠2.
  c Find the measure of ∠3.
  d Find the measure of ∠4.
  e Will a regular pentagon fit at ∠5?

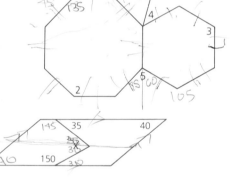

20 Given: Parallelogram as marked
Find: x

21 Given: WXYZ is an isosceles trapezoid,
        with $\overline{WZ} \cong \overline{XY}$.
        △PZY is isosceles.
Prove: P is the midpoint of $\overline{WX}$.

W   P   X

Z   Y

22 Given: $\overleftrightarrow{AC} \perp m$, $\overline{BC} \cong \overline{BA}$
Prove: D is the midpoint of $\overline{AC}$.

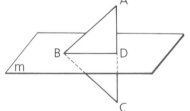

A
B   D
m
C

23 Find the length of a 45° arc of a circle whose radius is 8.

Problem Set B

24 What is the angle formed by the hands of a clock at

    a 11:30?   **b** 2:05?   **c** 3:24?

25 Given: Rectangle RECT in ⊙R,
             RT = 5, TQ = 2

    Find: ET

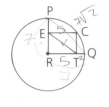
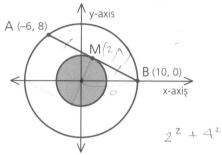

26 If M is the midpoint of $\overline{AB}$, what is the
area of the shaded region?

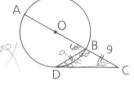

27 A woman walks 20 m west, 100 m south, another 8 m west, and
then 4 m north. How far is she from her starting point?

28 Given: ⊙O, CB = 9,
             ∠C = 30°, $\overline{BC} \cong \overline{BD}$;
             $\overleftrightarrow{CD}$ is tangent to ⊙O.

    Find: **a** m$\widehat{AD}$ **b** CD   **c** The radius of ⊙O

29 Given: The radius of ⊙O is 0.7.
             The radius of ⊙P is 1.1.
             $\overleftrightarrow{AB}$ is a common internal tangent.
             AB = 2.4

    Find: **a** OP

          b The distance between the circles

30 Given: Diagram as marked, with $\overleftrightarrow{PA}$ and
             $\overleftrightarrow{PD}$ tangent to ⊙O

    Find: **a** $\widehat{AD}$

          b m∠P

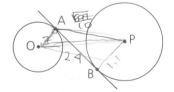
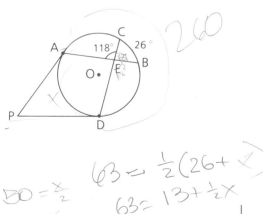

31 Given: Triangle as marked

Find: m∠WYA

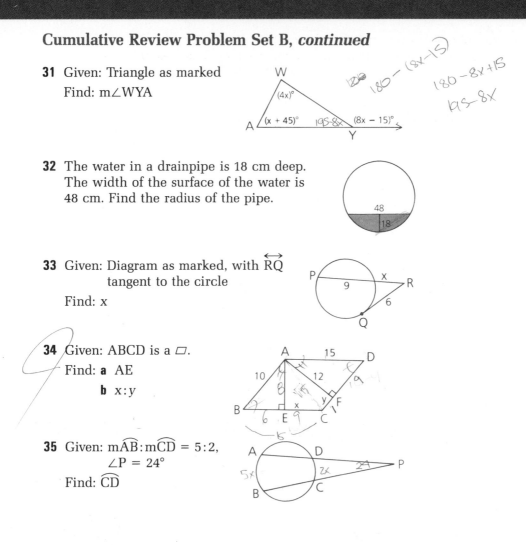

32 The water in a drainpipe is 18 cm deep. The width of the surface of the water is 48 cm. Find the radius of the pipe.

33 Given: Diagram as marked, with $\overleftrightarrow{RQ}$ tangent to the circle

Find: x

34 Given: ABCD is a ▱.

Find: **a** AE

b x:y

35 Given: m$\overset{\frown}{AB}$:m$\overset{\frown}{CD}$ = 5:2, ∠P = 24°

Find: $\overset{\frown}{CD}$

Problem Set C

36 A sled dog traveled 6 mi east, then 6 mi northeast, then another 6 mi east. How far was the dog from her starting point?

37 Given: $\overline{BC}$ is the base of isosceles △ABC.

$\overline{DE}$ is the base of isosceles △AED.

∠BAE = 40°

Find: m∠DEC

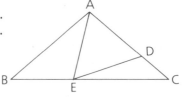

38 In this set of three semicircles, B can be any point between A and C. Prove that the shaded area is equal to π times the product of the radii of the unshaded semicircles.

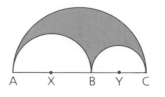

39 Two sides of one triangle are congruent to two sides of a second triangle, and the included angles are supplementary. The area of one triangle is 41. Can the area of the second triangle be found?

40 Given: In quadrilateral QUAD, $\overline{QU} \cong \overline{AD}$, $\angle A$ is supp. to $\angle Q$, and $\overline{QD} \not\cong \overline{AU}$.

Prove: QUAD is an isosceles trapezoid.

41 The lengths of the sides of a hexagon are in an arithmetic progression. The hexagon's perimeter is 30, and its longest side measures 7. Find the length of the next longest side.

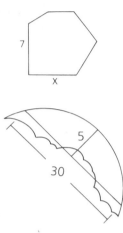

42 Clarence bragged that he ate most of a pizza, but he could not remember the pizza's diameter. On the remaining piece, however, he made the measurements shown. The distance from the midpoint of the arc to the midpoint of the corresponding chord was 5 cm. The chord measured 30 cm. Find the diameter of the pizza Clarence ate.

HISTORICAL SNAPSHOT

THE SHAPE OF THE UNIVERSE
Kepler and the orbits of the planets

The ancient Greeks discovered that of all the possible polyhedra, only five consist of faces that are congruent regular polygons. In the *Timaeus*, a dialogue on the creation of the universe, the philosopher Plato used these regular polyhedra to explain the mathematical structure of the cosmos. He associated the cube and the regular icosahedron, octahedron, and tetrahedron with the four elements that were thought to make up all substances—earth, water, air, and fire. The fifth—the regular dodecahedron—he thought to represent the form of the whole universe. Perhaps this was because it is nearly a sphere, to the Greeks the most perfect of all solids.

In the late 1500's, the astronomer Johannes Kepler began to think about the distances between the planets. He recalled the *Timaeus* and the regular polyhedra. Only six planets were known in Kepler's time, so it occurred to him that their orbits might correspond to a series of circles alternately circumscribed about and inscribed in the five regular solids (see illustration).

Kepler was unable to devise an accurate model of the solar system based on regular polyhedra. But he later discovered one of the fundamental laws of the solar system: that the square of the time it takes a planet to complete an orbit is directly proportional to the cube of the planet's distance from the sun.

COORDINATE GEOMETRY EXTENDED

These massive sections of a coordinate grid show a Yale professor's playful conception.

GRAPHING EQUATIONS

Objective

After studying this section, you will be able to
- Draw lines and circles that represent the solutions of equations

Part One: Introduction

Throughout your work with this book, you have seen problems involving coordinate geometry. You have dealt extensively with the formulas used to determine midpoints, slopes, and distances on the coordinate plane. In this section, you will review what you learned about graphing equations in your algebra studies and prepare yourself for the topics covered later in the chapter.

Part Two: Sample Problems

Problem 1 *Draw a graph of the equation*
$y = 2x - 1$.

Solution To make a graph, we frequently construct a ***table of values***. We choose values for either x or y and then substitute each value in the equation to find the other member of each ordered pair. For example, if $x = -1$, then $y = 2(-1) - 1 = -3$.

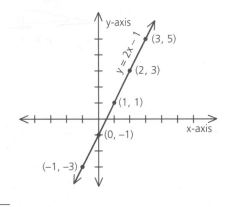

Table of Values for $y = 2x - 1$

x	-1	0	1	2	3
y	-3	-1	1	3	5

We then plot each ordered pair and draw a line through these points. This line represents the solution set of the equation.

Problem 2   *Draw a graph of the equation x = 4.*

Solution   Notice that no *y* appears in the equation x = 4. Thus, *y* can have any real value, but *x* is always equal to 4. The graph is the vertical line shown.

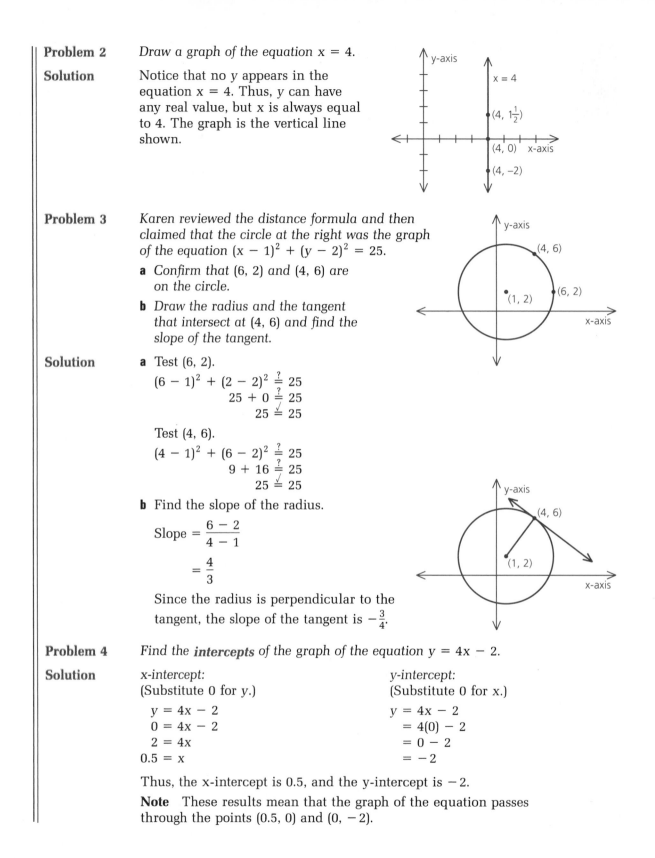

Problem 3   *Karen reviewed the distance formula and then claimed that the circle at the right was the graph of the equation $(x - 1)^2 + (y - 2)^2 = 25$.*

   a *Confirm that (6, 2) and (4, 6) are on the circle.*

   b *Draw the radius and the tangent that intersect at (4, 6) and find the slope of the tangent.*

Solution   **a** Test (6, 2).
$$(6 - 1)^2 + (2 - 2)^2 \overset{?}{=} 25$$
$$25 + 0 \overset{?}{=} 25$$
$$25 \overset{\checkmark}{=} 25$$

   Test (4, 6).
$$(4 - 1)^2 + (6 - 2)^2 \overset{?}{=} 25$$
$$9 + 16 \overset{?}{=} 25$$
$$25 \overset{\checkmark}{=} 25$$

   b Find the slope of the radius.
$$\text{Slope} = \frac{6 - 2}{4 - 1}$$
$$= \frac{4}{3}$$

   Since the radius is perpendicular to the tangent, the slope of the tangent is $-\frac{3}{4}$.

Problem 4   *Find the **intercepts** of the graph of the equation y = 4x − 2.*

Solution

x-intercept:
(Substitute 0 for *y*.)
$$y = 4x - 2$$
$$0 = 4x - 2$$
$$2 = 4x$$
$$0.5 = x$$

y-intercept:
(Substitute 0 for *x*.)
$$y = 4x - 2$$
$$= 4(0) - 2$$
$$= 0 - 2$$
$$= -2$$

Thus, the *x*-intercept is 0.5, and the *y*-intercept is −2.

Note   These results mean that the graph of the equation passes through the points (0.5, 0) and (0, −2).

Part Three: Problem Sets

Problem Set A

1 Make a table of values for each of the following equations and graph the two equations on the same set of axes.

$$y = x + 3 \qquad y = x - 1$$

2 Make a table of values for each of the following equations and graph the two equations on the same set of axes.

$$y = 2x - 5 \qquad y = 2x - 7$$

3 Graph $y - 1 = 2x$.

4 Graph $y - 1 = 2(x + 1)$.

5 Verify that the three points shown lie on the circle whose equation is $x^2 + y^2 = 9$.

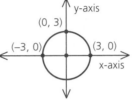

6 Verify that the three points shown lie on the circle whose equation is $x^2 + y^2 = 16$.

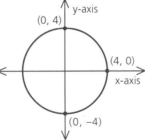

7 Find the x- and y-intercepts of the graph of $y = 2x - 6$.

8 Is (5, 4) on the graph of $y = 2x - 3$?

9 Is $(-4, 6)$ on the V-shaped graph of $y = |x - 2|$?

10 Consider the equations of three lines:

$$y = x + 4 \qquad y = 3x \qquad y = 2x - 2$$

If two of the three lines are selected at random, what is the probability that both contain the point (2, 6)?

Problem Set A, *continued*

11 Is (6, 8) on the graph of $x^2 + y^2 = 100$?

Problem Set B

12 Write an equation that represents the circle shown.

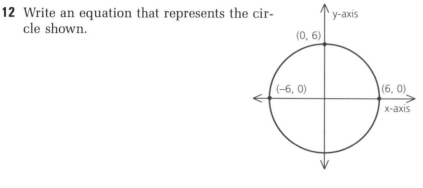

13 Find the area of a triangle with vertices $(-2, 0)$, $(4, 0)$, and $(2, 3)$.

14 The vertices of a right triangle are $(0, 0)$, $(3, 0)$, and $(3, 4)$.
  a Find the lengths of the three sides.
  b Find the length of the altitude to the hypotenuse.
  c Find the length of the median to the hypotenuse.

15 Consider the isosceles trapezoid shown.
  a Find the coordinates of vertex B.
  b Find the lengths of the bases.
  c Find the length of the median.
  d Find the trapezoid's area.

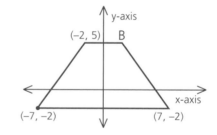

16 A parallelogram has vertices $(-5, -1)$, $(4, -1)$, and $(7, 6)$. Find the fourth vertex if two sides are parallel to the x-axis.

17 Find, to the nearest tenth, the area of the shaded region.

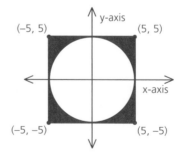

18 If $y = mx + b$, $(x, y) = (2, 4)$, and $m = -3$, find b.

19 If a line containing point (x_1, y_1) and having slope m can represent the equation $y - y_1 = m(x - x_1)$, find an equation that corresponds to the line containing point $(5, 2)$ and having a slope of 6.

20 In the diagram, the point $(2, 3)$ is the center of the circle. What is the slope of the tangent to the circle at $(7, 8)$?

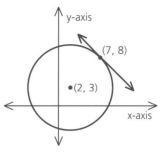

Problem Set C

21 $\overleftrightarrow{PT}$ is tangent to circle O at P.

   a Find the slope of $\overleftrightarrow{PT}$.

   b Verify that $y - 9 = -\frac{5}{8}(x - 8)$ is an equation that represents $\overleftrightarrow{PT}$.

   c Verify that $y = -\frac{5}{8}x + 14$ is an equation that represents $\overleftrightarrow{PT}$.

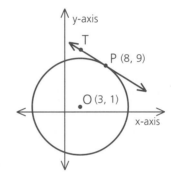

22 Given that $A = (10, 1)$ and $B = (2, 9)$, reflect B across the y-axis to its image B′. If $\overline{AB'}$ intersects the y-axis at C, verify that the slope of $\overline{AC}$ is $-\frac{2}{3}$.

23 Find, to the nearest tenth, the area of the shaded region.

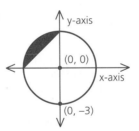

24 △OBD is *encased* in rectangle OACE as shown.

   a Find the areas of regions I, II, and III.

   b Find the area of △OBD.

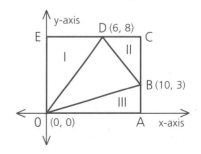

EQUATIONS OF LINES

Objectives

After studying this section, you will be able to
- Write equations that correspond to nonvertical lines
- Write equations that correspond to horizontal lines
- Write equations that correspond to vertical lines
- Identify various forms of linear equations

Part One: Introduction

Equations of Nonvertical Lines

Consider a line with a y-intercept of b and a slope of m. You know that $(0, b)$ is one point on the line. Let (x, y) represent any other point on the line and substitute the two sets of coordinates in the slope formula.

$$\frac{y - b}{x - 0} = m$$
$$y - b = mx + 0$$
$$y = mx + b$$

Theorem 123 **The *y-form*, or *slope-intercept form*, of the equation of a nonvertical line is**

$$y = mx + b$$

where b is the y-intercept of the line and m is the slope of the line.

Example *Use the y-form to write an equation of the line containing $(-1, 4)$ and $(1, 8)$.*

First we find the slope:
$$m = \frac{8 - 4}{1 - (-1)} = \frac{4}{2} = 2.$$
Since the line has a slope, we use the y-form, $y = mx + b$.
We now substitute 2 for m and $(1, 8)$ for (x, y).

$$8 = 2(1) + b$$
$$6 = b$$

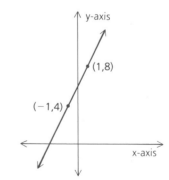

Therefore, the equation is $y = 2x + 6$. You will get the same equation if you use $(-1, 4)$ instead of $(1, 8)$ for (x, y). Try it and see!

Equations of Horizontal Lines

Since a horizontal line is nonvertical, the y-form can be used to develop a formula for the equation of any horizontal line.

$\overleftrightarrow{AB}$ is a horizontal line. Every point has the same y-coordinate (ordinate). The y-intercept is 4, so $b = 4$. The slope of a horizontal line is zero, so $m = 0$.

$y = mx + b$
$y = 0 \cdot x + 4$
The equation of $\overleftrightarrow{AB}$ is $y = 4$.

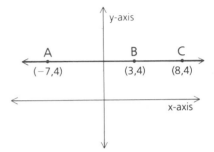

In general, all the points on a horizontal line have the same y-coordinate, b, but their x-coordinates are the set of real numbers. Since the slope m is zero, x does not appear in the equation of the line.

Theorem 124   *The formula for an equation of a horizontal line is*

$y = b$

where b is the y-coordinate of every point on the line.

The trick is to recognize a horizontal line, which may be disguised in a problem.

Example   *Find an equation that corresponds to*

a *The line containing (2, 5) and (24, 5)*
$y = 5$

b *The x-axis*
$y = 0$

c *The line $7\frac{1}{2}$ units below the x-axis*
$y = -7\frac{1}{2}$

d *The line perpendicular to the y-axis and passing through $(11, \sqrt{3})$*
$y = \sqrt{3}$

Equations of Vertical Lines

A vertical line has no slope. Therefore, the previous formulas cannot apply. However, every point on a vertical line has the same x-coordinate (abscissa), while its y-coordinate may be any real number.

Theorem 125 *The formula for the equation of a vertical line is*

$$x = a$$

where a is the x-coordinate of every point on the line.

The trick is to recognize when a line is vertical.

Example *Find an equation that corresponds to*

a *The line containing* $(-1, 6)$ *and* $(-1, 7)$

$x = -1$

b *The line having an x-intercept of 8 and passing through* $\left(8, 5\sqrt{2}\right)$

$x = 8$

c *The line that contains* $(-10, 4)$ *and is perpendicular to the graph of* $y = 7$

$x = -10$

Forms of the Equations of Lines

In this book, we shall emphasize the y-form, but you may find other forms listed in the following table helpful.

Equations of Lines		
Form	**Formula**	**Used for**
Slope-intercept (*y-form*)	$y = mx + b$ (m = slope; b = y-intercept)	Nonvertical lines only
Point-slope	$y - y_1 = m(x - x_1)$ [m = slope; (x_1, y_1) = known point]	Nonvertical lines only
Two-point	$\dfrac{y - y_1}{x - x_1} = \dfrac{y_2 - y_1}{x_2 - x_1}$ [(x_1, y_1) and (x_2, y_2) are known points.]	Nonvertical lines only
General linear	$ax + by + c = 0$ (a, b, and c are real numbers.)	Any line
Intercept	$\dfrac{x}{a} + \dfrac{y}{b} = 1$ (a = x-intercept; b = y-intercept)	Lines not passing through the origin (nonzero intercepts)

Part Two: Sample Problems

Problem 1   Write an equation of the line containing $(7, -3)$ and $(4, 1)$.

Solution   First find the slope.

$$m = \frac{1 - (-3)}{4 - 7} = \frac{4}{-3} = -\frac{4}{3}$$

Then substitute values in the y-form formula, using either $(7, -3)$ or $(4, 1)$ for (x, y).

$$y = mx + b$$
$$1 = -\tfrac{4}{3}(4) + b$$

$$\frac{3}{3} = -\frac{16}{3} + b$$

$$\frac{19}{3} = b$$

Thus, $y = -\tfrac{4}{3}x + \tfrac{19}{3}$ is an equation of the line.

Problem 2   Find an equation of the line with a slope of 3 and an x-intercept of 5.

Solution   If the line has an x-intercept of 5, it must contain the point $(5, 0)$. Therefore, $(5, 0)$ can be substituted for (x, y) and the given slope for m in the y-form formula.

$$y = mx + b$$
$$0 = 3(5) + b$$
$$0 = 15 + b$$
$$-15 = b$$

An equation of the line is $y = 3x - 15$.

Problem 3   **a** Find an equation of the line passing through $(2, 5)$ and $(17, 5)$.

b Find an equation of the line that is parallel to the y-axis and contains $\left(-\sqrt{6}, 1\right)$.

Solution   **a** The line is horizontal, so it corresponds to the equation $y = 5$.

b The line is vertical, so it corresponds to the equation $x = -\sqrt{6}$.

Problem 4   In △ABC, A = (−3, 2), B = (9, 4), and C = (5, 12).

a *Find an equation of the median to* $\overline{AB}$.

b *Find an equation of the perpendicular bisector of* $\overline{AB}$.

c *Find an equation of the altitude to* $\overline{AB}$.

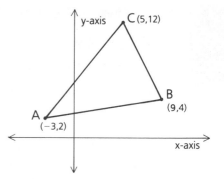

Solution   **a** By using the midpoint formula, we can find that the midpoint of $\overline{AB}$ is (3, 3). Let (3, 3) = (x_1, y_1) and (5, 12) = (x_2, y_2) in the two-point formula.

$$\frac{y - y_1}{x - x_1} = \frac{y_2 - y_1}{x_2 - x_1}$$

$$\frac{y - 3}{x - 3} = \frac{12 - 3}{5 - 3} = \frac{9}{2}$$

$$2y - 6 = 9x - 27$$
$$2y = 9x - 21$$

$$y = \frac{9}{2}x - \frac{21}{2}$$

Note   Actually, $y = \frac{9}{2}x - \frac{21}{2}$ is the equation of the *line containing* the median. The median itself is a segment. Unless otherwise stated, when we refer to the equation of a segment or ray, we mean the equation of the containing line.

b Slope of $\overleftrightarrow{AB} = \dfrac{4 - 2}{9 - (-3)} = \dfrac{1}{6}$

Since the slopes of two perpendicular lines are opposite reciprocals (except in the case of a horizontal and a vertical line), the slope of the perpendicular bisector is −6. Let the midpoint (3, 3) = (x_1, y_1) in the point-slope formula.

$$y - y_1 = m(x - x_1)$$
$$y - 3 = -6(x - 3)$$

Note   Since a line has infinitely many points, the point-slope formula does not produce a unique equation.

c The altitude contains C = (5, 12) and has a slope of −6 (it is perpendicular to $\overline{AB}$.) We can use the y-form formula or the point-slope formula.

y-form:

$$y = mx + b$$
$$12 = -6(5) + b$$
$$42 = b$$
$$y = -6x + 42$$

Point-slope form:

$$y - y_1 = m(x - x_1)$$
$$y - 12 = -6(x - 5)$$

The two equations are equivalent, so either is acceptable.

Part Three: Problem Sets

Problem Set A

1 Find the slope and the y-intercept of the graph of each equation.

a $y = 3x + 7$

b $y = 4x$

c $y = \frac{1}{2}x - \sqrt{3}$

d $y = 13 - 6x$

e $y = -5x - 6$

f $y = 7$

2 Rewrite each equation in y-form and find the slope and the y-intercept of its graph.

a $y - 3x = 1$

b $y + 5x = 2$

c $2x + 3y = 6$

d $7 - (6 - 2x) = 4y$

3 Write an equation of a line 6 units below, and parallel to, the x-axis.

4 Write an equation of a line that is perpendicular to the x-axis and passes through (8, 1).

5 Which two of the following three lines are parallel?

a $y = 5x - 1$ **b** $y = 7x + 2$ **c** $y = 2 + 5x$

6 Write a y-form equation of each line.

a y-intercept of 2; slope = 4

b $m = 5$; passes through $(0, -2)$

c Parallel to graph of $y = 10x - 6$; y-intercept of 1

d Perpendicular to graph of $2y = x + 16$; passes through $(0, -5)$

e y-intercept of 2; perpendicular to line containing $(-4, 6)$ and $(1, 11)$

7 Use the graph to find

a The slope of $\overleftrightarrow{AB}$

b An equation of $\overleftrightarrow{AB}$

c The slope of $\overleftrightarrow{CD}$

d An equation of $\overleftrightarrow{CD}$

Problem Set A, *continued*

8 Write (if possible, in point-slope form) an equation of the line
  a Containing (2, 1) and (3, 4)
  b Containing (− 6, 3) and (2, − 1)
  c Containing (1, 5) and (− 3, 5)
  d With an x-intercept of 2 and a slope of 7
  e That has an x-intercept of 3 and passes through (1, 8)
  f That passes through (− 3, 6) and (− 3, 10)
  g That passes through (8, 7) and is perpendicular to the graph of $3y = -2x + 24$

Problem Set B

9 The line that represents the equation $y = 8x - 1$ contains the point $(k, 5)$. Find k.

10 Line $\overleftrightarrow{CD}$ is perpendicular to the graph of $2x + 3y = 8$. If $C = (1, 4)$, find the equation of $\overleftrightarrow{CD}$.

11 Show that $-\frac{a}{b}$ is the slope of the graph of $ax + by + c = 0$.

12 Show that $-\frac{c}{b}$ is the y-intercept of the graph of $ax + by + c = 0$.

In problems 13–17, use △ABC in the diagram.

13 Write, in point-slope form, an equation of a line through C parallel to $\overleftrightarrow{AB}$.

14 Write an equation of the perpendicular bisector of $\overline{AB}$.

15 Write an equation of the altitude from C to $\overline{AB}$.

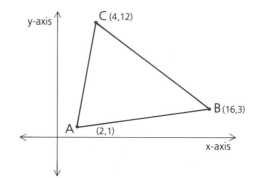

16 Write an equation of the median from C to $\overline{AB}$.

17 Find the slope of the line passing through the midpoints of $\overline{AC}$ and $\overline{BC}$.

18 A line passes through a point 3 units to the left of and 2 units above the origin. Write an equation of the line if it is parallel to
  a The x-axis   **b** The y-axis

19 If P = (−2, 5) and R = (0, 9), write, in point-slope form, an equation of the perpendicular bisector of $\overline{PR}$.

Problem Set C

20 Two numbers x and y (not necessarily different) are chosen at random from the set {0, 1, 2, 3}. The possible pairs (x, y) are illustrated by dots. Copy the graph.

    a How many pairs of numbers are there?

    b What is the probability that x = y?

    c Show the points on the graph for which x < y.

    d What is the probability that x < y?

21 Does the point (12, −3) lie on the line whose slope is $-\frac{3}{4}$ and whose y-intercept is 5? Support your answer.

22 A line has a y-intercept of 2 and forms a 60° angle with the x-axis. Find equations of the two possible lines.

23 Find an equation of the line whose intercepts are twice those of the graph of 2x + 5y = 10.

24 In △ABC, A = (0, 0), B = (4, 0), and C = (2, 6). Show that the medians of △ABC all intersect at (2, 2).

    Note It can be shown that the medians of any triangle are concurrent at a point called the *centroid* of the triangle.

25 Find the center of the circle containing D = (−3, 5), E = (3, 3), and F = (11, 19).

    Note The center of this circle is called the *circumcenter* of △DEF.

26 Find the reflection of the point (−9, 7) over the reference line y = x.

27 Find an equation of the reflection of the graph of $y = \frac{3}{4}x - 1$ over

    a The x-axis   **b** The y-axis   **c** The line y = x

SYSTEMS OF EQUATIONS

Objective

After studying this section, you will be able to

- Use two methods to solve systems of equations

Part One: Introduction

When two linear equations are graphed on the same coordinate plane, the resulting lines may be

Parallel (a ∥ b)
Intersecting (c intersects d.)
Identical (e and f coincide.)

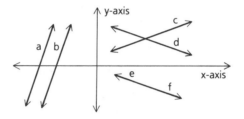

Each pair of lines may be represented by a ***system of equations***.

Systems of Equations		
System	**Graph**	**Intersection**
$\begin{cases} y = x + 8 \\ y = x + 13 \end{cases}$	Parallel lines	Empty set
$\begin{cases} y = x + 3 \\ y = -2x + 21 \end{cases}$	Intersecting lines	One point
$\begin{cases} y = \frac{1}{2}x - 10 \\ 2x - 4y = 40 \end{cases}$	Identical lines	All points on the line

Most of the problems in this section require solving a system of two linear equations. The sample problems illustrate two methods of solving such systems:

1 Addition or subtraction
2 Substitution

Part Two: Sample Problems

Problem 1   *Find the intersection of the two lines corresponding to x = 4 and*
y = 2x + 8.

Solution   *Substitution method:* Since x = 4 is the first equation, we can substitute 4 for x in the second equation.

$y = 2x + 8$
$y = 2(4) + 8$
$y = 8 + 8$
$y = 16$

Thus, the intersection is (4, 16).

Problem 2   *Find the intersection of the lines corresponding to the following system.*
$$\begin{bmatrix} 8x - 3y = 7 \\ 10x + 4y = 1 \end{bmatrix}$$

Solution   *Addition-subtraction method:*

$32x - 12y = 28$ Multiply both sides of first equation by 4.
$\underline{30x + 12y = 3}$ Multiply both sides of second equation by 3.
$62x + 0 = 31$ Add the equations.

$$x = \frac{1}{2}$$

Now substitute $\frac{1}{2}$ for x in the first or the second equation.

$8x - 3y = 7$
$8\left(\frac{1}{2}\right) - 3y = 7$
$y = -1$

The lines intersect at $\left(\frac{1}{2}, -1\right)$.

Problem 3   *Find the intersection of the lines corresponding to the following system.*
$$\begin{bmatrix} y = 3x + 1 \\ 6x - 2y = -2 \end{bmatrix}$$

Solution   *Substitution method:*

Substitute 3x + 1 for y in the second equation.

$6x - 2y = -2$
$6x - 2(3x + 1) = -2$
$6x - 6x - 2 = -2$
$-2 = -2$

Since the statement $-2 = -2$ is always true, the intersection is the entire graph of the first equation, which is therefore identical to the graph of the second equation. The solution set is {(x, y) : y = 3x + 1}.

Part Three: Problem Sets

Problem Set A

1 Determine the point of intersection of the graphs of each system.

a $\begin{cases} x + y = 10 \\ x - y = 2 \end{cases}$ **b** $\begin{cases} y = 5 \\ x + y = 7 \end{cases}$ **c** $\begin{cases} y = 2x - 1 \\ y = 4x + 5 \end{cases}$ **d** $\begin{cases} x + 2y = 7 \\ 4x - y = 10 \end{cases}$

2 Determine the intersection of the graphs of each system.

a $\begin{cases} x = 4 \\ x^2 + y^2 = 25 \end{cases}$ **b** $\begin{cases} y = 3 \\ |y - 2| = x \end{cases}$

3 Where do the lines intersect?

a $\begin{cases} x + 2y = 12 \\ x\text{-axis} \end{cases}$ **b** $\begin{cases} y = 3x - 7 \\ 9x - 3y = 21 \end{cases}$

4 Find the points each pair of lines has in common.

a $\begin{cases} 2x + y = 10 \\ 8x + 4y = 17 \end{cases}$ **b** $\begin{cases} y = 4x + 1 \\ \text{The line to the right of the y-axis,} \\ \text{parallel to it, and 4 units from it} \end{cases}$

Problem Set B

5 Where does $\overleftrightarrow{DE}$ intersect $\overleftrightarrow{FH}$?

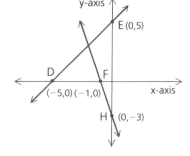

6 Find the intersection of the graphs of
$x = a$ and $3x + 2y = 12$.

7 Show that the graphs of the following three equations are concurrent (intersect at a single point). What are the coordinates of the point of intersection?
$$\begin{cases} 2x + 3y = 2 \\ y = 2x - 10 \\ 3x - y = 14 \end{cases}$$

8 The graph of $x^2 + y^2 = 25$ is a circle. (Circular graphs will be studied later in this chapter.) The graph of $x^2 - y^2 = 7$ is a hyperbola. (Hyperbolas are normally studied in a later math course.) Use one of the methods of solving a system of equations to find the intersection of the circle and the hyperbola.

9 Find, in point-slope form, an equation of the line containing (2, 1) and the point of intersection of the graphs of $3x - y = 3$ and $x + 2y = 15$.

10 Find an equation of the line that is parallel to the graph of $2x + 3y = 5$ and contains the point of intersection of the graphs of $y = 4x + 8$ and $y = x + 5$.

11 Find the point of intersection of the graphs of $y - 3 = \frac{1}{2}(x - 1)$ and $y + 1 = -\frac{3}{2}(x - 1)$.

12 Consider the line corresponding to $y = 2x + 1$. Line 2 contains (5, 3) and is parallel to the given line. Line 3 contains (5, 16) and has the same y-intercept as the given line. Find the intersection of lines 2 and 3.

Problem Set C

13 If the equations $ax + by = c$ and $dx + ey = f$ represent two intersecting lines, what are the coordinates of their point of intersection?

14 In $\triangle ABC$, A = (5, −1), B = (1, 1), and C = (5, −11). Find the length of the altitude from A to $\overline{BC}$.

15 Find the distance between the parallel lines corresponding to $y = 2x + 3$ and $y = 2x + 7$. (Hint: Start by choosing a convenient point on one of the lines.)

16 Find the intersection of the V-shaped graph of $y = |x - 3|$ and the graph of $y = 2x + 1$.

17 Find the area of the triangle whose sides lie on the graphs of $3x + y + 1 = 0$, $x + 4y - 7 = 0$, and $-5x + 2y + 13 = 0$.

18 Find the reflection of the point (−6, 5) over the graph of $2y - x = 6$.

GRAPHING INEQUALITIES

Objective

After studying this section, you will be able to
- Graph inequalities

Part One: Introduction

Inequalities and systems of inequalities can be graphed by means of the following procedure.

Two-Part Procedure for Graphing Inequalities

1 Pretend that the inequality is an equation. Graph this equation as a ***boundary line.***
2 In the inequality, test the coordinates of points in the various regions separated by the boundary line. Shade the region(s) whose points satisfy the inequality.

In the final graph, the boundary line is dashed if it is not included in the graph of the inequality.

Study the following sample problems closely.

Part Two: Sample Problems

Problem 1   Graph $y > 2x + 8$.

Solution   *Boundary line:* Pretend that $y = 2x + 8$.

x	y
0	8
1	10
-1	6
-2	4

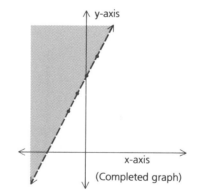

(Completed graph)

The boundary line is dashed, since there is no equal sign in the original inequality.

Test of Regions: In the inequality, test a convenient point not on the boundary line—for instance, (0, 0).

$y > 2x + 8$ Since $0 > 8$ is false, do not shade the
Is $0 > 2(0) + 8$? region to the right of the line.
Is $0 > 8$?

Now test a point in the other region, such as $(-10, 10)$.

Is $10 > 2(-10) + 8$? Since $10 > -12$ is true, do shade the
$10 > -12$ region containing $(-10, 10)$.

Problem 2   *Graph $y \geq |x - 2|$.*

Solution   *Boundary line: $y = |x - 2|$.*

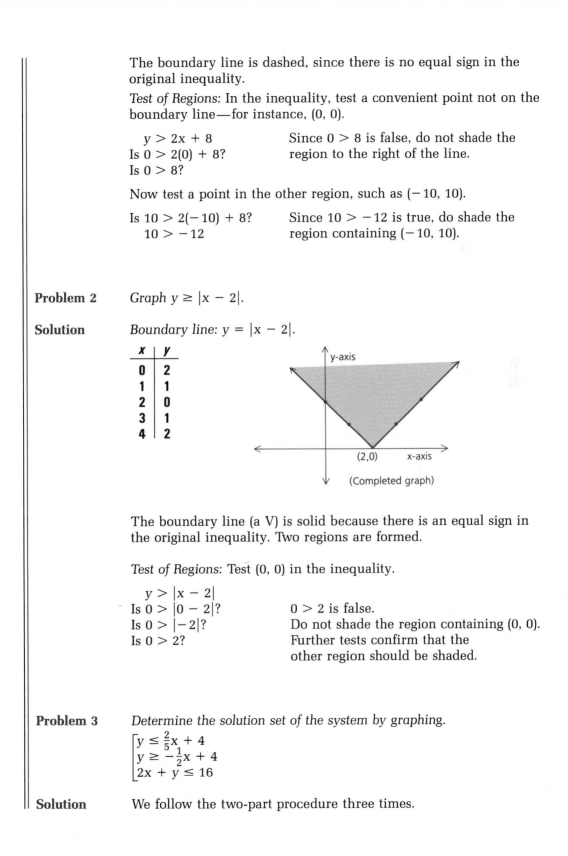

x	y
0	2
1	1
2	0
3	1
4	2

(Completed graph)

The boundary line (a V) is solid because there is an equal sign in the original inequality. Two regions are formed.

Test of Regions: Test (0, 0) in the inequality.

$y > |x - 2|$
Is $0 > |0 - 2|$? $0 > 2$ is false.
Is $0 > |-2|$? Do not shade the region containing (0, 0).
Is $0 > 2$? Further tests confirm that the
other region should be shaded.

Problem 3   *Determine the solution set of the system by graphing.*
$$\begin{cases} y \leq \frac{2}{5}x + 4 \\ y \geq -\frac{1}{2}x + 4 \\ 2x + y \leq 16 \end{cases}$$

Solution   We follow the two-part procedure three times.

Boundary line:	Boundary line:	Boundary line:
$y = \frac{2}{5}x + 4$	$y = -\frac{1}{2}x + 4$	$2x + y = 16$

x	y
0	4
5	6
10	8
15	10

x	y
0	4
2	3
4	2
6	1

x	y
0	16
1	14
2	12
3	10

After testing regions, we shade below the boundary line.

After testing regions, we shade above the boundary line.

After testing regions, we shade below the boundary line.

The solution consists of the union of the triangle and its interior, as shown in the final graph.

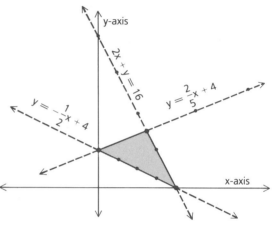

Part Three: Problem Sets

Problem Set A

1 Graph each inequality.

a $2x - 3y < 6$ **c** $5x + 2y \geq 10$ **e** $y \geq 2x + 3$

b $y < \frac{1}{2}x - 1$ **d** $x < -2$

2 Write the inequality represented by each graph.

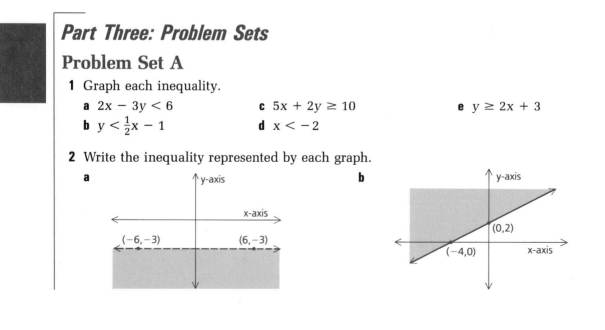

3 Graph each of the following.

a $y \geq |x + 1|$

c $\{(x, y):5 < y < 7\}$

b $\{(x, y):x > 2 \text{ or } x < -1\}$

d $\{(x, y):|x| < 3\}$

Problem Set B

4 Determine the intersection of the solution sets of the two inequalities $y > 2$ and $x + 2y < 6$ by graphing.

5 Graph the solution of each system of inequalities.

a $\begin{bmatrix} y \geq x + 4 \\ y \leq -2x + 6 \end{bmatrix}$

c $\begin{bmatrix} x + y > 12 \\ x - y \leq 4 \end{bmatrix}$

e $\begin{bmatrix} y > |x - 1| \\ x + 3y < 12 \end{bmatrix}$

b $\begin{bmatrix} x + y \leq 4 \\ 2x - y \leq 6 \\ x \geq 0 \end{bmatrix}$

d $\begin{bmatrix} 4y - 3x < 6 \\ y < 3x \\ 2x < 6 - 3y \end{bmatrix}$

f $\begin{bmatrix} y < 2x + 5 \\ 2x - y < 3 \end{bmatrix}$

6 Determine the *union* of the solution sets of the inequalities $x + y > 4$ and $y < 2x - 6$.

Problem Set C

7 Graph the solution set of each system of inequalities.

a $\begin{bmatrix} y < x^2 + 8 \\ y > -x + 12 \end{bmatrix}$

b $\begin{bmatrix} x^2 + y^2 \leq 25 \\ y \geq |x| \end{bmatrix}$

c $\begin{bmatrix} xy < 12 \\ x^2 + y^2 < 16 \end{bmatrix}$

8 Graph each inequality.

a $|x + y| \leq 4$

b $|x| + |y| \leq 4$

9 The graph of $y = x^2$ for the values of $0 \leq x \leq 3$ is shown.

a Find the coordinates of A, B, and C.

b We can estimate the area of the region between the graph of $y = x^2$ and the x-axis (when $0 \leq x \leq 3$) by adding the areas of $\triangle AOD$, trapezoid ABED, and trapezoid BCFE. Find this sum.

Note If you study calculus, you will learn that the actual area of this region is 9.

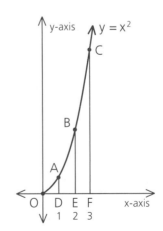

THREE-DIMENSIONAL GRAPHING AND REFLECTIONS

Objectives

After studying this section, you will be able to
- Graph in three dimensions
- Apply the properties of reflections

Part One: Introduction

Three-Dimensional Graphing

As an extension to graphing in a coordinate plane, here is a brief introduction to three-dimensional graphing.

In a three-dimensional coordinate system, there are three axes that are mutually perpendicular. The point P = (3, 4, 12) may be graphed in "3-D" by drawing the axis system shown. A rectangular box should be drawn as an aid in locating and visualizing the point. The sides of the box are drawn parallel to the axes. The x-axis is drawn at an angle but should be visualized as being perpendicular to the plane of the paper.

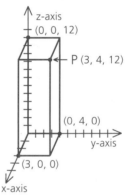

The distance between two points in space can be found with the **3-D distance formula,** which is a logical extension of the two-dimensional distance formula.

Theorem 126   *If P = (x_1, y_1, z_1) and Q = (x_2, y_2, z_2) are any two points, then the distance between them can be found with the formula*

$$PQ = \sqrt{(x_2 - x_1)^2 + (y_2 - y_1)^2 + (z_2 - z_1)^2}$$

Reflections

Since the beginning of this book, you have been solving problems involving rotations, reflections, and translations of points. Now you will work with a few applications of reflections that you might find useful.

Many of you have probably played miniature golf. In the diagram to the right, you see a type of hole you may have encountered. Obviously, it won't work to aim directly for the hole. You must aim to hit the barrier so that the ball will bounce off at the proper angle.

To find the point to shoot for, you can reflect point E (the pre-image) over the barrier to point E′ (the image). If you aim at point E′, the ball should strike the barrier at N and bounce directly to E. If your aim is good, you will have a hole in ONE.

Aim at E′.
The path is
O–N–E

Why does this reflection work? The answer depends on a law of physics. By the principles of reflection, $\overline{E'S} \cong \overline{ES}$ and $\angle ESN \cong \angle E'SN$. Since $\overline{SN} \cong \overline{SN}$, $\triangle SNE' \cong \triangle SNE$ by SAS. Hence, $\angle 2 \cong \angle 3$ by CPCTC. Since $\angle 1 \cong \angle 3$ (vertical angles), $\angle 1 \cong \angle 2$. A law of physics states that the angle of incidence ($\angle 1$) is equal in measure to the angle of reflection ($\angle 2$). Thus, your ball should bounce directly into the hole.

We can also use this diagram to prove an interesting physical fact: The path of the ball from O to N to E is the shortest possible path from O to E.

Pick any other point on the barrier, such as P, and consider the hypothetical path from O to P to E. By CPCTC, $\overline{PE'} \cong \overline{PE}$ and $\overline{NE'} \cong \overline{NE}$. So the path from O to P to E has the same length as the path from O to P to E′. In the same way, the distance from O to N to E is the same as that from O to N to E′. But $\overline{ONE'}$ is a straight line segment, so its length must be less than OP + PE′ by the triangle-inequality principle.

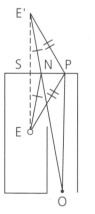

ON + NE′ < OP + PE′

You can also solve situations involving several reflections over several barriers, such as the complicated hole shown in Figure 1 at the right. First determine which barriers you wish the ball to strike. Then reflect the target point over these barriers, one by one, as shown in Figure 2. (Reflect E over the lower barrier to F; then reflect F over the line containing the left-hand barrier to G; then reflect G over the line containing the upper barrier to H.) If you putt the ball in the direction of point H, it should follow a path from A to R to N to I to E. You may not want to go to this much trouble when actually playing, but it is fun to know the principle involved.

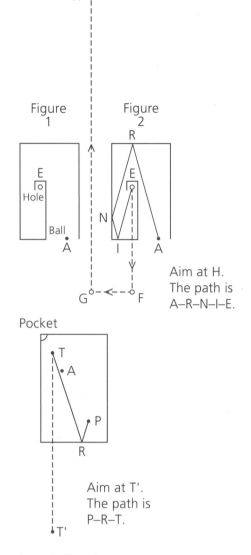

Figure 1

Figure 2

Aim at H.
The path is
A–R–N–I–E.

The reflection principle can be extended to the game of pool, or pocket billiards. With the cue ball at P, use the principles of reflection to knock the ball at T into the pocket.

One way is to reflect T to T′ as shown. If you aim the cue ball at T′, it should travel from P to R to T. There are some complications, however. You must strike T in such a way that

- T goes into the pocket
- The cue ball does not go into a pocket (If it does, you have "scratched" and lost your turn.)

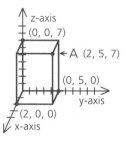

Aim at T'.
The path is
P–R–T.

Reflections are also useful in the game of three-cushion billiards.

The concepts of rotations and reflections are important in such mathematical studies as trigonometry and calculus. In addition, many professionals—structural engineers and architects, for example—use these concepts extensively in their work.

Part Two: Sample Problems

Problem 1 *Graph the point A = (2, 5, 7) on a 3-D graph.*

Solution Use a rectangular box as shown to aid you in locating and visualizing point A at (2, 5, 7).

Problem 2   *Find the distance from A = (2, 5, 7) to B = (3, −2, 4).*

Solution   Use the 3-D distance formula.

$$AB = \sqrt{(x_2 - x_1)^2 + (y_2 - y_1)^2 + (z_2 - z_1)^2}$$
$$= \sqrt{(3 - 2)^2 + (-2 - 5)^2 + (4 - 7)^2}$$
$$= \sqrt{59}$$
$$\approx 7.68$$

Problem 3   *Show where the ball should strike the barrier for you to have the best chance of making a hole in one.*

Solution   Reflect the hole at E over the barrier to E′. Then aim the ball at the imaginary E′ so that it strikes the barrier at N.

Problem 4   *On the miniature-golf hole shown, the ball is at J and the hole is at Y. Jan wants the ball to strike the barrier at y = 8, the barrier at x = 0, and the barrier at y = −1 before it goes into the hole at (4, 2).*

a *Show the reflections from the pre-image Y to the image at Y‴, where the ball should be aimed.*

b *Find the coordinates of Y‴.*

c *Find the coordinates of A, the point at which the ball should strike the first barrier.*

Solution   **a** Reflect Y over the line y = −1 to Y′ = (4, −4). Then reflect Y′ over the y-axis to Y″ = (−4, −4). Finally, reflect Y″ over the line y = 8 to Y‴ = (−4, 20).

b See part **a**.

c Since J, A, and Y‴ are collinear, use slopes. Let A = (x, 8).
Slope of $\overleftrightarrow{JY'''}$ = slope of $\overleftrightarrow{JA}$

$$\frac{20 - 0}{-4 - 6} = \frac{8 - 0}{x - 6}$$
$$20(x - 6) = -10(8)$$
$$20x - 120 = -80$$
$$20x = 40$$
$$x = 2$$

So the coordinates of A are (2, 8).

Part Three: Problem Sets

Problem Set A

1 Graph the point A = (2, 4, 6) on a 3-D graph. Use a rectangular box as an aid in locating and visualizing point A.

2 Find the distance from P = (3, 4, 12) to the origin.

3 Find, to the nearest tenth, the distance from P = (3, 4, 12) to D = (−1, −2, 9).

4 Find, to the nearest tenth, the perimeter of a triangle with vertices at (0, 0, 6), (0, 8, 0), and (15, 0, 0).

5 On a 3-D graph, draw the rectangular solid whose base has vertices at D = (0, 0, 0), A = (4, 0, 0), B = (4, 5, 0), and C = (0, 5, 0) and whose height is 7.

  a Find the area of the base.

  b Find the volume of the solid.

  c Find the diagonal of the solid.

  d Is (4, 5, 7) a vertex of the solid?

  e If the solid were rotated 90° downward about $\overline{AB}$, what would the new coordinates of the vertex be?

6 Two famous geometry teachers, Mr. Ripple and Mr. Wood, were playing the miniature-golf hole shown at the right. Mr. Wood shot first, hitting the barrier at W but missing the hole. After a moment of reflection, Mr. Ripple hit his ball to strike the barrier at R, and the ball bounced straight into the hole.

"How'd you do that?" asked Mr. Wood. "You just need the right image," Mr. Ripple replied. Draw a diagram to show Mr. Wood what Mr. Ripple meant.

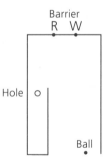

7 Reflect the hole over the barrier and give the coordinates of the image of the hole.

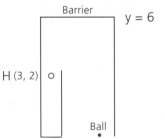

8 Are you more likely to make a hole in one by aiming at A, at B, at C, or at D? Show the reflections on a diagram to justify your answer.

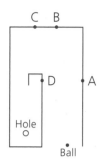

Problem Set B

9 Consider the points A = (2, 3, −5), B = (8, 9, 1), and C = (3, 17, 1).

   a Find the midpoint of $\overline{AB}$.

   b Find, to the nearest tenth, the length of the median from C to $\overline{AB}$.

10 Suppose that P = (3, 5) and that point P is reflected over the graph of x = 1 to P′. Find in point-slope form, the equation of $\overleftrightarrow{JP'}$, if J = (5, 6).

11 Point Q′ = (3, 7) is the image of a point after reflection over the y-axis. Find the pre-image.

12 Verify that if the path from S to H to O is the shortest distance from S to the y-axis to O, then H = (0, 6).

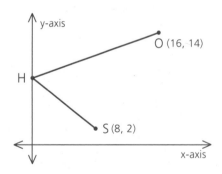

13 In a circle whose center is at P, the image of A = (4, 6) over P is (−2, −2). Find the image of B = (−3, 5) over P.

Problem Set C

14 The base of a triangular pyramid has vertices at (6, 0, 0), (0, 6, 0), and (0, 0, 6). If the peak of the pyramid is at (0, 0, 0), find the volume of the pyramid.

Problem Set C, *continued*

15 A square with vertices at A = (1, 1), B = (0, 4), C = (3, 5), and D = (4, 2) is reflected over the x-axis to produce a new square with vertices A′, B′, C′, and D′.

    a Find the area of square A′B′C′D′.

    b Find, in y-form, the equation of $\overleftrightarrow{A'C'}$.

16 If H = (10, 2) and K = (18, 17) and if J is any point on the graph of x = 2, find, to the nearest tenth, the minimum distance from H to J to K.

17 On a miniature-golf course, the ball is at (8, 1) and the hole is at (4, 2). A player can make a hole in one by hitting the ball along the path indicated by the arrows. Find the coordinates of point R.

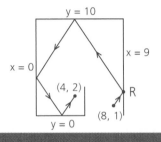

IMAGE-PRODUCING WAVES
Sound in the coordinate plane

Sound travels in waves. The number of wave cycles that pass a given point in one second is the *frequency* of the wave. Human ears are capable of hearing frequencies from about 16 cycles per second to 20,000 cycles per second. Sound with a frequency greater than 20,000 is *ultrasound*. The reflection of ultrasound waves directed into the body produces a moving image that can be useful in diagnostic medicine.

Kathy Gurnee is an ultrasonographer at Lovelace Medical Center in Albuquerque, New Mexico. She reads ultrasound echoes using a grid that resembles three-dimensional coordinate axes. Height and width can be read directly. Depth and density can be gauged from the shading of the image. The sonographer can zoom in on objects with dimensions as small as 1 millimeter.

Gurnee finds her work extremely challenging. "Unlike an X-ray," she says, "an ultrasound image is a continuously moving picture. This makes it a much more powerful diagnostic tool."

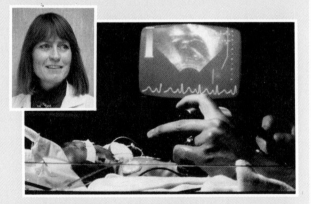

Originally from Yellow Springs, Ohio, Gurnee moved to Albuquerque, where she earned a degree in education from the University of New Mexico and then taught multiply-handicapped children for several years. She became interested in ultrasound when she learned that the technique had been used to diagnose the disabilities of some of her students before their births. After a year of further study at the University of New Mexico, she became a registered diagnostic medical sonographer.

13.6 | CIRCLES

Objective

After studying this section, you will be able to
- Write equations that correspond to circles

Part One: Introduction

The equation of a circle is based on the distance formula (Section 9.5) and the fact that all points on a circle are equidistant from the circle's center.

Theorem 127   *The equation of a circle whose center is (h, k) and whose radius is r is*

$$(x - h)^2 + (y - k)^2 = r^2$$

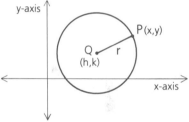

This *circle formula* may be used in several ways.

Example 1   *Find the equation of a circle whose center is (1, 5) and whose radius is 4.*

$$(x - 1)^2 + (y - 5)^2 = 16$$

Example 2   *Find the center and radius of the graph of $(x - 2)^2 + (y + 7)^2 = 64$.*

We rewrite the given equation in the same form as the circle equation.

$$(x - h)^2 + (y - k)^2 = r^2$$
$$(x - 2)^2 + [y - (-7)]^2 = 8^2$$

Hence, $h = 2$, $k = -7$, and $r = 8$. The center is $(2, -7)$ and the radius is 8.

The next example uses the circle formula in the same way as example 2, but the preparation is more complicated.

Example 3   Is $x^2 - 8x + y^2 - 10y = 8$ an equation of a circle?

We use the process of **completing the square,** which you have probably studied in algebra class, to rewrite the equation in the form of the circle equation.

$$x^2 - 8x + y^2 - 10y = 8$$
$$x^2 - 8x + \mathbf{16} + y^2 - 10y + \mathbf{25} = 8 + \mathbf{16} + \mathbf{25}$$

Key   Key
Number   Number

$$(x^2 - 8x + 16) + (y^2 - 10y + 25) = 49$$
$$(x - 4)^2 + (y - 5)^2 = 49$$

Yes, the solution set is a circle. The center is (4, 5) and the radius is 7. The two key numbers, 16 and 25, were introduced to complete the squares—to make the terms on the left-hand side of the equation form two perfect-square trinomials. Notice that 16 is the square of half of -8 and that 25 is the square of half of -10.

Part Two: Sample Problems

Problem 1   Find the equation of the circle with center $(0, -2)$ and a radius of 3.

Solution   Use the circle formula.

$$(x - h)^2 + (y - k)^2 = r^2$$
$$(x - 0)^2 + [y - (-2)]^2 = 3^2$$
$$x^2 + (y + 2)^2 = 9$$

Problem 2   Find, to the nearest tenth, the circumference of the circle represented by $3x^2 + 3y^2 + 6x - 18y = 15$.

Solution

$$3x^2 + 3y^2 + 6x - 18y = 15$$
$$x^2 + y^2 + 2x - 6y = 5 \qquad \text{Divide both sides by 3.}$$
$$x^2 + 2x + y^2 - 6y = 5 \qquad \text{Rearrange the terms.}$$
$$x^2 + 2x + 1 + y^2 - 6y + 9 = 5 + 1 + 9 \qquad \text{Complete the squares.}$$
$$(x + 1)^2 + (y - 3)^2 = 15$$

The radius is $\sqrt{15}$ and the circumference $= 2\pi r = 2\pi\sqrt{15} \approx 24.3$.

Problem 3   **a** Describe the graph of $(x - 2)^2 + (y + 5)^2 = 0$.

   b Describe the graph of $x^2 + (y - 4)^2 = -25$.

Solution   **a** The form of this equation indicates a circle with its center at $(2, -5)$ and a radius of 0. This is sometimes called a **point circle,** a circle that has shrunk to a single point—in this case, the point $(2, -5)$.

   b The form of this equation indicates a circle with its center at $(0, 4)$ and a radius of $\sqrt{-25}$. However, $\sqrt{-25}$ is not a real number, so such a circle cannot be drawn on the coordinate plane. The equation is said to represent an **imaginary circle.**

Part Three: Problem Sets

Problem Set A

1 Write an equation of each circle.

a Center $(0, 0)$; radius 4

b Center $(-2, 1)$; radius 5

c Center $(0, -2)$; radius $2\sqrt{3}$

d Center $(-6, 0)$; radius $\frac{1}{2}$

2 Graph each equation.

a $x^2 + y^2 = 9$

b $(x - 1)^2 + (y + 2)^2 = 16$

3 Find the center, the radius, the diameter, the circumference, and the area of the circle represented by each equation.

a $x^2 + y^2 = 36$

b $(x + 5)^2 + y^2 = \frac{9}{4}$

c $(x - 3)^2 + (y + 6)^2 = 100$

d $\frac{(x + 5)^2}{3} + \frac{(y - 2)^2}{3} = 27$

4 Write an equation of each circle. (Hint: Find the value of r and use the circle formula.)

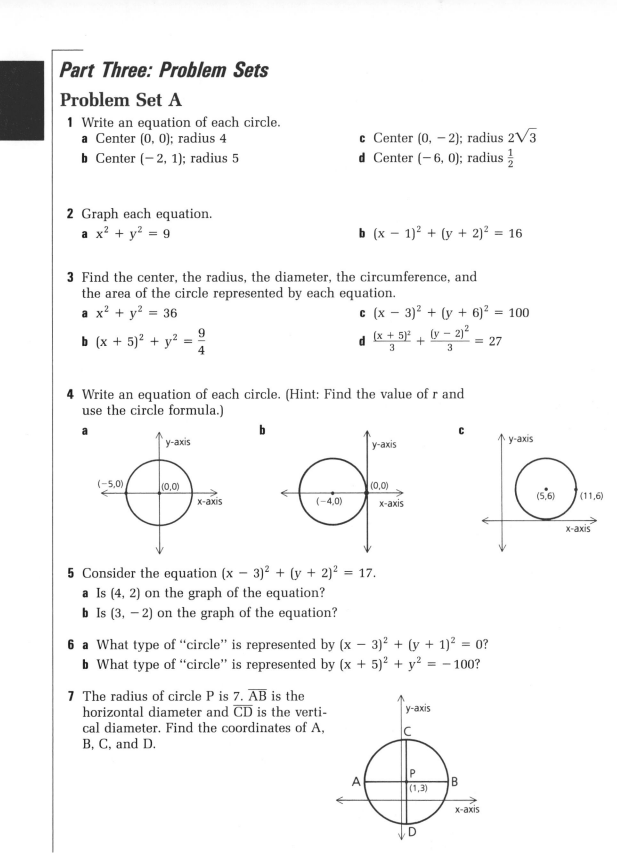

a

b

c

5 Consider the equation $(x - 3)^2 + (y + 2)^2 = 17$.

a Is $(4, 2)$ on the graph of the equation?

b Is $(3, -2)$ on the graph of the equation?

6 a What type of "circle" is represented by $(x - 3)^2 + (y + 1)^2 = 0$?

b What type of "circle" is represented by $(x + 5)^2 + y^2 = -100$?

7 The radius of circle P is 7. $\overline{AB}$ is the horizontal diameter and $\overline{CD}$ is the vertical diameter. Find the coordinates of A, B, C, and D.

Problem Set A, *continued*

8 Determine the equation of each circle.

  a The center is the origin, and the circle passes through $(0, -5)$.

  b The endpoints of a diameter are $(-2, 1)$ and $(8, 25)$.

  c The center is $(-1, 7)$, and the circle passes through the origin.

  d The center is $(2, -3)$, and the circle passes through $(3, 0)$.

9 For each given point, indicate whether the point is on, outside, or inside the circle with the given equation.

  a $(2, 5)$; $x^2 + y^2 = 29$ **c** Origin; $(x - 2)^2 + (y + 5)^2 = 16$

  b $(3, 0)$; $x^2 + y^2 = 100$ **d** $(-2, 1)$; $x^2 + (y + 6)^2 = 23$

10 Graph the solution of the system.
$$\begin{cases} x^2 + y^2 \geq 9 \\ x^2 + y^2 \leq 25 \end{cases}$$

Problem Set B

11 Find the center and the radius of the circle represented by each equation.

  a $x^2 + y^2 - 8y = 9$ **c** $x^2 + 10x + y^2 - 12y = -10$

  b $(x + 7)^2 + y^2 + 6y = 27$ **d** $x^2 + y^2 = 8x - 14y + 35$

12 Find the solution set of each system.

  a $\begin{cases} x^2 + y^2 = 25 \\ x = 3 \end{cases}$ **c** $\begin{cases} x^2 + y^2 = 34 \\ x + y = 8 \end{cases}$

  b $\begin{cases} x^2 + y^2 = 25 \\ x^2 - y^2 = 7 \end{cases}$ **d** $\begin{cases} |y| = 6 \\ x^2 + y^2 = 100 \end{cases}$

13 Find the distance between the points of intersection of the graph of $x^2 + y^2 = 17$ and the graph of $x + y = 3$.

14 Use the diagram of circle Q as marked to find

  a An equation of the tangent to the circle at $(6, 8)$

  b The circumference of the circle

  c The distance from A to Q

  d The distance from A to the circle (to the nearest tenth)

  e The area of the shaded sector (to the nearest tenth)

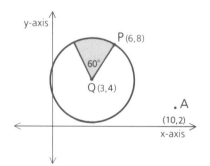

15 Consider the circle represented by $(x - 2)^2 + (y + 3)^2 = 61$. Write, in point-slope form, the equation of the tangent to the circle at point $(8, -8)$.

Problem Set C

16 Find the center and the radius of the graph of $3x^2 + 12x + 3y^2 - 5y = 2$.

17 Find the area of the circle shown.

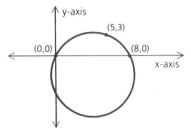

18 Find the equation of the path of a point that moves so that its distance from the point $(3, 0)$ is always twice its distance from the point $(-3, 0)$.

19 A marble was placed at point $\left(2, 4\sqrt{3}\right)$ and rolled clockwise around the graph of $x^2 - 12x + y^2 = 28$ until it stopped at the intersection of the circle with the positive x-axis.

  a Find the distance the marble traveled.

  b Find, to the nearest hundredth, the distance that would have been saved if the marble had rolled in a straight line.

Problem Set D

20 The quadrilateral region bounded by the graphs of $y = mx + 3$, $x = 2$, $x = 5$, and $y = 1$ has an area of 2. Find the maximum value of m.

COORDINATE-GEOMETRY PRACTICE

Objective

After studying this section, you will be able to
- Apply the principles of coordinate geometry in a variety of situations

The problems that follow will give you a chance to use what you have learned about coordinate geometry throughout your study of this book. As you examine each problem, try to determine which of the formulas and properties you have learned provides the best means of solving it. You will find that coordinate-geometry skills will become more and more important as you continue your study of mathematics.

Problem Sets

Problem Set A

1 Write an equation of circle P.

  a Find the area of the circle

  b Find the circle's circumference.

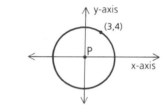

2 Find the area of the shaded sector.

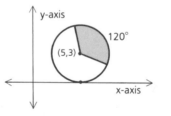

3 Find, to the nearest tenth, the area of the shaded region in each diagram.

  a ABCD is a square.

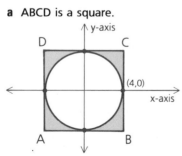

  b

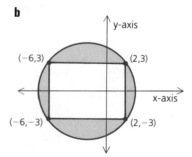

4 Find the area of the square with vertices at (1, 2), (6, 2), (6, 7), and (1, 7).

5 Given: Diagram as marked;
  M is the midpoint of $\overline{EF}$.
  Find: **a** OM
    b EM
    c FM

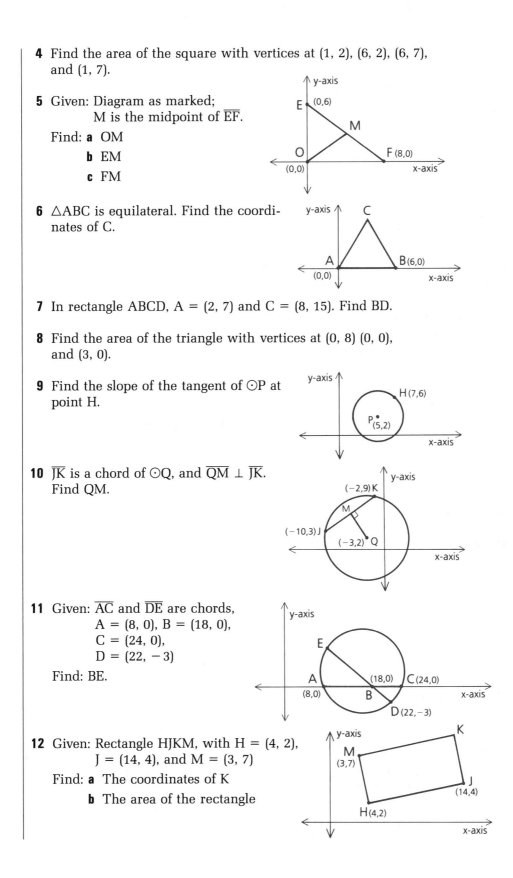

6 △ABC is equilateral. Find the coordinates of C.

7 In rectangle ABCD, A = (2, 7) and C = (8, 15). Find BD.

8 Find the area of the triangle with vertices at (0, 8) (0, 0), and (3, 0).

9 Find the slope of the tangent of ⊙P at point H.

10 $\overline{JK}$ is a chord of ⊙Q, and $\overline{QM} \perp \overline{JK}$. Find QM.

11 Given: $\overline{AC}$ and $\overline{DE}$ are chords,
    A = (8, 0), B = (18, 0),
    C = (24, 0),
    D = (22, −3)
  Find: BE.

12 Given: Rectangle HJKM, with H = (4, 2),
    J = (14, 4), and M = (3, 7)
  Find: **a** The coordinates of K
    b The area of the rectangle

Problem Set B

13 ⊙P is tangent to the x-axis and the y-axis at the points shown.

    a Find an equation of the circle.

    b Find, to the nearest tenth, the area of the shaded region bounded by the circle and the axes.

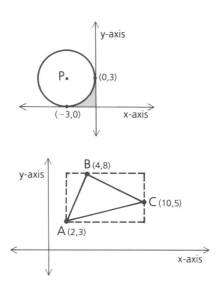

14 In the figure as marked, what is the area of △ABC? (Your solution should suggest a concept known as the *encasement principle*.)

15 In the figure as marked, what is the area of △DEF?

16 The point (13, 9) is on a circle centered at (7, 1).

    a Write an equation of the circle.

    b What is the circle's area?

    c What is the circle's circumference?

    d Find the coordinates of the point on the circle directly opposite (13, 9).

    e Write, in point-slope form, an equation of the line tangent to the circle at (13, 9).

    f Find the distance between (19, 6) and the center of the circle.

    g Find the distance between (19, 6) and the circle.

17 Find the area of the isosceles trapezoid with vertices at (4, 8), (2, 3), (14, 3), and (12, 8).

18 △ABC is an isosceles right triangle with base $\overline{AB}$. If A = (−3, −2) and B = (−3, 4), what are the two possibilities for the coordinates of C?

19 In △DEF, D = (1, 2), E = (7, 2), and F = (1, 10). Find the length of the altitude from D to $\overline{EF}$. (Hint: First find the area of △DEF.)

20 Consider the circle represented by $(x - 4)^2 + (y + 2)^2 = 50$. Let P be the center of the circle and T be a point on chord $\overline{AB}$ such that $\overline{PT}$ is perpendicular to $\overline{AB}$. If $A = (11, -1)$ and $B = (5, -9)$, what is

a PT?   **b** m∠TPA?

Problem Set C

21 $\overline{OA}$ is a fixed line segment. M can lie anywhere on a circle with a radius of 3 and its center at O. B moves so that M is always the midpoint of $\overline{AB}$. Find an equation of the circle on which B lies.

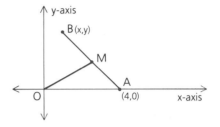

22 △AOB is placed on a coordinate system so that $A = (6, 12)$, $B = (21, 3)$, and $O = (0, 0)$. A segment, $\overline{CD}$, is drawn parallel to $\overline{OB}$ so that C lies on $\overline{AO}$, D lies on $\overline{AB}$, and $C = (4, 8)$.

a Find the coordinates of D.

b Find the ratio of the area of △ACD to the area of △AOB.

23 Find the distance between the lines represented by $y = 2x - 1$ and $y = 2x + 7$.

24 In △AOB, $A = (6, 0)$, $B = (0, 8)$, and $O = (0, 0)$.

a Find, to the nearest tenth, the volume of the solid formed by rotating the triangle about $\overline{OA}$.

b Find, to the nearest tenth, the volume of the solid formed by rotating the triangle about $\overline{OB}$.

c Find, to the nearest tenth, the volume and the total surface area of the solid formed by rotating the triangle about $\overline{AB}$.

25 Given the circles represented by $(x + 9)^2 + (y - 4)^2 = 52$ and $(x - 12)^2 + (y - 3)^2 = 13$, find the length of a

a Common internal tangent   **b** Common external tangent

26 Find the area of the quadrilateral with vertices at $(-3, 2)$, $(15, 6)$, $(7, 12)$, and $(-7, 8)$.

Problem Set D

27 A *lattice point* is a point whose coordinates are integers. How many lattice points are on the boundary and in the interior of the region bounded by the positive x-axis, the positive y-axis, the graph of $x^2 + y^2 = 25$, and the line passing through $(-3, 0)$ and $(0, 2)$?

28 A green billiard ball is located at $(3, 1)$, and a gray billiard ball at $(8, 9)$. Fats Tablechalk wants to strike the green ball so that it bounces off the y-axis and hits the gray ball. At what point on the y-axis should he aim? (Hint: Use the reflection principle.)

Problem Set D, *continued*

29 The points of $\overline{A_1 B_1}$ are "mapped" onto a new coordinate system (with shorter units) in such a way that $A_1 B_1$ is turned around, with A_1 becoming A_2 and B_1 becoming B_2.

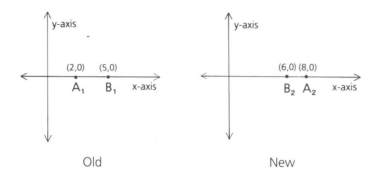

Old   New

a Find the coordinates of C_2, a point on the new coordinate system, if $C_1 = \left(3\frac{1}{2}, 0\right)$.

b Find the coordinates of D_2 if $D_1 = (4, 0)$.

c Find, in terms of x_1, the coordinates of E_2 if $E_1 = (x_1, 0)$.

THE SERPENT AND THE PEACOCK
A problem from medieval India

From ancient to medieval times, the scholars of Egypt, Mesopotamia, India, and China developed a variety of useful algebraic techniques. Unlike the Greeks, they showed little interest in the more abstract aspects of geometry.

Nevertheless, these scholars *were* aware of the Pythagorean Theorem and devised clever problems involving its application. The following is found in the treatise *Lilavati* of the Indian mathematician Bhaskara (A.D. 1114–c. 1185).

A peacock perched atop a pillar sees a snake slithering toward its den, which is at the base of the pillar. The snake is three times as far from its den as the pillar is high. If the peacock swoops down on the snake in a straight line and if the peacock and the snake travel equal distances before they meet, how far is the snake from its den when the peacock pounces on it?

Can you find a linear relationship between the height of the pillar and the distance *y* by which the snake fails to reach its den, for any height *x*?

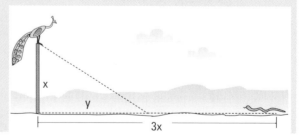

CHAPTER SUMMARY

CONCEPTS AND PROCEDURES

After studying this chapter, you should be able to

- Draw lines and circles that represent the solutions of equations (13.1)
- Write equations that correspond to nonvertical lines (13.2)
- Write equations that correspond to horizontal lines (13.2)
- Write equations that correspond to vertical lines (13.2)
- Identify various forms of linear equations (13.2)
- Use two methods to solve systems of equations (13.3)
- Graph inequalities (13.4)
- Graph in three dimensions (13.5)
- Apply the properties of reflections (13.5)
- Write equations that correspond to circles (13.6)
- Apply the principles of coordinate geometry in a variety of situations (13.7)

VOCABULARY

boundary line (13.4)
circle formula (13.6)
completing the square (13.6)
general linear form (13.2)
imaginary circle (13.6)
intercept (13.1)
intercept form (13.2)
point circle (13.6)

point-slope form (13.2)
slope-intercept form (13.2)
system of equations (13.3)
table of values (13.1)
3-D distance formula (13.5)
two-point form (13.2)
y-form (13.2)

REVIEW PROBLEMS

Problem Set A

1 Is the point (7, 5) on the graph of $2x + 3y = 62$?

2 In which quadrant are both coordinates negative?

3 If H is reflected over the barrier at $y = 10$ to H′, find the slope of $\overleftrightarrow{BH'}$.

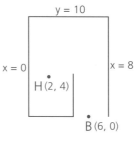

4 Find the coordinates of point D in each figure.

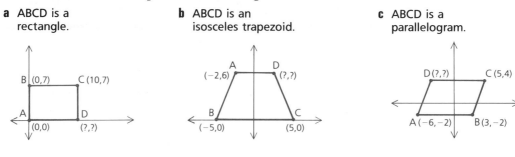

a ABCD is a rectangle.

b ABCD is an isosceles trapezoid.

c ABCD is a parallelogram.

5 If P = (4, −2) and Q = (10, 6), what is

a PQ? **b** The midpoint of $\overline{PQ}$? **c** The slope of $\overleftrightarrow{PQ}$?

6 Use the diagram of △ABC to find

a The slope of $\overline{AC}$

b The midpoint of $\overline{AC}$

c The slope of the median from B

d The length of the median from B

e The slope of the altitude from B

f The slope of a line through A and parallel to $\overleftrightarrow{BC}$

g The slope of the perpendicular bisector of $\overline{AC}$

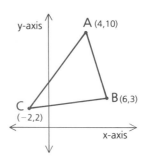

7 Find the area of each shaded region.

a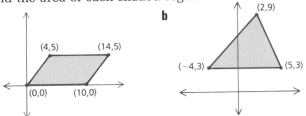

b

c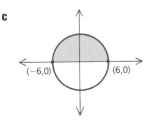

8 Write an equation of each circle.

   a Center at $(2, -3)$; radius of 4

   b Center at origin; passes through $(6, 8)$

   c Endpoints of a diameter are $(0, 0)$ and $(10, 0)$.

9 Write an equation of each line.

   a Slope of 2; y-intercept of 1

   b Contains the points $(2, 3)$ and $(2, 7)$

   c Parallel to, and 5 units to the left of, the y-axis

   d Contains the points $(2, 4)$ and $(6, 16)$

   e Slope of $\frac{1}{2}$; x-intercept of 4

   f Parallel to the graph of $y = 3x + 1$, with the same y-intercept as the graph of $y = 2x - 7$

   g x-intercept of 6; y-intercept of -3

10 Find the slope of the graph of each equation. Are the lines perpendicular, parallel, or neither?

   a $x + 2y = 10$ **b** $y = 2x + 3$

11 Are the points $(2, 4)$, $(5, 13)$, and $(26, 76)$ collinear?

12 Find the slope of $\overleftrightarrow{AB}$.

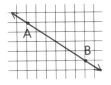

Problem Set B

13 Find the x-intercept of the line joining $(-2, 3)$ and $(5, 7)$.

14 The points $(2, 1)$, $(4, 0)$, and $(-4, k^2)$ are collinear. What is the value of k?

15 $A = (-6, 1)$ and $B = (2, 3)$. If B is the midpoint of $\overline{AC}$, find C.

16 Find the coordinates of the point one-fourth of the way from $(-5, 0)$ to $(7, 8)$.

Review Problem Set B, *continued*

17 In △ABC, A = (2, 3), B = (12, 5), and C = (9, 8).

  a Find the length of the median from C to $\overline{AB}$.

  b Write an equation of the median to $\overline{AB}$.

  c Write, in point-slope form, an equation of the perpendicular bisector of $\overline{AB}$.

  d Write, in point-slope form, an equation of the altitude from C to $\overline{AB}$.

  e Write, in point-slope form, an equation of the line containing C and parallel to $\overline{AB}$.

18 **a** Write an equation of circle P.

  b What is the area of circle P?

  c What are the coordinates of V?

  d Write, in point-slope form, an equation of the tangent $\overleftrightarrow{RT}$.

  e Find PT.

  f Find, to the nearest tenth, the distance from T to the circle.

  g What is the area of △PRT?

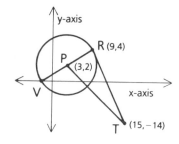

19 Graph the solution of each of the following systems of inequalities.

  a $\begin{bmatrix} y \ge 2x + 1 \\ x^2 + y^2 \le 25 \end{bmatrix}$
      b $\begin{bmatrix} y \ge 0 \\ x \le 0 \\ x - 3y \le 6 \end{bmatrix}$

20 If two of the five points (2, 1), (6, 4), (5, 17), (− 2, − 2), and (2, 10) are selected at random, what is the probability that

  a Both points lie in Quadrant I?

  b The two points will be collinear with one of the other points?

21 Find the intersection of the graphs of the equations in each system.

  a $\begin{bmatrix} y = 4x - 1 \\ y = 2x + 3 \end{bmatrix}$
    b $\begin{bmatrix} x - 3y = 10 \\ 2x + y = 13 \end{bmatrix}$
    c $\begin{bmatrix} y = 4 \\ (x - 1)^2 + (y - 5)^2 = 17 \end{bmatrix}$

22 Find the center and the radius of the graph of
$x^2 + 6x + y^2 - 4y = 12$.

23 Find, to the nearest tenth, the distance between the centers of the circles represented by $(x - 5)^2 + (y - 2)^2 = 29$ and $x^2 + 8x + y^2 = 31$.

24 The bases of an isosceles trapezoid are parallel to the y-axis. If three vertices are (5, 2), (5, 12), and (− 1, 10), find the trapezoid's area.

25 Describe the graph of $x^2 + 2x + y^2 - 6y = -10$.

26 Quadrilateral PQRS has vertices $(3, 1)$, $(15, -3)$, $(9, 7)$, and $(5, 7)$.

    a Find the quadrilateral's area by using the encasement principle. (See Section 13.7, problem 14.)

    b What is true about the diagonals?

Problem Set C

27 Consider the graph of $2x - 5y = 10$. In which quadrant(s) is there a point that is on this line and equidistant from the x-axis and the y-axis? Find the point(s).

28 Use a triangle with vertices at $(0, 0)$, $(2a, 0)$, and $(0, 2b)$ to show that the midpoint of the hypotenuse of any right triangle is equidistant from the vertices of the triangle.

29 If $A = (0, -17)$, $B = (4, -5)$, and $C = (12, -1)$, what is the length of the altitude from C to $\overline{AB}$?

30 Find the distance between the graphs of $y = 3x - 8$ and $y = 3x + 2$.

31 A triangle with vertices at $(0, 0)$, $(6, 0)$, and $\left(0, 6\sqrt{3}\right)$ is rotated around its longest side. Find, to the nearest tenth, the volume of the solid formed.

32 If $A = (-8, 5)$ and $B = (7, -3)$, where is the point R that divides $\overline{AB}$ so that $AR:RB = 3:2$?

33 In $\square$PQRS, M, N, and X are midpoints of $\overline{PQ}$, $\overline{PS}$, and $\overline{QR}$ respectively. Find the intersection of $\overline{MN}$ and $\overline{PX}$ if $P = (-8, 1)$, $Q = (0, 5)$, and $S = (4, 1)$.

34 How many lattice points are in the intersection of this system?

$$\begin{bmatrix} x > 0 \\ y > 0 \\ y < -|x - 4| + 10 \end{bmatrix}$$

35 $A = (2, 10)$ and $C = (8, 4)$. Find point B if it lies on the x-axis and $AB + BC$ is a minimum.

36 Find the image of point $(-5, 10)$ when it is reflected over

    a The x-axis   **b** The point $(-3, 1)$ **c** The graph of $y = 2x$

37 Find the intersection.

$$\begin{bmatrix} x + y = 16 \\ y = |2x + 10| \end{bmatrix}$$

CHAPTER

14 | Locus and Constructions

Every home in each locus of summer homes in the small community of Brøndbyvester, Denmark, is equidistant from a parking lot.

LOCUS

Objective

After studying this section, you will be able to
- Use the four-step locus procedure to solve locus problems

Part One: Introduction

Mathematicians sometimes find it convenient to describe a figure as a **locus**. (*Locus* is a Latin word meaning "place" or "position." Its plural form is *loci*.)

Definition   A **locus** is a set consisting of all the points, and only the points, that satisfy specific conditions.

In this book, all loci are to be considered sets of *coplanar* points unless specified otherwise.

Example 1   *Find the locus of points that are 1 in. from a given point O.*

Find one point, P₁, that is 1 in. from O. Then find a second such point, P₂. Continue finding such points until a pattern is formed—in this case, a circle.

Draw the circle and finish with a written description: "The locus of points 1 in. from a given point O is a circle having O as its center and a radius of 1 in."

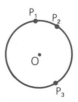

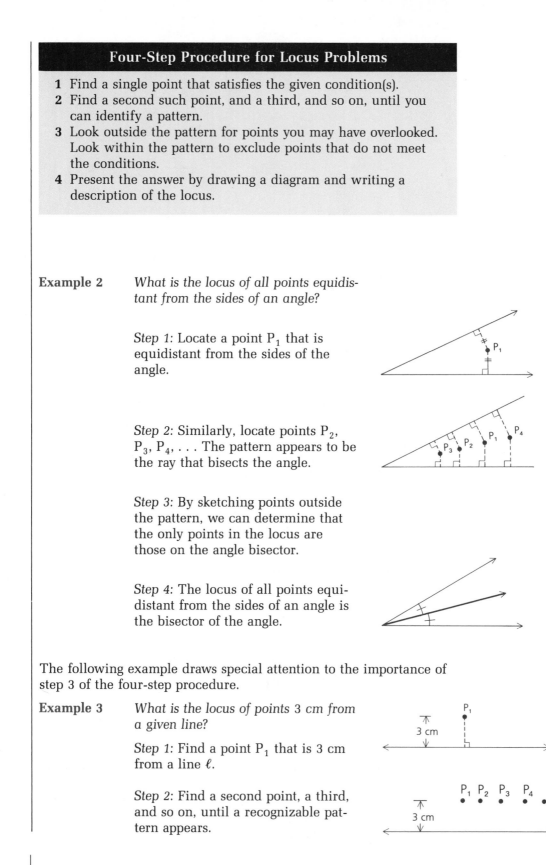

Four-Step Procedure for Locus Problems

1 Find a single point that satisfies the given condition(s).
2 Find a second such point, and a third, and so on, until you can identify a pattern.
3 Look outside the pattern for points you may have overlooked. Look within the pattern to exclude points that do not meet the conditions.
4 Present the answer by drawing a diagram and writing a description of the locus.

Example 2   *What is the locus of all points equidistant from the sides of an angle?*

Step 1: Locate a point P_1 that is equidistant from the sides of the angle.

Step 2: Similarly, locate points P_2, P_3, P_4, . . . The pattern appears to be the ray that bisects the angle.

Step 3: By sketching points outside the pattern, we can determine that the only points in the locus are those on the angle bisector.

Step 4: The locus of all points equidistant from the sides of an angle is the bisector of the angle.

The following example draws special attention to the importance of step 3 of the four-step procedure.

Example 3   *What is the locus of points 3 cm from a given line?*

Step 1: Find a point P_1 that is 3 cm from a line ℓ.

Step 2: Find a second point, a third, and so on, until a recognizable pattern appears.

Step 3: The pattern appears to be a line parallel to ℓ and 3 cm above it. But by checking other points, we can see that points 3 cm below ℓ are also in the locus.

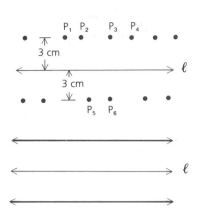

Step 4: The locus of points 3 cm from a given line is two lines parallel to the given line, 3 cm on either side of it.

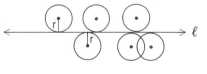

Part Two: Sample Problems

Remember that loci are plane figures unless specified otherwise.

Problem 1   *What is the locus of points 2 in. from a given circle whose radius is 5 in.?*

Answer   The locus of points 2 in. from the given circle is two circles that are concentric with that circle and have radii of 3 in. and 7 in.

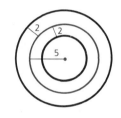

Problem 2   *Find the locus of points less than 3 cm from a given point A.*

Answer   The locus of points less than 3 cm from a given point A is the *interior* of a circle with its center at A and a radius of 3 cm. (The circle itself is not part of the locus. Do you see why?)

Problem 3   *What is the locus of the centers of all circles that have a fixed radius r and are tangent to a given line ℓ?*

Solution   Sketch a few circles tangent to the given line ℓ. Then consider the pattern of their centers only.

The locus of the centers of all circles that have a fixed radius r and are tangent to a given line ℓ is two parallel lines on opposite sides of ℓ, each at the distance r from ℓ.

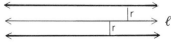

Problem 4   *Write the equation of the locus of points equidistant from points A = (1, 4) and B = (7, 8).*

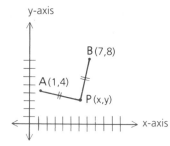

Solution   *Method One:* If P = (x, y) is any point on the locus, then PA = PB.

$$\sqrt{(x-1)^2 + (y-4)^2} = \sqrt{(x-7)^2 + (y-8)^2}$$
$$(x-1)^2 + (y-4)^2 = (x-7)^2 + (y-8)^2$$
$$x^2 - 2x + 1 + y^2 - 8y + 16 = x^2 - 14x + 49 + y^2 - 16y + 64$$
$$-2x - 8y + 17 = -14x - 16y + 113$$
$$y = -\frac{3}{2}x + 12$$

Method Two: We know that the locus of all points equidistant from A and B is the perpendicular bisector of $\overline{AB}$.

Midpoint of $\overline{AB}$ = (4, 6), and slope of $\overline{AB} = \frac{8-4}{7-1} = \frac{2}{3}$.

∴Slope of perpendicular bisector = $-\frac{3}{2}$.

$$y = mx + b$$
$$6 = -\frac{3}{2}(4) + b$$
$$12 = b$$
$$y = -\frac{3}{2}x + 12$$

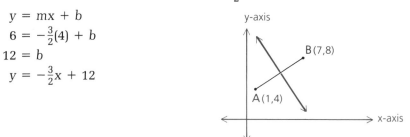

Part Three: Problem Sets

Problem Set A

Remember that loci are plane figures unless specified otherwise.

In problems 1–8, draw a sketch and write a description of each locus.

1 The locus of points that are 3 cm from a given line, $\overleftrightarrow{AB}$

2 The locus of the midpoints of the radii of a given circle

3 The locus of points equidistant from two given points

4 The locus of points occupied by the center of a dime as it rolls around the edge of a quarter

5 The locus of points that are 10 in. from a circle with a radius of 1 ft

6 The locus of the centers of all circles tangent to both of two given parallel lines

7 The locus of points equidistant from two given concentric circles (If the radii of the circles are 3 and 8, what is the size of the locus?)

8 The locus of points less than or equal to 14 units from a fixed point P

9 Write an equation for the locus of points that are 4 units from the origin.

10 a Find the locus of points that are 5 units from both a and b.
    b Find the locus of points that are 4 units from both a and b.

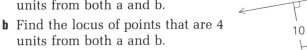

Problem Set B

11 What is the locus of the midpoints of all chords that can be drawn from a given point of a given circle?

12 What is the locus of the midpoints of all chords congruent to a given chord of a given circle?

13 Determine the locus of centers of all circles passing through two given points. Give an accurate, simple description of the locus.

14 Write an equation for the locus of points 6 units from $(-1, 3)$.

15 What is the locus of the midpoints of all segments drawn from one vertex of a triangle to the opposite side of the triangle?

16 What is the locus *in space* of points that are
   a 5 units from a given point?
   b 5 units from a given line?

17 Write an equation for the locus of points equidistant from the lines whose equations are $x = -2$ and $x = 7$

18 Find the locus of points that are 5 units from both the x-axis and the y-axis.

19 Given a circle Q with a radius of 9, find the locus of points 9 units from the circle Q.

20 a Sketch the locus of points 5 units from a segment, $\overline{PQ}$.
   b Find the area of the locus sketched in part **a** if PQ = 6.
   c Sketch the locus *in space* of points 5 units from segment $\overline{PQ}$.
   d Find the volume of the locus sketched in part **c** if PQ = 6.

21 Point P is 4 units above plane m. Find the locus of points that lie in plane m and are 5 units from P.

22 Write an equation for the locus of points equidistant from (3, 5) and (1, -9).

23 Points T and V are fixed. Find the locus of P such that $\overline{PT} \perp \overline{PV}$.

Problem Set C

24 Write an equation for the locus of points each of which is the vertex of the right angle of a right triangle whose hypotenuse is the segment joining (-1, 0) and (1, 0). Describe the set geometrically.

25 a The locus of points equidistant from the vertices of a triangle is the point of intersection of the __?__ of the triangle.
   b The locus of points equidistant from the sides of a triangle is the point of intersection of the __?__ of the triangle.

26 Write an equation for the locus of points (x, y) such that the area of the triangle with vertices (x, y), (0, 0), and (3, 0) is 2.

27 Given: P = (−3, 4)

    a Sketch the locus of points that are 2 or more units from P and at the same time are no more than 5 units from P.

    b Describe the locus algebraically.

    c Find the area of the locus.

28 A ladder 6 m long leans against a wall. Describe the locus of the midpoint of the ladder in all possible positions. Prove that your answer is correct.

29 Write an equation for the locus of points each of which is twice as far from (−2, 0) as it is from (1, 0).

30 PQRS is a rectangle with $\overline{PQ}$ twice as long as $\overline{QR}$. T is the midpoint of $\overline{RS}$. $\overline{TQ}$ is drawn. Sketch the locus of the midpoints of segments that are parallel to $\overline{TQ}$ and end on the sides of the rectangle.

HISTORICAL SNAPSHOT

THE GEOMETRY OF MUSIC
Pythagoras and the harmonious blacksmiths

The philosopher Pythagoras (c. 540 B.C.) and his followers believed that the whole numbers were the key to the structure of the universe. In part, this belief was based on discoveries they made about mathematical relationships among the tones of the musical scale.

As the sixth-century writer Macrobius tells the story, one day Pythagoras was walking by a workshop where two blacksmiths were beating out a piece of hot iron. Noticing that the workers' hammers rang with different but harmonious sounds, Pythagoras went inside to investigate the reason. He determined that the tones produced by the hammers depended not on the force with which the hammers were wielded but only on their sizes and weights.

In later experiments, the Pythagoreans plucked stretched strings to produce musical tones. It was discovered that by treating a string as a line segment and dividing it in ratios corresponding to quotients of whole numbers, all the tones of the musical scale can be produced. For instance, if a string is bisected, each half sounds a tone one octave higher than that produced by the whole string. Similarly, when a string is divided in the ratio 2:3, each part sounds the musical interval known as a fifth. The ratio 3:4 produces the interval known as a fourth.

The Pythagoreans' research forms the basis for the construction of many modern musical instruments. It is important, however, as one of the earliest cases in which mathematics was used to explain natural phenomena.

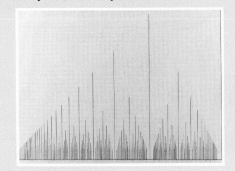

COMPOUND LOCUS

Objective

After studying this section, you will be able to
- Apply the compound-locus procedure

Part One: Introduction

Many locus problems involve combining two or more loci in one *compound locus*.

Example   If points A and B are 5 units apart, what is the locus of points 3 units from A and 4 units from B?

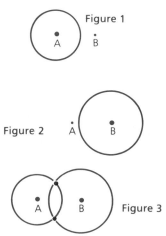

Figure 1

Figure 2

Figure 3

The locus of points 3 units from A is the circle shown in Figure 1.

The locus of points 4 units from B is the circle shown in Figure 2.

The locus of points that are both 3 units from A and 4 units from B is the two blue points in Figure 3.

Notice that the compound locus illustrated in Figure 3 is the *inter-section* of the loci in Figure 1 and Figure 2.

Compound-Locus Procedure

1 Solve each part of the compound locus problem separately.
2 Find all possible intersections of the loci.

Part Two: Sample Problems

Problem 1   Find the locus of points that are a fixed distance from a given line and lie on a given circle.

Solution   Follow the compound-locus procedure.

Step 1: Find each locus individually.

The locus of points that are a fixed distance from a given line is two lines that are parallel to the given line.

The locus of points that lie on a given circle is simply the circle itself.

Step 2: Find all possible intersections of the loci. Thus, the locus of points that are a fixed distance from a given line and lie on a given circle is 4 points, 3 points, 2 points, 1 point, or the empty set.

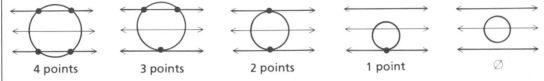

| 4 points | 3 points | 2 points | 1 point | ∅ |

Note To solve a compound-locus problem, keep any fixed distance or fixed figure the same in all drawings. Change given distances and the size and position of given figures to show all possible situations.

Problem 2 *Find the locus in space of points that are a fixed distance from a given plane and a given distance from a fixed point on the plane.*

Solution Follow the compound-locus procedure.

Step 1: Find each locus individually.

The locus of points that are a fixed distance from a given plane is two planes that are parallel to the given plane.

The locus in space of points that are a given distance r from a fixed point P is a sphere with center P and radius r.

Step 2: Find all possible intersections of the two loci.

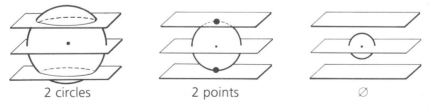

| 2 circles | 2 points | ∅ |

Thus, the locus in space of points that are a fixed distance from a given plane and a given distance from a fixed point on the plane is two circles or two points or the empty set.

Part Three: Problem Sets

Problem Set A

1 Sketch all possible intersections for each compound locus. Then describe the compound locus.

   a The locus of points equidistant from two given points and lying on a given circle

   b The locus of points that are a given distance from a point A and another given distance from a point B

   c The locus of points on both the graph of $y = 5$ and the graph of $x^2 + y^2 = r^2$, where $r > 0$

   d The locus of points equidistant from two parallel lines and lying on a third line

   e The locus of points equidistant from two intersecting lines and a fixed distance from their point of intersection

   f The locus of points equidistant from the sides of an angle and equidistant from two parallel lines

2 Find the locus of points that are 1 cm from a 4-cm-long segment and 2 cm from the midpoint of the segment.

3 How many points are equidistant from two given parallel lines and equidistant from two fixed points on one of those lines?

4 Given a regular hexagon, find the locus of points that are a given distance from its center and lie on the vertices of the hexagon.

Problem Set B

5 a What is the locus of points that are less than or equal to a fixed distance from a given point and lie on a given line?

   b What is the locus of points that are less than a fixed distance from a given point and lie on a given line?

6 Find the locus of points equidistant from two concentric circles and on a diameter of the larger circle.

7 Find all the points on a given line that are a fixed distance from a given circle if the fixed distance is less than the circle's radius.

8 Find the locus of points 10 units from the origin of a coordinate system and 6 units from the y-axis.

9 Transversal t intersects parallel lines m and n. Find the locus of points equidistant from m and n and 1 unit from t.

10 Given a regular pentagon, find the locus of points that are a given distance from its center and lie on it.

Problem Set C

11 Given three points, A, B, and C, find the locus of points equidistant from all three points.

12 a Find the locus *in space* of points that are 3 in. from a given plane and 5 in. from a fixed point on the plane.

b Find the area of the figure(s) found in part **a**.

13 Find all the points equidistant from two given points and at a given distance from a given circle.

14 Find the locus *in space* of points that are equidistant from two given points and at a given distance from a given line.

15 Find the locus of points that lie on a given square and also lie on a given circle with its center in the interior of the square.

16 Given ∠A and ∠B, find the locus of points that are equidistant from the sides of ∠A and the sides of ∠B.

17 Find the locus *in space* of a line segment revolving about its midpoint.

THE CONCURRENCE THEOREMS

Objective

After studying this section, you will be able to
- Identify the circumcenter, the incenter, the orthocenter, and the centroid of a triangle

Part One: Introduction

Lines that have exactly one point in common are said to be **concurrent**.

Definition   *Concurrent lines* are lines that intersect in a single point.

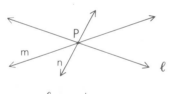

ℓ, m and n are
Concurrent at P.

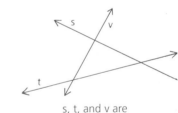

s, t, and v are
not Concurrent.

With this definition and an understanding of compound loci, we can investigate some theorems of advanced geometry.

Theorem 128   *The perpendicular bisectors of the sides of a triangle are concurrent at a point that is equidistant from the vertices of the triangle. (The point of concurrency of the perpendicular bisectors is called the* **circumcenter** *of the triangle.)*

Given: ℓ is the ⊥ bisector of $\overline{BC}$.
  m is the ⊥ bisector of $\overline{AC}$.
  n is the ⊥ bisector of $\overline{AB}$.

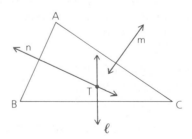

Prove: **a** ℓ, m, and n are concurrent at point T.

b T is equidistant from A, B, and C.

Proof: Let T be the point of intersection of ℓ and n.
(How do we know that ℓ and n intersect?)
We must show that m passes through T.

Because T is on line ℓ, the perpendicular bisector of $\overline{BC}$, T is equidistant from points B and C. (Any point on the perpendicular bisector of a line segment is equidistant from the endpoints of that segment.)

Similarly, T is equidistant from points A and B because it lies on n, the perpendicular bisector of $\overline{AB}$.

By transitivity, T is equidistant from A and C. Since m is the locus of *all* points equidistant from A and C, T must lie on m.

The bisectors of the angles of a triangle are also concurrent. This statement is formalized in the following theorem, which is presented without proof.

Theorem 129   ***The bisectors of the angles of a triangle are concurrent at a point that is equidistant from the sides of the triangle. (The point of concurrency of the angle bisectors is called the*** incenter ***of the triangle.)***

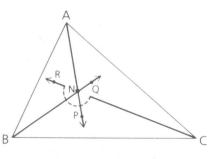

Given: $\overrightarrow{AP}$ bisects ∠BAC.

$\overrightarrow{BQ}$ bisects ∠ABC.

$\overrightarrow{CR}$ bisects ∠ACB.

Prove: **a** $\overrightarrow{AP}$, $\overrightarrow{BQ}$, and $\overrightarrow{CR}$ are concurrent at point N.

b N is equidistant from $\overline{AB}$, $\overline{BC}$, and $\overline{AC}$.

The proof of Theorem 129 depends on the fact that the locus of all points equidistant from the sides of an angle is the bisector of the angle (example 2 in Section 14.1). The organization of the proof is much like that of Theorem 128.

Theorem 130   ***The lines containing the altitudes of a triangle are concurrent. (The point of concurrency of the lines containing the altitudes is called the*** orthocenter ***of the triangle.)***

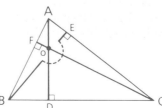

Given: $\overline{AD}$ is the altitude to $\overline{BC}$.

$\overline{BE}$ is the altitude to $\overline{AC}$.

$\overline{CF}$ is the altitude to $\overline{AB}$.

Prove: $\overleftrightarrow{AD}$, $\overleftrightarrow{BE}$, and $\overleftrightarrow{CF}$ are concurrent at O.

The proof of this theorem is asked for in Problem Set C, problem 19.

Note   The orthocenter of a triangle is not always inside the triangle, as you can see in the following figures.

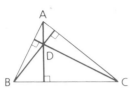

△ABC is an acute △.
D is the orthocenter.

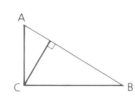

△ABC is a right △.
C is the orthocenter.

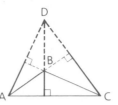

△ABC is an obtuse △.
D is the orthocenter.

Theorem 131   ***The medians of a triangle are concurrent at a point that is two thirds of the way from any vertex of the triangle to the midpoint of the opposite side. (The point of concurrency of the medians of a triangle is called the*** *centroid* ***of the triangle.)***

Given: Medians $\overline{AM}$, $\overline{BN}$, and $\overline{CP}$

Prove: **a** $\overline{AM}$, $\overline{BN}$, and $\overline{CP}$ are concurrent at T.

   b $\dfrac{AT}{AM} = \dfrac{CT}{CP} = \dfrac{BT}{BN} = \dfrac{2}{3}$

The proof of Theorem 131 is asked for in Problem Set D, problem 21. The centroid of a triangle is important in physics because it is the *center of gravity* of the triangle.

Part Two: Sample Problem

Problem   In △PQR, *medians* $\overline{QT}$ *and* $\overline{PS}$ *are concurrent at C.*
PC = 4x − 6,
CS = x
Find: **a** x   **b** PS

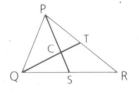

Solution   **a** The medians of a triangle are concurrent at a point that is two thirds of the way from any vertex of the triangle to the midpoint of the opposite side. Thus,
PC = $\frac{2}{3}$(PS), or PC = 2(CS).

$$4x - 6 = 2x$$
$$x = 3$$

b $PC = 4x - 6$
   $= 4(3) - 6$
   $= 12 - 6$
   $= 6$

Thus, $PS = PC + CS = 6 + 3 = 9$.

Part Three: Problem Sets

Problem Set A

1 Trace △ABC on a piece of paper. Use a ruler to locate the centroid of △ABC.

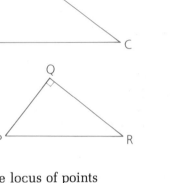

2 Find the orthocenter of right triangle PQR.

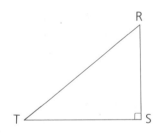

3 Given scalene △ DEF, explain how to find the locus of points equidistant from $\overline{DE}$, $\overline{EF}$, and $\overline{DF}$.

4 Trace right △ RST on a piece of paper.

   a Use a ruler to estimate the location of the circumcenter.

   b Use your result in part **a** to guess the exact location of the circumcenter of any right triangle.

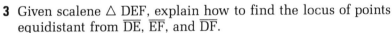

5 Every triangle has a circumcenter, an orthocenter, a centroid, and an incenter. Which of the four points will always lie in the interior of the triangle?

6 Given: △ABC, with medians $\overline{AM}$, $\overline{BN}$, and $\overline{CP}$.

   a If AM = 9, find AT.

   b If TN = 5, find BN.

   c If TC = 8, find PT.

   d If BN = $\sqrt{18}$, find TN.

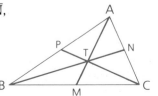

Problem Set A, *continued*

7 If a triangle is cut from cardboard and the circumcenter, the orthocenter, the centroid, and the incenter are located, upon which point could the triangle be balanced?

Problem Set B

8 In what kind of triangle is the orthocenter a vertex of the triangle?

9 In what kind of triangle is the orthocenter the same point as the circumcenter?

10 In what kind of triangle does the centroid lie outside the triangle?

11 Sketch three noncollinear points. Then sketch and describe the locus of points equidistant from all three points.

12 Given: △RST with medians
$\overline{RM}$ and $\overline{TN}$ intersecting at P,
RP = 2y − x, TP = 2y,
PM = y − 2, PN = x + 2

Find: The longer of the two medians

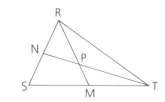

13 Given: △PLO with centroid V,
VT = 6, AT = 9, OT = 18

Find: **a** PA

   b The area of △PLO

   c The area of △POT

   d m∠APT

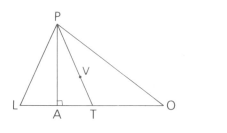

14 Given △PQR, with P = (0, 0), Q = (5, 12), and R = (10, 0), find the coordinates of its centroid.

Problem Set C

15 Given △ABC, with A = (1, 3), B = (7, −3), and C = (9, 5), find the circumcenter of the triangle.

16 Given △RST, with R = (−3, 2), S = (4, 5), and T = (7, −2), find the coordinates of its orthocenter.

17 Recall that the coordinates of the midpoint of a side of a triangle are the averages of the coordinates of the endpoints. As an extension of this idea, it can be shown that the coordinates of the centroid of a triangle are the averages of the coordinates of the three vertices of the triangle.

Given: $\triangle ABC$, with A = $(-2, 8)$, B = $(-6, -2)$, and C = $(12, 6)$

Find: **a** The coordinates of the centroid of $\triangle ABC$

   b The coordinates of the centroid of the triangle formed by joining the midpoints of the sides of $\triangle ABC$

18 Given: $\triangle ABC$, with median $\overline{AM}$ and centroid P

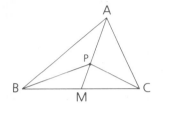

   a Using $\overline{BC}$ as the base of each triangle, prove that the altitude of $\triangle PBC$ is one third of the altitude of $\triangle ABC$.

   b Find the ratio of the area of $\triangle PBC$ to the area of $\triangle ABC$.

19 Given: $\triangle ABC$

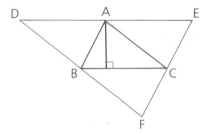

   Prove: The lines containing the altitudes of $\triangle ABC$ are concurrent (Theorem 130). (Hint: Through each vertex of the triangle, draw a line parallel to the opposite side, obtaining the diagram shown. Then apply Theorem 128.)

20 Sketch a triangle and its medians. As you know, the centroid of the triangle is one of the trisection points of each median. Now form another triangle by joining the *other* trisection points of the medians.

   a Find the ratio of the area of this triangle to the area of the original triangle.

   b What is the relationship of this triangle to the triangle formed by joining the midpoints of the sides of the original triangle.

Problem Set D

21 Given: $\triangle ABC$

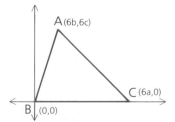

   Prove: The medians of $\triangle ABC$ are concurrent at a point that is two thirds of the way from any vertex of $\triangle ABC$ to the midpoint of the opposite side (Theorem 131). (Hint: Use the coordinates shown in the diagram.)

BASIC CONSTRUCTIONS

Objectives

After studying this section, you will be able to
- Identify the tools and procedures used in constructions
- Interpret the shorthand notation used in describing constructions
- Perform six basic constructions

Part One: Introduction

Constructions

A *construction* is a drawing made with the help of only two simple tools. The procedures used for constructions are based on ones developed by ancient Greek geometricians. The two tools needed are

1 A compass, to construct circles or arcs of circles
2 A straightedge, to draw lines or rays (A straightedge differs from a ruler only by the absence of marks for measuring distances.)

These tools can produce accurate drawings when correctly used. (A sharp pencil and good paper on flat, firm cardboard are necessities.) Admittedly, modern drafting machines can produce more-accurate drawings in less time, but constructions are still worth studying for reasons such as the following:

- The tools are simple and portable.
- There is an orderly progression of steps. Nothing is accepted just because the result looks correct.
- Analyzing constructions strengthens understanding of theorems.
- The restrictions on equipment and the strictly defined rules make producing constructions a challenging game, one enjoyed by most people who learn it. The game has a practical bonus for some, because users of drafting machines must analyze problems, and their analyses are often the same as those used for constructions.

Shorthand Notation for Constructions

So that the step-by-step instructions will be clear and concise, the following notation for constructions will be used in this book:

1 ⊙ **(P, PB)** represents a circle with center P and radius of length PB.

2 **arc (P, PB)** represents an arc with center P and radius of length PB.

Six Basic Constructions

The following six constructions are the basis of all further work with constructions. Because a construction has meaning only in terms of how it is developed, we urge you to redraw these constructions, following the instructions step by step.

Construction 1: Segment Copy

Construction of a line segment congruent to a given segment.

Given: $\overline{AB}$ (In the setup on your paper, draw segment $\overline{AB}$ of any length you want.)

Construct: A segment $\overline{PQ}$ that is congruent to $\overline{AB}$

Procedure:
1 Draw a *working line*, w.
2 Let P be any point on w.
3 On the given segment, construct arc (A, AB).
4 Construct arc (P, AB) intersecting w at some point Q.
5 $\overline{PQ} \cong \overline{AB}$

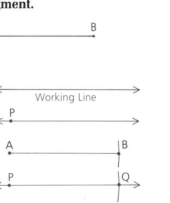

Notice that in constructions lengths are not measured with rulers; they are matched by compass settings.

Your finished paper should look something like this:

Given: $\overline{AB}$

Construct: $\overline{PQ}$, $\cong$ to $\overline{AB}$ $\therefore \overline{PQ} = \overline{AB}$

Note   Do not erase any arc marks in any construction problems.

Construction 2: Angle Copy

Construction of an angle congruent to a given angle.

Given: $\angle ABC$ (Make your setup big enough for easy use of the compass, yet not so big that everything won't fit on your paper.)

Construct: An angle PQR that is congruent to $\angle ABC$

Procedure:

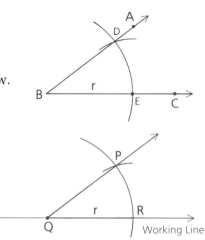

1. On the setup, use any radius *r* to construct arc (B, r) intersecting ∠ABC at two points. Call them D and E.
2. Let Q be any point on a working line, w.
3. Construct arc (Q, r) to intersect w at some point R.
4. Construct arc (E, ED).
5. Construct arc (R, ED) intersecting arc (Q, r) at some point P.
6. Draw $\overrightarrow{QP}$.
7. ∠PQR ≅ ∠ABC

If we drew $\overline{DE}$ and $\overline{PR}$, we would form △BDE and △QPR. Do you see how SSS is the basis of this construction?

Construction 3: Angle Bisection

Construction of the bisector of a given angle.

Given: ∠ABC

Construct: $\overrightarrow{BP}$, the bisector of ∠ABC

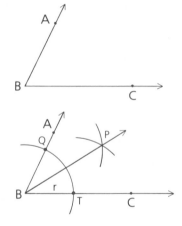

Procedure:

1. Use any radius r to construct arc (B, r) intersecting the sides of ∠ABC at two points, Q and T.
2. Use any radius s (which may or may not be equal to r) to construct arc (Q, s) and arc (T, s), intersecting each other at a point P.
3. Draw $\overrightarrow{BP}$.
4. $\overrightarrow{BP}$ bisects ∠ABC.

If we drew $\overline{QP}$ and $\overline{PT}$, each would be s units long. Can you see how SSS is the basis of this construction?

Construction 4: Perpendicular Bisector

Construction of the perpendicular bisector of a given line segment.

Given: $\overline{AB}$

Construct: $\overleftrightarrow{PQ}$, the perpendicular bisector of $\overline{AB}$

A   B

Procedure:
1 Use any radius *r* that is more than half the length of $\overline{AB}$ to construct arc (A, *r*).
2 Construct arc (B, *r*) intersecting arc (A, *r*) at P and Q.
3 Draw $\overleftrightarrow{PQ}$.
4 $\overleftrightarrow{PQ}$ is the perpendicular bisector of $\overline{AB}$.

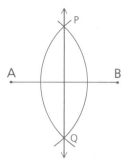

Construction 5: Erecting a Perpendicular

Construction of a line perpendicular to a given line at a given point on the line.

Given: $\overleftrightarrow{AB}$ and point P on the line

Construct: $\overleftrightarrow{PQ}$ perpendicular to $\overleftrightarrow{AB}$ at P

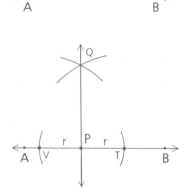

Procedure:
1 Use any radius *r* to construct arc (P, *r*) intersecting $\overleftrightarrow{AB}$ at V and T.
2 Use any radius *s* that is greater than *r* to construct arc (V, *s*) and arc (T, *s*), intersecting each other at a point Q.
3 Draw $\overleftrightarrow{PQ}$.
4 $\overleftrightarrow{PQ} \perp \overleftrightarrow{AB}$.

Construction 6: Dropping a Perpendicular

Construction of a line perpendicular to a given line from a given point not on the line.

Given: $\overleftrightarrow{AB}$ and point P not on $\overleftrightarrow{AB}$

Construct: $\overleftrightarrow{PQ}$ perpendicular to $\overleftrightarrow{AB}$

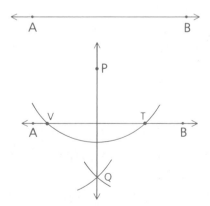

Procedure:
1 Use any radius *r* to construct arc (P, *r*) intersecting $\overleftrightarrow{AB}$ at V and T.
2 Use any radius *s* (which may or may not be equal to *r*) to construct arc (V, *s*) and arc (T, *s*), intersecting each other at a point Q.
3 Draw $\overleftrightarrow{PQ}$.
4 $\overleftrightarrow{PQ} \perp \overleftrightarrow{AB}$.

Part Two: Sample Problems

Problem 1   Given: ∠A and ∠B as shown

Construct: An angle whose measure is
equal to (x + y)

Solution   1 On a working line w, use the
angle-copy procedure to construct
∠VTS ≅ to ∠A.
2 With $\overleftrightarrow{TV}$ as a new working line,
use the angle-copy procedure to
construct ∠QTV ≅ to ∠B.
3 ∠QTS is the required angle.

Problem 2   Given: ⊙P and point A on the circle
Construct: The tangent to ⊙P at point A

Solution   Make a freehand sketch of the required construction. Analyze the
geometric relationships between the parts of the sketch to determine
the required procedure.
    For this problem, the sketch will
look like the one at the right. Do you
see what needs to be done?
1 Draw $\overrightarrow{PA}$.
2 Construct the ⊥ to $\overleftrightarrow{PA}$ at A. (See
Construction 5.)
3 $\overleftrightarrow{TA}$ is the required tangent.

Problem 3   Given: ⊙O and point P outside the circle
Construct: A tangent to ⊙O from point P

Solution   At the point of tangency, a radius and the required tangent will
form a right angle. (See Problem Set D, problem 19.)
1 Draw $\overline{OP}$.
2 Find the midpoint M of $\overline{OP}$ by the
perpendicular-bisector procedure.
3 Construct ⊙ (M, MP).
4 Label A and B, the intersections of
⊙O and ⊙M.
5 Draw $\overline{PA}$.
6 $\overline{PA}$ is tangent to ⊙O.

Part Three: Problem Sets

Problem Set A

1 Construct the locus of points equidistant from two fixed points A and B.

2 Draw two segments, $\overline{AB}$ and $\overline{CD}$, with AB > CD.
  a Construct a segment whose length is the sum of AB and CD.
  b Construct a segment whose length is the difference of AB and CD.
  c Locate the midpoint of $\overline{AB}$ by construction.
  d Construct an equilateral triangle whose sides are congruent to $\overline{CD}$.
  e Construct an isosceles triangle, making its base congruent to $\overline{CD}$ and each leg congruent to $\overline{AB}$.
  f Construct a square whose sides are congruent to $\overline{AB}$.
  g Construct a circle whose diameter is congruent to $\overline{CD}$.

3 Draw an acute angle ABC and an obtuse angle WXY.
  a Construct ∠FGH congruent to ∠WXY.
  b Construct the complement of ∠ABC.
  c Construct the supplement of ∠WXY.
  d Construct an angle whose measure is the difference of ∠WXY and ∠ABC.
  e Construct an angle whose measure is double that of ∠ABC.

4 Construct the following angles.
  a 90°   **b** 45°   **c** 60°   **d** 75°

5 Draw an obtuse triangle. Construct the bisector of each angle.

Problem Set B

6 If a and b are the lengths of two segments and $a < b$, construct a segment whose length is equal to $\frac{1}{2}(b - a)$.

7 Given ∠A and ∠B, construct an angle equal to $\frac{1}{2}(m\angle A + m\angle B)$.

8 Construct an angle with each given measure.
  a 135   **b** $112\frac{1}{2}$ **c** 165

9 Inscribe a square in a given circle. (Hint: Use the diagonals.)

10 Construct the three medians of a given △PQR.

11 Construct the three altitudes of an acute △ABC.

Problem Set B, *continued*

12 Given circle P with point Q in the interior of the circle, construct a chord of the circle having Q as its midpoint.

13 ∠A is the vertex angle of an isosceles triangle. Find, by construction, one of the base angles of the triangle. (Can you do this without drawing a triangle?)

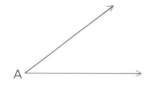

Problem Set C

14 Draw any triangle. Construct a second triangle similar to the first such that the ratio of the perimeters is 1:2.

15 Construct a square whose diagonal is equal to AB.

16 Explain how you would construct each angle.
    a $32\frac{1}{2}°$ (if given an angle of 80°)   **b** $41\frac{1}{4}°$

17 Construct two parallel lines.

18 Construct a line, $\overleftrightarrow{CD}$, that is parallel to $\overleftrightarrow{AB}$ and tangent to ⊙O.

Problem Set D

19 Write a paragraph proof to show that the construction of a tangent to a circle from an external point, as shown in sample problem 3, is valid.

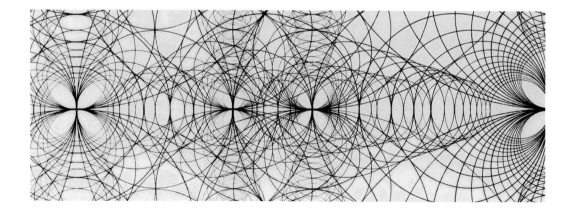

APPLICATIONS OF THE BASIC CONSTRUCTIONS

Objective

After studying this section, you will be able to
- Perform four other useful constructions

Part One: Introduction

The six basic constructions may be used to develop more-complicated constructions. Four of these are presented in this section. Once you have mastered all ten constructions, you will enjoy the challenge of future problem sets.

Construction 7: Parallels

Construction of a line parallel to a given line through a point not on the given line.

Given: $\overleftrightarrow{AB}$ with point P not on $\overleftrightarrow{AB}$

Construct: A line, $\overleftrightarrow{PQ}$, that is parallel to $\overleftrightarrow{AB}$

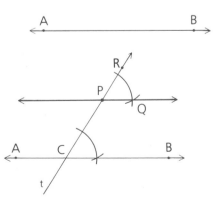

Procedure:
1. Draw any line t through P, intersecting $\overleftrightarrow{AB}$ at some point C.
2. Use the angle-copy procedure to construct ∠QPR ≅ to ∠PCB.
3. $\overleftrightarrow{PQ} \parallel \overleftrightarrow{AB}$ by corr. ∠s ≅ ⟹ ∥ lines.

Construction 8: Segment Division

Division of a segment into a given number of congruent segments.

Given: $\overline{AB}$

Construct: Points that divide $\overline{AB}$ into any
number of congruent segments
(In this construction we will divide
$\overline{AB}$ into three congruent segments.)

If parallel lines cut off ≅ segments on some
transversal, they cut off ≅ segments on any
other. Work backwards, transversals first.
$\overleftrightarrow{AB}$ is the "any other" transversal. On some
other line through A, mark off three ≅
segments of any length. Call their sum AR.
Then $\overleftrightarrow{RB}$ determines the direction of the parallel lines.

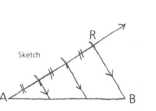

Procedure:
1. Draw any line ℓ through point A.
2. With a radius r, construct arc (A, r)
   intersecting line ℓ at a point P.
3. Construct arc (P, r) intersecting ℓ at Q.
4. Construct arc (Q, r) intersecting ℓ at R.
5. Draw $\overline{RB}$.
6. Using Construction 7, construct lines through P and Q parallel
   to $\overleftrightarrow{RB}$. Call the intersections of these lines with $\overline{AB}$ points S and T.
7. $\overline{AS} \cong \overline{ST} \cong \overline{TB}$. (Do you know the reason why?)

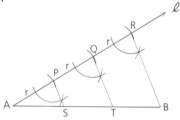

Construction 9: Mean Proportional

**Construction of a segment whose length is the mean proportional
between the lengths of two given segments.**

Given: $\overline{AB}$ and $\overline{CD}$

Construct: $\overline{VR}$ such that $(VR)^2 = (AB)(CD)$

Mean proportional suggests an altitude on a hypotenuse. We can find
h if we recall that an angle inscribed in a semicircle is a right angle.

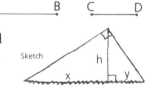

Procedure:
1. On a working line w, use the segment-
   copy procedure to construct a segment
   of length AB + CD. (Make TV = AB
   and VZ = CD.)
2. Use the perpendicular-bisector procedure to find the midpoint M of $\overline{TZ}$.
3. Construct semicircle (M, MT).
4. At V, erect a perpendicular to $\overleftrightarrow{TZ}$. The
   perpendicular will intersect ⊙M at R,
   and ∠TRZ will be a right angle.
5. $h^2 = xy$, so $(VR)^2 = (AB)(CD)$.

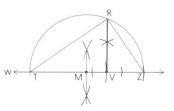

Construction 10: Fourth Proportional

Construction of a segment whose length is the fourth proportional to the lengths of three given segments.

Given: $\overline{AB}$ _____ a _____| $\overline{CD}$ ___ b ___| $\overline{EF}$ ___ c ___|

Construct: $\overline{TV}$ such that $\dfrac{a}{b} = \dfrac{c}{TV}$

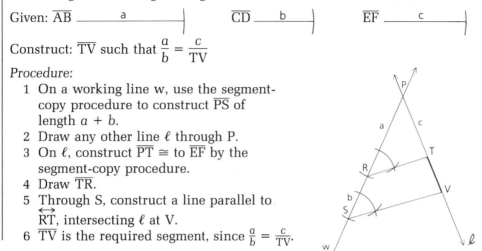

Procedure:

1 On a working line w, use the segment-copy procedure to construct $\overline{PS}$ of length $a + b$.
2 Draw any other line ℓ through P.
3 On ℓ, construct $\overline{PT} \cong$ to $\overline{EF}$ by the segment-copy procedure.
4 Draw $\overline{TR}$.
5 Through S, construct a line parallel to $\overleftrightarrow{RT}$, intersecting ℓ at V.
6 $\overline{TV}$ is the required segment, since $\dfrac{a}{b} = \dfrac{c}{TV}$.

Part Two: Sample Problems

Problem 1   *Inscribe a circle in a given △ABC.*

Solution   The center of an inscribed circle is equidistant from the sides, so it is the point of concurrency of the angle bisectors.

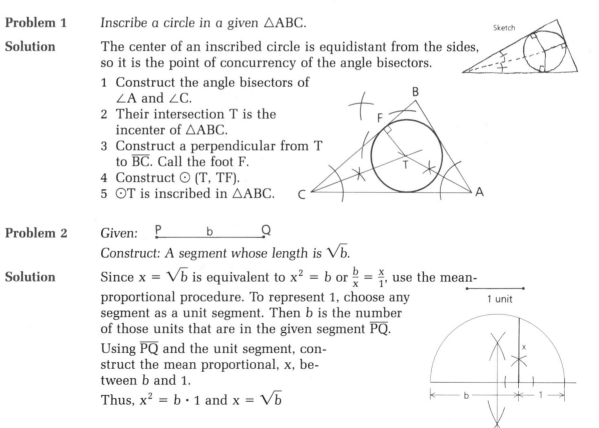

Sketch

1 Construct the angle bisectors of ∠A and ∠C.
2 Their intersection T is the incenter of △ABC.
3 Construct a perpendicular from T to $\overline{BC}$. Call the foot F.
4 Construct ⊙(T, TF).
5 ⊙T is inscribed in △ABC.

Problem 2   *Given:* P •_____ b _____• Q
   Construct: A segment whose length is $\sqrt{b}$.

Solution   Since $x = \sqrt{b}$ is equivalent to $x^2 = b$ or $\dfrac{b}{x} = \dfrac{x}{1}$, use the mean-proportional procedure. To represent 1, choose any segment as a unit segment. Then b is the number of those units that are in the given segment $\overline{PQ}$.

Using $\overline{PQ}$ and the unit segment, construct the mean proportional, x, between b and 1.

Thus, $x^2 = b \cdot 1$ and $x = \sqrt{b}$

Part Three: Problem Sets

Problem Set A

1 Given △ABC, construct a line parallel to $\overleftrightarrow{AB}$ and passing through C.

2 Given △PQR, trisect $\overline{QR}$.

3 Given $\overline{AB}$, with point C between A and B, construct a segment whose length is the mean proportional between AC and BC.

4 Given acute ∠DEF, with H between E and F, find by construction a point J between E and D such that $\frac{EJ}{JD} = \frac{EH}{HF}$.

5 Construct an equilateral triangle and its inscribed circle.

6 Construct a parallelogram, given two sides and an angle.

7 Construct an isosceles right triangle and its circumscribed circle.

8 Construct a rectangle, given the base and a diagonal.

9 Construct the centroid of a given triangle.

10 Use an object with a circular surface to trace the outline of a circle. By construction, locate the center of the circle.

11 Given a point P anywhere on a line w, construct a circle of radius r that is tangent to w at P.

Problem Set B

12 Given a segment of length b (make it about 14 cm long), solve $5x = b$ for x by a geometric method.

13 Construct a rhombus, given its diagonals.

14 Construct an isosceles trapezoid, given the bases and the altitude.

15 Given three noncollinear points, construct a circle that passes through all three points.

16 Given □ABCD as shown, construct
  a A rectangle with the same area as □ABCD
  b A triangle with the same area as □ABCD

17 Where should a straight fence be located to divide a given triangular field into two fields whose areas are in the ratio 2:1?

18 Given a segment of length a, construct the geometric mean between $2a$ and $3a$.

19 Given △ABC, find by construction a point M on $\overline{AC}$ that divides $\overline{AC}$ in a ratio equal to $\frac{AB}{BC}$.

Problem Set C

20 Given: a   1 ——————

Construct: A segment whose length is $\frac{1}{a}$

21 Given a unit segment, construct a segment whose length is $\sqrt{3}$.

22 Find the centroid, the circumcenter, and the orthocenter of a large scalene triangle. What seems to be true about these three points?

23 Construct a square equal in area to a given parallelogram.

24 Construct a square that has an area twice as great as the area of a given square.

25 Circumscribe a regular hexagon about a given circle.

Problem Set D

26 Suppose you wanted to construct a triangle equal in area to the given quadrilateral PQRS.

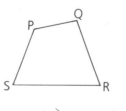

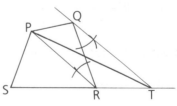

Procedure:
  1 Draw diagonal $\overline{PR}$.
  2 Construct a line parallel to $\overline{PR}$ through Q, intersecting $\overleftrightarrow{SR}$ at some point T.
  3 Draw $\overline{PT}$.
  4 Area (△PST) = area (quad PQRS)

  a Write a paragraph proof showing that this procedure is valid.

  b Construct a triangle that is equal in area to a given pentagon.

TRIANGLE CONSTRUCTIONS

Objective

After studying this section, you will be able to
- Construct triangles with given side lengths and angle measures

Part One: Introduction

In this section, you will construct triangles, given various combinations of parts and conditions. The following notation for parts and their associated measures will be helpful:

Side lengths: a, b, c
Angles: A, B, C
Altitudes: h_a, h_b, h_c
Medians: m_a, m_b, m_c
Angle bisectors: t_a, t_b, t_c

The side opposite vertex A is a units long.
The side opposite vertex B is b units long.
The side opposite vertex C is c units long.
The length of the altitude to the side opposite vertex A is h_a.
The length of the altitude to the side opposite vertex B is h_b.
Medians and angle bisectors have similar labeling.

The sample problems illustrate the importance of beginning with a sketch that shows the given parts and conditions.

Part Two: Sample Problems

Problem 1   *Construct:* $\triangle$ABC, given {a, C, b}.

Given: **a** ————————————

b ————————

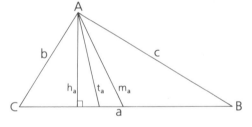

Construct: $\triangle$ABC

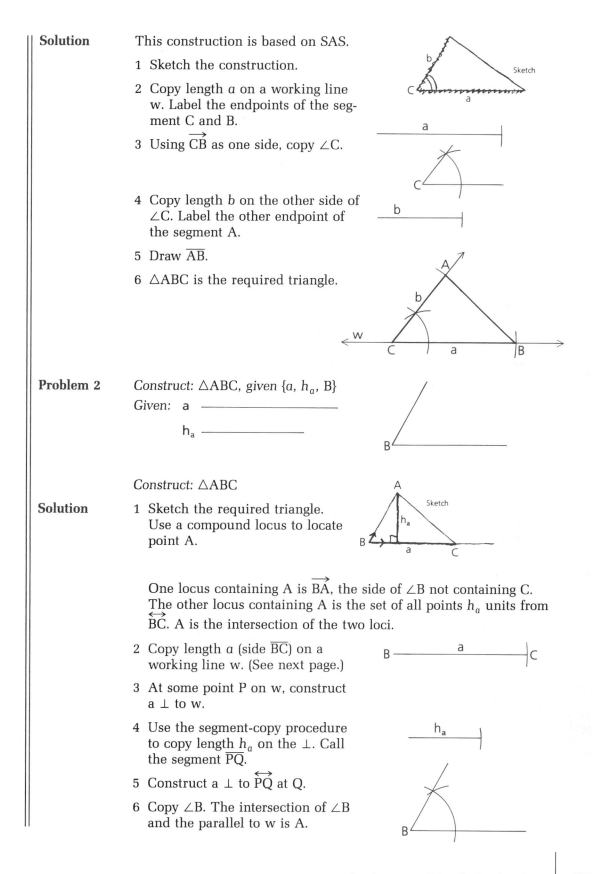

Solution   This construction is based on SAS.

1 Sketch the construction.

2 Copy length a on a working line w. Label the endpoints of the segment C and B.

3 Using $\overrightarrow{CB}$ as one side, copy $\angle C$.

4 Copy length b on the other side of $\angle C$. Label the other endpoint of the segment A.

5 Draw $\overline{AB}$.

6 $\triangle ABC$ is the required triangle.

Problem 2   *Construct:* $\triangle ABC$, given $\{a, h_a, B\}$

Given: **a** ———————

   h_a ———————

Construct: $\triangle ABC$

Solution

1 Sketch the required triangle. Use a compound locus to locate point A.

One locus containing A is $\overrightarrow{BA}$, the side of $\angle B$ not containing C. The other locus containing A is the set of all points h_a units from $\overleftrightarrow{BC}$. A is the intersection of the two loci.

2 Copy length a (side $\overline{BC}$) on a working line w. (See next page.)

3 At some point P on w, construct a $\perp$ to w.

4 Use the segment-copy procedure to copy length h_a on the $\perp$. Call the segment $\overline{PQ}$.

5 Construct a $\perp$ to $\overleftrightarrow{PQ}$ at Q.

6 Copy $\angle B$. The intersection of $\angle B$ and the parallel to w is A.

7 Draw $\overline{AC}$.

8 △ABC is the required triangle.

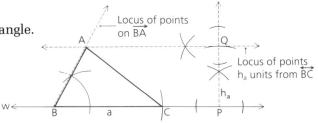

Part Three: Problem Sets

Problem Set A

1 In sample problem 1, a triangle was constructed by SAS. In a similar manner, construct a triangle by each of these methods.

  a ASA (Hint: Draw two different angles and a segment. Then construct a triangle in which the segment is the side included by the angles.)

  b SSS

  c HL

2 Construct an isosceles triangle, given

  a The vertex angle and a leg

  b The base and the altitude to the base

3 Construct an isosceles right triangle, given

  a A leg

  b The hypotenuse

4 Construct a triangle equal in area to a given square.

5 Construct a $30°-60°-90°$ triangle.

6 Given △ABC, construct a triangle whose area is twice as great as the area of △ABC.

7 Given a triangle, construct a triangle that is similar but not congruent to the given triangle.

Problem Set B

8 Construct a $30°-60°-90°$ triangle, given the hypotenuse.

9 Construct an isosceles triangle, given the length b of the base and the radius R of its circumscribed circle, where $b < 2R$.

10 Construct an isosceles triangle, given the length b of the base and the radius r of its inscribed circle, where $b > 2r$.

11 Construct an isosceles right triangle, given the median to the hypotenuse.

12 Construct a triangle by AAS. (Hint: Begin by constructing the third angle of the triangle.)

13 Construct an isosceles triangle, given the vertex angle and the altitude to the base.

14 For each given set, construct a triangle.
  a $\{a, c, m_c\}$ **d** $\{a, b, h_c\}$
  b $\{A, B, h_a\}$ **e** $\{A, B, h_c\}$
  c $\{h_b, t_b, a\}, h_b < t_b < a$ **f** $\{a, c, h_c\}$

15 Construct an isosceles triangle equal in area to a given triangle.

16 Construct an equilateral triangle, given the altitude.

Problem Set C

17 Construct an isosceles right triangle equal in area to a given triangle.

18 Construct a right triangle, given the hypotenuse and the altitude to the hypotenuse.

19 For each given set, construct a triangle.
  a $\{B, C, t_b\}$ **b** $\{a, m_b, m_c\}$ **c** $\{h_a, m_a, B\}$

20 Construct $\triangle ABC$, given a, b, and the point on the given length b where t_b intersects side $\overline{AC}$.

21 By construction, divide a given scalene triangle into a triangle and a trapezoid such that the ratio of the area of the triangle to the area of the trapezoid is $1:8$.

Problem Set D

22 Construct a triangle, given the three medians.

23 Construct a regular hexagon. Then construct an equilateral triangle whose area is equal to that of the hexagon.

Problem Set E

24 Given an acute angle with a point P in the interior of the angle, construct a circle that is tangent to the sides of the angle and passes through P.

CHAPTER SUMMARY

CONCEPTS AND PROCEDURES

After studying this chapter, you should be able to
- Use the four-step locus procedure to solve locus problems (14.1)
- Apply the compound-locus procedure (14.2)
- Identify the circumcenter, the incenter, the orthocenter, and the centroid of a triangle (14.3)
- Identify the tools and procedures used in constructions (14.4)
- Interpret the shorthand notation used in describing constructions (14.4)
- Perform six basic constructions (14.4)
- Perform four other useful constructions (14.5)
- Construct triangles with given side lengths and angle measures (14.6)

VOCABULARY

center of gravity (14.3)
centroid (14.3)
circumcenter (14.3)
compound locus (14.2)
concurrent lines (14.3)

construction (14.4)
incenter (14.3)
locus (14.1)
orthocenter (14.3)

REVIEW PROBLEMS

Problem Set A

1 Given segment $\overline{AB}$, find the locus of points that are the vertices of isosceles triangles having $\overline{AB}$ as a base.

2 Find the locus of the centers of all circles that pass through two fixed points.

3 Find the locus of points 3 units from a given line and 5 units from a given point on the line.

4 What is the name of the surface *in space* every point of which is a fixed distance from a given line?

5 What is the locus of points 2 in. from a circle with a radius of 2 in.?

6 A circle of given radius rolls around the perimeter of a given equilateral triangle. Sketch the locus of its center.

7 Write the equation of the locus of points 5 units from the origin in the coordinate plane.

8 Given scalene △ ABC, construct each of the following.
  a The incenter **b** The circumcenter **c** The centroid **d** The orthocenter

9 Given a 3-cm line segment, draw the locus of points 1 cm from the segment. (Each point of the locus must be 1 cm from the point of the segment nearest to it.)

10 Construct a parallelogram, given two sides and the angle they form.

11 Given a segment, construct an equilateral triangle with a perimeter equal to the segment's length.

12 What is the locus of points that are a fixed distance from a fixed point and equidistant from two given points.

Problem Set B

13 Write the equation of the locus of points for which the ordinate is 5 more than 3 times the abscissa.

14 What is the locus *in space* of points equidistant from all the points on a given circle?

15 Given segment $\overline{PQ}$, find the locus of points each of which is the intersection of the diagonals of a rectangle that has $\overline{PQ}$ as a base.

16 Given a circle with center P and a radius of 10 cm, find the locus of the midpoints of all possible 12-cm chords in the circle.

17 Find the locus of midpoints of all chords of a circle that have a fixed point of the circle as an endpoint.

18 A point outside a square 3 units on a side moves so that it is always 2 units from the point of the square nearest to it. Find the area enclosed by the locus of this moving point.

19 If the radius of a given circle is 10 cm, describe the locus of points 2 cm from the circle and equidistant from the endpoints of a given diameter of the circle.

20 Using coordinate-geometry methods, find the locus of points 5 units from the origin and 4 units from the y-axis.

21 Inscribe a regular octagon in a given circle.

22 Construct a parallelogram, given two sides and an altitude.

23 Explain how to construct an angle with each measure.
  a 30   **b** $18\frac{3}{4}$

24 Given three points A, B, and C, describe the locus of points that are equidistant from A and B and also equidistant from B and C.

Problem Set C

25 Find the locus of the intersections of the diagonals of all possible rhombuses having a fixed segment $\overline{PQ}$ as a side.

26 Prove that the angle bisectors of a kite are concurrent.

27 Given a chord of a circle, construct another chord parallel to the given chord and half its length.

28 Given scalene △ ABC, construct in the exterior of the triangle a circle that is tangent to one side and to extensions of the other two sides.

29 Construct a square whose area is equal to the sum of the areas of two given squares.

30 Given two parallel lines and a point P between them, construct a circle that is tangent to both lines and passes through point P.

31 Inscribe a square in a given rhombus.

Problem Set D

32 Given two circles, construct a common external tangent.

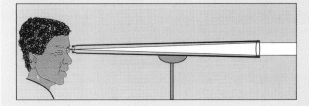

INEQUALITIES

H ow these sprinklers in a painting by
David Hockney represent inequalities may
seem a mystery. But consider the consequences of
changing the angle of the spray.

NUMBER PROPERTIES

Objective

After studying this section, you will be able to
- Use algebraic properties of inequality to solve inequalities

Part One: Introduction

The statement $a < b$ (a is less than b) is an inequality involving the numbers a and b. $a < b$ is equivalent to $b > a$ (b is greater than a).
  Here is a review of some of the properties of inequality.

Postulate   ***For any two real numbers x and y, exactly one of the following statements is true: x < y, x = y, or x > y. (Law of Trichotomy)***

Postulate   ***If a > b and b > c, then a > c. Similarly, if x < y and y < z, then x < z. (Transitive Property of Inequality)***

If the lengths of $\overline{AB}$, $\overline{PQ}$, and $\overline{XY}$ are such that $AB < PQ$ and $PQ < XY$, then $AB < XY$.

A ———— B

P ————— Q

X —————— Y

Postulate   ***If a > b, then a + x > b + x. (Addition Property of Inequality)***

If $4 > -7$, then $4 + 9 > -7 + 9$
$$13 > 2$$

Postulate   **If x < y and a > 0, then a · x < a · y. (*Positive Multiplication Property of Inequality*)**

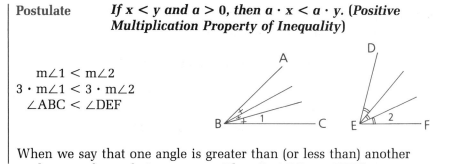

$$m\angle 1 < m\angle 2$$
$$3 \cdot m\angle 1 < 3 \cdot m\angle 2$$
$$\angle ABC < \angle DEF$$

When we say that one angle is greater than (or less than) another angle, we refer to their measures. Thus "$\angle ABC < \angle DEF$" means that $m\angle ABC < m\angle DEF$.

Postulate   **If x < y and a < 0, then a · x > a · y. (*Negative Multiplication Property of Inequality*)**

Notice that the direction of the inequality sign reverses.

$$-5x < 15$$
$$-\tfrac{1}{5}(-5x) > -\tfrac{1}{5}(15)$$
$$x > -3$$

Part Two: Sample Problem

Problem   A given angle is greater than twice its supplement. Find the possible measures of the given angle.

Solution   Let x = the measure of the given angle and $180 - x$ = the measure of the supplement.

$$x > 2(180 - x)$$
$$x > 360 - 2x$$
$$x + 2x > 360 - 2x + 2x \quad \text{Addition Property of Inequality}$$
$$3x > 360$$
$$\tfrac{1}{3}(3x) > \tfrac{1}{3}(360) \qquad \text{Positive Multiplication Property of Inequality}$$
$$x > 120$$

Thus, the given angle is greater than 120°. Since it has a supplement, the given angle is also less than 180°. Therefore, $120 < x < 180$.

Part Three: Problem Sets

Problem Set A

1 Solve each inequality for x.

  a $\frac{3}{5}x > 15$

  b $5x - 4 > 26$

  c $-4x \le 28$

  d $10 - x < 8x - (2x - 3)$

2 a If $x + y < 30$ and $y = 12$, what is true about x?

  b If $x + y = 30$ and $y < 12$, what is true about x?

3 If x exceeds y by 5 and y exceeds z by 3, how is x related to z?

4 If x is twice y and y is three times z, how is x related to z?

5 If $\angle A = \angle 1 + \angle 2$, what is the relation between $\angle A$ and $\angle 2$?

6 a If X is between P and Q, how is PX related to PQ?

  b If X is the midpoint of $\overline{PQ}$, write the relation between PX and PQ as an inequality.

  c Using the situation in part **b,** write the relation between PX and PQ as an equality.

Problem Set B

7 The complement of an angle is smaller than the angle. Find the restrictions on the measure of the original angle.

8 If $\angle X < \angle Y$, what is the relation between their complements?

9 If $\frac{1}{x} > 5$, what two numbers is x between?

10 An angle is greater than twice its complement. Find the restrictions on the angle and on the complement.

11 If $x \not< 3$ and $x \neq 3$, what can be concluded about x?

12 a What is the relation between an exterior angle of a triangle and the two remote interior angles?

  b What, then, is the relation between an exterior angle and one of the remote interior angles?

13 Given: $\angle ABC > \angle ACB$,

  $\overrightarrow{BD}$ bisects $\angle ABC$.

  $\overrightarrow{CD}$ bisects $\angle ACB$.

  Find and justify the relation between $\angle DBC$ and $\angle DCB$.

Problem Set C

14 Given: Real numbers a, b, and c, with $a > b$

  Prove: $c - a < c - b$ (Special Subtraction Property)

15 Solve $x^2 + x < 6$.

16 If $x > 3y + 7$ and $y > 6 - x$, find the restrictions on

  a x **b** y

Problem Set C, *continued*

17 If x exceeds y by 20% and y exceeds z by 20%, by what percentage does x exceed z?

18 Solve $18 - 3x > 3$ over the positive even integers.

19 ∠A is greater than its complement, and the complement of ∠A is greater than ∠B.

    a Compare the complement of ∠A with the complement of ∠B.

    b Compare the complement of ∠B with ∠A.

    c List ∠A, ∠B, and their complements in order of size, from largest to smallest.

Problem Set D

20 Solve $|2x - 7| > |x + 20| - 4$ for x.

DEDUCTIONS FROM SEISMIC WAVES

Yvonna Pardus unravels the mysteries contained in rocks

The earth's crust is composed of a complex series of rock layers, or *strata*, one pile atop the next. Within the rock are spaces that are filled with petroleum, the end product of the decay of plants that were deposited there millions of years ago. To find the petroleum, some of which may be thousands of feet below the surface, petroleum geologists set off explosive charges. They then record the reflected seismic waves at receivers distributed over a certain area.

Geologist Yvonna Pardus explains: "Seismic waves act like light waves. They reflect off discontinuities between rock strata. By analyzing the angle of reflection, and other characteristics of the reflected wave, we can learn a great deal about the nature of the rock the wave has traveled through."

Pardus points out that the velocity of the wave depends on the density of the rock. Compiling a complete picture of what Pardus calls "the subsurface geometry of the earth" requires a series of seismic shots and reflections recorded on as many as forty-eight receivers.

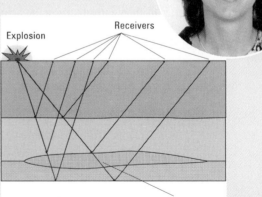

Yvonna Pardus attended Murray State University in Murray, Kentucky, where she earned a bachelor's degree in geology. A geologist needs a strong background in mathematics and physics, she says.

15.2 INEQUALITIES IN A TRIANGLE

Objectives

After studying this section, you will be able to
- Apply the Triangle Inequality Postulate
- Apply the Exterior-Angle-Inequality Theorem
- Use the Pythagorean Theorem test to classify a triangle as acute, right, or obtuse
- Recognize the relationships between the side lengths and the angle measures of a triangle

Part One: Introduction

The Triangle Inequality Postulate

The following postulate is a formal expression of an idea we have been using throughout this book.

Postulate   *The sum of the measures of any two sides of a triangle is always greater than the measure of the third side.*

In other words, traveling from A to B along $\overline{AB}$ is shorter than going first to X along $\overline{AX}$ and then to B along $\overline{XB}$—that is, AX + XB > AB.

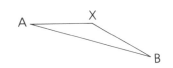

Exterior Angle Inequality

The following theorem, introduced in Section 5.2, can now be more easily proved.

Theorem 30   *The measure of an exterior angle of a triangle is greater than the measure of either remote interior angle. (**Exterior-Angle-Inequality Theorem**)*

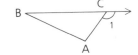

Given: △ABC, with exterior ∠1

Prove: ∠1 > ∠A and ∠1 > ∠B

Proof: In Chapter 7 you learned that ∠1 = ∠A + ∠B. Clearly, ∠A + ∠B > ∠A, so ∠1 > ∠A by substitution. In a similar manner, ∠A + ∠B > ∠B, so ∠1 > ∠B.

Classifying Triangles

As you discovered in Section 9.4, the converse of the Pythagorean Theorem can be used to prove that a triangle is a right triangle. You may recall that it also suggested the following way of finding whether a triangle is acute, right, or obtuse.

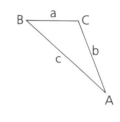

The Pythagorean Theorem Test

To classify a triangle as acute, right, or obtuse, compute a^2, b^2, and c^2, where c is the longest of the three sides a, b, and c.

If $a^2 + b^2 = c^2$, then $\triangle ABC$ is right ($\angle C$ is right).
If $a^2 + b^2 > c^2$, then $\triangle ABC$ is acute.
If $a^2 + b^2 < c^2$, then $\triangle ABC$ is obtuse ($\angle C$ is obtuse).

Side and Angle Relationships

The following theorems, the inverses of Theorems 20 and 21, were presented in Chapter 3. Now we are in a position to prove them.

Theorem 132 *If two sides of a triangle are not congruent, then the angles opposite them are not congruent, and the larger angle is opposite the longer side. (If ⟁, then ⟁.)*

Given: $\triangle ABC$,
$\qquad AC > AB$
Conclusion: $\angle B > \angle C$

Proof: Since $AC > AB$, extend $\overline{AB}$ to a point D so that AD = AC. Draw $\overline{DC}$.
$\qquad \angle ABC > \angle D$ by the Exterior-Angle-Inequality Theorem.
$\qquad \angle D \cong \angle ACD$ (If ⟁, then ⟁.)
$\qquad \angle ABC > \angle ACD$ by substitution.
$\qquad \angle ACD > \angle ACB$ (See diagram.)
$\qquad \therefore \angle ABC > \angle ACB$ by the Transitive Property of Inequality.

Theorem 133 *If two angles of a triangle are not congruent, then the sides opposite them are not congruent, and the longer side is opposite the larger angle. (If ⟁, then ⟁.)*

Given: $\triangle ABC$,
$\qquad \angle B > \angle C$
Conclusion: AB < AC

Proof: According to the Law of Trichotomy there are exactly three possible conclusions: AB > AC, AB = AC, or AB < AC. We must test them.

Case 1: If AB > AC, then by Theorem 132, ∠C > ∠B, which contradicts the given information.
Thus, AB > AC cannot be the correct conclusion.
Case 2: If AB = AC, then ∠C ≅ ∠B (If △, then △.)
The given information is again contradicted.
Thus, AB = AC cannot be the correct solution.

All that is left is AB < AC, which must be true by the Law of Trichotomy.

A simple extension of Theorem 133 enables us to say that the longest side of any triangle is the side opposite the largest angle.

Part Two: Sample Problems

Problem 1   *Does a triangle with sides 2, 5, and 10 exist?*

Solution   The sum of any two sides must be greater than the third side, and $2 + 5 \not> 10$. Therefore, the answer is no.

Problem 2   *Find the restrictions on ∠A.*

Solution $50 > m∠A$ because an exterior angle of a triangle exceeds either remote interior angle. An angle of a triangle must be greater than 0°, so $m∠A > 0$. Thus, $0 < m∠A < 50$.

Problem 3   *In △ABC, ∠A = 40° and ∠B = 65°. List the sides in order of their lengths, starting with the smallest.*

Solution   Draw a diagram listing all the angles. (∠C is easily found to be 75°.) The shortest side, $\overline{BC}$, is opposite the smallest angle, ∠A. The longest side, $\overline{BA}$, is opposite the largest angle, ∠C. Therefore, the correct order is $\overline{BC}$, $\overline{AC}$, $\overline{BA}$.

Problem 4   *Given:* $\triangle ABC$, *with* AB < AC;
$\overrightarrow{BD}$ *bisects* $\angle ABC$.
$\overrightarrow{CD}$ *bisects* $\angle ACB$.

Prove: BD < DC

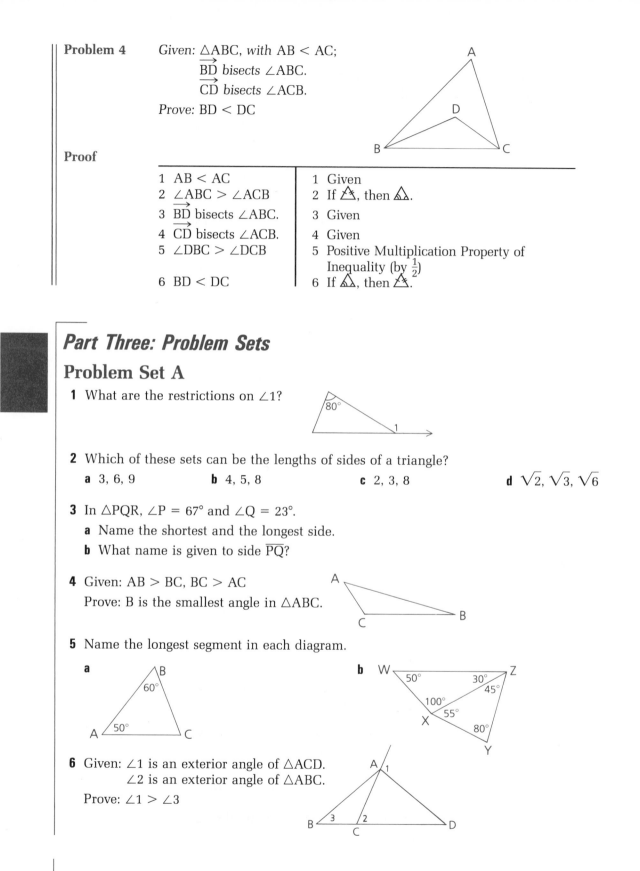

Proof

1 AB < AC	1 Given
2 $\angle ABC > \angle ACB$	2 If △, then △.
3 $\overrightarrow{BD}$ bisects $\angle ABC$.	3 Given
4 $\overrightarrow{CD}$ bisects $\angle ACB$.	4 Given
5 $\angle DBC > \angle DCB$	5 Positive Multiplication Property of Inequality (by $\frac{1}{2}$)
6 BD < DC	6 If △, then △.

Part Three: Problem Sets

Problem Set A

1 What are the restrictions on $\angle 1$?

2 Which of these sets can be the lengths of sides of a triangle?

   a 3, 6, 9   **b** 4, 5, 8   **c** 2, 3, 8   **d** $\sqrt{2}, \sqrt{3}, \sqrt{6}$

3 In $\triangle PQR$, $\angle P = 67°$ and $\angle Q = 23°$.

   a Name the shortest and the longest side.

   b What name is given to side $\overline{PQ}$?

4 Given: AB > BC, BC > AC

   Prove: B is the smallest angle in $\triangle ABC$.

5 Name the longest segment in each diagram.

   a   **b**

6 Given: $\angle 1$ is an exterior angle of $\triangle ACD$.
                $\angle 2$ is an exterior angle of $\triangle ABC$.

   Prove: $\angle 1 > \angle 3$

Problem Set B

7 A scalene triangle has a 60° angle. Is this angle opposite the longest, the shortest, or the other side?

8 The sides of a triangle are 14, 6, and x. Find the set of possible values of x.

9 Vertex angle A of isosceles triangle ABC is between 40° and 88°. Find the possible values for ∠B.

10 a Name the longest segment in the figure below.

b Name the shortest segment in the figure below.

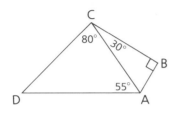

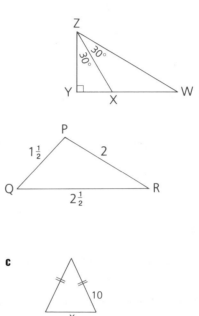

11 a List the angles in order of size, beginning with the smallest.

    b At which vertex is the exterior angle the largest?

12 Find the restrictions on x.

    a

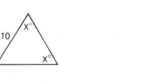

    c

    b

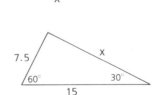

    d

13 A stick 8 cm long is cut into three pieces of integral lengths to be assembled as a triangle. What is the length of the shortest piece?

14 For each set of numbers, tell whether the numbers represent the lengths of the sides of an acute triangle, a right triangle, an obtuse triangle, or no triangle.

    a 12, 13, 14   **b** 11, 5, 18   **c** 9, 15, 18   **d** $\frac{1}{2}$, $1\frac{1}{5}$, $1\frac{3}{10}$

15 Prove that an altitude of an acute triangle is shorter than either side that is not the base.

Problem Set B, *continued*

16 Prove that if ABCD is a quadrilateral, then AB + BC + CD > AD.

17 Given the diagram shown, prove or dis-prove that ∠2 > ∠1.

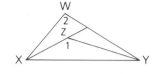

18 Given: $\overrightarrow{AC}$ bisects ∠BAD.
 Prove: AD > CD

19 The pattern shown can be folded to form a prism with a regular hexagonal base. Find, to the nearest tenth of a unit, the prism's

 a Lateral surface area

 b Total surface area

 c Volume

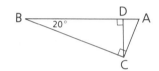

Problem Set C

20 ∠ACB and ∠CDB are right ∠s, and ∠B = 20°.

 a List $\overline{AC}$, $\overline{CB}$, $\overline{AB}$, $\overline{AD}$, and $\overline{CD}$ in order of size, starting with the smallest.

 b Where would $\overline{DB}$ fit into this list?

21 Given a point P in the interior of △XYZ, prove that PY + PZ < XY + XZ.

22 If two sides of a triangle have lengths x and y, what is the range of possible values of the length of the third side?

23 Prove: The shortest segment between a point and a line is the segment perpendicular to the line.

24 Given a point P in the interior of △XYZ, prove that ∠XPZ > ∠Y.

25 Deanna watched a spider crawl over the interior surfaces of a room from point (2, 0, 8) to point (5, 10, 0). The next day, she asked three of her classmates if they knew the length of the shortest path the spider could have taken.
 Abigail said, "12 + $\sqrt{89}$ ≈ 21.43."
 Ben said, "10 + $\sqrt{125}$ ≈ 21.18."
 Carol said, "8 + $\sqrt{109}$ ≈ 18.44."
 Deanna responded, "Actually, it was ≈ 16.40." Explain the reasoning of each student.

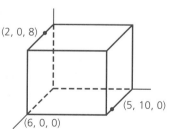

<table>
<tr><td>15.3</td><td></td></tr>
</table>

THE HINGE THEOREMS

Objective

After studying this section, you will be able to

- Use the hinge theorems to determine the relative measures of sides and angles

Part One: Introduction

Thus far we have discussed inequalities involving the sides and the angles of a single triangle. We now turn our attention to two triangles. If the size of angle AHC is changed from that in Figure 1 to that in Figure 2, what happens to the length of a spring connecting A and C?

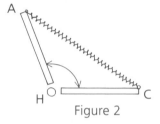

Figure 1   Figure 2

Theorem 134   **The Hinge Theorem:** *If two sides of one triangle are congruent to two sides of another triangle and the included angle in the first triangle is greater than the included angle in the second triangle, then the remaining side of the first triangle is greater than the remaining side of the second triangle. (SAS ≠)*

The following setup of Theorem 134 should help you see how the theorem can be applied.

Given: $\overline{AB} \cong \overline{XY}$,
    $\overline{BC} \cong \overline{YZ}$,
    $\angle B > \angle Y$
Conclusion: AC > XZ

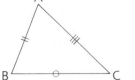

The converse of the Hinge Theorem is also true.

Theorem 135   **The Converse Hinge Theorem:** *If two sides of one triangle are congruent to two sides of another triangle and the third side of the first triangle is greater than the third side of the second triangle, then the angle opposite the third side in the first triangle is greater than the angle opposite the third side in the second triangle. (SSS ≠)*

Given: $\overline{AB} \cong \overline{WX}$,
    $\overline{BC} \cong \overline{XY}$,
    AC > WY
Conclusion: $\angle B > \angle X$

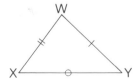

Part Two: Sample Problems

Problem 1

Given: $\overline{BD}$ is a median.
          $AD > CD$

Which is greater, $\angle 1$ or $\angle 2$?

Solution

Since $\overline{BD}$ is a median, $\overline{AB} \cong \overline{BC}$.
Also, $\overline{BD} \cong \overline{BD}$ and $\overline{AD} > \overline{CD}$.
Thus, by the Converse Hinge Theorem, $\angle 1 > \angle 2$.

Problem 2

Given: $\triangle ABC$ is isosceles, with base $\overline{BC}$.
          C is the midpoint of $\overline{BD}$.

Prove: $AD > AB$

Proof

1 C is the midpoint of $\overline{BD}$.	1 Given
2 $\overline{BC} \cong \overline{CD}$	2 A midpoint divides a segment into two congruent segments.
3 $\triangle ABC$ is isosceles, with base $\overline{BC}$.	3 Given
4 $\overline{AB} \cong \overline{AC}$	4 The legs of an isosceles $\triangle$ are $\cong$.
5 $\angle 1 > \angle 2$	5 Exterior-Angle-Inequality Theorem ($\angle 1$, $\triangle ABC$)
6 $AD > AC$	6 Hinge Theorem (SAS$\neq$)
7 $AD > AB$	7 Substitution (4 in 6)

Problem 3

Given: ABCD is a parallelogram.
          $\angle BAD > \angle ADC$

Which diagonal is longer, $\overline{AC}$ or $\overline{BD}$?

Solution

Consider the overlapping triangles as shown.

$\overline{AB} \cong \overline{DC}$ because the opposite sides of a parallelogram are $\cong$.
Also, $\overline{AD} \cong \overline{AD}$ and $\angle BAD > \angle ADC$.
So, $BD > AC$ by the Hinge Theorem.

Part Three: Problem Sets

Problem Set A

1 Which is longer, $\overline{AC}$ or $\overline{DF}$?

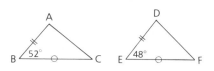

2 Which is larger, ∠R or ∠Y?

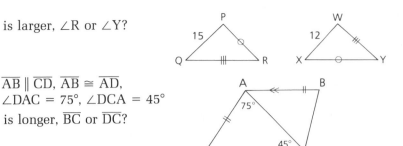

3 Given: $\overline{AB} \parallel \overline{CD}$, $\overline{AB} \cong \overline{AD}$,
  ∠DAC = 75°, ∠DCA = 45°
  Which is longer, $\overline{BC}$ or $\overline{DC}$?

4 Compare AB in △ABC with XZ in △XYZ, where BC = 7,
AC = 9, ∠C = 75°, YZ = 7, XY = 9, and ∠Y = 80°.

5 Given: $\overline{WX} \cong \overline{WZ}$,
  ∠XWY > ∠ZWY
  Prove: XY > ZY

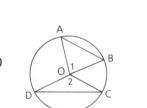

6 Given: ⊙O,
  AB < CD
  Prove: ∠1 < ∠2

7 In △WXY, WX = 10, WY = 4, and XY = 7.
  a Name the largest and the smallest angle.
  b Is the triangle acute, right, or obtuse?

Problem Set B

8 Given: ▱WXYZ, XZ > WY
  Prove: **a** ∠XWZ > ∠WZY (Use a two-column proof.)
  b ∠XWZ is obtuse. (Use a paragraph proof.)

9 Given: $\overline{PQ} \cong \overline{PR} \cong \overline{RS}$
  Prove: QR < PS

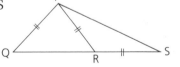

10 △WXY and △ABC are isosceles, with bases $\overline{WY}$ and $\overline{AB}$ respectively.
  If ∠X and ∠B are each 50° and $\overline{WX} \cong \overline{BC}$, which triangle has
  a The longer base?   **b** The longer altitude to the base?

11 Given: $\overline{AB}$ and $\overline{BC}$ are tangent to ⊙Q.
  AD > DC
  Conclusion: ∠ABD > ∠DBC

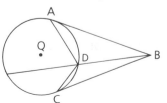

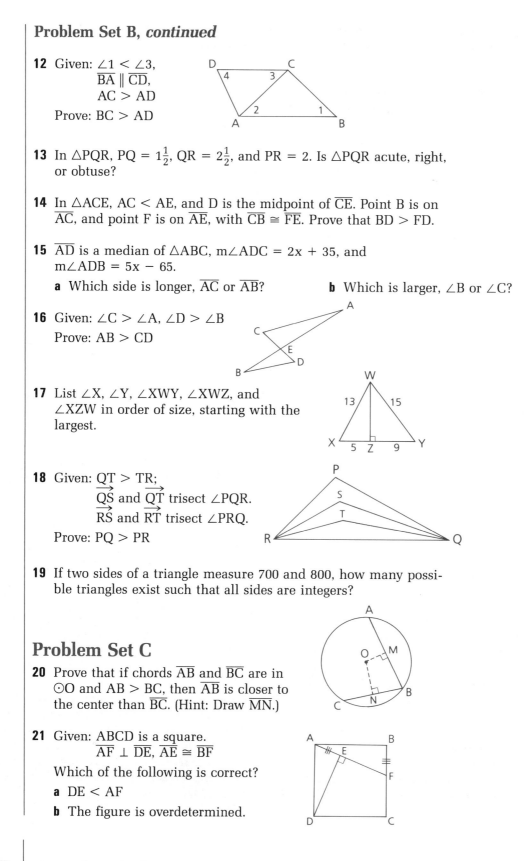

12 Given: $\angle 1 < \angle 3$,
$\overline{BA} \parallel \overline{CD}$,
$AC > AD$
Prove: $BC > AD$

13 In $\triangle PQR$, $PQ = 1\frac{1}{2}$, $QR = 2\frac{1}{2}$, and $PR = 2$. Is $\triangle PQR$ acute, right, or obtuse?

14 In $\triangle ACE$, $AC < AE$, and D is the midpoint of $\overline{CE}$. Point B is on $\overline{AC}$, and point F is on $\overline{AE}$, with $\overline{CB} \cong \overline{FE}$. Prove that $BD > FD$.

15 $\overline{AD}$ is a median of $\triangle ABC$, $m\angle ADC = 2x + 35$, and $m\angle ADB = 5x - 65$.

a Which side is longer, $\overline{AC}$ or $\overline{AB}$?   **b** Which is larger, $\angle B$ or $\angle C$?

16 Given: $\angle C > \angle A$, $\angle D > \angle B$
Prove: $AB > CD$

17 List $\angle X$, $\angle Y$, $\angle XWY$, $\angle XWZ$, and $\angle XZW$ in order of size, starting with the largest.

18 Given: $QT > TR$;
$\overrightarrow{QS}$ and $\overrightarrow{QT}$ trisect $\angle PQR$.
$\overrightarrow{RS}$ and $\overrightarrow{RT}$ trisect $\angle PRQ$.
Prove: $PQ > PR$

19 If two sides of a triangle measure 700 and 800, how many possible triangles exist such that all sides are integers?

Problem Set C

20 Prove that if chords $\overline{AB}$ and $\overline{BC}$ are in $\odot O$ and $AB > BC$, then $\overline{AB}$ is closer to the center than $\overline{BC}$. (Hint: Draw $\overline{MN}$.)

21 Given: ABCD is a square.
$\overline{AF} \perp \overline{DE}$, $\overline{AE} \cong \overline{BF}$

Which of the following is correct?

a $DE < AF$

b The figure is overdetermined.

22 $\overline{WX}$ is a diameter of a circle with center P, and $\overline{YZ}$ is a diameter of a larger concentric circle. W, X, Y, and Z are noncollinear. Prove that $\angle YWZ > \angle XYW$.

23 Given: B, C, and D lie on plane m.
          $\triangle BCD$ is isosceles, with base $\overline{CD}$.
          $\angle ABD > \angle ABC$

    Conclusion: $\angle ACD > \angle ADC$

24 Given: $\overset{\frown}{AD} \cong \overset{\frown}{CD}$,
          $AE < EC$
    Prove: $\overset{\frown}{AB} < \overset{\frown}{BC}$

25 Given: $\overline{AD}$ is a median.
          $\angle ABD > \angle ACD$

    Conclusion: $\angle 1 > \angle 4$

26 Given: $AC > CE$,
          $\overline{AB} \cong \overline{DE}$
    Prove: $AD > BE$

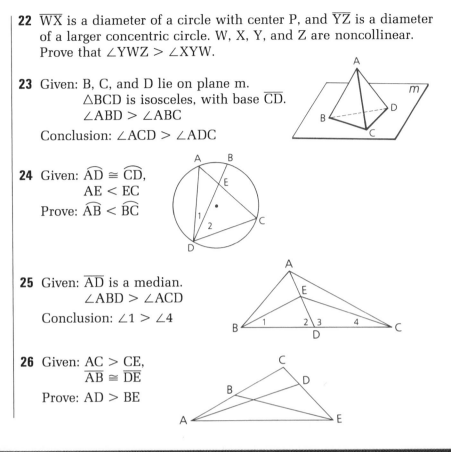

INEQUALITIES
A bicycle excursion

Triangle inequalities help explain why your bicycle feels and handles the way it does. Geometrically speaking, you can see from the diagram that a bicycle frame and rider form three triangles (one with an understood side) and a quadrilateral that is nearly a triangle. The properties of these triangles govern responsiveness, traction, riding position, and handling for a given bicycle. In general, racing bikes are more responsive, but handling is better on road bikes.

Some measurements that affect a bicycle's characteristics are shown on the diagram. *Chainstay length* affects uphill traction. *Wheelbase, fork rake,* and *head-tube angle* all determine how responsive the bicycle will be. A

more responsive bike is more difficult to handle. *Top-tube length* determines how far the rider must lean over to reach the handlebars. Notice that the top tube and the rider's upper body and arms also form a triangle. Describe the effects on angles increasing and decreasing lengths of parts of the frame.

CHAPTER SUMMARY

CONCEPTS AND PROCEDURES

After studying this chapter, you should be able to
- Use algebraic properties of inequality to solve inequalities (15.1)
- Apply the Triangle Inequality Postulate (15.2)
- Apply the Exterior-Angle-Inequality Theorem (15.2)
- Use the Pythagorean Theorem test to classify a triangle as acute, right, or obtuse. (15.2)
- Recognize the relationships between the side lengths and the angle measures of a triangle (15.2)
- Use the hinge theorems to determine the relative measures of sides and angles (15.3)

Properties of Inequality

- For any two real numbers x and y, exactly one of the following statements is true: $x < y$, $x = y$, or $x > y$. (15.1)
- If $a > b$ and $b > c$, then $a > c$. Similarly, if $x < y$ and $y < z$, then $x < z$. (15.1)
- If $a > b$, then $a + x > b + x$. (15.1)
- If $x < y$ and $a > 0$, then $a \cdot x < a \cdot y$. (15.1)
- If $x < y$ and $a < 0$, then $a \cdot x > a \cdot y$. (15.1)
- If $a > b$, then $c - a < c - b$. (15.1)

REVIEW PROBLEMS

Problem Set A

1 In △ABC, AB > AC > BC. List the angles in order, from smallest to largest.

2 In each case, decide which of the segments named is longest and state the reason for your decision.

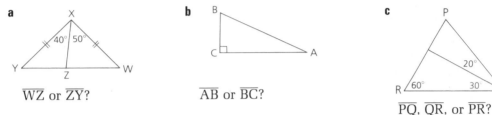

a

WZ or ZY?

b

AB or BC?

c

PQ, QR, or PR?

3 In each case, tell which angle is largest and give the reason.

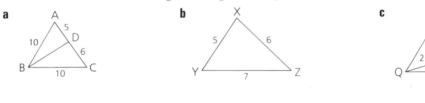

a

∠ABD or ∠CBD?

b

∠X, ∠Y, or ∠Z?

c

∠1, ∠2, or ∠P?

4 If x > 4 and x < y, what is the relationship between y and 4?

5 If x ≠ 6 and x ≮ 6, what can we conclude?

6 a Name all pairs of segments that we know to be congruent.
  b Which is shorter, BE or EC?
  c What is the name of side BC in △BEC?
  d Which is longer, AE or DE?
  e Which is the shortest segment in the figure?

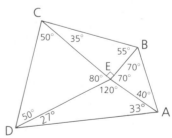

7 Which of these sets cannot represent the sides of a triangle?
  a 20, 40, 20 **b** 30, 40, 20 **c** 20, 20, 20 **d** 30, 40, 50

8 Given: $\overline{PQ} \cong \overline{RS}$
Prove: PS > QR

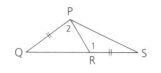

Problem Set B

9 Given △ABC as shown, list $\overline{AB}$, $\overline{AC}$, and $\overline{BC}$ in order of size, from longest to shortest.

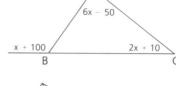

10 What are the restrictions on x?

11 △ABC is isosceles, with ∠C obtuse and AB = 6.
   a Which side is longest?
   b The perimeter must be between what two numbers?

12 In △ABC, AB > BC, m∠C = 4x − 4, and m∠A = x + 9. Find the minimum integral value of x.

13 A triangle has vertices P = (−1, −2), Q = (4, 1), and R = (6, −2).
   a Find PQ, QR, and PR.
   b Is △PQR acute, right, or obtuse?
   c List the angles in order of size, smallest first.

14 Given: AB < AD,
   $\overrightarrow{BE}$ bisects ∠ABC.
   $\overrightarrow{DE}$ bisects ∠ADC.
   Prove: ED > EB

15 Given: $\overline{AB} \cong \overline{AD}$
   Prove: AC < AD

16 Given: PR < QS,
   $\overline{PQ} \cong \overline{SR}$
   Prove: ∠PQR < ∠SRQ

17 Given: $\overline{BC} \cong \overline{EC}$,
        $\angle A \cong \angle C$
  Prove: AE < EC

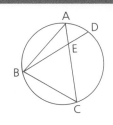

Problem Set C

18 In an obtuse triangle, the side opposite the obtuse angle is 6. If all sides are integral, how many such triangles exist?

19 Given △ABC as shown, list the sides $\overline{AB}$, $\overline{AC}$, $\overline{AD}$, $\overline{BC}$, $\overline{BD}$, and $\overline{CD}$ in order, from longest to shortest.

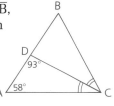

20 Prove that the measure of the median of a triangle is less than half of the sum of the measures of the two adjacent sides— that is, prove AM $< \frac{1}{2}$(AB + AC). (Hints: [1] Draw an appropriate midline, or [2] extend $\overline{AM}$ to point P so that $\overline{AM} \cong \overline{MP}$, then form $\square$ABPC.)

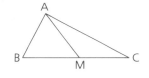

21 Prove that in any quadrilateral, the perimeter is greater than the sum of the diagonals.

22 Given: $\overline{ZX} \cong \overline{ZY}$,
        WX < WY
  Conclusion: XV > VY

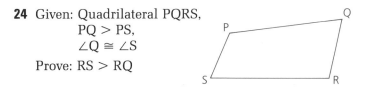

23 The sides of triangle ABC are integers, with AB = 5 and AC = 13. If one of the possible values of BC is picked at random, what is the probability that the resulting triangle will be obtuse?

24 Given: Quadrilateral PQRS,
        PQ > PS,
        $\angle Q \cong \angle S$
  Prove: RS > RQ

25 P is any point inside quadrilateral WXYZ. Prove that the sum of the distances from P to the four vertices (PW + PX + PY + PZ) is greater than or equal to the sum of the diagonals. (Consider all three cases for the position of point P within the quadrilateral.)

CUMULATIVE REVIEW
CHAPTERS 1–15

Problem Set A

1 Find the volume and the total surface area of a circular cone with a height of 4 and a base radius of 3.

2 If you graphed the equation $2x + 3y = 12$,
   a What would the graph's x-intercept be?
   b What would the graph's slope be?
   c Would the point $(37, -21)$ lie on the graph?

3 Given: Concentric circles, with $\overset{\frown}{CD} = 70°$ and $\overset{\frown}{QR} = 54°$
   Find: $\overset{\frown}{AB}$

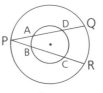

4 How far from the center of a circle with a diameter of 26 is a chord with a length of 24?

5 If the length of tangent $\overline{JM}$ is 10 and JP = 4, find PQ.

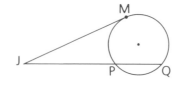

6 Solve for x.

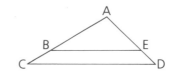

7 In $\triangle ADC$, $\overline{BE} \parallel \overline{CD}$, AB = 8, BC = 4, AE = 6, and BE = 9.
   a Find DE.
   b Find CD.
   c Is $\triangle ABE$ a right triangle?

8 Given: ABCD is a trapezoid, with AD ∥ BC.
   Prove: $AE \cdot BE = DE \cdot EC$

9 B and E are midpoints of $\overline{AC}$ and $\overline{AD}$ respectively. Find CD.

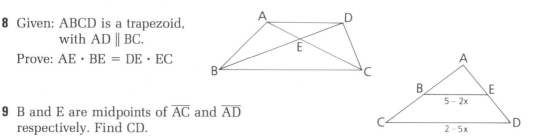

10 If a base angle of an isosceles triangle is twice the vertex angle, then find the measure of the vertex angle.

11 Draw a graph of △ABC with vertices A = (3, 8), B = (8, −4), and C = (−6, −4).

   a Find the lengths and the slopes of $\overline{AB}$, $\overline{BC}$, and $\overline{AC}$.

   b Is △ABC acute, right, or obtuse?

   c Find the equation of $\overleftrightarrow{AC}$ and its x- and y-intercepts.

   d Find the equation of $\overleftrightarrow{BC}$.

   e Where does the altitude to $\overline{BC}$ intersect $\overline{BC}$?

   f What is the equation of the altitude to $\overline{BC}$?

   g Find the length of the altitude to $\overline{BC}$.

   h Find the midpoint of $\overline{CB}$ and the slope of the median to $\overline{CB}$.

   i Find the area of △ABC.

12 Two regular pentagons have areas 8 and 18. What is the ratio of their perimeters?

13 Each interior angle of a regular polygon is 160°. Find the number of diagonals.

14 Find the area of the sector formed by the hands of a clock at 2 o'clock if the diameter of the clock is 12 in.

15 Find the area of an equilateral triangle whose height is 6.

16 Write the converse, the inverse, and the contrapositive of the statement, "If a parallelogram is inscribed in a circle, then it is not a 'plain old parallelogram.'"

17 Given: ∠X ≇ ∠Z;
            W is the midpoint of $\overline{XZ}$.
   Prove: $\overline{WY}$ is not an altitude to $\overline{XZ}$.

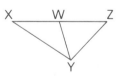

Problem Set B

18 Find, to the nearest tenth,

   a The area of the shaded region (a half washer)

   b The figure's perimeter (Hint: There are two semicircles and two segments.)

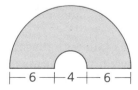

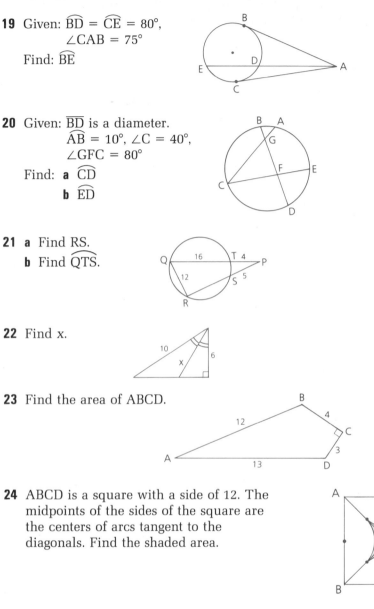

19 Given: $\overset{\frown}{BD} = \overset{\frown}{CE} = 80°$,
  $\angle CAB = 75°$
  Find: $\overset{\frown}{BE}$

20 Given: $\overline{BD}$ is a diameter.
  $\overset{\frown}{AB} = 10°$, $\angle C = 40°$,
  $\angle GFC = 80°$
  Find: **a** $\overset{\frown}{CD}$
  b $\overset{\frown}{ED}$

21 a Find RS.
  b Find $\overset{\frown}{QTS}$.

22 Find x.

23 Find the area of ABCD.

24 ABCD is a square with a side of 12. The midpoints of the sides of the square are the centers of arcs tangent to the diagonals. Find the shaded area.

25 The vertices of △ABC are A = (5, 4), B = (11, 6), and C = (9, 10).
  a Find the length of the median to $\overline{AB}$.
  b Find the equation of the median to $\overline{AB}$.
  c Find the equation of the altitude to $\overline{AB}$.
  d Find the equation of the perpendicular bisector of $\overline{AB}$.

26 Given a kite with diagonals 6 and 14, find, to the nearest tenth, the length of the segment joining the midpoints of two opposite sides.

27 Roger is 2 m tall. He is standing atop a tower, and the total length of his shadow and the tower's shadow is 14 m. If he were standing on the ground, his shadow would be 1 m long. How high is the tower?

28 The diagonals of a rhombus are 8 and 12. Find its altitude.

29 Quadrilateral PQRS is inscribed in ⊙O. The measures of $\overarc{PQ}$, $\overarc{QR}$, $\overarc{RS}$, and $\overarc{SP}$ are in the ratio 7:12:6:5. Find the acute angle formed by the diagonals of the quadrilateral.

30 Find the equation of the circle with center (2, 4) that passes through (1, 7).

31 Is △ARO acute, right, or obtuse?

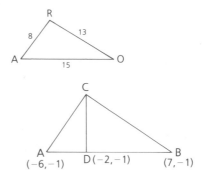

32 $\overline{CD}$ is the altitude to the hypotenuse of △ABC. The coordinates of points A, B, and D are given. Find the coordinates of point C.

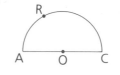

33 Find the ratio of the length of arc ARC to the length of diameter $\overline{AC}$.

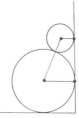

34 How far above the ground does the small ball touch the wall if the balls have radii of 4 cm and 9 cm?

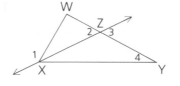

35 Given: Diagram as shown
Prove: ∠1 > ∠4

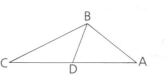

36 Given: $\overline{AD} \cong \overline{DC}$,
∠ADB < ∠BDC
Prove: ∠A > ∠C

37 Describe the locus of points a fixed distance from a given point and equidistant from the sides of an angle.

38 Two pipes are used to fill a pool with water. Their diameters are 12 and 16. Peter Plumber is hired to replace the two pipes with a single pipe having the same capacity as the other two combined.

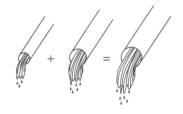

  a What is the diameter of the pipe that Peter must put in?

  b What general relationship exists between the diameters of the three pipes?

39 a Prove that ABCD is a kite.

  b Prove analytically that the figure formed by joining consecutive midpoints of the sides of ABCD is a rectangle.

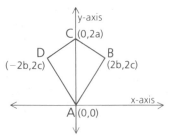

40 What can we conclude from the following statements?

  If *r* is red, then *b* is blue.
  If *q* is not green, then *y* is yellow.
  If *r* is not red, then *y* is not yellow.
  b is not blue.

Problem Set C

41 Describe the locus of points that are centers of congruent circles of a given radius if the circles are tangent to a given line and their centers lie on a given angle.

42 Circles O, P, Q, and R are tangent as shown. If the radius of ⊙R is 11, find the difference between the areas of the shaded regions above and below $\overline{XY}$.

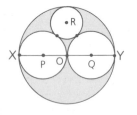

43 Prove: If two tangent segments are drawn to a circle from an external point, the triangle formed by these two tangents and any tangent to the minor arc included by them has a perimeter equal to the sum of the measures of the two original tangent segments.

44 In square ABCD, $\overline{HF} \perp \overline{AC}$. If the perimeter of the square is 32 and $FC = BC$, find the perimeter of quadrilateral HFEB.

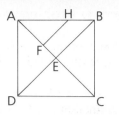

45 The diagonals of a parallelogram have measures of 8 and 10 and intersect at a 60° angle. Find the area of the parallelogram.

46 Sixty-four $1 \times 1 \times 1$ cubes are stacked together to form a $4 \times 4 \times 4$ cube. The large cube is painted and then broken up into the original sixty-four cubes. If two of the small cubes are selected at random, what is the probability that

a Exactly ten of the twelve faces will be unpainted?

b At least ten of the twelve faces will be unpainted?

47 a What is the locus in space of points generated by obtuse $\triangle ABC$ if it is rotated about the altitude from A to $\overleftrightarrow{BC}$?

b Find the volume of the locus.

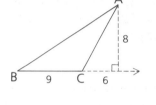

48 Prove that the shortest segment from an exterior point P to the circle is the segment along the line from P to O.

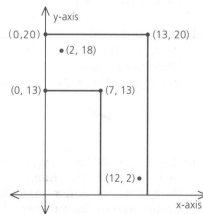

49 The point $A = (-3, 3)$ is rotated 90° clockwise about the origin to A'. If $C = (-2, 8)$ and $D = (16, 4)$, how far is A' from the midpoint of $\overline{CD}$?

50 On a miniature-golf course, the hole is at (2, 18) and the ball is at (12, 2), with barriers as shown.

a You can make a hole in one by bouncing the ball off the barrier $y = 20$ to the barrier $y = 13$ and into the hole. At what point must the ball strike the barrier $y = 20$?

b Can you go directly to the barrier $y = 20$ and then directly into the hole?

CHAPTER

16 ENRICHMENT TOPICS

O pen the wrought-iron-and-bronze
gates to discover enrichment topics
in geometry.

THE POINT–LINE DISTANCE FORMULA

Objective

After studying this section, you will be able to
- Use a formula to determine the distance from a point to a line in the coordinate plane

Part One: Introduction

In this chapter, we shall present some advanced geometry topics that you may enjoy exploring. Unlike the problem sets in the other chapters of this book, those in this chapter are not divided into A, B, and C groups.

We shall begin by developing a formula that you will find useful in solving a variety of coordinate-geometry problems. As you know, it is easy to determine the distance from a given point to a horizontal or vertical line in the coordinate plane. The *point-line distance formula,* however, can be used to find the distance from a given point to *any* line in the plane.

Theorem 136 **The distance d from any point $P = (x_1, y_1)$ to a line whose equation is in the form $ax + by + c = 0$ can be found with the formula**

$$d = \frac{|ax_1 + by_1 + c|}{\sqrt{a^2 + b^2}}$$

Proof: Remember, the distance from a point to a line is the length of the perpendicular segment from the point to the line. In the diagram, $Q = (x_2, y_2)$ is the foot of the perpendicular from point P to the line represented by $ax + by + c = 0$. The slope of the given line is $-\frac{a}{b}$, so the slope of $\overleftrightarrow{PQ}$ is $\frac{b}{a}$. Thus, we can write the system

$$\begin{cases} y - y_1 = \frac{b}{a}(x - x_1) & (\text{Equation of } \overleftrightarrow{PQ}) \\ ax + by + c = 0 & (\text{Equation of given line}) \end{cases}$$

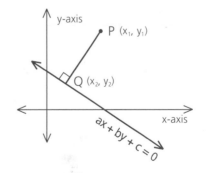

Now, by substituting x_2 and y_2 for x and y in the two equations and solving the system, we can express the coordinates of Q in terms of x_1 and y_1.

$$x_2 = \frac{b^2 x_1 - aby_1 - ac}{a^2 + b^2}$$

$$y_2 = \frac{-abx_1 + a^2 y_1 - bc}{a^2 + b^2}$$

Using these expressions in the distance formula to determine the distance from P to Q, we find that

$$d = \sqrt{\frac{a^2(ax_1 + by_1 + c)^2}{(a^2 + b^2)^2} + \frac{b^2(ax_1 + by_1 + c)^2}{(a^2 + b^2)^2}}$$

$$= \frac{|ax_1 + by_1 + c|}{\sqrt{a^2 + b^2}}$$

Part Two: Sample Problems

Problem 1   *Find the distance from the point $(2, -3)$ to the graph of $3x + 4y - 10 = 0$.*

Solution $d = \dfrac{|ax_1 + by_1 + c|}{\sqrt{a^2 + b^2}}$

$$= \frac{|3(2) + 4(-3) - 10|}{\sqrt{3^2 + 4^2}}$$

$$= \frac{16}{5}$$

Problem 2   *Find, to the nearest hundredth, the distance between the graphs of $y = 3x - 10$ and $y = 3x + 1$.*

Solution   Each of the two lines has a slope of 3, so the lines are parallel. We can choose a point on the first line—for example, $(0, -10)$—rewrite the second line's equation as $3x - y + 1 = 0$, and use the point-line distance formula.

$$d = \frac{|ax_1 + by_1 + c|}{\sqrt{a^2 + b^2}}$$

$$= \frac{|3(0) - (-10) + 1|}{\sqrt{3^2 + (-1)^2}}$$

$$= \frac{11}{\sqrt{10}}, \text{ or } \approx 3.48$$

Problem 3   *Write equations of the two lines that are parallel to the graph of*
5x − 12y = 17 and tangent to the circle whose center is at (4, − 3)
and whose radius is 5.

Solution   Since the lines are parallel to the graph of $5x - 12y = 17$, the slope
of each is $\frac{5}{12}$. Their equations are therefore of the form $5x - 12y +$
$c = 0$. We can substitute the coefficients of this equation, the coordinates of the circle's center, and the distance between the center and
the required lines (the circle's radius) in the point-line distance
formula.

$$d = \frac{|ax_1 + by_1 + c|}{\sqrt{a^2 + b^2}}$$

$$5 = \frac{|5(4) - 12(-3) + c|}{\sqrt{5^2 + 12^2}}$$

$$65 = |56 + c|$$

$$65 = 56 + c \text{ or } 65 = -56 - c$$
$$c = 9 \text{ or } c = -121$$

The lines can thus be represented by the equations
$5x - 12y + 9 = 0$ and $5x - 12y - 121 = 0$.

Part Three: Problem Set

1 Find the distance from the origin to the graph of
$4x - 3y + 15 = 0$.

2 Find the distance from the point (4, 2) to the graph of
$3x + 4y - 10 = 0$.

3 Find the distance from the point (2, 3) to the graph of
$7x - 24y + 2 = 0$.

4 Find the distance from the point (6, − 4) to the graph of
$3x - 4y = 14$.

5 Find, to the nearest hundredth, the distance from the point
(− 2, 6) to the line having a slope of 2 and passing through the
point (2, 1).

6 Find, to the nearest hundredth, the distance from the point
(− 2, 4) to the graph of $x \cos 30° + y \sin 30° - 8 = 0$.

7 Find, to four significant digits, the distance between the graphs
of $2x - 3y + 4 = 0$ and $2x - 3y + 15 = 0$.

8 Show that the graph of $12x + 5y = 12$ is tangent to the circle
having its center at (6, 1) and passing through (9, − 3).

Problem Set, *continued*

9 If the graph of $3x - 4y + k = 0$ is tangent to the circle with a radius of 2 and a center at (5, 1), what is the value of k?

10 It can be shown that in three dimensions, the distance from a point (x_1, y_1, z_1) to the plane represented by the equation $ax + by + cz + d = 0$ can be found with the formula

$$d = \frac{|ax_1 + by_1 + cz_1 + d|}{\sqrt{a^2 + b^2 + c^2}}$$

Find, to four significant digits, the distance from the point (5, 2, 1) to the graph of $3x - 7y + 5z + 13 = 0$.

11 Write equations of the bisectors of the angles formed by the graphs of $x - 2y + 5 = 0$ and $2x - y - 3 = 0$.

12 Find the possible values of b if the point (3, 4) is six units from the graph of $2x + by + 3 = 0$.

PLANETARY PORTRAITS
Kim Poor paints the heavens

Kim Poor is a landscape painter, but the landscapes he paints in his Tucson, Arizona, studio are of places no one has ever visited. He creates scenes showing planets and moons as they would appear to a cosmic explorer.

To make his works as realistic as possible, Kim regularly travels to Kitt Peak Observatory and the University of Arizona, where he makes sketches based on his conversations with astronomers and his reading in the observatories' libraries. Back in his studio, he carefully plans a painting, using trigonometry to determine how large each object in the picture would appear from the point of view he has selected. Then he gets to work with his airbrush.

According to Kim, the most important shape for the space artist is the ellipse, because circular features on the planets appear elliptical when viewed at an oblique angle. He gives an example: "We see Saturn's rings as anything from a line segment to an ellipse corresponding to a 20° tilt. And if the rings are shown as 20° ellipses, the cloud bands on the planet must also be 20° ellipses or the painting will look wrong." Kim uses protractors, compasses, and a variety of drafting techniques to produce the most accurate representations he can.

Kim's work can be seen in planetariums, magazines, encyclopedias, and textbooks. Along with his fellow space artists, he plays an important role in the interpretation and communication of the latest discoveries in planetary and stellar astronomy.

16.2 TWO OTHER USEFUL FORMULAS

Objectives

After studying this section, you will be able to
- Use a formula to find the area of a triangle when only the coordinates of its vertices are known
- Use a formula to find the diameter of a triangle's circumscribed circle

Part One: Introduction

Area of a Triangle

In Chapter 13, you used the encasement principle to find the areas of triangles in the coordinate plane. (See, for example, Section 13.7, problem 14.) Now we can use the point-line distance formula to develop a general formula for the area of a triangle with given vertices.

Theorem 137   ***The area A of a triangle with vertices at (x_1, y_1), (x_2, y_2), and (x_3, y_3) can be found with the formula***

$$A = \frac{1}{2}|x_1y_2 + x_2y_3 + x_3y_1 - x_1y_3 - x_2y_1 - x_3y_2|$$

Proof: The point-slope form of the equation of $\overleftrightarrow{BC}$ in the diagram at the right is

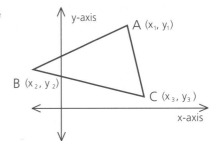

$$y - y_2 = \frac{y_3 - y_2}{x_3 - x_2}(x - x_2)$$

which can be rewritten as

$$x(y_2 - y_3) + y(x_3 - x_2) + x_2y_3 - x_3y_2 = 0$$

We can now find the distance from $A = (x_1, y_1)$ to $\overleftrightarrow{BC}$ (the altitude to base $\overline{BC}$) by using the point-line distance formula.

$$d = \frac{|(y_2 - y_3)x_1 + (x_3 - x_2)y_1 + x_2y_3 - x_3y_2|}{\sqrt{(y_2 - y_3)^2 + (x_3 - x_2)^2}}$$

Substituting this length and the length of base $\overline{BC}$ (determined by means of the distance formula) in the familiar formula for the area of a triangle, we find that

$$A = \frac{1}{2}bh$$

$$= \frac{1}{2}\sqrt{(y_3 - y_2)^2 + (x_3 - x_2)^2} \cdot \frac{|(y_2 - y_3)x_1 + (x_3 - x_2)y_1 + x_2y_3 - x_3y_2|}{\sqrt{(y_2 - y_3)^2 + (x_3 - x_2)^2}}$$

$$= \frac{1}{2}|x_1y_2 + x_2y_3 + x_3y_1 - x_1y_3 - x_2y_1 - x_3y_2|$$

Note If you are familiar with determinants, you may recognize that the formula in Theorem 137 can be written in the form

$$A = \frac{1}{2}\left\| \begin{array}{ccc} 1 & x_1 & y_1 \\ 1 & x_2 & y_2 \\ 1 & x_3 & y_3 \end{array} \right\|$$

Diameter of a Circumscribed Circle

In solving certain problems, it is useful to be able to calculate the diameter of a circle circumscribed about a triangle (the triangle's *circumcircle*). The theorem that follows is an extension of the Law of Sines, which was presented in Section 9.10, problem 2.1. (Recall that when we describe the parts of a triangle, we use a to represent the length of the side *opposite* vertex A, and so forth.)

Theorem 138 *In any triangle ABC, with side lengths a, b, and c,*

$$\frac{a}{\sin \angle A} = D \qquad \frac{b}{\sin \angle B} = D \qquad \frac{c}{\sin \angle C} = D$$

where D is the diameter of the triangle's circumcircle.

Proof: The diagrams below show the five possible cases for $\angle A$ in an inscribed triangle.

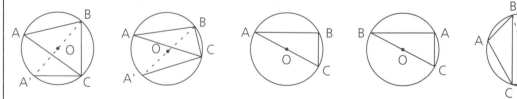

In the first two cases, we have drawn diameter $\overline{A'B}$, forming right triangle A'BC. (Remember, an angle inscribed in a semicircle is a right angle.) Since inscribed angles A and A' intercept the same arc, they are congruent, and therefore $\sin \angle A = \sin \angle A' = \frac{a}{D}$. Thus,

$$\frac{a}{\sin \angle A} = \frac{a}{\frac{a}{D}} = D$$

In the third case, we can obtain the same result without drawing an auxiliary line, since △ABC is already a right triangle.

In the fourth case, ∠A = 90°. From trigonometry, we know that sin 90° = 1, so the formula follows immediately.

In the last case, where ∠A is obtuse, we again draw diameter $\overline{A'B}$. Since opposite angles of an inscribed quadrilateral are supplementary, ∠A is supplementary to ∠A'. It is a basic principle of trigonometry that the sine of any angle is equal to the sine of its supplement, so sin ∠A = sin ∠A'. Hence, we obtain the same result as in the first two cases.

Similar reasoning can be used to show that for any ∠B and ∠C in an inscribed triangle, $\frac{b}{\sin \angle B} = D$ and $\frac{c}{\sin \angle C} = D$.

Part Two: Sample Problems

Problem 1   *Find, to the nearest tenth, the diameter of the circle circumscribed about △ABC.*

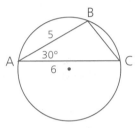

Solution   According to the Law of Cosines (see Section 9.10, problem 20),

$(BC)^2 = 5^2 + 6^2 - 2(5)(6)(\cos 30°)$

$= 25 + 36 - \dfrac{60\sqrt{3}}{2}$

$= 61 - 30\sqrt{3}$

$BC \approx 3.006$

We now use the formula for the diameter of a circumcircle.

$D = \dfrac{a}{\sin \angle A}$

$\approx \dfrac{3.006}{\sin 30°}$

$\approx \dfrac{3.006}{\frac{1}{2}} \approx 6.0$

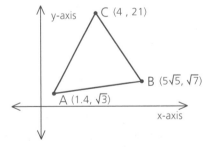

Problem 2   *Find the area of △ABC to the nearest tenth.*

Solution   We use the formula for the area of a triangle (Theorem 137).

$A = \dfrac{1}{2}|x_1y_2 + x_2y_3 + x_3y_1 - x_1y_3 - x_2y_1 - x_3y_2|$

$= \dfrac{1}{2}|1.4\sqrt{7} + 5\sqrt{5}(21) + 4\sqrt{3} - 1.4(21) - 5\sqrt{5}\sqrt{3} - 4\sqrt{7}|$

≈ 93.0

Part Three: Problem Set

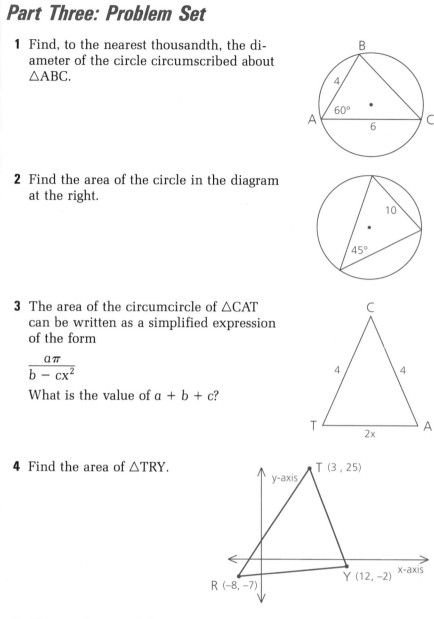

1 Find, to the nearest thousandth, the diameter of the circle circumscribed about △ABC.

2 Find the area of the circle in the diagram at the right.

3 The area of the circumcircle of △CAT can be written as a simplified expression of the form

$$\frac{a\pi}{b - cx^2}$$

What is the value of $a + b + c$?

4 Find the area of △TRY.

5 The coordinates of the vertices of a triangle are $(-2, 6)$, $(4, 17)$, and $(x, 11)$, and the triangle's area is 42. Find the possible values of x.

STEWART'S THEOREM

Objective

After studying this section, you will be able to
- Recognize a relationship among the parts of a triangle with a segment drawn from a vertex to the opposite side

Part One: Introduction

The following theorem is usually called Stewart's Theorem, after the eighteenth-century Scottish mathematician Matthew Stewart, although forms of the theorem were known as long ago as the fourth century A.D.

Theorem 139 *In any triangle ABC, with side lengths a, b, and c,*

$$a^2n + b^2m = cd^2 + cmn$$

where d is the length of a segment from vertex C to the opposite side, dividing that side into segments with lengths m and n. (Stewart's Theorem)

Given: Diagram as marked

Prove: $a^2n + b^2m = cd^2 + cmn$

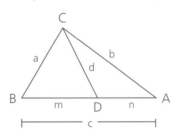

Proof: We draw $\overline{CE}$ perpendicular to $\overline{AB}$ and use the Pythagorean Theorem. In $\triangle BCE$, $a^2 = h^2 + (m - p)^2$, or $a^2 = h^2 + m^2 - 2mp + p^2$; and in $\triangle CED$, $d^2 = h^2 + p^2$. By subtraction, we find that $a^2 - d^2 = m^2 - 2mp$, or

$$a^2 = d^2 + m^2 - 2mp \qquad (1)$$

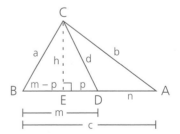

In $\triangle CEA$, $b^2 = h^2 + (p + n)^2$, or $b^2 = h^2 + p^2 + 2pn + n^2$. Since we know that $h^2 = d^2 - p^2$ (see the preceding paragraph), we can substitute $d^2 - p^2$ for h^2 to obtain the equation $b^2 = d^2 - p^2 + p^2 + 2pn + n^2$, or

$$b^2 = d^2 + 2pn + n^2 \qquad (2)$$

Equation (1) can be rewritten as $a^2n = d^2n + m^2n - 2mnp$, and equation (2) can be rewritten as $b^2m = d^2m + 2mnp + mn^2$. Adding these equations, we find that

$$a^2n + b^2m = d^2n + d^2m + m^2n + mn^2$$
$$= d^2(n + m) + mn(m + n)$$
$$= cd^2 + cmn$$

Part Two: Sample Problems

Problem 1   *If the sides of a triangle have measures of 3, 5, and 6, what is the length of the bisector of the angle included by the sides measuring 3 and 5?*

Solution   By the Angle Bisector Theorem (see Section 8.5),

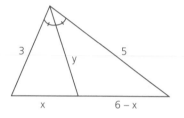

$$\frac{3}{5} = \frac{x}{6 - x}$$

$$5x = 18 - 3x$$

$$x = \frac{9}{4}$$

Therefore, $6 - x = \frac{15}{4}$. We now apply Stewart's Theorem.

$$3^2\left(\frac{15}{4}\right) + 5^2\left(\frac{9}{4}\right) = y^2(6) + 6\left(\frac{9}{4}\right)\left(\frac{15}{4}\right)$$

$$\frac{135}{4} + \frac{225}{4} = 6y^2 + \frac{405}{8}$$

$$y^2 = \frac{105}{16}$$

$$y = \frac{\sqrt{105}}{4}$$

Problem 2   *Prove that in a right triangle the sum of the squares of the segments from the vertex of the right angle to the trisection points of the hypotenuse is equal to five-ninths the square of the hypotenuse.*

Proof   According to Stewart's Theorem, in the diagram shown,

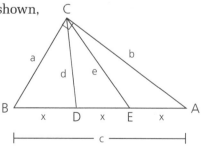

$$2a^2x + b^2x = d^2c + 2cx^2$$

and

$$a^2x + 2b^2x = ce^2 + 2cx^2$$

Adding these equations, we find that

$$3a^2x + 3b^2x = cd^2 + ce^2 + 4cx^2$$
$$3x(a^2 + b^2) = cd^2 + ce^2 + 4cx^2$$

By substituting c^2 for $a^2 + b^2$, we obtain

$$3xc^2 = c(d^2 + e^2 + 4x^2)$$

Now we substitute c for $3x$.

$$c^3 = c(d^2 + e^2 + 4x^2)$$
$$c^2 = d^2 + e^2 + 4x^2$$

Since $2x = \frac{2}{3}c$, we can substitute $\frac{4}{9}c^2$ for $4x^2$ to obtain

$$c^2 = d^2 + e^2 + \frac{4}{9}c^2$$

$$d^2 + e^2 = \frac{5}{9}c^2$$

Part Three: Problem Set

1 Find the value of x in the figure at the right.

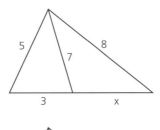

2 Find the value of y in the figure at the right.

3 A parallelogram has sides with measures of 7 and 9, and the measure of its shorter diagonal is 8. Find the measure of the parallelogram's longer diagonal.

4 Two sides of a triangle have measures of 9 and 18. If the bisector of the angle included by these sides has a measure of 8, what is the measure of the third side of the triangle?

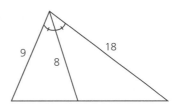

5 Find the measure of a side of a triangle if the other two sides and the bisector of the angle they include have measures of 3, 5, and 2 respectively.

PTOLEMY'S THEOREM

Objective

After studying this section, you will be able to

■ Recognize a relationship involving the sides and the diagonals of a cyclic quadrilateral

Part One: Introduction

Ptolemy's Theorem is named for a famous Alexandrian mathematician, astronomer, and geographer (often referred to by the Latin form of his name, Claudius Ptolemaeus) who lived from about 85 to 165 A.D.

Theorem 140 *If a quadrilateral is inscribable in a circle, the product of the measures of its diagonals is equal to the sum of the products of the measures of the pairs of opposite sides. (Ptolemy's Theorem)*

Given: Quadrilateral ABCD inscribed in ⊙O

Prove: (AC) (BD) = (AB) (CD) + (AD) (BC)

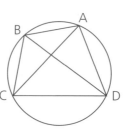

Proof: We extend $\overline{CD}$ to a point P so that ∠DAP ≅ ∠BAC. Since opposite angles of a cyclic quadrilateral are supplementary, ∠ABC is supplementary to ∠ADC; so ∠ABC ≅ ∠ADP because supplements of the same angle are congruent. Therefore, △BAC ~ △DAP (by AA), and

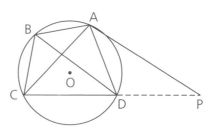

$$\frac{AB}{AD} = \frac{BC}{DP}$$

$$DP = \frac{(AD)\,(BC)}{AB} \qquad\qquad (1)$$

By the Addition Property, $\angle BAD \cong \angle CAP$; so $\angle ABD \cong \angle ACP$, since inscribed angles that intercept the same arc are congruent. Therefore, $\triangle ABD \sim \triangle ACP$ (by AA), and

$$\frac{AB}{AC} = \frac{BD}{CP}$$

$$CP = \frac{(AC)\,(BD)}{AB} \qquad\qquad (2)$$

We know that $CP = CD + DP$, and when we substitute the equivalent expressions from equations (1) and (2) for DP and CP in this equation, we obtain

$$\frac{(AC)\,(BD)}{AB} = CD + \frac{(AD)\,(BC)}{AB}$$

$$(AC)\,(BD) = (AB)\,(CD) + (AD)\,(BC)$$

Part Two: Sample Problems

Problem 1

Given: Inscribed quadrilateral ABCD,
AB = 3, BC = 5, CD = 4,
AD = 6, $AC = \dfrac{2\sqrt{1729}}{13}$

Find: BD

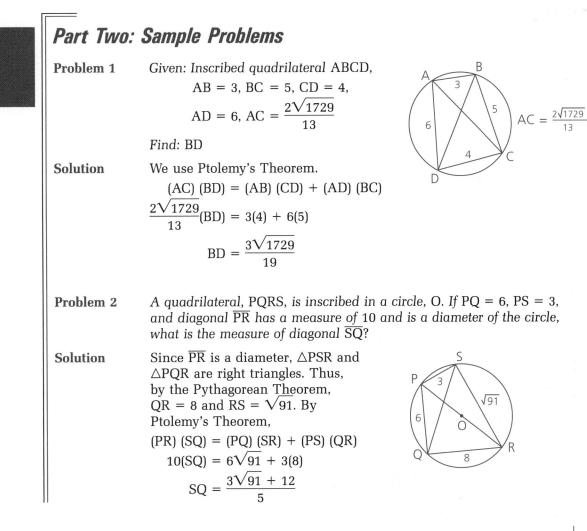

$AC = \dfrac{2\sqrt{1729}}{13}$

Solution

We use Ptolemy's Theorem.

$$(AC)\,(BD) = (AB)\,(CD) + (AD)\,(BC)$$

$$\frac{2\sqrt{1729}}{13}(BD) = 3(4) + 6(5)$$

$$BD = \frac{3\sqrt{1729}}{19}$$

Problem 2

A quadrilateral, PQRS, is inscribed in a circle, O. If PQ = 6, PS = 3, and diagonal $\overline{PR}$ has a measure of 10 and is a diameter of the circle, what is the measure of diagonal $\overline{SQ}$?

Solution

Since $\overline{PR}$ is a diameter, $\triangle PSR$ and $\triangle PQR$ are right triangles. Thus, by the Pythagorean Theorem, QR = 8 and RS = $\sqrt{91}$. By Ptolemy's Theorem,

$$(PR)\,(SQ) = (PQ)\,(SR) + (PS)\,(QR)$$

$$10(SQ) = 6\sqrt{91} + 3(8)$$

$$SQ = \frac{3\sqrt{91} + 12}{5}$$

Problem 3   ∠CFD *is inscribed in the circumcircle of rectangle ABCD, with* $\overline{CF}$ *intersecting* $\overline{DA}$ *at E. If DC = 6, DE = 6, and EA = 2, find BF.*

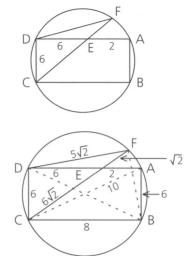

Solution   In right triangle CED, CE = 6√2. Because inscribed angles intercepting the same arc are congruent, ∠CAD ≅ ∠DFC and ∠FDA ≅ ∠FCA. Thus, △DEF ~ △CEA (by AA), and

$$\frac{6}{6\sqrt{2}} = \frac{DF}{10}$$

$$DF = 5\sqrt{2}$$

In a similar way, it can be shown that EF = √2. We now apply Ptolemy's Theorem to quadrilateral BCDF.

(BD) (CF) = (DC) (BF) + (DF) (BC)

10(7√2) = 6(BF) + 5√2(8)

BF = 5√2

Part Three: Problem Set

1 Given: Cyclic quadrilateral ABCD,
AB = 2, BC = 3, CD = 6,
AD = 8, BD = $\frac{18\sqrt{51}}{17}$

Find: AC

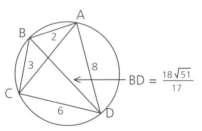

2 In the diagram at the right, ABCD is a square, and E is the point of intersection of its diagonals. If a point, F, is located in the exterior of the square so that △ABF is a right triangle with hypotenuse $\overline{AB}$, AF = 6, and BF = 8, what is distance EF? (Hint: Apply Ptolemy's Theorem to quadrilateral AEBF.)

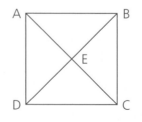

3 Given: $\odot$O, with inscribed quadrilateral
   EFGH, EF = 7, GH = 20, EH = 25

Find: The perimeter of EFGH

4 Diagonals $\overline{AC}$ and $\overline{BD}$ of quadrilateral
   ABCD intersect at E. If AE = 2, BE = 5,
   CE = 10, DE = 4, and BC = 7.5, what is
   distance AB? (Hint: Look for similar triangles that you can use to find AD and
   the ratio of AB to CD. Then apply
   Ptolemy's Theorem.)

5 A triangle is inscribed in a circle with a radius of 5. The measures of two of the triangle's sides are 5 and 6. What are the
   possible measures of the third side? (Hint: There are two possible
   triangles.)

HISTORICAL SNAPSHOT

DYNAMIC GEOMETRY
Buckminster Fuller and the geodesic dome

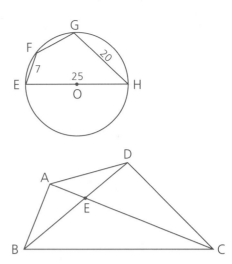

One day while serving in the United States Navy during World War I, young R. Buckminster Fuller stood observing the bubbles that boiled up in the wake of his ship. Noticing that they were constantly changing in shape, always approximating spheres but never settling into a stable spherical form, he concluded that "nature doesn't use pi." He decided that what governs the natural world is not the static figures and relationships of traditional geometry but the geometric interactions of forces that shape the objects around us.

Fuller was to base a new approach to architecture and design on this insight. He liked to call his approach "energetic-synergetic geometry." By studying the patterns of forces that hold molecules together, he developed a system of basic forms that could be used to produce structures that combine maximum strength with minimal materials. The most famous of these structures is the geodesic dome, an unsupport-ed framework of tensed triangular forms with a remarkable property: the larger the dome, the greater its total strength. Hence, there is no limit to the possible size of a geodesic dome. Fuller suggested that whole cities could be covered with domes to allow complete control of their climates.

While no domes large enough to cover cities have been constructed yet, the myriad ideas of Buckminster Fuller, who died in 1983, continue to exert influence in diverse fields from map-making to environmental science.

MASS POINTS

Objective

After studying this section, you will be able to
- Use the concept of mass points to solve problems

Part One: Introduction

Some people claim that the theory of **mass points** was developed by students in New York as a way of simplifying the solutions of many mathematics problems. The theory is based on what might be called the balance principle (or the fulcrum principle or the teeter-totter principle).

In the diagram of a lever above, w_1 and w_2 are weights, and d_1 and d_2 are their respective distances from the fulcrum. For the lever to be in balance, the product $w_1 d_1$ must be equal to the product $w_2 d_2$. Mass-point theory is simply an application of this physical principle to geometric problems. Consider, for example, a segment divided in the ratio $2:3$.

We can assign "weights" of 3 and 2 to points A and C respectively to "balance" the segment ($3 \cdot 2x = 2 \cdot 3x$). We can then assign a weight of 5—the sum of the weights of the endpoints—to point B, the "fulcrum." The completed mass-point diagram of the segment will look like this:

A	2x	B	3x	C
3		5		2

As the sample problems and the problem set in this section illustrate, the mass-point procedure can be used to solve a variety of problems in two or more dimensions. If you wish to investigate the topic of mass points further, you can consult the following two sources:

Hausner, Melvin. "The Center of Mass and Affine Geometry,"
   American Mathematical Monthly, Vol. 69 (1962), pp. 724–737.
Sitomer, Harry, and Steven R. Conrad. "Mass Points," *Eureka,*
   Vol. 2, No. 4 (April 1976), pp. 55–62.

Part Two: Sample Problems

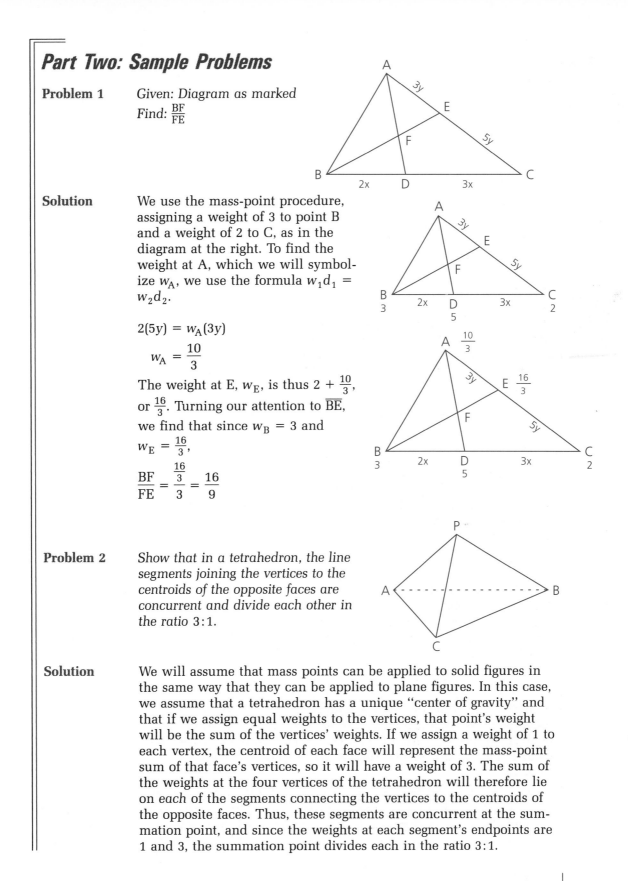

Problem 1

Given: Diagram as marked

Find: $\dfrac{BF}{FE}$

Solution

We use the mass-point procedure, assigning a weight of 3 to point B and a weight of 2 to C, as in the diagram at the right. To find the weight at A, which we will symbolize w_A, we use the formula $w_1 d_1 = w_2 d_2$.

$$2(5y) = w_A(3y)$$

$$w_A = \frac{10}{3}$$

The weight at E, w_E, is thus $2 + \frac{10}{3}$, or $\frac{16}{3}$. Turning our attention to $\overline{BE}$, we find that since $w_B = 3$ and $w_E = \frac{16}{3}$,

$$\frac{BF}{FE} = \frac{\frac{16}{3}}{3} = \frac{16}{9}$$

Problem 2

Show that in a tetrahedron, the line segments joining the vertices to the centroids of the opposite faces are concurrent and divide each other in the ratio 3:1.

Solution

We will assume that mass points can be applied to solid figures in the same way that they can be applied to plane figures. In this case, we assume that a tetrahedron has a unique "center of gravity" and that if we assign equal weights to the vertices, that point's weight will be the sum of the vertices' weights. If we assign a weight of 1 to each vertex, the centroid of each face will represent the mass-point sum of that face's vertices, so it will have a weight of 3. The sum of the weights at the four vertices of the tetrahedron will therefore lie on *each* of the segments connecting the vertices to the centroids of the opposite faces. Thus, these segments are concurrent at the summation point, and since the weights at each segment's endpoints are 1 and 3, the summation point divides each in the ratio 3:1.

Problem 3 In the figure shown, $\frac{AB}{BC} = \frac{3}{4}$ and $\frac{CD}{DE} = \frac{2}{5}$. Find $\frac{CG}{GF}$.

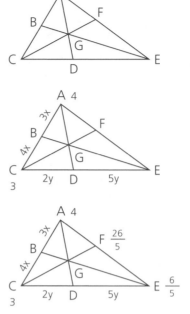

Solution We assign a weight of 4 to A and a weight of 3 to C so that $w_A(AB) = w_C(BC)$, as shown in the diagram at the right. We now find the weight at E.

$$3(2y) = w_E(5y)$$

$$w_E = \frac{6}{5}$$

Thus, $w_F = 4 + \frac{6}{5}$, or $\frac{26}{5}$. Since $w_C = 3$ and $w_F = \frac{26}{5}$,

$$\frac{CG}{GF} = \frac{\frac{26}{5}}{3} = \frac{26}{15}$$

Part Three: Problem Set

1 Given: $\overline{AE}$ is a median of $\triangle ABC$.
   AD:DC = 3:7
   Find: BF:FD

2 In the figure shown, $\frac{HG}{HF} = \frac{4}{9}$ and $\frac{FM}{MK} = \frac{2}{3}$.
   Find $\frac{HJ}{JK}$ and $\frac{FO}{FJ}$.

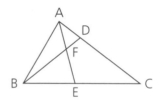

3 In a triangle ABC, $\overline{BD}$ is a median, F is a point on $\overline{AB}$, and $\overline{CF}$ intersects $\overline{BD}$ at E. If BE = 4(ED) and BF = 20, what is AF?

4 In a triangle ABC, $\angle A = 45°$, $\angle C = 60°$, and altitude $\overline{BH}$ intersects median $\overline{AM}$ at point P. If AP = 4, what is AM?

5 Given: Trapezoid ABCD ($\overleftrightarrow{AD} \parallel \overleftrightarrow{BC}$),
   $AD = \frac{1}{4}(BC)$, $\frac{DF}{FC} = \frac{2}{3}$
   Find: $\frac{GE}{GF}$

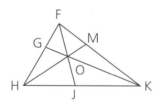

INRADIUS AND CIRCUMRADIUS FORMULAS

Objective

After studying this section, you will be able to

- Use formulas to calculate the radii of a triangle's inscribed circle and a triangle's circumscribed circle

Part One: Introduction

In Section 16.2, we presented a formula that can be used to find the diameter of a triangle's circumcircle when one angle and the measure of the side opposite that angle's vertex are known. In this section, you will work with two other useful formulas—one for determining the radius of a triangle's inscribed circle (the triangle's **inradius**) and the other for determining the radius of a triangle's circumscribed circle (the triangle's **circumradius**).

Theorem 141 **The inradius r of a triangle can be found with the formula**

$$r = \frac{A}{s}$$

where A is the triangle's area and s is the triangle's semiperimeter.

Given: $\triangle ABC$, with inscribed circle O and
       an inradius (r) drawn to each side

Prove: $r = \frac{A}{s}$

Proof: We draw $\overline{IA}$, $\overline{IC}$, and $\overline{IB}$. The area of $\triangle AIC$ is $\frac{1}{2}r(AC)$, the area of $\triangle AIB$ is $\frac{1}{2}r(AB)$, and the area of $\triangle BIC$ is $\frac{1}{2}r(BC)$. Thus, in $\triangle ABC$,

$$A = \frac{1}{2}r(AC) + \frac{1}{2}r(AB) + \frac{1}{2}r(BC)$$

$$= \frac{1}{2}r(AC + AB + BC)$$

$$= r\left[\frac{1}{2}(AC + AB + BC)\right]$$

$$= rs$$

Therefore, $r = \frac{A}{s}$.

Theorem 142   ***The circumradius R of a triangle can be found with
the formula***

$$R = \frac{abc}{4A}$$

***where a, b, and c are the lengths of the sides of the
triangle and A is the triangle's area.***

Given: $\triangle ABC$, with circumcircle O

Prove: $R = \frac{abc}{4A}$

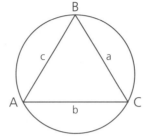

Proof: We draw diameter $\overline{BD}$ and chord $\overline{DC}$.
In $\triangle BDC$,

$$\sin \angle D = \frac{BC}{BD}$$

$$= \frac{a}{2R}$$

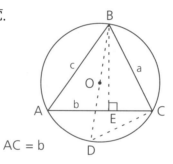

$AC = b$

Since $\angle A$ and $\angle D$ are inscribed angles intercepting the same arc,
they are congruent, so $\sin \angle A = \frac{a}{2R}$. We now draw altitude $\overline{BE}$, with
a length that we shall refer to as h_b. Therefore,

$$\sin \angle A = \frac{h_b}{c}$$

$$\frac{a}{2R} = \frac{h_b}{c}$$

$$R = \frac{ac}{2h_b}$$

$$= \frac{abc}{2h_b b} \qquad \left(\text{Multiplying by } \tfrac{b}{b} \right)$$

$$= \frac{abc}{2(2A)} \qquad \left(\text{Since } A = \tfrac{1}{2} bh_b \right)$$

$$= \frac{abc}{4A}$$

Part Two: Sample Problems

Problem 1   *Find the inradius and the circumradius of a (7, 8, 11) triangle.*

Solution   First, we use Hero's formula (see Section 11.8) to find the triangle's area.

$$A = \sqrt{13\,(6)\,(5)\,(2)} = 2\sqrt{195}$$

By the inradius formula,

$$r = \frac{A}{s} = \frac{2\sqrt{195}}{13}$$

By the circumradius formula,

$$R = \frac{abc}{4A} = \frac{7\,(8)\,(11)}{4\left(2\sqrt{195}\right)} = \frac{77\sqrt{195}}{195}$$

Problem 2   *Find the inradius and the circumradius of a (12, 35, 37) triangle.*

Solution   Be alert! By using the converse of the Pythagorean Theorem, we can establish that this is a right triangle. Therefore, $A = \frac{1}{2}(12)\,(35) = 210$. By the inradius formula,

$$r = \frac{A}{s} = \frac{210}{42} = 5$$

By the circumradius formula,

$$R = \frac{abc}{4A} = \frac{12\,(35)\,(37)}{4\,(210)} = \frac{37}{2}$$

In this problem, is it a coincidence that the circumradius is half the hypotenuse? Is it a coincidence that the inradius of this right triangle is $\frac{a + b - c}{2}$?

Part Three: Problem Set

1 Find the inradius and the circumradius of a (3, 5, 6) triangle.

2 Find the inradius and the circumradius of a (9, 40, 41) triangle.

3 Find the inradius and the circumradius of a (6, 8, 12) triangle.

4 Two of the sides of a triangle have measures of 10 and 12. If the triangle is inscribed in a circle with a diameter of 15, what is the altitude to the third side? (Hint: Substitute values in the circumradius formula.)

5 a Find the length of the third side of the triangle shown.

   b Find the circumradius of the triangle to four significant digits.

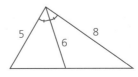

FORMULAS FOR YOU TO DEVELOP

Objective

After studying this section, you will be able to

■ Find or prove five additional formulas

In this section, you are asked to establish the validity of five formulas. In each case, there is a problem or two for you to solve by applying the formula.

Three Triangle Formulas

I. Consider a right triangle with legs a and b and hypotenuse c. Find a formula for the perimeter P of the triangle in terms of its hypotenuse and its area A.

    Now use your formula to find the perimeter of a right triangle if the triangle's area is 40 and the altitude to its hypotenuse is 5.

II. Find a formula relating a triangle's inradius, r, to its three altitudes, h_a, h_b, and h_c.

    Now use your formula to find the inradius of a triangle whose three altitudes are 4, 5, and 6.

III. Prove that the area A of any triangle ABC, with side lengths a, b, and c, can be found with the formula

$$A = \frac{1}{2}ab(\sin \angle C)$$

    Now use this formula to solve the following problems:

a Find the area of a regular dodecagon inscribed in a circle with a diameter of 20.

b Given: Diagram as marked

    Find: The area of △ADE

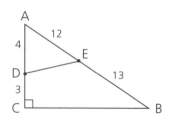

Ceva's Theorem

The following theorem is known as Ceva's Theorem, after the Italian mathematician Giovanni Ceva (c. 1647–1734).

Theorem 143   *If ABC is a triangle with D on $\overline{BC}$, E on $\overline{AC}$, and F on $\overline{AB}$, then the three segments $\overline{AD}$, $\overline{BE}$, and $\overline{CF}$ are concurrent if, and only if,*

$$\left(\frac{BD}{DC}\right)\left(\frac{CE}{EA}\right)\left(\frac{AF}{FB}\right) = 1$$

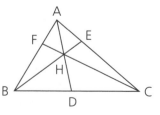

Copy the following proof of Ceva's Theorem and see if you can fill in the missing reasons.

Proof:

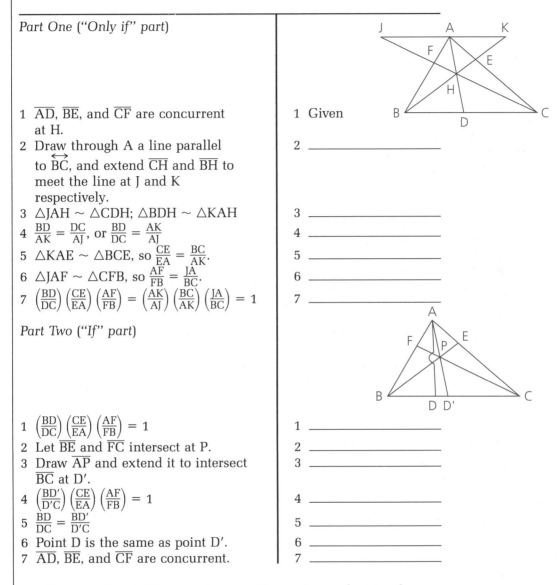

Part One ("Only if" part)

1 $\overline{AD}$, $\overline{BE}$, and $\overline{CF}$ are concurrent at H.

2 Draw through A a line parallel to $\overleftrightarrow{BC}$, and extend $\overline{CH}$ and $\overline{BH}$ to meet the line at J and K respectively.

3 $\triangle JAH \sim \triangle CDH$; $\triangle BDH \sim \triangle KAH$

4 $\frac{BD}{AK} = \frac{DC}{AJ}$, or $\frac{BD}{DC} = \frac{AK}{AJ}$

5 $\triangle KAE \sim \triangle BCE$, so $\frac{CE}{EA} = \frac{BC}{AK}$.

6 $\triangle JAF \sim \triangle CFB$, so $\frac{AF}{FB} = \frac{JA}{BC}$.

7 $\left(\frac{BD}{DC}\right)\left(\frac{CE}{EA}\right)\left(\frac{AF}{FB}\right) = \left(\frac{AK}{AJ}\right)\left(\frac{BC}{AK}\right)\left(\frac{JA}{BC}\right) = 1$

Part Two ("If" part)

1 $\left(\frac{BD}{DC}\right)\left(\frac{CE}{EA}\right)\left(\frac{AF}{FB}\right) = 1$

2 Let $\overline{BE}$ and $\overline{FC}$ intersect at P.

3 Draw $\overline{AP}$ and extend it to intersect $\overline{BC}$ at D'.

4 $\left(\frac{BD'}{D'C}\right)\left(\frac{CE}{EA}\right)\left(\frac{AF}{FB}\right) = 1$

5 $\frac{BD}{DC} = \frac{BD'}{D'C}$

6 Point D is the same as point D'.

7 $\overline{AD}$, $\overline{BE}$, and $\overline{CF}$ are concurrent.

1 Given

2 _____

3 _____

4 _____

5 _____

6 _____

7 _____

1 _____

2 _____

3 _____

4 _____

5 _____

6 _____

7 _____

Now use Ceva's Theorem to prove the medians of a triangle concurrent.

Theorem of Menelaus

The following theorem is known as the Theorem of Menelaus. (Menelaus was an Alexandrian mathematician of the first century A.D.) It is important to note that this theorem involves the concept of **sensed magnitudes**—that is, the measure of a segment in one direction is considered to be the opposite of its measure in the other direction. (For example, AB = −BA.)

Theorem 144 *If ABC is a triangle and F is on $\overline{AB}$, E is on $\overline{AC}$, and D is on an extension of $\overline{BC}$, then the three points D, E, and F are collinear if, and only if,*

$$\left(\frac{BD}{DC}\right)\left(\frac{CE}{EA}\right)\left(\frac{AF}{FB}\right) = -1$$

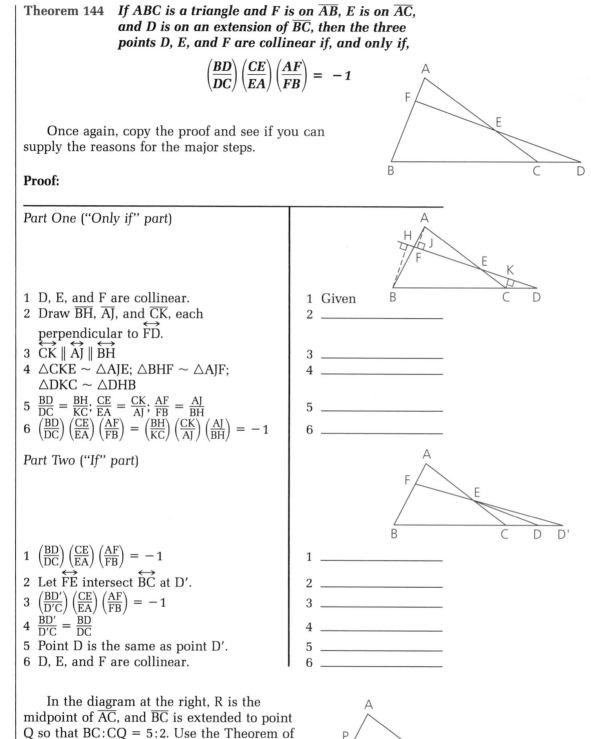

Once again, copy the proof and see if you can supply the reasons for the major steps.

Proof:

Part One ("Only if" part)

1 D, E, and F are collinear.
2 Draw $\overline{BH}$, $\overline{AJ}$, and $\overline{CK}$, each perpendicular to $\overleftrightarrow{FD}$.
3 $\overleftrightarrow{CK} \parallel \overleftrightarrow{AJ} \parallel \overleftrightarrow{BH}$
4 $\triangle CKE \sim \triangle AJE$; $\triangle BHF \sim \triangle AJF$; $\triangle DKC \sim \triangle DHB$
5 $\frac{BD}{DC} = \frac{BH}{KC}$; $\frac{CE}{EA} = \frac{CK}{AJ}$; $\frac{AF}{FB} = \frac{AJ}{BH}$
6 $\left(\frac{BD}{DC}\right)\left(\frac{CE}{EA}\right)\left(\frac{AF}{FB}\right) = \left(\frac{BH}{KC}\right)\left(\frac{CK}{AJ}\right)\left(\frac{AJ}{BH}\right) = -1$

1 Given
2 _____
3 _____
4 _____

5 _____

6 _____

Part Two ("If" part)

1 $\left(\frac{BD}{DC}\right)\left(\frac{CE}{EA}\right)\left(\frac{AF}{FB}\right) = -1$
2 Let $\overleftrightarrow{FE}$ intersect $\overleftrightarrow{BC}$ at D'.
3 $\left(\frac{BD'}{D'C}\right)\left(\frac{CE}{EA}\right)\left(\frac{AF}{FB}\right) = -1$
4 $\frac{BD'}{D'C} = \frac{BD}{DC}$
5 Point D is the same as point D'.
6 D, E, and F are collinear.

1 _____
2 _____
3 _____
4 _____
5 _____
6 _____

In the diagram at the right, R is the midpoint of $\overline{AC}$, and $\overline{BC}$ is extended to point Q so that BC:CQ = 5:2. Use the Theorem of Menelaus to find AP:PB.

CHAPTER SUMMARY

CONCEPTS AND PROCEDURES

After studying this chapter, you should be able to

- Use a formula to determine the distance from a point to a line in the coordinate plane (16.1)
- Use a formula to find the area of a triangle when only the coordinates of its vertices are known (16.2)
- Use a formula to find the diameter of a triangle's circumscribed circle (16.2)
- Recognize a relationship among the parts of a triangle with a segment drawn from a vertex to the opposite side (16.3)
- Recognize a relationship involving the sides and the diagonals of a cyclic quadrilateral (16.4)
- Use the concept of mass points to solve problems (16.5)
- Use formulas to calculate the radii of a triangle's inscribed circle and a triangle's circumscribed circle (16.6)
- Find or prove five additional formulas (16.7)

VOCABULARY

circumcircle (16.2)

circumradius (16.6)

inradius (16.6)

mass point (16.5)

point-line distance formula (16.1)

sensed magnitude (16.7)

16 REVIEW PROBLEMS

1 Use the figures below to solve for *x* and *y*.

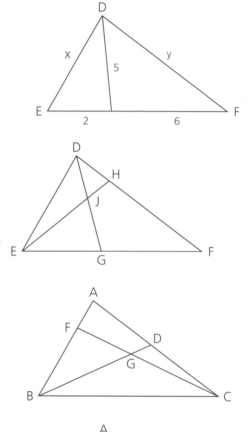

2 In the figure shown, EG:GF = 4:6 and DH:HF = 2:5. Find DJ:DG.

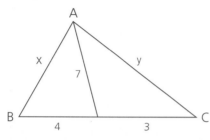

3 In the figure shown, AF = 12, AD:DC = 8:7, and $\overline{CF}$ intersects $\overline{BD}$ at G so that BG = 5(GD). Find BF.

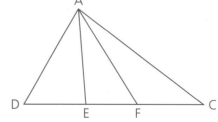

4 Given: ∠DAC = 90°,
$\overline{DE} \cong \overline{EF} \cong \overline{FC}$,
AE = 7, AF = 8

Find: DF, to four significant digits

5 The ratio of a triangle's inradius to its circumradius is $4:6\sqrt{2}$. If the triangle's area is 8 and the product of the measures of its sides is $64\sqrt{2}$, what is its semiperimeter?

6 A quadrilateral, RHOA, is inscribed in a circle, D. If RO = 12, AR = 5, RH = 2, and the radius of ⊙D is 6, what is AH?

7 In the diagram at the right, the measures of two sides and an angle bisector of a triangle are shown. Find the measure of the third side of the triangle.

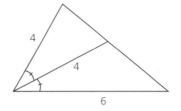

8 Find, to four significant digits, the distance from the point (− 2, 5) to the graph of x − 3y = 7.

9 Find the distance in space from the point (3, 4, 2) to the plane represented by 3x − 4y + 12z = 20.

10 Find the distance between the graphs of 3x − 4y + 10 = 0 and 6x − 8y + 15 = 0.

11 Write equations of the two lines that are parallel to the graph of x − 4y = 7 and three units from the point (5, 1).

12 Find the area of a triangle with vertices at (5, 1), (16, − 4), and (3, 12).

13 What is the area of the circle in the diagram at the right?

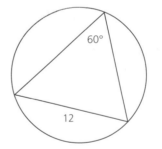

LIST OF POSTULATES AND THEOREMS

Postulates

Any segment or angle is congruent to itself. (Reflexive Property)	**112**
If there exists a correspondence between the vertices of two triangles such that three sides of one triangle are congruent to the corresponding sides of the other triangle, the two triangles are congruent. (SSS)	**116**
If there exists a correspondence between the vertices of two triangles such that two sides and the included angle of one triangle are congruent to the corresponding parts of the other triangle, the two triangles are congruent. (SAS)	**117**
If there exists a correspondence between the vertices of two triangles such that two angles and the included side of one triangle are congruent to the corresponding parts of the other triangle, the two triangles are congruent. (ASA)	**117**
Two points determine a line (or ray or segment).	**132**
If there exists a correspondence between the vertices of two right triangles such that the hypotenuse and a leg of one triangle are congruent to the corresponding parts of the other triangle, the two right triangles are congruent. (HL)	**156**
A line segment is the shortest path between two points.	**184**
Through a point not on a line there is exactly one parallel to the given line. (Parallel Postulate)	**224**
Three noncollinear points determine a plane.	**270**
If a line intersects a plane not containing it, then the intersection is exactly one point.	**271**
If two planes intersect, their intersection is exactly one line.	**271**
If there exists a correspondence between the vertices of two triangles such that the three angles of one triangle are congruent to the corresponding angles of the other triangle, then the triangles are similar. (AAA)	**339**
A tangent line is perpendicular to the radius drawn to the point of contact.	**459**
If a line is perpendicular to a radius at its outer endpoint, then it is tangent to the circle.	**459**
Circumference of a circle = $\pi \cdot$ diameter.	**499**
The area of a rectangle is equal to the product of the base and the height for that base.	**512**
Every closed region has an area.	**512**
If two closed figures are congruent, then their areas are equal.	**512**

If two closed regions intersect only along a common boundary, then the area of their union is equal to the sum of their individual areas. 512

The area of a circle is equal to the product of π and the square of the radius. 537

Total area of a sphere $= 4\pi r^2$, where r is the sphere's radius. 571

The volume of a right rectangular prism is equal to the product of its length, its width, and its height. 576

For any two real numbers x and y, exactly one of the following statements is true: $x < y$, $x = y$, or $x > y$. (Law of Trichotomy) 687

If $a > b$ and $b > c$, then $a > c$. Similarly, if $x < y$ and $y < z$, then $x < z$. (Transitive Property of Inequality) 687

If $a > b$, then $a + x > b + x$. (Addition Property of Inequality) 687

If $x < y$ and $a > 0$, then $a \cdot x < a \cdot y$. (Positive Multiplication Property of Inequality) 688

If $x < y$ and $a < 0$, then $a \cdot x > a \cdot y$. (Negative Multiplication Property of Inequality) 688

The sum of the measures of any two sides of a triangle is always greater than the measure of the third side. 691

Theorems

1   If two angles are right angles, then they are congruent. 24

2   If two angles are straight angles, then they are congruent. 24

3   If a conditional statement is true, then the contrapositive of the statement is also true. (If p, then $q \Leftrightarrow$ If $\sim q$, then $\sim p$.) 46

4   If angles are supplementary to the same angle, then they are congruent. 76

5   If angles are supplementary to congruent angles, then they are congruent. 77

6   If angles are complementary to the same angle, then they are congruent. 77

7   If angles are complementary to congruent angles, then they are congruent. 77

8   If a segment is added to two congruent segments, the sums are congruent. (Addition Property) 82

9   If an angle is added to two congruent angles, the sums are congruent. (Addition Property) 83

10   If congruent segments are added to congruent segments, the sums are congruent. (Addition Property) 83

List of Theorems, *continued*

11	If congruent angles are added to congruent angles, the sums are congruent. (Addition Property)	**83**
12	If a segment (or angle) is subtracted from congruent segments (or angles), the differences are congruent. (Subtraction Property)	**84**
13	If congruent segments (or angles) are subtracted from congruent segments (or angles), the differences are congruent. (Subtraction Property)	**84**
14	If segments (or angles) are congruent, their like multiples are congruent. (Multiplication Property)	**89**
15	If segments (or angles) are congruent, their like divisions are congruent. (Division Property)	**90**
16	If angles (or segments) are congruent to the same angle (or segment), they are congruent to each other. (Transitive Property)	**95**
17	If angles (or segments) are congruent to congruent angles (or segments), they are congruent to each other. (Transitive Property)	**95**
18	Vertical angles are congruent.	**101**
19	All radii of a circle are congruent.	**126**
20	If two sides of a triangle are congruent, the angles opposite the sides are congruent. (If △, then △.)	**148**
21	If two angles of a triangle are congruent, the sides opposite the angles are congruent. (If △, then △.)	**149**
22	If $A = (x_1, y_1)$ and $B = (x_2, y_2)$, then the midpoint $M = (x_m, y_m)$ of $\overline{AB}$ can be found by using the midpoint formula: $$M = (x_m, y_m) = \left(\frac{x_1 + x_2}{2}, \frac{y_1 + y_2}{2}\right)$$	**171**
23	If two angles are both supplementary and congruent, then they are right angles.	**180**
24	If two points are each equidistant from the endpoints of a segment, then the two points determine the perpendicular bisector of that segment.	**185**
25	If a point is on the perpendicular bisector of a segment, then it is equidistant from the endpoints of that segment.	**185**
26	If two nonvertical lines are parallel, then their slopes are equal.	**200**
27	If the slopes of two nonvertical lines are equal, then the lines are parallel.	**200**
28	If two lines are perpendicular and neither is vertical, each line's slope is the opposite reciprocal of the other's.	**200**
29	If a line's slope is the opposite reciprocal of another line's slope, the two lines are perpendicular.	**200**
30	The measure of an exterior angle of a triangle is greater than the measure of either remote interior angle.	**216**

31 If two lines are cut by a transversal such that two alternate interior angles are congruent, the lines are parallel. (Alt. int. ∠s ≅ ⇒ ∥ lines)   **217**

32 If two lines are cut by a transversal such that two alternate exterior angles are congruent, the lines are parallel. (Alt. ext. ∠s ≅ ⇒ ∥ lines)   **217**

33 If two lines are cut by a transversal such that two corresponding angles are congruent, the lines are parallel. (Corr. ∠s ≅ ⇒ ∥ lines)   **217**

34 If two lines are cut by a transversal such that two interior angles on the same side of the transversal are supplementary, the lines are parallel.   **218**

35 If two lines are cut by a transversal such that two exterior angles on the same side of the transversal are supplementary, the lines are parallel.   **218**

36 If two coplanar lines are perpendicular to a third line, they are parallel.   **218**

37 If two parallel lines are cut by a transversal, each pair of alternate interior angles are congruent. (∥ lines ⇒ alt. int. ∠s ≅)   **225**

38 If two parallel lines are cut by a transversal, then any pair of the angles formed are either congruent or supplementary.   **225**

39 If two parallel lines are cut by a transversal, each pair of alternate exterior angles are congruent. (∥ lines ⇒ alt. ext. ∠s ≅)   **226**

40 If two parallel lines are cut by a transversal, each pair of corresponding angles are congruent. (∥ lines ⇒ corr. ∠s ≅)   **226**

41 If two parallel lines are cut by a transversal, each pair of interior angles on the same side of the transversal are supplementary.   **226**

42 If two parallel lines are cut by a transversal, each pair of exterior angles on the same side of the transversal are supplementary.   **226**

43 In a plane, if a line is perpendicular to one of two parallel lines, it is perpendicular to the other.   **227**

44 If two lines are parallel to a third line, they are parallel to each other. (Transitive Property of Parallel Lines)   **227**

45 A line and a point not on the line determine a plane.   **271**

46 Two intersecting lines determine a plane.   **271**

47 Two parallel lines determine a plane.   **271**

48 If a line is perpendicular to two distinct lines that lie in a plane and that pass through its foot, then it is perpendicular to the plane.   **277**

49 If a plane intersects two parallel planes, the lines of intersection are parallel.   **283**

50 The sum of the measures of the three angles of a triangle is 180.   **295**

51 The measure of an exterior angle of a triangle is equal to the sum of the measures of the remote interior angles.   **296**

List of Theorems, *continued*

52	A segment joining the midpoints of two sides of a triangle is parallel to the third side, and its length is one-half the length of the third side. (Midline Theorem)	**296**
53	If two angles of one triangle are congruent to two angles of a second triangle, then the third angles are congruent. (No-Choice Theorem)	**302**
54	If there exists a correspondence between the vertices of two triangles such that two angles and a nonincluded side of one are congruent to the corresponding parts of the other, then the triangles are congruent. (AAS)	**302**
55	The sum S_i of the measures of the angles of a polygon with n sides is given by the formula $S_i = (n - 2)180$.	**308**
56	If one exterior angle is taken at each vertex, the sum S_e of the measures of the exterior angles of a polygon is given by the formula $S_e = 360$.	**308**
57	The number d of diagonals that can be drawn in a polygon of n sides is given by the formula $d = \frac{n(n-3)}{2}$.	**308**
58	The measure E of each exterior angle of an equiangular polygon of n sides is given by the formula $E = \frac{360}{n}$.	**315**
59	In a proportion, the product of the means is equal to the product of the extremes. (Means-Extremes Products Theorem)	**327**
60	If the product of a pair of nonzero numbers is equal to the product of another pair of nonzero numbers, then either pair of numbers may be made the extremes, and the other pair the means, of a proportion. (Means-Extremes Ratio Theorem)	**327**
61	The ratio of the perimeters of two similar polygons equals the ratio of any pair of corresponding sides.	**334**
62	If there exists a correspondence between the vertices of two triangles such that two angles of one triangle are congruent to the corresponding angles of the other, then the triangles are similar. (AA)	**339**
63	If there exists a correspondence between the vertices of two triangles such that the ratios of the measures of corresponding sides are equal, then the triangles are similar. (SSS~)	**340**
64	If there exists a correspondence between the vertices of two triangles such that the ratios of the measures of two pairs of corresponding sides are equal and the included angles are congruent, then the triangles are similar. (SAS~)	**340**
65	If a line is parallel to one side of a triangle and intersects the other two sides, it divides those two sides proportionally. (Side-Splitter Theorem)	**351**
66	If three or more parallel lines are intersected by two transversals, the parallel lines divide the transversals proportionally.	**351**
67	If a ray bisects an angle of a triangle, it divides the opposite side into segments that are proportional to the adjacent sides. (Angle Bisector Theorem)	**352**

68 If an altitude is drawn to the hypotenuse of a right triangle, then   **378**
   a. The two triangles formed are similar to the given right triangle and to each other
   b. The altitude to the hypotenuse is the mean proportional between the segments of the hypotenuse
   c. Either leg of the given right triangle is the mean proportional between the hypotenuse of the given right triangle and the segment of the hypotenuse adjacent to that leg (i.e., the projection of that leg on the hypotenuse)

69 The square of the measure of the hypotenuse of a right triangle is equal to the sum of the squares of the measures of the legs. (Pythagorean Theorem)   **384**

70 If the square of the measure of one side of a triangle equals the sum of the squares of the measures of the other two sides, then the angle opposite the longest side is a right angle.   **385**

71 If $P = (x_1, y_1)$ and $Q = (x_2, y_2)$ are any two points, then the distance between them can be found with the formula   **393**

$$PQ = \sqrt{(x_2 - x_1)^2 + (y_2 - y_1)^2} \text{ or } PQ = \sqrt{(\Delta x)^2 + (\Delta y)^2}$$

72 In a triangle whose angles have the measures 30, 60, and 90, the lengths of the sides opposite these angles can be represented by x, $x\sqrt{3}$, and $2x$ respectively. (30°–60°–90°–Triangle Theorem)   **405**

73 In a triangle whose angles have the measures 45, 45, and 90, the lengths of the sides opposite these angles can be represented by x, x, and $x\sqrt{2}$ respectively. (45°–45°–90°–Triangle Theorem)   **406**

74 If a radius is perpendicular to a chord, then it bisects the chord.   **441**

75 If a radius of a circle bisects a chord that is not a diameter, then it is perpendicular to that chord.   **441**

76 The perpendicular bisector of a chord passes through the center of the circle.   **441**

77 If two chords of a circle are equidistant from the center, then they are congruent.   **446**

78 If two chords of a circle are congruent, then they are equidistant from the center of the circle.   **446**

79 If two central angles of a circle (or of congruent circles) are congruent, then their intercepted arcs are congruent.   **453**

80 If two arcs of a circle (or of congruent circles) are congruent, then the corresponding central angles are congruent.   **453**

81 If two central angles of a circle (or of congruent circles) are congruent, then the corresponding chords are congruent.   **453**

82 If two chords of a circle (or of congruent circles) are congruent, then the corresponding central angles are congruent.   **453**

83 If two arcs of a circle (or of congruent circles) are congruent, then the corresponding chords are congruent.   **453**

List of Theorems, *continued*

102	The area of a trapezoid equals one-half the product of the height and the sum of the bases.	523
103	The measure of the median of a trapezoid equals the average of the measures of the bases.	524
104	The area of a trapezoid is the product of the median and the height.	524
105	The area of a kite equals half the product of its diagonals.	528
106	The area of an equilateral triangle equals the product of one-fourth the square of a side and the square root of 3.	531
107	The area of a regular polygon equals one-half the product of the apothem and the perimeter.	532
108	The area of a sector of a circle is equal to the area of the circle times the fractional part of the circle determined by the sector's arc.	537
109	If two figures are similar, then the ratio of their areas equals the square of the ratio of corresponding segments. (Similar-Figures Theorem)	544
110	A median of a triangle divides the triangle into two triangles with equal areas.	546
111	Area of a triangle $= \sqrt{s(s-a)(s-b)(s-c)}$, where a, b, and c are the lengths of the sides of the triangle and $s =$ semiperimeter $= \frac{a+b+c}{2}$. (Hero's formula)	550
112	Area of a cyclic quadrilateral $= \sqrt{(s-a)(s-b)(s-c)(s-d)}$, where a, b, c, and d are the sides of the quadrilateral and $s =$ semiperimeter $= \frac{a+b+c+d}{2}$. (Brahmagupta's formula)	550
113	The lateral area of a cylinder is equal to the product of the height and the circumference of the base.	571
114	The lateral area of a cone is equal to one-half the product of the slant height and the circumference of the base.	571
115	The volume of a right rectangular prism is equal to the product of the height and the area of the base.	576
116	The volume of any prism is equal to the product of the height and the area of the base.	576
117	The volume of a cylinder is equal to the product of the height and the area of the base.	577
118	The volume of a prism or a cylinder is equal to the product of the figure's cross-sectional area and its height.	577
119	The volume of a pyramid is equal to one third of the product of the height and the area of the base.	583
120	The volume of a cone is equal to one third of the product of the height and the area of the base.	584

List of Theorems, *continued*

121	In a pyramid or a cone, the ratio of the area of a cross section to the area of the base equals the square of the ratio of the figures' respective distances from the vertex.	**584**
122	The volume of a sphere is equal to four thirds of the product of π and the cube of the radius.	**589**
123	The y-form, or slope-intercept form, of the equation of a nonvertical line is $y = mx + b$, where b is the y-intercept of the line and m is the slope of the line.	**610**
124	The formula for an equation of a horizontal line is $y = b$, where b is the y-coordinate of every point on the line.	**611**
125	The formula for the equation of a vertical line is $x = a$, where a is the x-coordinate of every point on the line.	**612**
126	If $P = (x_1, y_1, z_1)$ and $Q = (x_2, y_2, z_2)$ are any two points, then the distance between them can be found with the formula $$PQ = \sqrt{(x_2 - x_1)^2 + (y_2 - y_1)^2 + (z_2 - z_1)^2}$$	**626**
127	The equation of a circle whose center is (h, k) and whose radius is r is $(x - h)^2 + (y - k)^2 = r^2$.	**633**
128	The perpendicular bisectors of the sides of a triangle are concurrent at a point that is equidistant from the vertices of the triangle. (The point of concurrency of the perpendicular bisectors is called the circumcenter of the triangle.)	**660**
129	The bisectors of the angles of a triangle are concurrent at a point that is equidistant from the sides of the triangle. (The point of concurrency of the angle bisectors is called the incenter of the triangle.)	**661**
130	The lines containing the altitudes of a triangle are concurrent. (The point of concurrency of the lines containing the altitudes is called the orthocenter of the triangle.)	**661**
131	The medians of a triangle are concurrent at a point that is two thirds of the way from any vertex of the triangle to the midpoint of the opposite side. (The point of concurrency of the medians of a triangle is called the centroid of the triangle.)	**662**
132	If two sides of a triangle are not congruent, then the angles opposite them are not congruent, and the larger angle is opposite the longer side. (If ⚠, then ⚠.)	**692**
133	If two angles of a triangle are not congruent, then the sides opposite them are not congruent, and the longer side is opposite the larger angle. (If ⚠, then ⚠.)	**692**
134	If two sides of one triangle are congruent to two sides of another triangle and the included angle in the first triangle is greater than the included angle in the second triangle, then the remaining side of the first triangle is greater than the remaining side of the second triangle. (SAS $\neq$)	**697**
135	If two sides of one triangle are congruent to two sides of another triangle and the third side of the first triangle is greater than the third side of the second triangle, then the angle opposite the third side in the first triangle is greater than the angle opposite the third side in the second triangle. (SSS $\neq$)	**697**

136 The distance d from any point $P = (x_1, y_1)$ to a line whose equation is in the form $ax + by + c = 0$ can be found with the formula   **713**

$$d = \frac{|ax_1 + by_1 + c|}{\sqrt{a^2 + b^2}}$$

137 The area A of a triangle with vertices at (x_1, y_1), (x_2, y_2), and (x_3, y_3) can be found with the formula   **717**

$$A = \frac{1}{2}|x_1y_2 + x_2y_3 + x_3y_1 - x_1y_3 - x_2y_1 - x_3y_2|$$

138 In any triangle ABC, with side lengths a, b, and c,   **718**

$$\frac{a}{\sin \angle A} = D \qquad \frac{b}{\sin \angle B} = D \qquad \frac{c}{\sin \angle D} = D$$

where D is the diameter of the triangle's circumcircle.

139 In any triangle ABC, with side lengths a, b, and c,   **721**

$$a^2n + b^2m = cd^2 + cmn$$

where d is the length of a segment from vertex C to the opposite side, dividing that side into segments with lengths m and n. (Stewart's Theorem)

140 If a quadrilateral is inscribable in a circle, the product of the measures of its diagonals is equal to the sum of the products of the measures of the pairs of opposite sides. (Ptolemy's Theorem)   **724**

141 The inradius r of a triangle can be found with the formula $r = \frac{A}{s}$, where A is the triangle's area and s is the triangle's semiperimeter.   **731**

142 The circumradius R of a triangle can be found with the formula $R = \frac{abc}{4A}$, where a, b, and c are the lengths of the sides of the triangle and A is the triangle's area.   **732**

143 If ABC is a triangle with D on $\overline{BC}$, E on $\overline{AC}$, and F on $\overline{AB}$, then the three segments $\overline{AD}$, $\overline{BE}$, and $\overline{CF}$ are concurrent if, and only if,   **734**

$$\left(\frac{BD}{DC}\right)\left(\frac{CE}{EA}\right)\left(\frac{AF}{FB}\right) = 1$$

144 If ABC is a triangle and F is on $\overline{AB}$, E is on $\overline{AC}$, and D is on an extension of $\overline{BC}$, then the three points D, E, and F are collinear if, and only if,   **736**

$$\left(\frac{BD}{DC}\right)\left(\frac{CE}{EA}\right)\left(\frac{AF}{FB}\right) = -1$$

SELECTED ANSWERS to ODD-NUMBERED PROBLEMS

1.1 Getting Started

1 $\overleftrightarrow{AB}$, $\overleftrightarrow{BA}$, line ℓ **3** No **5 a** B **b** $\overleftrightarrow{AC}$ or $\angle CEA$ **c** E **d** {} **e** $\overrightarrow{EC}$ **f** $\angle ABC$ **g** $\triangle BEC$ **9** J **11 a** $37\frac{1}{2}$ **b** 28

1.2 Measurement of Segments and Angles

1 a 61°40′ **b** 71°42′ **3** $\angle 1$ and $\angle 2$ **5 a** 87°10″ **b** 82°49′ **7 a** $\angle 5$ **b** Same size **c** $\angle 4$ **9 a** 90 **b** 45 **c** 100 **d** $142\frac{1}{2}$ **11** 51°53′50″ **13** 22 **15** $y = x + 17$ **17 a** $0 < m\angle P < 90$ **b** $20 < x < 50$ **19** No **21** −10; 40 **23** $72\frac{3}{8}°$

1.3 Collinearity, Betweenness, and Assumptions

1 134 **3 a** B and D **b** No; yes **c** $\overline{AB}$ and $\overline{BC}$ **d** Yes **e** Not necessarily **f** B **g** G **h** $\overline{AF}$ **i** $\overrightarrow{EB}$, $\overrightarrow{ED}$ **j** E and B **5** 7 **7 a** e.g., 33° and 40° **b** e.g., 60° and 70° **c** e.g., 45° and 45° **9** 135 **13 a** 15 **b** 3 **15** 80; 100; 80 **17** 1:05:27

1.4 Beginning Proofs

9 110° **13 b** Yes **c** It is the midpt. of $\overline{AA'}$.

1.5 Division of Segments and Angles

1 a $\overline{CO} \cong \overline{DO}$ **b** $\overline{WX} \cong \overline{WV}$ **3 a** $\overrightarrow{JG}$ **b** $\overrightarrow{OK}$ **5 a** 2;9 **b** 14 **7** 43 **9** Yes **19** 16 **21 a** 2 **b** No **23** 60

1.6 Paragraph Proofs

5 Cannot be proved

1.7 Deductive Structure

1 Undefined terms; assumptions (postulates); definitions; theorems and other conclusions **3 a** Yes **b** No
5 a i If B, then A.
  ii Wet $\Rightarrow$ ran
  iii If an angle is acute, then it is a 45° angle.
  iv If a point divides a segment into two congruent segments, it is the midpoint of the segment.
b i and ii are not necessarily true; iii is not true; iv, a definition, is true. **7** Not true if it is a "fair" coin. Probabilities don't "grow." **9** Not correct, since we do not know about $\angle C$. **11** Not correct, since we were reasoning from the reverse statement.

1.8 Statements of Logic

1 If a person is 18 years old, then (s)he may vote in federal elections. **b** If two angles are opposite angles of a parallelogram, then the two angles are congruent. **3 a 5 a** $d \Rightarrow f$ **b** $s \Rightarrow \sim p$ **c** If bobcats begin to browse, then horses head for home. **7** Original Statement: If a polygon is a square, then it is a quadrilateral with four congruent sides.
Converse: If a quadrilateral has four congruent sides, then it is a square.
Inverse: If a polygon is not a square, then it is not a quadrilateral with four congruent sides.
Contrapositive: If a quadrilateral does not have four congruent sides, then it is not a square. **9** $p \Rightarrow \sim g$

1.9 Probability

1 $\frac{3}{5}$ **3** $\frac{1}{5}$ **5** $\frac{1}{3}$ **7** $\frac{2}{5}$ **9** $\frac{9}{25}$ **11** $\frac{5}{12}$ **13** 18 **15 a** $\frac{1}{5}$ **b** $\frac{4}{5}$

Review Problems

1 a $\overleftrightarrow{AR}$, $\overleftrightarrow{AD}$, $\overleftrightarrow{RA}$, $\overleftrightarrow{RD}$, $\overleftrightarrow{DA}$, $\overleftrightarrow{DR}$ **b** $\overrightarrow{BA}$, $\overrightarrow{BC}$ **c** $\overrightarrow{DF}$ **d** $\overrightarrow{CB}$ **e** 60°; 52°; 120° **f** No **g** No angle can be called $\angle B$, since 3 angles have B as a vertex. **h** $\overleftrightarrow{AC}$ **i** $\overline{EF}$ **j** $\angle 1$ **k** A **l** $\overline{FE}$ **3 a** 69°4′35″ **b** 50°59′43″ **5 a** $\overline{BC} \cong \overline{RT}$ **b** $\angle A \cong \angle S$ **7** 20 **9** No **17 a** -3 **b** -13 **19 a** $\frac{2}{5}$ **b** $\frac{1}{10}$ **21 a** 30° **b** 140° **c** $127\frac{1}{2}°$ **23** 14 **25** 15 **29** 48°50′44″ **31 a** $\approx 44.5°$ **b** $\approx 44°33′$ **33** $7 < PR < 31$ **35 a** $90 < m\angle Q < 180$ **b** $59 < x < 104$ **37 a** $6 < w < 10$ **41** $\approx 3:32:44$ **43** $\approx 2:38:11$

2.1 Perpendicularity

1 a $\angle$s A, B, C, D **b** $\angle$s EHF, GHF, EFG **3 a** 21°42′26″ **b** 45 **5** (4, 0) **11** 15; 30; 45 **15 a** $\frac{9}{10}$ **b** $\frac{9}{10}$ **c** $\frac{4}{5}$

2.2 Complementary and Supplementary Angles

1 $\angle A$ and $\angle C$ **3** $(90 - y)°$ **5** 30 and 60 **11** 125 **13 a** Each angle is a right angle. (If $2x = 180$, then $x = 90$.) **b** Each angle is a 45° angle. (If $2x = 90$, then $x = 40$.) **15** ≈ 94.84 **19** 27 **21** 30 **23** 12 **25** 70

2.4 Congruent Supplements and Complements

1 a 49 **b** 131 **c** 49 **d** 41 **e** 139 **f** 41 **g** 139
5 35 and 55 **15** 37 or 61 **17** 165° **19** 98 **21** 3:2

2.5 Addition and Subtraction Properties

1 a $\overline{AD} \cong \overline{AC}$ **b** $\angle JFG \cong \angle JHG$ **9** 12; 21 **15** Bisector
of $\angle ABC$ **17 a** Yes **b** $\angle ABC = 180°$; $\overrightarrow{BF} \perp \overleftrightarrow{AC}$
19 $152\frac{1}{2}$

2.6 Multiplication and Division Properties

7 a $x = 6$ **b** $y = 8$ **9** (7, 2) **15** $x = -5$; $4 < y < 6$ or
$-4 < y < -2$

2.7 Transitive and Substitution Properties

9 70 **13 a** $180 - x - y$ **b** $180 - y$ **c** $180 - x$
17 Can be proved false **19** $\frac{1}{3}$

2.8 Vertical Angles

1 a $\overrightarrow{FE}$, $\overrightarrow{FC}$; $\overrightarrow{FD}$, $\overrightarrow{FA}$; $\overrightarrow{BA}$, $\overrightarrow{BC}$ **b** $\angle EFA$ and $\angle CFD$;
$\angle EFD$ and $\angle CFA$ **3** 43 **7** No **13** They are right $\angle$s.
15 $132\frac{3}{4}$ or 140

Review Problems

7 6 cm **13** $22\frac{1}{2}$ **15** 4 **17** (2, −5), (6, −11) **19 a** 1
b $\frac{1}{2}$ **21** 43°43′ **29** 50 **31** 110 **33 a** $x - 2y = y$ or
$x = 3y$ **b** $y = 124 - x$ **c** 31 **35 a** 28 **b** Same
37 $14

3.1 What Are Congruent Figures?

1 $\triangle TCR$; Reflexive Property **3** $\triangle YTW$; Vert. $\angle$s are $\cong$

3.2 Three Ways to Prove Triangles Congruent

1 a $\overline{GH} \cong \overline{KO}$, $\angle J \cong \angle M$ **b** $\overline{PS} \cong \overline{TR}$, $\angle PVS \cong \angle TVR$
c $\overline{BZ} \cong \overline{AX}$, $\angle BWZ \cong \angle AYX$ **21** $\angle 1 \cong \angle 2$

3.3 CPCTC and Circles

7 $A \approx 490.0$ sq cm; $C \approx 78.5$ cm **19 a** (18, 0) **b** 100π,
or ≈ 314

3.4 Beyond CPCTC

1 a Median **b** Altitude **c** Altitude **d** Both **13** At
any point (x, y) where $y = 11$ or $y = 1$

3.6 Types of Triangles

1 Scalene **3 a** Right **b** Obtuse **c** Right **d** Acute
e Right **f** Acute **11** $\overline{VY}$ **13** 4

3.7 Angle-Side Theorems

7 $\angle B$, $\angle A$, $\angle C$ **11** No **25** 22; 8; 60°

3.8 The HL Postulate

15 a (4, 0) **b** CPCTC **c** (10, 0) **d** 54

Review Problems

1 a S **b** A **c** N **d** N **e** N **7 a** 28; 60 **b** 114 **9** 8
15 $x = -5$ or $x = 11$ **17** 60

Cumulative Review Problems, Chapters 1–3

1 a C **b** $\overline{GJ}$ **c** $\angle FAB$ **d** D **e** ϕ **3** 46°42′09″ **5** 94
15 72; 60; 48 **17** −14; 28 **19** 35 m

4.1 Detours and Midpoints

5 (7, 2) **7** 6

4.3 A Right-Angle Theorem

5 (−1, 8) **7** ≈ 12.6 **15** 45°; 60°

4.4 The Equidistance Theorems

7 4 **9** (15, 3) **19 a** 6 units **b** (8, −2)

4.5 Introduction to Parallel Lines

1 a $\angle 3$ and $\angle 7$, $\angle 4$ and $\angle 8$ **b** $\angle 1$ and $\angle 5$, $\angle 2$ and $\angle 6$
c $\angle 1$ and $\angle 7$, $\angle 2$ and $\angle 4$, $\angle 3$ and $\angle 5$, $\angle 8$ and $\angle 6$
d $\angle 7$ and $\angle 8$, $\angle 3$ and $\angle 4$ **e** $\angle 1$ and $\angle 6$, $\angle 2$ and $\angle 5$
3 a (4, 8) **b** (9, 10) **c** Parallel **d** Congruent
e $\angle ANM$ and $\angle ACB$ **5 a** $\frac{5}{4}$ **b** $\frac{5}{4}$ **c** Parallel

4.6 Slope

1 a $\frac{8}{9}$ **b** $\frac{1}{7}$ **c** $\frac{11}{6}$ **d** 0 **e** No slope **f** $\frac{5c}{a}$ **3** −4
5 a $\frac{1}{4}$ **b** −4 **c** $-\frac{7}{2}$ **d** $\frac{1}{4}$ **9 a** $\frac{1}{2}$ **b** $\frac{1}{2}$ **c** Collinear
11 a $\angle ECD$ **b** $\angle CEB$ **13** $\overline{AC}$ **15** (7, 7)

Review Problems

9 a (9, 4) **b** $\frac{1}{2}$ **c** No; different slopes **d** −2
e 7 units **19** $m\angle Q = 90$

5.1 Indirect Proof

7 a (2a, 2b) **b** Yes **9 a** Corr. **b** Alt. int.

5.2 Proving That Lines Are Parallel

1 a Corr. $\angle$s $\cong \Rightarrow \parallel$ lines **b** Alt. int. $\angle$s $\cong \Rightarrow \parallel$ lines
c Alt. ext. $\angle$s $\cong \Rightarrow \parallel$ lines **3** (1, 5), (1, 7), (2, 6), (2, 8),
(3, 7), (3, 5), (4, 8), (4, 6) **5** $\overleftrightarrow{BC} \parallel \overleftrightarrow{DE}$; corr. $\angle$s $\cong \Rightarrow$
$\parallel$ lines **7** ≈ 0.4 **9** $\overleftrightarrow{BE} \parallel \overleftrightarrow{DF}$; alt. ext. $\angle$s $\cong \Rightarrow \parallel$ lines
11 $0 < x < 110$ **15** No, because the slopes are not
equal. **17** $16 < x < 66$ **23** No, because if $x = 25$,
then $\angle QBD$ supp. $\angle RCD$ and $\overleftrightarrow{PQ} \parallel \overleftrightarrow{RS}$, a contradiction

5.3 Congruent Angles Associated with Parallel Lines

5 41 **7** No **11** $\angle 2 \cong \angle 5$ **13** $x = 19.72$; $m\angle 1 = 42.2008$ **17** Yes; 60 **23** All but (4, 11)

5.4 Four-Sided Polygons

1 a–d **3** f **7 a** $\overline{ST}$ and $\overline{RV}$ **b** $\overline{SV}$ and $\overline{RT}$ **c** $\overline{RS}$ and $\overline{VT}$ **d** $\angle SRV$ and $\angle TVR$ **e** $\angle RST$ and $\angle VTS$ **f** $\angle STR \cong \angle VRT$, $\angle TSV \cong \angle RVS$ **9** A polygon consists entirely of segments. **11 a** 360 **b** 540 **19** 112 sq units **21 a** 0 **b** 2 **c** 5 **d** 9 **e** $n - 3$ **f** n **g** $\frac{n(n-3)}{2}$

5.5 Properties of Quadrilaterals

5 44 **7** 8; 5; 5 **11** 240 **13 a** m **b** p **c** q and r **19** 28 **21** $\overline{KI} \cong \overline{KE}$, $\overline{IT} \cong \overline{ET}$ **23 a** (19, 15) **b** Slope $\overleftrightarrow{HM} = -\frac{3}{2}$; slope $\overleftrightarrow{RO} = \frac{2}{3}$ **25** 1 **27** ≈ 22.7 **29 a** $a = 180 - y + x$ **b** $y - x < 90$

5.6 Proving That a Quadrilateral Is a Parallelogram

7 a Yes **b** Yes **c** Yes **9 a** 9 **b** 17 **c** 56 **11 a** S **b** S **c** A **d** A **17** 145 **21 a** $\frac{2}{7}$ **b** No. You will win $\frac{24}{49}$ of the time and lose $\frac{25}{49}$ of the time.

5.7 Proving That Figures Are Special Quadrilaterals

1 Rectangle **3** 21 **5 a** $18x^2 - 45x$ **b** $22x - 10$ **c** $A = 128.5$; $P = 82.4$ **13 a** Parallelogram **b** Trapezoid **c** Isosceles trapezoid **d** Rectangle **e** Rectangle **f** Rhombus **g** Kite **h** Quadrilateral **17 a** rhombus **b** kite **c** Square **19** $A = x^2 + 6x$; $P = 52$ m **21** ≈ 29.61 **23** $-\frac{1}{4}$; 4 **25** $\frac{1}{2}$ **29 a** $324 - x^2$ **b** $0 < \text{area} < 144$

Review Problems

1 a Parallelogram **b** Kite **c** Trapezoid **d** Square **e** Square **3** $0 < x < 25$ **7 a** Yes **b** No **c** Yes **13** $\frac{1}{3}$ **17** ≈ 78.540 sq units **19 a** S **b** A **c** S **d** S **25** 70 **27** $\frac{3}{5}$

6.1 Relating Lines to Planes

1 No; no **3** No; yes **11** Yes; no **13** Not necessarily **15** 7; ABC, ABP, BCP, CDP, DAP, ACP, BDP

6.2 Perpendicularity of a Line and a Plane

1 12

6.3 Basic Facts About Parallel Planes

1 a F **b** T **c** F **d** T **e** T **5** $\frac{1}{2}$; -2; right; the slopes are opposite reciprocals, so $\overline{EF} \perp \overline{FG}$.

Review Problems

1 a F **b** T **c** F **d** F **e** F **f** F **g** F **h** T **i** F **j** F **k** F **5** Not necessarily **7 a** No **b** No **c** Yes **9** a

Cumulative Review Problems, Chapters 1–6

1 a Rhombus **b** Parallelogram **c** Right triangle **d** Square **3** 131 **11 a** 140 **b** 58 **15** 110

7.1 Triangle Application Theorems

1 70 **3** 40; 140 **5** 48; 60; 72 **7** 9 **9 a** A **b** A **c** N **d** A **e** N **11** 40; 50 **15** 110 **17 a** 40 **b** Rhombus **21** $25\frac{5}{7}$

7.2 Two Proof-Oriented Triangle Theorems

9 50 **17 a** Rectangle **b** Rectangle **c** Square **d** Rhombus **e** Parallelogram **f** Parallelogram **g** Rhombus

7.3 Formulas Involving Polygons

1 a 360 **b** 900 **c** 1080 **d** 1800 **e** 16,380 **3 a** 5 **b** 9 **c** 2 **d** 0 **5 a** 70 **b** 45 **c** 65 **7** 3 **11 a** Quadrilateral **b** Hexagon **13 a** Heptagon **b** Decagon **c** 22-gon **15** $18 < x < 36$ **17** 48 **19** $\frac{3}{4}$ **23** 40; 50; 130

7.4 Regular Polygons

1 a 120 **b** 90 **c** 45 **d** 24 **e** $15\frac{15}{23}$ **3 a** 6 **b** 9 **c** 10 **d** 180 **e** 48 **7** Equiangular decagon **11** Pentagon **13 a** A **b** S **c** A **d** S **e** S **f** N **17** $x = 30$; $y = 12$

Review Problems

7 45 **9** 50 **11** 20 **13 a** 5580 **b** 360 **15** 90 **19 a** 32.5 **b** 122.5 **c** 25 **21 a** A **b** S **c** S **d** N **23** No **29** 32

8.1 Ratio and Proportion

1 a 9 **b** 4 and 9; 3 and 12 **3 a** 4 **b** $\frac{54}{7}$ **c** $\frac{47}{3}$ **5 a** $-\frac{1}{2}$ **b** $-\frac{1}{2}$ **c** Yes **7** $\frac{5}{36}$ **9** Rectangle **11 a** ± 10 **b** $\pm\sqrt{15}$ **c** $\pm\sqrt{ab}$ **13** 8; 12; 20; 28 **15** $\frac{8}{3}$ **17** 150 **19** $\frac{c + d}{a + b}$ **21** $\frac{x - 3}{x + 4}$ **25** 75 **27** $\frac{1}{3}$

8.2 Similarity

1 b, c, and d **3** 90; 30; 7.5 **5** 6; 9 **7** $\frac{5}{3}$ **9** 5.6; 7.5 **11** 205 **13** $\frac{11}{34}$ **15** 11 ft by 14 ft **17** 180 cm by 240 cm **19** $10\sqrt{3}$; $7.5\sqrt{3}$

8.3 Methods of Proving Triangles Similar

7 Cannot be proved. **19 a** Yes, by SAS~ **b** Yes, by corr. $\angle s \cong \Rightarrow \parallel$ lines

8.4 Congruences and Proportions in Similar Triangles

7 4; 14 **9** 25 m **17** $6\frac{6}{7}$ **19** 12 **21 a** SAS~ **b** $\angle$BDC **c** 18 **23** 6

8.5 Three Theorems Involving Proportions

1 a 8 **b** $\frac{35}{3}$ **3** 3; 9 **5** 1 **7** 9 **9** $\frac{5}{2}$; 10 **11** 51 **13** $\frac{27}{11}$; $\frac{72}{11}$ **19 a** 24 cm **b** 4x + 8 **21** 10.5; 17.5 **27** $8\frac{3}{4}$ m

Review Problems

1 b and c; a and d **3** ±10 **5** $\frac{4}{9}$ **7** $\frac{15}{2}$ **9** $\frac{2br}{3a}$ **11** 4; 15 **13** $\frac{20}{3}$ **15** $\approx$879 ft **19** $(-13, 0)$ **25** 30 **27** $\frac{104}{5}$ **29** 8; 9; 12 **31** 225 **35** 32

9.1 Review of Radicals and Quadratic Equations

1 a 2 **b** $3\sqrt{3}$ **c** $6\sqrt{2}$ **d** $4\sqrt{2}$ **e** $7\sqrt{2}$ **f** $10\sqrt{2}$ **g** $2\sqrt{5}$ **h** $2\sqrt{6}$ **3 a** $\frac{\sqrt{2}}{2}$ **b** $\frac{\sqrt{5}}{5}$ **c** $2\sqrt{2}$ **d** $2\sqrt{3}$ **5 a** ±5 **b** ±12 **c** ±13 **d** $\pm\frac{1}{2}$ **e** $\pm2\sqrt{3}$ **f** $\pm3\sqrt{2}$ **7 a** $\{6, -1\}$ **b** $\{2, -6\}$ **c** $\{5, 3\}$ **d** $\{6, -3\}$ **e** $\{12, -3\}$ **f** $\{9, -4\}$ **9 a** 20 **b** $2\sqrt{3}$ **c** ≈8.2 **11** $\{\frac{5}{2}, 5\}$ **13 a** $-h$ **b** $3 - x$ **c** pq **d** $-xy\sqrt{x}$

9.2 Introduction to Circles

1 $C = 19.6\pi$, or ≈61.58; $A = 96.04\pi$, or ≈301.72 **3 a** 180 **b** ≈12.6 **5** 12.5π, or ≈39.27 **7 a** 40 **b** 40 **9** (3, 3) **11 a** $(-3, 14)$ **b** -1 **13** (7, 1); $(-3, 7)$ **15** $2\frac{2}{5}$

9.3 Altitude-on-Hypotenuse Theorems

1 a $\sqrt{21}$ **b** $\sqrt{77}$ **c** 4 **3 a** 6 **b** 8 **c** $4\sqrt{3}$ **d** 4 **e** 9 **f** Impossible **5 a** 9 **b** 54 **c** $15 + 6\sqrt{3}$ **9** 25; 25; 25 **11** 25π, or ≈78.54 **13** 60; 30 **17 a** $2\sqrt{7}$ **b** $16\frac{2}{3}$ **c** $4\sqrt{6}$ **d** $7\frac{11}{12}$ **19** 1.8 **21** $2\sqrt{5}$

9.4 Geometry's Most Elegant Theorem

1 a $\sqrt{41}$ **b** 8 **c** 12 **d** 5 **e** 10 **f** 2 **g** $3\sqrt{2}$ **3** 40 km **5** 9 **7** 10 **9 a** (2, 3) **b** 8; 6 **c** 10 **d** Yes **11 a** $\sqrt{x^2 + y^2}$ **b** $\sqrt{4 + x^2}$ **c** $5a$ **d** $12c$ **13** 10 km **15** 60 **17** $\sqrt{5}$ **19** ≈5.56 m **21** $6\sqrt{5}$ **23 a** 1500 sq m **b** ≈36 m **25 a** 8 **b** No **27** 7 ft **29** 50 **31 a** Parallelogram **b** 54 **33** $12\sqrt{2}$ **35** $\frac{5}{12}$

9.5 The Distance Formula

1 a 2 **b** 4 **c** 5 **d** 10 **e** $\sqrt{29}$ **f** $2\sqrt{5}$ **5** 225π **7** $\frac{9}{2}$; 10 **11 a** 13π **b** ≈132.7 **13 a** ≈42.4 **b** ≈0.8 **15** ≈24.9; kite **21** 40 **27** $(4 + 2\sqrt{3}, 3 - 2\sqrt{3})$ or $(4 - 2\sqrt{3}, 3 + 2\sqrt{3})$

9.6 Families of Right Triangles

1 a 25 **b** 36 **c** 21 **d** $\frac{5}{3}$ **e** 60 **3 a** 250 **b** 48 **c** 28 **d** 2.4 **e** 264 **5 a** 12 **b** $2\sqrt{7}$ **c** 10 **d** 0.5 **e** 34 **f** $5\sqrt{7}$ **g** 72 **h** 45 **i** $12\sqrt{7}$ **7** 50 dm **9 a** 24 **b** $300\sqrt{5}$ **11** 40; 60 **13** ≈28 km **15 a** 144 **b** $\frac{3}{8}$ **c** $\sqrt{7}$ **17 a** Isosceles trapezoid **b** 48 **c** $4\sqrt{10}$ **21** 140 cm **23 a** $\frac{2}{5}$ **b** $\frac{4}{15}$ **25** (22, 99, 101); (20, 48, 52); (20, 21, 29); (15, 20, 25); (12, 16, 20)

9.7 Special Right Triangles

1 a 7; $7\sqrt{3}$ **b** 20; $10\sqrt{3}$ **c** 10; 5 **d** 346; $173\sqrt{3}$ **e** 114; $114\sqrt{3}$ **3 a** $2\sqrt{3}$ **b** $14\sqrt{3}$ **c** $13\sqrt{3}$ **5** $11\sqrt{2}$ **7** $3\sqrt{3}$ mm **9 a** $5\sqrt{2}$ **b** 13 **13 a** (1, 1) **b** 1 **c** 1 **15** 38 **17 a** $3\sqrt{3}$ **b** 9 **c** $6\sqrt{3}$ **d** 1:2 **19** ≈57.9 **21 a** 48 **b** $6 + 6\sqrt{2}$ **23** $(0, 2\sqrt{5})$ **25 a** $2 + 2\sqrt{3}$ **b** $2\sqrt{6}$ **27** $\frac{40(12 - 5\sqrt{3})}{23}$

9.8 The Pythagorean Theorem and Space Figures

1 a 5 **b** 13 **3** $5\sqrt{3}$; 10 **5 a** 14 **b** 7 **c** 25 **d** 56 **e** $14\sqrt{2}$ **7** $\overleftrightarrow{PB}$ and $\overleftrightarrow{PD}$ **9** 30 **11 a** $(-3, 0)$ **b** ≈7.1 **c** ≈4.7 **13 a** $5\sqrt{13}$ **b** $9\sqrt{11}$ **15** $2\sqrt{3}$ **17** 4 **19** $d = \sqrt{a^2 + b^2 + c^2}$ **21** Impossible

9.9 Introduction to Trigonometry

1 a $\frac{8}{17}$ **b** $\frac{15}{17}$ **c** $\frac{8}{15}$ **d** $\frac{15}{17}$ **e** $\frac{8}{17}$ **f** $\frac{15}{8}$ **3 a** $\frac{\sqrt{2}}{2}$ **b** $\frac{\sqrt{2}}{2}$ **c** 1 **5** $\frac{4}{5}$ **7 a** $2\sqrt{6}$ **b** $\frac{2\sqrt{6}}{7}$ **c** $\frac{5\sqrt{6}}{12}$ **9 a** $\frac{7}{25}$ **b** $\frac{8}{17}$ **c** $\frac{4}{5}$ **11 a** 45 **b** 30 **13 a** $\frac{2}{3}$ **b** $\frac{3\sqrt{13}}{13}$ **15** $\frac{4}{5}$ **21** $\frac{1}{6}$

9.10 Trigonometric Ratios

1 a ≈0.3584 **b** ≈1.2799 **c** ≈0.9962 **d** 1.0000 **e** ≈0.8660 **3 a** 45 **b** 30 **c** 60 **5** ≈15 **7** $\approx24°$ **9** $\approx37°$, $\approx53°$, 90° **11 a** $\approx67°$ **b** $5\sqrt{11}$ **13** 10 **15** ≈104 dm **17 a** ≈36.4 **b** ≈37.37 **c** $\approx74°$ **d** $\approx68°$ **19 a** $\frac{2}{3}$ **b** ≈34 **21 a** $\approx52°$ **b** ≈11 **d** $\frac{a}{\sin \angle A} = \frac{b}{\sin \angle B}$

Review Problems

1 a 9 **b** 8 **c** 5 **d** $\sqrt{13}$ **3 a** 30 **b** $5\sqrt{3}$; 5 **c** 7 **d** 15 **e** $4\sqrt{5}$ **f** 9 **g** $5\sqrt{3}$; $10\sqrt{3}$ **h** $\frac{25}{2}$ **i** 26 **j** $4\sqrt{2}$; $4\sqrt{2}$ **5** $3\sqrt{3}$ **7** 7 ft **9** 48 **11** $\sqrt{85}$ **13** 13 **15** ≈14.5 **17** 5 **19 a** 120 **b** 45 **c** 55 **21 a** 90 **b** 180 **c** 10π, or ≈31.42 **23** 75 km **25** Swim directly across and walk **27** 7.5 **29 a** 12 **b** $10\sqrt{13}$ **33** 1:2 **35** 7 **37 a** $\approx35°$ **b** 60°

Cumulative Review Problems, Chapters 1–9

1 $67\frac{1}{2}$ **3 a** 1260 **b** 30 **c** 14 **5** 14.4 m **7** 52 **9 a** $\pm\frac{7}{2}$

b $\frac{20}{3}$ **13 a** 55° **b** $5\frac{1}{2}$° **15** 15 **17** 27 **21 a** 7°

b $(2\sqrt{3},\ -4)$ **25** 25 **27** $\frac{2}{7}$ **29** No; opposite sides are

not of equal length **31** $\frac{1}{2}$

10.1 The Circle

5 8 mm **11** 8 m **17 a** 13 **b** 5 **c** 24 **23** 2 **25** 24

10.2 Congruent Chords

1 Same distance **7 a** ≈ 283.53 sq mm **b** ≈ 59.69 mm
11 a 8 **b** 5 **13** 10 **15 a** 8 **b** $24 + 6\sqrt{7}$

10.3 Arcs of a Circle

1 a 6 **b** 2 **c** 5 **d** 4 **e** 3 **f** 7 **g** 1 **3 a** 90 **b** 130
c 230 **d** 180 **e** 220 **9 a** $\frac{1}{45}$ **b** $\frac{2}{3}$ **c** $\frac{2}{5}$ **d** $\frac{7}{8}$ **11** 132
13 a 15π **b** 18π **19 a** $5\sqrt{2}$ **b** 135 **23 a** $\frac{n(n-1)}{2}$

b $n(n-1)$ **c** $\frac{360}{n}$

10.4 Secants and Tangents

1 17 cm **5 a** Q = (16, 0); S = (38, 0) **b** 3 **11 a** $2\sqrt{13}$,
or ≈ 7.21 **b** $-\frac{3}{2}$ **13 a** 12 cm **b** Yes **17 a** 9 **b** 17

19 a $\frac{2}{7}$ **b** $\frac{3}{7}$ **c** $\frac{2}{7}$ **23** 60 mm **25** 10 **27** $\frac{8\sqrt{10}}{3}$

29 $\frac{c-a+b}{2}$

10.5 Angles Related to a Circle

1 62 **3 a** 35 **b** 75 **5 a** 140 **b** 80 **c** 20 **d** $81\frac{1}{2}$ **e** 100

7 85°; 23° **9** 10° **11** 81° **13** 125° **15** 75 **17 a** $\frac{1}{2}$

b $\frac{5}{18}$ **c** $\frac{1}{6}$ **d** $\frac{11}{36}$ **19** 64; 120; 116 **21 a** 132 **b** 10 **c** 20

d 30 **23** 98° **25** 25° **27** $175\frac{1}{2}$ **29 a** 70 **b** 110

33 20° **35** 90

10.6 More Angle-Arc Theorems

3 10 mm **5** 97° **7** 137° **9** 42 **11 a** 6 cm
b $18 + 6\sqrt{3}$ cm **13** 15 **15** $10\sqrt{3}$ **17 a** 29° **b** 81°
23 4 **27** 47°

10.7 Inscribed and Circumscribed Polygons

1 113°; 76° **3 a** 70° **b** 110° **c** 85° **d** 80° **5** No
7 a Square **b** Isosceles **9 a** 65 **b** 85° **c** 85° **d** 95°
11 46 **15** 116 or 80 **17 a** Yes **b** No **c** Yes **19 a** 20
b $\frac{1}{2}$ **21 a** Midpoint of hypotenuse **b** Interior of △
c Exterior of △ **23 a** A **b** S **c** S **d** N **e** S **f** S
25 48 **27** If the equiangular polygon has an odd
number of sides, it will be equilateral.

10.8 The Power Theorems

1 a 15 **b** 8 **c** 25 **3 a** 20 **b** 21 **c** 48 **5** 3.5 **7** 6
9 1 or 6 **11** 5 **13** 2.5 **15** 900 mi **17** 26; 39 **19 a** 4
b $12 - 4\sqrt{5} < y < 8$

10.9 Circumference and Arc Length

1 a 21π mm; ≈ 65.97 mm **b** 12π mm; ≈ 37.70 mm

3 a 4π **b** 5π **c** $\frac{10\pi}{3}$ **d** 10π **5 a** $40 + 6\pi$ **b** $24 + 4\pi$

c $12 + 3\pi$ **d** $6 + 7\pi$ **7** 138 m **9 a** $4\pi\sqrt{3}$ **b** 6π

c 9π **11** ≈ 214 m **13** ≈ 96.5 m; ≈ 71.4 m **15** 10π in.
17 $(24\sqrt{3} + 22\pi)$ cm

Review Problems

1 a 94 **b** 94 **c** 43 **3 a** 16 **b** 8 **c** 4 **5** 125 **7 a** $\frac{3\pi}{2}$

b $12 + 1.5\pi$ **13** $4\frac{2}{3}$ **15 a** $\frac{2}{9}$ **b** $\frac{7}{12}$ **17** 45°, 105°, 135°, 75°

19 20 **23** 6; 18 **25** ≈ 258 cm **29** 8:5 **31** ≈ 16.68 ft

11.1 Understanding Area

1 a 207 **b** 78 **c** 80 **3 a** 120 **b** 84 **5 a** 144 **b** 50
c 7 **d** 36 **e** 81 **7 a** 10 **b** 7 **9** 256 sq cm

11 9 m by 15 m **13** (18, 8) **15** $1.3 < x < 2.3$ **17** $\frac{27}{65}$

11.2 Areas of Parallelograms and Triangles

1 a 198 sq mm **b** 102 sq cm **c** 35 **3 a** 35 **b** 144
5 48 **7** 14 **9 a** $18\sqrt{3}$ **b** 72 **c** $36\sqrt{3}$ **11 a** 84 **b** 128
13 12 **15** 85 **17** 33 **19 a** 168 **b** 180 **c** 81
21 a ≈ 72.7 **b** ≈ 120.2 **c** 120.0 **23** 12 **25 a** 30 **b** 12
27 a 6 **b** $A = \frac{s^2}{4}\sqrt{3}$ **29** 50 **31** 120

11.3 The Area of a Trapezoid

1 a 104 **b** 13 **3** 10.5; 73.5 **5** 11 **7 a** 396 **b** 78 **9** 24
11 89 **13** 72 **15** 16 sq units **17 a** $42\sqrt{3}$ **b** $27\sqrt{3}$

11.4 Areas of Kites and Related Figures

1 60 **3** 5 **5 a** 336 **b** 500 **7** 78 **9 a** 8; 28; 18 **b** 30

11.5 Areas of Regular Polygons

1 36 **3 a** $108\sqrt{3}$ **b** $48\sqrt{3}$ **c** $27\sqrt{3}$ **d** $36\sqrt{3}$ **5 a** 12
b $6\sqrt{3}$ **c** $216\sqrt{3}$ **7** 3 mm **9** 324 **11** $288\sqrt{3}$ **13 a** 11;
5.5 **b** 12 m; $2\sqrt{3}$ m **c** 4 cm; $2\sqrt{3}$ cm **15 a** $108\sqrt{3}$
b 288 **c** $216\sqrt{3}$ **17 a** $36 - 9\sqrt{3}$ **b** $27\sqrt{3}$ **c** $36\sqrt{3}$

19 a $450\sqrt{3}$ **b** 8 **c** $A = \frac{s^2\sqrt{3}}{2}$ **21 a** $150 + 100\sqrt{2}$
b $50 + 100\sqrt{2}$ **23** $1764\sqrt{3} - 3024$

25 a $\frac{1}{2}ab + \frac{1}{2}ab + \frac{1}{2}c^2$ **b** $\frac{1}{2}(a + b)(a + b)$
c $a^2 + b^2 = c^2$

11.6 Areas of Circles, Sectors, and Segments

1 a $\pi, 2\pi$ **b** $64\pi, 16\pi$ **c** $225\pi, 30\pi$ **3** 20π cm **5 a** π
b 32π **c** 2π **d** 27π **e** 75π **f** 9π **7** $150 + 25\pi$
9 a 24π **b** 12π **c** 8π **11 a** $16\pi - 32$ **b** $\frac{32\pi}{3} - 16\sqrt{3}$
c $12\pi - 9\sqrt{3}$ **13 a** $18\pi, 50\pi, 24\frac{1}{2}\pi$ **15** 12π
17 32 sq cm **19 a** $50\pi - 50\sqrt{3}$ **b** 10π **21 a** 120
b 120 **23** $\frac{33}{49}$

11.7 Ratios of Areas

1 a 1:1 **b** 1:2 **c** 15:8 **d** 5:6 **3 a** 1:1 **b** 1:2 **c** 2:1
5 3:4 **7** 1:16 **9 a** 64:225 **b** 1:2 **c** 1:1 **d** 4:9
11 5:4 **13** 250 **15** 16:81 **17** 4:9 **19 a** 4:1 **b** 8:1
c 1:1 **d** 1:2 **e** 30 **21** 5:6

11.8 Hero's and Brahmagupta's Formulas

1 a 6 **b** $2\sqrt{5}$ **c** $10\sqrt{2}$ **d** $6\sqrt{3}$ **e** 60 **f** 84 **3 a** 36
b $4\sqrt{15}$ **c** 24 **d** $16\sqrt{3}$ **5** ≈ 32.50 **9** $2\sqrt{6}$ **11 a** It
approaches a $\triangle$. **b** It becomes Hero's formula.
13 a $(6, 8 - 3\sqrt{3})$ **b** ≈ 37.7

Review Problems

1 a 84 **b** 42 **c** 75 **d** 52 **e** 20 **f** 8 **3 a** 70 **b** 24
c $16\sqrt{3}$ **5** $48\sqrt{3}$ **7** 18 **9** 196 **11** 81 sq m **13 a** 9π
b 16π **c** $100 - 25\pi$ **15 a** 5:8 **b** 9:16 **17** 360
19 120 **21** $A = 77\sqrt{3}$; $P = 50$ **23 a** 338 **b** 6
25 a $\frac{168}{5}$ **b** $27\sqrt{3} - 9\pi$ **c** $6 - \pi$ **27 a** $9\pi - 18$
b $6\pi - 9\sqrt{3}$ **29** Circle **31 a** (12, 13) **b** 156
33 $143\sqrt{3}$ **35** $18\pi\sqrt{2} - 9\pi$ **37** 432 **39** $72\sqrt{3} - 24\pi$
41 $11\frac{1}{4}\pi$ **43** 390 **45** ≈ 106.8

12.1 Surface Areas of Prisms

1 a 550 sq cm **b** 282 sq mm **c** 810 sq in. **3 a** 550
b 120 **c** 790 **5 a** 150 **b** 294 **7 a** L.A. = 480;
T.A. = 552 **b** L.A. = 120; T.A. = 132 **c** L.A. = 2500;
T.A. = 2620 **d** L.A. = 360; T.A. = $360 + 108\sqrt{3}$
9 L.A. = 616; T.A. = 712 **11 a** 0; 0; 0; 8; 12; 6; 1
b $\frac{20}{27}$ **c** 432 sq in.

12.2 Surface Areas of Pyramids

1 a 60 **b** 240 **c** 340 **3 a** The base is not regular.
b 936 **c** 1356 **5 a** 192 **b** 48 **c** 36 **d** 144 **e** 1:4
f 36 **7 a** 72 **b** 432 **c** 324 **d** 756 **9 a** 17; 10;
L.A. = 504; T.A. = 864 **b** 16 **11 a** $36\sqrt{3}$ **b** $2\sqrt{6}$
13 Cube

12.3 Surface Areas of Circular Solids

1 a 196π **b** 36π **c** 36π **d** 25π **3** 6 **5 a** $-2; \frac{1}{2}$
b Rhombus **7 a** 90π **b** 66π **c** 480π **9** 8π cm by
14 cm **11 a** 64 **b** 32 **13** 140π

12.4 Volumes of Prisms and Cylinders

1 a 300π **b** 720 **3** 357 **5 a** 343 **b** e^3 **c** 5 **7 a** ≈ 23
cu ft **b** ≈ 1456 lb **9** V = 600; T.A. = 620 **11** 6
13 $250\sqrt{2}$ **15** 189 **17 a** ≈ 621 cu in. **b** 439 sq in.
19 $V = \frac{2000}{3}\pi$; T.A. = $600 + \frac{1400}{9}\pi$ **21** 90π

12.5 Volumes of Pyramids and Cones

1 $490\sqrt{3}$ **3 a** 400 **b** 360 **5 a** 1080π **b** 369π **c** 450π
7 ≈ 1451 cu ft **9** 200 **11** 72π **13** 720 cu m
17 a $18\sqrt{2}$ **b** $\frac{s^3\sqrt{2}}{12}$ **19** 48

12.6 Volumes of Spheres

1 a 36π **b** 972π **c** $\frac{500}{3}\pi$ **3** ≈ 481 cu m **5** ≈ 523 cu ft
7 a 240π **b** 132π **9** ≈ 71 cu mm **11 a** 138π cu ft
b 105π sq ft **13 a** ≈ 524 cu m **b** ≈ 2721 cu m
15 $\approx 11\%$

Review Problems

1 a L.A. = 48; T.A. = 84 **b** L.A. = 56π, T.A. = 88π
3 a V = 360π, T.A. = 192π **b** V = 540; T.A. = 468
c V = 100π; T.A. = 90π **5 a** 5 **b** 6 **7** 562,500 cu cm
9 36π **11 a** 75π **b** $45\pi + 60$ **13** 35 **15** 5040
17 215 cu in. **19** $120 + 48\pi$ **21** $333\pi\sqrt{3}$

Cumulative Review Problems, Chapters 1–12

1 81 **5 a** 8 **b** $\frac{31}{5}$ **c** 44 **d** 12 **7 a** $\frac{50}{3}$ **b** $\frac{32}{3}$ **c** 8
9 89° **11 a** 60 **b** 83 **c** 50 **d** 78 **13 a** 25 **b** 16
15 64 **17** 36 **19 a** 60 **b** 135 **c** 120 **d** 45 **e** No
23 2π **25** 7 **27** 100 m **29 a** 3 **b** 1.2 **31** 35 **33** 3
35 32° **37** 20 **39** Yes **41** $6\frac{1}{5}$

13.1 Graphing Equations

7 x-intercept: 3; y-intercept: -6 **9** Yes **11** Yes **13** 9
15 a (2, 5) **b** 14 and 4 **c** 9 **d** 63 **17** ≈ 21.5
19 $y - 2 = 6(x - 5)$ **21 a** $-\frac{5}{8}$ **23** ≈ 2.6

13.2 Equations of Lines

1 a 3; 7 **b** 4; 0 **c** $\frac{1}{2}$; $-\sqrt{3}$ **d** -6; 13 **e** -5; -6
f 0; 7 **3** $y = -6$ **5** a and c **7 a** 1 **b** $y = x + 5$
c $-\frac{1}{2}$ **d** $y = -\frac{1}{2}x - \frac{5}{2}$ **9** $\frac{3}{4}$ **13** $y - 12 = \frac{1}{7}(x - 4)$
15 $y = -7x + 40$ **17** $\frac{1}{7}$ **19** $y - 7 = -\frac{1}{2}(x + 1)$
21 No **23** $y = -\frac{2}{5}x + 4$ **25** (3, 13)
27 a $y = -\frac{3}{4}x + 1$ **b** $y = -\frac{3}{4}x - 1$ **c** $y = \frac{4}{3}x + \frac{4}{3}$

13.3 Systems of Equations

1 a $(6, 4)$ **b** $(2, 5)$ **c** $(-3, -7)$ **d** $(3, 2)$ **3 a** $(12, 0)$
b $\{(x, y) \mid y = 3x - 7\}$ **5** $(-2, 3)$ **7** $(4, -2)$
9 $y - 1 = 5(x + 2)$ **11** $(-1, 2)$ **13** $\left(\frac{ce - bf}{ae - bd}, \frac{af - cd}{ae - bd}\right)$
15 $\frac{4\sqrt{5}}{5}$ **17** 11

13.4 Graphing Inequalities

9 a $(1, 1)$; $(2, 4)$; $(3, 9)$ **b** $9\frac{1}{2}$

13.5 Three-Dimensional Graphing and Reflections

3 ≈ 7.8 **5 a** 20 **b** 140 **c** $3\sqrt{10}$ **d** Yes **e** $(11, 5, 0)$ or
$(-3, 5, 0)$ **7** $(3, 10)$ **9 a** $(5, 6, -2)$ **b** ≈ 11.6
11 $(-3, 7)$ **13** $(5, -1)$ **15 a** 10 **b** $y = -2x + 1$
17 $\left(9, 2\frac{1}{2}\right)$

13.6 Circles

1 a $x^2 + y^2 = 16$ **b** $(x + 2)^2 + (y - 1)^2 = 25$
c $x^2 + (y + 2)^2 = 12$ **d** $(x + 6)^2 + y^2 = \frac{1}{4}$ **3 a** $(0, 0)$;
6; 12; 12π; 36π **b** $(-5, 0)$; $\frac{3}{2}$; 3; 3π; $\frac{9}{4}\pi$ **c** $(3, -6)$; 10;
20; 20π; 100π **d** $(-5, 2)$; 9; 18; 18π; 81π **5 a** Yes
b No **7** $(-6, 3)$; $(8, 3)$; $(1, 10)$; $(1, -4)$ **9 a** On
b Inside **c** Outside **d** Outside **11 a** $(0, 4)$; 5
b $(-7, -3)$; 6 **c** $(-5, 6)$; $\sqrt{51}$ **d** $(4, -7)$; 10 **13** $5\sqrt{2}$
15 $y + 8 = \frac{6}{5}(x - 8)$ **17** 17π **19 a** $\frac{16}{3}\pi$ **b** ≈ 2.90

13.7 Coordinate-Geometry Practice

1 $x^2 + y^2 = 25$ **a** 25π **b** 10π **3 a** ≈ 13.7 **b** ≈ 30.5
5 a 5 **b** 5 **c** 5 **7** 10 **9** -0.5 **11** 12
13 a $(x + 3)^2 + (y - 3)^2 = 9$ **b** ≈ 1.9 **15** 35 **17** 50
19 $\frac{24}{5}$ **21** $(x + 4)^2 + y^2 = 36$ **23** $\frac{8\sqrt{5}}{5}$ **25 a** $5\sqrt{13}$
b $\sqrt{429}$ **27** 20 **29 a** $(7, 0)$ **b** $\left(\frac{20}{3}, 0\right)$ **c** $\left(\frac{28 - 2x_1}{3}, 0\right)$

Review Problems

1 No **3** -4 **5 a** 10 **b** $(7, 2)$ **c** $\frac{4}{3}$ **7 a** 50 **b** 27
c 18π **9 a** $y = 2x + 1$ **b** $x = 2$ **c** $x = -5$
d $y = 3x - 2$ **e** $y = \frac{1}{2}x - 2$ **f** $y = 3x - 7$
g $y = \frac{1}{2}x - 3$ **11** Yes **13** $-\frac{29}{4}$ **15** $(10, 5)$ **17 a** $2\sqrt{5}$
b $y = 2x - 10$ **c** $y - 4 = -5(x - 7)$
d $y - 8 = -5(x - 9)$ **e** $y - 8 = \frac{1}{5}(x - 9)$ **21 a** $\{(2, 7)\}$
b $\{(7, -1)\}$ **c** $\{(-3, 4), (5, 4)\}$ **23** ≈ 9.2 **25** Point circle
27 III and IV; $\left(-\frac{10}{3}, -\frac{10}{3}\right)$ and $\left(\frac{10}{7}, -\frac{10}{7}\right)$ **29** $2\sqrt{10}$
31 ≈ 339.3 **33** $\left(-\frac{10}{3}, \frac{7}{3}\right)$ **35** $\left(\frac{44}{7}, 0\right)$ **37** $\{(2, 14),$
$(-26, 42)\}$

14.1 Locus

1 The locus is two lines parallel to $\overleftrightarrow{AB}$ and 3 cm on
each side of $\overleftrightarrow{AB}$. **3** The locus is the perpendicular
bisector of the segment joining the two given points.
5 The locus is two circles with the same center as the
given circle and with radii of 2 in. and 22 in. **7** The
locus is a circle concentric with the given circles and
with a radius equal to the average of the radii of the
given circles. If the radii of the given circles are 3 and
8, the radius of the locus is $5\frac{1}{2}$. **9** $x^2 + y^2 = 16$
11 The locus does not include the given point but
otherwise is a circle tangent internally to the given
circle at the given point and passing through the
center of the given circle. **13** The locus is the
perpendicular bisector of the segment joining the two
points. **15** The locus is a segment joining the
midpoints of the sides containing the given vertex.
17 $x = 2.5$ **19** The locus is the union of point Q and
the circle with center Q and radius 18. **21** The locus
is a circle with its center at the foot of the
perpendicular from P to m and with a radius of 3.
23 The locus does not include T and V but otherwise
is a circle with center at the midpoint of $\overline{TV}$ and
diameter TV. **25 a** Perpendicular bisectors of the
sides **b** Angle bisectors **29** $(x - 2)^2 + y^2 = 4$

14.2 Compound Locus

1 a ϕ, 1 point, or 2 points **b** ϕ, 1 point, or 2 points
c ϕ, 1 point, or 2 points **d** ϕ, 1 point, or a line **e** 4
points **f** ϕ, 1 point, or a ray **3** 1 point **5 a** ϕ, 1 point,
or a segment **b** ϕ or a segment **7** ϕ, 1 point, 2 points,
3 points, or 4 points **9** 2 points **11** ϕ or 1 point **13** ϕ,
1 point, 2 points, 3 points, or 4 points **15** ϕ, 1 point, 2
points, 3 points, . . . , or 8 points **17** A sphere and its
interior

14.3 The Concurrence Theorems

3 Find the incenter. **5** Centroid and incenter
7 Centroid **9** Equilateral **11** The locus is the
circumcenter of the triangle formed by joining the
three points. **13 a** $9\sqrt{3}$ **b** $162\sqrt{3}$ **c** $81\sqrt{3}$ **d** 30
15 $\left(\frac{28}{5}, \frac{8}{5}\right)$ **17 a** $\left(\frac{4}{3}, 4\right)$ **b** $\left(\frac{4}{3}, 4\right)$

Review Problems

1 The locus is the perpendicular bisector of $\overline{AB}$
(minus the midpoint of $\overline{AB}$). **3** 4 points **5** The locus
is a point and a circle. **7** $x^2 + y^2 = 25$ **13** $y = 3x + 5$
15 The locus is the perpendicular bisector of $\overline{PQ}$
(minus the midpoint of $\overline{PQ}$). **17** The locus is a circle
that is tangent internally to the given circle at the fixed
point and whose radius is half the original circle's but
which excludes the fixed point. **19** 4 points **25** The
locus does not include P and Q but otherwise is a
circle with $\overline{PQ}$ as diameter.

15.1 Number Properties

1 a $\{x|x > 25\}$ **b** $\{x|x > 6\}$ **c** $\{x|x \geq -7\}$ **d** $\{x|x > 1\}$
3 x exceeds z by 8. **5** $\angle A > \angle 2$ **7** $45 < x < 90$
9 $0 < x < \frac{1}{5}$ **11** $x > 3$ **13** $\angle DBC > \angle DCB$
15 $\{x|-3 < x < 2\}$ **17** 44 **19 a** Comp. $\angle B >$ comp.
$\angle A$ **b** Comp. $\angle B > \angle A$ **c** Comp. $\angle B$, $\angle A$, comp. $\angle A$,
$\angle B$

15.2 Inequalities in a Triangle

1 $80 < m\angle 1 < 180$ **3 a** $\overline{PR}$; $\overline{PQ}$ **b** Hypotenuse
5 a $\overline{AB}$ **b** $\overline{WZ}$ **7** The other **9** $46 < m\angle B < 70$
11 a $\angle R$, $\angle Q$, $\angle P$ **b** R **13** 2 cm **19 a** 714.0
b ≈ 968.6 **c** ≈ 2164.2

15.3 The Hinge Theorems

1 $\overline{AC}$ **3** $\overline{DC}$ **7 a** $\angle Y$; $\angle X$ **b** Obtuse **13** Right
15 a $\overline{AC}$ **b** $\angle B$ **17** $\angle XZW$, $\angle X$, $\angle XWY$, $\angle Y$, $\angle XWZ$
19 1399 **21** b

Review Problems

1 $\angle A$, $\angle B$, $\angle C$ **3 a** $\angle CBD$; Converse Hinge Theorem
b $\angle X$; If ⊿, then ⊿ **c** $\angle 1$; Exterior-Angle-Inequality
Theorem **5** $x > 6$ **7 a 9** $\overline{BC}$, $\overline{AC}$, $\overline{AB}$ **11 a** $\overline{AB}$
b $12 < P < 6 + 6\sqrt{2}$ **13 a** $\sqrt{34}$; $\sqrt{13}$; 7 **b** Obtuse
c $\angle P$, $\angle R$, $\angle Q$ **19** $\overline{AC}$, $AB \cong \overline{BC}$, $\overline{CD}$, $\overline{AD}$, $\overline{BD}$ **23** $\frac{7}{9}$

Cumulative Review Problems, Chapters 1–15

1 $V = 12\pi$, $A = 24\pi$ **3** $16°$ **5** 21 **7 a** 3 **b** $13\frac{1}{2}$ **c** No
9 42 **11 a** 13, 14, 15; $-\frac{12}{5}$, 0, $\frac{4}{3}$ **b** Acute
c $y = \frac{4}{3}x + 4$; -3; 4 **d** $y = -4$ **e** $(3, -4)$ **f** $x = 3$
g 12 **h** $(1, -4)$; 6 **i** 84 **13** 135 **15** $12\sqrt{3}$ **19** $175°$
21 a 11 **b** $180°$ **23** 36 **25 a** $\sqrt{26}$ **b** $y = 5x - 35$
c $y = 3x + 37$ **d** $y = -3x + 29$ **27** 26 m **29** $78°$
31 Acute **33** $\pi:2$ **37** ϕ, 1 point, or 2 points **41** ϕ, 1
point, 2 points, 3 points, 4 points, a ray, a ray and a
point, or a line **45** $20\sqrt{3}$ **47 a** A cone with a conical
hole in it **b** 504π **49** 5

16.1 The Point-Line Distance Formula

1 3 **3** $\frac{56}{25}$ **5** ≈ 5.81 **7** ≈ 3.051 **9** -1 or -21
11 $x + y - 8 = 0$ and $3x - 3y + 2 = 0$

16.2 Two Other Useful Formulas

1 ≈ 6.110 **3** 81 **5** $-\frac{76}{11}$ or $\frac{92}{11}$

16.3 Stewart's Theorem

1 $\frac{-11 + \sqrt{181}}{2}$ **3** 14 **5** $\frac{8\sqrt{165}}{15}$

16.4 Ptolemy's Theorem

1 $\frac{2\sqrt{51}}{3}$ **3** 60.8 **5** $3\sqrt{3} - 4$ or $3\sqrt{3} + 4$

16.5 Mass Points

1 10:3 **3** 10 **5** $\frac{4}{11}$

16.6 Inradius and Circumradius Formulas

1 $\frac{2\sqrt{14}}{7}$, $\frac{45\sqrt{14}}{56}$ **3** $\frac{\sqrt{455}}{13}$, $\frac{144\sqrt{455}}{455}$ **5 a** $\frac{13\sqrt{10}}{10}$ **b** ≈ 4.744

Review Problems

1 $x = \frac{\sqrt{165}}{3}$; $y = \sqrt{93}$ **3** 28 **5** 6 **7** $\frac{10\sqrt{3}}{3}$ **9** $\frac{3}{13}$
11 $x - 4y - 1 + 3\sqrt{17} = 0$ and
$x - 4y - 1 - 3\sqrt{17} = 0$ **13** 48π

GLOSSARY

acute angle An angle whose measure is greater than 0 and less than 90. (p. 11)

acute triangle A triangle in which all three angles are acute. (p. 143)

alternate exterior angles A pair of angles in the exterior of a figure formed by two lines and a transversal, lying on alternate sides of the transversal and having different vertices. (p. 194)

alternate interior angles A pair of angles in the interior of a figure formed by two lines and a transversal, lying on alternate sides of the transversal and having different vertices. (p. 193)

altitude (of triangle) A perpendicular segment from a vertex of a triangle to the opposite side, extended if necessary. (p. 132)

angle A figure formed by two rays with a common endpoint. (p. 5)

angle of depression The angle between a downward line of sight and the horizontal. (p. 423)

angle of elevation The angle between an upward line of sight and the horizontal. (p. 423)

annulus A region bounded by two concentric circles. (p. 540)

apothem A segment joining the center of a regular polygon to the midpoint of one of the polygon's sides. (p. 532)

arc A figure consisting of two points on a circle and all points on the circle needed to connect them by a single path. (p. 450)

area The number of square units of space within the boundary of a closed region. (p. 511)

arithmetic mean The average of two numbers. The arithmetic mean of the numbers a and b, for example, is $\frac{1}{2}(a + b)$. (p. 328)

auxiliary line A line introduced into a diagram for the purpose of clarifying a proof. (p. 132)

base (of isosceles triangle) In a nonequilateral isosceles triangle, the side that is congruent to neither of the other sides. (p. 142)

base (of trapezoid) Either of the two parallel sides of a trapezoid. (p. 236)

base angle In an isosceles triangle or trapezoid, the angle formed by a base and an adjacent side. (pp. 142, 236)

bisect To divide a segment or an angle into two congruent parts. (pp. 28, 29)

center (of arc) The center of the circle of which an arc is a part. (p. 450)

center (of circle) See *circle*.

central angle An angle whose vertex is at the center of a circle. (p. 450)

centroid The point of concurrency of the medians of a triangle. (p. 662)

chord A segment joining two points on a circle. (p. 440)

chord-chord angle An angle formed by two chords that intersect at a point inside a circle but not at the circle's center. (p. 470)

circle The set of all points in a plane that are a given distance from a given point in the plane. (That point is called the circle's *center*.) (p. 439)

circumcenter A point associated with a polygon, corresponding to the center of the polygon's circumscribed circle. (The circumcenter of a triangle is the point of concurrency of the perpendicular bisectors of the triangle's sides.) (p. 486)

circumference The perimeter of a circle. (p. 370)

circumscribed polygon A polygon each of whose sides is tangent to a circle. (p. 486)

collinear Lying on the same line. (p. 18)

common tangent A line tangent to two circles (not necessarily at the same point)—called a *common internal tangent* if it lies between the circles or a *common external tangent* if it does not. (p. 461)

complementary angles Two angles whose sum is 90° (a right angle). (p. 66)

compound locus The intersection of two or more loci. (p. 656)

concentric circles Two or more coplanar circles with the same center. (p. 439)

conclusion The "then" clause in a conditional statement. (p. 40)

concurrent lines Lines that intersect in a single point. (p. 660)

conditional statement A statement in the form "If p, then q," where p and q are declarative statements. (p. 40)

congruent angles Angles that have the same measure. (p. 12)

congruent arcs Arcs that have the same measure and are parts of the same circle or congruent circles. (p. 452)

congruent segments Segments that have the same length. (p. 12)

congruent triangles Triangles in which all pairs of corresponding parts (angles and sides) are congruent. (p. 111)

construction A drawing made with only a compass and a straightedge. (p. 666)

contrapositive A statement associated with a conditional statement "If p, then q," having the form "If not q, then not p." (p. 44)

converse A statement associated with a conditional statement "If p, then q," having the form "If q, then p." (p. 40)

convex polygon A polygon in which each interior angle has a measure less than 180. (p. 235)

coplanar Lying in the same plane. (p. 192)

corresponding angles In a figure formed by two lines and a transversal, a pair of angles on the same side of the transversal, one in the interior and one in the exterior of the figure, having different vertices. (p. 194)

cross section The intersection of a solid with a plane. (p. 577)

cyclic quadrilateral A quadrilateral that can be inscribed in a circle. (p. 550)

diagonal (*of polygon*) A segment that joins two nonconsecutive (nonadjacent) vertices of a polygon. (p. 235)

diagonal (*of rectangular solid*) A segment whose endpoints are vertices not in the same face of a rectangular solid. (p. 413)

diameter A chord that passes through the center of a circle. (p. 440)

distance The length of the shortest path between two objects. (p. 184)

equiangular Having all angles congruent. (p. 143)

equilateral Having all sides congruent. (p. 142)

exterior angle An angle that is adjacent to and supplementary to an interior angle of a polygon. (p. 296)

extremes   The first and fourth terms of a proportion. In the proportion $a:b = c:d$ $\left(\text{or } \frac{a}{b} = \frac{c}{d}\right)$, for example, a and d are the extremes. (p. 327)

face   One of the polygonal surfaces making up a polyhedron. (p. 413)

foot (of line)   The point of intersection of a line and a plane. (p. 270)

fourth proportional   The fourth term of a proportion. In the proportion $a:b = c:x$ $\left(\text{or } \frac{a}{b} = \frac{c}{x}\right)$, for example, x is the fourth proportional. (p. 328)

frustum   The portion of a pyramid or a cone that lies between the base and a cross section of the figure. (p. 585)

geometric mean   Either of the two means of a proportion in which the means are equal. Also called a *mean proportional.* (p. 327)

hypotenuse   The side opposite the right angle in a right triangle. (p. 143)

hypothesis   The "if" clause in a conditional statement. (p. 40)

incenter   A point associated with a polygon, corresponding to the center of the polygon's inscribed circle. (The incenter of a triangle is the point of concurrency of the triangle's angle bisectors.) (p. 487)

inscribed angle   An angle whose vertex is on a circle and whose sides are determined by two chords. (p. 469)

inscribed polygon   A polygon each of whose vertices lies on a circle. (p. 486)

inverse   A statement associated with a conditional statement "If p, then q," having the form "If not p, then not q." (p. 44)

isosceles trapezoid   A trapezoid in which the nonparallel sides are congruent. (p. 236)

isosceles triangle   A triangle in which at least two sides are congruent. (p. 142)

interior angle   An angle whose sides are determined by two consecutive sides of a polygon. (p. 308)

kite   A quadrilateral in which two disjoint pairs of consecutive sides are congruent. (p. 236)

lateral surface area   The sum of the areas of a solid's lateral faces. (p. 562)

leg (of isosceles trapezoid)   One of the nonparallel, congruent sides of an isosceles trapezoid. (p. 236)

leg (of isosceles triangle)   One of the two congruent sides of a nonequilateral isosceles triangle. (p. 142)

leg (of right triangle)   One of the sides that form the right angle in a right triangle. (p. 143)

locus   A set consisting of all the points, and only the points, that satisfy specific conditions. (p. 649)

major arc   An arc whose points are on or outside a central angle. (p. 451)

mean proportional   See *geometric mean.*

means   The second and third terms of a proportion. In the proportion $a:b = c:d$ $\left(\text{or } \frac{a}{b} = \frac{c}{d}\right)$, for example, b and c are the means. (p. 327)

median (of trapezoid)   A segment joining the midpoints of the nonparallel sides of a trapezoid. (p. 523)

median (of triangle)   A segment from a vertex of a triangle to the midpoint of the opposite side. (p. 131)

midpoint   A point that divides a segment or an arc into two congruent parts. (pp. 28, 453)

minor arc   An arc whose points are on or between the sides of a central angle. (p. 451)

oblique lines   Two intersecting lines that are not perpendicular. (p. 65)

obtuse angle   An angle whose measure is greater than 90 and less than 180. (p. 11)

obtuse triangle   A triangle in which one of the angles is obtuse. (p. 143)

opposite rays   Two collinear rays that have a common endpoint and extend in opposite directions. (p. 100)

orthocenter   The point of concurrency of the altitudes of a triangle. (p. 661)

parallel lines   Coplanar lines that do not intersect. (p. 195)

parallelogram   A quadrilateral in which both pairs of opposite sides are parallel. (p. 236)

perimeter   The sum of the lengths of the sides of a polygon. (p. 8)

perpendicular   Intersecting at right angles. (p. 61)

perpendicular bisector   A line that bisects and is perpendicular to a segment. (p. 185)

plane   A surface such that if any two points on the surface are connected by a line, all points of the line are also on the surface. (p. 192)

postulate   An unproved assumption. (p. 39)

prism   A solid figure that has two congruent parallel faces whose corresponding vertices are joined by parallel edges. (p. 561)

proportion   An equation stating that two or more ratios are equal. (p. 326)

protractor   An instrument, marked in degrees, used to measure angles. (p. 9)

pyramid   A solid figure that has a polygonal base and lateral edges that meet in a single point. (p. 565)

quadrilateral   A four-sided polygon. (p. 236)

radius (of circle)   A segment joining the center of a circle to a point on the circle. Also, the length of such a segment. (p. 439)

radius (of regular polygon)   A segment joining the center of a regular polygon to one of the polygon's vertices. (p. 532)

ratio   A quotient of two numbers. (p. 325)

ray   A straight set of points that begins at an endpoint and extends infinitely in one direction. (p. 4)

rectangle   A parallelogram in which at least one angle is a right angle. (p. 236)

rectangular solid   A prism with six rectangular faces. (p. 413)

regular polygon   A polygon that is both equilateral and equiangular. (p. 314)

rhombus   A parallelogram in which at least two consecutive sides are congruent. (p. 236)

right angle   An angle whose measure is 90. (p. 11)

right triangle   A triangle in which one of the angles is a right angle. (p. 143)

scalene triangle   A triangle in which no two sides are congruent. (p. 142)

secant   A line that intersects a circle at exactly two points. (p. 459)

secant-secant angle   An angle whose vertex is outside a circle and whose sides are determined by two secants. (p. 471)

secant segment   The part of a secant that joins a point outside the circle to the farther point of intersection of the secant and the circle. (p. 460)

secant-tangent angle   An angle whose vertex is outside a circle and whose sides are determined by a secant and a tangent. (p. 471)

sector   A region bounded by two radii and an arc of a circle. (p. 537)

segment (*of circle*)   A region bounded by a chord of a circle and its corresponding arc. (p. 538)

semicircle   An arc whose endpoints are the endpoints of a diameter. (p. 451)

similar polygons   Polygons in which the ratios of the measures of corresponding sides are equal and corresponding angles are congruent. (p. 333)

skew lines   Two lines that are not coplanar. (p. 283)

slant height   A perpendicular segment from the vertex of a pyramid to a side of the pyramid's base. (p. 413)

square   A parallelogram that is both a rhombus and a rectangle. (p. 236)

straight angle   An angle whose measure is 180. (p. 11)

supplementary angles   Two angles whose sum is 180° (a straight angle). (p. 67)

tangent   A line that intersects a circle at exactly one point. (p. 459)

tangent-chord angle   An angle whose vertex is on a circle and whose sides are determined by a tangent and a chord that intersect at the tangent's point of contact. (p. 469)

tangent circles   Circles that intersect at exactly one point. (p. 460)

tangent segment   The part of a tangent line between the point of contact and a point outside the circle. (p. 460)

tangent-tangent angle   An angle whose vertex is outside a circle and whose sides are determined by two tangents. (p. 471)

theorem   A mathematical statement that can be proved. (p. 23)

transversal   A line that intersects two coplanar lines in two distinct points. (p. 192)

trapezoid   A quadrilateral with exactly one pair of parallel sides. (p. 236)

triangle   A three-sided polygon. (p. 5)

trisect   To divide a segment or an angle into three congruent parts. (pp. 29, 30)

vertex (*of angle*)   The common endpoint of the two rays that form an angle. (p. 5)

vertex (*of polygon*)   The common endpoint of two sides of a polygon. (p. 6)

vertex angle   The angle opposite the base of a nonequilateral isosceles triangle. (p. 142)

vertical angles   A pair of angles such that the rays forming the sides of one and the rays forming the sides of the other are opposite rays. (p. 100)

volume   The number of cubic units of space contained by a solid figure. (p. 575)

INDEX

K

Kite, 189, 190, 236, 256
    area of, 528
    properties of, 242

L

Lateral area
    of cone, 571
    of cylinder, 570–71
    of prism, 562
    of pyramid, 566
Lateral edge, 561, 562, 565
Lattice point, 641
Law of Cosines, 427, 719
Law of Sines, 427, 718
Law of Trichotomy, 687
Legs
    of isosceles trapezoid, 236,
        242
    of isosceles triangle, 142
    of right triangle, 143, 156,
        384, 418–19
Line of centers, 461
Lines, 3
    auxiliary, 132
    concurrence of, 660
    coplanar, 192, 269–70
    determination of, 132
    distances from points to,
        174, 713–14
    equations of, 610–12
    feet of, 270, 276–77, 565
    horizontal
        equations of, 611
        slope of, 199
    intersecting, 61, 62, 100, 192,
        271, 618
    intersection of, with planes,
        269–270, 271, 276–77
    number, 3–4, 62
    oblique, 65
    parallel, 195, 200, 217–18,
        224–27, 271, 283,
        351–52
    parallel to plane, 282, 283
    perpendicular, 61–62, 180,
        185, 200, 218, 227
    perpendicular to plane,
        276–77, 283
    secant, 459
    skew, 195, 274, 282–83
    slopes of, 198–200
    tangent, 459, 461
    vertical
        equations of, 611–12
        slope of, 199
    working, 667
Line segments. *See* Segments.
Locus, 649–51
    compound, 656
Logic, 41, 44–46. *See also* Proof.
Lunes of Hippocrates, 542

M

Major arc, 451
Masères, rule of, 403
Mass points, 728
Mathematical Excursions, 17,
        81, 130, 318, 383, 492,
        536, 701
Mean
    arithmetic, 328, 383
    geometric, 327–28, 383. *See
        also* Mean
        proportional.
    harmonic, 383
Mean proportional, 327, 377–78
    construction of, 674
Means (of proportion), 327
Means-Extremes Products
        Theorem, 327, 345
Means-Extremes Ratio
        Theorem, 327
Measures
    of angles, 9–10, 11–12
    of arcs, 371, 451–52
    of exterior angles of polygon,
        216, 296, 308, 315, 691
    of interior angles of polygon,
        216, 295, 296, 308, 691
    of segments, 9
Median(s)
    of trapezoid, 523–24
    of triangle, 31, 131, 132, 546,
        662
Midline Theorem, 296–97
Midpoint
    of arc, 453
    of segment, 28–29, 170–71
    of side of polygon, 131,
        296–97, 523
Midpoint formula, 170–71
Minor arc, 451
Minute (angle measure), 11–12
Missing diagram, 176–77
Multiplication property
    of inequality, 688
    for segments and angles, 89

N

Negation, 44
n-gon, 307
No-Choice Theorem, 302
Nonagon, 307
Nonconvex polygon, 235, 312
Number line, 3–4, 62

O

Oblique lines, 65
Obtuse angle, 11
Obtuse triangle, 143
    test for, 385, 692
Octagon, 307
Octahedron, 569
Opposite rays, 100

Opposite reciprocals, 200, 257,
        614
Ordered pair, 62, 605
Ordinate, 611
Orthocenter, 661–62
Overlapping triangles, 138

P

Paragraph proof, 36–37
Parallelism
    of line and plane, 282, 283
    of lines, 195, 200, 217–18,
        224–27, 271, 283,
        351–52
    of planes, 282–83
Parallel Postulate, 224, 295
Parallelogram, 203, 219, 236,
        249, 487–88
    area of, 516–17
    properties of, 241
Pentadecagon, 307
Pentagon, 307
Pentagonal prism, 561, 562
Perimeter(s), 8
    circumference as, 370
    ratios of, 334
    of right triangle, 734
Perpendicular bisector, 185,
        440, 660
    construction of, 668–69
Perpendicularity. *See also*
        Perpendicular bisector.
    of line and plane, 276–77,
        283
    of lines, 61–62, 180, 200,
        218, 227
Pi, 126, 499
Planes, 192, 269
    determination of, 270–71
    intersection of, 271, 283
    intersection of, with lines,
        269–70, 271, 276–77
    parallel, 282–83
Plato, rule of, 403
Point circle, 634
Point-line distance formula,
        713–14
Point of tangency, 459
Points, 3
    betweenness of, 18
    bisection. *See* Midpoint.
    collinear, 18, 19, 735–36
    coordinates of, 62
    coplanar, 192, 269–70, 649
    distances between, 184,
        392–93, 626
    distances to lines, 179,
        713–14
    equidistant, 184–85
    lattice, 641
    loci of, 649–51, 656
    mass, 728
    trisection, 29

Credits, continued

210: © Georg Gerster/Comstock, New York; 211: Merrick/Hedrich-Blessing, Chicago; 227: Superstock, New York; 249: H. Armstrong Roberts, Chicago; 268: Myron Goldsmith/Skidmore, Owings & Merrill, Chicago, Courtesy of Hedrich-Blessing, Chicago; 275: Skidmore, Owings & Merrill, Chicago; 281: Historical Pictures Service Chicago; 287: *Winter Window*, 1941, Charles Sheeler, Collection of James Maroney; 294: Adam Woolfitt/ Susan Griggs Agency, London; 295: The Granger Collection, New York; 301: © Georg Gerster/Comstock, New York; 306: © 1985 Sidney Harris, New Haven, Connecticut; 313: Birlauf Steen Photo, Denver, Colorado; 318: (left and right) Annette Del Zoppo/© 1988 *Discover* Publications, New York; 324: *Titus Canyon*, Linda MacDonald; 338: Norman Prince, San Francisco; 344: (left and right) Photograph from *A Collector's Guide to Nesting Dolls* by Michelle Lyons Lefkowitz, Books Americana, Florence, Alabama; 359: (left and right) Linda MacDonald; 365: The Granger Collection, New York; 366: Adrienne McGrath, North Barrington, Illinois; 383: J.N. Hewitt, E.L. Turner, and B.F. Burke; 391: Adrienne McGrath, North Barrington, Illinois; 397: John Zoiner/Peter Arnold, Inc., New York; 404, 433: Adrienne McGrath, North Barrington, Illinois; 438: From *Art Forms from Photomicrography* by Lewis R. Wolberg; 458: *Campsite Round Waterhole*, Mick Namerari Tjapaltjarri, Aboriginal Artists Agency, Ltd., North Sydney, Australia, Courtesy of Lauraine Diggins Fine Art, Melbourne, Australia; 485: Algimantas Kezys, Stickney, Illinois; 492: (left and right) Adrienne McGrath, North Barrington, Illinois; 498: Courtesy of A.A. Jackson; 509: Robert Frerck/Odyssey Productions, Chicago; 510: *Abstraction*, Sonia Delaunay, Collection of Charles Gilman, Photograph by Roman Szechter, New York; 522: © 1985 Sidney Harris, New Haven, Connecticut; 542: (left and right) Courtesy of William Field; 559: *Nives II,* Victor Vassarely, Tate Gallery/Art Resource, New York; 560: © Pete Turner/Image Bank, Chicago; 588: Manfred Kage/Peter Arnold, Inc., New York; 597: *Cube*, Isamu Noguchi, Ezra Stoller/© Esto, Mamaroneck, New York; 603: The Granger Collection, New York; 604: *Piero's Piazza*, 1982, Al Held, Albright-Knox Gallery, Buffalo, New York, Gift of Seymour H. Knox, 1982; 621: © 1986 Sidney Harris, New Haven, Connecticut; 632: (left) Courtesy of Kathy Gurnee; 632: (right) Peter Arnold, Inc., New York; 637: Carl Warnecke & Assoc., San Francisco; 648: © Georg Gerster/Comstock, New York; 655: (above) The Granger Collection, New York; (below) *Harmonic Circles*, Glenn Branca, New York; 659: Sunken Garden for Chase Manhattan Bank Plaza, New York, 1961–64, Isamu Noguchi, Isamu Noguchi Foundation, New York; 666: Superstock, New York; 672: (detail) *Classical Space*, Glenn Branca, New York; 673: Superstock, New York; 685: Courtesy of Anne Dunn; 686: *A Lawn Being Sprinkled*, 1967, David Hockney; 687: *Stairway to the Studio*, Charles Sheeler, Philadelphia Museum of Art, Bequest of Mrs. Earl Horter; 690: Courtesy of Yvonna Pardus; 702: *Farewell to New York—All That Is Beautiful*, Ben Shahn, Kennedy Galleries, New York; 712: Entrance Gates to the Executive Suite, 52nd Floor, Chanin Building, New York, René Chambellon; 716: *Saturn from Dione*, Kim Poor/Novagraphics, Tucson, Arizona; 727: UPI/Bettmann Newsphotos, New York.

Illustrations
Pawel Bodytko: 17, 43, 94, 137, 215, 255, 281, 383, 498, 536, 642, 685, 690, 701.

Phil Kantz: 446, 447, 472, 480, 611.

Carol Tornatore: 130, 240, 313, 569.

McDougal, Littell and Company has made every effort to locate the copyright holders for the images used in this book and to make full acknowledgment for their use.

Symbols Used in Geometry

$\overline{AB}$	segment $\overline{AB}$	$=$	is equal to
$\overleftrightarrow{AB}$	line AB	$\neq$	is not equal to
$\overrightarrow{AB}$	ray AB	$>$	is greater than
$\overset{\frown}{AB}$	arc AB	$<$	is less than
AB	length of $\overline{AB}$	$\not>$	is not greater than
$\angle s$	angles	$\geq$	is greater than or equal to
$\angle A$	angle A	$\leq$	is less than or equal to
$m\angle A$	measure of $\angle$ A	$\approx$	is approximately equal to
$\triangle$	triangle	$\Longleftrightarrow$	is equivalent to
$\triangle\!\!\!\triangle$	triangles	$\Longrightarrow$	implies
$\odot$	circle	$\sim p$	not p or p is false
$\circledS$	circles	$\therefore$	therefore
$\not{C}$	cross-sectional area	$\{\ \}$	set
$\square$	parallelogram	$\varnothing$	null set
$\cong$	congruent	$\cup$	union
$\not\cong$	not congruent	$\cap$	intersection
$\vdash\!\!\!\!-\!\!\!\!\dashv$	congruent segments	$\sqrt{x}$	square root of x
$\angle\!\!\angle$	congruent angles	$\lvert a \rvert$	absolute value of a
$\perp$	perpendicular	$\triangle x$	change in x
$\not\perp$	not perpendicular	π	pi
$\llcorner$	right angle	$\circ$	degrees
$\parallel$	parallel	$'$	minutes
$\nparallel$	not parallel	$''$	seconds
$\nearrow\!\!\nearrow$	parallel lines	$\frac{a}{b}$	$a \div b$, $a\!:\!b$; ratio of a to b
$\sim$	similar		